CRYPTOGRAPHY'S
ROLE
IN
SECURING THE
INFORMATION
SOCIETY

Kenneth W. Dam and Herbert S. Lin, *Editors*

Committee to Study National Cryptography Policy
Computer Science and Telecommunications Board
Commission on Physical Sciences, Mathematics, and Applications

National Research Council

NATIONAL ACADEMY PRESS
Washington, D.C.   1996

Nᴀᴛɪᴏɴᴀʟ Aᴄᴀᴅᴇᴍʏ Pʀᴇss 2101 Constitution Avenue, NW Washington, DC 20418

NOTICE: The project that is the subject of this report was approved by the Governing Board of the National Research Council, whose members are drawn from the councils of the National Academy of Sciences, the National Academy of Engineering, and the Institute of Medicine. The members of the committee responsible for the report were chosen for their special competences and with regard for appropriate balance.

This report has been reviewed by a group other than the authors according to procedures approved by a Report Review Committee consisting of members of the National Academy of Sciences, the National Academy of Engineering, and the Institute of Medicine.

Support for this project was provided by the Department of Defense (under contract number DASW01-94-C-0178) and the Department of Commerce (under contract number 50SBNB4C8089). Any opinions, findings, conclusions, or recommendations expressed in this material are those of the authors and do not necessarily reflect the views of the sponsors.

Library of Congress Catalog Card Number 96-68943
International Standard Book Number 0-309-05475-3

The Computer Science and Telecommunications Board (CSTB) will be glad to receive comments on this report. Please send them via Internet e-mail to CRYPTO@NAS.EDU, or via regular mail to CSTB, National Research Council, 2101 Constitution Avenue NW, Washington, DC 20418.

COMMITTEE TO STUDY
NATIONAL CRYPTOGRAPHY POLICY

KENNETH W. DAM, University of Chicago Law School, *Chair*
W.Y. SMITH, Institute for Defense Analyses (retired), *Vice Chair*
LEE BOLLINGER, Dartmouth College
ANN CARACRISTI, National Security Agency (retired)
BENJAMIN R. CIVILETTI, Venable, Baetjer, Howard and Civiletti
COLIN CROOK, Citicorp
SAMUEL H. FULLER, Digital Equipment Corporation
LESLIE H. GELB, Council on Foreign Relations
RONALD GRAHAM, AT&T Bell Laboratories
MARTIN HELLMAN, Stanford University
JULIUS L. KATZ, Hills & Company
PETER G. NEUMANN, SRI International
RAYMOND OZZIE, Iris Associates
EDWARD C. SCHMULTS, General Telephone and Electronics (retired)
ELLIOT M. STONE, Massachusetts Health Data Consortium
WILLIS H. WARE, RAND Corporation

Staff

MARJORY S. BLUMENTHAL, Director
HERBERT S. LIN, Study Director and Senior Staff Officer
JOHN M. GODFREY, Research Associate
FRANK PITTELLI, Consultant to CSTB
GAIL E. PRITCHARD, Project Assistant

The National Academy of Sciences is a private, nonprofit, self-perpetuating society of distinguished scholars engaged in scientific and engineering research, dedicated to the furtherance of science and technology and to their use for the general welfare. Upon the authority of the charter granted to it by the Congress in 1863, the Academy has a mandate that requires it to advise the federal government on scientific and technical matters. Dr. Bruce Alberts is president of the National Academy of Sciences.

The National Academy of Engineering was established in 1964, under the charter of the National Academy of Sciences, as a parallel organization of outstanding engineers. It is autonomous in its administration and in the selection of its members, sharing with the National Academy of Sciences the responsibility for advising the federal government. The National Academy of Engineering also sponsors engineering programs aimed at meeting national needs, encourages education and research, and recognizes the superior achievements of engineers. Dr. William A. Wulf is interim president of the National Academy of Engineering.

The Institute of Medicine was established in 1970 by the National Academy of Sciences to secure the services of eminent members of appropriate professions in the examination of policy matters pertaining to the health of the public. The Institute acts under the responsibility given to the National Academy of Sciences by its congressional charter to be an adviser to the federal government and, upon its own initiative, to identify issues of medical care, research, and education. Dr. Kenneth I. Shine is president of the Institute of Medicine.

The National Research Council was organized by the National Academy of Sciences in 1916 to associate the broad community of science and technology with the Academy's purposes of furthering knowledge and advising the federal government. Functioning in accordance with general policies determined by the Academy, the Council has become the principal operating agency of both the National Academy of Sciences and the National Academy of Engineering in providing services to the government, the public, and the scientific and engineering communities. The Council is administered jointly by both Academies and the Institute of Medicine. Dr. Bruce Alberts and Dr. William A. Wulf are chairman and interim vice chairman, respectively, of the National Research Council.

Preface

INTRODUCTION

For most of history, cryptography—the art and science of secret writing—has belonged to governments concerned about protecting their own secrets and about asserting their prerogatives for access to information relevant to national security and public safety. In the United States, cryptography policy has reflected the U.S. government's needs for effective cryptographic protection of classified and other sensitive communications as well as its needs to gather intelligence for national security purposes, needs that would be damaged by the widespread use of cryptography. National security concerns have motivated such actions as development of cryptographic technologies, development of countermeasures to reverse the effects of encryption, and control of cryptographic technologies for export.

In the last 20 years, a number of developments have brought about what could be called the popularization of cryptography. First, some industries—notably financial services—have come to rely on encryption as an enabler of secure electronic funds transfers. Second, other industries have developed an interest in encryption for protection of proprietary and other sensitive information. Third, the broadening use of computers and computer networks has generalized the demand for technologies to secure communications down to the level of individual citizens and assure the privacy and security of their electronic records and transmissions. Fourth, the sharply increased use of wireless communications (e.g., cellular telephones) has highlighted the greater vulnerability of such communications to unauthorized intercept as well as the difficulty of detecting these intercepts.

As a result, efforts have increased to develop encryption systems for private sector use and to integrate encryption with other information technology products. Interest has grown in the commercial market for cryptographic technologies and systems incorporating such technologies, and the nation has witnessed a heightened debate over individual need for and access to technologies to protect individual privacy.

Still another consequence of the expectation of widespread use of encryption is the emergence of law enforcement concerns that parallel, on a civilian basis, some of the national security concerns. Law enforcement officials fear that wide dissemination of effective cryptographic technologies will impede their efforts to collect information necessary for pursuing criminal investigations. On the other side, civil libertarians fear that controls on cryptographic technologies will give government authorities both in the United States and abroad unprecedented and unwarranted capabilities for intrusion into the private lives of citizens.

CHARGE OF THE COMMITTEE TO STUDY
NATIONAL CRYPTOGRAPHY POLICY

At the request of the U.S. Congress in November 1993, the National Research Council's Computer Science and Telecommunications Board (CSTB) formed the Committee to Study National Cryptography Policy. In accordance with its legislative charge (Box P.1), the committee undertook the following tasks:

• *Framing the problem.* What are the technology trends with which national cryptography policy must keep pace? What is the political environment? What are the significant changes in the post-Cold War environment that call attention to the need for, and should have an impact on, cryptography policy?

• *Understanding the underlying technology issues and their expected development and impact on policy over time.* What is and is not possible with current cryptographic (and related) technologies? How could these capabilities have an impact on various U.S. interests?

• *Describing current cryptography policy.* To the committee's knowledge, there is no single document, classified or unclassified, within the U.S. government that fully describes national cryptography policy.

• *Articulating a framework for thinking about cryptography policy.* The interests affected by national cryptography policy are multiple, varied, and related: they include personal liberties and constitutional rights, the maintenance of public order and national security, technology develop-

---

BOX P.1
Legislative Charge to the National Research Council

Public Law 103-160
Defense Authorization Bill for Fiscal Year 1994
Signed November 30, 1993

SEC. 267. COMPREHENSIVE INDEPENDENT STUDY OF NATIONAL CRYPTOGRAPHY POLICY.

(a) **Study by National Research Council.**—Not later than 90 days after the date of the enactment of this Act, the Secretary of Defense shall request the National Research Council of the National Academy of Sciences to conduct a comprehensive study of cryptographic technologies and national cryptography policy.

(b) **Matters To Be Assessed in Study.**—The study shall assess—
　　(1) the effect of cryptographic technologies on—
　　　　(A) national security interests of the United States Government;
　　　　(B) law enforcement interests of the United States Government;
　　　　(C) commercial interests of United States industry; and
　　　　(D) privacy interests of United States citizens; and
　　(2) the effect on commercial interests of United States industry of export controls on cryptographic technologies.

(c) **Interagency Cooperation With Study.**—The Secretary of Defense shall direct the National Security Agency, the Advanced Research Projects Agency, and other appropriate agencies of the Department of Defense to cooperate fully with the National Research Council in its activities in carrying out the study under this section. The Secretary shall request all other appropriate Federal departments and agencies to provide similar cooperation to the National Research Council.

---

ment, and U.S. economic competitiveness and markets. At a minimum, policy makers (and their critics) must understand how these interests interrelate, although they may decide that one particular policy configuration better serves the overall national interest than does another.

• *Identifying a range of feasible policy options.* The debate over cryptography policy has been hampered by an incomplete analysis and discussion of various policy options—both proponents of current policy and of alternative policies are forced into debating positions in which it is difficult or impossible to acknowledge that a competing view might have some merit. This report attempts to discuss fairly the pros and cons of a number of options.

• *Making recommendations regarding cryptography policy.* No cryptography policy will be stable for all time. That is, it is unrealistic to imagine that this committee or any set of policy makers could craft a policy that would not have to evolve over time as the technological and political milieu itself changes. Thus, the committee's recommendations are framed in the context of a transition, from a world characterized by slowly evolving technology, well-defined enemies, and unquestioned U.S. technological, economic, and geopolitical dominance to one characterized by rapidly evolving technology, fuzzy lines between friend and foe, and increasing technological, economic, and political interdependencies between the United States and other nations of the world.

Given the diverse applications of cryptography, national cryptography policy involves a very large number of important issues. Important to national cryptography policy as well are issues related to the deployment of a large-scale infrastructure for cryptography and legislation and regulations to support the widespread use of cryptography for authentication and data integrity purposes (i.e., collateral applications of cryptography), even though these issues have not taken center stage in the policy debate.

The committee focused its efforts primarily on issues related to cryptography for confidentiality, because the contentious problem that this committee was assembled to address at the center of the public policy debate relates to the use of cryptography in confidentiality applications. It also addressed issues of cryptography policy related to authentication and data integrity at a relatively high level, casting its findings and recommendations in these areas in fairly general terms. However, it notes that detailed consideration of issues and policy options in these collateral areas requires additional study at a level of detail and thoroughness comparable to that of this report.

In preparing this report, the committee reviewed and synthesized relevant material from recent reports, took written and oral testimony from government, industry, and private individuals, reached out extensively to the affected stakeholders to solicit input, and met seven times to discuss the input from these sources as well as the independent observations and findings of the committee members themselves. In addition, this study built upon three prior efforts to examine national cryptography policy: the Association for Computing Machinery report *Codes, Keys, and Conflicts: Issues in U.S. Crypto Policy*,[1] the Office of Technology Assessment report *Information Security and Privacy in Network Environments*,[2] and

---

[1]Susan Landau et al., *Codes, Keys, and Conflicts: Issues in U.S. Crypto Policy*, Association for Computing Machinery Inc., New York, 1994.

[2]Office of Technology Assessment, *Information Security and Privacy in Network Environments*, OTA-TCT-606, U.S. Government Printing Office, Washington, D.C., September 1994.

the JASON encryption study.[3] A number of other examinations of cryptography and/or information security policy were also important to the committee's work.[4] (Appendix N contains source documents (e.g., statutes, regulations, memorandums of understanding), relevant to the national debate over cryptography policy.)

WHAT THIS REPORT IS NOT

The subject of national cryptography policy is quite complex, as it figures importantly in many areas of national interest. To keep the project manageable within the time, resources, and expertise available, the committee chose not to address in detail a number of issues that arose with some nontrivial frequency during the course of its study.

• This report is not a comprehensive study of the grand trade-offs that might be made in other dimensions of national policy to compensate for changes in cryptography policy. For example, this report does not address matters such as relaxing exclusionary rules that govern the court admissibility of evidence or installing video cameras in every police helmet as part of a package that also eliminates restrictions on cryptography, though such packages are in principle possible. Similarly, it does not address options such as increasing the budget for counterterrorist operations as a quid pro quo for relaxations on export controls of cryptography. The report does provide information that would help to assess the impact of various approaches to cryptography policy, although how that impact should be weighed against the impact of policies related to other areas is outside the scope of this study and the expertise of the committee assembled for it.

• This report is not a study on the future of the National Security Agency (NSA) in the post-Cold War era. A determination of what mis-

---

[3]JASON Program Office, *JASON Encryption/Privacy Study,* Report JSR-93-520 (unpublished), MITRE Corporation, McLean, Va., August 18, 1993.

[4]These works include *Global Information Infrastructure,* a joint report by the European Association of Manufacturers of Business Machines and Information Technology Industry, the U.S. Information Technology Industry Council, and the Japan Electronic Industry Development Association (EUROBIT-ITI-JEIDA), developed for the G-7 Summit on the Global Information Society, GII Tripartite Preparatory Meeting, January 26-27, 1995, Brussels; the U.S. Council for International Business statement titled "Business Requirements for Encryption," October 10, 1994, New York; and the International Chamber of Commerce position paper "International Encryption Policy," Document No. 373/202 Rev. and No. 373-30/9 Rev., Paris, undated. Important source documents can be found in Lance J. Hoffman (ed.), *Building in Big Brother: The Cryptographic Policy Debate,* Springer-Verlag, New York, 1995, and in the cryptography policy source books published annually by the Electronic Privacy Information Center in Washington, D.C.

sions the NSA should be pursuing and/or how it should pursue those missions was not in the committee's charge. The report does touch lightly on technological trends that affect the ability to undertake the missions to which cryptography is relevant, but only to the extent necessary to frame the cryptography issue.

At the same time, this report does address certain conditions of the political, social, and technological environment that will affect the answers that anyone would formulate to these questions, such as the potential impact on policy of a world that offers many users the possibilities of secure communications.

• This report is not a study of computer and communications security, although of course cryptography is a key element of such security. Even the strongest cryptography is not very useful unless it is part of a secure *system*, and those responsible for security must be concerned about everything from the trustworthiness of individuals writing the computer programs to be used to the physical security of terminals used to access the system. A report that addressed system dimensions of computer security was the National Research Council report *Computers at Risk;*[5] this current study draws on that report and others to the extent relevant for its analysis, findings, and conclusions about cryptography policy.

• This report is not a study of the many patent disputes that have arisen with respect to national cryptography policy in the past several years. While such disputes may well be a sign that the various holders expect cryptography to assume substantial commercial importance in the next several years, such disputes are in principle resolvable by the U.S. Congress, which could simply legislate ownership by eminent domain or by requiring compulsory licensing. Moreover, since many of the key patents will expire in any case in the relatively near future (i.e., before any infrastructure that uses them becomes widely deployed), the issue will become moot in any case.

• This report is not exclusively a study of national policy associated with the Clipper chip. While the Clipper chip has received the lion's share of press and notoriety in the past few years, the issues that this study was chartered to address go far beyond those associated simply with the Clipper chip. This study addresses the larger context and picture of which the Clipper chip is only one part.

---

[5]Computer Science and Telecommunications Board, National Research Council, *Computers at Risk: Safe Computing in the Information Age,* National Academy Press, Washington, D.C., 1991.

ON SECRECY AND REPORT TIME LINE

For most of history, the science and technologies associated with cryptography have been the purview of national governments and/or heads of state. It is only in the last 25 years that cryptographic expertise has begun to diffuse into the nongovernment world. Thus, it is not surprising that much of the basis and rationale underlying national cryptography policy has been and continues to be highly classified. Indeed, in a 1982 article, then-Deputy Director of the Central Intelligence Agency Bobby R. Inman wrote that

> [o]ne sometimes hears the view that publication should not be restrained because "the government has not made its case," almost always referring to the absence of specific detail for public consumption. This reasoning is circular and unreasonable. It stems from a basic attitude that the government and its public servants cannot be trusted. Specific details about why information must be protected are more often than not even more sensitive than the basic technical information itself. Publishing examples, reasons and associated details would certainly damage the nation's interests. Public review and discussion of classified information which supports decisions is not feasible or workable.[6]

Secrecy is a two-edged sword for a democratic nation. On the one hand, secrecy has a legitimate basis in those situations in which fundamental national interests are at stake (e.g., the preservation of American lives during wartime). Moreover, the history of intelligence reveals many instances in which the revelation of a secret, whether intentional or inadvertent, has led to the compromise of an information source or the loss of a key battle.[7]

On the other hand, secrecy has sometimes been used to stifle public debate and conceal poorly conceived and ill-informed national policies, and mistrust is therefore quite common among many responsible critics

---

[6]Bobby Inman, "Classifying Science: A Government Proposal . . . ," *Aviation Week and Space Technology*, February 8, 1982, p. 10.

[7]For example, following press reports of deciphered Libyan messages before and after a bombing in West Berlin in which an American soldier died, Libya changed its communications codes. A senior American official was quoted as saying that the subsequent Libyan purchase of advanced cryptographic equipment from a Swiss firm was "one of the prices [the United States is] paying for having revealed, in order to marshal support of our allies and public opinion, that intercepted communications traffic provided evidence that Libya was behind the bombing of the Berlin disco." See "Libyans Buy Message-Coding Equipment," *Washington Post*, April 22, 1986, p. A8.

of government policy. A common refrain by defenders of policies whose origins and rationales are secret is that "if you knew what we knew, you would agree with us." Such a position may be true or false, but it clearly does not provide much reassurance for those not privy to those secrets for one very simple reason: those who fear that government is hiding poorly conceived policies behind a wall of secrecy are not likely to trust the government, yet in the absence of the substantive argument being called for, the government's claim is essentially a plea for trust.

In pursuing this study, the committee has adopted the position that some secrets are still legitimate in today's global environment, but that its role is to illuminate as much as possible without compromising those legitimate interests. Thus, the committee has tried to act as a surrogate for well-intentioned and well-meaning people who fear that the worst is hiding behind the wall of secrecy—it has tried to ask the questions that these people would have asked if they could have done so. Public Law 103-160 called for all defense agencies, including the National Security Agency, to cooperate fully with the National Research Council in this study.

For obvious reasons, the committee cannot determine if it did not hear a particular piece of information because an agency withheld that information or because that piece of information simply did not exist. But for a number of reasons, the committee believes that to the best of its knowledge, the relevant agencies have complied with Public Law 103-160 and other agencies have cooperated with the committee. One important reason is that several members of the committee have had extensive experience (on a classified basis) with the relevant agencies, and these members heard nothing in the briefings held for the committee that was inconsistent with that experience. A second reason is that these agencies had every motivation and self-interest to make the best possible case for their respective positions on the issues before the committee. Thus, on the basis of agency assurances that the committee has indeed received all information relevant to the issue at hand, they cannot plausibly argue that "if the committee knew what Agency X knew, it would agree with Agency X's position."

This unclassified report does not have a classified annex, nor is there a classified version of it. After receiving a number of classified briefings on material relevant to the subject of this study, the fully cleared members of the committee (13 out of the total of 16) agree that these details, while necessarily important to policy makers who need to decide tomorrow what to do in a specific case, are not particularly relevant to the larger issues of why policy has the shape and texture that it does today nor to the general outline of how technology will and policy should evolve in the future. For example, the committee was briefed on certain intelligence activities of various nations. Policy makers care that the activities of nation X (a friendly nation) fall into certain categories and that those of nation Y (an unfriendly nation) fall into other categories, because they must craft a policy toward nation X in one way and one toward nation Y in another way. But for analytical purposes, the exact names of the nations involved are much less relevant than the fact that there will always be nations friendly and unfriendly to the United States. Committee members are prepared to respond on a classified basis if necessary to critiques and questions that involve classified material.[8]

As for the time line of this study, the committee was acutely aware of the speed with which the market and product technologies evolve. The legislation called for a study to be delivered within 2 years after the full processing of all necessary security clearances, and the study committee accelerated its work schedule to deliver a report in 18 months from its first meeting (and only 13 months from the final granting of the last clearance). The delivery date of this study was affected by the fact that the contract to fund this study was signed by the Department of Defense on September 30, 1994.

A NOTE FROM THE CHAIR

The title of this report is *Cryptography's Role in Securing the Information Society*. The committee chose this title as one best describing our inquiry and report—that is, the committee has tried to focus on the role that cryptography, as one of a number of tools and technologies, can play in providing security for an information age society through, among other means, preventing computer-enabled crimes and enhancing national security. At the same time, the committee is not unaware of the acronym for this report—CRISIS—and it believes that the acronym is apt.

From my own standpoint as chair of the NRC Committee to Study National Cryptography Policy, I believe that the crisis is a *policy* crisis, rather than a technology crisis, an industry crisis, a law enforcement crisis, or an intelligence-gathering crisis.

It is not a technology crisis because technologies have always been two-edged swords. All technologies—cryptography included—can be used for good or for ill. They can be used to serve society or to harm it, and cryptography will no doubt be used for both purposes by different groups. Public policy will determine in large measure not just the net balance of benefit and loss but also how much benefit will be derived from constructive uses of this remarkable technology.

---

[8]The point of contact within the National Research Council for such inquiries is the Computer Science and Telecommunications Board, National Research Council, 2101 Constitution Avenue, N.W., Washington, DC 20418 (telephone 202-334-2605 or e-mail CSTB@NAS.EDU).

It is not an industry crisis, nor a law enforcement crisis, nor an intelligence-gathering crisis, because industry, law enforcement, and the intelligence establishment have all had to cope with rapid technological change, and for the most part the vitality of these enterprises within the nation is a testament to their successes in so coping.

But a policy crisis is upon the nation. In the face of an inevitably growing use of cryptography, our society, acting as it must through our government as informed by the manifold forums of our democratic processes, has been unable to develop a consensus behind a coherent national cryptography policy, either within government or with the private stakeholders throughout society—the software industry, those concerned with computer security, the civil liberties community, and so on. Indeed, the committee could not even find a clear written statement of national cryptography policy that went beyond some very general statements.

To be sure, a number of government proposals have seen the light of day. The best known of these proposals, the Clipper initiative, was an honest attempt to address some of the issues underlying national cryptography policy, but one of its primary effects was to polarize rather than bring together the various stakeholders, both public and private. On the other hand, it did raise public awareness of the issue. In retrospect, many Administration officials have wished that the discourse on national cryptography policy could have unfolded differently, but in fairness we recognize that the government's task is not easy in view of the deep cleavages of interest reviewed in this report. In this context, we therefore saw it as our task, commanded by our statutory charge, to analyze the underlying reasons for this policy crisis and the interests at stake, and then to propose an intelligent, workable, and acceptable policy.

The Committee to Study National Cryptography Policy is a group of 16 individuals with very diverse backgrounds, a broad range of expertise, and differing perspectives on the subject. The committee included individuals with extensive government service and also individuals with considerable skepticism about and suspicion of government; persons with great technical expertise in computers, communications, and cryptography; and persons with considerable experience in law enforcement, intelligence, civil liberties, national security, diplomacy, international trade, and other fields relevant to the formation of policy in this area. Committee members were drawn from industry, including telecommunications and computer hardware and software, and from users of cryptography in the for-profit and not-for-profit sectors; serving as well were academics and think-tank experts.[9] The committee was by design highly heteroge-

---

[9]Note that the committee was quite aware of potential financial conflicts of interest among several of its members. In accordance with established National Research Council proce-

neous, a characteristic intended to promote discussion and synergy among its members.

At first, we wondered whether these different perspectives would allow us to talk among ourselves at all, let alone come to agreement. But the committee worked hard. The full committee met for a total of 23 days in which we received briefings and argued various points; ad hoc subcommittees attended a dozen or so additional meetings to receive even more briefings; members of the committee and staff held a number of open sessions in which testimony from the interested public was sought and received (including a very well attended session at the Fifth Annual Conference on Computers, Freedom, and Privacy in San Francisco in early 1995 and an open session in Washington, D.C., in April 1995); and the committee reviewed nearly a hundred e-mail messages sent in response to its Internet call for input. The opportunity to receive not only written materials but also oral briefings from a number of government agencies, vendors, trade associations, and assorted experts, as well as to participate in the first-ever cryptography policy meeting of the Organization for Economic Cooperation and Development and of its Business Industry Advisory Council, provided the occasion for extended give-and-take discussions with government officials and private stakeholders.

Out of this extended dialogue, we found that coming to a consensus among ourselves—while difficult—was not impossible. The nature of a consensus position is that it is invariably somewhat different from a position developed, framed, and written by any one committee member, particularly before our dialogue and without comments from other committee members. Our consensus is a result of the extended learning and interaction process through which we lived rather than any conscious effort to compromise or to paper over differences. The committee stands fully behind its analysis, findings, and recommendations.

We believe that our report makes some reasonable proposals for national cryptography policy. But a proposal is just that—a proposal for action. What is needed now is a public debate, using and not sidestepping the full processes of government, leading to a judicious resolution of pressing cryptography policy issues and including, on some important points, legislative action. Only in this manner will the policy crisis come to a satisfactory and stable resolution.

---

dures, these potential financial conflicts of interest were thoroughly discussed by the committee; no one with a direct and substantial financial stake in the outcome of the report served on the committee.

ACKNOWLEDGMENTS

The full list of individuals (except for those who explicitly requested anonymity) who provided input to the committee and the study project is contained in Appendix A. However, a number of individuals deserve special mention. Michael Nelson, Office of Science and Technology Policy, kept us informed about the evolution of Administration policy. Dorothy Denning of Georgetown University provided many useful papers concerning the law enforcement perspective on cryptography policy. Clinton Brooks and Ron Lee from the National Security Agency and Ed Roback and Raymond Kammer from the National Institute of Standards and Technology acted as agency liaisons for the committee, arranging briefings and providing other information. Marc Rotenberg from the Electronic Privacy Information Center and John Gilmore from Cygnus Support provided continuing input on a number of subjects as well as documents released under Freedom of Information Act requests. Rebecca Gould from the Business Software Alliance, Steve Walker from Trusted Information Systems, and Ollie Smoot from the Information Technology Industry Council kept the committee informed from the business perspective. Finally, the committee particularly acknowledges the literally hundreds of suggestions and criticisms provided by the reviewers of an early draft of this report. Those inputs helped the committee to sharpen its message and strengthen its presentation, but of course the content of the report is the responsibility of the committee.

The committee also received a high level of support from the National Research Council. Working with the Special Security Office of the Office of Naval Research, Kevin Hale and Kimberly Striker of the NRC's National Security Office had the complex task of facilitating the prompt processing of security clearances necessary to complete this study in a timely manner and otherwise managing these security clearances. Susan Maurizi worked under tight time constraints to provide editorial assistance. Acting as primary staff for the committee were Marjory Blumenthal, John Godfrey, Frank Pittelli, Gail Pritchard, and Herb Lin. Marjory Blumenthal directs the Computer Science and Telecommunications Board, the program unit within the National Research Council to which this congressional tasking was assigned. She sat with the committee during the great majority of its meetings, providing not only essential insight into the NRC process but also an indispensable long-term perspective on how this report could build on other CSTB work, most notably the 1991 NRC report *Computers at Risk*. John Godfrey, research associate for CSTB, was responsible for developing most of the factual material in most of the appendixes as well as for tracking down hundreds of loose ends; his prior work on a previous NRC report on standards also provided an important point of departure for the committee's discussion on standards as they apply to cryptography policy. Frank Pittelli is a consultant to CSTB, whose prior experience in computer and information security was invaluable in framing a discussion of technical issues in cryptography policy. Gail Pritchard, project assistant for CSTB, handled logistical matters for the committee with the utmost skill and patience as well as providing some research support to the committee. Finally, Herb Lin, senior staff officer for CSTB and study director on this project, arranged briefings, crafted meeting agendas, and turned the thoughts of committee members into drafts and then report text. It is fair to say that this study could not have been carried out nor this report written, especially on our accelerated schedule, without his prodigious energy and his extraordinary talents as study director, committee coordinator, writer, and editor.

Kenneth W. Dam, *Chair*
Committee to Study
National Cryptography Policy

Contents

EXECUTIVE SUMMARY   1

A ROAD MAP THROUGH THIS REPORT   15

PART I—FRAMING THE POLICY ISSUES

1   GROWING VULNERABILITY IN THE
    INFORMATION AGE   19
    1.1   The Technology Context of the Information Age, *19*
    1.2   Transition to an Information Society—Increasing
          Interconnections and Interdependence, *22*
    1.3   Coping with Information Vulnerability, *27*
    1.4   The Business and Economic Perspective, *30*
          1.4.1   Protecting Important Business Information, *30*
          1.4.2   Ensuring the Nation's Ability to Exploit
                  Global Markets, *38*
    1.5   Individual and Personal Interests in Privacy, *40*
          1.5.1   Privacy in an Information Economy, *41*
          1.5.2   Privacy for Citizens, *44*
    1.6   Special Needs of Government, *46*
    1.7   Recap, *48*

2   CRYPTOGRAPHY: ROLES, MARKET, AND
    INFRASTRUCTURE   51
    2.1   Cryptography in Context, *51*
    2.2   What Is Cryptography and What Can It Do?, *52*
    2.3   How Cryptography Fits into the Big Security Picture, *57*
          2.3.1   Factors Inhibiting Access to Information, *58*
          2.3.2   Factors Facilitating Access to Information, 60
    2.4   The Market for Cryptography, *65*
          2.4.1   The Demand Side of the Cryptography
                  Market, *66*
          2.4.2   The Supply Side of the Cryptography Market, *72*
    2.5   Infrastructure for Widespread Use of Cryptography, *74*
          2.5.1   Key Management Infrastructure, *74*
          2.5.2   Certificate Infrastructures, *75*
    2.6   Recap, *77*

3   NEEDS FOR ACCESS TO ENCRYPTED INFORMATION   79
    3.1   Terminology, *79*
    3.2   Law Enforcement: Investigation and Prosecution, *81*
          3.2.1   The Value of Access to Information for
                  Law Enforcement, *81*
          3.2.2   The Legal Framework Governing Surveillance, *84*
          3.2.3   The Nature of the Surveillance Needs of
                  Law Enforcement, *88*
          3.2.4   The Impact of Cryptography and New Media
                  on Law Enforcement (Stored and Communicated
                  Data), *90*
    3.3   National Security and Signals Intelligence, *94*
          3.3.1   The Value of Signals Intelligence, *95*
          3.3.2   The Impact of Cryptography on Signals
                  Intelligence, *101*
    3.4   Similarities in and Differences Between Foreign
          Policy/National Security and Law Enforcement
          Needs for Communications Monitoring, *102*
          3.4.1   Similarities, *102*
          3.4.2   Differences, *104*
    3.5   Business and Individual Needs for Exceptional Access
          to Protected Information, *104*
    3.6   Other Types of Exceptional Access to Protected
          Information, *108*
    3.7   Recap, *109*

PART II—POLICY INSTRUMENTS

4 EXPORT CONTROLS 113
  4.1 Brief Description of Current Export Controls, *113*
    4.1.1 The Rationale for Export Controls, *113*
    4.1.2 General Description, *114*
    4.1.3 Discussion of Current Licensing Practices, *122*
  4.2 Effectiveness of Export Controls on Cryptography, *127*
  4.3 The Impact of Export Controls on U.S. Information
      Technology Vendors, *134*
    4.3.1 De Facto Restrictions on the Domestic
          Availability of Cryptography, *134*
    4.3.2 Regulatory Uncertainty Related to Export
          Controls, *138*
    4.3.3 The Size of the Affected Market for
          Cryptography, *145*
    4.3.4 Inhibiting Vendor Responses to User Needs, *152*
  4.4 The Impact of Export Controls on U.S. Economic and
      National Security Interests, *153*
    4.4.1 Direct Economic Harm to U.S. Businesses, *153*
    4.4.2 Damage to U.S. Leadership in Information
          Technology, *155*
  4.5 The Mismatch Between the Perceptions of Government/
      National Security and Those of Vendors, *157*
  4.6 Export of Technical Data, *159*
  4.7 Foreign Policy Considerations, *162*
  4.8 Technology-Policy Mismatches, *163*
  4.9 Recap, *165*

5 ESCROWED ENCRYPTION AND RELATED ISSUES 167
  5.1 What Is Escrowed Encryption?, *167*
  5.2 Administration Initiatives Supporting Escrowed
      Encryption, *169*
    5.2.1 The Clipper Initiative and the Escrowed
          Encryption Standard, *170*
    5.2.2 The Capstone/Fortezza Initiative, *176*
    5.2.3 The Relaxation of Export Controls on Software
          Products Using "Properly Escrowed" 64-bit
          Encryption, *177*
    5.2.4 Other Federal Initiatives in Escrowed
          Encryption, *179*
  5.3 Other Approaches to Escrowed Encryption, *179*

5.4 The Impact of Escrowed Encryption on Information Security, *181*

5.5 The Impact of Escrowed Encryption on Law Enforcement, *184*

    5.5.1 Balance of Crime Enabled vs. Crime Prosecuted, *184*

    5.5.2 Impact on Law Enforcement Access to Information, *185*

5.6 Mandatory vs. Voluntary Use of Escrowed Encryption, *187*

5.7 Process Through Which Policy on Escrowed Encryption Was Developed, *188*

5.8 Affiliation and Number of Escrow Agents, *189*

5.9 Responsibilities and Obligations of Escrow Agents and Users of Escrowed Encryption, *193*

    5.9.1 Partitioning Escrowed Information, *193*

    5.9.2 Operational Responsibilities of Escrow Agents, *194*

    5.9.3 Liabilities of Escrow Agents, *197*

5.10 The Role of Secrecy in Ensuring Product Security, *201*

    5.10.1 Algorithm Secrecy, *201*

    5.10.2 Product Design and Implementation Secrecy, *204*

5.11 The Hardware/Software Choice in Product Implementation, *208*

5.12 Responsibility for Generation of Unit Keys, *211*

5.13 Issues Related to the Administration Proposal to Relax Export Controls on 64-bit Escrowed Encryption in Software, *213*

    5.13.1 The Definition of "Proper Escrowing," *213*

    5.13.2 The Proposed Limitation of Key Lengths to 64 Bits or Less, *214*

5.14 Recap, *215*

6 OTHER DIMENSIONS OF NATIONAL CRYPTOGRAPHY POLICY   216

6.1 The Communications Assistance for Law Enforcement Act, *216*

    6.1.1 Brief Description of and Stated Rationale for the CALEA, *217*

    6.1.2 Reducing Resource Requirements for Wiretaps, *218*

    6.1.3 Obtaining Access to Digital Streams in the Future, *220*

6.1.4 The CALEA Exemption of Information Service Providers and Distinctions Between Voice and Data Services, *221*
6.2 Other Levers Used in National Cryptography Policy, *221*
6.2.1 Federal Information Processing Standards, *222*
6.2.2 The Government Procurement Process, *224*
6.2.3 Implementation of Policy: Fear, Uncertainty, Doubt, Delay, Complexity, *225*
6.2.4 R&D Funding, *227*
6.2.5 Patents and Intellectual Property, *228*
6.2.6 Formal and Informal Arrangements with Various Other Governments and Organizations, *231*
6.2.7 Certification and Evaluation, 232
6.2.8 Nonstatutory Influence, *234*
6.2.9 Interagency Agreements Within the Executive Branch, *235*
6.3 Organization of the Federal Government with Respect to Information Security, *237*
6.3.1 Role of National Security vis-à-vis Civilian Information Infrastructures, *237*
6.3.2 Other Government Entities with Influence on Information Security, *241*
6.4 International Dimensions of Cryptography Policy, *243*
6.5 Recap, *244*

PART III—POLICY OPTIONS, FINDINGS, AND RECOMMENDATIONS

7 POLICY OPTIONS FOR THE FUTURE 249
7.1 Export Control Options for Cryptography, *249*
7.1.1 Dimensions of Choice for Controlling the Export of Cryptography, *249*
7.1.2 Complete Elimination of Export Controls on Cryptography, *251*
7.1.3 Transfer of All Cryptography Products to the Commerce Control List, *254*
7.1.4 End-use Certification, *256*
7.1.5 Nation-by-Nation Relaxation of Controls and Harmonization of U.S. Export Control Policy on Cryptography with Export/Import Policies of Other Nations, *256*
7.1.6 Liberal Export for Strong Cryptography with Weak Defaults, *257*

7.1.7   Liberal Export for Cryptographic Applications
        Programming Interfaces, *259*
7.1.8   Liberal Export for Escrowable Products with
        Encryption Capabilities, *262*
7.1.9   Alternatives to Government Certification of Escrow
        Agents Abroad, *263*
7.1.10 Use of Differential Work Factors in
        Cryptography, *264*
7.1.11 Separation of Cryptography from Other Items
        on the U.S. Munitions List, *264*

7.2   Alternatives for Providing Government Exceptional
      Access to Encrypted Data, *265*
7.2.1   A Prohibition on the Use and Sale of Cryptography
        Lacking Features for Exceptional Access, *265*
7.2.2   Criminalization of the Use of Cryptography in the
        Commission of a Crime, *273*
7.2.3   Technical Nonescrow Approaches for Obtaining
        Access to Information, *274*
7.2.4   Network-based Encryption, *278*
7.2.5   Distinguishing Between Encrypted Voice
        and Data Communications Services for
        Exceptional Access, *281*
7.2.6   A Centralized Decryption Facility for Government
        Exceptional Access, *284*

7.3   Looming Issues, *286*
7.3.1   The Adequacy of Various Levels of Encryption
        Against High-Quality Attack, *286*
7.3.2   Organizing the U.S. Government for Better
        Information Security on a National Basis, *289*

7.4   Recap, *292*

8   SYNTHESIS, FINDINGS, AND RECOMMENDATIONS   293
8.1   Synthesis and Findings, *293*
8.1.1   The Problem of Information Vulnerability, *293*
8.1.2   Cryptographic Solutions to Information
        Vulnerabilities, *296*
8.1.3   The Policy Dilemma Posed by Cryptography, *297*
8.1.4   National Cryptography Policy for the
        Information Age, *298*

8.2   Recommendations, *303*
8.3   Additional Work Needed, *338*
8.4   Conclusion, *339*

APPENDIXES

A   CONTRIBUTORS TO THE NRC PROJECT ON NATIONAL
     CRYPTOGRAPHY POLICY   343
     A.1   Committee Members, *343*
     A.2   Additional Contributors to the Project, *349*

B   GLOSSARY   353

C   A BRIEF PRIMER ON CRYPTOGRAPHY   364
     C.1   A Very Short History of Cryptography, *364*
     C.2   Capabilities Enabled by Cryptography, *365*
           C.2.1   Ensuring the Integrity of Data, *365*
           C.2.2   Authentication of Users, *367*
           C.2.3   Nonrepudiation, *370*
           C.2.4   Preservation of Confidentiality, *371*
     C.3   Basic Constructs of Cryptography, *374*
     C.4   Attacks on Cryptographic Systems, *378*
     C.5   Elements of Cryptographic Security, *383*
     C.6   Expected Lifetimes of Cryptographic Systems, *384*
           C.6.1   Background, *385*
           C.6.2   Asymmetric Cryptographic Systems, *385*
           C.6.3   Conventional Cryptographic Systems, *388*
           C.6.4   Timing Attacks, *390*
           C.6.5   Skipjack/Clipper/EES, *391*
           C.6.6   A Warning, *391*
           C.6.7   Quantum and DNA Computing, *392*
           C.6.8   Elliptic Curve Cryptographic Systems, *394*
           C.6.9   Quantum Cryptography, *394*

D   AN OVERVIEW OF ELECTRONIC SURVEILLANCE:
     HISTORY AND CURRENT STATUS   396
     D.1   The Legal Framework for Domestic Law Enforcement
           Surveillance, *396*
           D.1.1   The General Prohibition on Electronic
                   Surveillance, *396*
           D.1.2   Title III of the Omnibus Crime Control and
                   Safe Streets Act of 1968 and the Electronic
                   Communications Privacy Act of 1986, *396*
           D.1.3   The Foreign Intelligence Surveillance Act, *403*
     D.2   Historical Overview of Electronic Surveillance, *410*

E A BRIEF HISTORY OF CRYPTOGRAPHY POLICY   414
   E.1 Export Controls, *414*
   E.2 Academic Research and the Control of Information
       About Cryptography, *415*
   E.3 Commercial Cryptography, *417*
   E.4 Recent Developments, *419*

F A BRIEF PRIMER ON INTELLIGENCE   421
   F.1 The Intelligence Mission, *423*
   F.2 The Intelligence Cycle, *425*
       F.2.1 Planning, *426*
       F.2.2 Collection, *426*
       F.2.3 Processing, *428*
       F.2.4 Analysis, *428*
       F.2.5 Dissemination, *429*

G THE INTERNATIONAL SCOPE OF CRYPTOGRAPHY
   POLICY   430
   G.1 International Dimensions of Cryptography Policy, *430*
   G.2 Similarities in and Differences Between the United States
       and Other Nations with Respect to Cryptography, *431*
   G.3 Foreign Export Control Regimes, *434*
   G.4 Foreign Import and Use Control Regimes, *436*
   G.5 The State of International Affairs Today, *438*
   G.6 Obtaining International Cooperation on Policy Regarding
       Secure Communications, *439*
   G.7 The Fundamental Questions of International Cryptography
       Policy, *444*
       G.7.1 Who Holds the Keys?, *444*
       G.7.2 Under What Circumstances Does the Key Holder
           Release the Keys to Other Parties?, *444*
       G.7.3 How Will Nations Reach Consensus on
           International Cryptography Policy Regarding
           Exports and Use?, *447*

H SUMMARY OF IMPORTANT REQUIREMENTS FOR A
   PUBLIC-KEY INFRASTRUCTURE   450

I INDUSTRY-SPECIFIC DIMENSIONS OF SECURITY   455
   I.1 Banking and Financial Services, *455*
   I.2 Medical Consultations and Health Care, *457*
   I.3 Manufacturing, *461*

I.4 The Petroleum Industry, *463*
I.5 The Pharmaceutical and Chemical Industries, *465*
I.6 The Entertainment Industry, *466*
I.7 Government, *466*

J EXAMPLES OF RISKS POSED BY UNPROTECTED INFORMATION 469
    J.1 Risks Addressed by Cryptography for Authentication, *469*
    J.2 Risks Addressed by Cryptography for Confidentiality, *470*
    J.3 Risks Addressed by Cryptography for Both Authentication and Confidentiality, *471*
    J.4 Risks Addressed by Cryptography for Data Integrity, *472*

K CRYPTOGRAPHIC APPLICATIONS PROGRAMMING INTERFACES 474

L OTHER LOOMING ISSUES RELATED TO CRYPTOGRAPHY POLICY 477
    L.1 Digital Cash, *477*
        L.1.1 Anonymity and Criminal Activity, *480*
        L.1.2 Public Trust, *480*
        L.1.3 Taxation, *482*
        L.1.4 Cross-Border Movements of Funds, *482*
    L.2 Cryptography for Protecting Intellectual Property, *482*

M FEDERAL INFORMATION PROCESSING STANDARDS 485

N LAWS, REGULATIONS, AND DOCUMENTS RELEVANT TO CRYPTOGRAPHY 489
    N.1 Statutes, *489*
        N.1.1 Wire and Electronic Communications Interception and Interception of Oral Communications (U.S. Code, Title 18, Chapter 119), *489*
        N.1.2 Foreign Intelligence Surveillance (U.S. Code, Title 50, Chapter 36), *511*
        N.1.3 Pen Register and Traffic Analysis (U.S. Code, Title 18, Chapters 121 and 206), *526*
        N.1.4 Communications Assistance for Law Enforcement Act of 1995, *540*
        N.1.5 Computer Security Act of 1987, *551*
        N.1.6 Arms Export Control Act (U.S. Code, Title 22, Chapter 39), *558*

N.2   Executive Orders, *573*
        N.2.1   Executive Order 12333 (U.S. Intelligence
                  Activities), *573*
        N.2.2   Executive Order 12958 (Classified National
                  Security Information), *589*
        N.2.3   Executive Order 12472 (Assignment of National
                  Security and Emergency Preparedness
                  Telecommunications Functions), *612*
        N.2.4   National Security Directive 42 (National Policy for the
                  Security of National Security Telecommunications
                  and Information Systems), *620*
N.3   Memorandums of Understanding (MOU) and Agreement
        (MOA), *627*
        N.3.1   National Security Agency/National Institute of
                  Standards and Technology MOU, *627*
        N.3.2   National Security Agency/Federal Bureau of
                  Investigation MOU, *630*
        N.3.3   National Security Agency/Advanced Research
                  Projects Agency/Defense Information Systems
                  Agency MOA, *632*
N.4   Regulations, *636*
        N.4.1   International Traffic in Arms Regulations
                  (22 CFR, Excerpts from Parts 120-123, 125,
                  and 126), *636*
        N.4.2   Export Administration Regulations, *655*

INDEX   677

CRYPTOGRAPHY'S ROLE IN SECURING THE INFORMATION SOCIETY

National cryptography policy entails a complex juggling act among a number of different interests. A member of the National Research Council's Committee to Study National Cryptography Policy, Ronald Graham (pictured above) is also a member of the National Academy of Sciences and a past president of the International Juggling Association. Photograph by Ché Graham.

Executive Summary

In an age of explosive worldwide growth of electronic data storage and communications, many vital national interests require the effective protection of information. When used in conjunction with other approaches to information security, cryptography is a very powerful tool for protecting information. Consequently, current U.S. policy should be changed to promote and encourage the widespread use of cryptography for the protection of the information interests of individuals, businesses, government agencies, and the nation as a whole, while respecting legitimate national needs of law enforcement and intelligence for national security and foreign policy purposes to the extent consistent with good information protection.

BASIC POLICY ISSUES

The Information Security Problem

Today's information age requires U.S. businesses to compete on a worldwide basis, sharing sensitive information with appropriate parties while protecting that information against competitors, vandals, suppliers,

---

BOX ES.1
The Foreign Threat to U.S. Business Interests

Of the wide variety of information risks facing U.S. companies operating internationally, those resulting from electronic vulnerabilities appear to be the most significant. The National Counterintelligence Center (NACIC), an arm of the U.S. intelligence community established in 1994 by presidential directive, concluded that "specialized technical operations (including computer intrusions, telecommunications targeting and intercept, and private-sector encryption weaknesses) account for the largest portion of economic and industrial information lost by U.S. corporations." Specifically, the NACIC noted that

> [b]ecause they are so easily accessed and intercepted, corporate telecommunications—particularly international telecommunications—provide a highly vulnerable and lucrative source for anyone interested in obtaining trade secrets or competitive information. Because of the increased usage of these links for bulk computer data transmission and electronic mail, intelligence collectors find telecommunications intercepts cost-effective. For example, foreign intelligence collectors intercept facsimile transmissions through government-owned telephone companies, and the stakes are large—approximately half of all overseas telecommunications are facsimile transmissions. Innovative "hackers" connected to computers containing competitive information evade the controls and access companies' information. In addition, many American companies have begun using electronic data interchange, a system of transferring corporate bidding, invoice, and pricing data electronically overseas. Many foreign government and corporate intelligence collectors find this information invaluable.

SOURCE: National Counterintelligence Center, *Annual Report to Congress on Foreign Economic Collection and Industrial Espionage*, July 1995, pp. 16–17.

---

customers, and foreign governments (Box ES.1). Private law-abiding citizens dislike the ease with which personal telephone calls can be tapped, especially those carried on cellular or cordless telephones. Elements of the U.S. civilian infrastructure such as the banking system, the electric power grid, the public switched telecommunications network, and the air traffic control system are central to so many dimensions of modern life that protecting these elements must have a high priority. The federal government has an important stake in assuring that its important and sensitive political, economic, law enforcement, and military information, both classified and unclassified, is protected from foreign governments or other parties whose interests are hostile to those of the United States.

Cryptographic Dimensions of Information Security Solutions

Information vulnerabilities cannot be eliminated through the use of any single tool. For example, it is impossible to prevent with technical means a party authorized to view information from improperly disclosing that information to someone else. However, as part of a comprehensive approach to addressing information vulnerabilities, cryptography is a powerful tool that can help to assure the confidentiality and integrity of information in transit and in storage and to authenticate the asserted identity of individuals and computer systems. Information that has been properly encrypted cannot be understood or interpreted by those lacking the appropriate cryptographic "key"; information that has been integrity-checked cannot be altered without detection. Properly authenticated identities can help to restrict access to information resources to those properly authorized individuals and to take fuller advantage of audit trails to track down parties who have abused their authorized access.

Law Enforcement and National Security Dilemmas Posed by Cryptography

For both law enforcement and national security, cryptography is a two-edged sword. The public debate has tended to draw lines that frame the policy issues as the privacy of individuals and businesses against the needs of national security and law enforcement. While such a dichotomy does have a kernel of truth, when viewed in the large, this dichotomy is misleading. If cryptography can protect the trade secrets and proprietary information of businesses and thereby reduce economic espionage (which it can), it also supports in a most important manner the job of law enforcement. If cryptography can help protect nationally critical information systems and networks against unauthorized penetration (which it can), it also supports the national security of the United States. Framing discussion about national cryptography policy in this larger law enforcement and national security context would help to reduce some of the polarization among the relevant stakeholders.

On the other hand, cryptography intended primarily to maintain the confidentiality of information that is available to the general public for legitimate purposes such as defending against information theft is also available for illegitimate purposes such as terrorism. Encryption thus does pose a threat to the capability that law enforcement authorities may seek under appropriate legal authorization to gain access to information for the purpose of investigating and prosecuting criminal activity. Encryption also poses a threat to intelligence gathering for national security and foreign policy purposes, an activity that depends on access to information of foreign governments and other foreign entities.

Note that other applications of cryptography—for purposes of assuring data integrity and authenticating identities of users and computer systems—do not pose dilemmas for law enforcement and national security in the same way that confidentiality does.

National Cryptography Policy for the Information Age

For many years, concern over foreign threats to national security has been the primary driver of a national cryptography policy that has sought to maximize the protection of U.S. military and diplomatic communications while denying the confidentiality benefits of cryptography to foreign adversaries through the use of export controls on cryptography and related technical data. More recently, the U.S. government has aggressively promoted the domestic use of a certain kind of cryptography—escrowed encryption—that would provide strong protection for legitimate uses but would permit access by law enforcement officials when authorized by law. Today, these and other dimensions of current national cryptography policy generate considerable controversy.

All of the various stakes are legitimate: privacy for individuals, protection of sensitive or proprietary information for businesses, ensuring the continuing reliability and integrity of nationally critical information systems and networks, law enforcement access to stored and communicated information for purposes of investigating and prosecuting crime, and national security access to information stored or communicated by foreign powers or other entities and organizations whose interests and intentions are relevant to the national security and the foreign policy interests of the United States. Informed public discussion of the issues must begin by acknowledging the legitimacy both of information gathering for law enforcement and national security purposes and of information security for law-abiding individuals and businesses.

The conduct of the debate regarding national cryptography policy has been complicated because a number of participants have often invoked classified information that cannot be made public. However, the cleared members of the National Research Council's Committee to Study National Cryptography Policy (13 of the 16 committee members) concluded that **the debate over national cryptography policy can be carried out in a reasonable manner on an unclassified basis.** Classified material is often important to operational matters in specific cases, but it is neither essential to the big picture of why cryptography policy is the way it is nor required for the general outline of how technology will and policy should evolve in the future.

BOX ES.2
The Past and Future World Environment

Past	Future Trends
Computing and communications were expensive and rare.	Computing and information acquisition, retrieval, and processing are inexpensive and ubiquitous. Rapid growth is evident in the development and deployment of diverse technology-enabled services.
Communications networks were analog and voice oriented; communications made heavy use of dedicated lines.	Communications networks are digital and oriented toward video and data transmissions.
	Communications make heavy use of shared infrastructure and multiple channels of different media (e.g., satellites, wireless). Passive eavesdropping is thus harder to detect.
Telecommunications was controlled by a small number of players.	Telecommunications involves a large number of players.
The U.S. economy was unquestionably dominant in the world.	The U.S. economy is important but not dominant in the world, and it is increasingly interlinked with allies, customers, suppliers, vendors, and competitors all over the world.
The economy was oriented toward material production.	The economy is oriented toward information and services.
The security threat was relatively homogeneous (Soviet Union and Cold War).	Security threats are much more heterogeneous than in the Cold War, both in origin and in nature.
Cryptography was used primarily for military and diplomatic purposes. Government had a relative monopoly on cryptographic expertise and capability.	Cryptography has important applications throughout all aspects of society. Nongovernmental entities have significant expertise and capability built on an open, public, and expanding base of scientific and technical knowledge about cryptography.

The problems of information vulnerability, the legitimacy of the various national interests described above, and trends such as those outlined in Box ES.2 point to the need for a concerted effort to protect vital information assets of the United States. Cryptography is one important element of a comprehensive U.S. policy for better information security.

The committee believes that **U.S. national policy should be changed to support the broad use of cryptography in ways that take into account competing U.S. needs and desires for individual privacy, international economic competitiveness, law enforcement, national security, and**

world leadership. Because cryptography is an important tool for protecting information and because it is very difficult for governments to control, the committee believes that widespread nongovernment use of cryptography in the United States and abroad is inevitable in the long run. Accordingly, the proper role of national cryptography policy is to facilitate a judicious transition between today's world of high information vulnerability and a future world of greater information security, while to the extent possible meeting the legitimate needs of law enforcement and information gathering for national security and foreign policy purposes.

The committee found that **current national cryptography policy is not adequate to support the information security requirements of an information society.** Indeed, current policy discourages the use of cryptography, whether intentionally or not, and in so doing impedes the ability of the nation to use cryptographic tools that would help to remediate certain important vulnerabilities. National cryptography policy should support three objectives:

1. Broad availability of cryptography to all legitimate elements of U.S. society;

2. Continued economic growth and leadership of key U.S. industries and businesses in an increasingly global economy, including but not limited to U.S. computer, software, and communications companies; and

3. Public safety and protection against foreign and domestic threats.

Objectives 1 and 2 argue for a policy that places few government restrictions on the use of cryptography and actively promotes the use of cryptography on a broad front. Objective 3 argues that some kind of government policy role in the deployment and use of cryptography for confidentiality may continue to be necessary for public safety and national security reasons. These three objectives can be met within a framework recognizing that **on balance, the advantages of more widespread use of cryptography outweigh the disadvantages.**

The recommendations below address several critical policy areas. In the interests of brevity, only short rationales for the recommendations are given here. The reader is urged to read Chapter 8 of the report for essential qualifications, conditions, and explanations.

A FRAMEWORK FOR NATIONAL CRYPTOGRAPHY POLICY

The framework for national cryptography policy should provide coherent structure and reduce uncertainty for potential vendors and for nongovernment and government users of cryptography in ways that policy does not do today.

Recommendation 1: **No law should bar the manufacture, sale, or use of any form of encryption within the United States.** Specifically, a legislative ban on the use of unescrowed encryption would raise both technical and legal or constitutional issues. Technically, many methods are available to circumvent such a ban; legally, constitutional issues, especially those related to free speech, would be almost certain to arise, issues that are not trivial to resolve. Recommendation 1 is made to reinforce this particular aspect of the Administration's cryptography policy.

Recommendation 2: **National cryptography policy should be developed by the executive and legislative branches on the basis of open public discussion and governed by the rule of law.** Only a national discussion of the issues involved in national cryptography policy can result in the broadly acceptable social consensus that is necessary for any policy in this area to succeed. A consensus derived from such deliberations, backed by explicit legislation when necessary, will lead to greater degrees of public acceptance and trust, a more certain planning environment, and better connections between policy makers and the private sector on which the nation's economy and social fabric rest.

Recommendation 3: **National cryptography policy affecting the development and use of commercial cryptography should be more closely aligned with market forces.** As cryptography has assumed greater importance to nongovernment interests, national cryptography policy has become increasingly disconnected from market reality and the needs of parties in the private sector. Experience with technology deployment suggests that reliance on market forces is generally the most effective way to promote the widespread use of a new technology. Since the committee believes that widespread deployment and use of cryptography are in the national interest, it believes that national cryptography policy should align itself with user needs and market forces to the maximum feasible extent. Accordingly, national cryptography policy should emphasize the freedom of domestic users to determine cryptographic functionality, protection, and implementations according to their security needs as they see fit; encourage the adoption of cryptographic standards by the federal government and private parties that are consistent with prevailing industry practice; and support the use of algorithms, product designs, and product implementations that are open to public scrutiny.

EXPORT CONTROLS

For many years, the United States has controlled the export of cryptographic technologies, products, and related technical information as munitions (on the U.S. Munitions List administered by the State Department). However, the current export control regime for cryptography is an increasing impediment to the information security efforts of U.S. firms competing and operating in world markets, developing strategic alliances internationally, and forming closer ties with foreign customers and suppliers. Export controls also have had the effect of reducing the domestic availability of products with strong encryption capabilities. Looking to the future, both U.S. and foreign companies have the technical capability to integrate high-quality cryptographic features into their products and services. U.S. export controls may stimulate the growth of significant foreign competition for U.S. vendors to the detriment of both U.S. national security interests and U.S. business and industry.

Some relaxation of today's export controls on cryptography is warranted. Relaxation would create an environment in which U.S. and multinational firms and individuals could use the same security products in the United States and abroad, thereby supporting better information security for U.S. firms operating internationally. It would also increase the availability of good cryptography products in the United States. Finally, it would help to solidify U.S. leadership in a field critical to national security and economic competitiveness.

At the same time, cryptography is inherently dual-use in character, with important applications to both civilian and military purposes. Because cryptography is a particularly critical military application for which few technical alternatives are available, retention of some export controls on cryptography will mitigate the loss to U.S. national security interests in the short term, allow the United States to evaluate the impact of relaxation on national security interests before making further changes, and "buy time" for U.S. national security authorities to adjust to a new technical reality.

Recommendation 4: **Export controls on cryptography should be progressively relaxed but not eliminated.**

Recommendation 4.1—Products providing confidentiality at a level that meets most general commercial requirements should be easily exportable.[1] **Today, products with encryption capabilities that incorporate the 56-bit DES algorithm provide this level of confidentiality and**

---

[1]For purposes of Recommendation 4.1, a product that is "easily exportable" will automatically qualify for treatment and consideration (i.e., commodity jurisdiction, or CJ) under the Commerce Control List (CCL). Automatic qualification refers to the same procedure under which software products using RC2 or RC4 algorithms for confidentiality with 40-bit key sizes currently qualify for the CCL.

should be easily exportable. As a condition of export, vendors of products covered under this Recommendation 4.1 (and 4.2 below) would be required to provide to the U.S. government full technical specifications of their product and reasonable technical assistance upon request in order to assist the U.S. government in understanding the product's internal operations.

Recommendation 4.2—Products providing stronger confidentiality should be exportable on an expedited basis to a list of approved companies if the proposed product user is willing to provide access to decrypted information upon legally authorized request. Firms on the list would agree to abide by a set of requirements described in Chapter 8 that would help to ensure the ability of the U.S. government to obtain the plaintext of encrypted information upon presentation of a proper law enforcement request. (Plaintext is the information that was initially encrypted.)

Recommendation 4.3—The U.S. government should streamline and increase the transparency of the export licensing process for cryptography. Greater efforts in this area would reduce uncertainty regarding rules, time lines, and the criteria used in making decisions about the exportability of particular products. Chapter 8 describes specific possible steps that might be taken.

ADJUSTING TO NEW TECHNICAL REALITIES

As noted above, cryptography is helpful to some dimensions of law enforcement and national security and harmful to others. The committee accepts that the onset of an information age is likely to create many new challenges for public safety, among them the greater use of cryptography by criminal elements of society. If law enforcement authorities are unable to gain access to the encrypted communications and stored information of criminals, some criminal investigations and prosecutions will be significantly impaired. For these reasons, specific steps should be taken to mitigate these difficulties. In the realm of national security, new capabilities are needed to better cope with the challenges that cryptography presents.

Since 1993, the approach of the U.S. government to these problems has been an aggressive promotion of escrowed encryption (see Chapter 5) as a pillar of the technical foundation for national cryptography policy, primarily in response to the law enforcement concerns described above. Initiatives promoted by the U.S. government include the Escrowed Encryption Standard (a voluntary Federal Information Processing Standard for secure voice telephony), the Capstone/Fortezza initiative that provides escrowed encryption capabilities for secure data storage and communications, and a recent proposal to liberalize export controls on certain encryption products if the keys are "properly escrowed."

The committee understands the Administration's rationale for promoting escrowed encryption but believes that escrowed encryption should be only one part of an overall strategy for dealing with the problems that encryption poses for law enforcement and national security. The committee's view of an appropriate overall strategy is described below, and escrowed encryption is the focus of Recommendation 5.3.

Recommendation 5: The U.S. government should take steps to assist law enforcement and national security to adjust to new technical realities of the information age. Over the past 50 years, both law enforcement and national security authorities have had to cope with a variety of changing technological circumstances. For the most part, they have coped with these changes quite well. Today, however, "business as usual" will not suffice to bring agencies responsible for law enforcement and national security into the information age. At the same time, both law enforcement and national security have demonstrated considerable adaptability to new environments; this record of adaptability provides considerable confidence that they can adapt to a future of digital communications and stored data as well.

The specific subrecommendations that follow attempt to build on this record. They are intended to support law enforcement and national security missions in their totality—for law enforcement, in both crime prevention and crime prosecution and investigation; and for national security, in both the defense of nationally critical information systems and the collection of intelligence information.

Recommendation 5.1—The U.S. government should actively encourage the use of cryptography in nonconfidentiality applications such as user authentication and integrity checks. These applications are particularly important in addressing vulnerabilities of nationally critical information systems and networks. Furthermore, these applications of cryptography are important crime-fighting measures. To date, national cryptography policy has not fully supported such nonconfidentiality uses. Some actions have been taken in this area, but these actions have sometimes conflicted with government concerns about confidentiality. As importantly, government has expressed considerably more concern in the public debate regarding the deleterious impact of widespread cryptography used for confidentiality than over the deleterious impact of not deploying cryptographic capabilities for user authentication and data integrity. Chapter 8 provides a number of illustrative examples to demonstrate what specific actions government can take to promote nonconfidentiality applications of cryptography.

Recommendation 5.2—The U.S. government should promote the security of the telecommunications networks more actively. At a minimum, the U.S. government should promote the link encryption of cellular communications[2] and the improvement of security at telephone switches. Such steps would not diminish government access for lawfully authorized wiretaps through the requirements imposed on carriers today to cooperate with law enforcement in such matters. Furthermore, by addressing public demands for greater security in voice communications that are widely known to be nonsecure through the telecommunications service providers, these measures would also reduce the demand for (and thus the availability of) devices used to provide end-to-end encryption of voice communications. Without a ready supply of such devices, a criminal user would have to go to considerable trouble to obtain a device that could thwart a lawfully authorized wiretap.

Recommendation 5.3—To better understand how escrowed encryption might operate, the U.S. government should explore escrowed encryption for its own uses. To address the critical international dimensions of escrowed communications, the U.S. government should work with other nations on this topic. Escrowed encryption has both benefits and risks. The benefits for law enforcement and national security are that when escrowed encryption is properly implemented and widely deployed, law enforcement and national security authorities will be able to obtain access to escrow-encrypted data in specific instances when authorized by law. Escrowed encryption also enables end users to recover encrypted stored data to which access has been inadvertently lost. The risk to end users is that escrowed encryption provides a potentially lower degree of confidentiality because it is specifically designed to permit exceptional access by parties not originally intended to have access to the encrypted data.

Aggressive government promotion of escrowed encryption is not appropriate at this time for several reasons: the lack of operational experi-

---

[2]"Link encryption" refers to the practice of encrypting information being communicated in such a way that it is encrypted only in between the node from which it is sent and the node where it is received; while the information is at the nodes themselves, it is unencrypted. In the context of link encryption for cellular communications, a cellular call would be encrypted between the mobile handset and the ground station. When carried on the landlines of the telephone network, the call would be unencrypted.

ence with how a large-scale infrastructure for escrowed encryption would work; the lack of demonstrated evidence that escrowed encryption will solve the most serious problems that law enforcement authorities face; the likely harmful impact on the natural market development of applications made possible by new information services and technologies; and the uncertainty of the market response to such aggressive promotion. At the same time, many policy benefits can be gained by an operational exploration of escrowed encryption by the U.S. government for government applications; such exploration would enable the U.S. government to develop the base of experience on which to build a more aggressive promotion of escrowed encryption should circumstances develop in such a way that encrypted communications come to pose a significant problem for law enforcement.

Recommendation 5.4—Congress should seriously consider legislation that would impose criminal penalties on the use of encrypted communications in interstate commerce with the intent to commit a federal crime. The purpose of such a statute would be to discourage the use of cryptography for illegitimate purposes, thus focusing the weight of the criminal justice system on individuals who were in fact guilty of criminal activity rather than on law-abiding citizens and criminals alike. Any statute in this area should be drawn narrowly.

Recommendation 5.5—High priority should be given to research, development, and deployment of additional technical capabilities for law enforcement and national security for use in coping with new technological challenges. Such R&D should be undertaken during the time that it will take for cryptography to become truly ubiquitous. These new capabilities are almost certain to have a greater impact on future information collection efforts than will aggressive attempts to promote escrowed encryption to a resistant market.

THE POLICY RELATIONSHIP BETWEEN INFORMATION SECURITY AND CRYPTOGRAPHY

Although this report is concerned primarily with national cryptography policy, any such policy is only one component of a national information security policy. Without a forward-looking and comprehensive national information security policy, changes in national cryptography policy may have little operational impact on U.S. information security.

Recommendation 6: The U.S. government should develop a mechanism to promote information security in the private sector. As is widely acknowledged, the U.S. government is not well organized to meet the challenges presented by an information society, and no government agency has the responsibility to promote information security in the private sector. Absent a coordinated approach to promoting information security, the needs of many stakeholders may well be given inadequate attention and notice; those who are pursuing enhanced information security and those who have a need for legal access to stored or communicated information must both be included in a robust process for managing the often-competing issues and interests that will inevitably arise over time. Government has an important role in actively promoting the security of information systems and networks critical to the nation's welfare (e.g., the banking and financial system, the public switched telecommunications network, the air traffic control system, the electric power grid). In other sectors of the economy, the role of the U.S. government should be limited to providing information and expertise. Chapter 8 provides some illustrative examples of what the government might do to promote information security in the private sector.

CONCLUSION

The committee believes that its recommendations will lead to enhanced confidentiality and protection of information for individuals and companies, thereby reducing economic and financial crimes and economic espionage from both domestic and foreign sources. In addition, they will result in improved security and assurance for the information systems and networks used by the nation—a more secure national information infrastructure. While the recommendations will in these ways contribute to the prevention of crime and enhance national security, the committee recognizes that the spread of cryptography will increase the burden of those in government charged with carrying out certain specific law enforcement and intelligence activities. It believes that widespread commercial and private use of cryptography in the United States and abroad is inevitable in the long run and that its advantages, on balance, outweigh its disadvantages. Thus, the committee concluded that the overall interests of the government and the nation would best be served by a policy that fosters a judicious transition toward the broad use of cryptography.

A Road Map Through This Report

This report responds to a request made in the Defense Authorization Act of FY 1994 by the U.S. Congress for the National Research Council to conduct a comprehensive study of national cryptography policy, a subject that has generated considerable controversy in the past few years.

This report is organized into three parts. Part I frames the policy issues. Chapter 1 outlines the problem of growing information vulnerability and the need for technology and policy to mitigate this problem. Chapter 2 describes possible roles for cryptography in reducing information vulnerability and places cryptography into context as one element of an overall approach to ensuring information security. Chapter 3 discusses needs for access to encrypted information and related public policy issues, specifically those related to information gathering for law enforcement and national security purposes.

Part II of this report describes the instruments and goals of current U.S. cryptography policy and some of the issues raised by current policy. Chapter 4 is concerned primarily with export controls on cryptography, a powerful tool that has long been used in support of national security objectives but whose legitimacy has come under increasing fire in the last several years. Chapter 5 addresses escrowed encryption, an approach aggressively promoted by the federal government as a technique for balancing national needs for information security with those of law enforcement and national security for information gathering. Chapter 6 discusses other dimensions of national cryptography policy, including the Digital Telephony Act of 1995 (also known as the Communications Assistance for Law Enforcement Act) and a variety of other levers used in national cryptography policy that do not often receive much attention in the debate.

Part III has two goals—enlarging the space of possible policy options and offering findings and recommendations. Chapter 7 discusses a variety of options for cryptography policy, some of which have been suggested or mentioned in different forums (e.g., in public and/or private input received by the committee, or by various members of the committee). These policy options include alternative export control regimes for cryptography and alternatives for providing exceptional access capabilities when necessary. In addition, Chapter 7 addresses several issues related to or affected by cryptography that will appear on the horizon in the foreseeable future. Chapter 8 describes the committee's findings and recommendations.

A set of appendixes provides more detail where needed.

PART I

Framing the Policy Issues

PART I IS INTENDED TO EXPLICATE *the fundamental issues underlying national cryptography policy. Chapter 1 outlines basic elements of a critical problem facing the nation—the increasing vulnerability of information, a commodity that has become essential to national well-being and future opportunity. This vulnerability results from a number of trends, including the explosive growth of digital communications and data storage, the increasingly international dimensions of business, and the growing dependence of the nation on a number of critical information systems and networks. Chapter 2 describes how cryptography can play an important role in reducing the information vulnerability of the nation, of businesses, and of private individuals. Chapter 2 also places cryptography into context, as one element of an overall approach to information security, as a product that responds to factors related to both supply and demand, and as a technology whose large-scale use requires a supporting infrastructure. Chapter 3 discusses public policy issues raised by the need for access to encrypted information. The prospect of near-absolute confidentialty of information—a prospect enabled by modern cryptography—is reassuring to some and quite disturbing to others. Important public policy issues are raised by law enforcement authorities, who regard the ability to obtain information surreptitiously but legally as essential to their crime-fighting abilities, and by national security authorities, who place a high value on the ability to monitor the communications of potential adversaries. Even private individuals, who might wish to encrypt records securely, may face the need to recover their data as though they were outsiders if they have forgotten how to gain "legitimate" access; the same is true for businesses in many situations.*

1

Growing Vulnerability in the Information Age

Chapter 1 frames a fundamental problem facing the United States today—the need to protect against the growing vulnerability of information to unauthorized access and/or change as the nation makes the transition from an industrial age to an information age. Society's reliance on a changing panoply of information technologies and technology-enabled services, the increasingly global nature of commerce and business, and the ongoing desire to protect traditional freedoms as well as to ensure that government remains capable of fulfilling its responsibilities to the nation all suggest that future needs for information security will be large. These factors make clear the need for a broadly acceptable national cryptography policy that will help to secure vital national interests.

1.1 THE TECHNOLOGY CONTEXT OF THE INFORMATION AGE

The information age is enabled by computing and communications technologies (collectively known as information technologies) whose rapid evolution is almost taken for granted today. Computing and communications systems appear in virtually every sector of the economy and increasingly in homes and other locations. These systems focus economic and social activity on information—gathering, analyzing, storing, presenting, and disseminating information in text, numerical, audio, image,

19

and video formats—as a product itself or as a complement to physical or tangible products.[1]

Today's increasingly sophisticated information technologies cover a wide range of technical progress:

• *Microprocessors and workstations* are increasingly important to the computing infrastructure of companies and the nation. Further increases in speed and computational power today come from parallel or distributed processing with many microcomputers and processors rather than faster supercomputers.

• *Special-purpose electronic hardware* is becoming easier to develop. Thus, it may make good sense to build specialized hardware optimized for performance, speed, or security with respect to particular tasks; such specialized hardware will in general be better adapted to these purposes than general-purpose machines applied to the same tasks.

• *Media* for transporting digital information are rapidly becoming faster (e.g., fiber optics instead of coaxial cables), more flexible (e.g., the spread of wireless communications media), and less expensive (e.g., the spread of CD-ROMs as a vehicle for distributing digital information). Thus, it becomes feasible to rely on the electronic transmission of larger and larger volumes of information and on the storage of such volumes on ever-smaller physical objects.

• *Convergence* of technologies for communications and for computing. Today, the primary difference between communications and computing is the distance traversed by data flows: in communications, the traversed distance is measured in miles (e.g., two people talking to each other), while in computing the traversed distance is measured in microns (e.g., between two subcomponents on a single integrated circuit). A similar convergence affects companies in communications and in computing—their boundaries are blurring, their scopes are changing, and their production processes overlap increasingly.

• *Software* is increasingly carrying the burden of providing functionality in information technology. In general, software is what gives hardware its functional capabilities, and different software running on the same hardware can change the functionality of that hardware entirely. Since software is intangible, it can be deployed widely on a very short

---

[1]Citations to a variety of press accounts can be found in Computer Science and Telecommunications Board (CSTB), National Research Council, *Information Technology and Manufacturing: A Research Agenda,* National Academy Press, Washington, D.C., 1993; CSTB, *Information Technology in the Service Society: A Twenty-First Century Lever,* 1993; CSTB, *Realizing the Information Future: The Internet and Beyond,* 1994; CSTB, *Keeping the Computer and Communications Industry Competitive: Convergence of Computing, Communications, and Entertainment,* 1995; and CSTB, *The Unpredictable Certainty: Information Infrastructure Through 2000,* 1996.

BOX 1.1
Communications and Computing Devices
and the Role of Software

Communications and computing devices can be dedicated to a single purpose or may serve multiple purposes. Dedicated single-purpose devices are usually (though not always) hardware devices whose functionality cannot be easily altered. Examples include unprogrammable pocket calculators, traditional telephones, walkie-talkies, pagers, fax machines, and ordinary telephone answering machines.

A multipurpose device is one whose functionality can be altered by the end user. In some instances, a hardware device may be "reprogrammed" to perform different functions simply by the physical replacement of a single chip by another chip or by the addition of a new circuit board. Open bus architectures and standard hardware interfaces such as the PC card are intended to facilitate multipurpose functionality.

Despite such interfaces and architectures for hardware, software is the primary means for implementing multipurpose functionality in a hardware device. With software, physical replacement of a hardware component is unnecessary—a new software program is simply loaded and executed. Examples include personal computers (which do word processing or mathematical calculations, depending on what software the user chooses to run), programmable calculators (which solve different problems, depending on the programming given to them), and even many modern telephones (which can be programmed to execute functions such as speed dialing). In these instances, the software is the medium in which the expectations of the user are embedded.

Today, the lines between hardware and software are blurring. For example, some "hardware" devices are controlled by programs stored in semi-permanent read-only memory. "Read-only memory" (ROM) originally referred to memory for storing instructions and data that could never be changed, but this characteristic made ROM-controlled devices less flexible. Thus, the electronics industry responded with "read-only" memory whose contents take special effort to change (such as exposing the memory chip to a burst of ultraviolet light or sending only a particular signal to a particular pin on the chip). The flexibility and cheapness of today's electronic devices make them ubiquitous. Most homes now have dozens of microprocessors in coffee makers, TVs, refrigerators, and virtually anything that has a control panel.

---

time scale compared to that of hardware. Box 1.1 contains more discussion of this point.

As these examples suggest, information technologies are ever more affordable and ubiquitous. In all sectors of the economy, they drive demand for information systems; such demand will continue to be strong and experience significant growth rates. High-bandwidth and/or wireless media are becoming more and more common. Interest in and use of the Internet and similar public networks will continue to grow rapidly.

1.2 TRANSITION TO AN INFORMATION SOCIETY— INCREASING INTERCONNECTIONS AND INTERDEPENDENCE

As the availability and use of computer-based systems grow, so, too, does their interconnection. The result is a shared infrastructure of information, computing, and communications resources that facilitates collaboration at a distance, geographic dispersal of operations, and sharing of data. With the benefits of a shared infrastructure also come costs. Changes in the technology base have created more vulnerabilities, as well as the potential to contain them. For example, easier access for users in general implies easier access for unauthorized users.

The design, mode of use, and nature of a shared infrastructure create vulnerabilities for all users. For national institutions such as banking, new risks arise as the result of greater public exposure through such interconnections. For example, a criminal who penetrates one bank interconnected to the world's banking system can steal much larger amounts of money than are stored at that one bank. (Box 1.2 describes a recent electronic bank robbery.) Reducing vulnerability to breaches of security will depend on the ability to identify and authenticate people, systems, and processes and to assure with high confidence that information is not improperly manipulated, corrupted, or destroyed.

Although society is entering an era abounding with new capabilities, many societal practices today remain similar to those of the 1960s and 1970s, when computing was dominated by large, centralized mainframe computers. In the 1980s and 1990s, they have not evolved to reflect the introduction of personal computers, portable computing, and increasingly ubiquitous communications networks. Thus, people continue to relinquish control over substantial amounts of personal information through credit card transactions, proliferating uses of Social Security numbers, and participation in frequent-buyer programs with airlines and stores. Organizations implement trivial or no protection for proprietary data and critical systems, trusting policies to protect portable storage media or relying on simple passwords to protect information.

These practices have endured against a backdrop of relatively modest levels of commercial and individual risk; for example, the liability of a credit card owner for credit card fraud perpetrated by another party is limited by law to $50. Yet most computer and communications hardware and software systems are subject to a wide range of vulnerabilities, as described in Box 1.3. Moreover, information on how to exploit such vulnerabilities is often easy to obtain. As a result, a large amount of information that people say they would like to protect is in fact available through entirely legal channels (e.g., purchasing a credit report on an individual) or in places that can be accessed improperly through technical attacks requiring relatively modest effort.

BOX 1.2
An Attempted Electronic Theft from Citicorp

Electronic money transfers are among the most closely guarded activities in banking. In 1994, an international group of criminals penetrated Citicorp's computerized electronic transfer system and moved about $12 million from legitimate customer accounts to their own accounts in banks around the world. According to Citicorp, this is the first time its computerized cash-management system has been breached. Corporate customers access the system directly to transfer funds for making investments, paying bills, and extending loans, among other purposes. The Citicorp system moves about $500 billion worldwide each day. Authority to access the system is verified with a cryptographic code that only the customer knows.

The case began in June 1994, when Vladimir Levin of St. Petersburg, Russia, allegedly accessed Citicorp computers in New York through the international telephone network, posing as one of Citicorp's customers. He moved some customer funds to a bank account in Finland, where an accomplice withdrew the money in person. In the next few months, Levin moved various Citicorp customers' funds to accomplices' personal or business accounts in banks in St. Petersburg, San Francisco, Tel Aviv, Rotterdam, and Switzerland.

Accomplices had withdrawn a total of about $400,000 by August 1994. By that time, bank officials and their customers were on alert. Citicorp detected subsequent transfers quickly enough to warn the banks into which funds were moved to freeze the destination accounts. (Bank officials noted that they could have blocked some of these transfers, but they permitted and covertly monitored them as part of the effort to identify the perpetrators.) Other perpetrators were arrested in Tel Aviv and Rotterdam; they revealed that they were working with someone in St. Petersburg. An examination of telephone company records in St. Petersburg showed that Citicorp computers had been accessed through a telephone line at AO Saturn, a software company. A person arrested after attempting to make a withdrawal from a frozen account in San Francisco subsequently identified Levin, who was an AO Saturn employee. Russia has no extradition treaty with the United States; however, Levin traveled to Britain in March 1995 and was arrested there. As of September 1995, proceedings to extradite him for trial in the United States were in progress.

Levin allegedly penetrated Citicorp computers using customers' user identifications and passwords. In each case, Levin electronically impersonated a legitimate customer, such as a bank or an investment capital firm. Some investigators suspect that an accomplice inside Citicorp provided Levin with necessary information; otherwise, it is unclear how he could have succeeded in accessing customer accounts. He is believed to have penetrated Citicorp's computers 40 times in all. Citicorp says it has upgraded its system's security to prevent future break-ins.

SOURCES: William Carley and Timothy O'Brien, "Cyber Caper: How Citicorp System Was Raided and Funds Moved Around World," *Wall Street Journal*, September 12, 1995, p. A1; Saul Hansell, "A $10 Million Lesson in the Risks of Electronic Banking," *New York Times*, August 19, 1995, p. 31.

BOX 1.3
Vulnerabilities in Information Systems and Networks

Information systems and networks can be subject to four generic vulnerabilities:

1. *Eavesdropping or data browsing.* By surreptitiously obtaining the confidential data of a company or by browsing a sensitive file stored on a computer to which one has obtained improper access, an adversary could be in a position to undercut a company bid, learn company trade secrets (e.g., knowledge developed through proprietary company research) that would eliminate a competitive advantage of the company, or obtain the company's client list in order to steal customers. Moreover, damage can occur independent of the use of stealth—many companies would be damaged if their sensitive data were disclosed, even if they knew that such a disclosure had occurred.

2. *Clandestine alteration of data.* By altering a company's data clandestinely, an adversary could destroy the confidence of the company's customers in the company, disrupt internal operations of the company, or subject the company to shareholder litigation.

3. *Spoofing.* By illicitly posing as a company, an adversary could place false orders for services, make unauthorized commitments to customers, defraud clients, and cause no end of public relations difficulties for the company. Similarly, an adversary might pose as a legitimate customer, and a company—with an interest in being responsive to user preferences to remain anonymous under a variety of circumstances—could then find itself handicapped in seeking proper confirmation of the customer's identity.

4. *Denial of service.* By denying access to electronic services, an adversary could shut down company operations, especially time-critical ones. On a national scale, critical infrastructures controlled by electronic networks (e.g., the air traffic control system, the electrical power grid) involving many systems linked to each other are particularly sensitive.

Today, the rising level of familiarity with computer-based systems is combining with an explosion of experimentation with information and communications infrastructure in industry, education, health care, government, and personal settings to motivate new uses of and societal expectations about the evolving infrastructure. A key feature of the new environment is connection or exchange: organizations are connecting internal private facilities to external public ones; they are using public networks to create virtual private networks, and they are allowing outsiders such as potential and actual customers, suppliers, and business allies to access their systems directly. One vision of a world of electronic commerce and what it means for interconnection is described in Box 1.4.

Whereas a traditional national security perspective might call for keeping people out of sensitive stores of information or communications networks, national economic and social activity increasingly involves the

BOX 1.4
Electronic Commerce and the Implications for Interconnectivity

A number of reports have addressed the potential nature and impact of electronic commerce.[1] Out of such reports, several common elements can be distilled:

- The interconnection of geographically dispersed units into a "virtual" company.
- The linking of customers, vendors, and suppliers through videoconferencing, electronic data interchange, and electronic networks.
- The creation of temporary or more permanent strategic alliances for business purposes.
- A vast increase in the on-line availability of information and information products, both free and for a fee, that are useful to individuals and organizations.
- The electronic transaction of retail business, beginning with today's toll-free catalog shopping and extending to electronic network applications that enable customers to:
—apply for bank loans;
—order tangible merchandise (e.g., groceries) for later physical delivery;
—order intangible merchandise (e.g., music, movies) for electronic delivery;
—obtain information and electronic documents (e.g., official documents such as driver's licenses and birth certificates).
- The creation of a genuinely worldwide marketplace that matches buyers to sellers largely without intermediaries.
- New business opportunities for small entrepreneurs that could sell low-value products to the large numbers of potential customers that an electronic marketplace might reach.

In general, visions of electronic commerce writ large attempt to leverage the competitive edge that information technologies can provide for commercial enterprises. Originally used exclusively to facilitate internal communications, information technology is now used by corporations to connect directly with their suppliers and business partners.[2] In the future, corporate networks will extend all the way to customers, enabling improvements in customer service and more direct channels for customer feedback. Furthermore, information technologies will facilitate the formation of ad hoc strategic alliances among diverse enterprises and even among competitors on a short time scale, driven by changes in business conditions that demand prompt action. This entire set of activities is already well under way.

---

[1]See, for example, Cross-Industry Working Team, *Electronic Cash, Tokens, and Payments in the National Information Infrastructure*, Corporation for National Research Initiatives, 1895 Preston White Drive, Suite 100, Reston, Virginia 22091-5434 (Internet: info-xiwt@cnri.reston.va.us; Tel: 703/620-8990), 1994; Office of Technology Assessment, *Electronic Enterprises: Looking to the Future*, U.S. Government Printing Office, Washington, D.C., July 1994.

[2]For example, in manufacturing, collaborative information technologies can help to improve the quality of designs and reduce the cost and time needed to revise designs; product designers will be able to create a "virtual" product, make extensive computer simulations of its behavior without supplying all of

continued

BOX 1.4 *continued*

its details, and "show" it to the customer for rapid feedback. Networks will enable the entire manufacturing enterprise to be integrated all along the supply chain, from design shops to truck fleets that deliver the finished products. (See Computer Science and Telecommunications Board, National Research Council, *Information Technology and Manufacturing: A Research Agenda,* National Academy Press, Washington, D.C., 1995.)

In the delivery of services, the more effective use and transmission of information have had dramatic effects. Today's air transportation system would not exist without rapid and reliable information flows regarding air traffic control, sales, marketing, maintenance, safety, and logistics planning. Retailers and wholesalers depend on the rapid collection and analysis of sales data to plan purchasing and marketing activities, to offer more differentiated services to customers, and to reduce operational costs. The insurance industry depends on rapid and reliable information flows to its sales force and to customize policies and manage risks. (See Computer Science and Telecommunications Board, National Research Council, *Information Technology in the Service Society: A Twenty-First Century Lever,* National Academy Press, Washington, D.C., 1994.)

BOX 1.5
Tensions Between Security and Openness

Businesses have long been concerned about the tension between openness and security. An environment that is open to everyone is not secure, while an environment that is closed to everyone is highly secure but not useful. A number of trends in business today tend to exacerbate this conflict. For example:

• Modern competitive strategies emphasize openness to interactions with potential customers and suppliers. For example, such strategies would demand that a bank present itself as willing to do business with anyone, everywhere, and at any time. However, such strategies also offer potential adversaries a greater chance of success, because increasing ease of access often facilitates the penetration of security protections.

• Many businesses today emphasize decentralized management that pushes decision-making authority toward the customer and away from the corporate hierarchy. Yet security often has been (and is) approached from a centralized perspective. (For example, access controls are necessarily hierarchical (and thus centralized) if they are to be maintained uniformly.)

• Many businesses rely increasingly on highly mobile individuals. When key employees were tied to one physical location, it made sense to base security on physical presence, e.g., to have a user present a photo ID card to an operator at the central corporate computer center. Today, mobile computing and communications are common, with not even a physical wire to ensure that the person claiming to be an authorized user is accessing a computer from an authorized location or to prevent passive eavesdropping on unencrypted transmissions with a radio scanner.

exact opposite: inviting people from around the world to come in—with varying degrees of recognition that all who come in may not be benevolent. Box 1.5 describes some of the tensions between security and openness. Such a change in expectations and perspective is unfolding in a context in which controls on system access have typically been deficient, beginning with weak operating system security. The distributed and internetworked communications systems that are emerging raise questions about protecting information regardless of the path traveled (end-to-end security), as close to the source and destination as possible.

The international dimensions of business and the growing importance of competitiveness in the global marketplace complicate the picture further. Although "multinationals" have long been a feature of the U.S. economy, the inherently international nature of communications networks and the growing capabilities for distributing and accessing information worldwide are helping many activities and institutions to transcend national boundaries. (See Box 1.6.)

At the same time, export markets are at least as important as domestic U.S. markets for a growing number of goods and service producers, including producers of information technology products as well as a growing variety of high- and low-technology products. The various aspects of globalization—identifying product and merchandising needs that vary by country; establishing and maintaining employment, customer, supplier, and distribution relationships by country; coordinating activities that may be dispersed among countries but result in products delivered to several countries; and so on—place new demands on U.S.-based and U.S.-owned information, communication, organizational, and personal resources and systems.

1.3 COPING WITH INFORMATION VULNERABILITY

Solutions to cope with the vulnerabilities described above require both appropriate technology and user behavior and are as varied as the needs of individual users and organizations. Cryptography—a technology described more fully in Chapter 2 and Appendix C—is an important element of many solutions to information vulnerability that can be used in a number of different ways. National cryptography policy—the focus of this report—concerns how and to what extent government affects the development, deployment, and use of this important technology. To date, public discussion of national cryptography policy has focused on one particular application of cryptography, namely its use in protecting the confidentiality of information and communications.

Accordingly, consideration of national cryptography policy must take into account two fundamental issues:

BOX 1.6
International Dimensions of Business and Commerce Today

U.S. firms increasingly operate in a global environment, obtaining goods and services from companies worldwide, participating in global virtual corporations, and working as part of international strategic alliances. One key dimension of increasing globalization has been the dismantling of barriers to trade and investment. In the past 40 years, tariffs among developed countries have been reduced by more than two-thirds. After the Uruguay Round reductions are phased in, tariffs in these countries will be under 4%, with 43% of current trade free of any customs duties.

While tariffs of developing countries are at higher levels, they have recently begun to decline substantially. After the Uruguay Round, tariffs in these countries will average 12.3% by agreement and will be even lower as a result of unilateral reductions. In response to the reductions in trade barriers, trade has grown rapidly. From 1950 to 1993, U.S. and world trade grew at an average compound rate of 10% annually.

Investment has also grown rapidly in recent years, stimulated by the removal of restrictions and by international rules that provide assurances to investors against discriminatory or arbitrary treatment. U.S. foreign direct investment also has grown at almost 10% annually during the past 20 years and now totals about half a trillion dollars. Foreign direct investment in the United States has risen even faster over the same period—at almost 19% annually—and now also totals almost $500 billion.

The expansion of international trade and investment has resulted in a much more integrated and interdependent world economy. For the United States, this has meant a much greater dependence on the outside world. More than a quarter of the U.S. gross domestic product is now accounted for by trade in goods and services and returns on foreign investment. Over 11 million jobs are now directly or indirectly related to our merchandise trade.

Because the U.S. economy is mature, the maintenance of a satisfactory rate of economic growth requires that the United States compete vigorously for international markets, especially in the faster growing regions of the world. Many sectors of our economy are now highly dependent on export markets. This is particularly the case for, but is not limited to, high-technology goods, as indicated in Table 1.1.

A second international dimension is the enormous growth in recent years of multinational enterprises. Such firms operate across national boundaries, frequently in multiple countries. According to the 1993 World Investment Report of the United

TABLE 1.1 Dependence of U.S. Business Sectors on Export Markets

Area of Export	Exports as a Percentage of U.S. Output
Electronic computing and parts	52
Semiconductors and related devices	47
Magnetic and optical recording media (includes software products)	40

SOURCE: U.S. Department of Commerce, *Commerce News*, August 9, 1995.

Nations, transnational corporations (TNCs) with varying degrees of integration account for about a third of the world's private sector productive assets.

The number of TNCs has more than tripled in the last 20 years. At the outset of this decade, about 37,000 U.S. firms had a controlling equity interest in some 170,000 foreign affiliates. This does not include nonequity relationships, such as management contracts, subcontracting, franchising, or strategic alliances. There are some 300 TNCs based in the United States and almost 15,000 foreign affiliates, of which some 10,000 are nonbank enterprises.

The strategies employed by TNCs vary among firms. They may be based on trade in goods and services alone or, more often, involve more complex patterns of integrated production, outsourcing, and marketing. One measure of the extent of integration by U.S. firms is illustrated by the U.S. Census Bureau, which reported that in 1994, 46% of U.S. imports and 32% of U.S. exports were between related firms. Of U.S. exports to Canada and Mexico, 44% were between related parties; for the European Union and Japan, the share was 37%.

With respect to imports, the shares of related-party transactions were 75.5% for Japan, 47.2% for the European Union, 44.6% for Canada, and 69.2% for Mexico. Among those sectors with the highest levels of interparty trade are data processing equipment, including computers, and parts and telecommunications equipment, ranging from 50% to 90%.

- If the public information and communications infrastructure continues to evolve with very weak security throughout, reflecting both deployed technology and user behavior, the benefits from cryptography for confidentiality will be significantly less than they might otherwise be.
- The vulnerabilities implied by weak security overall affect the ability of specific mechanisms such as cryptography to protect not only confidentiality but also the integrity of information and systems and the availability of systems for use when sought by their users. Simply protecting (e.g., encrypting) sensitive information from disclosure can still leave the rest of a system open to attacks that can undermine the encryption (e.g., the lack of access controls that could prevent the insertion of malicious software) or destroy the sensitive information.

Cryptography thus must be considered in a wider context. It is not a panacea, but it is extremely important to ensuring security and can be used to counter several vulnerabilities.

Recognition of the need for system and infrastructure security and demand for solutions are growing. Although demand for solutions has yet to become widespread, the trend is away from a marketplace in which the federal government[2] was the only meaningful customer. Growing reliance

---

[2]The more general statement is that the market historically involved national governments in several countries as the principal customers.

on a shared information and communications infrastructure means that all individuals and organizations should be, and the committee believes will become, the dominant customers for better security. That observation is inherent in the concept of infrastructure as something on which people rely.

What may be less obvious is that as visions of ubiquitous access and interconnection are increasingly realized, individual, organizational, and governmental needs may become aligned. Such an alignment would mark a major change from the past. Again, sharing of a common infrastructure is the cause: everyone, individual or organization, public or private sector, is a user. As significantly, all of these parties face a multitude of threats to the security of information (Box 1.7). Consideration of the nation's massive dependence on the public switched telecommunications network, which is one of many components of the information and communications infrastructure, provides insight into the larger set of challenges posed by a more complex infrastructure (Box 1.8).

To illustrate the broad panorama of stakeholder interests in which national cryptography policy is formulated, the next several sections examine different aspects of society from the standpoint of needs for information security.

1.4 THE BUSINESS AND ECONOMIC PERSPECTIVE

For purposes of this report, the relationship of U.S. businesses to the information society has two main elements. One element is that of protecting information important to the success of U.S. businesses in a global marketplace. The second element is ensuring the nation's continuing ability to exploit U.S. strengths in information technology on a worldwide basis.

1.4.1 Protecting Important Business Information

A wide range of U.S. companies operating internationally are threatened by foreign information-collection efforts. The National Counterintelligence Center (NACIC) reports that "the U.S. industries that have been the targets in most cases of economic espionage and other foreign collection activities include biotechnology; aerospace; telecommunications; computer hardware/software, advanced transportation and engine technology; advanced materials and coatings; energy research; defense and armaments technology; manufacturing processes; and semiconductors."[3] Foreign col-

---

[3]National Counterintelligence Center, *Annual Report to Congress on Foreign Economic Collection and Industrial Espionage*, Washington, D.C., July 1995, p. 15.

lectors target proprietary business information such as bid, contract, customer, and strategy information, as well as corporate financial and trade data.

Of all of the information vulnerabilities facing U.S. companies internationally (see Box 1.7), electronic vulnerabilities appear to be the most significant. For example, the NACIC concluded that "specialized technical operations (including computer intrusions, telecommunications targeting and intercept, and private-sector encryption weaknesses) account for the largest portion of economic and industrial information lost by U.S. corporations." The NACIC noted,

> Because they are so easily accessed and intercepted, corporate telecommunications—particularly international telecommunications—provide a highly vulnerable and lucrative source for anyone interested in obtaining trade secrets or competitive information. Because of the increased usage of these links for bulk computer data transmission and electronic mail, intelligence collectors find telecommunications intercepts cost-effective. For example, foreign intelligence collectors intercept facsimile transmissions through government-owned telephone companies, and the stakes are large—approximately half of all overseas telecommunications are facsimile transmissions. Innovative "hackers" connected to computers containing competitive information evade the controls and access companies' information. In addition, many American companies have begun using electronic data interchange, a system of transferring corporate bidding, invoice, and pricing data electronically overseas. Many foreign government and corporate intelligence collectors find this information invaluable.[4]

Why is electronic information so vulnerable? The primary reason is that it is computer readable and thus much more vulnerable to automated search than are intercepted voice or postal mail transmissions. Once the information is collected (e.g., through an existing wiretap or a protocol analyzer on an Internet router), it is relatively simple for computers to search streams of electronic information for word combinations of interest (e.g., "IBM," "research," and "superconductivity" in the same message). As the cost of computing drops, the cost of performing such

---

[4]From the National Counterintelligence Center, *Annual Report to Congress on Foreign Economic Collection and Industrial Espionage,* July 1995. Further, intelligence collections by foreign powers are facilitated when a hostile government interested in eavesdropping controls the physical environment in which a U.S. company may be operating. For example, the U.S. company may be in a nation in which the telecommunications system is under the direct control of the government. When a potentially hostile government controls the territory on which a company must operate, many more compromises are possible.

BOX 1.7
Threat Sources

• *Foreign national agencies (including intelligence services).* Foreign intelligence operations target key U.S. businesses. For example, two former directors of the French intelligence service have confirmed publicly that the French intelligence service collects economic intelligence information, including classified government information and information related to or associated with specific companies of interest.[1] Foreign intelligence agencies may break into facilities such as the foreign offices of a U.S. company or the hotel suite of a U.S. executive and copy computer files from within that facility (e.g., from a laptop computer in a hotel room, or a desktop computer connected to a network in an office).[2] Having attained such access, they can also insert malicious code that will enable future information theft.

• *Disgruntled or disloyal employees that work "from the inside."* Such parties may collude with outside agents. Threats involving insiders are particularly pernicious because insiders are trusted with critical information that is not available to outsiders. Such information is generally necessary to understand the meaning of various data flows that may have been intercepted, even when those data flows are received in the clear.

• *Network hackers and electronic vandals* that are having fun or making political statements through the destruction of intellectual property without the intent of theft. Information terrorists may threaten to bring down an information network unless certain demands are met; extortionists may threaten to bring down an information network unless a ransom is paid. Disgruntled customers seeking revenge on a company also fall into this category.

• *Thieves* attempting to steal money or resources from businesses. Such individuals may be working for themselves or acting as part of a larger conspiracy (e.g., in association with organized crime). The spreading of electronic commerce will increase the opportunities for new and different types of fraud, as illustrated by the large increase in fraud seen as the result of increased electronic filing to the Internal Revenue Service. Even worse, customers traditionally regarded as the first line of defense against fraud (because they check their statements and alert the merchants or banks involved to problems) may become adversaries as they seek to deny a signature on a check or alter the amount of a transaction.

It is difficult to know the prevalence of such threats, because many companies do not discuss for the record specific incidents of information theft. In some cases, they fear stockholder ire and losses in customer confidence over security breaches; in others, they are afraid of inspiring "copy-cat" attacks or revealing security weaknesses. In still other cases, they simply do not know that they have been the victim of such theft. Finally, only a patchwork of state laws apply to the theft of trade secrets and the like (and not all states have such laws). There is no federal statute that protects trade secrets or that addresses commercial information theft, and federal authorities probing the theft of commercial information must rely on proving violations of other statutes, such as wire and mail fraud laws, interstate transport of stolen property, conspiracy, or computer fraud and abuse laws; as a result, documentation of what would be a federal offense if such a law were present is necessarily spotty.

For all of these reasons, what is known on the public record about economic losses from information theft almost certainly understates the true extent of the problem.

---

[1]Two former directors of the DGSE (the French intelligence service), have publicly stated that one of the DGSE's top priorities was to collect economic intelligence. During a September 1991 NBC news program, Pierre Marion, former DGSE Director, revealed that he had initiated an espionage program against US businesses for the purpose of keeping France internationally competitive. Marion justified these actions on the grounds that the United States and France, although political and military allies, are economic and technological competitors. During an interview in March 1993, then DGSE Director Charles Silberzahn stated that political espionage was no longer a real priority for France but that France was interested in economic intelligence, "a field which is crucial to the world's evolution." Silberzahn advised that the French had some success in economic intelligence but stated that much work is still needed because of the growing global economy. Silberzahn advised during a subsequent interview that theft of classified information, as well as information about large corporations, was a long-term French Government policy. These statements were seemingly corroborated by a DGSE targeting document prepared in late 1989 and leaked anonymously to the US Government and the press in May 1993. It alleged that French intelligence had targeted numerous US Government agencies and corporations to collect economic and industrial information. Industry leaders such as Boeing, General Dynamics, Hughes Aircraft, Lockheed, McDonnell Douglas, and Martin Marietta all were on the list. Heading the US Government listing was the Office of the US Trade Representative.

The above unclassified paragraph can be found in the secret version of *Annual Report to Congress on Foreign Economic Collection and Industrial Espionage,* National Counterintelligence Center, Washington, D.C., July 1995.
[2]According to a report from the National Communications System, countries that currently have significant intelligence operations against the United States for national security and/or economic purposes include Russia, the People's Republic of China, Cuba, France, Taiwan, South Korea, India, Pakistan, Israel, Syria, Iran, Iraq, and Libya. "All of the intelligence organizations listed [above] have the capability to target telecommunications and information systems for information or clandestine attacks. The potential for exploitation of such systems may be significantly larger." See National Communications System (NCS), *The Electronic Intrusion Threat to National Security and Emergency Preparedness Telecommunications: An Awareness Document,* 2nd ed., NCS, Alexandria, Va., December 5, 1994, pp. 2-20.

BOX 1.8
Vulnerability of the Public Switched Telecommunications Network

The nation's single most critical national-level component of information infrastructure vulnerable to compromise is the public switched telecommunications network (PSTN). The PSTN provides information transport services for geographically dispersed and national assets such as the banking system and financial markets,[1] and the air traffic control system.[2] Even the traditional military[3] is highly dependent on the PSTN. Parties connected to the PSTN are therefore vulnerable to failure of the PSTN itself and to attacks transmitted over the PSTN.

The fundamental characteristic of the PSTN from the standpoint of information vulnerability is that it is a highly interconnected network of heterogeneously controlled and operated computer-based switching stations. Network connectivity implies that an attacker—which might range from a foreign government to a teen-aged hacker—can in principle connect to any network site (including sites of critical importance for the entire network) from any other network site (which may be geographically remote and even outside the United States).[4] The sites of critical importance for the PSTN are the switching nodes that channel the vast majority of telecommunications traffic in the United States. Access to these critical nodes, and to other switching facilities, is supposed to be limited to authorized personnel, but in practice these nodes are often vulnerable to penetration. Once in place on a critical node, hostile and unauthorized users are in a position to disrupt the entire network.

The systemic vulnerabilities of the PSTN are the result of many factors. One is the increasing accessibility of network software to third parties other than the common carriers, resulting from the Federal Communications Commission requirement that the PSTN support open, equal access for third-party providers of enhanced services as well as for the common carriers; such accessibility offers intruders many opportunities to capture user information, monitor traffic, and remotely manipulate the network. A second reason is that service providers are allowing customers more direct access to network elements, in order to offer customer-definable services such as call forwarding. A third reason is that advanced services made possible by Signaling System 7 are dependent on a common, out-of-band signaling system for control of calls through a separate packet-switched data network that adds to network vulnerability.[5] Finally, space-based PSTN components (i.e., satellites) have few control centers, are susceptible to electronic attack, and generally do not encrypt their command channels, making the systems vulnerable to hackers copying their commands and disrupting service.[6] These conditions imply that the PSTN is a system that would benefit from better protection of system integrity and availability.

Threats to the PSTN affect all national institutions whose ability to function fully and properly depends on being able to communicate, be it through telephony, data transmission, video, or all of these. Indeed, many data networks operated "privately" by large national corporations or national institutions such as those described above are private only in the sense that access is supposed to be limited to corporate purposes; in fact, national institutions or corporations generally use all forms of communications, including those physically carried by the PSTN.[7] However, the physical and computational infrastructure of these networks is in general owned by the telecommunications service provider, and this infrastructure is part of the larger PSTN infrastructure. Thus, like the Internet, the "private" data network of a national corporation is in general *not* physically independent of the PSTN. Similarly, it is dependence on the PSTN that has led to failures in the air traffic control system and important financial markets:

- In January 1991, the accidental severing of an AT&T fiber-optic cable in Newark, New Jersey, led to the disruption of Federal Aviation Administration (FAA) air traffic control communications in the Boston-Washington corridor and the shutdown of the New York Mercantile Exchange and several commodities exchanges. In May 1991, the severing of a fiber-optic cable led to the shutdown of four of the FAA's 20 major air traffic control centers with "massive operational impact."[8]
- The 1991 failure of a PSTN component in New York caused the loss of connectivity between a major securities house and the Securities Industry Automation Corporation, resulting in an inability to settle the day's trades over the network.[9]

Examples of small-scale activities by the computer "underground" against the PSTN demonstrate capabilities that, if coupled to an intent to wage serious information warfare against the United States, pose a serious threat to the U.S. information infrastructure:

- In 1990, several members of the Legion of Doom's Atlanta branch were charged with penetrating and disrupting telecommunications network elements. They were accused of planting "time bomb" programs in network elements in Denver, Atlanta, and New Jersey; these were designed to shut down major switching hubs but were defused by telephone carriers before causing damage.[10]
- Members of a group known as MOD were indicted on July 8, 1992, on 11 accounts. It is significant that they appear to have worked as a team. Among their alleged activities were developing and unleashing "programmed attacks" (see below) on telephone company computers and accessing telephone company computers to create new circuits and add services with no billing records.[11]
- Reported (but not well documented) is a growing incidence of "programmed attacks."[12] These have been detected in several networks and rely on customized software targeting specific types of computers or network elements. They are rarely destructive, but rather seek to add or modify services. "The capability illustrated by this category of attacks has not fully matured. However, if a coordinated attack using these types of tools were directed at the PSTN with a goal of disrupting national security/emergency preparedness (NS/EP) telecommunications, the result could be significant."[13] (The same point probably applies to the goal of disrupting other kinds of telecommunications beyond those used for NS/EP.)

A number of reports and studies[14] have called attention to the vulnerability of components of the national telecommunications infrastructure.

---

[1]These private networks for banking include Fedwire (operated by the Federal Reserve banks), the Clearinghouse for Interbank Payment Systems (CHIPS; operated by New York Clearinghouse, an association of money center banks), the Society for Worldwide Interbank Financial Telecommunication (SWIFT; an international messaging system that carries instructions for wire transfers between pairs of correspondent banks), and the Automated Clearing House (ACH)

continued

BOX 1.8 *continued*

systems for domestic transfers, typically used for routine smaller purchases and payments. In the 1980s, several U.S. banks aggressively developed global networks with packet switches, routers, and so on, to interconnect their local and wide area networks; or, they used third-party service providers to interconnect. In the 1990s, there are signs that U.S. international banks are moving to greater use of carrier-provided or hybrid networks because of the availability of virtual private networks from carriers. Carrier-provided networks are more efficient than networks built on top of dedicated leased lines, because they can allocate demand dynamically among multiple customers.

[2] The air traffic control system uses leased lines to connect regional air traffic control centers.

[3] Over 95% of U.S. military and intelligence community voice and data communications are carried over facilities owned by public carriers. (See Joint Security Commission, *Redefining Security: A Report to the Secretary of Defense and the Director of Central Intelligence*, February 28, 1994, Chapter 8.) Of course, the 95% figure includes some noncritical military communications; however, only 30% of the telecommunications networks that would be used during wartime operate in the classified environment (and are presumably more secure), while the other 70% are based on the use of unclassified facilities of public carriers. See Richard Powers, *Information Warfare: A CSI Special Report*, Computer Security Institute, Washington, D.C., Fall 1995.

[4] Clifford Stoll, *The Cuckoo's Egg*, Pocket Books, New York, 1989.

[5] National Research Council, *Growing Vulnerability of the Public Switched Networks: Implications for National Security and Emergency Preparedness* (National Academy Press, Washington, D.C., 1989), p. 36; Reliability and Vulnerability Working Group, Telecommunications Policy Committee, Information Infrastructure Task Force, *Reliability and Vulnerability of the NII: Capability Assessments*, from the National Communications System home page at http://164.117.147.223/nc-ia/html.

[6] Reliability and Vulnerability Working Group, Telecommunications Policy Committee, Information Infrastructure Task Force, *Reliability and Vulnerability of the NII: Capability Assessments*, from the National Communications System home page at http://164.117.147.223/nc-ia/html.

[7] Both shared circuits and private networks are expected to grow dramatically in the next several years. See, for example, Michael Csenger, "Private Lines Dead? Don't Buy Those Flowers Just Yet," *Network World*, May 1, 1995, p. 1.

[8] Software Engineering Notes, Volume 17, January 1992, as cited in Peter G. Neumann, *Computer-Related Risks*, Addison-Wesley, New York, 1995, p. 17.

[9] See Office of Technology Assessment, *U.S. Congress, U.S. Banks and International Telecommunications—Background Paper*, OTA-BP-TCT-100, U.S. Government Printing Office, Washington, D.C., September 1992, pp. 32-33.

[10] National Communications System (NCS), *The Electronic Intrusion Threat to National Security and Emergency Preparedness Telecommunications: An Awareness Document*, 2nd ed., NCS, Alexandria, Va., December 5, 1994, p. 2-5.

[11] NCS, *The Electronic Intrusion Threat to National Security and Emergency Preparedness Telecommunications*, 1994, pp. 2-8 to 2-9.

[12] NCS, *The Electronic Intrusion Threat to National Security and Emergency Preparedness Telecommunications*, 1994, p. 2-6.

[13] NCS, *The Electronic Intrusion Threat to National Security and Emergency Preparedness Telecommunications*, 1994, p. 2-6.

[14]Joint Security Commission, *Redefining Security: A Report to the Secretary of Defense and the Director of Central Intelligence*, Washington, D.C., February 28, 1994; National Research Council, *Growing Vulnerability of the Public Switched Networks: Implications for National Security and Emergency Preparedness*, 1989; NCS, *The Electronic Intrusion Threat to National Security and Emergency Preparedness Telecommunications*, 1994; Reliability and Vulnerability Working Group, Telecommunications Policy Committee, Information Infrastructure Task Force, *Reliability and Vulnerability of the NII: Capability Assessments*, from the National Communications System home page at http://164.117.147.223/nc-ia/html.

searches drops.[5] The threat posed by automated search, coupled with the sensitivity of certain communications that are critical for nongovernment users, is at the root of nongovernment demand for security.[6]

Note that solutions for coping with information-age vulnerabilities may well create new responsibilities for businesses. For example, businesses may have to ensure that the security measures they take are appropriate for the information they are protecting, and/or that the information they are protecting remains available for authorized use. Failure to discharge these responsibilities properly may result in a set of liabilities that these businesses currently do not face.

---

[5]As a rough rule of thumb, Martin Hellman estimates that 10 billion (10^{10}) words can be searched for $1. This estimate is based on an experiment in which Hellman used the Unix utility program "fgrep" to search a 1 million (10^6) character file for a specific string of 10 characters known to be at the end of the file and nowhere else. It took the NeXT workstation on which this experiment was run approximately 1 second to find these last 10 characters. Since there are approximately 10^5 seconds in a day and 10^3 days (about 3 years) in the useful life of the workstation, it can search roughly 10^{13} over its life. Since such a workstation is worth on the order of $1,000 today, this works out to 10^{10} words searched for $1. (With the use of specialized hardware, this cost could be reduced significantly. For example, in the 1976 Book IV of the Senate Select Committee on Intelligence Report, R.L. Garwin describes the use of "match registers" to efficiently implement queries against a database; see Frank Church et al., U.S. Congress, *Senate Select Committee to Study Governmental Operations with Respect to Intelligence Activities*, U.S. Government Printing Office, Washington, D.C., 1976, Volume 4.)

[6]Other noncomputer-based technology for the clandestine gathering of information is widely available on the retail market. In recent years, concern over the ready availability of such equipment has grown. See, for example, Ross E. Milloy, "Spying Toys for Adults or Supplies for Crimes?," *New York Times*, August 28, 1995, p. A10; Pam Belluck, "A Shadow over the Spy-Shop Business," *New York Times*, September 22, 1995, p. B3; and James C. McKinley, Jr., "U.S. Agents Raid Stores in 24 Cities to Seize Spy Gear," *New York Times*, April 6, 1995, p. A1.

Appendix I of this report elaborates issues of information vulnerability in the context of key industries such as banking and financial services, health care, manufacturing, the petroleum industry, pharmaceuticals, the entertainment industry, and government.

1.4.2 Ensuring the Nation's Ability to Exploit Global Markets

With the increasing globalization of business operations, information technology plays a key role in maintaining the competitive strengths of U.S. business. In particular, U.S. businesses have proven adept at exploiting information and information technologies to create new market niches and expand old ones. This pattern has deep roots. For example, beginning in the 1960s, American Airlines pioneered in computerized reservations systems and extended use of the information captured and stored in such systems, generating an entire new business that is more profitable than air transport services. More recently, creative uses of information technology have advanced U.S. leadership in the production of entertainment products (e.g., movies and videos, recorded music, on-line services) for the world.

U.S. innovation in using information technology reflects in part the economic vitality that makes new technology affordable. It also reflects proximity to the research and production communities that supply key information technology products, communities with which a variety of U.S. industries have successfully exchanged talent, communicated their needs as customers, and collaborated in the innovation process. In other words, it is not an accident that innovation in both use and production of information technology has blossomed in the United States.

The business advantages enjoyed by U.S. companies that use information technology are one important reason that the health of U.S. computer, telecommunications, and information industries is important to the economy as a whole. A second important reason is the simple fact that the U.S. information technology sector (the set of industries that supply information technology goods and services) is the world's strongest.[7] The industry has an impressive record of product innovation; key U.S.

---

[7]For example, a staff study by the U.S. International Trade Commission found that 8 of the world's top 10 applications software vendors, 7 of the world's top 10 systems software vendors, the top 5 systems integration firms, and 8 of the top 10 custom programming firms are U.S. firms; the top 9 global outsourcing firms have headquarters in the United States. See Office of Industries, U.S. International Trade Commission, *Global Competitiveness of the U.S. Computer Software and Service Industries*, Staff Research Study #21, Washington, D.C., June 1995, Chapter 5.

products are de facto world standards; U.S. marketing and distribution capabilities for software products are unparalleled; and U.S. companies have considerable strengths in the manufacture of specialized semiconductor technologies and other key components. A strong information technology sector makes a significant contribution to the U.S. balance of payments and is responsible for large numbers of high-paying jobs. These strengths establish a firm foundation for continued growth in sales for U.S. information technology products and services as countries worldwide assimilate these technologies into their economies.

Finally, because of its technological leadership the United States should be better positioned to extend that lead, even if the specific benefits that may result are not known in advance. The head start in learning how to use information technology provides a high baseline on which U.S. individuals and organizations can build.

The committee believes that information technology is one of a few high-technology areas (others might include aerospace and electronics) that play a special role in the economic health of the nation, and that leadership in this area is one important factor underlying U.S. economic strength in the world today.[8] To the extent that this belief is valid, the economic dimension of national security and perhaps even traditional national security itself may well depend critically on a few key industries that are significant to military capabilities, the industrial base, and the overall economic health of the nation. Policy that acts against the health and global viability of these industries or that damages the ability of the private sector to exploit new markets and identify niches globally thus deserves the most careful scrutiny.

Because it is inevitable that other countries will expand their installed information technology bases and develop their own innovations and

---

[8]The committee acknowledges that there is a wide range of judgment among responsible economists on this matter. Some argue that the economy is so diverse that the fate of a single industry or even a small set of industries has a relatively small effect on broader economic trends. Others argue that certain industries are important enough to warrant subsidy or industrial policy to promote their interests. The committee discussed this specific issue to a considerable extent and found a middle ground between these two extremes—that information technology is one important industry among others, and that the health and well-being of that industry are important to the nation. This position is also supported by the U.S. government, which notes that telecommunications and computer hardware/software are among a number of industries that are of "strategic interest to the United States . . . because they produce classified products for the government, produce dual use technology used in both the public and private sectors, and are responsible for leading-edge technologies critical to maintaining U.S. economic security" (National Counterintelligence Center, *Annual Report to Congress on Foreign Economic Collection and Industrial Espionage*, Washington, D.C., July 1995, p. 15).

entrepreneurial strengths, U.S. leadership is not automatic. Already, evidence of such development is available, as these nations build on the falling costs of underlying technologies (e.g., microprocessors, aggregate communications bandwidth) and worldwide growth in relevant skills. The past three decades of information technology history provide enough examples of both successful first movers and strategic missteps to suggest that U.S. leadership can be either reinforced or undercut: leadership is an asset, and it is sensitive to both public policy and private action.

Public and private factors affecting the competitive health of U.S. information technology producers are most tightly coupled in the arena of foreign trade.[9] U.S. producers place high priority on ease of access to foreign markets. That access reflects policies imposed by U.S. and foreign governments, including governmental controls on what can be exported to whom. Export controls affect foreign trade in a variety of hardware, software, and communications systems.[10] They are the subject of chronic complaints from industry, to which government officials often respond by pointing to other, industry-centered explanations (e.g., deficiencies in product design or merchandising) for observed levels of foreign sales and market shares. Chapter 4 addresses export controls in the context of cryptography and national cryptography policy.

1.5 INDIVIDUAL AND PERSONAL INTERESTS IN PRIVACY

The emergence of the information age affects individuals as well as businesses and other organizations. As numerous reports argue, the nation's information infrastructure promises many opportunities for self-education, social exchange, recreation, personal business, cost-effective delivery of social programs, and entrepreneurship.[11] Yet the same tech-

---

[9]Of course, many intrafirm and intraindustry factors shape competitive strength, such as good management, adequate financing, good fit between products and consumer preferences, and so on.

[10]See, for example, John Harvey et al., *A Common-Sense Approach to High-Technology Export Controls*, Center for International Security and Arms Control, Stanford University, Stanford, Calif., March 1995; National Research Council, *Finding Common Ground: U.S. Export Controls in a Changed Global Environment*, National Academy Press, Washington, D.C., 1991; Computer Science and Technology Board, National Research Council, *Global Trends in Computer Technology and Their Impact on Export Control*, National Academy Press, Washington, D.C., 1988.

[11]See, for example, Computer Science and Telecommunications Board (CSTB), National Research Council, *The Unpredictable Certainty: Information Infrastructure Through 2000*, National Academy Press, Washington, D.C., 1996; CSTB, *White Papers: The Unpredictable Certainty*, 1996; and CSTB, *The Changing Nature of Telecommunications/Information Infrastructure*, 1995.

nologies that enable such benefits may also convey unwanted side effects. Some of those can be considered automated versions of problems seen in the paper world; others are either larger in scale or different in kind. For individuals, the area relevant to this report is privacy and the protection of personal information. Increasing reliance on electronic commerce and the use of networked communication for all manner of activities suggest that more information about more people will be stored in network-accessible systems and will be communicated more broadly and more often, thus raising questions about the security of that information.

Privacy is generally regarded as an important American value, a right whose assertion has not been limited to those "with something to hide." Indeed, assertion of the right to privacy as a matter of principle (rather than as an instrumental action) has figured prominently in U.S. political and social history; it is not merely abstract or theoretical.

In the context of an information age, an individual's privacy can be affected on two levels: privacy in the context of personal transactions (with businesses or other institutions and with other individuals), and privacy vis-à-vis governmental units. Both levels are affected by the availability of tools, such as cryptography in the context of information and communications systems, that can help to preserve privacy. Today's information security technology, for example, makes it possible to maintain or even raise the cost of collecting information about individuals. It also provides more mechanisms for government to help protect that information. The Clinton Administration has recognized concerns about the need to guard individual privacy, incorporating them into the security and privacy guidelines of its Information Infrastructure Task Force.[12] These guidelines represent an important step in the process of protecting individual privacy.

1.5.1 Privacy in an Information Economy

Today, the prospect of easier and more widespread collection and use of personal data as a byproduct of ordinary activities raises questions about inappropriate activities by industry, nosy individuals, and/or criminal elements in society. Criminals may obtain sensitive financial information to defraud individuals (credit card fraud, for example, amounts to approximately $20 per card per year). Insurance companies may use health data collected on individuals to decide whether to provide or deny health insurance—putting concerns about business profit-

---

[12]Information Infrastructure Task Force, National Information Infrastructure Security Issues Forum, *NII Security: The Federal Role,* Washington, D.C., June 5, 1995.

ability in possible conflict with individual and public health needs. On the other hand, much of the personal data in circulation is willingly divulged by individuals for specific purposes; the difficulty is that once shared, such information is available for additional uses. Controlling the further dissemination of personal data is a function both of procedures for how information should be used and of technology (including but not limited to cryptography) and procedures for restricting access to those authorized.

Given such considerations, individuals in an information age may wish to be able to:

• *Keep specific information private.* Disclosure of information of a personal nature that could be embarrassing if known, whether or not such disclosure is legal, is regarded as an invasion of privacy by many people. A letter to Ann Landers from a reader described his inadvertent eavesdropping on some very sensitive financial transactions being conducted on a cordless telephone.[13] A staff member of this study committee has heard broadcasts of conversations that apparently emanate from a next-door baby monitor whose existence has been forgotten. Home banking services using telephone lines or network connections and personal computers will result in the flow on public networks of large amounts of personal information regarding finances. Even the ad copy in some of today's consumer catalogues contains references to information security threats.[14]

• *Ensure that a party with whom they are transacting business is indeed the party he or she claims to be.* Likewise, they may seek to authenticate their own identity with confidence that such authentication will be accepted by other parties, and that anyone lacking such authentication will be denied the ability to impersonate them.[15] Such a capability is needed

---

[13]Ann Landers, "Ann Landers," *Washington Post,* Creators Syndicate, October 20, 1995, p. D5.

[14]For example, a catalogue from Comtrad Industries notes that "burglars use 'Code Grabbers' to open electric garage doors and break into homes," defining "code grabbers" as "devices that can record and play back the signal produced from your garage door remote control" (Comtrad Industries catalogue, 1995, p. 20). The Herrington catalogue advertises the "Enigma" phone scrambler by noting that "[a] recent *Wall Street Journal* article documents the increasing acceptance and prevalence of industrial espionage" and mentions as an "example of the alarming intrusion of the federal government into citizens' private lives" the fact that "the FBI petitioned Congress to further expand its wiretapping authority" (Herrington catalogue, Winter 1996, p. 13). Note that both of these mail-order firms cater to mainstream consumer sentiment.

[15]For example, a journalist who had reported on the trafficking of illegally copied software on America Online was the victim of hackers who assumed his on-line identity, thereby intercepting his e-mail messages and otherwise impersonating him. See Peter

to transfer money among mutual funds with a telephone call or to minimize unauthorized use of credit card accounts.[16] In an electronic domain without face-to-face communications or recognizable indicators such as voices and speech patterns (as used today in telephone calls), forgery of identity becomes increasingly easy.

• *Prevent the false repudiation of agreed-to transactions.* It is undesirable for a party to a transaction to be able to repudiate (deny) his agreement to the terms of the transaction. For example, an individual may agree to pay a certain price for a given product; he or she should not then be able to deny having made that agreement (as he or she might be tempted to do upon finding a lower price elsewhere).

• *Communicate anonymously* (i.e., carry out the opposite of authenticated communication). Individuals may wish to communicate anonymously to criticize the government or a supervisor, report illegal or unethical activity without becoming further involved, or obtain assistance for a problem that carries a social stigma. In other instances, they may simply wish to speak freely without fear of social reprisal or for the entertainment value of assuming a new digital identity in cyberspace.

• *Ensure the accuracy of data relevant to them.* Many institutions such as banks, financial institutions, and hospitals keep records on individuals. These individuals often have no personal control of the records, even though the integrity of the data in these records can be of crucial significance. Occasional publicity attests to instances of the inaccuracy of such data (e.g., credit records) and to the consequences for individuals.

Practical safeguards for privacy such as those outlined above may be more compelling than abstract or principled protection of a right to privacy.

Lewis, "Security Is Lost in Cyberspace," *New York Times*, February 22, 1995, p. D1. Other cases of "stolen identities" have been reported in the press, and while these cases remain relatively isolated, they are still a matter of public concern. Thieves forge signatures and impersonate the identities of law-abiding citizens to steal money from bank accounts and to obtain credit cards in the name of those citizens; see Charles Hall, "A Personal Approach to Stealing," *Washington Post*, April 1, 1996, p. A1.

[16]For example, a recent press article calls attention to security concerns raised by the ease of access to 401(k) retirement accounts (for which there is no cap on the liability incurred if a third party with unauthorized access transfers funds improperly). See Timothy Middleton, "Will Thieves Crack Your Automated Nest Egg?," *New York Times*, March 10, 1996, Business Section, p. 10. Another article describes a half-dozen easy-to-apply methods that can be used by criminals to undertake fraud. See Albert Crenshaw, "Creative Credit Card Crooks Draw High-Tech Response," *Washington Post*, August 6, 1995, Business Section, p. H1.

1.5.2 Privacy for Citizens

Public protection of privacy has been less active in the United States than in other countries, but the topic is receiving increasing attention. In particular, it has become an issue in the political agenda of people and organizations that have a wide range of concerns about the role and performance of government at all levels; it is an issue that attracts advocates from across the spectrum of political opinion. The politicization of privacy may inhibit the orderly consideration of relevant policy, including cryptography policy, because it revolves around the highly emotional issue of trust in government. The trust issue surfaced in the initial criticisms of the Clipper chip initiative proposal in 1993 (Chapter 5) and continues to color discussion of privacy policy generally and cryptography policy specifically.

To many people, freedom of expression and association, protection against undue governmental, commercial, or public intrusion into their personal affairs, and fair treatment by various authorities are concerns shaped by memories of highly publicized incidents in which such rights were flouted.[17] It can be argued that such incidents were detectable and correctable precisely because they involved government units that were obligated to be publicly accountable—and indeed, these incidents prompted new policies and procedures as well as greater public vigilance. It is also easy to dismiss them as isolated instances in a social system that for the most part works well. But where these episodes involve government, many of those skeptical about government believe that they demonstrate a capacity of government to violate civil liberties of

---

[17]Some incidents that are often cited include the surveillance of political dissidents, such as Martin Luther King, Jr., Malcolm X, and the Student Non-Violent Coordinating Committee in the mid to late 1960s; the activities of the Nixon "plumbers" in the late 1960s, including the harassment and surveillance of sitting and former government officials and journalists and their associates in the name of preventing leaks of sensitive national security information; U.S. intelligence surveillance of the international cable and telephone communications of U.S. citizens from the early 1940s through the early 1970s in support of FBI and other domestic law enforcement agencies; and the creation of FBI dossiers on opponents of the Vietnam War in the mid-1960s. The description of these events is taken largely from Frank J. Donner, *The Age of Surveillance*, Alfred A. Knopf, New York, 1980 (surveillance of political dissidents, pp. 244-248; plumbers, pp. 248-252; FBI dossiers on antiwar protesters, pp. 252-256; NSA surveillance, pp. 276-277). Donner's book documents many of these events. See also *Final Report of the Senate Select Committee to Study Governmental Operations with Respect to Intelligence Activities*, Book II, April 26, 1974, U.S. Government Printing Office, Washington, D.C., p. 12.

Americans who are exercising their constitutional rights.[18] This perception is compounded by attempts to justify past incidents as having been required for purposes of national security. Such an approach both limits public scrutiny and vitiates policy-based protection of personal privacy.

It is hard to determine with any kind of certainty the prevalence of the sentiments described in this section. By some measures, over half of the public is skeptical about government in general,[19] but whether that skepticism translates into widespread public concern about government surveillance is unclear. The committee believes that most people acting as private individuals feel that their electronic communications are secure and do not generally consider it necessary to take special precautions against threats to the confidentiality of those communications. These attitudes reflect the fact that most people, including many who are highly knowledgeable about the risks, do not give much conscious thought to these issues in their day-to-day activities.

At the same time, the committee acknowledges the concerns of many law-abiding individuals about government surveillance. It believes that such concerns and the questions they raise about individual rights and government responsibilities must be taken seriously. It would be inappropriate to dismiss such individuals as paranoid or overly suspicious. Moreover, even if only a minority is worried about government surveillance, it is an important consideration, given the nation's history as a

---

[18]For example, at the 4th Conference on Computers, Freedom, and Privacy in Chicago, Illinois, held in 1994, a government speaker asked the audience if they were more concerned about government abuse and harassment or about criminal activity that might be directed at them. An overwhelming majority of the audience indicated greater concern about the first possibility. For recent accounts that give the flavor of concerns about malfeasance by law enforcement officials, see Ronald Smothers, "Atlanta Holds Six Policemen in Crackdown," *New York Times*, September 7, 1995, p. 9; George James, "Police Officer Is Arrested on Burglary Charges in Sting Operation," *New York Times*, September 7, 1995, p. B5; Kenneth B. Noble, "Many Complain of Bias in Los Angeles Police," *New York Times*, September 4, 1995, p. 11; Kevin Sack, "Racism of a Rogue Officer Casts Suspicion on Police Nationwide," *New York Times*, September 4, 1995, p. 1; Gordon Witkin, "When the Bad Guys Are Cops," *U.S. News & World Report*, September 11, 1995, p. 20; Barry Tarlow, "Doing the Fuhrman Shuffle," *Washington Post*, August 27, 1995, p. C2; and David W. Dunlap, "F.B.I. Kept Watch on AIDS Group During Protest Years," *New York Times*, May 16, 1995, p. B3.

[19]For example, a national Harris poll in January 1994 asked "Which type of invasions of privacy worry you the most in America today—activities of government agencies or businesses?" Fifty-two percent said that government agencies were their greater worry, while 40% selected business. See Center for Social and Legal Research, *Privacy & American Business*, Volume 1(3), Hackensack, N.J., 1994, p. 7.

democracy,[20] for determining whether and how access to and use of cryptography may be considered a citizen's right (Chapter 7).

1.6 SPECIAL NEEDS OF GOVERNMENT

Government encompasses many functions that generate or depend on information, and current efforts to reduce the scope and size of government depend heavily on information technology. In many areas of government, the information and information security needs resemble those of industry (see Appendix I). Government also has important responsibilities beyond those of industry, including those related to public safety. For two of the most important and least understood in detail, law enforcement and national security, the need for strong information security has long been recognized.

Domestic law enforcement authorities in our society have two fundamental responsibilities: preventing crime and prosecuting individuals who have committed crimes. Crimes committed and prosecuted are more visible to the public than crimes prevented (see Chapter 3).

The following areas relevant to law enforcement require high levels of information security:

• *Prevention of information theft from businesses and individuals*, consistent with the transformation of economic and social activities outlined above.

• *Tactical law enforcement communications*. Law enforcement officials working in the field need secure communications. At present, police scanners available at retail electronics stores can monitor wireless com-

---

[20]Protecting communications from government surveillance is a time-honored technique for defending against tyranny. A most poignant example is the U.S. insistence in 1945 that the postwar Japanese constitution include protection against government surveillance of the communications of Japanese citizens. In the aftermath of the Japanese surrender in World War II, the United States drafted a constitution for Japan. The initial U.S. draft contained a provision saying that "[n]o censorship shall be maintained, nor shall the secrecy of any means of communication be violated." The Japanese response to this provision was a revised provision stating that "[t]he secrecy of letter and other means of communication is guaranteed to all of the people, provided that necessary measures to be taken for the maintenance of public peace and order, shall be provided by law." General Douglas MacArthur, who was supervising the drafting of the new Japanese constitution, insisted that the original provision regarding communications secrecy and most other provisions of the original U.S. draft be maintained. The Japanese agreed, this time requesting only minor changes in the U.S. draft and accepting fully the original U.S. provision on communications secrecy. See Osamu Nishi, *Ten Days Inside General Headquarters (GHQ): How the Original Draft of the Japanese Constitution Was Written in 1946*, Seibundo Publishing Co. Ltd., Tokyo, 1989.

munications channels used by police; criminals eavesdropping on such communications can receive advance warning of police responding to crimes being committed.

• *Efficient use by law enforcement officials of the large amounts of information compiled on criminal activity.* Getting the most use from such information implies that it be remotely accessible and not be improperly modified (assuming its accuracy and proper context, a requirement that in itself leads to much controversy[21]).

• *Reliable authentication of law enforcement officials.* Criminals have been known to impersonate law enforcement officials for nefarious purposes, and the information age presents additional opportunities.

In the domain of national security, traditional missions involve protection against military threats originating from other nation-states and directed against the interests of the United States or its friends and allies. These traditional missions require strong protection for vital information:

• U.S. military forces require secure communications. Without cryptography and other information security technologies in the hands of friendly forces, hostile forces can monitor the operational plans of friendly forces to gain an advantage.[22]

• Force planners must organize and coordinate flows of supplies, personnel, and equipment. Such logistical coordination involves databases whose integrity and confidentiality as well as remote access must be maintained.

• Sensitive diplomatic communications between the United States and its representatives or allies abroad, and/or between critical elements

---

[21]See, for example, U.S. General Accounting Office (GAO), *National Crime Information Center: Legislation Needed to Deter Misuse of Criminal Justice Information*, GAO/T-GGD-93-41, GAO, Washington, D.C., 1993.

[22]For example, the compromise of the BLACK code used by Allied military forces in World War II enabled German forces in Africa in 1942, led by General Erwin Rommel, to determine the British order of battle (quantities, types, and locations of forces), estimate British supply and morale problems, and know the tactical plans of the British. The compromise of one particular message enabled Rommel to thwart a critical British counterattack. In July of that year, the British switched to a new code, thus denying Rommel an important source of strategic intelligence. Rommel was thus surprised at the Battle of Alamein, widely regarded as a turning point in the conflict in the African theater. See David Kahn, *The Codebreakers: The Story of Secret Writing*, MacMillan, New York, 1967, pp. 472-477.

of the U.S. government, must be protected as part of the successful conduct of foreign affairs, even in peacetime.[23]

In addition, the traditional missions of national security have expanded in recent years to include protection against terrorists[24] and international criminals, especially drug cartels.[25] Furthermore, recognition has been growing that in an information age, economic security is part of national security.

More broadly, there is a practical convergence under way among protection of individual liberties, public safety, economic activity, and military security. For example, the nation is beginning to realize that critical elements of the U.S. civilian infrastructure—including the banking system, the air traffic control system, and the electric power grid—must be protected against the threats described above, as must the civilian information infrastructure that supports the conduct of sensitive government communications. Because civilian infrastructure provides a significant degree of functionality on which the military and defense sector depends, traditional national security interests are at stake as well, and concerns have grown about the implications of what has come to be known as information warfare (Box 1.9). More generally, the need for more secure systems, updated security policies, and effective procedural controls is taking on truly nationwide dimensions.

1.7 RECAP

Chapter 1 underscores the need for attention to protecting vital U.S. interests and values in an information age characterized by a number of trends:

- The world economy is in the midst of a transition from an indus-

---

[23]An agreement on Palestinian self-rule was reached in September 1995. According to public reports, the parties involved, Yasir Arafat (leader of the Palestinian Liberation Organization) and Shimon Peres (then Foreign Minister of Israel), depended heavily on the telephone efforts of Dennis Ross, a U.S. negotiator, in mediating the negotiations that led to the agreement. Obviously, in such circumstances, the security of these telephone efforts was critical. See Steven Greenhouse, "Twist to Shuttle Diplomacy: U.S. Aide Mediated by Phone," *New York Times*, September 25, 1995, p. 1.

[24]Terrorist threats generally emanate from nongovernmental groups, though at times involving the tacit or implicit (but publicly denied) support of sponsoring national governments. Furthermore, the United States is regarded by many parties as a particularly important target for political reasons by virtue of its prominence in world affairs. Thus, terrorists in confrontation with a U.S. ally may wish to make a statement by attacking the United States directly rather than its ally.

[25]See, for example, Phil Williams, "Transnational Criminal Organizations and International Security," *Survival*, Volume 36(1), Spring 1994, pp. 96-113.

BOX 1.9
Information Warfare

"Information warfare" (IW) is a term used in many different ways. Of most utility for this report is the definition of IW as hostile action that targets the information systems and information infrastructure of an opponent (i.e., offensive actions that attack an opponent's communications, weapon systems, command and control systems, intelligence systems, information components of the civil and societal infrastructure such as the power grid and banking system) coupled with simultaneous actions seeking to protect U.S. and allied systems and infrastructure from such attacks. Other looser uses of the term IW include the following:

• The use of information and tactical intelligence to apply weapon systems more effectively. IW may be used in connection with information-based suppression of enemy air defenses or "smart" weapons using sensor data to minimize the volume of ordnance needed to destroy a target.
• The targeting of companies' information systems for IW attacks. As industrial espionage spreads and/or international competitiveness drives multinational corporations into military-like escapades, the underlying notion of information-based probing of and attack on a competitor's information secrets could take on a flavor of intergovernment military or intelligence activities.
• The fight against terrorism, organized crime, and even street crime, which might be characterized as IW to the extent that information about these subjects is used to prosecute the battle. This usage is not widespread, although it may develop in the future.

Usage of the term has shifted somewhat as federal agencies, notably the Department of Defense, struggle to fully appreciate this new domain of warfare (or low-intensity conflict) and to create relevant policy and doctrine for it. Conversely, there is some discussion of the vulnerabilities of the U.S. civil information infrastructure to such offense. A broad range of activities can take place in information warfare:

• Physical destruction of information-handling facilities to destroy or degrade functionality;
• Denial of use of an opponent's important information systems;
• Degradation of effectiveness (e.g., accuracy, speed of response) of an opponent's information systems;
• Insertion of spurious, incorrect, or otherwise misleading data into an opponent's information systems (e.g., to destroy or modify data, or to subvert software processes via improper data inputs);
• Withdrawal of significant tactical or strategic data from an opponent's information systems;
• Insertion of malicious software into an opponent's system to affect its intended behavior in various ways and, perhaps, to do so at a time controlled by the aggressor; and
• Subversion of an opponent's software and/or hardware installation to make it an in-place self-reporting mole for intelligence purposes.

As an operational activity, information warfare clearly is related closely to, but yet is distinct from, intelligence functions that are largely analytical. IW is also related to information security, since its techniques are pertinent both to prosecution of offensive IW and to protection for defensive IW.

trial to an information age in which information products are extensively bought and sold, information assets provide leverage in undertaking business activities, and communications assume ever-greater significance in the lives of ordinary citizens. At the same time, national economies are increasingly interlinked across national borders, with the result that international dimensions of public policy are important.

• Trends in information technology suggest an ever-increasing panoply of technologies and technology-enabled services characterized by high degrees of heterogeneity, enormous computing power, and large data storage and transmission capabilities.

• Given the transition to a global information society and trends in information technology, the future of individuals and businesses alike is likely to be one in which information of all types plays a central role. Electronic commerce in particular is likely to become a fundamental underpinning of the information future.

• Government has special needs for information security that arise from its role in society, including the protection of classified information and its responsibility for ensuring the integrity of information assets on which the entire nation depends.

Collectively, these trends suggest that future needs for information security will be large. Threats to information security will emerge from a variety of different sources, and they will affect the confidentiality and integrity of data and the reliable authentication of users; these threats do and will affect businesses, government, and private individuals.

Chapter 2 describes how cryptography may help to address all of these problems.

2

Cryptography:
Roles, Market, and Infrastructure

Cryptography is a technology that can play important roles in addressing certain types of information vulnerability, although it is not sufficient to deal with all threats to information security. As a technology, cryptography is embedded into products that are purchased by a large number of users; thus, it is important to examine various aspects of the market for cryptography. Chapter 2 describes cryptography as a technology used in products, as a product within a larger market context, and with reference to the infrastructure needed to support its large-scale use.

2.1 CRYPTOGRAPHY IN CONTEXT

Computer system security, and its extension network security, are intended to achieve many purposes. Among them are safeguarding physical assets from damage or destruction and ensuring that resources such as computer time, network connections, and access to databases are available only to individuals—or to other systems or even software processes—authorized to have them.[1] Overall information security is dependent on many factors, including various technical safeguards, trustworthy and capable personnel, high degrees of physical security, competent administrative oversight, and good operational procedures. Of the avail-

---

[1] The term "information security" and shortened versions such as INFOSEC, COMPSEC, and NETSEC are also in use.

able technical safeguards, cryptography has been one of the least utilized to date.[2]

In general, the many security safeguards in a system or network not only fulfill their principal task but also act collectively to mutually protect one another. In particular, the protection or operational functionality that can be afforded by the various cryptographic safeguards treated in this report will inevitably require that the hardware or software in question be embedded in a secure environment. To do otherwise is to risk that the cryptography might be circumvented, subverted, or misused—hence leading to a weakening or collapse of its intended protection.

As individual stand-alone computer systems have been incorporated into ever larger networks (e.g., local area networks, wide area networks, the Internet), the requirements for cryptographic safeguards have also increased. For example, users of the earliest computer systems were almost always clustered in one place and could be personally recognized as authorized individuals, and communications associated with a computer system usually were contained within a single building. Today, users of computer systems can be connected with one another worldwide, through the public switched telecommunications network, a local area network, satellites, microwave towers, and radio transmitters. Operationally, an individual or a software process in one place can request service from a system or a software process in a far distant place. Connectivity among systems is impromptu and occurs on demand; the Internet has demonstrated how to achieve it. Thus, it is now imperative for users and systems to identify themselves to one another with a high degree of certainty and for distant systems to know with certainty what privileges for accessing databases or software processes a remote request brings. Protection that could once be obtained by geographic propinquity and personal recognition of users must now be provided electronically and with extremely high levels of certainty.

2.2 WHAT IS CRYPTOGRAPHY AND WHAT CAN IT DO?

The word "cryptography" is derived from Greek words that mean secret writing. Historically, cryptography has been used to hide informa-

---

[2]Other safeguards, in particular software safeguards, are addressed in various standard texts and reports. See, for example, National Institute of Standards and Technology, *An Introduction to Computer Security*, NIST Special Publication 800-12, Department of Commerce, Washington, D.C., October 1995; Department of Defense, *Trusted Computer System Evaluation Criteria*, August 15, 1983; Computer Science and Telecommunications Board, National Research Council, *Computers at Risk: Safe Computing in the Information Age*, National Academy Press, Washington, D.C., 1991.

tion from access by unauthorized parties, especially during communications when it would be most vulnerable to interception. By preserving the secrecy, or confidentiality, of information, cryptography has played a very important role over the centuries in military and national affairs.[3]

In the traditional application of cryptography for confidentiality, an originator (the *first party*) creates a message intended for a recipient (the *second party*), protects (*encrypts*) it by a cryptographic process, and transmits it as *ciphertext*. The receiving party *decrypts* the received ciphertext message to reveal its true content, the *plaintext*. Anyone else (the *third party*) who wishes undetected and unauthorized access to the message must penetrate (by *cryptanalysis*) the protection afforded by the cryptographic process.

In the classical use of cryptography to protect communications, it is necessary that both the originator and the recipient(s) have common knowledge of the cryptographic process (the *algorithm* or *cryptographic algorithm*) and that both share a secret common element—typically, the key or cryptographic key, which is a piece of information, not a material object. In the encryption process, the algorithm transforms the plaintext into the ciphertext, using a particular key; the use of a different key results in a different ciphertext. In the decryption process, the algorithm transforms the ciphertext into the plaintext, using the key that was used to encrypt[4] the original plaintext. Such a scheme, in which both communicating parties must have a common key, is now called *symmetric cryptography* or *secret-key cryptography*; it is the kind that has been used for centuries and written about widely.[5] It has the property, usually an operational disadvantage, of requiring a safe method of distributing keys to relevant parties (*key distribution* or *key management*).

It can be awkward to arrange for symmetric and secret keys to be available to all parties with whom one might wish to communicate, especially when the list of parties is large. However, a scheme called *asymmetric cryptography* (or, equivalently, *public-key cryptography*), developed in the mid-1970s, helps to mitigate many of these difficulties through the use

---

[3]The classic work on the history of cryptography is David Kahn, *The Codebreakers*, MacMillan, New York, 1967.

[4]This report uses the term "encrypt" to describe the act of using an encryption algorithm with a given key to transform one block of data, usually plaintext, into another block, usually ciphertext.

[5]Historical perspective is provided in David Kahn, *Kahn on Codes*, MacMillan, New York, 1983; F.W. Winterbotham, *The Ultra Secret*, Harper & Row, New York, 1974; and Ronald Lewin, *Ultra Goes to War*, Hutchinson & Co., London, 1978. A classic reference on the fundamentals of cryptography is Dorothy Denning, *Cryptography and Data Security*, Addison-Wesley, Reading, Mass., 1982.

of different keys for encryption and decryption.[6] Each participant actually has two keys. The public key is published, is freely available to anyone, and is used for encryption; the private key is held in secrecy by the user and is used for decryption.[7] Because the two keys are inverses, knowledge of the public key enables the derivation of the private key in theory. However, in a well-designed public-key system, it is computationally infeasible in any reasonable length of time to derive the private key from knowledge of the public key.

A significant operational difference between symmetric and asymmetric cryptography is that with asymmetric cryptography anyone who knows a given person's public key can send a secure message to that person. With symmetric cryptography, only a selected set of people (those who know the private key) can communicate. While it is not mathematically provable, all known asymmetric cryptographic systems are slower than their symmetric cryptographic counterparts, and the more public nature of asymmetric systems lends credence to the belief that this will always be true. Generally, symmetric cryptography is used when a large amount of data needs to be encrypted or when the encryption must be done within a given time period; asymmetric cryptography is used for short messages, for example, to protect key distribution for a symmetric cryptographic system.

Regardless of the particular approach taken, the applications of cryptography have gone beyond its historical roots as secret writing; today, cryptography serves as a powerful tool in support of system security. Cryptography can provide many useful capabilities:

• *Confidentiality*—the characteristic that information is protected from being viewed in transit during communications and/or when stored in an information system. With cryptographically provided confidentiality, encrypted information can fall into the hands of someone not authorized to view it without being compromised. It is almost entirely the confidentiality aspect of cryptography that has posed public policy dilemmas.

The other capabilities, described below, can be considered collectively as *nonconfidentiality* or *collateral* uses of cryptography:

---

[6]Gustavus J. Simmons (ed.), *Contemporary Cryptology: The Science of Information Integrity*, IEEE Press, Piscataway, N.J., 1992; Whitfield Diffie, "The First Ten Years of Public-Key Cryptography," *Proceedings of the IEEE*, Volume 76, 1988, pp. 560-577.

[7]The seminal paper on public-key cryptography is Whitfield Diffie and Martin Hellman, "New Directions in Cryptography," *IEEE Transactions on Information Theory*, Volume IT-22, 1976, pp. 644-654.

- *Authentication*—cryptographically based assurance that an asserted identity is valid for a given person (or computer system). With such assurance, it is difficult for an unauthorized party to impersonate an authorized one.
- *Integrity check*—cryptographically based assurance that a message or computer file has not been tampered with or altered.[8] With such assurance, it is difficult for an unauthorized party to alter data.
- *Digital signature*—cryptographically based assurance that a message or file was sent or created by a given person. A digital signature cryptographically binds the identity of a person with the contents of the message or file, thus providing *nonrepudiation*—the inability to deny the authenticity of the message or file. The capability for nonrepudiation results from encrypting the digest (or the message or file itself) with the private key of the signer. Anyone can verify the signature of the message or file by decrypting the signature using the public key of the sender. Since only the sender should know his or her own private key, assurance is provided that the signature is valid and the sender cannot later repudiate the message. If a person divulges his or her private key to any other party, that party can impersonate the person in all electronic transactions.
- *Digital date/time stamp*—cryptographically based assurance that a message or file was sent or created at a given date and time. Generally, such assurance is provided by an authoritative organization that appends a date/time stamp and digitally signs the message or file.

These cryptographic capabilities can be used in complementary ways. For example, authentication is basic to controlling access to system or network resources. A person may use a password to authenticate his own identity; only when the proper password has been entered will the system allow the user to "log on" and obtain access to files, e-mail, and so on.[9] But passwords have many limitations as an access control measure (e.g., people tell others their passwords or a password is learned via eavesdropping), and cryptographic authentication techniques can provide

---

[8]Digital signatures and integrity checks use a condensed form of a message or file—called a digest—which is created by passing the message or file through a one-way hash function. The digest is of fixed length and is independent of the size of the message or file. The hash function is designed to make it highly unlikely that different messages (or files) will yield the same digest, and to make it computationally very difficult to modify a message (or file) but retain the same digest.

[9]An example more familiar to many is that the entry of an appropriate personal identification number into an automatic teller machine (ATM) gives the ATM user access to account balances or cash.

much better and more effective mechanisms for limiting system or resource access to authorized parties.

Access controls can be applied at many different points within a system. For example, the use of a dial-in port on an information system or network can require the use of cryptographic access controls to ensure that only the proper parties can use the system or network at all. Many systems and networks accord privileges or access to resources depending on the specific identity of a user; thus, a hospital information system may grant physicians access that allows entering orders for patient treatment, whereas laboratory technicians may not have such access. Authentication mechanisms can also be used to generate an audit trail identifying those who have accessed particular data, thus facilitating a search for those known to have compromised confidential data.

In the event that access controls are successfully bypassed, the use of encryption on data stored and communicated in a system provides an extra layer of protection. Specifically, if an intruder is denied easy access to stored files and communications, he may well find it much more difficult to understand the internal workings of the system and thus be less capable of causing damage or reading the contents of encrypted inactive data files that may hold sensitive information. Of course, when an application opens a data file for processing, that data is necessarily unencrypted and is vulnerable to an intruder that might be present at that time.

Authentication and access control can also help to protect the privacy of data stored on a system or network. For example, a particular database application storing data files in a specific format could allow its users to view those files. If the access control mechanisms are set up in such a way that only certain parties can access that particular database application, then access to the database files in question can be limited and the privacy of data stored in those databases protected. On the other hand, an unauthorized user may be able to obtain access to those files through a different, uncontrolled application, or even through the operating system itself. Thus, encryption of those files is necessary to protect them against such "back-door" access.[10]

The various cryptographic capabilities described above may be used within a system in order to accomplish a set of tasks. For example, a

---

[10]The measure-countermeasure game can continue indefinitely. In response to file encryption, an intruder can insert into an operating system a Trojan horse program that waits for an authorized user to access the encrypted database. Since the user is authorized, the database will allow the decryption of the relevant file, and the intruder can simply "piggyback" on that decryption. Thus, those responsible for system security must provide a way to check for Trojan horses, and so the battle goes round.

banking system may require confidentiality and integrity assurances on its communications links, authentication assurances for all major processing functions, and integrity and authentication assurances for high-value transactions. On the other hand, merchants may need only digital signatures and date/time stamps when dealing with external customers or cooperating banks when establishing contracts. Furthermore, depending on the type of capability to be provided, the underlying cryptographic algorithms may or may not be different.

Finally, when considering what cryptography can do, it is worth making two practical observations. First, the initial deployment of any technology often brings out unanticipated problems, simply because the products and artifacts embodying that technology have not had the benefit of successive cycles of failure and repair. Similarly, human procedures and practices have not been tested against the demands of real-life experience. Cryptography is unlikely to be any different, and so it is probable that early large-scale deployments of cryptography will exhibit exploitable vulnerabilities.[11]

The second point is that against a determined opponent that is highly motivated to gain unauthorized access to data, the use of cryptography may well simply lead that opponent to exploit some other vulnerability in the system or network on which the relevant data is communicated or stored, and such an exploitation may well be successful. But the use of cryptography can help to raise the cost of gaining improper access to data and may prevent a resource-poor opponent from being successful at all.

More discussion of cryptography can be found in Appendix C.

2.3 HOW CRYPTOGRAPHY FITS INTO THE BIG SECURITY PICTURE

In the context of confidentiality, the essence of information security is a battle between information protectors and information interceptors. Protectors—who may be motivated by "good" reasons (if they are legitimate businesses) or "bad" reasons (if they are criminals)—wish to restrict access to information to a group that they select. Interceptors—who may also be motivated by "bad" reasons (if they are unethical business competitors) or "good" reasons (if they are law enforcement agents investigating serious crimes)—wish to obtain access to the information being protected whether or not they have the permission of the information protectors. It is this dilemma that is at the heart of the public policy controversy and is addressed in greater detail in Chapter 3.

---

[11]For a discussion of this point, see Ross Anderson, "Why Cryptosystems Fail," *Communications of the ACM*, Volume 37(11), November 1994, pp. 32-40.

From the perspective of the information interceptor, encryption is only one of the problems to be faced. In general, the complexity of today's information systems poses many technical barriers (Section 2.3.1). On the other hand, the information interceptor may be able to exploit product features or specialized techniques to gain access (Section 2.3.2).

2.3.1 Factors Inhibiting Access to Information[12]

Compared to the task of tapping an analog telephone line, obtaining access to the content of a digital information stream can be quite difficult. With analog "listening" (traditional telephony or radio interception), the technical challenge is obtaining access to the communications channel. When communications are digitized, gaining access to the channel is only the first step: one must then unravel the digital format, a task that can be computationally very complex. Furthermore, the complexity of the digital format tends to increase over time, because more advanced information technology generally implies increased functionality and a need for more efficient use of available communications capacity.

Increased complexity is reflected in particular in the interpretation of the digital stream that two systems might use to communicate with each other or the format of a file that a system might use to store data. Consider, for example, one particular sequence of actions used to communicate information. The original application in the sending system might have started with a plaintext message, and then compressed it (to make it smaller); encrypted it (to conceal its meaning); and appended error-control bits to the compressed, encrypted message (to prevent errors from creeping in during transmission).[13] Thus, a party attempting to intercept a communication between the sender and the receiver could be faced with a data stream that would represent the combined output of many different operations that transform the data stream in some way. The interceptor would have to know the error-control scheme and the decompression algorithms as well as the key and the algorithm used to encrypt the message.

When an interceptor moves onto the lines that carry bulk traffic, iso-

---

lating the bits associated with a particular communication of interest is itself quite difficult.[14] A high-bandwidth line (e.g., a long-haul fiber-optic cable) typically carries hundreds or thousands of different communications; any given message may be broken into distinct packets and intermingled with other packets from other contemporaneously operating applications.[15] The traffic on the line may be encrypted "in bulk" by the line provider, thus providing an additional layer of protection against the interceptor. Moreover, since a message traveling from point A to point B may well be broken into packets that traverse different physical paths en route, an interceptor at any given point between A and B may not even see all of the packets pass by.

Another factor inhibiting access to information is the use of technologies that facilitate anonymous communications. For the most part, intercepted communications are worthless if the identity of the communicating parties is not known. In telephony, call forwarding and pager callbacks from pay telephones have sometimes frustrated the efforts of law enforcement officials conducting wiretaps. In data communications, so-called anonymous remailers can strip out all identifying information from an Internet e-mail message sent from person A to person B in such a way that person B does not know the identity of person A. Some remailers even support return communications from person B to person A without the need for person B to know the identity of person A.

Access is made more difficult because an information protector can switch communications from one medium to another very easily without changing end-user equipment. Some forms of media may be easily accessed by an interceptor (e.g., conventional radio), whereas other forms may be much more challenging (e.g., fiber-optic cable, spread-spectrum radio). The proliferation of different media that can interoperate smoothly even at the device level will continue to complicate the interceptor's attempts to gain access to communications.

Finally, obtaining access also becomes more difficult as the number of service providers increases (Box 2.1). In the days when AT&T held a

---

[14]This point is made independently in a report that came to the attention of the committee as this report was going to press. A staff study of the Permanent Select Committee on Intelligence, U.S. House of Representatives, concluded that "the ability to filter through the huge volumes of data and to extract the information from the layers of formatting, multiplexing, compression, and transmission protocols applied to each message is the biggest challenge of the future, [while] increasing amounts and sophistication of encryption add another layer of complexity" (*IC21: Intelligence Community in the 21st Century*, U.S. Government Printing Office, Washington, D.C., p. 121).

[15]Paul Haskell and David G. Messerschmitt, "In Favor of an Enhanced Network Interface for Multimedia Services," submitted to *IEEE Multimedia Magazine*.

BOX 2.1
The Evolution of the Telecommunications Industry

Prior to 1984, the U.S. telecommunications industry was dominated by one primary player—AT&T. An elaborate regulatory structure had evolved in the preceding decades to govern what had become an essential national service on which private citizens, government, and business had come to rely.

By contrast, the watchword in telecommunications a mere decade later has become competition. AT&T is still a major player in the field, but the regional Bell operating companies (RBOCs), separated from AT&T as part of the divestiture decision of 1984, operate entirely independently, providing local services. Indeed, the current mood in Congress toward deregulation is already causing increasingly active competition and confrontation among all of the players involved, including cable TV companies, cellular and mobile telephone companies, the long-distance telecommunications companies (AT&T, MCI, Sprint, and hundreds of others), the RBOCs and other local exchange providers, TV and radio broadcast companies, entertainment companies, and satellite communications companies. Today, all of these players compete for a share of the telecommunications pie in the same geographic area; even railroads and gas companies (which own geographic rights of way along which transmission lines can be laid) and power companies (which have wires going to every house) have dreams of profiting from the telecommunications boom. The playing field is even further complicated by the fact of reselling—institutions often buy telecommunications services from "primary" providers in bulk to serve their own needs and resell the excess to other customers.

In short, today's telecommunications industry is highly heterogeneous and widely deployed with multiple public and private service providers, and will become more so in the future.

---

monopoly on voice communications and criminal communications could generally be assumed to be carried on AT&T-operated lines, law enforcement and national security authorities needed only one point of contact with whom to work. As the telecommunications industry becomes increasingly heterogeneous, law enforcement authorities may well be uncertain about what company to approach about implementing a wiretap request.

2.3.2 Factors Facilitating Access to Information

System or Product Design

Unauthorized access to protected information can inadvertently be facilitated by product or system features that are intended to provide legitimate access but instead create unintentional loopholes or weaknesses that can be exploited by an interceptor. Such points of access may be deliberately incorporated into product or system designs, and they include the following:

- *Maintenance and monitoring ports.*[16] For example, many telephone switches and computer systems have dial-in ports that are intended to facilitate monitoring and remote maintenance and repair by off-site technicians.
- *Master keys.* A product can have a single master key that allows its possessor to decrypt all ciphertext produced by the product.
- *Mechanisms for key escrow or key backup.* A third party, for example, may store an extra copy of a private key or a master key. Under appropriate circumstances, the third party releases the key to the appropriate individual(s), who is (are) then able to decrypt the ciphertext in question. This subject is discussed at length in Chapter 5.
- *Weak encryption defaults.* A product capable of providing very strong encryption may be designed in such a way that users invoke those capabilities only infrequently. For example, encryption on a secure telephone may be designed so that the use of encryption depends on the user pressing a button at the start of a telephone call. The requirement to press a button to invoke encryption is an example of a weak default, because the telephone could be designed so that encryption is invoked automatically when a call is initiated; when weak defaults are designed into systems, many users will forget to press the button.

Despite the good reasons for designing systems and products with these various points of access (e.g., facilitating remote access through maintenance ports to eliminate travel costs of system engineers), any such point of access can be exploited by unauthorized individuals as well.

Methods Facilitating Access to Information

Surreptitious access to communications can also be gained by methods such as the following:

- *Interception in the ether.* Many point-to-point communications make use of a wireless (usually radio) link at some point in the process. Since it is impossible to ensure that a radio broadcast reaches only its intended receiver(s), communications carried over wireless links—such as those involving cellular telephones and personal pagers—are vulnerable to interception by unauthorized parties.

---

[16]A port is a point of connection to a given information system to which another party (another system, an individual) can connect.

- *Use of pen registers.* Telephone communications involve both the content of a call and call-setup information such as numbers called, originating number, time and length of call, and so on. Setup information is often easily accessible, some of it even to end users.[17]

- *Wiretapping.* To obtain the contents of a call carried exclusively by nonwireless means, the information carried on a circuit (actually, a replica of the information) is sent to a monitoring station. A call can be wiretapped when an eavesdropper picks up an extension on the same line, hooks up a pair of alligator clips to the right set of terminals, or obtains the cooperation of telephone company officials in monitoring a given call at a chosen location.

- *Exploitation of related data.* A great deal of useful information can be obtained by examining in detail a digital stream that is associated with a given communication. For example, people have developed communications protocol analyzers that examine traffic as it flows by a given point for passwords and other sensitive information.

- *Reverse engineering* (discussed in greater detail in Chapter 5). Decompilation or disassembly of software can yield deep understanding of how that software works. One implication is that any algorithm built into software cannot be assumed to be secret for very long, since disassembly of the software will inevitably reveal it to a technically trained individual.

- *Cryptanalysis* (discussed in greater detail in Appendix C). Cryptanalysis is the task of recovering the plaintext corresponding to a given ciphertext without knowledge of the decrypting key. Successful cryptanalysis can be the result of:

— *Inadequately sized keys.* A product with encryption capabilities that implements a strong cryptographic algorithm with an inadequately sized key is vulnerable to a "brute-force" attack.[18] Box 2.2 provides more detail.

—*Weak encryption algorithms.* Some encryption algorithms have weaknesses that, if known to an attacker, require the testing of only a small fraction of the keys that could in principle be the proper key.

- *Product flaws.* Like weak encryption, certain design choices such as limits on the maximum size of a password, the lack of a reasonable lower bound on the size of a password, or use of a random number generator that is not truly random may lead to a product that presents a work factor

---

[17]"Caller ID," a feature that identifies the number of the calling party, makes use of call-setup information carried on the circuit.

[18]A brute-force attack against an encryption algorithm is a computer-based test of all possible keys for that algorithm undertaken in an effort to discover the key that actually has been used. Hence, the difficulty and time to complete such attacks increase markedly as the key length grows (specifically, the time doubles for every bit added to the key length).

BOX 2.2
Fundamentals of Cryptographic Strength

Cryptographic strength depends on two factors: the size of the key and the mathematical structure of the algorithm itself. For well-designed symmetric cryptographic systems, "brute-force" exhaustive search—trying all possible keys with a given decryption algorithm until the (meaningful) plaintext appears—is the best publicly known cryptanalytic method. For such systems the work factor (i.e., the time to cryptanalyze) grows exponentially with key size. Hence, with a sufficiently long key, even an eavesdropper with very extensive computing resources would have to take a very long time (longer than the age of the universe) to test all possible combinations. Adding one binary digit (bit) to the length of a key doubles the length of time it takes to undertake a brute-force attack while adding only a very small increment (or sometimes none at all) to the time it takes to encrypt the plaintext.

How long is a "long" key? To decipher by brute force a message encrypted with a 40-bit key requires 2^{40} (approximately 10^{12}) tests. If each test takes 10^{-6} seconds to conduct, 1 million seconds of testing time on a single computer are required to conduct a brute-force attack, or about 11.5 days. A 56-bit key increases this time by a factor of 2^{16}, or 65,536; under the same assumptions, a brute-force attack on a message encrypted with a 56-bit key would take over 2,000 years.

Two important considerations mitigate the bleakness of this conclusion from the perspective of the interceptor. One is that computers can be expected to grow more powerful over time. Speed increases in the underlying silicon technology have exhibited a predictable pattern for the past 50 years—computational speed doubles every 18 months (Moore's law), equivalent to increasing by a factor of 10 every 5 years. Thus, if a single test takes 10^{-6} seconds today, in 15 years it can be expected to take 10^{-9} seconds. Additional speedup is possible using parallel processing. Some supercomputers use tens of thousands of microprocessors in parallel, and cryptanalytic problems are particularly well suited to parallel processing. But even 1,000 processors working in parallel, each using the underlying silicon technology of 15 years hence, would be able to decrypt a single 56-bit encrypted message in 18 hours.

As for the exploitation of alternatives to brute-force search, all known asymmetric (i.e., public-key) cryptographic systems allow shortcuts to exhaustive search. Because more information is public in such systems, it is also likely that shortcut attacks will exist for any new systems invented. Shortcut attacks also exist for poorly designed symmetric systems. Newly developed shortcut attacks constitute unforeseen breakthroughs, and so by their very nature introduce an unpredictable "wild card" into the effort to set a reasonable key size. Because such attacks are applicable primarily to public-key systems, larger key sizes and larger safety margins are needed for such systems than for symmetric cryptographic systems. For example, factoring a 512-bit number by exhaustive search would take 2^{256} tests (since at least one factor must be less than 2^{256}); known shortcut attacks would allow such numbers to be factored in approximately 2^{65} operations, a number on the order of that required to undertake a brute-force exhaustive search of a message encrypted with a 64-bit symmetric cryptographic system. While symmetric 64-bit systems are considered relatively safe, fear of future breakthroughs in cryptanalyzing public-key systems has led many cryptographers to suggest a minimum key size of 1,024 bits for public-key systems, thereby providing in key length a factor-of-two safety margin over the safety afforded by 512-bit keys.

More discussion of this topic can be found in Appendix C.

for an attacker that is much smaller than the theoretical strength implied by the algorithm it uses.[19]

• *Monitoring of electronic emissions.* Most electronic communications devices emit electromagnetic radiation that is highly correlated with the information carried or displayed on them. For example, the contents of an unshielded computer display or terminal can in principle be read from a distance (estimates range from tens of meters to hundreds of meters) by equipment specially designed to do so. Coined by a U.S. government program, TEMPEST is the name of a class of techniques to safeguard against monitoring of emissions.

• *Device penetration.* A software-controlled device can be penetrated in a number of ways. For example, a virus may infect it, making a clandestine change. A message or a file can be sent to an unwary recipient who activates a hidden program when the message is read or the file is opened; such a program, once active, can record the keystrokes of the person at the keyboard, scan the mass storage media for sensitive data and transmit it, or make clandestine alterations to stored data.

• *Infrastructure penetration.* The infrastructure used to carry communications is often based on software-controlled devices such as routers. Router software can be modified as described above to copy and forward all (or selected) traffic to an unauthorized interceptor.

The last two techniques can be categorized as invasive, because they alter the operating environment in order to gather or modify information. In a network environment, the most common mechanisms of invasive attacks are called viruses and Trojan horses. A virus gains access to a system, hides within that system, and replicates itself to infect other systems. A Trojan horse exploits a weakness from within a system. Either approach can result in intentional or unintentional denial of services for the host system.[20] Modern techniques for combining both techniques to covertly exfiltrate data from a system are becoming increasingly powerful

---

[19]"Work factor" is used in this report to mean a measure of the difficulty of undertaking a brute-force test of all possible keys against a given ciphertext (and known algorithm). A 40-bit work factor means that a brute-force attack must test at most 2^{40} keys to be certain that the corresponding plaintext message is retrieved. In the literature, the term "work factor" is also used to mean the ratio of work needed for brute-force cryptanalysis of an encrypted message to the work needed to encrypt that message.

[20]On November 2, 1988, Robert T. Morris, Jr., released a "worm" program that spread itself throughout the Internet over the course of the next day. At trial, Morris maintained that he had not intended to cause the effects that had resulted, a belief held by many in the Internet community. Morris was convicted on a felony count of unauthorized access. See Peter G. Neumann, *Computer-Related Risks*, Addison-Wesley, Reading, Mass., 1995, p. 133.

and difficult to detect.[21] Such attacks will gain in popularity as networks become more highly interconnected.

2.4 THE MARKET FOR CRYPTOGRAPHY

Cryptography is a product as well as a technology. Products offering cryptographic capabilities can be divided into two general classes:

• *Security-specific* or *stand-alone* products that are generally add-on items (often hardware, but sometimes software) and often require that users perform an operationally separate action to invoke the encryption capabilities. Examples include an add-on hardware board that encrypts messages or a program that accepts a plaintext file as input and generates a ciphertext file as output.

• *Integrated* (often "general-purpose") products in which cryptographic functions have been incorporated into some software or hardware application package as part of its overall functionality. An integrated product is designed to provide a capability that is useful in its own right, as well as encryption capabilities that a user may or may not use. Examples include a modem with on-board encryption or a word processor with an option for protecting (encrypting) files with passwords.[22]

---

[21]The popular World Wide Web provides an environment in which an intruder can act to steal data. For example, an industrial spy wishing to obtain data stored on the information network of a large aerospace company can set up a Web page containing information of interest to engineers at the aerospace company (e.g., information on foreign aerospace business contracts in the making), thereby making the page an attractive site for those engineers to visit through the Web. Once an engineer from the company has visited the spy's Web page, a channel is set up by which the Web page can send back a Trojan horse (TH) program for execution on the workstation being used to look at the page. The TH can be passed as part of any executable program (Java and Postscript provide two such vehicles) that otherwise does useful things but on the side collects data resident on that workstation (and any other computers to which it might be connected). Once the data is obtained, it can be sent back to the spy's Web page during the same session, or e-mailed back, or sent during the next session used to connect to that Web page. Furthermore, because contacts with a Web page by design provide the specific address from which the contact is coming, the TH can be sent only to the aerospace company (and to no one else), thus reducing the likelihood that anyone else will stumble upon it. Furthermore, the Web page contact also provides information about the workstation that is making the contact, thus permitting a customized and specially debugged TH to be sent to that workstation.

[22]From a system design perspective, it is reasonable to assert that word processing and database applications do not have an intrinsic requirement for encryption capabilities and that such capabilities could be better provided by the operating system on which these applications operate. But as a practical matter, operating systems often do not provide such capabilities, and so vendors have significant incentives to provide encryption capabilities that are useful to customers who want better security.

In addition, an integrated product may provide sockets or hooks to user-supplied modules or components that offer additional cryptographic functionality. An example is a software product that can call upon a user-supplied package that performs certain types of file manipulation such as encryption or file compression. Cryptographic sockets are discussed in Chapter 7 as cryptographic applications programming interfaces.

A product with cryptographic capabilities can be designed to provide data confidentiality, data integrity, and user authentication in any combination; a given commercial cryptographic product may implement functionality for any or all of these capabilities. For example, a PC card may integrate cryptographic functionality for secure authentication and for encryption onto the same piece of hardware, even though the user may choose to invoke these functions independently. A groupware program for remote collaboration may implement cryptography for confidentiality (by encrypting messages sent between users) and cryptography for data integrity and user authentication (by appending a digital signature to all messages sent between users). Further, this program may be implemented in a way that these features can operate independently (either, both, or neither may be operative at the same time).

Because cryptography is usable only when it is incorporated into a product, whether integrated or security-specific, issues of supply and demand affect the use of cryptography. The remainder of this section addresses both demand and supply perspectives on the cryptography market.

2.4.1 The Demand Side of the Cryptography Market

Chapter 1 discussed vulnerabilities that put the information assets of businesses and individuals at risk. But despite the presence of such risks, many organizations do not undertake adequate information security efforts, whether those efforts involve cryptography or any other tool. This section explores some of the reasons for this behavior.

Lack of Security Awareness (and/or Need)

Most people who use electronic communications behave as though they regard their electronic communications as confidential. Even though they may know in some sense that their communications are vulnerable to compromise, they fail to take precautions to prevent breaches in communications security. Even criminals aware that they may be the subjects of wiretaps have been overheard by law enforcement officials to say,

"This call is probably being wiretapped, but . . . ," after which they go on to discuss incriminating topics.[23]

The impetus for thinking seriously about security is usually an event that is widely publicized and significant in impact.[24] An example of responding to publicized problems is the recent demand for encryption of cellular telephone communications. In the past several years, the public has been made aware of a number of instances in which traffic carried over cellular telephones was monitored by unauthorized parties (Appendix J). In addition, cellular telephone companies have suffered enormous financial losses as the result of "cloning," an illegal practice in which the unencrypted ID numbers of cellular telephones are recorded off the air and placed into cloned units, thereby allowing the owner of the cloned unit to masquerade as the legitimate user.[25] Even though many users today are aware of such practices and have altered their behavior somewhat (e.g., by avoiding discussion of sensitive information over cellular telephone lines), more secure systems such as GSM (the European standard for mobile telephones) have gained only a minimal foothold in the U.S. market.

A second area in which people have become more sensitive to the need for information security is in international commerce. Many international business users are concerned that their international business communications are being monitored, and indeed such concerns motivate a considerable amount of today's demand for secure communications.

It is true that the content of the vast majority of telephone communications in the United States (e.g., making a dinner date, taking an ordi-

---

[23]A case in point is that the officers charged in the Rodney King beating used their electronic communications system as though it were a private telephone line, even though they had been warned that all traffic over that system was recorded. In 1992, Rodney King was beaten by members of the Los Angeles Police Department. A number of transcripts of police radio conversations describing the incident were introduced as evidence at the trial. Had they been fully cognizant at the moment of the fact that all conversations were being recorded as a matter of department policy, the police officers in question most likely would not have said what they did (personal communication, Sara Kiesler, Carnegie Mellon University, 1993).

[24]It is widely believed that only a few percent of computer break-ins are detected. See, for example, Jane Bird, "Hunting Down the Hackers," *Management Today*, July, 1994, p. 64 (reports that 1% of attacks are detected); Bob Brewin, "Info Warfare Goes on Attack," *Federal Computer Week*, Volume 9(31), October 23, 1995, p. 1 (reports 2% detection); and Gary Anthes, "Hackers Try New Tacks," *ComputerWorld*, January 30, 1995, p. 12 (reports 5% detection).

[25]See, for example, Bryan Miller, "Web of Cellular Phone Fraud Widens," *New York Times*, July 20, 1995, p. C1; and George James, "3 Men Accused of Stealing Cellular Phone ID Numbers," *New York Times*, October 19, 1995, p. B3.

nary business call) and data communications (e.g., transferring a file from one computer to another, sending an e-mail message) is simply not valuable enough to attract the interest of most eavesdroppers. Moreover, most communications links for point-to-point communications in the United States are hard wired (e.g., fiber-optic cable) rather than wireless (e.g., microwave); hard-wired links are much more secure than wireless links.[26] In some instances, compromises of information security do not directly damage the interests of the persons involved. For example, an individual whose credit card number is improperly used by another party (who may have stolen his wallet or eavesdropped on a conversation) is protected by a legal cap on the liability for which he is responsible.

Other Barriers Influencing Demand for Cryptography

Even when a user is aware that communications security is threatened and wishes to take action to forestall the threat, a number of practical considerations can affect the decision to use cryptographic protection. These considerations include the following:

• *Lack of critical mass.* A secure telephone is not of much use if only one person has it. Ensuring that communications are secure requires collective action—some critical mass of interoperable devices is necessary in order to stimulate demand for secure communications. To date, such a critical mass has not yet been achieved.

• *Uncertainties over government policy.* Policy often has an impact on demand. A number of government policy decisions on cryptography have introduced uncertainty, fear, and doubt into the marketplace and have made it difficult for potential users to plan for the future. Seeing the controversy surrounding policy in this area, potential vendors are reluctant to bring to market products that support security, and potential users are reluctant to consider products for security that may become obsolete in the future in an unstable legal and regulatory environment.

• *Lack of a supporting infrastructure.* The mere availability of devices is not necessarily sufficient. For some applications such as secure interpersonal communications, a national or international infrastructure for managing and exchanging keys could be necessary. Without such an

---

[26]A major U.S. manufacturer reported to the committee that in the late 1980s, it was alerted by the U.S. government that its microwave communications were vulnerable. In response, this manufacturer took steps to increase the capacity of its terrestrial communications links, thereby reducing its dependence on microwave communications. A similar situation was faced by IBM in the 1970s. See William Broad, "Evading the Soviet Ear at Glen Cove," *Science*, Volume 217(3), 1982, pp. 910-911.

infrastructure, encryption may remain a niche feature that is usable only through ad hoc methods replicating some of the functions that an infrastructure would provide and for which demand would thus be limited. Section 2.5 describes some infrastructure issues in greater detail.

- *High cost.* To date, hardware-based cryptographic security has been relatively expensive, in part because of the high cost of stand-alone products made in relatively small numbers. A user that initially deploys a system without security features and subsequently wants to add them can be faced with a very high cost barrier, and consequently there is a limited market for add-on security products.

On the other hand, the marginal cost of implementing cryptographic capabilities in software at the outset is rapidly becoming a minor part of the overall cost, and so cryptographic capabilities are likely to appear in all manner and types of integrated software products where there might be a need.

- *Reduced performance.* The implementation of cryptographic functions often consumes computational resources (e.g., time, memory). In some cases, excessive consumption of resources makes encryption too slow or forces the user to purchase additional memory. For example, if encrypting the communications link over which a conversation is carried delays that conversation by more than a few tenths of a second, users may well choose not to use the encryption capability.

- *A generally insecure environment.* A given network or operating system may be so inherently insecure that the addition of cryptographic capabilities would do little to improve overall security. Moreover, retrofitting security measures atop an inherently insecure system is generally difficult.

- *Usability.* A product's usability is a critical factor in its market acceptability. Products with encryption capabilities that are available for use but are in fact unused do not increase information security. Such products may be purchased but not used for the encryption they provide because such use is too inconvenient in practice, or they may not be purchased at all because the capabilities they provide are not aligned well with the needs of their users. In general, the need to undertake even a modest amount of extra work or to tolerate even a modest inconvenience for cryptographic protection that is not directly related to the primary function of the device is likely to discourage the use of such protection.[27] When cryptographic features are well integrated in a way that does not

---

[27]For example, experience with current secure telephones such as the STU-III suggests that users of such phones may be tempted, because of the need to contact many people, to use them in a nonsecure mode more often than not.

demand case-by-case user intervention, i.e., when such capabilities can be invoked transparently to the average user, demand may well increase.

• *Lack of independent certification or evaluation of products.* Certification of a product's quality is often sought by potential buyers who lack the technical expertise to evaluate product quality or who are trying to support certain required levels of security (e.g., as the result of bank regulations). Many potential users are also unable to detect failures in the operation of such products.[28] With one exception discussed in Chapter 6, independent certification for products with integrated encryption capabilities is not available, leading to market uncertainty about such products.

• *Electronic commerce.* An environment in which secure communications were an essential requirement would do much to increase the demand for cryptographic security.[29] However, the demand for secure communications is currently nascent.

• *Uncertainties arising from intellectual property issues.* Many of the algorithms that are useful in cryptography (especially public-key cryptography) are protected by patents. Some vendors are confused by the fear, uncertainty, and doubt caused by existing legal arguments among patent holders. Moreover, even when a patent on a particular algorithm is undisputed, many users may resist its use because they do not wish to pay the royalties.[30]

• *Lack of interoperability and standards.* For cryptographic devices to be useful, they must be interoperable. In some instances, the implementation of cryptography can affect the compatibility of systems that may have interoperated even though they did not conform strictly to interoperability standards. In other instances, the specific cryptographic algorithm used is yet another function that must be standardized in order for two products to interoperate. Nevertheless, an algorithm is only one piece of a cryptographic device, and so two devices that implement the

---

[28]Even users who do buy security products may still be unsatisfied with them. For example, in two consecutive surveys in 1993 and 1994, a group of users reported spending more and being less satisfied with the security products they were buying. See Dave Powell, "Annual Infosecurity Industry Survey," *Infosecurity News,* March/April, 1995, pp. 20-27.

[29]AT&T plans to take a nontechnological approach to solving some of the security problems associated with retail Internet commerce. AT&T has announced that it will insure its credit card customers against unauthorized charges, as long as those customers were using AT&T's service to connect to the Internet. This action was taken on the theory that the real issue for consumers is the fear of unauthorized charges, rather than fears that confidential data per se would be compromised. See Thomas Weber, "AT&T Will Insure Its Card Customers on Its Web Service," *Wall Street Journal,* February 7, 1996, p. B5.

[30]See, for example, James Bennett, "The Key to Universal Encryption," *Strategic Investment,* December 20, 1995, pp. 12-13.

same cryptographic algorithm may still not interoperate.[31] Only when two devices conform fully to a single interoperability standard (e.g., a standard that would specify how keys are to be exchanged, the formatting of the various data streams, the algorithms to be used for encryption and decryption, and so on) can they be expected to interoperate seamlessly.

An approach gaining favor among product developers is protocol negotiation,[32] which calls for two devices or products to mutually negotiate the protocol that they will use to exchange information. For example, the calling device may query the receiving device to determine the right protocol to use. Such an approach frees a device from having to conform to a single standard and also facilitates the upgrading of standards in a backward-compatible manner.

- *The heterogeneity of the communications infrastructure.* Communications are ubiquitous, but they are implemented through a patchwork of systems and technologies and communications protocols rather than according to a single integrated design. In some instances, they do not conform completely to the standards that would enable full interoperability. In other instances, interoperability is achieved by intermediate conversion from one data format to another. The result can be that transmission of encrypted data across interfaces interferes with achieving connectivity among disparate systems. Under these circumstances, users

---

[31]Consider the Data Encryption Standard (DES) as an example. DES is a symmetric encryption algorithm, first published in 1975 by the U.S. government, that specifies a unique and well-defined transformation when given a specific 56-bit key and a block of text, but the various details of operation within which DES is implemented can lead to incompatibilities with other systems that include DES, with stand-alone devices incorporating DES, and even with software-implemented DES.

Specifically, how the information is prepared prior to being encrypted (e.g., how it is blocked into chunks) and after the encryption (how the encrypted data is modulated on the communications line) will affect the interoperability of communications devices that may both use DES. In addition, key management may not be identical for DES-based devices developed independently. DES-based systems for file encryption generally require a user-generated password to generate the appropriate 56-bit DES key, but since the DES standard does not specify how this aspect of key management is to be performed, the same password used on two independently developed DES-based systems may not result in the same 56-bit key. For these and similar reasons, independently developed DES-based systems cannot necessarily be expected to interoperate.

[32]Transmitting a digital bit stream requires that the hardware carrying that stream be able to interpret it. Interpretation means that regardless of the content of the communications (e.g., voice, pictures), the hardware must know what part of the bit stream represents information useful to the ultimate receiver and what part represents information useful to the carrier. A communications protocol is an agreed-upon convention about how to interpret any given bit stream and includes the specification of any encryption algorithm that may be used as part of that protocol.

may be faced with a choice of using unencrypted communications or not being able to communicate with a particular other party at all.[33]

2.4.2 The Supply Side of the Cryptography Market

The supply of products with encryption capabilities is inherently related to the demand for them. Cryptographic products result from decisions made by potential vendors and users as well as standards determined by industry and/or government. Use depends on availability as well as other important factors such as user motivation, relevant learning curves, and other nontechnical issues. As a general rule, the availability of products to users depends on decisions made by vendors to build or not to build them, and all of the considerations faced by vendors of all types of products are relevant to products with encryption capabilities.

In addition to user demand, vendors need to consider the following issues before deciding to develop and market a product with encryption capabilities:

• *Accessibility of the basic knowledge underlying cryptography.* Given that various books, technical articles, and government standards on the subject of cryptography have been published widely over the past 20 years, the basic knowledge needed to design and implement cryptographic systems that can frustrate the best attempts of anyone (including government intelligence agencies) to penetrate them is available to government and nongovernment agencies and parties both here and abroad. For example, because a complete description of DES is available worldwide, it is relatively easy for anyone to develop and implement an encryption system that involves multiple uses of DES to achieve much stronger security than that provided by DES alone.

• *The skill to implement basic knowledge of cryptography.* A product with encryption capabilities involves much more than a cryptographic algorithm. An algorithm must be implemented in a system, and many design decisions affect the quality of a product even if its algorithm is mathematically sound. Indeed, efforts by multiple parties to develop products with encryption capabilities based on the same algorithm could result in a variety of manufactured products with varying levels of quality and resistance to attack.

---

[33]An analogous example is the fact that two Internet users may find it very difficult to use e-mail to transport a binary file between them, because the e-mail systems on either end may well implement standards for handling binary files differently, even though they may conform to all relevant standards for carrying ASCII text.

For example, although cryptographic protocols are not part and parcel of a cryptographic algorithm per se, these protocols specify how critical aspects of a product will operate. Thus, weaknesses in cryptographic protocols—such as a key generation protocol specifying how to generate and exchange a specific encryption key for a given message to be passed between two parties or a key distribution protocol specifying how keys are to be distributed to users of a given product—can compromise the confidentiality that a real product actually provides, even though the cryptographic algorithm and its implementation are flawless.[34]

• *The skill to integrate the cryptography into a usable product.* Even a product that implements a strong cryptographic algorithm in a competent manner is not valuable if the product is unusable in other ways. For integrated products with encryption capabilities, the noncryptographic functions of the product are central, because the primary purpose of an integrated product is to provide some useful capability to the user (e.g., word processing, database management, communications) that does *not* involve cryptography per se; if cryptography interferes with this primary functionality, it detracts from the product's value.

In this area, U.S. software vendors and system integrators have distinct strengths,[35] even though engineering talent and cryptographic expertise are not limited to the United States. For example, foreign vendors do not market integrated products with encryption capabilities that are sold as mass-market software, whereas many such U.S. products are available.[36]

• *The cost of developing, maintaining, and upgrading an economically viable product with encryption capabilities.* The technical aspects of good encryption are increasingly well understood. As a result, the incremental

---

[34]An incident that demonstrates the importance of the nonalgorithm aspects of a product is the failure of the key-generation process for the Netscape Navigator Web browser that was discovered in 1995; a faulty random number generation used in the generation of keys would enable an intruder exploiting this flaw to limit a brute-force search to a much smaller number of keys than would generally be required by the 40-bit key length used in this product. See John Markoff, "Security Flaw Is Discovered in Software Used in Shopping," *New York Times*, September 19, 1995, p. A1. A detailed discussion of protocol failures can be found in Gustavus Simmons, "Cryptanalysis and Protocol Failures," *Communications of the ACM*, Volume 37(11), 1994, pp. 56-65.

[35]Computer Science and Telecommunications Board, National Research Council, *Keeping the U.S. Computer Industry Competitive: Systems Integration*, National Academy Press, Washington, D.C., 1992.

[36]For example, the Department of Commerce and the National Security Agency found no general-purpose software products with encryption capability from non-U.S. manufacturers. See Department of Commerce and National Security Agency, *A Study of the International Market for Computer Software with Encryption*, released January 11, 1996, p. III-9.

cost of designing a software product so that it can provide cryptographic functionality to end users is relatively small. As cost barriers to the inclusion of cryptographic functionality are reduced dramatically, the long-term likelihood increases that most products that process digital information will include some kinds of cryptographic functionality.

• *The suitability of hardware vs. software* as a medium in which to implement a product with encryption capabilities. The duplication and distribution costs for software are very low compared to those for hardware, and yet, trade secrets embedded in proprietary hardware are easier to keep than those included in software. Moreover, software cryptographic functions are more easily disabled.

• *Nonmarket considerations and export controls.* Vendors may withhold or alter their products at government request. For example, a well-documented instance is the fact that AT&T voluntarily deferred the introduction of its 3600 Secure Telephone Unit (STU) at the behest of government (see Appendix E on the history of current cryptography policy and Chapter 6 on government influence). Export controls also affect decisions to make products available even for domestic use, as described in Chapter 4.

2.5 INFRASTRUCTURE FOR WIDESPREAD USE OF CRYPTOGRAPHY

The widespread use of cryptography requires a support infrastructure that can service organizational or individual user needs with regard to cryptographic keys.

2.5.1 Key Management Infrastructure

In general, to enable use of cryptography across an enterprise, there must be a mechanism that:

• Periodically supplies all participating locations with keys (typically designated for use during a given calendar or time period—the crypto-period) for either stored materials or communications; or
• Permits any given location to generate keys for itself as needed (e.g., to protect stored files); or
• Can securely generate and transmit keys among communicating parties (e.g., for data transmissions, telephone conversations).

In the most general case, any given mechanism will have to perform all three functions. With symmetric systems, the movement of keys from place to place obviously must be done securely and with a level of protection adequate to counter the threats of concern to the using parties. Whatever the distribution system, it clearly must protect the keys with appropriate safeguards and must be prepared to identify and authenticate the source. The overall task of securely assuring the availability of keys for symmetric applications is often called key management.

If all secure communications take place within the same corporation or among locations under a common line of authority, key management is an internal or possibly a joint obligation. For parties that communicate occasionally or across organizational boundaries, mutual arrangements must be formulated for managing keys. One possibility might be a separate trusted entity whose line of business could be to supply keys of specified length and format, on demand and for a fee.

With asymmetric systems, the private keys are usually self-generated, but they may also be generated from a central source, such as a corporate security office. In all cases, however, the handling of private keys is the same for symmetric and asymmetric systems; they must be guarded with the highest levels of security. Although public keys need not be kept secret, their integrity and association with a given user are extremely important and should also be supported with extremely robust measures.

The costs of a key management infrastructure for national use are not known at this time. One benchmark figure is that the cost of the Defense Department infrastructure needed to generate and distribute keys for approximately 320,000 STU-III telephone users is somewhere in the range of $10 million to $13 million per year.[37]

2.5.2 Certificate Infrastructures

The association between key information (such as the name of a person and the related public key) and an individual or organization is an extremely important aspect of a cryptographic system. That is, it is undesirable for one person to be able to impersonate another. To guard against impersonation, two general types of solutions have emerged: an organization-centric approach consisting of *certificate authorities* and a user-centric approach consisting of a *web of trust*.

A certificate authority serves to validate information that is associated with a known individual or organization. Certificate authorities can exist within a single organization, across multiple related organizations, or across society in general. Any number of certificate authorities can coexist, and they may or may not have agreements for cross-certification,

---

[37]William Crowell, Deputy Director, National Security Agency, personal communication, April 1996.

whereby if one authority certifies a given person, then another authority will accept that certification within its own structure. Certificate authority hierarchies are defined in the Internet RFCs 1421-1424, the X.509 standard, and other emerging commercial standards, such as that proposed by MasterCard/Visa. A number of private certificate authorities, such as VeriSign, have also begun operation to service secure mass-market software products, such as the Netscape Navigator Web browser.

Among personal acquaintances validation of public keys can be passed along from person to person or organization to organization, thus creating a web of trust in which the entire ensemble is considered to be trusted based on many individual instances of trust. Such a chain of trust can be established between immediate parties, or from one party to a second to establish the credentials of a third. This approach has been made popular by the Pretty Good Privacy (PGP) software product; all users maintain their own "key-ring," which holds the public keys of everyone with whom they want to communicate.

Importantly, it should be noted that both the certificate authority approach and the web of trust approach replicate the pattern of trust that already exists among participating parties in societal and business activities. In a sense, the certificate infrastructure for cryptography simply formalizes and makes explicit what society and its institutions are already accustomed to.

At some point, banks, corporations, and other organizations already generally trusted by society will start to issue certificates. At that time, individuals especially may begin to feel more comfortable about the cryptographic undergirding of society's electronic infrastructure, at which point the webs of trust can be expected to evolve according to individual choices and market forces. However, it should be noted that different certificates will be used for different functions, and it is unlikely that a single universal certificate infrastructure will satisfy all societal and business needs. For example, because an infrastructure designed to support electronic commerce and banking may do no more than identify valid purchasers, it may not be useful for providing interpersonal communication or corporate access control.

Certificate authorities already exist within some businesses, especially those that have moved vigorously into an electronic way of life. Generally, there is no sense of a need for a legal framework to establish relationships among organizations, each of which operates its own certificate function. Arrangements exist for them to cross-certify one another; in general, the individual(s) authorizing the arrangement will be a senior officer of the corporation, and the decision will be based on the existence of other legal agreements already in place, notably, contracts that define the relationships and obligations among organizations.

For the general business world in which any individual or organization wishes to conduct a transaction with any other individual or organization, such as the sale of a house, a formal certificate infrastructure has yet to be created. There is not even one to support just a digital signature application within government. Hence, it remains to be seen how, in the general case, individuals and organizations will make the transition to an electronic society.

Certificate authorities currently operate within the framework of contractual law. That is, if some problem arises as the result of improper actions on the part of the certification authority, its subscribers will have to pursue a civil complaint. As certificate authorities grow in size and service a greater part of society, it will probably be necessary to regulate their actions under law, much like those of any major societal institutions.[38] It is interesting to observe that the legal and operational environment that will have to exist for certificate organizations involves the same set of issues that are pertinent to escrow organizations (as discussed in Chapter 5).

2.6 RECAP

Cryptography provides important capabilities that can help deal with the vulnerabilities of electronic information. Cryptography can help to assure the integrity of data, to authenticate the identity of specific parties, to prevent individuals from plausibly denying that they have signed something, and to preserve the confidentiality of information that may have improperly come into the possession of unauthorized parties. At the same time, cryptography is not a silver bullet, and many technical and human factors other than cryptography can improve or detract from information security. In order to preserve information security, attention must be given to all of these factors. Moreover, people can use cryptography only to the extent that it is incorporated into real products and systems; unimplemented cryptographic algorithms cannot contribute to information security. Many factors other than raw mathematical knowledge contribute to the supply of and demand for products with cryptographic functionality. Most importantly, the following aspects influence the demand for cryptographic functions in products:

- Critical mass in the marketplace,

---

[38]Shimshon Berkovits et al., *Public Key Infrastructure Study: Final Report,* National Institute of Standards and Technology, Gaithersburg, Md., April 1994. Performed under contract to MITRE Corporation, this study is summarized in Appendix H.

- Government policy,
- Supporting infrastructure,
- Cost,
- Performance,
- Overall security environment,
- Usability,
- Quality certification and evaluation, and
- Interoperability standards.

Finally, any large-scale use of cryptography, with or without key escrow (discussed later in Chapter 5), depends on the existence of a substantial supporting infrastructure, the deployment of which raises a different set of problems and issues.

3

Needs for Access to Encrypted Information

Information protected for confidentiality (i.e., encrypted information) is stored or communicated for later use by certain parties with the authorization of the original protector. However, it may happen for various legitimate and lawfully authorized reasons that other parties may need to recover this information as well. This chapter discusses needs for access to encrypted information under exceptional circumstances for legitimate and lawfully authorized purposes from the perspectives of businesses, individuals, law enforcement, and national security. Businesses and individuals may want access to encrypted data or communications for their own purposes and thus may cooperate in using products to facilitate such access, while law enforcement and national security authorities may want access to the encrypted data or communications of criminals and parties hostile to the United States.

3.1 TERMINOLOGY

It is useful to conceptualize data communications and data storage using the language of transactions. For example, one individual may telephone another; the participants in the transaction are usually referred to as the calling party and the called party. Or, a person makes a purchase; the participants are called the buyer and seller. Or, a sender mails something to the recipient. Adopting this construct, consider communications in which the first party (Party A) sends a message and the second party (Party B) receives it. "Party" does not necessarily imply a person; a "party" can be a computer system, a communication system, a software process. In the case of data storage, Party A stores the data, while Party B retrieves it. Note that Party A and Party B can be the same party (as is the case when an individual stores a file for his or her own later use).

Under some circumstances, a third party may be authorized for access to data stored or being communicated. For example, law enforcement authorities may be granted legal authorization to obtain surreptitious access to a telephone conversation or a stored data file or record without the knowledge of Parties A or B. The employer of Party A may have the legal right to read all data files for which Party A is responsible or to monitor all communications in which Party A participates. Party A might inadvertently lose access to a data file and wish to recover that access.

In cases when the data involved is unencrypted, the procedures needed to obtain access can be as simple as identifying the relevant file name or as complex as seeking a court order for legal authorization. But when the data involved is encrypted, the procedures needed to obtain access will require the possession of certain critical pieces of information, such as the relevant cryptographic keys.

Third-party access has many twists and turns. When it is necessary for clarity of exposition or meaning, this report uses the phrase "exceptional access" to stress that the situation is not one that was included within the intended bounds of the original transaction, but is an unusual subsequent event. Exceptional access refers to situations in which an authorized party needs and can obtain the plaintext of encrypted data (for storage or communications). The word "exceptional" is used in contrast to the word "routine" and connotes something unusual about the circumstances under which access is required.

Exceptional access can be divided into three generic categories:

• *Government exceptional access* refers to the case in which government has a need for access to information under specific circumstances authorized by law. For example, a person might store data files that law enforcement authorities need to prosecute or investigate a crime. Alternatively, two people may be communicating with each other in the planning or commission of a serious crime. Government exceptional access thus refers to the government's need to obtain the relevant information under circumstances authorized by law, and requires a court order (for access to voice or data communications) or a subpoena or search warrant (for access to stored records). Government exceptional access is the focus of Section 3.2. The related signals intelligence need is discussed in Section 3.3.

• *Employer (or corporate) exceptional access* refers to the case in which an employer (i.e., the corporate employer) has the legal right to access to information encrypted by an employee. If an employee who has encrypted a file is indisposed on a certain day, for example, the company may need exceptional access to the contents of the file. Alternatively, an employee may engage in communications whose content the company may have a legitimate need to know (e.g., the employee may be leaking proprietary information). Employer exceptional access would then refer to the company's requirement to obtain the key necessary to obtain the contents of the file or communications, and may require the intervention of another institutional entity. Employer or corporate exceptional access is the focus of Section 3.5.

- *End-user exceptional access* refers to the case in which the parties primarily intended to have access to plaintext have lost the means to obtain such access. For example, a single user may have stored a file for later retrieval, but encrypted it to ensure that no other party would have access to it while it was in storage. However, the user might also lose or forget the key used to encrypt that file. End-user exceptional access refers to such a user's requirement to obtain the proper key, and may require that the individual who has lost a key prove his identify to a party holding the backup key and verify his authorization to obtain a duplicate copy of his key. End-user exceptional access is also discussed in Section 3.5.

The need for exceptional access when the information stored or communicated is encrypted has led to an examination of a concept generically known as escrowed encryption (the subject of Chapter 5), which, loosely speaking, uses agents other than the parties participating in the communication or data storage to hold copies of or otherwise have access to relevant cryptographic keys "in escrow" so that needs for end-user, corporate, and government exceptional access can be met; these agents are called escrow agents.

3.2 LAW ENFORCEMENT: INVESTIGATION AND PROSECUTION

Obtaining information (both evidence and intelligence) has always been a central element in the conduct of law enforcement investigations and prosecutions. Accordingly, criminals have always wished to protect the information relevant to their activities from law enforcement authorities.

3.2.1 The Value of Access to Information for Law Enforcement

Many criminals keep records related to their activities; such records can be critical to the investigation and prosecution of criminal activity.

BOX 3.1
Examples of the Utility of Wiretaping

• The El Rukn Gang in Chicago, acting as a surrogate for the Libyan government and in support of terrorism, planned to shoot down a commercial airliner within the United States using a stolen military weapon. This act of terrorism was prevented through the use of telephone wiretaps.

• The 1988 "Ill Wind" public corruption and Defense Department fraud investigation relied heavily on court-ordered telephone wiretaps. To date, this investigation has resulted in the conviction of 65 individuals and more than a quarter of a billion dollars in fines, restitutions, and recoveries.

• Numerous drug trafficking and money laundering investigations, such as the "Polar Cap" and "Pizza Connection" cases, utilized extensive telephone wiretaps in the successful prosecution of large-scale national and international drug trafficking organizations. "Polar Cap" resulted in the arrest of 33 subjects and the recovery of $50 million in assets seized. Additionally, in a 1992 Miami raid, which directly resulted from wiretaps, agents confiscated 15,000 pounds of cocaine and arrested 22 subjects.

• The investigation of convicted spy Aldrich Ames relied heavily on wiretaps ordered under Foreign Intelligence Surveillance Act authority.

• In a 1990 "Sexual Exploitation of Children" investigation, the FBI relied heavily on wiretaps to prevent violent individuals from abducting, torturing, and murdering a child in order to make a "snuff murder" film.

SOURCE: Federal Bureau of Investigation.

For example, criminals engaged in white-collar crimes such as fraud often leave paper trails that detail fraudulent activities; drug dealers often keep accounting records of clients, drop-offs, supplies, and income. Reconstruction of these paper trails is often a critical element in building a case against these individuals. The search-and-seizure authority of law enforcement to obtain paper records is used in a large fraction of criminal cases.

As for communications, law enforcement officials believe that wiretapping is a crucial source of information that could not be obtained in any other way or obtained only at high risk (Box 3.1). For example, the Federal Bureau of Investigation (FBI) has testified that

> [w]ithout law enforcement's ability to effectively execute court orders for electronic surveillance, the country would be unable to protect itself against foreign threats, terrorism, espionage, violent crime, drug trafficking, kidnapping, and other crimes. We may be unable to intercept a terrorist before he sets off a devastating bomb; unable to thwart a for-

eign spy before he can steal secrets that endanger the entire country; and unable to arrest drug traffickers smuggling in huge amounts of drugs that will cause widespread violence and death. Court-approved electronic surveillance is of immense value, and often is the only way to prevent or solve the most serious crimes facing today's society.[1]

Criminals often discuss their past criminal activity and plans for future criminal activity with other parties. Obtaining "inside information" on such activities is often a central element of building a case against the perpetrators. A defendant who describes in his own words how he committed a crime or the extent to which he was involved in it gives prosecutors a powerful weapon that juries tend to perceive as fair.[2]

Other methods of obtaining "inside information" have significant risks associated with them:

• Informants are often used to provide inside information. However, the credibility of informants is often challenged in court, either because the informants have shady records themselves or because they may have made a deal with prosecutors by agreeing to serve as informants in return for more lenient treatment.[3] By contrast, challenges to evidence obtained through wiretaps are based far more frequently on their admissibility in court rather than their intrinsic credibility. Informants may also be difficult to find when a criminal group is small in size.

• Surreptitiously planted listening devices are also used to obtain inside information. However, they generally obtain only one side of a conversation (use of a speaker-phone presents an exception). Further, since listening devices require the use of an agent to plant them, installation of such devices is both highly intrusive (arguably more so than wiretapping) for the subject of the device and risky for the planting agent. Requests for the use of such devices are subject to the same judicial oversight and review as wiretaps.

---

[1]Statement of James K. Kallstrom, Special Agent in Charge, Special Operations Division, New York Field Division, Federal Bureau of Investigation, on "Security Issues in Computers and Communications," before the Subcommittee on Technology, Environment, and Aviation of the Committee on Science, Space, and Technology, U.S. House of Representatives, May 3, 1994.

[2]For example, see Edward Walsh, "Reynolds Guilty on All Counts," *Washington Post*, August 23, 1995, p. 1.

[3]See, for example, Sharon Walsh, "Whistle-Blower Quandary: Will Testimony Fly?," *Washington Post*, August 23, 1995, p. F3; Richard Perez-Pena, "An Informer's Double Life: Blows Come from 2 Sides," *New York Times*, October 15, 1995, p. 35; Joseph P. Fried, "Undermining a Bomb-Trial Witness," *New York Times*, April 9, 1995, p. 42; and Stephen Labaton, "The Price Can Be High for Talk That's Cheap," *New York Times*, Week in Review, April 2, 1995, p. 3.

This discussion is not intended to suggest that wiretaps are a perfect source of information and always useful to law enforcement. An important difficulty in using wiretaps is that context is often difficult for listeners to establish when they are monitoring a telephone conversation that assumes shared knowledge between the communicators.[4]

Because of the legal framework regulating wiretaps, and the fact that communications are by definition transient whereas records endure, wiretapping is used in far fewer criminal cases than is seizure of records. Although the potential problems of denying law enforcement access to communications has been the focus of most of the public debate, encryption of data files in a way that denies law enforcement authorities access to data files relevant to criminal activity arguably presents a much larger threat to their capabilities.

3.2.2 The Legal Framework Governing Surveillance

An evolving legal framework governs the authority of government authorities to undertake surveillance of communications that take place within the United States or that involve U.S. persons. Surveillance within the United States is authorized only for certain legislatively specified purposes: the enforcement of certain criminal statutes and the collection of foreign intelligence. A more extended description of this framework (with footnoted references) is contained in Appendix D.

Domestic Communications Surveillance
for Domestic Law Enforcement Purposes

Communications surveillance can involve surveillance for traffic analysis and/or surveillance for content; these separate activities are governed by different laws and regulations. Traffic analysis, a technique that establishes patterns of connections and communications, is performed with the aid of pen registers that record the numbers dialed from a target telephone, and trap-and-trace devices that identify the numbers of telephones from which calls are placed to the target telephone. Orders for the

---

[4]Indeed, in some instances, wiretap evidence has been used to *exculpate* defendants. See, for example, Peter Marks, "When the Best Defense Is the Prosecution's Own Tapes," *New York Times,* June 30, 1995, p. D20. According to Roger Shuy, professor of linguistics at Georgetown University, there are many difficulties in ascribing meaning to particular utterances that may be captured on tape recordings of conversations. See Roger Shuy, *Language Crimes*, Blackwell Publishers, Cambridge, Mass., 1993. Shuy's book is mostly focused on tapes made by "wires" carried by informants or "bugs" placed near a subject, but the basic principle is the same.

use of these devices may be requested by any federal attorney and granted by any federal district judge or magistrate, and are granted on a more or less pro forma basis.

Surveillance of communications for content for purposes of domestic law enforcement is governed by Title 18, U.S. Code, Sections 2510-2521, concerning "wire and electronic communications interceptions and interception of all communications," generally known as Title III. These sections of the U.S. Code govern the use of listening devices (usually known as "bugs"); wiretaps of communications involving human speech (called "oral communications" in Title III) carried over a wire or wire-like cable, including optical fiber; and other forms of electronically transmitted communication, including various forms of data, text, and video that may be communicated between or among people as well as computers or communications devices. Under Title III, only certain federal crimes may be investigated (e.g., murder, kidnapping, child molestation, racketeering, narcotics offenses) through the interception of oral communications. In addition, 37 states have passed laws that are similar to Title III, but they include such additional restrictions as allowing only a fixed number of interceptions per year (Connecticut) or only for drug-related crimes (California). State wiretaps account for the majority of wiretaps in the United States.

Surveillance of oral communications governed under Title III in general requires a court order (i.e., a warrant) granted at the discretion of a judge.[5] Because electronic surveillance of oral communications is both inherently intrusive and clandestine, the standards for granting a warrant for such surveillance are more stringent than those required by the Fourth Amendment. These additional requirements are specified in Title III and are enforced by criminal and civil penalties applicable to law enforcement officials or private citizens, and by a statutory exclusionary rule that violations of the central features of requirements may lead to suppression of evidence in a later trial, even if such evidence meets the relevant Fourth Amendment test.

Because of the resources required, the administrative requirements for the application procedure, and the legal requirement that investigators exhaust other means of obtaining information, wiretaps are not often used. Approximately 1,000 orders (both federal and state) are authorized yearly (a number small compared to the number of felonies investigated,

---

[5]Emergency intercepts may be performed without a warrant in certain circumstances, such as physical danger to a person or conspiracy against the national security. There has been "virtually no use" of the emergency provision, and its constitutionality has not been tested in court (Wayne R. LaFave and Jerold H. Israel, *Criminal Procedure*, West Publishing Company, St. Paul, Minn., 1992, p. 254).

even if such felonies are limited to those specified in Title III as eligible for investigation with wiretaps).[6] About 2,500 conversations are intercepted per order, and the total number of conversations intercepted is a very small fraction of the annual telephone traffic in the United States.

Surveillance of nonvoice communications, including fax and electronic communications, is also governed by Title III.[7] The standard for obtaining an intercept order for electronic communications is less stringent than that for intercepting voice communications. For example, any federal felony may be investigated through electronic interception. In addition, the statutory exclusionary rule of Title III for oral and wire communications does not apply to electronic communications.

Despite the legal framework outlined above, it is nevertheless possible that unauthorized or unlawful surveillance, whether undertaken by rogue law enforcement officials or overzealous private investigators, occurs. Concerns over such activity are often expressed by critics of the current Administration policy, and they focus on two scenarios:

• With current telephone technology, it is sometimes technically possible for individuals (e.g., private investigators, criminals, rogue law enforcement personnel) to undertake wiretaps on their own initiative (e.g., by placing alligator clips on the proper terminals in the telephone box of an apartment building). Such wiretaps would subject the personnel involved to Title III criminal penalties, but detection of such wiretaps might well be difficult. On the other hand, it is highly unlikely that such a person could obtain the cooperation of major telephone service providers without a valid warrant or court order, and so these wiretaps would have to be conducted relatively close to the target's telephone, and not in a telephone switching office.

• Information obtained through a wiretap in violation of Title III can

---

[6]Some analysts critical of the U.S. government position on wiretaps have suggested that the actual distribution of crimes investigated under Title III intercept or surveillance orders may be somewhat inconsistent with government claims of the high value of such orders. (See, for example, testimony of David B. Kopel, Cato Institute, "Hearings on Wiretapping and Other Terrorism Proposals," Committee on the Judiciary, U.S. Senate, May 24, 1995; also available on-line at http://www.cato.org/ct5-24-5.html.) For example, Table D.3 in Appendix D indicates that no cases involving arson, explosives, or weapons were investigated using Title III wiretaps in 1988. The majority of Title III orders have involved drug and gambling crimes.

[7]Note that when there is no reasonable expectation of privacy, law enforcement officials are not required to undertake any special procedure to monitor such communications. For example, a law enforcement official participating in an on-line "chat" group is not required to identify himself as such, nor must he obtain any special permission at all to monitor the traffic in question. However, as a matter of policy, the FBI does not systematically monitor electronic forums such as Internet relay chats.

be suppressed in court, but such evidence may still be useful in the course of an investigation. Specifically, such evidence may cue investigators regarding specific areas that would be particularly fruitful to investigate, and if the illegal wiretap is never discovered, a wiretap that provides no court-admissible evidence may still prove pivotal to an investigation.[8] (Even if it is discovered, different judges apply the doctrine of discarding "the fruit of the poisonous tree" with different amounts of rigor.)

The extent to which these and similar scenarios actually occur is hard to determine. Information provided by the FBI to the committee indicates a total of 187 incidents of various types (including indictments/complaints and convictions/pretrial diversions) involving charges of illegal electronic surveillance (whether subsequently confirmed or not) over the past 5 fiscal years (1990 through 1994).[9]

Domestic Communications Surveillance for Foreign Intelligence Purposes

The statute governing interception of electronic communications for purposes of protecting national security is known as the Foreign Intelligence Surveillance Act (FISA), which has been codified as Sections 1801 to 1811 in Title 18 of the U.S. Code. Passed in 1978, FISA was an attempt to balance Fourth Amendment rights against the constitutional responsibility of the executive branch to maintain national security. FISA is relevant only to communications occurring at least partly within the United States (wholly, in the case of radio communications), although listening stations used by investigating officers may be located elsewhere, and FISA surveillance may be performed only against foreign powers or their agents. Interception of communications, when the communications occur entirely outside the United States, whether or not the participants include U.S. persons, is not governed by FISA, Title III, or any other statute. However, when a U.S. person is outside the United States, Executive Order 12333 governs any communications intercepts targeted against such individuals.

---

[8]Such concerns are raised by reports of police misconduct as described in Chapter 1.

[9]The committee recognizes the existence of controversy over the question of whether such reports should be taken at face value. For example, critics of the U.S. government who believe that law enforcement authorities are capable of systematically abusing wiretap authority argue that law enforcement authorities would not be expected to report figures that reflected such abuse. Alternatively, it is also possible that cases of improper wiretaps are in fact more numerous than reported and have simply not come to the attention of the relevant authorities. The committee discussed such matters and concluded that it had no reason to believe that the information it received on this subject from law enforcement authorities was in any way misleading.

The basic framework of FISA is similar to that of Title III, with certain important differences, among which are the following:

• The purpose of FISA surveillance is to obtain foreign intelligence information, defined in terms of U.S. national security, including defense against attack, sabotage, terrorism, and clandestine intelligence activities, among others. The targeted communications need not relate to any crime or be relevant as evidence in court proceedings.

• In most instances, a FISA surveillance application requires a warrant based on probable cause that foreign intelligence information will be collected.[10] Surveillance of a U.S. person (defined as a U.S. citizen, U.S. corporation or association, or legal resident alien) also requires probable cause showing that the person is acting as a foreign agent. Political and other activities protected by the First Amendment may not serve as the basis for treating a U.S. person as a foreign agent.

• Targets of FISA surveillance might never be notified that communications have been intercepted.

Since 1979, there have been an average of over 500 FISA orders per year. In 1992, 484 were issued. Other information about FISA intercepts is classified.

3.2.3 The Nature of the Surveillance Needs of Law Enforcement

In cooperation with the National Technical Investigators Association, the FBI has articulated a set of requirements for its electronic surveillance needs (Box 3.2). Of course, access to surveillance that does not meet all of these requirements is not necessarily useless. For example, surveillance that does not meet the transparency requirement may still be quite useful in certain cases (e.g., if the subjects rationalize the lack of transparency as "static on the line"). The basic point is that these requirements constitute a set of continuous metrics by which the quality of a surveillance capability can be assessed, rather than a list that defines what is or is not useful surveillance.

Of these requirements, the real-time requirement is perhaps the most demanding. The FBI has noted that

---

[10]Surveillance may take place without a court order for up to 1 year if the Attorney General certifies that there is very little likelihood of intercepting communications involving U.S. persons and that the effort will target facilities used exclusively by foreign powers. Under limited circumstances, emergency surveillance may be performed before a warrant is obtained (Clifford S. Fishman, *Wiretapping and Eavesdropping: Cumulative Supplement*, Clark Boardman Callaghan, Deerfield, Ill., November 1994, sections 361, 366).

BOX 3.2
Law Enforcement Requirements for the Surveillance of
Electronic Communications

• Prompt and expeditious access both to the contents of the electronic communications and "setup" information necessary to identify the calling and called parties
• Real-time, full-time monitoring capability for intercepts. Such capability is particularly important in an operational context, in which conversations among either criminal conspirators (e.g., regarding a decision to take some terrorist action) or criminals and innocent third parties (e.g., regarding a purchase order for explosives from a legitimate dealer) may have immediate significance
• Delivery of intercepted communications to specified monitoring facilities
• Transparent access to the communications, i.e., access that is undetectable to all parties to the communications (except to the monitoring parties) and implementation of safeguards to restrict access to intercept information
• Verification that the intercepted communications are associated with the intercept subject
• Capabilities for some number of simultaneous intercepts to be determined through a cooperative industry/law enforcement effort
• Reliability of the services supporting the intercept at the same (or higher) level of the reliability of the communication services provided to the intercept subject
• A quality of service for the intercept that complies with the performance standards of the service providers

---

SOURCE: Law Enforcement Requirements for the Surveillance of Electronic Communications, Federal Bureau of Investigation in cooperation with the National Technical Investigators Association, June 1994.

---

[s]ome encryption products put at risk efforts by federal, state and local law enforcement agencies to obtain the contents of intercepted communications by precluding real-time decryption. Real-time decryption is often essential so that law enforcement can rapidly respond to criminal activity and, in many instances, prevent serious and life-threatening criminal acts.[11]

---

[11]Statement of James K. Kallstrom, Special Agent in Charge, Special Operations Division, New York Field Division, Federal Bureau of Investigation, on "Security Issues in Computers and Communications," before the Subcommittee on Technology, Environment, and Aviation of the Committee on Science, Space, and Technology, U.S. House of Representatives, May 3, 1994. An illustrative example is an instance in which the FBI was wiretapping police officers who were allegedly guarding a drug shipment. During that time, the FBI overheard a conversation between the police chief and several other police officials that the FBI believes indicated a plot to murder a certain individual who had previously filed a police brutality complaint against the chief. (However, the FBI was unable to decode the police chief's "street slang and police jargon" in time to prevent the murder.) See Paul Keegan, "The Thinnest Blue Line," *New York Times Magazine*, March 31, 1996, pp. 32-35.

Real-time surveillance is generally less important for crimes that are prosecuted or investigated than for crimes that are prevented because of the time scales involved. Prosecutions and investigations take place on the time scales of days or more, whereas prevention may take place on the time scale of hours. In some instances, the longer time scale is relevant: because Title III warrants can be issued only when "probable cause" exists that a crime has been committed, the actual criminal act is committed before the warrant is issued, and thus prevention is no longer an issue. In other instances, information obtained under a valid Title III warrant issued to investigate a specific criminal act can be used to prevent a subsequent criminal act, in which case the shorter time scale may be relevant. The situation is similar under FISA, in which warrants need not necessarily be obtained in connection with any criminal activity. A good example is terrorism cases, in which it is quite possible that real-time surveillance could provide actionable information useful in thwarting an imminent terrorist act.

3.2.4 The Impact of Cryptography and New Media on Law Enforcement (Stored and Communicated Data)

Cryptography can affect information collection by law enforcement officials in a number of ways. However, for perspective, it is important to keep in mind a broader context—namely that advanced information technologies (of which cryptography is only one element) have potential impacts across many different dimensions of law enforcement; Box 3.3 provides some discussion of this point.

Encrypted Communications

As far as the committee has been able to determine, criminal use of digitally encrypted voice communications has not presented a significant problem to law enforcement to date.[12] On rare occasions, law enforcement officials conducting a wiretap have encountered "unknown signals" that could be encrypted traffic or simply a data stream that was unrecognizable to the intercept equipment. (For example, a high-speed fax transmission might be transported on a particular circuit; a monitoring agent

---

[12]In this regard, it is important to distinguish between "voice scramblers" and encrypted voice communications. Voice scramblers are a relatively old and widely available technology for concealing the contents of a voice communication; they transform the analog waveform of a voice and have nothing to do with encryption per se. True encryption is a transformation of digitally represented data. Voice scramblers have been used by criminals for many years, whereas devices for digital encryption remain rare.

might be unable to distinguish between the signal of the fax and an encrypted voice signal with the equipment available to him.)

The lack of criminal use of encryption in voice communications most likely reflects the lack of use of encryption by the general public. Moreover, files are more easily encrypted than communications, simply because the use of encrypted communications presumes an equally sophisticated partner, whereas only one individual must be knowledgeable to encrypt files. As a general rule, criminals are most likely to use what is available to the general public, and the encryption available to and usable by the public has to date been minimal. At the same time, sophisticated and wealthy criminals (e.g., those associated with drug cartels) are much more likely to have access to and to use cryptography.[13]

In data communications, one of the first publicized instances of law enforcement use of a Title III intercept order to monitor a suspect's electronic mail occurred in December 1995, when the customer of an on-line service provider was the subject of surveillance during a criminal investigation.[14] E-mail is used for communications; a message is composed at one host, sent over a communications link, and stored at another host. Two opportunities exist to obtain the contents of an e-mail message—the first while the message is in transit over the communications link, and the second while it is resident on the receiving host. From a technical perspective, it is much easier to obtain the message from the receiving host, and this is what happened in the December 1995 instance. (Appendix D contains more detail on how electronic communications are treated under Title III.)

Federal law enforcement authorities believe that encryption of communications (whether voice or data) will be a significant problem in the future. FBI Director Louis Freeh has argued that "unless the issue of encryption is resolved soon, criminal conversations over the telephone and other communications devices will become indecipherable by law enforcement. This, as much as any issue, jeopardizes the public safety and national security of this country. Drug cartels, terrorists, and kidnappers will use telephones and other communications media with impunity

---

[13]For example, police raids in Colombia on offices of the Cali cartel resulted in the seizure of advanced communications devices, including radios that distort voices, videophones to provide visual authentication of callers' identities, and devices for scrambling computer modem transmissions. The Colombian defense minister was quoted as saying that the CIA had told him that the technological sophistication of the Cali cartel was about equal to that of the KGB at the time of the Soviet Union's collapse. See James Brooke, "Crackdown Has Cali Drug Cartel on the Run," *New York Times*, June 27, 1995, p. A1.

[14]See Gautam Naik, "U.S., Using E-Mail Tap, Charges Three with Operating Cellular-Fraud Ring," *Wall Street Journal*, January 2, 1996, p. B16.

BOX 3.3
**How Noncryptography Applications of Information Technology
Could Benefit Law Enforcement**

As acknowledged in the main text, encryption in ubiquitous use would create certain difficulties for law enforcement. Nevertheless, it is important to place into context the overall impact on law enforcement of the digital information technologies that enable encryption and other capabilities that are not the primary subject of this report. Chapter 2 suggested how encryption capabilities can be a positive force for more effective law enforcement (e.g., secure police communications). But information technology is increasingly ubiquitous and could appear in a variety of other applications less obvious than encryption. For example:

• Video technology has become increasingly inexpensive. Thus, it is easy to imagine police cruisers with video cameras that are activated upon request when police are responding to an emergency call. Monitoring those cameras at police headquarters would provide a method for obtaining timely information regarding the need of the responding officers for backup. Equipping individual police officers with even smaller video cameras attached to their uniforms and recording such transmissions would provide objective evidence to corroborate (or refute) an officer's description of what he saw at a crime scene.

• The number of users of cellular telephones and wide-area wireless communications services will grow rapidly. As such technologies enable private citizens to act as responsible eyes and ears that observe and report emergencies in progress, law enforcement officials will be able to respond more quickly. (See, for example, Chana Schoenberger, "The Pocket-Size Protector; Feeling Safe, not Stylish, with Cellular Phones," *Washington Post*, August 29, 1995, p. B5.)

• Electronically mediated sting operations help to preserve cover stories of law enforcement officials. For example, the Cybersnare sting operation resulted in the arrest of six individuals who allegedly stole cellular telephone numbers en masse

---

knowing that their conversations are immune from our most valued investigative technique."[15] In addition, the initial draft of the digital telephony bill called for telephone service providers to deliver the plaintext of any encrypted communications they carried, a provision that was dropped in later drafts of the bill.[16]

---

[15]See the Prepared Statement of Louis J. Freeh, Director, Federal Bureau of Investigation, for the Federal Drug Law Enforcement Hearing before the House Judiciary Committee, Subcommittee on Crime, U.S. House of Representatives, March 30, 1995.

[16]The final bill provides that "a telecommunications carrier shall not be responsible for decrypting, or ensuring the government's ability to decrypt, any communication encrypted by a subscriber or customer, unless the encryption was provided by the carrier and the carrier possesses the information necessary to decrypt the communication."

from major companies, resulting in millions of dollars of industry losses. Cybersnare was based on an underground bulletin board that appealed to cellular telephone and credit card thieves. Messages were posted offering for sale cellular telephone "cloning" equipment and stolen cellular telephone numbers, and included contact telephone numbers that were traced to the individuals in question. (See Gautam Naik, "Secret Service Agents Arrest Six Hackers in Cellular-Phone Sting in Cyberspace," *Wall Street Journal*, September 12, 1995, p. B6.)

- The locations of automobiles over a metropolitan area could be tracked automatically, either passively or actively. An active technique might rely on a coded beacon that would localize the position of the automobile on which it was mounted. A passive technique might rely on automatic scanning for license plates that were mounted on the roofs of cars. As an investigative technique, the ability to track the location of a particular automobile over a period of time could be particularly important.

Even today, information technology enables law enforcement officials to conduct instant background checks for handgun purchases and arrest records when a person is stopped for a traffic violation. Retail merchants guard against fraud by using information technology to check driving records when cars are rented and credit checks for big purchases. The Department of the Treasury uses sophisticated information technology to detect suspicious patterns that might indicate large-scale money laundering by organized crime.

All such possibilities involve important social as well as technical issues. For example, the first two examples featured above seem relatively benign, while the last two raise serious entrapment and privacy issues. Even the "instant background checks" of gun buyers have generated controversy. The mention of these applications (potential and actual) is not meant as endorsement, recommendation, or even suggestion; they do, however, place into better context the potentialities of information technology in some overall sense to improve the capabilities of law enforcement while at the same time illustrating that concerns about excessive government power are not limited to the issue of cryptography.

Encrypted Data Files

Encryption by criminals of computer-based records that relate to their criminal activity is likely to pose a significant problem for law enforcement in the future. FBI Director Freeh has noted publicly[17] two instances in which encrypted files have already posed a problem for law enforcement authorities: a terrorist case in the Philippines involving a plan to blow up a U.S. airliner as well as a plan to assassinate the Pope in late 1994,[18] and the "Innocent Images" child pornography case of 1995 in

---

[17]Speech of FBI Director Louis Freeh, before the International Cryptography Institute 1995 conference, Washington, D.C., September 21, 1995.

[18]A general discussion of this case is found in Phillip Shenon, "World Trade Center Suspect Linked to Plan to Blow Up 2 Planes," *New York Times*, March 26, 1995, p. 37.

which encrypted images stood in the way of grand jury access procedures.[19] Furthermore, Director Freeh told the committee that the use of
stored records in criminal prosecutions and investigations was much more
frequent than the use of wiretaps.

The problem of encrypted data files is similar to the case in which a
criminal keeps books or records in a code or a language that renders them
unusable to anyone else—in both instances, the cooperation of the criminal (or someone else with access to the key) is necessary to decipher the
records. The physical records as well as any recorded version of the key,
if such a record exists, are available through a number of standard legal
mechanisms, including physical search warrants and subpoenas. On the
other hand, while the nature of the problem itself is the same in both
instances, the ease and convenience of electronic encryption, especially if
performed automatically, may increase the frequency with which encryption is encountered and/or the difficulties faced by law enforcement in
cryptanalyzing the material in question without the cooperation of the
criminal.

Finally, the problem of exceptional access to stored encrypted information is more easily solved than the problem of exceptional access to
encrypted communications. The reason is that for file decryption, the
time constraints are generally less stringent. A file may have existed for
many days or weeks or even years, and the time within which decryption
is necessary (e.g., to build a criminal case) is measured on the time scale of
investigatory activities; by contrast, the relevant time scale in the case of
decrypting communications may be the time scale of operations, which
might be as short as minutes or hours.

3.3 NATIONAL SECURITY AND SIGNALS INTELLIGENCE[20]

Cryptography is a two-edged sword for U.S. national security interests. Cryptography is important in maintaining the security of U.S. classified information (Appendix I), and the U.S. government has developed
its own cryptographic systems to meet these needs. At the same time, the
use of cryptography by foreign adversaries also hinders U.S. acquisition

---

[19]A general discussion of the Innocent Images case is found in Kara Swisher, "On-Line
Child Pornography Charged as 12 Are Arrested," *Washington Post*, September 14, 1995, p. 1.

[20]One note on terminology: In the signals intelligence community, the term "access" is
used to refer to obtaining the desired signals, whether those signals are encrypted or not.
This use conflicts with the usage adopted in this report, in which "access" generally means
obtaining the information contained in a signal (or message or file).

of communications intelligence. This section discusses the latter. (Appendix F contains a short primer on intelligence.)

3.3.1 The Value of Signals Intelligence[21]

Signals intelligence (SIGINT) is a critically important arm of U.S. intelligence, along with imagery intelligence (IMINT) and intelligence information collected directly by people, i.e., human intelligence (HUMINT). SIGINT also provides timely tip-off and guidance to IMINT and HUMINT collectors and is, in turn, tipped off by them. As in the case of law enforcement, the information contained in a communications channel treated by an opponent as secure is likely to be free of intentional deception.

The committee has received both classified and unclassified assessments of the current value of SIGINT and finds that the level of reporting reflects a continuing capability to produce both tactical and strategic information on a wide range of topics of national intelligence interest. SIGINT production is responding to the priorities established by Presidential Decision Directive 35. As publicly described by President Bill Clinton in remarks made to the staff of the CIA and intelligence community, the priorities are as follows:

- "First, the intelligence need of our military during an operation . . . ,
- Second, political, economic and military intelligence about countries hostile to the United States. We must also compile all-source information on major political and economic powers with weapons of mass destruction who are potentially hostile to us,
- Third, intelligence about specific trans-national threats to our security, such as weapons proliferation, terrorism, drug trafficking, organized crime, illicit trade practices and environmental issues of great gravity."[22]

SIGINT is one valuable component of the overall U.S. intelligence capability. It makes important contributions to ensure an informed, alert, and secure environment for U.S. war fighters and policy makers.

---

[21]This report deals only with the communications intelligence (COMINT) aspects of SIGINT; see Appendix F for a discussion of electronic intelligence (ELINT) and its relationship to COMINT.

[22]Office of the Press Secretary, The White House, "Remarks by the President to Staff of the CIA and Intelligence Community," Central Intelligence Agency, McLean, Va., July 14, 1995.

SIGINT Support of Military Operations

SIGINT is important to both tactical and strategic intelligence. Tactical intelligence provides operational support to forces in the field, whether these forces are performing military missions or international law enforcement missions (e.g., as in drug eradication raids in Latin America conducted in cooperation with local authorities). The tactical dimensions were most recently demonstrated in the Gulf War through a skillfully orchestrated interaction of SIGINT, IMINT, and HUMINT that demonstrated the unequaled power of U.S. intelligence. SIGINT produced timely command and control intelligence and specific signal information to support electronic warfare; IMINT provided precise locating information to permit precision bombing, together with HUMINT; SIGINT and IMINT provided the field commands with an unprecedented degree of battlefield awareness.

History also demonstrates many instances in which SIGINT has proven decisive in the conduct of tactical military operations. These instances are more easily identified now because the passage of time has made the information less sensitive.

- The American naval victory at the Battle of Midway and the destruction of Japanese merchant shipping resulted, in part, from Admiral C.W. Nimitz's willingness to trust the SIGINT information he received from his intelligence staff. General George Marshall wrote that as a result of this SIGINT information, "we were able to concentrate our limited forces to meet [the Japanese] naval advance on Midway when otherwise we almost certainly would have been some 3,000 miles out of place."[23]

- The shoot-down in April 1943 of the commander-in-chief of the Japanese Navy, Admiral Isoroku Yamamoto, was the direct result of a signals intercept that provided his detailed itinerary for a visit to the Japanese front lines.[24]

- The U.S. Navy was able to compromise the operational code used by German U-boats in the Atlantic in 1944, with the result that large numbers of such boats were sunk.[25]

- Allied intercepts of German army traffic were instrumental in the defense of the Anzio perimeter in Italy in February 1944, a defense that some analysts believe was a turning point in the Italian campaign; these intercepts provided advance knowledge of the German timing, direction,

---

[23]A good discussion of these topics is given in David Kahn, *The Codebreakers*, MacMillan, New York, 1967, pp. 561-573 (Midway) and pp. 593-594 (merchant shipping).

[24]See Kahn, *The Codebreakers*, 1967, pp. 595-601.

[25]Kahn, *The Codebreakers*, 1967, pp. 504-507.

and weight of assault, and enabled Allied generals to concentrate their resources in the appropriate places.[26]

While these examples are 50 years old, the nature of warfare is not so different today as to invalidate the utility of successful SIGINT. A primary difference between then and now is that the speed of warfare has increased substantially, placing a higher premium on real-time or near-real-time intercepts. Since the end of World War II, SIGINT has provided tactical support to every military operation involving U.S. forces.

Other types of tactical intelligence to which SIGINT can contribute include indications and warning efforts (detecting an adversary's preparations to undertake armed hostilities); target identification, location, and prioritization (what targets should be attacked, where they are, and how important they are); damage assessment (how much damage an attacked target sustained); and learning the enemy's rules of engagement (under what circumstances an adversary is allowed to engage friendly forces).

SIGINT Support of Strategic Intelligence

Strategic (or national) intelligence is intended to provide analytical support to senior policy makers rather than field commanders. In this role, strategic or national intelligence serves foreign policy, national security, and national economic objectives. Strategic intelligence focuses on foreign political and economic events and trends, as well as on strategic military concerns such as plans, doctrine, scientific and technical resources, weapon system capabilities, and nuclear program development. History also demonstrates the importance of SIGINT in a diplomatic, counterintelligence, and foreign policy context:

- In the negotiations following World War I over a treaty to limit the tonnage of capital ships (the Washington Conference on Naval Arms Limitations), the U.S. State Department was able to read Japanese diplomatic traffic instructing its diplomats. One particular decoded intercept provided the bottom line in the Japanese position, information that was useful in gaining Japanese concessions.[27]
- Recently, Director of Central Intelligence John Deutch unveiled the so-called VENONA material, decrypted Soviet intelligence service messages of the mid-1940s that revealed Soviet espionage against the U.S.

---

[26]See Ralph Bennett, *Ultra and Mediterranean Strategy*, William Morrow and Company, New York, 1989, pp. 265-269.

[27]See Kahn, *The Codebreakers*, 1967, pp. 358-359.

atomic program.[28] Intelligence about the Cuban missile crisis has been released. Although primarily a story about U-2 photography, the role of SIGINT is included as well.

• Decrypted intercepts of allied communications in the final months of World War II played a major role in assisting the United States to achieve its goals at the conference called to decide on the United Nations charter. American policy makers knew the negotiating positions of nearly all of the participating nations and thus were able to control the debate to a considerable degree.[29]

• During the Cold War, SIGINT provided information about adversary military capabilities, weapons production, command and control, force structure and operational planning, weapons testing, and activities of missile forces and civil defense.

In peacetime as in combat, each of the intelligence disciplines can contribute critical information in support of national policy. Former Director of Central Intelligence Admiral Stansfield Turner has pointed out that "[e]lectronic intercepts may be even more useful [than human agents] in discerning intentions. For instance, if a foreign official writes about plans in a message and the United States intercepts it, or if he discusses it and we record it with a listening device, those verbatim intercepts are likely to be more reliable than second-hand reports from an agent."[30] He also noted that "as we increase emphasis on securing economic intelligence, we will have to spy on the more developed countries—our allies and friends with whom we compete economically—but to whom we turn first for political and military assistance in a crisis. This means that rather than instinctively reaching for human, on-site spying, the United States will want to look to those impersonal technical systems, primarily satellite photography and intercepts."[31]

Today, the United States conducts the largest SIGINT operation in the world in support of information relevant to conventional military threats; the proliferation of weapons of mass destruction; terrorism; enforcement

---

[28]Center for Cryptologic History, National Security Agency, *Introductory History of VENONA and Guide to the Translations*, Fort George G. Meade, Md., undated. VENONA material is also available from the Web site of the National Security Agency at http://www.nsa.gov:8080/docs/venona/venona.html.

[29]Stephen Schlesinger, "Cryptanalysis for Peacetime: Codebreaking and the Birth and Structure of the United Nations," *Cryptologia*, Volume 19(3), July 1995, pp. 217-235.

[30]Stansfield Turner, "Intelligence for a New World Order," *Foreign Affairs,* Fall 1991, pp. 150-166.

[31]Turner, "Intelligence for a New World Order," 1991, pp. 150-166.

of international sanctions; protection of U.S. economic and trade interests; and political and economic developments abroad.

- U.S. intelligence has been used to uncover unfair trade practices (as determined by U.S. law and custom) of other nations whose industries compete with U.S. businesses, and has helped the U.S. government to ensure the preservation of a level economic playing field. According to the National Security Agency (NSA), the economic benefits of SIGINT contributions to U.S. industry taken as a whole have totaled tens of billions of dollars over the last several years.
- In sanctions monitoring and enforcement, intelligence intercepts of Serbian communications are reported to have been the first indication for U.S. authorities that an F-16 pilot enforcing a no-fly zone over Serbia and shot down in June 1995 was in fact alive,[32] and an important element in his rescue. If the pilot had indeed been captured, U.S. options in Serbia could have been greatly constrained.
- SIGINT that has been made public or that has been tacitly acknowledged includes information about the shoot-down of the Korean airliner KAL 007 on September 1, 1983, and the bombing of La Belle Discotheque in West Berlin ordered by Libya in April 1986.
- In foreign policy, accurate and timely intelligence has been, and remains, vital to U.S. efforts to avert conflicts between nations.
- In September 1988, President Ronald Reagan made the decision to disclose NSA decrypts of Iraqi military communications "to prove that, despite their denials, Iraqi armed forces had used poison gas against the Kurds."[33]

The information provided by SIGINT has helped to produce information on weapons proliferation, providing indications of violations of treaties or embargo requirements. SIGINT has collected information on international terrorism and foreign drug trafficking, thereby assisting in the detection of drug shipments intended for delivery to the United States. Similarly, such information will continue to be a source of important economic intelligence.

In conducting these intelligence-gathering operations, a wide variety of sources may be targeted, including the communications of governments, nongovernment institutions, and individuals. For example, banking is an international enterprise, and the U.S. government may need to

---

[32]Daniel Williams, "'I'm Ready to Get the Hell Out of Here,'" *Washington Post*, July 9, 1995, p. A1.

[33] Christopher Andrew, *For the President's Eyes Only*, HarperCollins, New York, 1995.

know about flows of money for purposes of counterterrorism or sanctions monitoring.

Although the value of SIGINT to military operations and to law enforcement is generally unquestioned, senior decision makers have a wide range of opinions on the value of strategic and/or political intelligence. Some decision makers are voracious consumers of intelligence reports. They believe that the reports they receive provide advance notice of another party's plans and intentions, and that their own decisions are better for having such information. These decision makers find that almost no amount of information is too much and that any given piece of information has the potential to be helpful.

To illustrate the value of SIGINT to some senior policy makers, it is helpful to recall President Clinton's remarks to the intelligence community on July 14, 1995, at the CIA: he said that "in recent months alone you warned us when Iraq massed its troops against the Kuwaiti border. You provided vital support to our peacekeeping and humanitarian missions in Haiti and Rwanda. You helped to strike a blow at a Colombian drug cartel. You uncovered bribes that would have cheated American companies out of billions of dollars." On a previous occasion, then-President George Bush gave his evaluation of SIGINT when he said that ". . . over the years I've come to appreciate more and more the full value of SIGINT. As President and Commander-in-Chief, I can assure you, signals intelligence is a prime factor in the decision making process by which we chart the course of this nation's foreign affairs."[34]

Some policy makers, generally less senior than the President, have stated that while intelligence reports are occasionally helpful, they do not in general add much to their decision-making ability because they contribute to information overload, are not sufficiently timely in the sense that the information is revealed shortly in any event, lack necessary context-setting information, or do not provide much information beyond that available from open sources. Even among the members of the committee who have served in senior government positions, this range of opinion is represented.[35]

The perceived value of strategic SIGINT (as with many other types of intelligence) depends largely on the judgment and position of the particu-

---

[34]*Public Papers of the Presidents*, U.S. Government Printing Office, Washington, D.C., 1991, as quoted by Andrew in *For the President's Eyes Only*, 1995, p. 526.

[35]For an open-source report on the value of intelligence as perceived by different policy makers, see David E. Sanger, "Emerging Role for the C.I.A.: Economic Spy," *New York Times*, October 15, 1995, p. 1; and David E. Sanger, "When Spies Look Out for the Almighty Buck," *New York Times*, October 22, 1995, p. 4.

lar individuals whom the intelligence community is serving. These individuals change over time as administrations come and go, but intelligence capabilities are built up over a time scale longer than the election cycle. The result is that the intelligence community gears itself to serve those decision makers who will demand the most from it, and is loath to surrender sources and/or capabilities that may prove useful to decision makers.

Since the benefits of strategic intelligence are so subjective, formal cost-benefit analysis cannot be used to justify a given level of support for intelligence. Rather, intelligence tends to be supported on a "level-of-effort" basis, that is, a political judgment about what is "reasonable," given other defense and nondefense pressures on the overall national budget.

3.3.2 The Impact of Cryptography on Signals Intelligence

Cryptography poses a threat to SIGINT for two separate but related reasons:

• Strong cryptography can prevent any given message from being read or understood. Strong cryptography used primarily by foreign governments with the discipline to use those products on a regular and consistent basis presents the United States with a formidable challenge. Some encrypted traffic regularly intercepted by the United States is simply undecipherable by any known means.

• Even weak cryptography, if practiced on a widespread basis by foreign governments or other entities, increases the cost of exploitation dramatically.[36] When most messages that are intercepted are unencrypted, the cost to determine whether an individual message is interesting is quite low. However, if most intercepted messages are encrypted, each one has to be cryptanalyzed individually, because the interceptor does not know if it is interesting or not.[37]

According to Administration officials who testified to the committee,

---

[36]This point is echoed in Susan Landau et al., *Codes, Keys, and Conflicts: Issues in U.S. Crypto Policy*, 1994, p. 25.

[37]For example, assume that 1 out of every 1,000 messages is interesting and that the cost of intercepting a message is X and the cost of decrypting a message is Y. Thus, each interesting message is acquired at a cost of $1,000 X + Y$. However, if every message is encrypted, the cost of each interesting message is $1,000 (X + Y)$, which is approximately $1,000 Y$ larger. In other words, the cryptanalyst must do 1,000 times more work for each interesting message.

the acquisition and proper use of cryptography by a foreign adversary could impair the national security interests of the United States in a number of ways:

• Cryptography used by adversaries on a wide scale would significantly increase the cost and difficulty of intelligence gathering across the full range of U.S. national security interests.
• Cryptography used by governments and foreign companies can increase an adversary's capability to conceal the development of missile delivery systems and weapons of mass destruction.
• Cryptography can improve the ability of an adversary to maintain the secrecy of its military operations to the detriment of U.S. or allied military forces that might be similarly engaged.

The above comments suggest that the deployment of strong cryptography that is widely used will diminish the capabilities of those responsible for SIGINT. Today, there is a noticeable trend toward better and cheaper encryption that is steadily closing the window of exploitation of unencrypted communications. The growth of strong encryption will reduce the availability of such intelligence. Using capabilities and techniques developed during the Cold War, the SIGINT system will continue its efforts to collect against countries and other entities newly hostile to the United States. Many governments and parties in those nations, however, will be potential customers for advanced cryptography as it becomes available on world markets. In the absence of improved cryptanalytic methods, cooperative arrangements with foreign governments, and new ways of approaching the information collection problem, it is likely that losses in traditional SIGINT capability would result in a diminished effectiveness of the U.S. intelligence community.

3.4 SIMILARITIES IN AND DIFFERENCES BETWEEN FOREIGN POLICY/NATIONAL SECURITY AND LAW ENFORCEMENT NEEDS FOR COMMUNICATIONS MONITORING

It is instructive to consider the similarities in and differences between national security and law enforcement needs for communications monitoring.

3.4.1 Similarities

• *Secrecy*. Both foreign policy and law enforcement authorities regard surreptitiously intercepted communications as a more reliable source than information produced through other means. Surveillance targets usually believe (however falsely) that their communications are private; therefore, eavesdropping must be surreptitious and the secrecy of monitoring maintained. Thus, the identity and/or nature of specific SIGINT sources are generally very sensitive pieces of information, and are divulged only for good cause.

• *Timeliness.* For support of tactical operations, near-real-time information may be needed (e.g., when a crime or terrorist operation is imminent, when hostile forces are about to be engaged).

• *Resources available to targets.* Many parties targeted for electronic surveillance for foreign policy reasons or by law enforcement authorities lack the resources to develop their own security products, and are most likely to use what they can purchase on the commercial market.

• *Allocation of resources for collection.* The size of the budget allocated to law enforcement and to the U.S. intelligence community is not unlimited. Available resources constrain both the amount of surveillance law enforcement officials can undertake and the ability of the U.S. SIGINT system to respond to the full range of national intelligence requirements levied upon it.

—Electronic surveillance, although in many cases critical, is only one of the tools available to U.S. law enforcement. Because it is manpower intensive, it is a tool used sparingly; thus, it represents a relatively small percentage of the total investment. The average cost of a wiretap order is $57,000 (see Appendix D) or approximately one-half of a full-time-equivalent agent-year.

—The U.S. SIGINT system is a major contributor to the overall U.S. intelligence collection capability and represents a correspondingly large percentage of the foreign intelligence budget. Although large, the U.S. system is by no means funded to "vacuum clean" the world's communications. It is sized to gather the most potentially lucrative foreign signals and targeted very selectively to collect and analyze only those communications most likely to yield information relating to high-priority intelligence needs.

• *Perceptions of the problem.* The volume of electronic traffic and the use of encryption are both expected to grow, but how the growth of one will compare to that of the other is unclear at present. If the overall growth in the volume of unencrypted electronic traffic lags the growth in the use of cryptography, those conducting surveillance for law enforcement or foreign policy reasons may perceive a loss in access because the fraction of intercepts available to them will decrease, even if the absolute amount of information intercepted has increased as the result of larger volumes of information. Of course, if the communicating parties take special care to encrypt their sensitive communications, the absolute amount of useful information intercepted may decrease as well.

3.4.2 Differences

• *Protection of sources.* While the distinction is not hard and fast, law enforcement authorities conducting an electronic surveillance are generally seeking specific items of evidence that relate to a criminal act and that can be presented in open court, which implies that the source of such information (i.e., the wiretap) will be revealed (and possibly challenged for legal validity). By contrast, national security authorities are usually seeking a body of intelligence information over a longer period of time and are therefore far more concerned with preserving the secrecy of sources and methods.

• *Definition of interests.* There is a consensus, expressed in law, about the specific types of domestic crimes that may be investigated through the use of wiretapping. Even internationally, there is some degree of consensus about what activities are criminal; the existence of this consensus enables a considerable amount of law enforcement cooperation on a variety of matters. National security interests are defined differently and are subject to refinement in a changing world, and security interests often vary from nation to nation. However, a community of interest among NATO allies and between the United States and the major nations of the free world makes possible fruitful intelligence relationships, even though the United States may at times target a nation that is both ally and competitor.

• *Volume of potentially relevant communications.* The volume of communications of interest to law enforcement authorities is small compared to the volume of interest to national security authorities.

• *Legal framework.* Domestic law enforcement authorities are bound by constitutional protections and legislation that limit their ability to conduct electronic surveillance. National security authorities operate under far fewer legal constraints in monitoring the communications of foreign parties located outside the United States.

• *Perceptions of vulnerability to surveillance.* Parties targeted by national security authorities are far more likely to take steps to protect their communications than are most criminals.

3.5 BUSINESS AND INDIVIDUAL NEEDS FOR EXCEPTIONAL ACCESS TO PROTECTED INFORMATION

As noted above in Section 3.1, an employer may need access to data that has been encrypted by an employee. Corporations that use cryptography for confidentiality must always be concerned with the risk that keys will be lost, corrupted, required in some emergency situation, or be otherwise unavailable, and they have a valid interest in defending their interests in the face of these eventualities.[38]

Cryptography can present problems for companies attempting to satisfy their legitimate business interests in access to stored and communicated information:

• *Stored data.* For entirely legitimate business reasons, an employee might encrypt business records, but due to circumstances such as vacation or sick leave, the employer might need to read the contents of these records without the employee's immediate assistance. Then again, an employee might simply forget the relevant password to an encrypted file, or an employee might maliciously refuse to provide the key (e.g., if he has a grudge against his employer), or might keep records that are related to improper activities but encrypt them to keep them private; a business undertaking an audit to uncover or investigate these activities might well need to read these records without the assistance of the employee. For example, in a dispute over alleged wrongdoing of his superiors, a Washington, D.C., financial analyst changed the password on the city's computer and refused to share it.[39] In another incident, the former chief financial officer of an insurance company, Golden Eagle Group Ltd., installed a password known only to himself and froze out operations. He demanded a personal computer that he claimed was his, his final paycheck, a letter of reference, and a $100 fee—presumably for revealing the password.[40] While technical fixes for these problems are relatively easy, they do demonstrate the existence of motivation to undertake such actions. Furthermore, it is poor management practice that allows a single employee to control critical data, but that issue is beyond the scope of this study.

• *Communications.* A number of corporations provided input to the committee indicating that for entirely legitimate business reasons (e.g., for resolution of a dispute between the corporation and a customer), an employer might need to learn about the content of an employee's communications. Alternatively, an employee might use company communications facilities as a means for conducting improper activities (e.g., leaking company-confidential information, stealing corporate assets, engaging in

---

[38]While users may lose or corrupt keys used for user authentication, the procedures needed in this event are different than if the keys in question are for encryption. For example, a lost authentication key creates a need to *revoke* the key, so that another party that comes into possession of the authentication key cannot impersonate the original owner. By contrast, an encryption key that is lost creates a need to *recover* the key.

[39]Peter G. Neumann, *Computer-Related Risks*, Addison-Wesley, New York, 1995, p. 154.

[40]Neumann, *Computer-Related Risks*, 1995, p. 154.

kickback or fraud schemes, inappropriately favoring one supplier over another). A business undertaking an audit to uncover or investigate these activities might well need to monitor these communications without the consent of the employee (Box 3.4)[41] but would be unable to do so if the communications were encrypted. In other instances, a company might wish to assist law enforcement officials in investigating information crimes against it[42] but would not be able to do so if it could not obtain access to unsanctioned employee-encrypted files or communications. Many, though certainly not all, businesses require prospective employees to agree as a condition of employment that their communications are subject to employer monitoring under various circumstances.[43]

It is a generally held view among businesses that provisions for cor-porate exceptional access to stored data are more important than such provisions for communications.[44] For individuals, the distinction is even

---

[41]For example, employees with Internet access may spend so much time on nonwork-related Internet activities that their productivity is impaired. Concerns about such prob-lems have led some companies to monitor the Internet activities of their employees, and spawned products that covertly monitor and record Internet use. See Laurie Flynn, "Find-ing On-line Distractions, Employers Strive to Keep Workers in Line," *New York Times*, No-vember 6, 1995, p. D5.

[42]A number of examples of such cooperation can be found in Peter Schweizer, *Friendly Spies*, Atlantic Monthly Press, New York, 1993.

[43]The legal ramifications of employer access to on-the-job communications of employees are interesting, though outside the scope of this report. For example, a company employee may communicate with another company employee using cryptography that denies em-ployer access to the content of those communications; such use may be contrary to explicit company policy. May an employee who has violated company policy in this manner be discharged legally? In general, employer access to on-the-job communications raises many issues of ethics and privacy, even if such access is explicitly permitted by contract or policy.

[44]This distinction becomes somewhat fuzzy when considering technologies such as e-mail that serve the purpose of communications but that also involve data storage. Greater clarity is possible if one distinguishes between the electronic bits of a message in transit (e.g., on a wire) and the same bits that are at rest (e.g., in a file). With e-mail, the message is sent and then stored; thus, e-mail can be regarded as a stored communication. These comments suggest that a need for exceptional access to e-mail is much more similar to that for storage than for communications, because it is much more likely that a need will arise to read an e-mail message after it has been stored than while it is in transit. A likely scenario of exceptional access to e-mail is that a user may receive e-mail encrypted with a public key for which he no longer has the corresponding private key (that would enable him to de-crypt incoming messages). While this user could in principle contact the senders and in-form them of a new public key, an alternative would be to develop a system that would permit him to obtain exceptional access without requiring such actions.

BOX 3.4
Examples of Business Needs for Exceptional Access to Communications

• A major Fortune 1000 corporation was the subject of various articles in the relevant trade press. These articles described conditions within the corporation (e.g., employee morale) that were based on information supplied by employees of this corporation acting in an unauthorized manner and contrary to company policy; moreover, these articles were regarded by corporate management as being highly embarrassing to the company. The employees responsible were identified through a review of tapes of all their telephone conversations in the period immediately preceding publication of the damaging articles, and were summarily dismissed. As a condition of employment, these employees had given their employer permission to record their telephone calls.

• Executives at a major Fortune 1000 corporation had made certain accommodations in settling the accounts of a particular client that, while legal, materially distorted an accounting audit of the books of that client. A review of the telephone conversations in the relevant period indicated that these executives had done so knowingly, and they were dismissed. As a condition of employment, these executives had given their employer permission to record their telephone calls.

• Attempting to resolve a dispute about the specific terms of a contract to sell oil at a particular price, a multinational oil company needed to obtain all relevant records. Given the fact that oil prices fluctuate significantly on a minute-by-minute basis, most such trades are conducted and agreed to by telephone. All such calls are recorded, in accordance with contracts signed by traders as a condition of employment. Review of these voice records provided sufficient information to resolve the dispute.

• A multinational company was notified by a law enforcement agency in Nation A regarding its suspicions that an employee of the company was committing fraud against the company. This employee was a national of Nation B. The company began an investigation of this individual in cooperation with law enforcement authorities in Nation B, and in due course, legal authorization for a wiretap on this individual using company facilities was obtained. The company cooperated with these law enforcement authorities in the installation of the wiretap.

SOURCE: Anonymous testimony to the Committee to Study National Cryptography Policy.

sharper. Private individuals as well as businesses have a need to retrieve encrypted data that is stored and for which they may have lost or forgotten the key. For example, a person may have lost the key to an encrypted will or financial statement and wish to retrieve the data. However, it is much more difficult to imagine circumstances under which a person might have a legitimate need for the real-time monitoring of communications.

3.6 OTHER TYPES OF EXCEPTIONAL ACCESS TO PROTECTED INFORMATION

The discussion of exceptional access above involves *only* the question of encryption for confidentiality. While it is possible to imagine legitimate needs for exceptional access to encrypted data (for purposes of ensuring secrecy), it is nearly impossible to imagine a legitimate need for exceptional access to cryptography used for the purposes of user authentication, data integrity, or nonrepudiation. In a business context, these cryptographic capabilities implement or support longstanding legal precepts that are essential to the conduct of commerce.

• Without unforgeable digital signatures, the concept of a binding contract is seriously weakened.
• Without trusted digitally notarized documents, questions of time precedence might not be legally resolvable.
• Without unforgeable integrity checks, the notion of a certifiably accurate and authentic copy of digital documents is empty.
• Without strong authentication and unquestionable nonrepudiation, the analog of registered delivery in postal systems is open to suspicion.[45]

With exceptional access to the cryptography implementing such features or to the private keys associated with them, the legal protection that such features are intended to provide might well be called into question. At a minimum, there would likely be a questioning of the validity or integrity of the protective safeguards, and there might be grounds for legal challenge. For example, a businessperson might have to demonstrate to the satisfaction of a court or jury that he has properly and adequately protected the private keys used to digitally sign his contracts.

It is conceivable that the government, for national security purposes, might seek exceptional access to such capabilities for offensive information warfare (see Chapter 2); however, public policy should not promote these capabilities, because such access could well undermine public confidence in such cryptographic mechanisms.

---

[45]In fact, digital signatures and nonrepudiation provide a stronger guarantee than does registered delivery; the former can be used to assure the delivery of the contents of an "envelope," whereas postal registered delivery can only be used to assure the delivery of the envelope.

3.7 RECAP

In general, cryptography for confidentiality involves a party undertaking an encryption (to protect information by generating ciphertext from plaintext) and a party authorized by the encryptor to decrypt the ciphertext and thus recover the original plaintext. In the case of information that is communicated, these parties are in general different individuals. In the case of information that is stored, the first party and the second party are in general the same individual. However, circumstances can and do arise in which third parties (i.e., decrypting parties that are not originally authorized or intended by the encrypting party to recover the information involved) may need access to such information. These needs for exceptional access to encrypted information may arise from businesses, individuals, law enforcement, and national security, and these needs are different depending on the parties in question. Encryption that renders such information confidential threatens the ability of these third parties to obtain the necessary access.

How the needs for confidentiality and exceptional access are reconciled in a policy context is the subject of Part II.

PART II

Policy Instruments

TO THE BEST OF THE COMMITTEE'S KNOWLEDGE, *the goals of U.S. cryptography policy have not been explicitly formalized and articulated within the government. However, senior government officials have indicated that U.S. cryptography policy seeks to promote the following objectives:*

- *Deployment of encryption adequate and strong enough to protect electronic commerce that may be transacted on the future information infrastructure;*
- *Development and adoption of global (rather than national) standards and solutions;*
- *Widespread deployment of products with encryption capabilities for confidentiality that enable legal access for law enforcement and national security purposes; and*
- *Avoidance of the development of de facto cryptography standards (either domestically or globally) that do not permit access for law enforcement and national security purposes, thus ensuring that the use of such products remains relatively limited.*

Many analysts believe that these goals are irreconcilable. To the extent that this is so, the U.S. government is thus faced with a policy problem requiring a compromise among these goals that is tolerable, though by assumption not ideal with respect to any individual goal. Such has always been the case with many issues that generate social controversy—balancing product safety against the undesirability of burdensome regulation on product vendors, public health against the rights of individuals to refuse medical treatment, and so on.

111

As of this writing, U.S. cryptography policy is still evolving, and the particular laws, regulations, and other levers that government uses to influence behavior and policy are under review or are being developed.

Chapter 4 is devoted to the subject of export controls, which dominate industry concerns about national cryptography policy. Many senior executives in the information technology industry perceive these controls as a major limitation on their ability to export products with encryption capabilities. Furthermore, because exports of products with encryption capabilities are governed by the regime applied to technologies associated with munitions, reflecting the importance of cryptography to national security, they are generally subject to more stringent controls than are exports of other computer-related technologies.

Chapter 5 addresses the subject of escrowed encryption. Escrowed encryption is a form of encryption intended to provide strong protection for legitimate uses but also to permit exceptional access by government officials, by corporate employers, or by end users under specified circumstances. Since 1993, the Clinton Administration has aggressively promoted escrowed encryption as a basic pillar of national cryptography policy. Public concerns about escrowed encryption have focused on the possibilities for failure in the mechanisms intended to prevent improper access to encrypted information, leading to losses of confidentiality.

Chapter 6 addresses a variety of other aspects of national cryptography policy and public concerns that these aspects have raised.

4

Export Controls

Export controls on cryptography and related technical data have been a pillar of national cryptography policy for many years. Increasingly, they have generated controversy because they pit the needs of national security to conduct signals intelligence against the information security needs of legitimate U.S. businesses and the markets of U.S. manufacturers whose products might meet these needs. Chapter 4 describes the current state of export controls on cryptography and issues that these controls raise, including their effectiveness in achieving their stated objectives; negative effects that the export control regime has on U.S. businesses and U.S. vendors of information technology that must be weighed against the positive effects of reducing the use of cryptography abroad; the mismatch between vendor and government perceptions of export controls; and various other aspects of the export control process as it is experienced by those subject to it.

4.1 BRIEF DESCRIPTION OF CURRENT EXPORT CONTROLS

Many advanced industrialized nations maintain controls on exports of cryptography, including the United States. The discussion below focuses on U.S. export controls; Appendix G addresses foreign export control regimes on cryptography.

4.1.1 The Rationale for Export Controls

On the basis of discussion with senior government officials and its own deliberations, the committee believes that the current U.S. export control regime on products with encryption capabilities for confidentiality is intended to serve two primary purposes:

- To delay the spread of strong cryptographic capabilities and the use of those capabilities throughout the world. Senior intelligence officials recognize that in the long run, the ability of intelligence agencies to engage in signals intelligence will inevitably diminish due to a variety of technological trends, including the greater use of cryptography.[1]
- To give the U.S. government a tool for monitoring and influencing the commercial development of cryptography. Since any U.S. vendor that wishes to export a product with encryption capabilities for confidentiality must approach the U.S. government for permission to do so, the export license approval process is an opportunity for the U.S. government to learn in detail about the capabilities of such products. Moreover, the results of the license approval process have influenced the cryptography that is available on the international market.

4.1.2 General Description[2]

Authority to regulate imports and exports of products with cryptographic capabilities to and from the United States derives from two items of legislation: the Arms Export Control Act (AECA) of 1949 (intended to regulate munitions) and the Export Administration Act (EAA; intended to regulate so-called dual-use products[3]). The AECA is the legislative basis for the International Traffic in Arms Regulations (ITAR), in which the U.S. Munitions List (USML) is defined and specified. Items on the USML are regarded for purposes of import and export as munitions, and the ITAR are administered by the Department of State. The EAA is the legislative basis for the Export Administration Regulations (EAR), which

---

[1]Although the committee came to this conclusion on its own, it is consistent with that of the Office of Technology Assessment, *Information Security and Privacy in Network Environments*, U.S. Government Printing Office, Washington, D.C., September 1994.

[2]Two references that provide detailed descriptions of the U.S. export control regime for products with encryption capability are a memorandum by Fred Greguras of the law firm Fenwick & West (Palo Alto, Calif.), dated March 6, 1995, and titled "Update on Current Status of U.S. Export Administration Regulations on Software" (available at http://www.batnet.com:80/oikoumene/SftwareEU.html), and a paper by Ira Rubinstein, "Export Controls on Encryption Software," in *Coping with U.S. Export Controls 1994*, Commercial Law & Practice Course Handbook Series No. A-733, Practicing Law Institute, October 18, 1995. The Greguras memorandum focuses primarily on the requirements of products controlled by the Commerce Control List, while the Rubinstein paper focuses primarily on how to move a product from the Munitions List to the Commerce Control List.

[3]A dual-use item is one that has both military and civilian applications.

define dual-use items on a list known as the Commerce Control List (CCL);[4] the EAR are administered by the Department of Commerce. The EAA lapsed in 1994 but has been continued under executive order since that time. Both the AECA and the EAA specify sanctions that can be applied in the event that recipients of goods exported from the United States fail to comply with all relevant requirements, such as agreements to refrain from reexport (Box 4.1).

At present, products with encryption capabilities can be imported into the United States without restriction, although the President does have statutory authority to regulate such imports if appropriate. Exports are a different matter. Any export of an item covered by the USML requires a specific affirmative decision by the State Department's Office of Defense Trade Controls, a process that can be time-consuming and cumbersome from the perspective of the vendor and prospective foreign purchaser.

The ITAR regulate and control exports of all "cryptographic systems, equipment, assemblies, modules, integrated circuits, components or software with the capability of maintaining secrecy or confidentiality of information or information systems"; in addition, they regulate information about cryptography but not implemented in a product in a category known as "technical data."[5]

Until 1983, USML controls were maintained on all cryptography products. However, since that time, a number of relaxations in these controls have been implemented (Box 4.2), although many critics contend that such relaxation has lagged significantly behind the evolving marketplace. Today, the ITAR provide a number of certain categorical exemptions that allow for products in those categories to be regulated as dual-use items and controlled exclusively by the CCL. For products that do not fall into these categories and for which there is some question about whether it is the USML or the CCL that governs their export, the ITAR also provide for a procedure known as commodity jurisdiction,[6] under which potential exporters can obtain judgments from the State Department about which list governs a specific product. A product granted commodity jurisdiction to the CCL falls under the control of the EAR and the Department of Commerce. Note that commodity jurisdiction to the CCL is generally granted for products with encryption capabilities using 40-bit keys regardless of the algorithm used, although these decisions are made on a

---

[4]The CCL is also commonly known as the Commodity Control List.

[5]However, encryption products intended for domestic Canadian use in general do not require export licenses.

[6]Commodity jurisdiction is also often known by its acronym, CJ.

BOX 4.1
Enforcing Compliance with End-Use Agreements

In general, a U.S. Munitions List (USML) license is granted to a U.S. exporter for the shipping of a product, technical data, or service covered by the USML to a particular foreign recipient for a set of specified end uses and subject to a number of conditions (e.g., restrictions on reexport to another nation, nontransfer to a third party). The full range of ITAR sanctions is available against the U.S. exporter and the foreign recipient outside the United States.

The ITAR specify that as a condition of receiving a USML license, the U.S. exporter must include in the contract with the foreign recipient language that binds the recipient to abide by all appropriate end-use restrictions. Furthermore, the U.S. exporter that does not take reasonable steps to enforce the contract is subject to ITAR criminal and civil sanctions. But how can end-use restrictions be enforced for a foreign recipient?

A number of sanctions are available to enforce the compliance of foreign recipients of USML items exported from the United States. The primary sanctions available are the criminal and civil liabilities established by the Arms Export Control Act (AECA); the foreign recipient can face civil and/or criminal charges in U.S. federal courts for violating the AECA. Although different U.S. courts have different views on extraterritoriality claims asserted for U.S. law, a criminal conviction or a successful civil lawsuit could result in the imposition of criminal penalties on individuals involved and/or seizure of any U.S. assets of the foreign recipient. (When there are no U.S. assets, recovering fines or damages can be highly problematic, although some international agreements and treaties provide for cooperation in such cases.) Whether an individual could be forced to return to the United States for incarceration would depend on the existence of an appropriate extradition treaty between the United States and the foreign nation to whose jurisdiction the individual is subject.

A second avenue of enforcement is that the foreign recipient found to be in violation can be denied all further exports from the United States. In addition, the foreign violator can be denied permission to compete for contracts with the U.S. government. From time to time, proposals are made to apply sanctions against violators that would deny privileges for them to export products to the United States, though such proposals often create political controversy.

A third mechanism of enforcement may proceed through diplomatic channels. Depending on the nation to whose jurisdiction the foreign recipient is subject, the U.S. government may well approach the government of that nation to seek its assistance in persuading or forcing the recipient to abide by the relevant end-use restrictions.

A fourth mechanism of enforcement is the sales contract between the U.S. exporter and the foreign recipient, which provides a mechanism for civil action against the foreign recipient. A foreign buyer who violates the end-use restrictions is in breach of contract with the U.S. exporter, who may then sue for damages incurred by the U.S. company. Depending on the language of the contract, the suit may be carried out in U.S. or foreign courts; alternatively, the firms may submit to binding arbitration.

The operation of these enforcement mechanisms can be cumbersome, uncertain, and slow. But they exist, and they are used. Thus, while some analysts believe that they do not provide sufficient protection for U.S. national security interests, others defend them as a reasonable but not perfect attempt at defending those interests.

BOX 4.2
Licensing Relaxations on Cryptography: A Short History

Prior to 1983, all cryptography exports required individual licenses from the State Department. Since then, a number of changes have been proposed and mostly implemented.

Year   *Change*

1983   Distribution licenses established allowing exports to multiple users under a
        single license
1987   Nonconfidentiality products moved to Department of Commerce (DOC) on
        a case-by-case basis
1990   International Traffic in Arms Regulations amended—all nonconfidentiality
        products under DOC jurisdiction
1990   Mass-market general-purpose software with encryption for confidentiality
        moved to DOC on case-by-case basis
1992   Software Publishers Association agreement providing for 40-bit RC2/RC4-
        based products under DOC jurisdiction
1993   Mass-market hardware products with encryption capabilities moved to DOC
        on case-by-case basis
1994   Reforms to expedite license processing at Department of State
1995   Proposal to move to DOC software products with 64-bit cryptography for
        confidentiality with "properly escrowed" keys
1996   "Personal use" exemption finalized

SOURCE: National Security Agency.

---

product-by-product basis. In addition, when a case-by-case export licensing decision results in CCL jurisdiction for a software product, it is usually only the object code, which cannot be modified easily, that is transferred; the source code of the product (embedding the identical functionality but more easily modified) generally remains on the USML.

As described in Box 4.3, key differences between the USML and the CCL have the effect that items on the CCL enjoy more liberal export consideration than items on the USML. (This report uses the term "liberal export consideration" to mean treatment under the CCL.) Most importantly, a product controlled by the CCL is reviewed only once by the U.S. government, thus drastically simplifying the marketing and sale of the product overseas.

The most important of these explicit categorical exemptions to the USML for cryptography are described in Box 4.4. In addition, the current export control regime provides for an individual case-by-case review of USML licensing applications for products that do not fall under the jurisdiction of the CCL. Under current practice, USML licenses to acquire and

BOX 4.3
Important Differences Between the U.S. Munitions List and the Commerce Control List

For Items on U.S. Munitions List (USML)	For Items on Commerce Control List (CCL)
Department of State has broad leeway to take national security considerations into account in licensing decisions; indeed, national security and foreign policy considerations are the driving force behind the Arms Export Control Act.	Department of Commerce may limit exports only to the extent that they would make "a significant contribution to the military potential of any other country which would prove detrimental to the national security of the United States" or "where necessary to further significantly the foreign policy of the United States." The history of the Export Administration Act strongly suggests that its national security purpose is to deny dual-use items to countries of Communist Bloc nations, nations of concern with respect to proliferation of weapons of mass destruction, and other rogue nations.
Items are included on the USML if the item is "inherently military in character"; the end use is irrelevant in such a determination. Broad categories of product are included.	Performance parameters rather than broad categories define included items.
Decisions about export can take as long as necessary.	Decisions about export must be completed within 120 days.
Export licenses can be denied on very general grounds (e.g., the export would be against the U.S. national interest).	Export licenses can be denied only on very specific grounds (e.g., high likelihood of diversion to proscribed nations).

Individually validated licenses are generally required, although distribution and bulk licenses are possible.[1]	General licenses are often issued, although general licenses do not convey blanket authority for export.[2]
Prior government approval is needed for export.	Prior government approval is generally not needed for export.
Licensing decisions are not subject to judicial review.	Licensing decisions are subject to judicial review by a federal judge or an administrative law judge.
Foreign availability may or may not be a consideration in granting a license at the discretion of the State Department.	Foreign availability of items that are substantially equivalent is, by law, a consideration in a licensing decision.
Items included on the USML are not subject to periodic review.	Items included on the CCL must be reviewed periodically.
A Shipper's Export Declaration (SED) is required in all instances.	A SED may be required, unless exemption from the requirement is granted under the Export Administration Regulations.

[1] Bulk licenses authorize multiple shipments without requiring individual approval. Distribution licenses authorize multiple shipments to a foreign distributor. In each case, record-keeping requirements are imposed on the vendor. In practice, a distribution license shifts the burden of export restrictions from vendor to distributor. Under a distribution license, enforcement of restrictions on end use and on destination nations and post-shipment record-keeping requirements are the responsibility of the distributor; vendors need not seek an individual license for each specific shipment.

[2] Even if an item is controlled by the CCL, U.S. exporters are not allowed to ship such an item if the exporter knows that it will be used directly in the production of weapons of mass destruction or ballistic missiles by a certain group of nations. Moreover, U.S. exports from the CCL are prohibited entirely to companies and individuals on a list of "Specially Designated Nationals" designated as agents of Cuba, Libya, Iraq, North Korea, or Yugoslavia or to a list of companies and individuals on the Bureau of Export Administration's Table of Denial Orders (including some located in the United States and Europe).

BOX 4.4
Categorical Exemptions on the USML for Products Incorporating Cryptography and Informal Practices Governing Licensing

Categorical Exemptions

The International Traffic in Arms Regulations (ITAR) provide for a number of categorical exemptions, including:

- Mass-market software products that use 40-bit key lengths with the RC2 or RC4 algorithm for confidentiality.[1]
- Products with encryption capabilities for confidentiality (of any strength) that are specifically intended for use only in banking or money transactions. Products in this category may have encryption of arbitrary strength.
- Products that are limited in cryptographic functionality to providing capabilities for user authentication, access control, and data integrity.

Products in these categories are automatically granted commodity jurisdiction to the Commerce Control List (CCL).

Informal Noncodified Exemptions

The current export control regime provides for an individual case-by-case review of U.S. Munitions List (USML) licensing applications for products that do not fall under the jurisdiction of the CCL. Under current practice, certain categories of firms will generally be granted a USML license through the individual review process to acquire and export for their own use products with encryption capabilities stronger than that provided by 40-bit RC2/RC4 encryption:[2]

- A U.S.-controlled firm (i.e., a U.S. firm operating abroad, a U.S.-controlled foreign firm, or a foreign subsidiary of a U.S. firm);
- Banks and financial institutions (including stock brokerages and insurance companies), whether U.S.-controlled or -owned or foreign-owned, if the products involved are intended for use in internal communications and communications with other banks even if these communications are not limited strictly to banking or money transactions.

---

[1]The RC2 and RC4 algorithms are symmetric-key encryption algorithms developed by RSA Data Security Inc. (RSADSI). They are both proprietary algorithms, and manufacturers of products using these algorithms must enter into a licensing arrangement with RSADSI. RC2 and RC4 are also trademarks owned by RSADSI, although both algorithms have appeared on the Internet. A product with capabilities for confidentiality will be automatically granted commodity jurisdiction to the CCL if it meets a certain set of requirements, the most important of which are the following:

a. The software includes encryption for data confidentiality and uses the RC4 and/or RC2 algorithms with a key space of 40 bits.

b. If both RC4 and RC2 are used in the same software, their functionality must be separate; that is, no data can be operated on by both routines.

c. The software must not allow the alteration of the data encryption mechanism and its associated key spaces by the user or by any other program.

d. The key exchange used in the data encryption must be based on either a public-key algorithm with a key space less than or equal to a 512-bit modulus and/or a symmetrical algorithm with a key space less than or equal to 64 bits.
e. The software must not allow the alteration of the key management mechanism and its associated key space by the user or any other program.

To ensure that the software has properly implemented the approved encryption algorithm(s), the State Department requires that the product pass a "vector test," in which the vendor receives test data (the vector) and a random key from the State Department, encrypts the vector with the product using the key provided, and returns the result to the State Department; if the product-computed result is identical to the known correct answer, the product automatically qualifies for jurisdiction under the CCL.

Note that the specific technical requirements described in this footnote are not contained in the *Federal Register*; rather, they were described in a State Department document, any change in which is not subject to an official procedure for public comment. (These conditions were first published in "Defense Trade News," Volume 3(4), October 1992, pp. 11-15. "Defense Trade News" is a newsletter published by the Office of Defense Trade Controls at the Department of State.)

[2]See Footnote 7 in the main text of this chapter.

export for internal use products with encryption capabilities stronger than that provided by 40-bit RC2/RC4 encryption (hereafter in this chapter called "strong encryption"[7]) are generally granted to U.S.-controlled firms (i.e., U.S. firms operating abroad, U.S.-controlled foreign firms, or foreign subsidiaries of a U.S. firm). In addition, banks and financial institutions (including stock brokerages and insurance companies), whether U.S.-controlled or -owned or foreign-owned, are generally granted USML licenses for strong encryption for use in internal communications and communications with other banks even if these communications are not limited strictly to banking or money transactions.

In September 1994, the Administration promulgated regulations that provided for U.S. vendors to distribute approved products with encryption capabilities for confidentiality directly from the United States to foreign customers without using a foreign distributor and without prior

[7]How much stronger than 40-bit RC2/RC4 is unspecified. Products incorporating the 56-bit DES algorithm are often approved for these informal exemptions, and at times even products using larger key sizes have been approved. But the key size is not unlimited, as may be the case under the explicit categorical exemptions specified in the ITAR.

State Department approval for each export.[8] It also announced plans to finalize a "personal use exemption" to allow license-free temporary exports of products with encryption capabilities when intended for personal use; a final rule on the personal use exemption was announced in early 1996 and is discussed below in Section 4.3.2. Lastly, it announced a number of actions intended to streamline the export control process to provide more rapid turnaround for certain "preapproved" products.

In August 1995, the Administration announced a proposal to liberalize export controls on software products with encryption capabilities for confidentiality that use algorithms with a key space of 64 or fewer bits, provided that the key(s) required to decrypt messages and files are "properly escrowed"; such products would be transferred to the CCL. However, since an understanding of this proposal requires some background in escrowed encryption, discussion of it is deferred to Chapter 5.

4.1.3 Discussion of Current Licensing Practices

Categorical Exemptions

The categorical exemptions described in Box 4.4 raise a number of issues:

- In the case of the 40-bit limitation, the committee was unable to find a specific analytical basis for this figure. Most likely, it was the result of a set of compromises that were politically driven by all of the parties involved.[9] However, whatever the basis for this key size, recent success-

---

[8]Prior to this rule, almost every encryption export required an individual license. Only those exports covered by a distribution arrangement could be shipped without an individual license. This distribution arrangement required a U.S. vendor of products with cryptographic capabilities to export to a foreign distributor that could then resell them to multiple end users. The distribution arrangement had to be approved by the State Department and included some specific language. Under the new rule, a U.S. vendor without a foreign distributor can essentially act as his own distributor, and avoid having to obtain a separate license for each sale. Exporters are required to submit a proposed arrangement identifying, among other things, specific items to be shipped, proposed end users and end use, and countries to which the items are destined. Upon approval of the arrangement, exporters are permitted to ship the specified products directly to end users in the approved countries based on a single license. See Bureau of Political-Military Affairs, Department of State, "Amendment to the International Traffic in Arms Regulations," *Federal Register*, September 2, 1994.

[9]It is worth noting a common argument among many nongovernment observers that any level of encryption that qualifies for export (e.g., that qualifies for control by the CCL, or that is granted an export license under the USML) must be easily defeatable by NSA, or else

ful demonstrations of the ability to undertake brute-force cryptanalysis on messages encrypted with a 40-bit key (Box 4.5) have led to a widespread perception that such key sizes are inadequate for meaningful information security.

- In the case of products intended for use only in banking or money transactions, the exemption results from the recognition by national security authorities that the integrity of the world's financial system is worth protecting with high levels of cryptographic security. Given the primacy of the U.S. banking community in international financial markets, such a conclusion makes eminent sense. Furthermore, at the time this exemption was promulgated, the financial community was the primary customer for products with encryption capabilities.

This rationale for protecting banking and money transactions naturally calls attention to the possibilities inherent in a world of electronic commerce, in which routine communications will be increasingly likely to include information related to financial transactions. Banks (and retail shops, manufacturers, suppliers, end customers, and so on) will engage in such communications across national borders. In a future world of electronic commerce, connections among nonfinancial institutions may become as important as the banking networks are today. At least one vendor has been granted authority to use strong encryption in software intended for export that would support international electronic commerce (though under the terms of the license, strong encryption applies only to a small portion of the transaction message).[10]

- In the case of products useful only for user authentication, access control, and data integrity, the exemption resulted from a judgment that the benefits of more easily available technology for these purposes outweigh whatever costs there might be to such availability. Thus, in principle, these nonconfidentiality products from U.S. vendors should be available overseas without significant restriction.

In practice, however, this is not entirely the case. Export restrictions on confidentiality have some "spillover" effects that reduce somewhat

---

NSA would not allow it to leave the country. The subtext of this argument is that such a level of encryption is per force inadequate. Of course, taken to its logical conclusion, this argument renders impossible any agreement between national security authorities and vendors and users regarding acceptable levels of encryption for export.

[10]"Export Approved for Software to Aid Commerce on Internet," *New York Times*, May 8, 1995, p. D7.

BOX 4.5
Successful Challenges to 40-bit Encryption

In the summer of 1995, a message encoded with the 40-bit RC4 algorithm was successfully decrypted without prior knowledge of the key by Damien Doligez of the INRIA organization in France. The message in question was a record of an actual submission of form data that was sent to Netscape's electronic shop order form in "secure" mode (including a fictitious name and address). The challenge was posed to break the encryption and recover the name and address information entered in the form and sent securely to Netscape. Breaking the encryption was accomplished by a brute-force search on a network of about 120 workstations and a few parallel computers at INRIA, Ecole Polytechnique, and ENS. The key was found after scanning a little more than half the key space in 8 days, and the message was successfully decrypted. Doligez noted that many people have access to the amount of computing power that he used, and concluded that the exportable Secure Sockets Layer protocol is not strong enough to resist the attempts of amateurs to decrypt a "secure" message.

In January 1996, a Massachusetts Institute of Technology undergraduate student used a single $83,000 graphics computer to perform the same task in 8 days. Testing keys at an average rate of more than 830,000 keys per second, the program running on this computer would take 15 days to test every key.

---

the availability of products that are intended primarily for authentication.[11]

Another spillover effect arises from a desire among vendors and users to build and use products that integrate multiple cryptographic capabilities (for confidentiality and for authentication/integrity) with general-

---

[11]For example, Kerberos is an application designed to enhance operating system security by providing strong cryptographic authentication of users (and hence strong access control for system resources). As a secondary feature, Kerberos was designed with the capability to provide confidentiality, both as a subroutine library (called by application programmers) and as a set of user programs run by users (e.g., the remote-login program offers an option to encrypt the network connection involved). Typically, Kerberos is distributed in the United States in source code through the Internet to increase its usability on a wide range of platforms, to accommodate diverse user needs, and to increase maintainability; source code distribution is a common practice on the Internet.

Only a small amount of Kerberos code is used to support user-invocable confidentiality. However, in order to prevent running afoul of export regulations, most sites from which Kerberos is available strip out *all* of the cryptographic source code, including the DES module used as the cryptographic engine to support both the authentication and the confidentiality features and every system call to the module for either authentication or confidentiality purposes.

purpose functionality. In many instances, it is possible for cryptography for authentication/integrity and cryptography for confidentiality to draw on the same algorithm. Export control regulations may require that a vendor weaken or even eliminate the encryption capabilities of a product that also provides authentication/integrity capabilities, with all of the consequent costs for users and vendors (as described in Section 4.3).

Such spillover effects suggest that government actions that discourage capabilities for confidentiality may also have some negative impact on the development and use of products with authentication/integrity capabilities even if there is no direct prohibition or restriction on export of products with capabilities only for the latter.

Informal Noncodified Practices

As described above, it is current practice to grant USML licenses for exports of strong cryptography to firms in a number of categories described in Box 4.4. However, the fact that this practice is not explicitly codified contributes to a sense of uncertainty among vendors and users about the process and in practice leads to unnecessary delays in license processing.

In addition, there is uncertainty about whether or not a given foreign company is "controlled" by a U.S. firm. Specifically, vendors often do not know (and cannot find out in advance) whether a proposed sale to a particular foreign company falls under the protection of this unstated exemption. As a practical rule, the U.S. government has a specific set of

---

Thus, export controls on confidentiality have inhibited the use of Kerberos for its intended authentication purposes. However, because no one (to the committee's knowledge) has actually obtained a formal decision on the status of a source-code version of Kerberos without confidentiality capabilities but with authentication capabilities, it is an open question whether such a version would qualify for commodity jurisdiction to the CCL under the authentication exception.

A second example was provided in testimony to the committee from a company that had eliminated all cryptographic capabilities from a certain product because of its perceptions of the export control hurdles to be overcome. The capabilities eliminated included those for authentication. While it can be argued that the company was simply ignorant of the exemptions in the ITAR for products providing authentication capabilities, the fact remains that much of the vendor community is either not familiar with the exemptions or does not believe that they represent true "fast-track" or "automatic" exceptions.

Note: The committee appreciates John Gilmore's assistance in correcting the information provided about Kerberos in the prepublication version of this report.

guidelines that are used to make this determination.[12] But these rules require considerable interpretation and thus do not provide clear guidance for U.S. vendors.

A third issue that arises with current practice is that the lines between "foreign" and "U.S." companies are blurring in an era of transnational corporations, ad hoc strategic alliances, and close cooperation between suppliers and customers of all types. For example, U.S. companies often team with foreign companies in global or international ventures. It would be desirable for U.S. products with encryption capabilities to be used by both partners to conduct business related to such alliances without requiring a specific export licensing decision.[13]

In some instances, USML licenses have granted U.S. companies the authority to use strong encryption rather freely (e.g., in the case of a U.S. company with worldwide suppliers). But these licenses are still the result of a lengthy case-by-case review whose outcome is uncertain.

Finally, the State Department and NSA explicitly assert control over products without any cryptographic capability at all but developed with "sockets," or, more formally, cryptographic applications programming

---

[12]Under Defense Department guidelines for determining foreign ownership, control, or influence (FOCI), a U.S. company is considered under FOCI "whenever a foreign interest has the power, direct or indirect, whether or not exercised, and whether or not exercisable through the ownership of the U.S. company's securities, by contractual arrangements or other means, to direct or decide matters affecting the management or operations of that company in a manner which may result in unauthorized access to classified information or may affect adversely the performance of classified contracts." A FOCI determination for a given company is made on the basis of a number of factors, including whether a foreign person occupies a controlling or dominant minority position and the identification of immediate, intermediate, and ultimate parent organizations. (See Department of Defense, *National Industrial Security Program Operating Manual*, DOD-5220.22-M, January 1995, pp. 2-3-1 to 2-3-2.) According to ITAR Regulation 122.2, "ownership" means that more than 50 percent of the outstanding voting securities of the firm are owned by one or more foreign persons. "Control" means that one or more foreign persons have the authority or ability to establish or direct the general policies or day-to-day operations of the firm. Control is presumed to exist where foreign persons own 25 percent or more of the outstanding voting securities if no U.S. persons control an equal or larger percentage. The standards for control specified in 22 CFR 60.2(c) also provide guidance in determining whether control in fact exists. Defense Department Form 4415, August 1990, requires answers to 11 questions in order for the Defense Department to make a FOCI determination for any given company.

[13]In one instance reported to the committee, a major multinational company with customer support offices in China experienced a break-in in which Chinese nationals apparently copied paper documents and computer files. File encryption would have mitigated the impact associated with this "bag job." Then-current export restrictions hampered deployment of encryption to this site because the site was owned by a foreign (Chinese) company rather than a U.S.-controlled company and therefore not easily covered under then-current practice.

interfaces into which a user can insert his own cryptography. Such products are regarded as having an inherent cryptographic capability (although such capability is latent rather than manifest) and as such are controlled by the USML, even though the text of the ITAR does not mention these items explicitly.[14] In general, vendors and users understand this to be the practice and do not challenge it, but they dislike the fact that it is not explicit.

4.2 EFFECTIVENESS OF EXPORT CONTROLS ON CRYPTOGRAPHY

One of the most contentious points in the debate over export controls on cryptography concerns their effectiveness in delaying the spread of strong cryptographic capabilities and the use of those capabilities throughout the world. Supporters of the current export control regime believe that these controls have been effective, and they point to the fact that encryption is not yet in widespread commercial use abroad and that a significant fraction of the traffic intercepted globally is unencrypted. Further, they argue that U.S. products with encryption capabilities dominate the international market to an extent that impeding the distribution of U.S. products necessarily affects worldwide usage.

Critics of current policy assert that export controls have not been effective in limiting the availability of cryptography abroad. For example, based on its ongoing survey of cryptography products worldwide (a study widely cited by critics of current policy), Trusted Information Systems Inc. has noted that

> [w]e have now identified 1181 products worldwide [as of March 30, 1996], and we're continuing to learn about new products, both domestic and foreign, on a daily basis. We've also obtained numerous products from abroad and are examining these products to assess their functionality and security. The survey results show that cryptography is indeed widespread throughout the world. Export controls outside of the U.S.

---

[14]Specifically, the ITAR place on the USML "cryptographic devices, software, and components specifically designed or modified therefor, including: cryptographic (including key management) systems, equipment, assemblies, modules, integrated circuits, components or software with the capability of maintaining secrecy or confidentiality of information or information systems." Note that these categories do not explicitly mention systems without cryptography but with the capability of accepting "plug-in" cryptography.

appear to be less restrictive. The quality of foreign products seems to be comparable to that of U.S. products.[15]

Furthermore, critics of U.S. export controls argue that sources other than U.S. commercial vendors (specifically foreign vendors, the in-house expertise of foreign users, Internet software downloads, and pirated U.S. software) are capable of providing very good cryptography that is usable by motivated foreign users.

In assessing the arguments of both supporters and critics of the current export control regime, it is important to keep in mind that the ultimate goal of export controls on cryptography is to keep strong cryptography out of the hands of potential targets of signals intelligence. Set against this goal, the committee believes that the arguments of both supporters and critics have merit but require qualification.

The supporters of the current export regime are right in asserting that U.S. export controls have had a nontrivial impact in retarding the use of cryptography worldwide. This argument is based on three linked factors:

• U.S. export controls on cryptography have clearly limited the sale of U.S. products with encryption capabilities in foreign markets; indeed, it is this fact that drives the primary objection of U.S. information technology vendors to the current export control regime on cryptography.

• Very few foreign vendors offer integrated products with encryption capabilities.[16] U.S. information technology products enjoy a very high reputation for quality and usability, and U.S. information technology vendors, especially those in the mass-market software arena, have marketing and distribution skills that are as yet unparalleled by their foreign counterparts. As a result, foreign vendors have yet to fill the void left by an absence of U.S. products.

• U.S. information technology products account for a large fraction of global sales. For example, a recent U.S. International Trade Commission staff report points out that over half of all world sales in information

---

[15]Available on-line from the TIS home page, http://www.tis.com; at the time of its presentation to the committee, TIS had identified 450 such products available from foreign nations. Testimony on this topic was first presented by Steven Walker, president of Trusted Information Systems, to the House Committee on Foreign Affairs, Subcommittee on Economic Policy, Trade, and Environment, on October 12, 1993. TIS briefed the study committee on December 15, 1994, and July 19, 1995. The survey mentioned in testimony to the committee continues, and regularly updated figures can be found on the TIS Web page (http://www.tis.com/crypto-survey).

[16]The Department of Commerce and the National Security Agency found no general-purpose software products with encryption capability from non-U.S. manufacturers. See Department of Commerce and National Security Agency, *A Study of the International Market for Computer Software with Encryption*, released January 11, 1996, p. III-9.

technology come from the United States.[17] Actions that impede the flow of U.S. products to foreign consumers are bound to have significant effects on the rate at which those products are purchased and used.

On the other hand, it is also true that some foreign targets of interest to the U.S. government today use encryption that is for all practical purposes unbreakable; major powers tend to use "home-grown" cryptography that they procure on the same basis that the United States procures cryptography for its own use, and export controls on U.S. products clearly cannot prevent these powers from using such cryptography.

Furthermore, the fact that cryptography is not being widely used abroad does not necessarily imply that export controls are effective—or will be in the near future—in restraining the use of cryptography by those who desire the protection it can provide. The fact is that cryptography is not used widely either in the United States or abroad, and so it is unclear whether it is the lack of information security consciousness described in Chapter 2 or the U.S. export control regime for cryptography that is responsible for such non-use; most probably, it is some combination of these two factors.

Critics of the current export regime are right in asserting that foreign suppliers of cryptography are many and varied, that software products with encryption capabilities are quite easily available through the Internet (probably hundreds of thousands of individuals have the technical skill needed to download such products), and that cryptography does pose special difficulties for national authorities wishing to control such technology (Box 4.6). Yet, most products with encryption capabilities available on the Internet are not integrated products; using security-specific products is generally less convenient than using integrated products (as described in Chapter 2), and because such products are used less often, their existence and availability pose less of a threat to the collection of signals intelligence.

Furthermore, Internet products are, as a general rule, minimally supported and do not have the backing of reputable and established vendors.[18] Users who download software from the Internet may or may not

---

[17]Office of Industries, U.S. International Trade Commission, *Global Competitiveness of the U.S. Computer Software and Service Industries*, Staff Research Study #21, Washington, D.C., June 1995, executive summary.

[18]Whether major vendors will continue to avoid the Internet as a distribution medium remains to be seen. Even today, a number of important products, including Adobe's Acrobat Reader, Microsoft's Word Viewer and Internet Assistant, and the Netscape Navigator are distributed through the Internet. Some vendors make products freely available in limited functionality versions as an incentive for users to obtain full-featured versions; others make software products freely available to all takers in order to stimulate demand for other products from that vendor for which customers pay.

BOX 4.6
Difficulties in Controlling Cryptography

Hardware products with encryption capabilities can be controlled on approximately the same basis as traditional munitions. But software products with encryption capabilities are a different matter. A floppy disk containing programs involving cryptography is visually indistinguishable from one containing any other type of program or data files. Furthermore, software products with encryption capabilities can be transported electronically, with little respect for physical barriers or national boundaries, over telephone lines and the Internet with considerable ease. Cryptographic algorithms, also controlled by the International Traffic in Arms Regulations as "technical data," represent pure knowledge that can be transported over national borders inside the heads of people or via letter.

As is true for all other software products, software products with encryption capabilities are infinitely reproducible at low cost and with perfect fidelity; hence, a controlled item can be replicated at a large number of points. This fact explains how vast amounts of software piracy can occur both domestically and abroad. In principle, one software product with encryption capabilities taken abroad can serve as the seed for an unlimited number of reproductions that can find their way to hostile parties. Finally, it can be argued that the rogue nations that pose the most important targets for U.S. signals intelligence collection are also the least likely to refrain from pirating U.S. software.

---

know exactly what code the product contains and may not have the capability to test it to ensure that it functions as described.[19] Corporate customers, the primary driver for large-scale deployment of products, are unlikely to rely on products that are not sold and supported by reputable vendors, and it is products with a large installed base (i.e., those created by major software vendors) that would be more likely to have the high-quality encryption that poses a threat to signals intelligence. Table 4.1 indicates the primary differences between commercial products and "freeware" available on the Internet.

The committee's brief survey of product literature describing foreign stand-alone security-specific products with encryption capabilities (Box 4.7) also indicated many implementations that were unsound from a security standpoint, even taking for granted the mathematical strength of the algorithms involved and the proper implementation of the indicated algorithms.[20] The committee has no reason to believe that the stand-alone

---

[19]Indeed, the lack of quality control for Internet-available software provides an opportunity for those objecting to the proliferation of good products with encryption capability to flood the market with their own products anonymously or pseudonymously; such products may include features that grant clandestine access with little effort.

[20]The committee's analysis of foreign stand-alone products for cryptography was based on material provided to the committee by TIS, which TIS had collected through its survey.

TABLE 4.1 Key Differences Between Commercial Products and "Freeware"

	Products from Major Commercial Vendors	"Freeware" Products
Stake in reputation of product offerer	Higher	Lower
Scale of operation	Larger	Smaller
Cost of distribution	Higher	Lower
Support for products	Greater	Lesser
Role of profit-making motive	Greater	Lesser
Ability to integrate cryptography into useful and sophisticated general-purpose software	Greater	Lesser
Vulnerability to regulatory and legal constraints	Higher	Lower
Likelihood of market "staying power"	Higher	Lower
Likelihood of wide distribution and use	Higher	Lower
Financial liability for poor product performance	Higher	Lower
Cost of entry into markets	Higher	Lower

NOTE: All of the characterizations listed are tendencies rather than absolutes and are relative (i.e., determined by comparing products from major commercial vendors to "freeware" products).

security-specific products with encryption capabilities made by U.S. vendors are on average better at providing security,[21] although the large

---

This material was limited to product brochures and manuals that the committee believes put the best possible face on a product's quality. Thus, the committee's identification of security defects in these products is plausibly regarded as a minimum estimate of their weaknesses—more extensive testing (e.g., involving disassembly) would be likely to reveal additional weaknesses, since implementation defects would not be written up in a product brochure. Moreover, the availability of a product brochure does not ensure the availability of the corresponding product; TIS has brochures for all of the 800-plus products identified in its survey, but due to limited resources, it has been able to obtain physical versions (e.g., a disk, a circuit board) of fewer than 10 percent of the products described in those brochures.

[21]An "amateur" review of encryption for confidentiality built into several popular U.S. mass-market software programs noted that the encryption facilities did not provide particularly good protection. The person who reviewed these programs was not skilled in cryptography but was competent in his understanding of programming and how the Macintosh manages files. By using a few commonly available programming tools (a file compare program, a "debugger" that allows the user to trace the flow of how a program executes, and a "disassembler" that turns object code into source code that can be examined), the reviewer was able to access in less than two hours the "protected" files generated

---

BOX 4.7
A Partial Survey of Foreign Encryption Products on the TIS Survey

• A British product manual notes that "a key can be any word, phrase, or number from 1 to 78 characters in length, though for security purposes keys shorter than six characters are not recommended." Only alphanumeric characters are used in the key, and alpha characters do not distinguish between upper and lower case. While the longer pass phrases can produce keys with the full 56 bits of uncertainty [changing "can" to "do" would require more extensive tests], passwords of even 6 characters are woefully inadequate. It is dangerous to allow users to enter such keys, much less the single-character keys allowed by this product.

• One British product is a DES implementation that recommends cipher block chaining but uses electronic codebook (ECB) mode as the default. The use of ECB as the default is dangerous because ECB is less secure than cipher block chaining.

• A Danish product uses DES with an 8-character key, but limits each character to alphanumeric and punctuation symbols. Hence the key is less than a full 56 bits long. With this restriction, many users are likely to use only upper or lower case alpha characters, resulting in a key less than 40 bits long.

• A foreign product uses the FEAL algorithm as well as a proprietary algorithm. Aside from the question of algorithm strength, the key is 1 to 8 characters long and does not distinguish between upper and lower case. The result is a ridiculously short key, a problem that is compounded by the recommendation in the manual to use a 6- to 8-letter artificial word as the key (e.g., it suggests that for the name Bill, "bill-bum" might be used as the key).

• A product from New Zealand uses DES plus a public-key system similar to RSA, but based on Lucas functions. The public-key portion limits the key size to 1,024 bits, but does not seem to have a lower bound, a potentially dangerous situation. The DES key can be 1 to 24 characters in length. If the key is 1 to 8 characters,

---

established software vendors in the United States do have reputations for providing relatively high quality in their products for features unrelated to security.[22] Without an acceptable product certification service, most users have no reliable way of determining the quality of any given product for themselves.

---

by four out of eight programs. See Gene Steinbert, "False Security," *MACWORLD*, November 1995, pp. 118-121.

One well-publicized cryptographic security flaw found in the Netscape Corporation's Navigator Web browser is discussed in footnote 34 in Chapter 2. Because of a second flaw, Netscape Navigator could also enable a sophisticated user to damage information stored on the host computer to which Navigator is connected. (See Jared Sandberg, "Netscape Software for Cruising Internet Is Found to Have Another Security Flaw," *Wall Street Journal*, September 25, 1995, p. B12.)

[22]In addition, a product with a large installed base is subject to a greater degree of critical examination than is a product with a small installed base, and hence flaws in the former are more likely to be noticed and fixed. Large installed bases are more characteristic of products produced by established vendors than of freeware or shareware products.

then single DES is used; otherwise triple DES is used. The lack of a lower bound on key length is dangerous.

• An Israeli product uses DES or QUICK, a proprietary algorithm. The minimum key length is user selectable between 0 and 8 characters. Allowing such small lower bounds on key length is dangerous. The product also has a "super-password" supplied by the vendor, another potentially dangerous situation. This product is available both in hardware and in software.

• A German hardware product has user-settable S-boxes, and the key can be entered either as 8 characters or 16 hexadecimal characters to yield a true 64-bit key (which will be reduced by the algorithm to 56 bits). The use of 16 hexadecimal character keys will result in higher security, but if the key can also be entered as 8 alphanumeric characters, many users are likely to do so, thus severely reducing the security level. User-selectable S-boxes can have advantages (if they are unknown to a cryptanalyst) and disadvantages (if they are poorly chosen and either are known to or can be guessed by a cryptanalyst). On balance, the danger is arguably greater than the advantage.

• A British product recommends one master key per organization so that files can be shared across personal computers. This practice is very dangerous.

To summarize, the defects in these products are related to poor key management practices, because they either employ or allow poor key management that would enable a determined and knowledgeable adversary to penetrate with relative ease the security they offer. As noted in Section 4.2 of the text, U.S. products are not necessarily more secure.

SOURCE: Committee examination and synthesis of materials provided by Trusted Information Systems Inc.

As a general rule, a potential user of cryptography faces the choice of buying commercially available products with encryption capabilities on the open market (perhaps custom-made, perhaps produced for a mass market) or developing and deploying those products independently. The arguments discussed above suggest that global dissemination of knowledge about cryptography makes independent development an option, but the problems of implementing knowledge as a usable and secure product drive many potential users to seek products available from reputable vendors. In general, the greater the resources available to potential users and the larger the stakes involved, the more likely they are to attempt to develop their own cryptographic resources. Thus, large corporations and First World governments are, in general, more likely than small corporations and Third World governments to develop their own cryptographic implementations.

Finally, the text of the ITAR seems to allow a number of entirely legal actions that could have results that the current export control regime is

---

BOX 4.8
Circumventions of the ITAR

Current export controls on cryptography can apparently be circumvented in a number of entirely legal and/or hard-to-detect ways. For example:

• A U.S. company can develop a product without encryption capabilities and then sell the source code of the product to a friendly foreign company that incorporates additional source code for encryption into the product for resale from that foreign country (assuming that that country has no (or weaker) export controls on cryptography).

• A U.S. company possessing products with encryption capabilities can be bought by a foreign company; in general, no attempt is made to recover those products.

• A U.S. company can work with legally independent counterparts abroad that can incorporate cryptographic knowledge available worldwide into products.

---

intended to prevent (Box 4.8). For example, RSA Data Security Inc. has announced a partnership with the Chinese government to fund an effort by Chinese government scientists to develop new encryption software. This software may be able to provide a higher degree of confidentiality than software that qualifies today for liberal export consideration under the CCL.[23]

4.3 THE IMPACT OF EXPORT CONTROLS ON U.S. INFORMATION TECHNOLOGY VENDORS

U.S. export controls have a number of interrelated effects on the economic health of U.S. vendors and on the level of cryptographic protection available to U.S. firms operating domestically. (The impact of foreign import controls on U.S. vendors is discussed in Chapter 6 and Appendix G.)

4.3.1 De Facto Restrictions on the Domestic Availability of Cryptography

Current law and policy place no formal restrictions whatever on products with encryption capabilities that may be sold or used in the United States. In principle, the domestic market can already obtain any type of cryptography it wants. For stand-alone security-specific products, this principle is true in practice as well. But the largest markets are not for

---

[23]See Don Clark, "China, U.S. Firm Challenge U.S. on Encryption-Software Exports," *Wall Street Journal*, February 8, 1996, p. A10.

stand-alone security-specific products, but rather for integrated products with encryption capabilities.

For integrated products with encryption capabilities, export controls do have an effect on domestic availability. For example:

• The Netscape Communications Corporation distributes a version of Netscape Navigator over the Internet and sells a version as shrink-wrapped software. Because the Internet version can be downloaded from abroad, its encryption capabilities are limited to those that will allow for liberal export consideration; the shrink-wrapped version is under no such limitation and in fact is capable of much higher levels of encryption.[24] Because it is so much more convenient to obtain, the Internet version of Netscape Navigator is much more widely deployed in the United States than is the shrink-wrapped version, with all of the consequences for information security that its weaker encryption capability implies.

• The Microsoft Corporation recently received permission to ship Windows NT Version 4, a product that incorporates a cryptographic applications programming interface approved by the U.S. government for commodity jurisdiction to the CCL. However, this product is being shipped worldwide with a cryptographic module that provides encryption capabilities using 40-bit RC4.[25] While domestic users may replace the default module with one providing stronger encryption capabilities, many will not, and the result is a weaker encryption capability for those users.

• A major U.S. software vendor distributes its major product in modular form in such a way that the end user can assemble a system configuration in accordance with local needs. However, since the full range of USML export controls on encryption is applied to modular products into which cryptographic modules may be inserted, this vendor has not been able to find a sensible business approach to distributing the product in such a way that it would qualify for liberal export consideration. The result has been that the encryption capabilities provided to domestic users of this product are much less than they would otherwise be in the absence of export controls.

What factors underlie the choices made by vendors that result in the

---

[24] The shrink-wrapped version of Netscape Navigator sold within the United States and Canada supports several different levels of encryption, including 40-bit RC4, 128-bit RC4, 56-bit DES, and triple-DES. The default for a domestic client communicating with a domestic server is 128-bit RC4 (Jeff Weinstein, Netscape Communications Corporation, Mountain View, Calif., personal communication, February 1996).

[25] See Jason Pontin, "Microsoft Encryption API to Debut in NT Workstation Beta," *Infoworld*, January 29, 1996, p. 25.

outcomes described above? At one level, the examples above are simply the result of market decisions and preferences. At a sufficiently high level of domestic market demand, U.S. vendors would find it profitable and appropriate to develop products for the domestic market alone. Similarly, given a sufficiently large business opportunity in a foreign country (or countries) that called for a product significantly different from that used by domestic users, vendors would be willing to develop a customized version of a product that would meet export control requirements. Furthermore, many other manufacturers of exportable products must cope with a myriad of different requirements for export to different nations (e.g., differing national standards for power, safety, and electromagnetic interference), as well as differing languages in which to write error messages or user manuals. From this perspective, export controls are simply one more cost of doing business outside the United States.

On the other hand, the fact that export controls *are* an additional cost of doing business outside the United States is not an advantage for U.S. companies planning to export products. A vendor incurs less expense and lower effort for a single version of a product produced for both domestic and foreign markets than it does when multiple versions are involved. While the actual cost of *developing* two different versions of a product with different key lengths and different algorithms is relatively small, a much larger part of the expense associated with multiple versions relates to marketing, manufacture, support, and maintenance of multiple product versions after the initial sale has been made.[26]

Since a vendor may be unable to export a given product with encryption capabilities to foreign markets, domestic market opportunities must be that much greater to warrant a domestic-only version. (Given that about half of all sales of U.S. information technology vendors are made to foreign customers,[27] the loss of foreign markets can be quite damaging to a U.S. vendor.) When they are not, vendors have every incentive to develop products with encryption capabilities that would easily qualify

---

[26]Note that development and support concerns are even more significant when a given product is intended for cross-platform use (i.e., for use in different computing environments such as Windows, Mac OS, Unix, and so on), as is the case for many high-end software products (such as database retrieval systems): when a product is intended for use on 50 different platforms, multiplying by a factor of two the effort required on the part of the vendor entails much more of an effort by the vendor than if the product were intended for use on only one platform.

[27]See footnote 17.

for liberal export consideration. As a result, the domestic availability of products with strong encryption capability is diminished. While a sufficiently high level of domestic market demand would make it profitable for U.S. vendors to develop products for the domestic market alone, the "sufficiently" qualifier is a strong one indeed, given the realities of the market into which vendors must sell and compete, and one infrequently met in practice.

Users are also affected by an export control regime that forces foreign and domestic parties in communication with each other to use encryption systems based on different algorithms and/or key lengths. In particular, an adversary attempting to steal information will seek out the weakest point. If that weakest point is abroad because of the weak cryptography allowed for liberal export, then that is where the attack will be. In businesses with worldwide network connections, it is critical that security measures be taken abroad, even if key information repositories and centers of activity are located in the continental United States. Put differently, the use of weak cryptography abroad means that sensitive information communicated by U.S. businesses to foreign parties faces a greater risk of compromise abroad because stronger cryptography integrated into U.S. information technology is not easily available abroad.

Finally, the export licensing process can have a significant impact on how a product is developed. For example, until recently, products developed to permit the *user* to substitute easily his own cryptography module were subject to the USML and the ITAR.[28] One vendor pointed out to the committee that its systems were designed to be assembled "out of the box" by end users in a modular fashion, depending on their needs and computing environment. This vendor believed that such systems would be unlikely to obtain liberal export consideration, because of the likelihood that a foreign user would be able to replace an "export-approved" cryptography module with a cryptography module that would not pass export review. Under these circumstances, the sensible thing from the export control perspective would be to deny exportability for the modu-

---

[28]Note, however, that the use of object-oriented software technology can in general facilitate the use of applications programming interfaces that provide "hooks" to modules of the user's choosing. A number of vendors have developed or are developing general-purpose applications programming interfaces that will allow the insertion of a module to do almost anything. Since these programming interfaces are not specialized for cryptography, but instead enable many useful functions (e.g., file compression, backups), it is very difficult to argue the basis on which applications incorporating these interfaces should be denied export licenses simply because they *could* be used to support encryption.

A further discussion of recent developments involving cryptography modules and cryptographic applications programming interfaces is contained in Chapter 7.

larized product even if its capabilities did fall within the "safe harbor" provisions for products with encryption capabilities.

The considerations above led the committee to conclude that U.S. export controls have had a negative impact on the cryptographic strength of many integrated products with encryption capabilities available in the United States.[29] Export controls tend to drive major vendors to a "lowest common denominator" cryptographic solution that will pass export review as well as sell in the United States. The committee also believes that export controls have had some impact on the availability of cryptographic authentication capabilities around the world. Export controls distort the global market for cryptography, and the product decisions of vendors that might be made in one way in the absence of export controls may well be made another way in their presence.

Some of the reasons for this vendor choice are explored in Section 4.3.2.

4.3.2 Regulatory Uncertainty Related to Export Controls

A critical factor that differentiates the costs of complying with export controls from other costs of doing business abroad is the unpredictability of the export control licensing process. (Other dimensions of uncertainty for vendors not related to export controls are discussed in Chapter 6.) A company must face the possibility that despite its best efforts, a USML export license or a commodity jurisdiction to the CCL will not be granted for a product. Uncertainties about the decisions that will emerge from the export control regime force vendors into very conservative planning scenarios. In estimating benefits and costs, corporate planners must take into account the additional costs that could be incurred in developing two largely independent versions of the same product or limit the size of the potential market to U.S. purchasers. When such planning requirements are imposed, the number of product offerings possible is necessarily reduced.

USML licensing is particularly unpredictable, because the reasons that a license is denied in any given instance are not necessarily made available to the applicant; in some cases, the rationale for specific licensing decisions is based on considerations that are highly classified and by law cannot be made available to an uncleared applicant. Since such ration-

---

[29]A similar conclusion was reached by the FBI, whose testimony to the committee noted that "the use of export controls may well have slowed the speed, proliferation, and volume of encryption products sold in the U.S." (written statement, "FBI Input to the NRC's National Cryptographic Study Committee," received December 1, 1995).

ales cannot be discussed openly, an atmosphere of considerable uncertainty pervades the development process for vendors seeking to develop products for overseas markets. Furthermore, there is no independent adjudicating forum to which a negative licensing decision can be appealed.

Since USML licensing is undertaken on a case-by-case basis, it requires the exercise of judgment on the part of the regulatory authorities. A judgment-based approach has the disadvantage that it requires a considerable degree of trust between the regulated and the regulator.[30] To the extent that an individual regulated party believes that the regulator is acting in the best interests of the entire regulated community, it is natural that it would be more willing to accept the legitimacy of the process that led to a given result. However, in instances in which those who are regulated do not trust the regulator, the judgments of the regulator are much more likely to be seen as arbitrary and capricious.[31]

This situation currently characterizes the relationship between cryptography vendors/users and national security authorities responsible for implementing the U.S. export control regime for cryptography. In input received by the committee, virtually all industry representatives, from large to small companies, testified about the unpredictability of the process. From the vendor point of view, the resulting uncertainty inhibits product development and allows negative decisions on export to be rendered by unknown forces and/or government agencies with neither explanation nor a reasonable possibility of appeal.

The need to stay far away from the vague boundaries of what might or might not be acceptable is clearly an inhibitor of technological progress and development. Vendor concerns are exacerbated in those instances in which export control authorities are unwilling to provide a specific reason for the denial of an export license or any assurance that a similarly but not identically configured product with encryption capabilities would pass export review. Even worse from the vendor perspective, product parameters are not the only determinant of whether a licensing decision

---

[30]In contrast to a judgment-based approach, a clarity-based approach would start from the premise that regulations and laws should be as clear as possible, so that a party that may be affected knows with a high degree of certainty what is and is not permitted or proscribed. The downside of a clarity-based approach is that affected parties tend to go "right up to the line" of what is prohibited and may seek ways to "design around" any stated limitations. Furthermore, a clarity-based approach would require the specification, in advance, of all acts that are prohibited, even when it may not be possible to define in advance all acts that would be undesirable.

[31]For example, critics of the uncertainty engendered by the export regime point out that uncertainty is helpful to policy makers who wish to retain flexibility to modify policy without the work or publicity required for a formal regulatory change.

will be favorable except in a very limited and narrow range of cryptographic functionality.

The uncertainty described above is not limited to new and inexperienced vendors encountering the U.S. export control regime for the first time; large and sophisticated institutions with international connections have also encountered difficulties with the current export control regime. For example, a representative from a major U.S. bank with many international branches reported that export controls affect internally developed bank software with encryption capabilities; a U.S. citizen who works on bank software with encryption capabilities in England may "taint" that software so that it falls under U.S. export control guidelines. Thus, despite the fact that the current export control regime treats banks and other financial institutions relatively liberally, major banks have still struggled under its limitations.

The situation is worse for smaller companies. While large companies have experience and legal staffs that help them to cope with the export control regime, small companies do not. New work on information technology often begins in garage-shop operations, and the export control regime can be particularly daunting to a firm with neither the legal expertise nor the contacts to facilitate compliance of a product with all of the appropriate regulations. These companies in particular are the ones most likely to decide in the end to avoid entirely the inclusion of cryptographic features due to concern about running afoul of the export control rules.

The following three examples illustrate how the unpredictability of the export control licensing process has affected U.S. vendors and their products.

Modularity

As noted above, cryptographic applications programming interfaces that are directly and easily accessible to the user are in general subject to USML licensing. However, even "closed" interfaces that are not easily accessible to the user are sometimes perceived to pose a risk for the vendor. One major product vendor reported to the committee that it was reluctant to use modular development for fear that even an internal module interface could keep a product from passing export control review. Any software product that uses modular techniques to separate the basic product functionality from the cryptography has a well-defined interface between the two. Even when the software product is converted to object code, that interface is still present (though it is hidden from the casual user). However, the interface cannot in general be hidden from a person with strong technical skills, and such a person would be able to find it and tamper with it in such a way that a different cryptography module could be used.[32] A number of similar considerations apply for hardware products, in which the cryptographic capabilities might be provided by a "plug-in" chip.

The alternative to the use of modular techniques in the development of integrated products would complicate the "swap-in/swap-out" of cryptographic capabilities: lines of code (if software) and wires (if hardware) that implemented cryptographic capabilities would be highly interwoven with lines of code and wires that implemented the primary capabilities of the product. On the other hand, this approach would be tantamount to the development of two largely distinct products with little overlap in the work that was required to produce them.

The NSA has spoken publicly about its willingness to discuss with vendors from the early stages of product design features and capabilities of proposed products with encryption capabilities for confidentiality so that the export license approval process can be facilitated, and also its willingness to abide by nondisclosure agreements to reassure vendors that their intellectual property rights will be protected.[33] Nonetheless, the receipt of an export control license useful for business purposes is not guaranteed by such cooperation. For example, while decisions about commodity jurisdiction often provide CCL jurisdiction for object code and USML jurisdiction for source code (and thus need not inhibit modular product development if the product is to be distributed in object form only), the fact remains that such decisions are part of a case-by-case review whose outcome is uncertain. Different vendors are willing to tolerate different levels of risk in this regard, depending on the magnitude of the investments involved.

As a general rule, NSA does not appear willing to make agreements in advance that will assure licenses for a product that has not yet been instantiated or produced. Such a position is not unreasonable given NSA's stance toward products with encryption capabilities in general, and the fact that the true capabilities of a product may depend strongly on how it is actually implemented in hardware or software. Thus, vendors

---

[32]Of course, such considerations obviously apply to software products with cryptographic capabilities that are designed to be shipped in source code; not only can the cryptographic module be easily identified and replaced, but it can also be pulled out and adapted to other purposes. This point was also raised in footnote 11 of this chapter.

[33]For example, NSA representatives made comments to this effect at the RSA Data Security Conference in San Francisco in January 1995.

have no indemnification against the risk that a product might not be approved.[34]

The Definition of Export

There is uncertainty about what specific act constitutes the "export" of software products with encryption capabilities. It is reasonably clear that the act of mailing to a foreign country a disk with a product with encryption capabilities on it constitutes an export of that product. But if that product is uploaded to an Internet site located in the United States and is later downloaded by a user located in another country, is the act of export the upload or the download? What precautions must be taken by the uploader to remain on the legal side of the ITAR?

The committee has been unable to find any formal document that indicates answers to these questions. However, a March 1994 letter from the State Department's Office of Defense Trade Controls appears to indicate that a party could permit the posting of cryptographic software on an Internet host located in the United States if "(a) the host system is configured so that only people originating from nodes in the United States and Canada can access the cryptographic software, or (b) if the software is placed in a file or directory whose name changes every few minutes, and the name of the file or directory is displayed in a publicly known and readable file containing an explicit notice that the software is for U.S. and Canadian use only."[35] Of course, such a letter does not provide formal guidance to parties other than the intended addressee (indeed, under the ITAR, advisory opinions provided to a specific party with a given set of circumstances are not binding on the State Department even with respect to that party), and so the issue remains murky.

The Speed of the Licensing Process

Uncertainty is also generated by a lengthy licensing process without time lines that allow vendors to make realistic schedules. Box 4.9 describes some of the problems reported to the committee. To summarize,

---

[34]Although other industries also have to deal with the uncertainties of regulatory approval regarding products and services, the export control process is particularly opaque, because clear decisions and rationales for those decisions are often not forthcoming (and indeed are often classified and/or unrelated to the product per se).

[35]Letter from Clyde Bryant, Office of Defense Trade Controls, U.S. Department of State, Washington, D.C., to Daniel Appelman, Heller, Ehrman, White & McAuliffe, dated March 11, 1994.

BOX 4.9
Problems Arising from a Lengthy Export Licensing Process

• Some foreign customers know it will take a long time to obtain a positive licensing decision and as a consequence do not bother to approach U.S. vendors at all.

• Products to market are delayed; even when export licenses are eventually granted, they are often granted too late to be useful, because the area of information technology is so fast-moving.

• Rapid decisions are not rendered. In one instance reported to the committee, a U.S. information technology company wanted permission to use its own software (with strong encryption capabilities) to communicate with its foreign offices. Such cases are in theory expedited because of a presumptive approval in these circumstances; this vendor's government contacts agreed that "such an application would be no problem" and that an approval would be a rapid "rubber-stamp" one, but in fact, this vendor is still awaiting a license after more than a year.

• System integrators intending to ship complete systems rather than individual products face particular difficulties in obtaining a speedy turnaround, because the task for national security authorities involves an assessment of the entire system into which a given product (or products) with encryption capabilities will be integrated, rather than an assessment of just the products with encryption capabilities alone.

• Even vendors that manufacture cryptographic software not intended for export are required to register with the State Department's Office of Defense Trade Controls, primarily "to provide the U.S. government with necessary information on who is involved in certain manufacturing and exporting activities."[1]

---

[1]International Traffic in Arms Regulations, Section 122.1 (c).

---

the perceptions of many vendors about the excessive length of time it takes to obtain a license reflect the time required for discussions with NSA about a product before an application is formally submitted; the prospect of facing the export control process deters some vendors entirely from creating certain products. By contrast, NSA starts the clock only when it receives a formal application, and in fact the usual time between receipt of a formal application and rendering of a decision is relatively short (a few weeks). The reason that such a fast turnaround is possible is that by the time the application is received, enough is known about the product involved that processing is routine because there is no need for negotiation about how the product must be changed for a license to be approved.

In response to some of these concerns, the U.S. government has undertaken a number of reforms of the export control regime (described in Section 4.1) to reduce the hassle and red tape involved in obtaining export licenses.[36] These reforms are important. Nevertheless, the pace at which new information technology products develop and the increasing complexity of those products will complicate product review efforts in the future. Given relatively fixed staffing, these factors will tend to increase the length of time needed to conduct product reviews at a time when vendors are feeling pressures to develop and market products more rapidly.

One particular reform effort that deserves discussion is the "personal use" exemption. For many years, Americans traveling abroad were required under the ITAR to obtain "temporary export licenses" for products with encryption capabilities carried overseas for their personal use.[37] The complexity of the procedure for obtaining such a license was a considerable burden for U.S. businesspeople traveling abroad, and these individuals were subject to significant criminal penalties for an act that was widely recognized to be harmless and well within the intent of the export control regime.

In February 1994, the Administration committed itself to promulgating regulations to support a personal-use exemption from the licensing requirement. Two years later, on February 16, 1996, the *Federal Register* contained a notice from the Department of State, Bureau of Political-Military Affairs, announcing final rule of an amendment to the ITAR allowing U.S. persons to temporarily export cryptographic products for personal use without the need for an export license.[38]

Some critics of government policy have objected to the particular formulation of the record-keeping requirement. All parties involved—including senior Administration officials—have agreed that 2 years was far too long a period for promulgation of so simple a rule.

---

[36]For example, according to NSA, the detailing of an NSA representative to work with the State Department Office of Defense Trade Controls has resulted in a considerable reduction in the time needed to process a license.

[37]For a description of how this process worked in practice, see Matt Blaze, "My Life as an International Arms Courier," e-mail message circulated by Matt Blaze (mab@research.att.com) on January 6, 1995. A news article based on Blaze's story is contained in Peter H. Lewis, "Between a Hacker and a Hard Place: Data-Security Export Law Puts Businesses in a Bind," *New York Times*, April 10, 1995, p. D1.

[38]According to the regulation, the product must not be intended for copying, demonstration, marketing, sale, re-export, or transfer of ownership or control. It must remain in the possession of the exporting person, which includes being locked in a hotel room or safe. While in transit, it must be with the person's accompanying baggage. Exports to certain countries are prohibited—currently Cuba, Iran, Iraq, Libya, North Korea, Sudan, and Syria. The exporter must maintain records of each temporary export for 5 years. See Public Notice 2294, *Federal Register*, Volume 61(33), February 16, 1996, pp. 6111-6113.

4.3.3 The Size of the Affected Market for Cryptography

Since export controls on products with encryption capabilities constrain certain aspects of sales abroad, considerable public attention has focused on the size of the market that may have been affected by export controls. Vendors in particular raise the issue of market share with considerable force:

- "The only effect of the export controls is to cause economic harm to US software companies that are losing market share in the global cryptography market to companies from the many countries that do not have export controls."[39]
- "[The government's current policy on encryption] is anti-competitive. The government's encryption export policy jeopardizes the future of the software industry, one of the fastest growing and most successful industries."[40]

The size of the market for products with encryption capabilities cuts across many dimensions of cryptography policy, but since it is raised most often in the context of the export control debate, it is addressed in this section.

Plausible arguments can be made that the market ranges from no more than the value of the security-specific products sold annually (i.e., several hundred million dollars per year—a low-end estimate)[41] to the total value of all hardware and software products that might include encryption capabilities (many tens of billions of dollars—a high-end estimate).[42] The committee was unable to determine the size of the informa-

---

[39]Jim Hassert, Washington Connections, Software Publishers Association, Washington, D.C., Chapter 9. Available on-line at http://www.spa.org.

[40]Business Software Alliance, *Information and Data Security: The Encryption Update.* Available on-line at http://www.bsa.org.

[41]Department of Commerce and National Security Agency, *A Study of the International Market for Computer Software with Encryption*, released January 11, 1996, p. III-1. Note, however, that this report does not arrive at this estimate independently; rather, it cites other estimates made in the private sector.

[42]Of course, it is a matter of speculation what fraction of the information technology market (on the order of $193 billion in 1993; see below) might usefully possess encryption capabilities; good arguments can be made to suggest that this fraction is very small or very large. A number of information technology trade organizations have also made estimates. The Software Publishers Association cited a survey by the National Computer Security Association that quoted a figure of $160 million in aggregate known losses in 1993 because of export controls; see "Written Testimony of the Software Publishers Association to the National Research Council," Washington, D.C., July 19, 1995. In 1993, the Business Software Alliance estimated that "approximately $6-9 billion in U.S. company revenues are

tion technology market directly affected by export controls on encryption to within a factor of more than 100, a range of uncertainty that renders any estimate of the market quite difficult to use as the basis for a public policy decision.

Nevertheless, although it is not large enough to be decisive in the policy debate, the floor of such estimates—a few hundred million dollars per year—is not a trivial sum. Furthermore, all trends point to growth in this number, growth that may well be very large and nonlinear in the near future. To the extent that both of these observations are valid, it is only a matter of a relatively short time before even the floor of any estimate will be quite significant in economic terms.

The next three subsections describe some of the factors that confound the narrowing of the large range of uncertainty in any estimate of the size of the market affected by export controls.

Defining a "Lost Sale"

A number of vendors have pointed to specific instances of lost sales as a measure of the harm done to vendors as a result of export controls on

---

currently at risk because of the inability of those companies to be able to sell world wide generally available software with encryption capabilities employing DES or other comparable strength algorithms"; see testimony of Ray Ozzie, president, Iris Associates, on behalf of the Business Software Alliance, "The Impact on America's Software Industry of Current U.S. Government Munitions Export Controls," before the Economic Policy, Trade, and Environment Subcommittee, House Committee on Foreign Affairs, Washington, D.C., October 12, 1993. The Computer Systems Policy Project (CSPP) estimated that in 2000, the potential annual revenue exposure for U.S. information technology vendors would range from $3 billion to $6 billion on sales of cryptographic products, including both hardware and software; CSPP also estimated $30 billion to $60 billion in potential revenue exposure on sales of associated computer systems; see William F. Hagerty IV, The Management Advisory Group, Computer Systems Policy Project, *The Growing Need for Cryptography: The Impact of Export Control Policy on U.S. Competitiveness*, Study Highlights (viewgraphs), Bethesda, Md., December 15, 1995.

The $193 billion figure is taken from Department of Commerce, *U.S. Industrial Outlook, 1994*, and includes computers and peripherals ($62.5 billion, p. 26-1), packaged software ($32.0 billion, p. 27-1), information services ($13.6 billion, p. 25-1), data processing and network services ($46.4 billion, p. 25-1), and systems integration/custom programming services ($38.7 billion, p. 25-5). Note that this figure does not include some other industry sectors that could, in principle, be affected by regulations regarding secure communications; in 1993, U.S. companies provided telecommunications services valued at $10.4 billion to foreign nations (p. 29-1) and shipped $17.5 billion (1987 dollars) in telephone equipment worldwide (p. 30-3).

cryptography.[43] National security officials believe that these figures are considerably overstated. Administration officials and congressional staff have expressed considerable frustration in pinning down a reliable estimate of lost sales.

It is important to begin with the understanding that the concept of a "lost sale" is intrinsically soft. Trying to define the term "lost sales" raises a number of questions:

• What events count as a sale lost because of export restrictions? Several possibilities illustrate the complications:

—A U.S. vendor is invited along with foreign vendors to bid on a foreign project that involves cryptography, but declines because the bid requirements are explicit and the U.S. vendor knows that the necessary export licenses will not be forthcoming on a time scale compatible with the project.

—A U.S. vendor is invited along with foreign vendors to bid on a foreign project that involves cryptography. In order to expedite export licensing, the U.S. vendor offers a bid that involves 40-bit encryption (thus ignoring the bid requirements), and the bid is rejected.

—A U.S. vendor is invited along with foreign vendors to bid on a foreign project that involves cryptography. A foreign vendor emerges as the winner. The sale is certainly a lost sale, but since customers often make decisions with a number of reasons in mind and may not inform losing vendors of their reasons, it is difficult to determine the relationship of export controls to the lost sale.

—No U.S. vendor is invited to bid on a foreign project that involves cryptography. In such an instance, the potential foreign customer may have avoided U.S. vendors, recognizing that the cryptography would subject the sale to U.S. export control scrutiny, possibly compromising

---

[43]For example, in a presentation to the committee on July 19, 1995, the Software Publishers' Association documented several specific instances in which a U.S. company had lost a sale of a product involving cryptography to a foreign firm. These instances included a company that lost one-third of its total revenues because export controls on DES-based encryption prevented sales to a foreign firm; a company that could not sell products with encryption capability to a European company because that company resold products to clients other than financial institutions; a U.S. company whose European division estimated at 50 percent the loss of its business among European financial institutions, defense industries, telecommunications companies, and government agencies because of inadequate key sizes; and a U.S. company that lost the sale of a DES-based system to a foreign company with a U.S. subsidiary (Software Publishers' Association, "Presentation on Impacts of Export Control on Encryption Before the NRC National Cryptography Policy Committee," July 19, 1995).

sensitive information or delaying contract negotiations inordinately. On the other hand, the potential customer may have avoided U.S. vendors for other reasons, e.g., because the price of the U.S. product was too high.

• What part of a product's value is represented by the cryptographic functionality that limits a product's sales when export controls apply? As noted in Chapter 2, stand-alone products with encryption capabilities are qualitatively different from general-purpose products integrated with encryption capabilities. A security-specific stand-alone product provides no other functionality, and so the value of the cryptography is the entire cost of the product. But such sales account for a very small fraction of information technology sales. Most sales of information technology products with encryption capabilities are integrated products. Many word processing and spreadsheet programs may have encryption capabilities, but users do not purchase such programs for those capabilities—they purchase them to enhance their ability to work with text and numbers. Integrated products intended for use in networked environments (e.g., "groupware") may well have encryption capability, but such products are purchased primarily to serve collaboration needs rather than encryption functions. In these instances, it is the cost of the entire integrated product (which may not be exportable if encryption is a necessary but secondary feature) that counts as the value lost.

• How does a vendor discover a "lost sale"? In some cases, a specific rejection counts as evidence. But in general there is no systematic way to collect reliable data on the number or value of lost sales.

• An often-unnoticed dimension of "lost sales" does not involve product sales at all, but rather services whose delivery may depend on cryptographic protection. For example, a number of U.S. on-line service providers (e.g., America Online, Compuserve, Prodigy) intend to offer or expand access abroad;[44] the same is true for U.S. providers of telecommunications services.[45] To the extent that maintaining the security of foreign interactions with these service providers depends on the use of strong cryptography, the ability of these companies to provide these services may be compromised by export restrictions and thus sales of service potentially reduced.

---

[44]See, for example, Kara Swisher, "Old World, New Frontier in Cyberspace," *Washington Post*, December 12, 1995, p. C1; Victoria Shannon, "U.S. On-Line Services Fall Short on International Reach," *Washington Post*, April 3, 1995, Washington Business, p. 20. For more detail on AOL plans, see Elizabeth Cocoran, "America Online to Offer Access in Europe," *Washington Post*, May 19, 1995, p. F3.

[45]See, for example, Office of Technology Assessment, *U.S. Telecommunications Services in European Markets*, OTA-TCT-548, U.S. Government Printing Office, Washington, D.C., August 1993.

Latent vs. Actual Demand

In considering the size of the market for cryptography, it is important to distinguish between "actual" demand and "latent" demand.

• Actual demand reflects what users spend on products with encryption capabilities. While the value of "the market for cryptography" is relatively well defined in the case of stand-alone security-specific products (it is simply the value of all of the sales of such products), it is not well defined when integrated products with encryption capabilities are involved. The reason is that for such products, there is no demand for cryptography per se. Rather, users have a need for products that do useful things; cryptography is a feature added by designers to protect users from outside threats to their work, but as a purely defensive capability, cryptography does not so much add functional value for the user as protect against reductions in the value that the user sees in the product. Lotus Notes, for example, would not be a viable product in the communications software market without its encryption capabilities, but users buy it for the group collaboration capabilities that it provides rather than for the encryption per se.

• Latent demand (i.e., inherent demand that users do not realize or wish to acknowledge but that surfaces when a product satisfying this demand appears on the market) is even harder to measure or assess. Recent examples include Internet usage and faxes; in these instances, the underlying technology has been available for many years, but only recently have large numbers of people been able to apply these technologies for useful purposes. Lower prices and increasing ease of use, prompted in part by greater demand, have stimulated even more demand. To the extent that there is a latent demand for cryptography, the inclusion of cryptographic features in integrated products might well stimulate a demand for cryptography that grows out of knowledge and practice, out of learning by doing.

Determining the extent of latent demand is complicated greatly by the fact that latent demand can be converted into actual demand on a relatively short time scale. Indeed, such growth curves—very slow growth in use for a while and then a sudden explosion of demand—characterize many critical mass phenomena: some information technologies (e.g., networks, faxes, telephones) are valuable only if some critical mass of people use them. Once that critical mass is reached, other people begin to use those technologies, and demand takes off. Linear extrapolations 5 or 10 years into the future based on 5 or 10 years in the past miss this very nonlinear effect.

Of course, it is difficult to predict a surge in demand before it actually occurs. In the case of cryptography, market analysts have been predicting significantly higher demand for many years; today, growth rates are high, but demand for information security products including cryptography is not yet ubiquitous.

Two important considerations bearing directly on demand are increasing system complexity and the need for interoperability. Users must be able to count on a high degree of interoperability in the systems and software they purchase if they are to operate smoothly across national boundaries (as described in Chapter 1). Users understand that it is more difficult to make different products interoperate, even if they are provided by the same vendor, than to use a single product. For example, the complexity of a product generally rises as a function of the number of products with which it must interoperate, because a new product must interoperate with already-deployed products. Increased complexity almost always increases vulnerabilities in the system or network that connects those products. In addition, more complex products tend to be more difficult to use and require greater technical skill to maintain and manage; thus, purchasers tend to shy away from such products. This reluctance, in turn, dampens demand, even if the underlying need is still present.

From the supply side, vendors feel considerable pressure from users to develop interoperable products. But greater technical skills are needed by vendors to ensure interoperability among different product versions than to design a single product that will be used universally, just as they are for users involved in the operation and maintenance of these products. Requirements for higher degrees of technical skill translate into smaller talent pools from which vendors can draw and thus fewer products available that can meet purchasers' needs for interoperability.

Problems relating to interoperability and system complexity, as well as the size of the installed base, have contributed to the slow pace of demand to date for products with encryption capabilities.

Nevertheless, the committee believes it is only a matter of time until a surge occurs, at the same time acknowledging the similarity between this prediction and other previous predictions regarding demand. This belief is based on projections regarding the growth of networked applications[46]

---

[46]For example, a survey by the International Data Corporation indicated that the installed base of users for work-group applications (involving communications among physically separated users) is expected to grow at a rate of about 74 percent annually between 1993 and 1998. See Ann Palermo and Darby Johnson, Analysts, International Data Corporation, *Workgroup Applications Software: Market Review and Forecast, 1993-1998*, Framingham, Mass., 1993. It is true that a considerable amount of remote collaboration is done via e-mail without cryptographic protection, but work-group applications provide much higher degrees of functionality for collaboration because they are specifically designed for that purpose. As these applications become more sophisticated (e.g., as they begin to process large assemblies of entire documents rather than the short messages for which e-mail is best suited), the demand for higher degrees of protection is likely to increase.

and the trends discussed in Chapter 1—increasing demand for all kinds of information technology, increasing geographic dispersion of businesses across international boundaries, increasing diversity of parties wishing/needing to communicate with each other, and increasing diversity in information technology applications and uses in all activities of a business. Further, the committee believes that computer users the world over have approximately the same computing needs as domestic users, and so domestic trends in computing (including demand for more information security) will be reflected abroad, though perhaps later (probably years later but not decades later).

Market Development

A third issue in assessing the size of the market for cryptography is the extent to which judgments should be made on the basis of today's market conditions (which are known with a higher certainty) rather than markets that may be at risk tomorrow (which are known with a much lower degree of certainty).

The market for certain types of software tends to develop in a characteristic manner. In particular, the long-term success of infrastructure software (i.e., software that supports fundamental business operations such as operating systems or groupware) depends strongly on the product's market timing; once such software is integrated into the infrastructure of the installing organization, demands for backward-compatibility make it difficult for the organization to install any alternative.[47] In other words, an existing software infrastructure inhibits technological change even if better software might be available. It is for this reason that in some software markets, major advantages accrue to the first provider of a reasonable product.

These pressures complicate life for government policy makers who would naturally prefer a more deliberate approach to policy making, because it is only during a small window of time that their decisions are relevant—the sooner they act, the better. The longer they wait, the higher will be the percentage of companies that have already made their technol-

---

[47]Many products require backward-compatibility for marketplace acceptance. Demands for backward-compatibility even affect products intended for operation in a stand-alone environment—an institution with 2 million spreadsheet files is unlikely to be willing to switch to a product that is incompatible with its existing database unless the product provides reasonable translation facilities for migrating to the new product. Network components are even harder to change, because stations on a network must interoperate. For example, most corporate networks have servers deployed with workstations that communicate with those servers. Any change to the software for the servers must not render it impossible for those workstations to work smoothly with the upgrade.

ogy choices, and these companies will face large changeover costs if policy decisions entail incompatible alternatives to their currently deployed infrastructure. If the initial choices of companies involve putting non-U.S. software in place, U.S. vendors fear that they will have lost huge future market opportunities.[48]

4.3.4 Inhibiting Vendor Responses to User Needs

In today's marketing environment, volume sales (licensing) to large corporate or government customers, rather than purchases by individuals, tend to drive sales of business software products.[49] Since corporate customers have large leverage in the marketplace (because one purchasing decision can result in thousands of product sales to a single corporation), major software vendors are much more responsive to the needs of corporate users. Of particular relevance to the export control debate are three perceptions of corporate users:

• Corporate users do not see that different levels of encryption strength (as indicated, for example, by the key length of foreign and domestic versions of a product) provide differential advantages. Put differently, the market reality is that users perceive domestic-strength versions as the standard and liberally exportable versions of cryptography as weak, rather than seeing liberally exportable versions of cryptography as the standard and domestic-strength versions as stronger.

• Corporate users weigh all features of a product in deciding whether or not to buy it. Thus, the absence of a feature such as strong encryption that is desired but not easily available because of U.S. export controls counts as a distinct disadvantage for a U.S. product. Although other features may help to compensate for this deficiency, the deficiency may pose enough of a barrier to a product's acceptance abroad that sales are significantly reduced.

• Corporate users see cryptographic strength as an important parameter in their assessments of the information security that products offer. It is true that cryptography is only one dimension of information

---

[48]The deployment of Lotus Notes provides a good example. Lotus marketing data suggests fairly consistently that once Notes achieves a penetration of about 200 users in a given company, an explosion of demand follows, and growth occurs until Notes is deployed company-wide.

[49]The Department of Commerce noted that "civil use of software-based encryption will significantly increase in the next five years, with corporate customers dominating this new marketplace." See Department of Commerce and National Security Agency, *A Study of the International Market for Computer Software with Encryption*, released January 11, 1996, p. III-2.

security, that export controls do not affect certain approaches to increasing overall information security, and that vendors often do not address these other approaches. But cryptography is a visible aspect of the information security problem, and vendors feel an obligation to respond to market perceptions even if these perceptions may not be fully justified by an underlying technical reality. Moreover, many of the information security measures that do not involve export controls are more difficult and costly than cryptography to implement, and so it is natural for vendors to focus their concerns on export controls on cryptography.

U.S. vendors that are unable to respond in a satisfactory manner to these perceptions have a natural disadvantage in competing against vendors that are able to respond.

4.4 THE IMPACT OF EXPORT CONTROLS ON U.S. ECONOMIC AND NATIONAL SECURITY INTERESTS

By affecting U.S. industries abroad that might use cryptography to protect their information interests and U.S. vendors of a critical technology (namely, information technology), export controls have a number of potentially negative effects on national security that policy makers must weigh against the positive effects of reducing the use of cryptography by hostile parties.

4.4.1 Direct Economic Harm to U.S. Businesses

While acknowledging the economic benefits to U.S. business from signals intelligence (as described in Chapter 3), the committee notes that protection of the information interests of U.S. industries is also a dimension of national security, especially when the threats emanate from foreign sources.

If the potential value of proprietary information is factored into the debate over export controls, it dominates all other figures of merit. A figure of $280 billion to $560 billion was placed by the Computer Systems Policy Project on the value of future revenue opportunities as the result of electronic distribution and commerce and future opportunities to reengineer business processes by 2000.[50] Opponents of export controls on cryptography argue that if electronic channels and information systems

---

[50]William F. Hagerty IV, *The Growing Need for Cryptography: The Impact of Export Control Policy on U.S. Competitiveness*, Study Highlights (viewgraphs), December 15, 1995.

are perceived to be vulnerable, businesses may well be discouraged from exploiting these opportunities, thereby placing enormous potential revenues at risk.

On the other hand, it is essentially impossible to ascertain with any degree of confidence what fraction of proprietary information would be at risk in any practical sense if businesses did move to exploit these opportunities. Current estimates of industrial and economic espionage provide little guidance. The most authoritative publication on the subject to date, the *Annual Report to Congress on Foreign Economic Collection and Industrial Espionage*,[51] noted that

> [i]n today's world in which a country's power and stature are often measured by its economic/industrial capability, foreign government ministries—such as those dealing with finance and trade—and major industrial sectors are increasingly looked upon to play a more prominent role in their respective country's collection efforts. . . . An economic competitor steals a US company's proprietary business information or government trade strategies, [and] foreign companies and commercially oriented government ministries are the main beneficiaries of US economic information. The aggregate losses that can mount as a result of such efforts can reach billions of dollars per year, constituting a serious national security concern.

The report went on to say that "[t]here is no formal mechanism for determining the full qualitative and quantitative scope and impact of the loss of this targeted information. Industry victims have reported the loss of hundreds of millions of dollars, lost jobs, and lost market share."

Thus, even this report, backed by all of the counterintelligence efforts of the U.S. government, is unable to render a definitive estimate to within an order of magnitude. Of course, it may well be that these estimates of loss are low, because companies are reluctant to publicize occurrences of foreign economic and industrial espionage since such publicity can adversely affect stock values, customers' confidence, and ultimately competitiveness and market share, or also because clandestine theft of information may not be detected. Furthermore, because all business trends point to greater volumes of electronically stored and communicated information in the future, it is clear that the potential for information compromises will grow—the value of information that could be compromised through electronic channels is only going to increase.

---

[51]National Counterintelligence Center, *Annual Report to Congress on Foreign Economic Collection and Industrial Espionage*, Washington, D.C., July 1995.

4.4.2 Damage to U.S. Leadership in Information Technology

The strength of the U.S. information technology industry has been taken as a given for the past few decades. But as knowledge and capital essential to the creation of a strong information technology industry become more available around the world, such strength can no longer be taken for granted.[52] If and when foreign products become widely deployed and well integrated into the computing and communications infrastructure of foreign nations, even better versions of U.S. products will be unable to achieve significant market penetration. One example of such a phenomenon may be the growing interest in the United States in personal communications systems based on GSM, the European standard for

---

[52]Obviously, it is impossible to predict with certainty whether export controls will stimulate the growth of significant foreign competition for U.S. information technology vendors. But the historical evidence suggests some reason for concern. For example, a 1991 report (National Research Council, *Finding Common Ground: U.S. Export Controls in a Changed Global Environment*, National Academy Press, Washington, D.C., 1991) found that "unilateral embargoes on exports [of technologies for commercial aircraft and jet engines] to numerous countries not only make sales impossible but actually encourage foreign competitors to develop relationships with the airlines of the embargoed countries. By the time the U.S. controls are lifted, those foreign competitors may have established a competitive advantage" (p. 22). The same report also found that for computer technology, "marginal supplier disadvantages can lead to significant losses in market position, and it is just such marginal disadvantages that can be introduced by export controls" (p. 23). An earlier study (Charles Ferguson, "High Technology Product Life Cycles, Export Controls, and International Markets," in *Working Papers* of the National Research Council report *Balancing the National Interest, U.S. National Security Export Controls and Global Economic Competition*, National Academy Press, Washington, D.C., 1987) pointed out that the emergence of strong foreign competition in a number of high-technology areas appeared in close temporal proximity to the enforcement of strong export controls in these areas for U.S. vendors. While the correlation does not prove that export controls necessarily influenced or stimulated the growth of foreign competition, the history suggests that they may have had some causal relationship. In the financial arena (not subject to export controls), U.S. financial controls associated with the Trading-with-the-Enemy Act may have led to the rise of the Eurodollar market, a set of foreign financial institutions, markets, and instruments that eroded the monopoly held on dollar-denominated instruments and dollar-dominated institutions by U.S. firms.

The likelihood of foreign competition being stimulated for cryptography may be larger than suggested by some of these examples, because at least in the software domain, product development and distribution are less capital intensive than in traditional manufacturing industries; lower capital intensiveness would mean that competitors would be more likely to emerge.

Finally, while it is true that some foreign nations also impose export controls on cryptography, those controls tend to be less stringent than those of the United States, as discussed in Appendix G. In particular, it is more difficult to export encryption from the United States to the United Kingdom than the reverse, and the U.S. market is an important market for foreign vendors. Further, it takes only one nation with weak or nonexistent controls to spawn a competitor in an industry such as software.

digital cellular voice communications. Further, as the example of Microsoft vis-à-vis IBM in the 1980s demonstrated, industry dominance once lost is quite difficult to recover in rapidly changing fields.

The development of foreign competitors in the information technology industry could have a number of disadvantageous consequences from the standpoint of U.S. national security interests:

• Foreign vendors, by assumption, will be more responsive to their own national governments than to the U.S. government. To the extent that foreign governments pursue objectives involving cryptography that are different from those of the United States, U.S. interests may be adversely affected. Specifically, foreign vendors could be influenced by their governments to offer for sale to U.S. firms products with weak or poorly implemented cryptography. If these vendors were to gain significant market share, the information security of U.S. firms could be adversely affected. Furthermore, the United States is likely to have less influence and control over shipments of products with encryption capabilities between foreign nations than it has over similar U.S. products that might be shipped abroad; indeed, many foreign nations are perfectly willing to ship products (e.g., missile parts, nuclear reactor technology) to certain nations in contravention to U.S. or even their own interests. In the long run, the United States may have even less control over the products with encryption capabilities that wind up on the market than it would have if it promulgated a more moderate export control regime.

• Detailed information about the workings of foreign products with encryption capabilities is much less likely to be available to the U.S. government than comparable information about similar U.S. products that are exported. Indeed, as part of the export control administration process, U.S. products with encryption capabilities intended for export are examined thoroughly by the U.S. government; as a result, large amounts of information about U.S. products with encryption capabilities are available to it.[53]

Export controls on cryptography are not the only factor influencing the future position of U.S. information technology vendors in the world market. Yet, the committee believes that these controls do pose a risk to their future position that cannot be ignored, and that relaxation of controls will help to ensure that U.S. vendors are able to compete with foreign vendors on a more equal footing.

---

[53]For example, U.S. vendors are more likely than foreign vendors to reveal the source code of a program to the U.S. government (for purposes of obtaining export licenses). While it is true that the object code of a software product can be decompiled, decompiled object code is always much more difficult to understand than the original source code that corresponds to it.

4.5 THE MISMATCH BETWEEN THE PERCEPTIONS OF GOVERNMENT/NATIONAL SECURITY AND THOSE OF VENDORS

As the committee proceeded in its study, it observed what can only be called a disconnect between the perceptions of the national security authorities that administer the export control regulations on cryptography and the vendors that are affected by it. This disconnect was apparent in a number of areas:

• National security authorities asserted that export controls did not injure the interests of U.S. vendors in the foreign sales of products with encryption capabilities. U.S. vendors asserted that export controls had a significant negative effect on their foreign sales.

• National security authorities asserted that nearly all export license applications for a product with encryption capabilities are approved. Vendors told the committee that they refrained from submitting products for approval because they had been told on the basis of preliminary discussions that their products would not be approved for export.

• National security authorities presented data showing that the turn-around time for license decisions had been dramatically shortened (to a matter of days or a few weeks at most). Vendors noted that these data took into account only the time from the date of formal submission of an application to the date of decision, and did not take into account the much greater length of time required to negotiate product changes that would be necessary to receive approval. (See Section 4.3.2 for more discussion.)

• National security authorities asserted that they wished to promote good information security for U.S. companies, pointing out the current practice described in Section 4.1.2 that presumes the granting of USML licenses for stronger cryptography to U.S.-controlled companies and banking and financial institutions. Vendors pointed to actions taken by these authorities to weaken the cryptographic security available for use abroad, even in business ventures in which U.S. firms had substantial interests. Potential users often told the committee that even under presumptive approval, licenses were not forthcoming, and that for practical purposes, these noncodified categories were not useful.

• National security authorities asserted that they took into account foreign competition and the supply of products with encryption capabilities when making decisions on export licenses for U.S. products with encryption capabilities. Vendors repeatedly pointed to a substantial supply of foreign products with encryption capabilities.

• National security authorities asserted that they wished to maintain the worldwide strength and position of the U.S. information technology industry. Vendors argued that when they are prevented from exploiting their strengths—such as being the first to develop integrated products with strong encryption capabilities—their advantages are in fact being eroded.

The committee believes that to some extent these differences can be explained as the result of rhetoric by parties intending to score points in a political debate. But the differences are not merely superficial; they reflect significantly different institutional perspectives. For example, when national security authorities "take into account foreign supplies of cryptography," they focus naturally on what is available at the time the decision is being made. On the other hand, vendors are naturally concerned about incorporating features that will give their products a competitive edge, even if no exactly comparable foreign products with cryptography are available at the moment. Thus, different parties focus on different areas of concern—national security authorities on the capabilities available today, and vendors on the capabilities that might well be available tomorrow.

NSA perceptions of vendors and users of cryptography may well be clouded by an unwillingness to speak publicly about the full extent of vendor and user unhappiness with the current state of affairs. National security authorities asserted that their working relationships with vendors of products with encryption capabilities are relatively harmonious. Vendors contended that since they are effectively at the mercy of the export control regulators, they have considerable incentive to suppress any public expression of dissatisfaction with the current process. A lack (or small degree) of vendor outcry against the cryptography export control regime cannot be taken as vendor support for it. More specifically, the committee received input from a number of private firms on the explicit condition of confidentiality. For example:

• Companies with interests in cryptography affected by export control were reluctant to express fully their dissatisfaction with the current rules governing export of products with encryption capabilities or how these rules were actually implemented in practice. They were concerned that any explicit connection between critical comments and their company might result in unfavorable treatment of a future application for an export license for one of their products.

• Companies that had significant dealings with the Department of Defense (DOD) were reluctant to express fully their unhappiness with policy that strongly promoted classified encryption algorithms and government-controlled key-escrow schemes. These companies were concerned that expressing their unhappiness fully might result in unfavorable treatment in competing for future DOD business.

Many companies have expressed dissatisfaction publicly, although a very small number of firms did express to the committee their relative comfort with the way in which the current export control regime is managed. The committee did not conduct a systematic survey of all firms affected by export regulations, and it is impossible to infer the position of a company that has not provided input on the matter.[54]

4.6 EXPORT OF TECHNICAL DATA

The rules regarding "technical data" are particularly difficult to understand. A cryptographic algorithm (if described in a manner that is not machine-executable) is counted as technical data, whereas the same algorithm if described in machine-readable form (i.e., source or object code) counts as a product. Legally, the ITAR regulate products with encryption capabilities differently than technical data related to cryptography, although the differences are relatively small in nature. For example, technical data related to cryptography enjoys an explicit exemption when distributed to U.S.-controlled foreign companies, whereas products with encryption capabilities are in principle subject to a case-by-case review in such instances (although in practice, licenses for products with encryption capabilities under such circumstances are routinely granted).

Private citizens, academic institutions, and vendors are often unclear about the legality of actions such as:

- Discussing cryptography with a foreign citizen in the room;
- Giving away software with encryption capabilities over the Internet (see Section 4.8);
- Shipping products with encryption capabilities to a foreign company within the United States that is controlled but not owned by a U.S. company;
- Selling a U.S. company that makes products with strong encryption capabilities to a foreign company;
- Selling products with encryption capabilities to foreign citizens on U.S. soil;
- Teaching a course on cryptography that involves foreign graduate students;

---

[54]The Department of Commerce study is the most systematic attempt to date to solicit vendors' input on how they have been affected by export controls, and the solicitation received a much smaller response than expected. See Department of Commerce and National Security Agency, *A Study of the International Market for Computer Software with Encryption*, released January 11, 1996.

- Allowing foreign citizens residing in the United States to work on the source code of a product that uses embedded cryptography.[55]

Box 4.10 provides excerpts from the only document known to the committee that describes the U.S. government explanation of the regulations on technical data related to cryptography. In practice, these and other similar issues regarding technical data do not generally pose problems because these laws are for the most part difficult to enforce and in fact are not generally enforced. Nevertheless, the vagueness and broad nature of the regulations may well put people in jeopardy unknowingly.[56]

---

[55]For example, one vendor argues that because foreign citizens hired by U.S. companies bring noncontrolled knowledge back to their home countries anyway, the export control regulations on technical data make little sense as a technique for limiting the spread of knowledge. In addition, other vendors note that in practice the export control regulations on technical data have a much more severe impact on the employees that they may hire than on academia, which is protected at least to some extent by presumptions of academic freedom.

[56]A suit filed in February 1995 seeks to bar the government from restricting publication of cryptographic documents and software through the use of the export control laws. The plaintiff in the suit is Dan Bernstein, a graduate student in mathematics at the University of California at Berkeley. Bernstein developed an encryption algorithm that he wishes to publish and to implement in a computer program intended for distribution, and he wants to discuss the algorithm and program at open, public meetings. Under the current export control laws, any individual or company that exports unlicensed encryption software may be in violation of the export control laws that forbid the unlicensed export of defense articles, and any individual who discusses the mathematics of cryptographic algorithms may be in violation of the export control laws that forbid the unlicensed export of "technical data." The lawsuit argues that the export control scheme as applied to encryption software is an "impermissible prior restraint on speech, in violation of the First Amendment" and that the current export control laws are vague and overbroad in denying people the right to speak about and publish information about cryptography freely. A decision by the Northern District Court of California on April 15, 1996, by Judge Marilyn Patel, denied the government's motion to dismiss this suit, and found that for the purposes of First Amendment analysis, source code should be treated as speech. The outcome of this suit is unknown at the time of this writing (spring 1996). The full text of this decision and other related documents can be found at http://www.eff.org/pub/Legal/Cases/Bernstein_v_DoS/Legal.

The constitutionality of export controls on technical data has not been determined by the U.S. Supreme Court. A ruling by the U.S. Ninth Circuit Court of Appeals held that the ITAR, when construed as "prohibiting only the exportation of technical data significantly and directly related to specific articles on the Munitions List, do not interfere with constitutionally protected speech, are not overbroad and the licensing provisions of the Act are not an unconstitutional prior restraint on speech." (See 579 F.2d 516, U.S. vs. Edler, U.S. Court of Appeals, Ninth Circuit, July 31, 1978.) Another suit filed by Philip Karn directly challenging the constitutionality of the ITAR was dismissed by the U.S. District Court for the District of Columbia on March 22, 1996. The issue at hand was the fact that Karn had been denied CCL jurisdiction for a set of floppy diskettes containing source code for cryptographic confidentiality identical to that contained in Bruce Schneier's book *Applied Cryptography* (which the State Department had determined was not subject to cryptographic export controls of any kind). See http://www.qualcomm.com/people/pkarn/export/index.html

---

BOX 4.10
On the Export of Technical Data Related to Cryptography

"Cryptologic technical data . . . refers . . . only [to] such information as is designed or intended to be used, or which reasonably could be expected to be given direct application, in the design, production, manufacture, repair, overhaul, processing, engineering, development, operation, maintenance or reconstruction of items in such categories. This interpretation includes, in addition to engineering and design data, information designed or reasonably expected to be used to make such equipment more effective, such as encoding or enciphering techniques and systems, and communications or signal security techniques and guidelines, as well as other cryptographic and cryptanalytic methods and procedures. It does not include general mathematical, engineering or statistical information, not purporting to have or reasonably expected to be given direct application to equipment in such categories. It does not include basic theoretical research data. It does, however, include algorithms and other procedures purporting to have advanced cryptologic application.

"The public is reminded that professional and academic presentations and informal discussions, as well as demonstrations of equipment, constituting disclosure of cryptologic technical data to foreign nationals are prohibited without the prior approval of this office. Approval is not required for publication of data within the United States as described in Section 125.11(a)(1). Footnote 3 to section 125.11 does not establish a prepublication review requirement.

"The interpretation set forth in this newsletter should exclude from the licensing provisions of the ITAR most basic scientific data and other theoretical research information, except for information intended or reasonably expected to have a direct cryptologic application. Because of concerns expressed to this office that licensing procedures for proposed disclosures of cryptologic technical data contained in professional and academic papers and oral presentations could cause burdensome delays in exchanges with foreign scientists, this office will expedite consideration as to the application of ITAR to such disclosures. If requested, we will, on an expedited basis provide an opinion as to whether any proposed disclosure, for other than commercial purposes, of information relevant to cryptology, would require licensing under the ITAR."

SOURCE: Office of Munitions Control, Department of State, "Cryptography/ Technical Data," in *Munitions Control Newsletter*, Number 80, February 1980. (The Office of Munitions Control is now the Office of Defense Trade Controls.)

---

for the running story (Karn is appealing this decision); this Web page also contains the District Court's opinion on this lawsuit.) Some scholars argue to the contrary that export controls on technical data may indeed present First Amendment problems, especially if these controls are construed in such a way that they inhibit academic discussions of cryptography with foreign nationals or prevent academic conferences on cryptography held in the United States from inviting foreign nationals. See, for example, Allen M. Shinn, Jr., "First Amendment and Export Laws: Free Speech on Scientific and Technical Matters," *George Washington Law Review*, January 1990, pp. 368-403; and Kenneth J. Pierce, "Public Cryptography, Arms Export Controls, and the First Amendment: A Need for Legislation," *Cornell International Law Journal*, Volume 17(19), 1984, pp. 197-237.

4.7 FOREIGN POLICY CONSIDERATIONS

A common perception within the vendor community is that the National Security Agency is the sole "power behind the scenes" for enforcing the export control regime for cryptography. While NSA is indeed responsible for making judgments about the national security impact of exporting products with encryption capabilities, it is by no means the only player in the export license application process.

The Department of State plays a role in the export control process that is quite important. For example, makers of foreign policy in the U.S. government use economic sanctions as a tool for expressing U.S. concern and displeasure with the actions of other nations; such sanctions most often involve trade embargoes of various types. Violations of human rights by a particular nation, for example, represent a common issue that can trigger a move for sanctions. Such sanctions are sometimes based on presidential determinations (e.g., that the human rights record of country X is not acceptable to the United States) undertaken in accordance with law; in other cases, sanctions against specific nations are determined directly by congressional legislation; in still other cases, sanctions are based entirely on the discretionary authority of the President.

The imposition of sanctions is often the result of congressional action that drastically limits the discretionary authority of the State Department. In such a context, U.S. munitions or articles of war destined for particular offending nations (or to the companies in such nations) are the most politically sensitive, and in practice the items on the USML are the ones most likely to be denied to the offending nations. In all such cases, the State Department must determine whether a particular item on the USML should or should not qualify for a USML license. A specific example of such an action given to the committee in testimony involved the export of cryptography by a U.S. bank for use in a branch located in the People's Republic of China. Because of China's human rights record, the Department of State delayed the export, and the contract was lost to a Swiss firm. The sale of cryptographic tools that are intended to protect the interests of a U.S. company operating in a foreign nation was subject to a foreign policy stance that regarded such a sale as equivalent to supplying munitions to that nation.

Thus, even when NSA has been willing to grant an export license for a given cryptography product, the State Department has sometimes denied a license because cryptography is on the USML. In such cases, NSA takes the blame for a negative decision, even when it had nothing to do with it.

Critics of the present export control regime have made the argument that cryptography, as an item on the USML that is truly dual-use, should not necessarily be included in such sanctions. Such an argument has some intellectual merit, but under current regulations it is impossible to separate cryptography from the other items on the USML.

4.8 TECHNOLOGY-POLICY MISMATCHES

Two cases are often cited in the cryptography community as examples of the mismatch between the current export control regime and the current state of cryptographic technology (Box 4.11). Moreover, they are often used as evidence that the government is harassing innocent, law-abiding citizens.

Taken by themselves and viewed from the outside, both of the cases outlined in Box 4.11 suggest an approach to national security with evident weaknesses. In the first instance, accepting the premise that programs for cryptography cannot appear on the Internet because a foreigner might download them seems to challenge directly the use of the Internet as a forum for exchanging information freely even within the United States. Under such logic (claim the critics), international telephone calls would also have to be shut down because a U.S. person might discuss cryptography with a foreign national on the telephone. In the second instance, the information contained in the book (exportable) is identical to that on the disk (not exportable). Since it is the information about cryptography that is technically at issue (the export control regulations make no mention of the medium in which that information is represented), it is hard to see why one would be exportable and the other not.

On the other hand, taking the basic assumptions of the national security perspective as a given, the decisions have a certain logic that is not only the logic of selective prosecution or enforcement.

• In the case of Zimmermann, the real national security issue is not the program itself, but rather the fact that a significant PGP user base may be developing. Two copies of a good encryption program distributed abroad pose no plausible threat to national security. But 20 million copies might well pose a threat. The export control regulations as written do not mention potential or actual size of the user base, and so the only remaining leverage for the U.S. government is the broad language that brings cryptography under the export control laws.

• In the case of Schneier, the real national security issue relates to the nature of any scheme intended to deny capabilities to an adversary. Typing the book's source code into the computer is an additional step that an adversary must take to implement a cryptography program and a step at which an adversary could make additional errors. No approach to denial can depend on a single "silver bullet"; instead, denial rests on the erection

BOX 4.11
Two Export Control Cases

The Zimmermann PGP Case

Philip Zimmermann is the author of a software program known as PGP (for Pretty Good Privacy). PGP is a program that is used to encrypt mail messages end-to-end based on public-key cryptography. Most importantly, PGP includes a system for key management that enables two users who have never interacted to communicate securely based on a set of trusted intermediaries that certify the validity of a given public key. Across the Internet, PGP is one of the most widely used systems for secure e-mail communication.

Zimmermann developed PGP as a "freeware" program to be distributed via diskette. Another party subsequently posted PGP to a USENET "newsgroup."[1] (A commercial version licensed from but not supplied by Zimmermann has since emerged.) In 1993, it was determined that Zimmermann was the target of a criminal investigation probing possible violations of the export control laws.[2] Zimmermann was careful to state that PGP was not to be used or downloaded outside the United States, but of course international connections to the Internet made for easy access to copies of PGP located within the United States. In January 1996, the U.S. Department of Justice closed its investigation of Zimmermann without filing charges against him.[3]

The Bruce Schneier-*Applied Cryptography* Case

Bruce Schneier wrote a book called *Applied Cryptography*[4] that was well received in the cryptography community. It was also regarded as useful in a practical sense because it contained printed on its pages source code that could be entered into a computer and compiled into a working cryptography program. In addition, when distributed within the United States, the book contained a floppy disk that contained source code identical to the code found in the book. However, when another party (Philip Karn) requested a ruling on the exportability of the book, he (Karn) received permission to export the book but not the disk. This decision has been greeted with considerable derision in the academic cryptography community, with comments such as "They think that terrorists can't type?" expressing the general dismay of the community.

---

[1] A USENET newsgroup is in effect a mailing list to which individuals around the world may subscribe. Posting is thus an act of transmission to all list members.

[2] John Schwartz, "Privacy Program: An On-Line Weapon?," *Washington Post*, April 3, 1995, p. A1.

[3] Elizabeth Cocoran, "U.S. Closes Investigation in Computer Privacy Case," *Washington Post*, January 12, 1996, p. A11.

[4] Bruce Schneier, *Applied Cryptography*, John Wiley & Sons, New York, 1994.

of multiple barriers, all of which taken together are expected to result in at least a partial denial of a certain capability. Moreover, if one begins from the premise that export controls on software encryption represent appropriate national policy, it is clear that allowing the export of the source code to Schneier's book would set a precedent that would make it very difficult to deny permission for the export of other similar software products with encryption capabilities. Finally, the decision is consistent with a history of commodity jurisdiction decisions that generally maintain USML controls on the *source* code of a product whose *object* code implementation of confidentiality has been granted commodity jurisdiction to the CCL.

These comments are not intended to excoriate or defend the national security analysis of these cases. But the controversy over these cases does suggest quite strongly that the traditional national security paradigm of export controls on cryptography (one that is biased toward denial rather than approval) is stretched greatly by current technology. Put differently, when the export control regime is pushed to an extreme, it appears to be manifestly ridiculous.

4.9 RECAP

Current export controls on products with encryption capabilities are a compromise between (1) the needs of national security to conduct signals intelligence and (2) the needs of U.S. and foreign businesses operating abroad to protect information and the needs of U.S. information technology vendors to remain competitive in markets involving products with encryption capabilities that might meet these needs. These controls have helped to delay the spread of strong cryptographic capabilities and the use of those capabilities throughout the world, to impede the development of standards for cryptography that would facilitate such a spread, and to give the U.S. government a tool for monitoring and influencing the commercial development of cryptography. Export controls have clearly been effective in limiting the foreign availability of products with strong encryption capabilities made by U.S. manufacturers, although enforcement of export controls on certain products with encryption capabilities appears to have created many public relations difficulties for the U.S. government, and circumventions of the current regulations appear possible. The dollar cost of limiting the availability of cryptography abroad is hard to estimate with any kind of confidence, since even the definition of what counts as a cost is quite fuzzy. At the same time, a floor of a few hundred million dollars per year for the market affected by export controls on encryption seems plausible, and all indications are that this figure will only grow in the future.

A second consideration is the possibility that export controls on products with encryption capabilities may well have a *negative* impact on U.S. national security interests by stimulating the growth of important foreign competitors over which the U.S. government has less influence, and possibly by damaging U.S. competitive advantages in the use and development of information technology. In addition, the export control regime is clouded by uncertainty from the vendor standpoint, and there is a profound mismatch between the perceptions of government/national security and those of vendors on the impact of the export control regime. Moreover, even when a given product with encryption capabilities may be acceptable for export on national security grounds, nonnational security considerations may play a role in licensing decisions.

Partly in response to expressed concerns about export controls, the export regime has been gradually loosened since 1983. This relaxation raises the obvious question of how much farther and in what directions such loosening could go without significant damage to national security interests. This subject is addressed in Chapter 7.

5

Escrowed Encryption and Related Issues

This chapter describes a tool—escrowed encryption—that responds to the needs described in Chapter 3 for exceptional access to encrypted information. Escrowed encryption is the basis for a number of Administration proposals that seek to reconcile needs for information security against the needs of law enforcement and to a lesser extent national security. As in the case of export controls, escrowed encryption generates considerable controversy.

5.1 WHAT IS ESCROWED ENCRYPTION?

The term "escrow," as used conventionally, implies that some item of value (e.g., a trust deed, money, real property, other physical object) is delivered to an independent trusted party that might be a person or an organization (i.e., an escrow agent) for safekeeping, and is accompanied by a set of rules provided by the parties involved in the transaction governing the actions of the escrow agent. Such rules typically specify what is to be done with the item, the schedule to be followed, and the list of other events that have to occur. The underlying notion is that the escrow agent is a secure haven for temporary ownership or possession of the item, is legally bound to comply with the set of rules for its disposition, functions as a disinterested extratransaction party, and bears legal liability for malfeasance or mistakes.

Usually, the rules stipulate that when all conditions set forth in the escrow rules have been fulfilled, the item will eventually be delivered to a specified party (e.g., possibly the original depositing party, an estate, a judicial officer for custody, one or more individuals or organizations). In any event, the salient point is that all terms and conditions and functioning of an escrow process are, or can be, visible to the parties involved; moreover, the behavior and performance of formal escrow agents are governed by legally established obligations.

As it applies to cryptography, the term "escrow" was introduced by the U.S. government's April 1993 Clipper initiative in the context of encryption keys. Prior to this time, the term "escrow" had not been widely associated with cryptography, although the underlying concepts had been known for some time (as described below). The Clipper initiative promoting escrowed encryption was intended "to improve the security and privacy of telephone communications while meeting the legitimate needs of law enforcement."[1] In this original context, the term "escrowed encryption" had a very specific and narrow meaning: escrowed encryption was a mechanism that would assure law enforcement access to the voice communications underlying encrypted intercepts from wiretaps.

However, during 3 years of public debate and dialogue, "escrow," "key escrow," and "escrowed encryption" have become terms with a much broader meaning. Indeed, many different schemes for "escrowed encryption" are quite different from "escrowed encryption" as the term was used in the Clipper initiative.

As is so often the case in computer-related matters, terminology for escrowed systems is today not clearly established and can be confusing or misleading. While new terminology could be introduced in an effort to clarify meaning, the fact is that the present policy and public and technical dialogues all use "escrow" and "escrowed encryption" in a very generic and broad sense. It is no longer the very precise restricted concept embodied in the Clipper initiative and described in Section 5.2.1. Escrow as a concept now applies not only to the initial purpose of assuring law enforcement access to encrypted materials, but also to possible end-user or organizational requirements for a mechanism to protect against lost, corrupted, or unavailable keys. It can also mean that some process such as authority to decrypt a header containing a session key is escrowed with a trusted party, or it can mean that a corporation is ready to cooperate with law enforcement to access encrypted materials.

---

[1] See "Statement by the Press Secretary, The White House, April 16, 1993," reprinted in David Banisar (ed.), *1994 Cryptography and Privacy Sourcebook*, Part II, Electronic Privacy Information Center, Diane Publishing, Upland, Pa., 1994. The name "Clipper" initially selected as the name of this effort proved later to be a trademark whose holder relinquished it to public use.

This report conforms to current usage, considering escrowed encryption as a broad concept that can be implemented in many ways; Section 5.3 addresses forms of escrowed encryption other than that described in the Clipper initiative. Also, escrowed encryption is only one of several approaches to providing exceptional access to encrypted information; nonescrow approaches to providing exceptional access are discussed in Chapter 7.[2]

Finally, the relationship between "strong encryption" and "escrowed encryption" should be noted. As stated above, escrowed encryption refers to an approach to encryption that enables exceptional access to plaintext without requiring a third party (e.g., government acting with legal authorization, a corporation acting in accordance with its contractual rights vis-à-vis its employees, an individual who has lost an encryption key) to perform a cryptanalytic attack. At the same time, escrowed encryption can involve cryptographic algorithms that are strong or weak and keys that are long or short. Some participants in the public debate appear to believe that escrowed encryption is necessarily equivalent to weak encryption, because it does not prevent third parties from having access to the relevant plaintext. But this is a mischaracterization of the intent behind escrowed encryption, since all escrowed encryption schemes proposed to date are intended to provide very strong cryptographic confidentiality (strong algorithms, relatively long keys) for users against *unauthorized* third parties, but no confidentiality at all against third parties who have *authorized* exceptional access.

5.2 ADMINISTRATION INITIATIVES SUPPORTING ESCROWED ENCRYPTION

Since inheriting the problem of providing law enforcement access to encrypted telephony from the outgoing Bush Administration in late 1992,

---

[2]In the more general meaning of escrowed encryption, exceptional access refers to access to plaintext by a party other than the originator and the recipient of encrypted communications. For the case of stored information, exceptional access may refer to access to the plaintext of an encrypted file by someone not designated by the original encryptor of the file to decrypt it or even by persons so designated who have forgotten how to do so. See also Chapter 3.

Contrast the meaning of third-party access in the original Clipper context, in which third-party access refers to assured access, under proper court authorization, by law enforcement to the plaintext of an encrypted voice conversation. The Clipper initiative was intended to support a system that provided a technically convenient means to assure fulfillment of such a requirement. Note that this meaning is much narrower than the use of the more general term "exceptional access" described in the previous paragraph.

Clinton Administration officials have said that as they considered the not-so-distant future of information technology and information security along with the stated needs of law enforcement and national security for access to information, they saw three alternatives:[3]

- To do nothing, resulting in the possible proliferation of products with encryption capabilities that would seriously weaken, if not wholly negate, the authority to wiretap embodied in the Wiretap Act of 1968 (Title III) and damage intelligence collection for national security and foreign policy reasons;
- To support an approach based on weak encryption, likely resulting in poor security and cryptographic confidentiality for important personal and business information; and
- To support an approach based on strong but escrowed encryption. If widely adopted and properly implemented, escrowed encryption could provide legitimate users with high degrees of assurance that their sensitive information would remain secure but nevertheless enable law enforcement and national security authorities to obtain access to escrow-encrypted data in specific instances when authorized under law. Moreover, the Administration hoped that by meeting legitimate demands for better information security, escrowed encryption would dampen the market for unescrowed encryption products that would deny access to law enforcement and national security authorities even when they sought access for legitimate and lawfully authorized purposes.

The Administration chose the last, and since April 1993, the U.S. government has advanced a number of initiatives to support the insertion of key escrow features into products with encryption capabilities that will become available in the future. These include the Clipper initiative and the Escrowed Encryption Standard, the Capstone/Fortezza initiative, and the proposal to liberalize export controls on products using escrowed encryption. These initiatives raise a number of important issues that are the focus of Sections 5.3 to 5.13.

5.2.1 The Clipper Initiative and the Escrowed Encryption Standard

As noted above, the Clipper initiative was conceived as a way for providing legal access by law enforcement authorities to encrypted tele-

---

[3]See, for example, statement of Raymond Kammer, Deputy Director, National Institute of Standards and Technology, before the Committee on the Judiciary, U.S. Senate, May 3, 1994. Available on-line at http://www.nist.gov/item/testimony/may94/encryp.html.

BOX 5.1
Key Technical Attributes of the Clipper Initiative

1. A chip-unique secret key—the "unit key" or "device key" or "master key"—would be embedded in the chip at the time of fabrication and could be obtained by law enforcement officials legally authorized to do so under Title III.

2. Each chip-unique device key would be split into two components.

3. The component parts would be deposited with and held under high security by two trusted third-party escrow agents proposed to be agencies of the U.S. government. Note: "Third-party" is used here to indicate parties other than those participating in the communication.

4. A law enforcement access field (LEAF) would be a required part of every transmission. The LEAF would contain (a) the current session key, encrypted with a combination of the device-unique master key and a different but secret "family key" also permanently embedded in the chip, and (b) the chip serial number, also protected by encryption with the family key.

5. Law enforcement could use the information in the LEAF to identify the particular device of interest, solicit its master-key components from the two escrow agents, combine them, recover the session key, and eventually decrypt the encrypted traffic.

6. The encryption algorithm on the chip would be secret.

7. The chip would be protected against reverse engineering and other attempts to access its technical details.

SOURCE: Dorothy Denning and Miles Smid, "Key Escrowing Today," *IEEE Communications*, Volume 32(9), September 1994, pp. 58-68. Available online at http://www.cosc.georgetown.edu/~denning/ crypto/Key-Escrowing-Today.txt.

phony.[4] The Escrowed Encryption Standard (EES; a Federal Information Processing Standard, FIPS-185) was promulgated in February 1994 as the key technological component of the Clipper initiative (Box 5.1). Specifically, the EES called for the integration of special microelectronic integrated circuit chips (called "Clipper chips") into devices used for voice communications; these chips, as one part of an overall system, provide voice confidentiality for the user and exceptional access to law enforcement authorities. To provide these functions, the Clipper chip was designed with a number of essential characteristics:

• Confidentiality would be provided by a classified algorithm known as Skipjack. Using an 80-bit key, the Skipjack algorithm would offer

---

[4]Dorothy Denning and Miles Smid, "Key Escrowing Today," *IEEE Communications,* Volume 32(9), September 1994, pp. 58-68. Available on-line at http://www.cosc. georgetown.edu/~denning/crypto/Key-Escrowing-Today.txt.

considerably more protection against brute-force attacks than the 56-bit DES algorithm (FIPS 46-1). The Skipjack algorithm was reviewed by several independent experts, all with the necessary security clearances. In the course of an investigation limited by time and resources, they reported that they did not find shortcuts that would significantly reduce the time to perform a cryptanalytic attack below what would be required by brute force.[5]

• The chip would be protected against reverse engineering and other attempts to access its technical details.

• The chip would be factory-programmed with a chip-unique secret key, the "unit key" or "device key,"[6] at the time of fabrication. Possession of this key would enable one to decrypt all communications sent to and from the telephone unit in which the chip was integrated.

• A law enforcement access field (LEAF) would be a required part of every transmission and would be generated by the chip. The LEAF would contain two items: (a) the current session key,[7] encrypted with a combination of the device-unique unit key, and (b) the chip serial number. The entire LEAF would itself be encrypted by a different but secret "family key" also permanently embedded in the chip. The family key would be the same in all Clipper chips produced by a given manufacturer; in practice, all Clipper chips regardless of manufacturer are programmed today by the Mykotronx Corporation with the same family key.

To manage the use of the LEAF, the U.S. government would undertake a number of actions:

---

[5]See Ernest Brickell et al., *SKIPJACK Review: Interim Report*, July 28, 1993. Posted to the "sci.crypt" newsgroup on August 1, 1993, by Dorothy Denning and available on-line at http://www.cosc.georgetown.edu/~denning/SKIPJACK.txt. Reprinted in Lance J. Hoffman (ed.), *Building in Big Brother: The Cryptographic Policy Debate*, Springer-Verlag, New York, 1995, pp. 119-130.

[6]The device key or unit key is used to open the encryption that protects a session key. Hence, possession of the unit key allows the decryption of *all* messages or files encrypted with that unit or device. "Session key" is defined in footnote 7.

[7]"Session," as in computer science, denotes a period of time during which one or more computer-based processes are operational and performing some function; typically two or more of systems, end users, or software processes are involved in a session. It is analogous to a meeting among these things. For cryptography, a session is the plaintext data stream on which the cryptographic process operates. The session key is the actual key that is needed to decrypt the resulting ciphertext. In the context of an encrypted data transmission or telephone call, the session key is the key needed to decrypt the communications stream. For encrypted data storage, it is the key needed to decrypt the file. Note that in the case of symmetric encryption (discussed in Chapter 2), the decryption key is identical to the encryption key. Since asymmetric encryption for confidentiality is efficient only for short messages or files, symmetric encryption is used for session encryption of telephony, data transmissions, and data storage.

- The unit key, known at the time of manufacture and unchangeable for the life of the chip, would be divided into two components, each of which would be deposited with and held under high security by two trusted government escrow agents located within the Departments of Commerce and Treasury.
- These escrow agents would serve as repositories for all such materials, releasing the relevant information to law enforcement authorities upon presentation of the unit identification and lawfully obtained court orders.

When law enforcement officials encountered a Clipper-encrypted conversation on a wiretap, they would use the LEAF to obtain the serial number of the Clipper chip performing the encryption and the encrypted session key.[8] Upon presentation of the serial number and court authorization for the wiretap to the escrow agents, law enforcement officials could then obtain the proper unit-key components, combine them, recover the session key, and eventually decrypt the encrypted voice communications.[9] Only one key would be required in order to obtain access to both sides of the Clipper-encrypted conversation. The authority for law enforcement to approach escrow agents and request unit-key components was considered to be that granted by Title III and the Foreign Intelligence Surveillance Act (FISA).[10]

As a FIPS, the EES is intended for use by the federal government and has no legal standing outside the federal government. Indeed, its use is

---

[8]Because the family key would be known to law enforcement officials, obtaining the unencrypted LEAF would present no problems.

[9]Questions have arisen about NSA access to escrowed keys. NSA has stated for the record to the committee that "key escrow does not affect either the authorities or restrictions applicable to NSA's signals intelligence activities. NSA's access to escrowed keys will be tied to collection against legitimate foreign intelligence targets. The key holder must have some assurance that NSA is involved in an authorized intelligence collection activity and that the collection activity will be conducted in accordance with the appropriate restrictions." For a description of these restrictions, see Appendix D of this report.

[10]Dorothy Denning and Miles Smid, "Key Escrowing Today," *IEEE Communications*, Volume 32(9), 1994, pp. 58-68. Available on-line at http://www.cosc.georgetown.edu/~denning/crypto/Key-Escrowing-Today.txt.

Given its initial intent to preserve law enforcement's ability to conduct wire taps, it follows that Clipper key escrow would be conducted without the knowledge of parties whose keys had been escrowed, and would be conducted according to a set of rules that would be publicly known but not changeable by the affected parties. Under the requirements of Title III, the affected parties would be notified of the tapping activity at its conclusion, unless the information were to become the basis for a criminal indictment or an ongoing investigation. In the latter case, the accused would learn of the wiretaps, and hence the law enforcement use of escrowed keys, through court procedures.

optional even by federal agencies. In other words, federal agencies with a requirement for secure voice communications have a choice about whether or not to adopt the EES for their own purposes. More importantly, the use of EES-compliant devices by private parties cannot in general be compelled by executive action alone; private consumers are free to decide whether or not to use EES-compliant devices to safeguard communications and are free to use other approaches to communications security should they so desire.[11] However, if consumers choose to use EES-compliant devices, they must accept key escrow as outlined in procedures promulgated by the government. This characteristic—that interoperability requires acceptance of key escrow—is a design choice; a different specification could permit the interoperability of devices with or without features for key escrow.

The EES was developed by communications security experts from the NSA, but the escrow features of the EES are intended to meet the needs of law enforcement—i.e., its needs for clandestine surveillance of electronic and wire communications as described in Chapter 3. NSA played this development role because of its technical expertise. EES-compliant devices are also approved for communicating classified information up to and including SECRET. In speaking with the committee, Administration officials described the Clipper initiative as more or less irrelevant to the needs of signals intelligence (SIGINT) (Box 5.2).

As of early 1996, AT&T had sold 10,000 to 15,000 units of the Surity Telephone Device 3600. These include four configurations: Model C, containing only the Clipper chip, which has been purchased primarily by U.S. government customers; Model F, containing only an AT&T-proprietary algorithm that is exportable; Model P, containing an AT&T-proprietary nonexportable algorithm in addition to the exportable algorithm; and Model S, with all three of the above. Only units with the Clipper chip have a key-escrow feature. All the telephones are interoperable—they negotiate with each other to settle on a mutually available algorithm at the beginning of a call.[12] In addition, AT&T and Cycomm International have agreed to jointly develop and market Clipper-compatible digital voice encryption attachments for Motorola's Micro-Tac series of handheld

---

[11]For example, an opinion issued by the Congressional Research Service argues that legislation would be required to mandate the use of the Clipper chip beyond federal computer systems. Memorandum from the American Law Division, Congressional Research Service, "Current Legal Authority to Mandate Adoption of 'Clipper Chip' Standards by Private Parties," Library of Congress, Washington, D.C., October 4, 1994.

[12]AT&T Secure Communications product literature, available on-line at http://www.att.com/press/0694/940613.pdb.html, and personal communication with Bruce Bailey, AT&T Secure Communications Systems, Greensboro, N.C., March 29, 1996.

BOX 5.2
The Relationship of Escrowed Encryption to Signals Intelligence

Escrowed encryption—especially the Escrowed Encryption Standard (EES) and the Clipper initiative—is a tool of law enforcement more than of signals intelligence (SIGINT). The EES was intended primarily for domestic use, although exports of EES-compliant devices have not been particularly discouraged. Given that the exceptional access feature of escrowed encryption has been openly announced, purchase by foreign governments for secure communications is highly unlikely.

On the other hand, the U.S. government has classified the Skipjack algorithm to keep foreign adversaries from learning more about good cryptography. In addition, wide deployment and use of escrowed encryption would complicate the task of signals intelligence, simply because individual keys would have to be obtained one by one for communications that might or might not be useful. (Still, EES devices would be better for SIGINT than unescrowed secure telephones, in the sense that widely deployed secure telephones without features for exceptional access would be much harder to penetrate.)

Finally, the impact of escrowed encryption on intelligence collection abroad depends on the specific terms of escrow agent certification. Even assuming that all relevant escrow agents are located within the United States (a question addressed at greater length in Appendix G), the specific regulations governing their behavior are relevant. Intelligence collections of digital data can proceed with few difficulties if regulations permit escrow agents to make keys available to national security authorities on an automated basis and without the need to request keys one by one. On the other hand, if the regulations forbid wholesale access to keys (and the products in question do not include a "universal key" that allows one key to decrypt messages produced by many devices), escrowed encryption would provide access primarily to specific encrypted communications that are known to be intrinsically interesting (e.g., known to be from a particular party of interest). However, escrowed encryption without wholesale access to keys would not provide significant assistance to intelligence collections undertaken on a large scale.

---

cellular telephones; these products are expected to be available in the second quarter of 1996.[13] Finally, AT&T makes no particular secret of the fact that its Surity line of secure voice communication products employs Clipper chip technology, but that fact is not featured in the product literature; potential consumers would have to know enough to ask a knowledgeable sales representative.

---

[13]AT&T news release, "AT&T, Cycomm International Develop Digital Voice Encryption," November 1, 1995. Available on-line at http://www.att.com/press/1195/951101. mma.html.

5.2.2 The Capstone/Fortezza Initiative[14]

The Capstone/Fortezza effort supports escrowed encryption for data storage and communications, although a FIPS for this application has not been issued. Specifically, the Capstone chip is an integrated-circuit chip that provides a number of encryption services for both stored computer data and data communications. For confidentiality, the Capstone chip uses the Skipjack algorithm, the same algorithm that is used in the Clipper chip (which is intended only for voice communications, including low-speed data and fax transmission across the public switched telephone network, and the same mechanism to provide for key escrowing. The agents used to hold Capstone keys are also identical to those for holding Clipper keys—namely, the Departments of Treasury and Commerce. In addition, the Capstone chip (in contrast to the Clipper chip) provides services that conform to the Digital Signature Standard (FIPS-186) to provide digital signatures that authenticate user identity and the Secure Hash Standard (FIPS-180); the chip also implements a classified algorithm for key exchange (usually referred to as the Key Exchange Algorithm (KEA)) and a random number generator.

The Capstone chip is the heart of the Fortezza card.[15] The Fortezza card is a PC-card (formerly known as a PCMCIA card) intended to be plugged into any computer with a PC-card expansion slot and appropriate support software; with the card in place, the host computer is able to provide reliable user authentication and encryption for confidentiality and certify data transmission integrity in any communication with any other computer so equipped. The Fortezza card is an example of a hardware token that can be used to ensure proper authentication.[16] Note also

---

[14]Technically speaking, Clipper and Capstone/Fortezza are not separate initiatives. The Capstone program had been under way for a number of years prior to the public announcement of the Clipper chip in 1993, and the Clipper chip is based entirely on technology developed under the Capstone program. The Clipper chip was developed when the incoming Clinton Administration felt it had to address the problem of voice encryption. However, while Clipper and Capstone/Fortezza are not technically separate programs, the public debate has engaged Clipper to a much greater degree than it has Capstone. For this reason, this report discusses Clipper and Capstone/Fortezza separately.

[15]The Fortezza card was previously named the Tessera card; the name was changed when previous trademark claims on "Tessera" were discovered.

[16]To ensure that the holder of the Fortezza card is in fact the authorized holder, a personal identification number (PIN) is associated with the card: only when the proper PIN is entered will the Fortezza card activate its various functions. While concerns have been raised in the security literature that passwords and PINs are not secure when transmitted over open communications lines, the PIN used by the Fortezza card is never used outside the confines of the user's system. That is, the PIN is never transmitted over any network link; the sole function of the PIN is to turn on the Fortezza card, after which an automated protocol ensures secure authentication.

that there are other hardware PC cards that provide cryptographic functionality similar to that of Fortezza but without the escrow features.[17]

To date, the NSA has issued two major solicitations for Fortezza cards, the second of which was for 750,000 cards.[18] These cards will be used by those on the Defense Messaging System, a communications network that is expected to accommodate up to 2 million Defense Department users in 2005. In addition, Fortezza cards are intended to be available for private sector use. The extent to which Fortezza cards will be acceptable in the commercial market remains to be seen, although a number of product vendors have decided to incorporate support for Fortezza cards in some products.[19]

5.2.3 The Relaxation of Export Controls on Software Products Using "Properly Escrowed" 64-bit Encryption

As noted in Chapter 4, the Administration has proposed to treat software products using a 64-bit encryption key as it currently treats products with encryption capabilities that are based on a 40-bit RC2 or RC4 algorithm, providing that products using this stronger encryption are "properly escrowed." This change is intended to facilitate the global sale of U.S. software products with significantly stronger cryptographic protection than is available from U.S. products sold abroad today.

To work out the details of what is meant by "properly escrowed," the National Institute of Standards and Technology held workshops in September and December 1995 at which the Administration released a number of draft criteria for export control (Box 5.3). These criteria are intended to ensure that a product's key escrow mechanism cannot be readily altered or bypassed so as to defeat the purposes of key escrowing. In early 1996, the Administration expressed its intent to move forward rapidly with its proposal and to finalize export criteria and make formal conforming modifications to the export regulations "soon."

---

[17]For example, such devices are made by Cylink and Telequip. See *Government Computer News*, "Security Device Is 007 in Your Pocket," August 7, 1995, p. 6.

[18]Paul Constance, "DoD Plans to Install 750,000 Fortezza Cards," *Government Computer News*, July 31, 1995, p. 1 for the solicitation.

[19]For example, the Netscape Communications Corporation has announced that it will support Fortezza in the next version of its Web browser, while the Oracle Corporation will support Fortezza in the next version of its Secure Network Services product. See Elizabeth Sikorovsky, "Netscape and Oracle Products Support Fortezza Card," *Federal Computer Week*, October 23, 1995, p. 36.

BOX 5.3
Administration's Draft Software Key Escrow Export Criteria
November 1995

Key Escrow Feature

1. The key(s) required to decrypt the product's key escrow cryptographic functions' ciphertext shall be accessible through a key escrow feature.

2. The product's key escrow cryptographic functions shall be inoperable until the key(s) is escrowed in accordance with #3.

3. The product's key escrow cryptographic functions' key(s) shall be escrowed with escrow agent(s) certified by the U.S. Government, or certified by foreign governments with which the U.S. Government has formal agreements consistent with U.S. law enforcement and national security requirements.

4. The product's key escrow cryptographic functions' ciphertext shall contain, in an accessible format and with a reasonable frequency, the identity of the key escrow agent(s) and information sufficient for the escrow agent(s) to identify the key(s) required to decrypt the ciphertext.

5. The product's key escrow feature shall allow access to the key(s) needed to decrypt the product's ciphertext regardless of whether the product generated or received the ciphertext.

6. The product's key escrow feature shall allow for the recovery of multiple decryption keys during the period of authorized access without requiring repeated presentations of the access authorization to the key escrow agent(s).

Key Length Feature

7. The product's key escrow cryptographic functions shall use an unclassified encryption algorithm with a key length not to exceed sixty-four (64) bits.

8. The product's key escrow cryptographic functions shall not provide the feature of multiple encryption (e.g., triple-DES).

Interoperability Feature

9. The product's key escrow cryptographic functions shall interoperate only with key escrow cryptographic functions in products that meet these criteria, and shall not interoperate with the cryptographic functions of a product whose key escrow encryption function has been altered, bypassed, disabled, or otherwise rendered inoperative.

Design, Implementation, and Operational Assurance

10. The product shall be resistant to anything that could disable or circumvent the attributes described in #1 through #9.

SOURCE: National Institute of Standards and Technology, *Draft Software Key Escrow Encryption Export Criteria*, November 6, 1995. Reprinted from text available on-line at http://csrc.ncsl.nist.gov/keyescrow/criteria.txt (November 1995 version; NIST Web page).

5.2.4 Other Federal Initiatives in Escrowed Encryption

In addition to the initiatives described above, the Administration has announced plans for new Federal Information Processing Standards in two other areas:

- FIPS-185 will be modified to include escrowed encryption for data in both communicated and stored forms. The modified FIPS is expected in late 1996; how this modification will relate to Capstone/Fortezza is as yet uncertain.
- A FIPS for key escrow will be developed that will, among other things, specify performance requirements for escrow agents and for escrowed encryption products. How this relates to the existing or modified FIPS-185 is also uncertain at this time.

Note: As this report goes to press from the prepublication version, the Administration has released a draft working paper entitled "Enabling Privacy, Commerce, Security and Public Safety in the Global Information Infrastructure"[20] that appears to call for one infrastructure for cryptography that would support both public-key authentication and key-escrowing functions.

5.3 OTHER APPROACHES TO ESCROWED ENCRYPTION

A general concept akin to escrowed encryption has long been familiar to some institutions, notably banks, that have for years purchased information systems allowing them to retrieve the plaintext of encrypted files or other stored information long after the immediate need for such information has passed.[21] However, only since the initial announcement of the Clipper initiative in April 1993 has escrowed encryption gained prominence in the public debate.

Denning and Branstad describe a number of different approaches to implementing an escrowed encryption scheme, all of which have been

---

[20]See "Enabling Privacy, Commerce, Security and Public Safety in the Global Information Infrastructure," Executive Office of the President, Office of Management and Budget, Washington, D.C., May 20, 1996.

[21]An example first announced in 1994 is Northern Telecom's "Entrust," which provides for file encryption and digital signature in a corporate network environment using RSA public-key cryptography. "Entrust" allows master access by a network administrator to all users' encrypted files, even after a user has left the company. A product review for a recent version of "Entrust" can be found in Stephen Cobb, "Encryption for the Enterprise," *Network World*, March 11, 1996, p. 57.

discussed publicly since 1993.[22] Those and other different approaches vary along the dimensions discussed below:

- *Number of escrow agents required to provide exceptional access.* For example, one proposal called for separation of Clipper unit keys into more than two components.[23] A second proposal called for the k-of-n arrangement described in Section 5.9.1.
- *Affiliation of escrow agents.* Among the possibilities are government in the executive branch, government in the judicial branch, commercial institutions, product manufacturers, and customers.
- *Ability of parties to obtain exceptional access.* Under the Clipper initiative, the key-escrowing feature of the EES is available only to law enforcement authorities acting under court order; users never have access to the keys.
- *Authorities vested in escrow agents.* In the usual discussion, escrow agents hold keys or components of keys. But in one proposal, escrow agents known as Data Recovery Centers (DRCs) do not hold user keys or user key components at all. Products escrowed with a DRC would include in the ciphertext of a transmission or a file the relevant session key encrypted with the public key of that DRC and the identity of the DRC in plaintext. Upon presentation of an appropriate request (e.g., valid court order for law enforcement authorities, a valid request by the user of the DRC-escrowed product), the DRC would retrieve the encrypted session key, decrypt it, and give the original session key to the authorized third party, who could then recover the data encrypted with that key.[24]
- *Hardware vs. software implementation of products.*
- *Partial key escrow.*[25] Under a partial key escrow, a product with encryption capabilities could use keys of any length, except that all but a certain number of bits would be escrowed. For example, a key might be 256 bits long, and 216 bits (256 − 40) of the key would be escrowed; 40 bits

---

[22]All of these examples are taken from Dorothy Denning and Dennis Branstad, "A Taxonomy of Key Escrow Encryption," *Communications of the ACM*, Volume 39, March 1996.

[23]This comment was probably made during the meetings of July, August, and September 1993 by the Computer System Security and Privacy Advisory Board to solicit public views on the Clipper initiative. Transcripts of the meetings are available from the National Institute of Standards and Technology.

[24]Stephen T. Walker et al., *Commercial Key Escrow: Something for Everyone Now and for the Future*, Report #541, Trusted Information Systems, Glenwood, Md., January 1995.

[25]Adi Shamir, "Partial Key Escrow: A New Approach to Software Key Escrow," summary of presentation at NIST FIPS Key Escrow Workshop, National Institute of Standards and Technology, Gaithersburg, Md., September 15, 1995. Available on-line at http://reality.sgi.com/employees/chrisr_corp/pkedc.html.

would remain private. Thus, decrypting ciphertext produced by this product would require a 256-bit work factor for those without the escrowed bits and a 40-bit work factor for those individuals in possession of the escrowed bits. Depending on the number of private bits used, this approach would protect users against disclosure of keys to those without access to the specialized decryption facilities required to conduct an exhaustive search against the private key (in this case, 40 bits).

Box 5.4 describes a number of other conceptual approaches to escrowed encryption.

5.4 THE IMPACT OF ESCROWED ENCRYPTION ON INFORMATION SECURITY

In the debate over escrowed encryption, the dimension of information security that has received the largest amount of public attention has been confidentiality. Judgments about the impact of escrowed encryption on confidentiality depend on the point of comparison. If the point of comparison is taken to be the confidentiality of data available today, then the wide use of escrowed encryption does improve confidentiality. The reason is that most information today is entirely unprotected.

Consider first information in transit (communications). Most communications today are unencrypted. For example, telephonic communications can be tapped in many different ways, including through alligator clips at a junction box in the basement of an apartment house or on top of a telephone pole, off the air when some part of a telephonic link is wireless (e.g., in a cellular call), and from the central switching office that is carrying the call. Calls made using EES-compliant telephones would be protected against such surveillance, except when surveillance parties (presumably law enforcement authorities) had obtained the necessary keys from escrow agents. As for information in storage, most files on most computers are unencrypted. Escrowed encryption applied to these files would protect them against threats such as casual snoops, although individuals with knowledge of the vulnerabilities of the system on which those files reside might still be able to access them.

On the other hand, if the point of comparison is taken to be the level of confidentiality that *could* be possible using unescrowed encryption, then escrowed encryption offers a lower degree of confidentiality. Escrowed encryption by design introduces a system weakness (i.e., it is deliberately designed to allow exceptional access), and so if the procedures that protect against improper use of that access somehow fail, infor-

BOX 5.4
Non-Clipper Proposals for Escrowed Encryption

AT&T CryptoBackup. CryptoBackup is an AT&T proprietary design for a commercial or private key-escrow encryption system. The data encryption key for a document is recovered through a backup recovery vector (BRV), which is stored in the document header. The BRV contains the document key encrypted under a master public key of the escrowed agent(s). (David P. Maher, "Crypto Backup and Key Escrow," *Communications of the ACM*, March 1996.)

Bankers Trust Secure Key Escrow Encryption System (SecureKEES). Employees of a corporation register their encryption devices (e.g., smart card) and private encryption keys with one or more commercial escrow agents selected by the corporation. (SecureKEES product literature, CertCo, Bankers Trust Company.)

Bell Atlantic Yaksha System. An on-line key security server generates and distributes session keys and file keys using a variant of the RSA algorithm. The server transmits the keys to authorized parties for data recovery purposes. (Ravi Ganesan, "The Yaksha Security System," *Communications of the ACM*, March 1996.)

Royal Holloway Trusted Third Party Services. This proposed architecture for a public key infrastructure requires that the trusted third parties associated with communicating users share parameters and a secret key. (Nigel Jefferies, Chris Mitchell, and Michael Walker, *A Proposed Architecture for Trusted Third Party Services,*" Royal Holloway, University of London, 1995.)

RSA Secure^{TM}. This file encryption product provides data recovery through an escrowed master public key, which can be split among up to 255 trustees using a threshold scheme. (RSA Secure^{TM}, product literature from RSA Data Security Inc.)

Nortel Entrust. This commercial product archives users' private encryption keys as part of the certificate authority function and public-key infrastructure support. (Warwick Ford, "Entrust Technical Overview," White Paper, Nortel Secure Networks, October 1994.)

National Semiconductor CAKE. This proposal combines a TIS Commercial Key Escrow (CKE) with National Semiconductor's PersonaCard^{TM}. (W.B. Sweet, "Commercial Automated Key Escrow (CAKE): An Exportable Strong Encryption Proposal," National Semiconductor, iPower Business Unit, June 4, 1995.)

TIS Commercial Key Escrow (CKE). This is a commercial key escrow system for stored data and file transfers. Data recovery is enabled through master keys held by a Data Recovery Center. (Stephen T. Walker, Stephen B. Lipner, Carl M. Ellison, and David M. Balenson, "Commercial Key Recovery," *Communications of the ACM*, March 1996.)

TECSEC VEIL^{TM}. This commercial product provides file (and object) encryption. Private key escrow is built into the key management infrastructure. (Edward M. Scheidt and Jon L. Roberts, "Private Escrow Key Management," TECSEC Inc., Vienna, Va. See also TECSEC VEIL^{TM}, product literature.)

Viacrypt PGP/BE (Business Edition). Viacrypt is a commercialized version of PGP, the free Internet-downloadable software package for encrypted communications. The Business Edition of Viacrypt optionally enables an employer to decrypt all encrypted files or messages sent or received by an employee by carrying the session key encrypted under a "Corporate Access Key" in the header for the file or message. (See http://www.viacrypt.com.)

SOURCE: Most of these examples are taken from Dorothy Denning and Miles Smid, "Key Escrowing Today," *IEEE Communications,* Volume 32(9), 1994, pp. 58-68. Available on-line at http://www.cosc.georgetown.edu/~denning/crypto/ Key-Escrowing-Today.txt.

mation is left unprotected.[26]   For example, EES-compliant telephones would offer *less* confidentiality for telephonic communications than would telephones that could be available with the same encryption algorithm and implementation but without the escrow feature, since such telephones could be designed to provide communications confidentiality against *all* eavesdroppers, including rogue police, private investigators, or (and this is the important point) legally authorized law enforcement officials.

More generally, escrowed encryption weakens the confidentiality provided by an encryption system by providing an access path that can be compromised.[27] Yet escrowed encryption also provides a hedge against the loss of access to encrypted data by those authorized for access; for example, a user may lose or forget a decryption key.   Assurances that encrypted data will be available when needed are clearly greater when a mechanism has been installed to facilitate such access. Reasonable people may disagree about how to make that trade-off in any particular case, thus underscoring the need for end users themselves to make their own risk-benefit assessments regarding the loss of authorized access (against which escrowed encryption can protect by guaranteeing key recovery) vs. the loss of confidentiality to unauthorized parties (whose likelihood is increased by the use of escrowed encryption).

A point more specifically related to EES is that escrowed encryption can also be used to enhance certain dimensions of Title III protection. For example, the final procedures for managing law enforcement access to EES-protected voice conversations call for the hardware providing exceptional access to be designed in such a way that law enforcement officials would decrypt communications only if the communications were occurring during the time window specified in the initial court authorization. The fact that law enforcement officials will have to approach escrow agents

---

[26]Even worse, it is not just future communications that are placed at risk, but past communications as well.   For example, if encrypted conversations are recorded and the relevant key is not available, they are useless. However, once the unit key is obtained, those recordings become decipherable if they are still available. Such recording would be illegal, because legal authorization for the wiretap would have been necessary to obtain the key, but since these circumstances presume a breakdown of escrow procedures in the first place, the fact of illegality is not particularly relevant.

[27]For example, if a party external to the corporation has the keys that provide access to that corporation's encrypted information, the corporation is more vulnerable to a loss of confidentiality, because the external party can become the target of theft, extortion, blackmail, and the like by unauthorized parties who are seeking that information. Of course, the corporation itself is vulnerable, but since only one target (either the corporation or any external key-holding party) needs to be compromised, more targets lead to greater vulnerability. Of course, if keys are split among a number of external parties, the likelihood of compromise through this route is reduced, but the overall risk of compromise is still increased.

to obtain the relevant key means that there will be an audit trail for wiretaps requiring decryption, thus deterring officials who might be tempted or able to act on their own in obtaining a wiretap without legal authorization.

5.5 THE IMPACT OF ESCROWED ENCRYPTION ON LAW ENFORCEMENT

Box 5.5 describes the requirements for escrowed encryption that law enforcement authorities (principally the FBI) would like product vendors to accommodate. But two additional high-level questions must be addressed before escrowed encryption is accepted as an appropriate solution to the stated law enforcement problem.

5.5.1 Balance of Crime Enabled vs. Crime Prosecuted

One question is the following: Does the benefit to law enforcement from access to encrypted information through an escrow mechanism outweigh the damage that might occur due to the failure of procedures intended to prevent unauthorized access to the escrow mechanism? Since government authorities believe that the implementation of these procedures can be made robust (and thus the anticipated expectation of failure is slight), they answer the question in the affirmative. Critics of government initiatives promoting escrowed encryption raise the concern that the risk of failure may be quite large, and thus their answer to the question ranges from "maybe" to "strongly negative." These parties generally prefer to rely on technologies and procedures that they fully understand and control to maintain the security of their information, and at best, they believe that any escrow procedures create a potentially serious risk of misuse that must be stringently counteracted, diligently monitored, and legally constrained. Moreover, they believe that reliance on government-established procedures to maintain proper access controls on escrowed keys invites unauthorized third parties to target those responsible for upholding the integrity of the escrow system.

History suggests that procedural risks materialize as real problems over the long run,[28] but in practice, a base of operational experience is necessary to determine if these risks are significant.

---

[28]See, for example, Peter G. Neumann, *Computer-Related Risks*, Addison-Wesley, New York, 1995; and Charles Perrow, *Normal Accidents: Living with High-Risk Technologies*, Basic Books, New York, 1984. Neumann describes a large number of computer-related reliability and safety problems and security vulnerabilities that have arisen from combinations of defective system implementation, flawed system design, and human error in executing procedures. Perrow describes a number of accidents that have occurred in other domains (e.g., maritime shipping, air traffic control, nuclear power plant operation) that have resulted from a similar set of problems.

BOX 5.5
Law Enforcement Requirements for Escrowed Encryption Products

Information Identification

• The product is unable to encrypt/decrypt data unless the necessary information to allow law enforcement to decrypt communications and stored information is available for release to law enforcement.
• A field is provided that readily identifies the information needed to decrypt each message, session, or file generated or received by the user of the product.
• Repeated involvement by key escrow agents (KEAs) is not required to obtain the information needed to decrypt multiple conversations and data messages (refer to expeditious information release by KEAs) during a period of authorized communications interception.

Provision of Subject's Information Only

• Only information pertaining to the communications or stored information generated by or for the subject is needed for law enforcement decryption.

Subversions of Decryption Capability

• The product is resistant against alterations that disable or bypass law enforcement decryption capabilities.
• Any alteration to the product to disable or bypass law enforcement's decryption capability requires a significant level of effort regardless of whether similar alterations have been made to any other identical version of that product.

Transparency

• The decryption of an intercepted communication is transparent to the intercept subject and all other parties to the communication except the investigative agency and the key escrow agent.

Access to Technical Details to Develop Decrypt Capability

• Law enforcement may need access to a product's technical details to develop a key escrow decrypt capability for that product.

SOURCE: Federal Bureau of Investigation, viewgraphs of presentation to International Cryptography Institute 1995 conference, September 22, 1995.

5.5.2 Impact on Law Enforcement Access to Information

Even if escrowed encryption were to achieve significant market penetration and were widely deployed, the question would still remain regarding the likely effectiveness of a law enforcement strategy to preserve wiretapping and data recovery capabilities through deployments of escrowed encryption built around voluntary use.[29] This question has surfaced most strongly in the debate over EES, but as with other aspects of the cryptography debate, the answer depends on the scenario in question:

• Many criminals will reach first for devices and tools that are readily at hand because they are so much more convenient to use than those that require special efforts to obtain. Criminals who have relatively simple and straightforward needs for secure communications may well use EES-compliant devices if they are widely available. In such cases, they will simply have forgotten (or not taken sufficient conscious account of) the fact that these "secure" devices have features that provide law enforcement access,[30] and law enforcement officials will obtain the same level and quality of information they currently obtain from legal wiretaps. Indeed, the level and quality of information might be even greater than what is available today because criminals speaking on EES-compliant devices might well have a false sense of security that they could not be wiretapped.

• Criminals whose judgment suggests the need for extra and non-routine security are likely to use secure communications devices without features for exceptional access. In these cases, law enforcement officials may be denied important information. However, the use of these communications devices is likely to be an ad hoc arrangement among participants in a criminal activity. Since many criminal activities often require participants to communicate with people outside the immediate circle of participants, "secondary" wiretap information might be available if nonsecure devices were used to communicate with others not directly associated with the activity.

Senior Administration officials have recognized that the latter scenario is inevitable—it is impossible to prevent all uses of strong unescrowed encryption by criminals and terrorists. However, the widespread deployment of strong encryption without features for exceptional access would mean that even the careless criminal would easily obtain unbreakable encryption, and thus the Administration's initiatives are directed primarily at the first scenario.

Similar considerations would apply to escrowed encryption products used to store data—many criminals will use products with encryption

---

[29]"Voluntary" has been used ambiguously in the public debate on key escrow. It can mean voluntary use of key escrow in any context or implementation, or it can mean voluntary use of EES-compliant products. In the latter situation, of course, the key-escrow feature would be automatic. Usually, the context of its use will clarify which interpretation of "voluntary" is intended.

[30]Cf. point in Chapter 2 regarding behavior of criminals with respect to wiretapped telephone calls.

capabilities that are easily available to store files and send e-mail. If these products are escrowed, law enforcement officials have a higher likelihood of having access to those criminal data files and e-mail. On the other hand, some criminals will hide or conceal their stored data through the use of unescrowed products or by storing them on remote computers whose location is known only to them, with the result that the efforts of law enforcement authorities to obtain information will be frustrated.

5.6 MANDATORY VS. VOLUNTARY USE OF ESCROWED ENCRYPTION

As noted above, the federal government cannot compel the private sector to use escrowed encryption in the absence of legislation, whether for voice communications or any other application. However, EES raised the very important public concern that the use of encryption without features for exceptional access might be banned by statute. The Administration has stated that it has no intention of outlawing the use of such cryptography or of regulating in any other way the domestic use of cryptography. Nevertheless, no administration can bind future administrations, and Congress can change a law at any time. More importantly, widespread acceptance of escrowed encryption, even if voluntary, would put into place an infrastructure that would support such a policy change. Thus, the possibility that a future administration and/or Congress might support prohibitions on unescrowed encryption cannot be dismissed. This topic is discussed in depth in Chapter 7.

With respect to the federal government's assertion of authority in the use of the EES by private parties, there are a number of gray areas. For example, a federal agency that has adopted the EES for secure telephonic communications clearly has the right to require all contractors that interact with it to use EES-compliant devices as a condition of doing business with the government;[31,32] this point is explored further in Chapter 6. More problematic is the question of whether an agency that interacts with the public at large without a contractual arrangement may require such use.

A second important gray area relates to the establishment of EES as a

---

[31]For example, at present the Department of Defense requires that contractors acquire and employ STU-III secure telephones for certain sensitive telephonic communications with DOD personnel. The Federal Acquisition Regulations (FAR) were modified to allow the costs of such telephones to be charged against contracts, to further encourage purchase of these telephones.

[32]One major manufacturer noted to the committee that meeting federal requirements for encryption also reduces its ability to standardize on a single solution in distributed networks. Government-mandated key escrow could differ substantially enough from key escrow systems required for commercial operations that two separate key escrow systems could be needed.

de facto standard for use in the private sector through mechanisms described in Chapter 6. In this area, Administration officials have expressed to the committee a hope that such would be the case. If EES-compliant devices were to become very popular, they might well drive potential competitors (specifically, devices for secure telephonic communications without features for exceptional access) out of the market for reasons of cost and scarcity. Under such circumstances, it is not clear that initially voluntary use of the EES would in the end leave room for a genuine choice for consumers.

5.7 PROCESS THROUGH WHICH POLICY ON ESCROWED ENCRYPTION WAS DEVELOPED

Much criticism of the Clipper initiative has focused on the process through which the standard was established. Specifically, the Clipper initiative was developed out of the public eye, with minimal if any connection to the relevant stakeholders in industry and the academic community, and appeared to be "sprung" on them with an announcement in the *New York Times*. Furthermore, a coherent approach to the international dimensions of the problem was not developed, a major failing since business communications are global in nature. After the announcement of the Clipper initiative, the federal government promulgated the EES despite a near-unanimous condemnation of the proposed standard in the public comments on it.

Similar comments have been expressed with respect to the August-September 1995 Administration proposal to relax export controls on 64-bit software products if they are properly escrowed. This proposal, advertised by the Administration as the follow-up to the Gore-Cantwell letter of July 1994,[33] emerged after about a year of virtual silence from the Administration during which public interactions with industry were minimal.

---

[33]On July 20, 1994, Vice President Al Gore wrote to Representative Maria Cantwell (D-Washington) expressing a willingness to enter into "a new phase of cooperation among government, industry representatives and privacy advocates with a goal of trying to develop a key escrow encryption system that will provide strong encryption, be acceptable to computer users worldwide, and address our national security needs as well." The Vice President went on to say that "we welcome the opportunity to work with industry to design a more versatile, less expensive system. Such a key escrow system would be implementable in software, firmware, hardware, or any combination thereof, would not rely upon a classified algorithm, would be voluntary, and would be exportable. . . . We also recognize that a new key escrow encryption system must permit the use of private-sector key escrow agents as one option. . . . Having a number of escrow agents would give individuals and businesses more choices and flexibility in meeting their needs for secure communications." Letter reprinted in Hoffman, *Building in Big Brother*, 1995, pp. 236-238.

The result has been a tainting of escrowed encryption that inhibits unemotional discussion of its pros and cons and makes it difficult to reach a rational and well-balanced decision.

5.8 AFFILIATION AND NUMBER OF ESCROW AGENTS

Any deployment of escrowed encryption on a large scale raises the question of who the escrow agents should be. (The equally important question of their responsibilities and liabilities is the subject of Section 5.9.) The original Clipper/Capstone escrow approach called for agencies of the executive branch to be escrow agents; at this writing, the Administration's position seems to be evolving to allow parties in the private sector to be escrow agents. Different types of escrow agents have different advantages and disadvantages.

The use of executive branch agencies as escrow agents has a number of advantages. Executive branch escrow agents can be funded directly and established quickly, rather than depending on the existence of a private sector market or business for escrow agents. Their continuing existence depends not on market forces but on the willingness of the Congress to appropriate money to support them. Executive branch escrow agents may well be more responsive than outside escrow agents to authorized requests from law enforcement for keys. Executive branch escrow agents can be enjoined more easily from divulging to the target of a surveillance the fact that they turned over a key to law enforcement officials, thereby helping to ensure that a surveillance can be performed surreptitiously. In the case of FISA intercepts, executive branch escrow agents may be more protective of associated classified information (such as the specific target of the intercept). Under sovereign immunity, executive branch escrow agents can disavow civil liability for unauthorized disclosure of keys.

Of course, from a different standpoint, most of these putative advantages can be seen as disadvantages. If direct government subsidy is required to support an escrow operation, by definition it lacks the support of the market.[34] The high speed with which executive branch escrow agents were established suggested to critics that the Administration was attempting to present the market with a fait accompli with respect to escrow. A higher degree of responsiveness to requests for keys may well

---

[34]The original Clipper/Capstone proposal made no provision for parties other than law enforcement authorities to approach escrow agents, and in this context could be regarded as a simple law enforcement initiative with no particular relevance to the private sector. However, in light of the Administration's arguments concerning the desirability of escrowed encryption to meet the key backup needs of the private sector, the importance of relevance to the private sector is obvious.

coincide with greater disregard for proper procedure; indeed, since one of the designated escrow agencies (the Treasury Department) also has law enforcement jurisdiction and the authority to conduct wiretaps under some circumstances, a Treasury escrow agent might well be faced with a conflict of interest in managing keys. The obligation to keep the fact of key disclosure secret might easily lead to circumvention and unauthorized disclosures. The lack of civil liability and of criminal penalties for improper disclosure might reduce the incentives for compliance with proper procedure. Most importantly, all executive branch workers are in principle responsible to a unitary source of authority (the President). Thus, concerns are raised that any corruption at the top levels of government might diffuse downward, as exemplified by past attempts by the Executive Office of the President to use the Internal Revenue Service to harass its political enemies. One result might be that executive branch escrow agents might divulge keys improperly; a second result might be that executive branch escrow agents could be more likely to reveal the fact of key disclosure to targets in the executive branch under investigation.

Some of the concerns described above could be mitigated by placement of escrow agents in the judiciary branch of government on the theory that since judicial approval is needed to conduct wiretaps, giving the judiciary control of escrowed keys would in fact give it a way of enforcing the Title III requirements for legal authorization. On the other hand, the judiciary branch would have to rule on procedures and misuse, thereby placing it at risk of a conflict of interest should alleged misdeeds in the judiciary branch come to light. Matters related to separation of powers between the executive and judicial branches of government are also relevant.

The best argument for government escrow agents is that government can be held politically accountable. When a government does bad things, the government can be replaced. Escrow agents must be trustworthy, and the question at root is whether it is more appropriate to trust government or a private party; the views on this point are diverse and often vigorously defended.

The committee believes that government-based escrow agents present few problems when used to hold keys associated with government work. Nonetheless, mistrust of government-based escrow agents has been one of the primary criticisms of the EES. If escrowed encryption is to serve broad social purposes across government and the private sector, it makes sense to consider other possible escrow agents in addition to government escrow agents:

- *Private organizations established to provide key registration services (on a fee-for-service basis).* Given that some business organizations have certain needs for data retrieval and monitoring of communications as described in Chapter 3, such needs might create a market for private escrow agents. Some organizations might charge more and provide users with bonding against failure or improper revelations of keys; other organizations might charge less and not provide such bonding.

• *Vendors of products with encryption capabilities and features for exceptional access.* Vendors acting as escrow agents would face a considerable burden in having to comply with registration requirements and might be exposed to liability.[35] At the same time, vendors could register keys at the time of manufacture or by default at some additional expense.[36]

• *Customers themselves.* In the case of a corporate customer, a specially trusted department within the corporation that purchases escrowed encryption products could act as an escrow agent for the corporation. Such "customer escrow" of a corporation's own keys may be sufficient for its needs; customer escrow would also enable the organization to know when its keys have been revealed. Since legal entities such as corporations will continue to be subject to extant procedures of the law enforcement court order or subpoena, law enforcement access to keys under authorized circumstances could be assured. In the case of individual customers who are also the end users of the products they purchase, the individual could simply store a second copy of the relevant keys as a form of customer escrow.

Note especially that site licenses[37] to corporations account for the

---

[35]For example, in the early days of an offering by AT&T to provide picture-phone meeting services, the question arose as to whether AT&T or the end user should provide security. The business decision at the time was that AT&T should not provide security because of the legal implications—a company that guaranteed security but failed to provide it was liable. (Ironically, at least one major computer vendor declined to provide encryption services for data communications and storage on the grounds that encryption would be provided by AT&T.) While today's AT&T support for the PictureTel product line for videoconferencing (which provides encryption capabilities) may suggest a different AT&T perspective on the issue of who is responsible for providing security, companies will have to decide for themselves their own tolerable thresholds of risk for liability.

[36]The cost of vendor registration would be high in the case of certain software products. Specifically, products that are distributed by CD-ROM must be identical, because it would be very expensive (relative to current costs) to ship CD-ROMs with unique serial numbers or keys. To some extent, the same is true of products distributed by network—it is highly convenient and desirable from the vendor's perspective to have just one file that can be downloaded upon user request, although it is possible and more expensive to provide numbered copies of software distributed by network.

[37]Under a site license, a corporation agrees with a vendor on a price for a certain (perhaps variable) number of licenses to use a given software package. Site licenses also include agreements on and conditions for support and documentation.

largest portion of vendor sales in software.[38] In a domestic context, corporations are entities that are subject to legal processes in the United States that permit law enforcement authorities to obtain information in the course of a criminal investigation. In a foreign context, exports to certain foreign corporations can be conditioned on a requirement that the foreign corporation be willing to escrow its key in such a manner that U.S. law enforcement authorities would be able to have access to that information under specified circumstances and in a manner to be determined by a contract binding on the corporation. (The use of contract law in this manner is discussed further in Chapter 7.) In short, sales of escrowed encryption to foreign and domestic corporate users could be undertaken in such a way that a very large fraction of the installed user base would in fact be subject to legal processes for obtaining information on keys.

Nongovernment escrow agents are subject to the laws of the government under whose jurisdiction they operate. In addition, they raise other separate questions. For example, a criminal investigation may target the senior officials of a corporation, who may themselves be the ones authorized for access to customer-escrowed keys; they might then be notified of the fact of being wiretapped. The same would be true of end users controlling their own copies of keys. Private organizations providing key-holding services might be infiltrated or even set up by criminal elements that would frustrate lawful attempts to obtain keys or would even use the keys in their possession improperly. Private organizations may be less responsive to government requests than government escrow agents. Finally, private organizations motivated by profit and tempted to cut corners might be less responsible in their conduct.

A second important issue regarding escrow agents deals with their number. Concentrating escrow arrangements in a few escrow agents may make law enforcement access to keys more convenient, but it also focuses the attention of those who may attempt to compromise those facilities—the "big, fat target" phenomenon—because the aggregate value of the keys controlled by these few agents is, by assumption, large.[39] On the other hand, given a fixed budget, concentrating resources on a few escrow agents may enable them to increase the security against compro-

---

[38]The dominance of corporate sales over sales to individuals was cited in Department of Commerce and National Security Agency, *A Study of the International Market for Computer Software with Encryption*, released January 11, 1996, p. III-2.

[39]Note also that maintaining the physical security of escrow agents, especially government escrow agents, may be especially critical; sabotage or destruction of an escrow agent facility might well be seen in some segments of society as a blow for freedom and liberty.

mise, whereas spreading resources among many escrow agents may leave each one much more open to compromise. Indeed, the security of a well-funded and well-supported escrow agent may be greater than that of the party that owns the encryption keys; in this case, the incremental risk that a key would be improperly compromised by the escrow agent would be negligible. Increasing the number of escrow agents so that each would be responsible for a relatively small number of keys reduces the value of compromising any particular escrow agent but increases the logistical burdens, overhead, and expense for the nation. The net impact on security against compromise of keys is very scenario-dependent.[40]

5.9 RESPONSIBILITIES AND OBLIGATIONS OF ESCROW AGENTS AND USERS OF ESCROWED ENCRYPTION

Regardless of who the escrow agents are, they will hold certain information and have certain responsibilities and obligations.[41] Users of escrowed encryption also face potential liabilities.

5.9.1 Partitioning Escrowed Information

Consider what precisely an escrow agent would hold. In the simplest case, a single escrow agent would hold all of the information needed to provide exceptional access to encrypted information. (In the Clipper case, two escrow agents would be used to hold the unit keys to all EES-compliant telephones.)

A single escrow agent for a given key poses a significant risk of single-point failure—that is, the compromise of only one party (the single escrow agent) places at risk all information associated with that key. The Clipper/Capstone approach addresses this point by designating two executive branch agencies (Commerce and Treasury), each holding one component (of two) of the unit key of a given Clipper/Capstone-compliant device. Reconstruction of a unit key requires the cooperation of both

---

[40]A similar issue arises with respect to certificate authorities for authentication. As discussed in Chapter 2, a cryptography-based authentication of an individual's identity depends on the existence of an entity—a certification authority—that is trusted by third parties as being able to truly certify the identity of the individual in question. Concentration of certification authority into a single entity would imply that an individual would be vulnerable to any penetration or malfeasance of the entity and thus to all of the catastrophic effects that tampering with an individual's digital identity would imply.

[41]Nothing in this discussion is intended to preclude the possibility that an organization serving as an escrow agent might also have responsibilities as a certification authority (for authentication purposes, as described in Chapter 2).

agencies. This approach was intended to give the public confidence that their keys were secure in the hands of the government.

In the most general case, an escrow system can be designed to separate keys into n components but with the mathematics of the separation process arranged so that exceptional access would be possible if the third party were able to acquire any k (for k less than or equal to n) of these components.[42] This approach is known as the "k-of-n" approach. For the single escrow agent, $k = 1$ and $n = 1$; for the Clipper/Capstone system, $k = 2$ and $n = 2$. But it is possible to design systems where k is any number less than n; for example, the consent of any three (k) of five (n) escrow agents could be sufficient to enable exceptional access. Obviously, the greater the number of parties that are needed to consent, the more cumbersome exceptional access becomes.

It is a policy or business decision as to what the specific values of k and n should be, or if indeed the choice about specific values should be left to users. The specific values chosen for k and n reflect policy judgments about needs for recovery of encrypted data relative to user concerns about improper exceptional access. Whose needs? If a national policy decision determines k and n, it is the needs of law enforcement and national security weighed against user concerns. If the user determines k and n, it is the needs of the user weighed against law enforcement and national security concerns.

5.9.2 Operational Responsibilities of Escrow Agents

For escrowed encryption to play a major role in protecting the information infrastructure of the nation and the information of businesses and individuals, users must be assured about the operational obligations and procedures of escrow agents. Clear guidelines will be required to regulate the operational behavior of escrow agents, and clear enforcement mechanisms must be set into place to ensure that the escrow agents comply with those guidelines. While these guidelines and mechanisms might come into existence through normal market forces or cooperative agreements within industries, they are more likely to require a legal setting that would also include criminal penalties for malfeasance.

Guidelines are needed to assure the public and law enforcement agencies of two points:

---

[42]See, for example, Silvio Micali, "Fair Public-Key Cryptosystems," in *Advances in Cryptology—Crypto '92*, Springer-Verlag, Heidelberg, 1993, pp. 113-138.

- That information relevant to exceptional access (the full key or a key fragment) will be divulged upon proper legal request and that an escrow agent will not notify the key owner of disclosure until it is legally permissible to do so, and
- That information relevant to exceptional access will be divulged only upon proper legal request.

Note that the fulfillment of the second requirement has both an "abuse of authority" component and a technical and procedural component. The first relates to an individual (an "insider") who is in a position to give out relevant information but also to abuse his position by giving out that information without proper authorization. The second relates to the fact that even if no person in the employ of an escrow agent improperly gives out relevant information, an "outsider" may be able to penetrate the security of the escrow agent and obtain the relevant information without compromising any particular individual. Such concerns are particularly relevant to the extent that escrow agents are connected electronically, since they would then be vulnerable in much the same ways that all other parties connected to a network are vulnerable. The security of networked computer systems is difficult to assure with high confidence,[43] and the security level required of escrow agents must be high, given the value of their holdings to unauthorized third parties.

Thus, those concerned about breaches of confidentiality must be concerned about technical and procedural weaknesses of the escrow agent infrastructure that would enable outsiders to connect remotely to these sites and obtain keys, as well as about insiders abusing their positions of trust. Either possibility could lead not just to individual keys being compromised, but also to wholesale compromise of all of the keys entrusted to escrow agents within that infrastructure. From a policy standpoint, it is necessary to have a contingency plan that would facilitate recovery from wholesale compromise.

Box 5.6 describes law enforcement views on the responsibilities of escrow agents. Box 5.7 describes draft Administration views on requirements for maintaining the integrity and security of escrow agents; Box 5.8 describes draft Administration views on requirements for assuring access to escrowed keys.

---

[43]See, for example, Computer Science and Telecommunications Board, National Research Council, *Computers at Risk: Safe Computing in the Information Age*, National Academy Press, Washington, D.C., 1991.

BOX 5.6
Law Enforcement Requirements for Escrow Agents

Information Availability

• The information necessary to allow law enforcement the ability to decrypt communications and stored information is available. KEAs [key escrow agents] should maintain or be capable of generating all the necessary decrypt (key) information.

• Key and/or related information needed to decrypt communications and stored information is retained for extended time periods. KEAs should be able to decrypt information encrypted with a device or product's current and/or former key(s) for a time period that may vary depending on the application (e.g., voice vs. stored files).

• A backup capability exists for key and other information needed to decrypt communications and stored information. Thus, a physically separate backup capability should be available to provide redundancy of resources should the primary capability fail.

Key Escrow Agent (KEA) Accessibility

• KEAs should be readily accessible. For domestic products, they should reside and operate in the United States. They should be able to process proper requests at any time; most requests will be submitted during normal business hours, but exigent circumstances (e.g., kidnappings, terrorist threats) may require submission of requests during nonbusiness hours.

Information Release by KEAs

• The information needed for decryption is expeditiously released upon receipt of a proper request. Since communications intercepts require the ability to decrypt multiple conversations and data messages sent to or from the subject (i.e., access to each session or message key) during the entire intercept period, only one initial affirmative action should be needed to obtain the relevant information. Exigent circumstances (e.g., kidnappings, terrorist threats) will require the release of decrypt information within a matter of hours.

Confidentiality and Safeguarding of Information

• KEAs should safeguard and maintain the confidentiality of information pertaining to the request for and the release of decrypt information. KEAs should protect the confidentiality of the person or persons for whom a key escrow agent holds keys or components thereof, and protect the confidentiality of the identity of the agency requesting decrypt information or components thereof and all information concerning such agency's access to and use of encryption keys or components thereof.

For law enforcement requests, KEA personnel knowledgeable of an interception or decryption should be of good character and have not been convicted of crimes of moral turpitude or otherwise bearing on their trustworthiness. For national security requests, KEA personnel viewing and/or storing classified requests must meet the applicable U.S. government requirements for accessing and/or storing classified information. Efforts are ongoing to examine unclassified alternatives.

• KEAs should be legitimate organizations without ties to criminal enterprises, and licensed to conduct business in the United States. KEAs for domestic products should not be a foreign corporation, a foreign country, or an entity thereof.

SOURCE: Federal Bureau of Investigation, viewgraphs of presentation to International Cryptography Institute 1995 conference, September 22, 1995.

BOX 5.7
**Proposed U.S. Government Requirements for Ensuring
Escrow Agent Integrity and Security**

1. Escrow agent entities shall devise and institutionalize policies, procedures, and mechanisms to ensure the confidentiality, integrity, and availability of key escrow related information.

a. Escrow agent entities shall be designed and operated so that a failure by a single person, procedure, or mechanism does not compromise the confidentiality, integrity or availability of the key and/or key components (e.g., two person control of keys, split keys, etc.)

b. Unencrypted escrowed key and/or key components that are stored and/or transmitted electronically shall be protected (e.g., via encryption) using approved means.

c. Unencrypted escrowed key and/or key components stored and/or transferred via other media/methods shall be protected using approved means (e.g., safes).

2. Escrow agent entities shall ensure due form of escrowed key access requests and authenticate the requests for escrowed key and/or key components.

3. Escrow agent entities shall protect against disclosure of information regarding the identity of the person/organization whose key and/or key components is requested, and the fact that a key and/or key component was requested or provided.

4. Escrow agent entities shall enter keys/key components into the escrowed key database immediately upon receipt.

5. Escrow agent entities shall ensure at least two copies of any key and/or key component in independent locations to help ensure the availability of such key and/or key components due to unforeseen circumstances.

6. Escrow agent entities that are certified by the U.S. government shall work with developers of key escrow encryption products and support a feature that allows products to verify to one another that the products' keys have been escrowed with a U.S.-certified agent.

SOURCE: National Institute of Standards and Technology, *Draft Key Escrow Agent Criteria*, December 1, 1995. Reprinted from text available on-line at http://csrc.ncsl.nist.gov/keyescrow/criteria.txt.

5.9.3 Liabilities of Escrow Agents

In order to assure users that key information entrusted to escrow agents remains secure and authorized third parties that they will be able to obtain exceptional access to encrypted data when necessary, escrow agents and their employees must be held accountable for improper behavior and for the use of security procedures and practices that are appropriate to the task of protection.

Liabilities can be criminal or civil (or both). For example, criminal penalties could be established for the disclosure of keys or key compo-

BOX 5.8
Proposed Requirements for Ensuring Key Access

7. An escrow agent entity shall employ one or more persons who possess a SECRET clearance for purposes of processing classified (e.g., FISA) requests to obtain keys and/or key components.

8. Escrow agent entities shall protect against unauthorized disclosure of information regarding the identity of the organization requesting the key or key components.

9. Escrow agent entities shall maintain data regarding all key escrow requests received, key escrow components released, database changes, system administration accesses, and dates of such events, for purposes of audit by appropriate government officials or others.

10. Escrow agent entities shall maintain escrowed keys and/or key components for as long as such keys may be required to decrypt information relevant to a law enforcement investigation.

11. Escrow agent entities shall provide key/key components to authenticated requests in a timely fashion and shall maintain a capability to respond more rapidly to emergency requirements for access.

12. Escrow agent entities shall possess and maintain a Certificate of Good Standing from the State of incorporation (or similar local/national authority).

13. Escrow agent entities shall provide to the U.S. government a Dun & Bradstreet/TRW number or similar credit report pointer and authorization.

14. Escrow agent entities shall possess and maintain an Errors & Omissions insurance policy.

15. Escrow agent entities shall provide to the U.S. government a written copy of, or a certification of the existence of a corporate security policy governing the key escrow agent entity's operation.

16. Escrow agent entities shall provide to the U.S. government a certification that the escrow agent will comply with all applicable federal, state, and local laws concerning the provisions of escrow agent entity services.

17. Escrow agent entities shall provide to the U.S. government a certification that the escrow agent entity will transfer to another approved escrow agent the escrow agent entity's equipment and data in the event of any dissolution or other cessation of escrow agent entity operations.

18. Escrow agent entities for products sold in the United States shall not be a foreign country or entity thereof, a national of a foreign country, or a corporation of which an alien is an officer or more than one-fourth of the stock which is owned by aliens or which is directly or indirectly controlled by such a corporation. Foreign escrow agent entities for products exported from the United States will be approved on a case by case basis as law enforcement and national security agreements can be negotiated.

19. Escrow agent entities shall provide to the U.S. government a certification that the escrow agent entity will notify the U.S. government in writing of any changes in the forgoing information.

20. Fulfillment of these and the other criteria are subject to periodic recertification.

NOTE: The material reprinted in this box is a continuation of the requirements listed in Box 5.7 and is extracted from the same source.

nents to unauthorized parties or for the refusal to disclose such information to appropriately authorized parties. It is worth noting that the implementing regulations accompanying the EES proposal run counter to this position in the sense that they do not provide specific penalties for failure to adhere to the procedures for obtaining keys (which only legislation could do). The implementing regulations specifically state that "these procedures do not create, and are not intended to create, any substantive rights for individuals intercepted through electronic surveillance, and noncompliance with these procedures shall not provide the basis for any motion to suppress or other objection to the introduction of electronic surveillance evidence lawfully acquired."[44]

Questions of civil liability are more complex. Ideally, levels of civil liability for improper disclosure of keys would be commensurate with the loss that would be incurred by the damaged party. For unauthorized disclosure of keys that encrypt large financial transactions, this level is potentially very large.[45] On the other hand, as a matter of public policy, it is probably inappropriate to allow such levels of damages. More plausible may be a construct that provides what society, as expressed through Congress, thinks is reasonable (Box 5.9). Users of escrow agents might also be able to buy their own insurance against unauthorized disclosure. Note that holding government agencies liable for civil damages might require an explicit change in the Federal Tort Claims Act that waives sovereign immunity in certain specified instances, or other legislative changes.

On the other hand, the amount of liability associated with compromising information related to data communications is likely to dwarf the analogous volume for voice communications. If escrowed encryption is adopted widely in data communications, compromise of escrow agents holding keys relevant to network encryption may be catastrophic, and may become easier as the number of access points that can be penetrated becomes larger.

Note that liability of escrow agents may be related to the voluntary use of escrow. A party concerned about large potential losses would have alternatives to escrowed encryption—namely, unescrowed encryption—that would protect the user against the consequences of improper key disclosure. Under these circumstances, a user whose key was compro-

---

[44]U.S. Department of Justice, *Authorization Procedures for Release of Encryption Key Components in Conjunction with Intercepts Pursuant to Title III and FISA*, February 4, 1994. Reprinted in Hoffman (ed.), *Building in Big Brother*, 1995, pp. 243-246.

[45]Even if these transactions are authenticated (as most large transactions would be), large transactions that are compromised could lead to loss of bids and the like by the firms involved in the transaction.

BOX 5.9
Statutory Limitations on Liability

Government can promote the use of specific services and products by assuming some of the civil liability risks associated with them. Three examples follow:

- The Atomic Energy Damages Act, also called the Price-Anderson Act, limits the liability of nuclear power plant operators for harm caused by a nuclear incident (such as an explosion or radioactive release). To operate a nuclear power plant, a licensee must show the U.S. Nuclear Regulatory Commission (U.S. NRC) that it maintains financial protection (such as private insurance, self-insurance, or other proof of financial responsibility) equal to the maximum amount of insurance available at reasonable cost and reasonable terms from private sources, unless the U.S. NRC sets a lower requirement on a case-specific basis. The U.S. NRC indemnifies licensees from all legal liability arising from a nuclear incident, including a precautionary evacuation, which is in excess of the required financial protection, up to a maximum combined licensee-and-government liability of $560 million. Incidents that cause more than $560 million in damage will trigger review by the Congress to determine the best means to compensate the public, including appropriating funds.
- The Commercial Space Launch Act provides similar protection to parties licensed to launch space vehicles or operate launch sites, but with a limit on the total liability the United States accepts. The licensee must obtain financial protection sufficient to compensate the maximum probable loss that third parties could claim for harm or damage, as determined by the secretary of transportation. The most that can be required is $500 million or the maximum liability insurance available from private sources, whichever is lower. The United States is obligated to pay successful claims by third parties in excess of the required protection, up to $1.5 billion, unless the loss is related to the licensee's willful misconduct. The law also requires licensees to enter into reciprocal waivers of claims with their contractors and customers, under which each party agrees to be responsible for losses it sustains.
- The swine flu vaccination program of 1976 provides an example in which the United States accepted open-ended liability and paid much more than expected. Doctors predicted a swine flu epidemic, and Congress appropriated money for the Department of Health, Education, and Welfare (HEW) to pay four pharmaceutical manufacturers for vaccines to be distributed nationwide. The manufacturers' inability to obtain liability insurance delayed the program until Congress passed legislation (P.L. 94-380) in which the United States assumed all liability other than manufacturer negligence. The government's liability could thus include, for example, harmful side effects. Claims against the United States would be processed under the Federal Tort Claims Act (which provides for trial by judge rather than jury and no punitive damages, among other distinctions). Some of the 45 million people who were immunized developed complications, such as Guillain-Barre syndrome; consequently, the program was canceled. By September 1977, 815 claims had been filed. The United States ultimately paid more than $100 million to settle claims, and some litigation is still pending today. Manufacturers, who by law were liable only for negligence, were not sued.

mised could be held responsible for his loss because he did not choose to use unescrowed encryption; an escrow agent's exposure to liability would be limited to the risks associated with parties that use its services. On the other hand, if escrowed encryption were the only cryptography permitted to be used, then by assumption the user would have no alternatives, and so in that case an escrow agent would shoulder a larger liability.

Another aspect of liability could arise if the escrow agents were also charged with the responsibilities of certificate authorities. Under some circumstances, it might be desirable for the functions of escrow agents and certificate authorities to be carried out by the same organization. Thus, these dual-purpose organizations would have all of the liabilities carried by those who must certify the authenticity of a given party.

5.10 THE ROLE OF SECRECY IN ENSURING PRODUCT SECURITY

The fact that EES and the Fortezza card involve classified algorithms has raised the general question of the relationship between secrecy and the maintenance of a product's trustworthiness in providing security. Specifically, the Clipper/Capstone approach is based on a secret (classified) encryption algorithm known as Skipjack. In addition, the algorithm is implemented in hardware (a chip) whose design is classified. The shroud of secrecy surrounding the hardware and algorithms needed to implement EES and Fortezza makes skeptics suspect that encrypted communications could be decrypted through some secret "back door" (i.e., without having the escrowed key).[46]

Logically, secrecy can be applied to two aspects of an encryption system: the algorithms used and the nature of the implementation of these algorithms. Each is addressed in turn below. Box 5.10 describes a historical perspective on cryptography and secrecy that is still valid today.

5.10.1 Algorithm Secrecy

The use of secret algorithms for encryption has advantages and disadvantages. From an information security standpoint, a third party who

---

[46]A kind of de facto secret back door can result from the fact that vendors of security products employing Clipper or Capstone technology are not likely to advertise the fact that the relevant encryption keys are escrowed with the U.S. government. Thus, even if the escrowing capability is "open" in the sense that no one involved makes any attempt to hide that fact, a user that does not know enough to ask about the presence or absence of escrowing features may well purchase such products without realizing their presence. Functionally, escrowing of which the user is ignorant is equivalent for that user to a "secret" back door.

BOX 5.10
Perspectives on Secrecy and System Security

The distinction between the general system (i.e., a product) and the specific key (of an encrypted message) was first articulated by Auguste Kerckhoffs in his historic book *La Cryptographie Militaire*, published in 1883. Quoting David Kahn in *The Codebreakers*:

Kerckhoffs deduced [that] . . . compromise of the system should not inconvenience the correspondents. . . . Perhaps the most startling requirement, at first glance, was the second . . . . Kerckhoffs explained that by "system" he meant "the material part of the system; tableaux, code books, or whatever mechanical apparatus may be necessary," and not "the key proper." Kerckhoffs here makes for the first time the distinction, now basic to cryptology, between the general system and the specific key. Why must the general system "not require secrecy"? . . . "Because," Kerckhoffs said, "it is not necessary to conjure up imaginary phantoms and to suspect the incorruptibility of employees or subalterns to understand that, if a system requiring secrecy were in the hands of too large a number of individuals, it could be compromised at each engagement. . . . This has proved to be true, and Kerckhoffs' second requirement has become widely accepted under a form that is sometimes called the fundamental assumption of military cryptography: that the enemy knows the general system. But he must still be unable to solve messages in it without knowing the specific key. In its modern formulation, the Kerckhoffs doctrine states that secrecy must reside solely in the keys."[1]

A more modern expression of this sentiment is provided by Dorothy Denning:

The security of a cryptosystem should depend only on the secrecy of the keys and not on the secrecy of the algorithms. . . . This requirement implies the algorithms must be inherently strong; that is, it should not be possible to break a cipher simply by knowing the method of encipherment. This requirement is needed because the algorithms may be in the public domain, or known to a cryptanalyst.[2]

---

[1]David Kahn, *The Codebreakers*, MacMillan, New York, 1967, p. 235.
[2]Dorothy Denning, *Cryptography and Data Security*, Addison-Wesley, Reading, Mass., 1982, p. 8.

---

knows the algorithm associated with a given piece of ciphertext has an enormous advantage over one who does not—if the algorithm is unknown, cryptanalysis is much more difficult. Thus, the use of a secret algorithm by those concerned about information security presents an additional (and substantial) barrier to those who might be eavesdropping. From a signals intelligence (SIGINT) standpoint, it is advantageous to keep knowledge of good encryption out of the hands of potential SIGINT targets. Thus, if an algorithm provides good cryptographic security, keeping the algorithm secret prevents the SIGINT target from implementing it. In addition, if an algorithm is known to be good, studying it in detail can reveal a great deal about what makes any algorithm good or bad. Algorithm secrecy thus helps to keep such information out of the public domain.[47]

On the other hand, algorithm secrecy entails a number of disadvantages as well. One is that independent analysis of a secret algorithm by the larger community is not possible. Without such analysis, flaws may remain in the algorithm that compromise the security it purports to provide. If these flaws are kept secret, users of the algorithm may unknowingly compromise themselves. Even worse, sophisticated users who need high assurances of security are unable to certify for themselves the security it provides (and thus have no sense of the risks they are taking if they use it). In most cases, the real issue is whether the user chooses to rely on members of the academic cryptography communities publishing in the open literature, or on members of the classified military community or members of the commercial cryptography community who are unable to fully disclose what they know about a subject because it is classified or proprietary.

A second disadvantage of algorithm secrecy is the fact that if a cryptographic infrastructure is based on the assumption of secrecy, public discovery of those secrets can compromise the ends to be served by that infrastructure. For example, if a cryptographic infrastructure based on a secret algorithm were widely deployed, and if that algorithm contained a secret and unannounced "back door" that allowed those with knowledge of this back door easy access to encrypted data, that infrastructure would be highly vulnerable and could be rendered untrustworthy in short order by the public disclosure of the back door.

A third disadvantage is that a secret algorithm cannot be implemented in software with any degree of assurance that it will remain secret. Software, as it exists ready for actual installation on a computer (so-called object code or executable code), can usually be manipulated with special software tools to yield an alternate form (namely, source code) reflecting the way the creating programmer designed it, and therefore revealing many, even most, of its operational details, including any algorithm em-

---

[47]Of course, if other strong algorithms are known publicly, the force of this argument is weakened from a practical standpoint. For example, it is not clear that the disclosure of Skipjack would be harmful from the standpoint of making strong algorithms public, because triple-DES is already publicly known, and triple-DES is quite strong.

bedded within it. This process is known as "decompiling" or "disassembly" and is a standard technique in the repertoire of software engineers.[48]

All of the previous comments apply to secrecy whether it is the result of government classification decisions or vendor choices to treat an algorithm as a trade secret. In addition, vendors may well choose to treat an algorithm as a trade secret to obtain the market advantages that proprietary algorithms often bring. Indeed, many applications of cryptography for confidentiality in use today are based on trade-secret algorithms such as RC2 and RC4.

5.10.2 Product Design and Implementation Secrecy

Product design and implementation secrecy has a number of advantages. For example, by obscuring how a product has been designed, secrecy makes it more difficult for an outsider to reverse-engineer the product in such a way that he could understand it better or, even worse, modify it in some way. Since vulnerabilities sometimes arise in implementation, keeping the implementation secret makes it harder for an attacker to discover and then exploit those vulnerabilities. Design and implementation secrecy thus protects any secrets that may be embedded in the product for a longer time than if they were to be published openly.

On the other hand, it is taken as an axiom by those in the security community that it is essentially impossible to maintain design or implementation secrecy indefinitely. Thus, the question of the time scale of reverse engineering is relevant—given the necessary motivation, how long will it take and how much in resources will be needed to reverse-engineer a chip or a product?

- For software, reverse engineering is based on decompilation or disassembly (as described in Section 5.10.1). The larger the software product, the longer it takes to understand the original program; even a small one can be difficult to understand, especially if special techniques have been used to obscure its functionality. Modification of the original program can present additional technical difficulties (the product may be designed in such a way that disassembling or decompiling the entire product is necessary to isolate critical features that one might wish to modify). Certain techniques can be used to increase the difficulty of

---

[48]As one example, the RC2 encryption algorithm, nominally a trade secret owned by RSA Data Security Inc. was posted to the Internet in early 1996, apparently as the result of an apparent "disassembly" of a product embedding that algorithm (personal communication, Robert Baldwin, RSA Data Security Inc., May 16, 1996).

making such modifications,[49] but there is virtual unanimity in the computer community that modification cannot be prevented forever. How robust must these anti-reverse-engineering features be? The answer is that they must be robust enough that the effort needed to overcome them is greater than the effort needed to develop an encryption system from scratch.

• For hardware, reverse engineering takes the form of physical disassembly and/or probing with x-rays of the relevant integrated circuit chips. Such chips can be designed to resist reverse engineering in a way that makes it difficult to understand what various components on the chip do. For example, the coating on a die used to fabricate a chip may be designed so that removal of the coating results in removal of one or more layers of the chip, thus destroying portions of what was to be reverse-engineered. The chip may also be fabricated with decoy or superfluous elements that would distract a reverse engineer. For all of these reasons, reverse engineering for understanding a chip's functions is difficult. However, it is not impossible, and under some circumstances, it is possible to modify a chip. In general, reverse engineering of the circuits and devices inside a chip requires significant expertise and access to expensive tools.[50]

An important factor that works against implementation secrecy is the wide distribution of devices or products whose implementation is secret. It is difficult to protect a device against reverse engineering when millions of those devices are distributed around the world without any physical barriers (except those on the implementation itself) to control access to them. Everyone with an EES-compliant telephone or a Foretzza card, for

---

[49]For example, Trusted Information Systems Inc. of Glenwood, Md., has advocated an approach to preventing modification that relies on the placement of integrity checks at strategic locations. With such an approach, a change to the disassembled source code would have to be reflected properly in all relevant integrity checks; doing so might well involve disassembly of an entire product rather than of just one module of the product. Nevertheless, such an approach cannot prevent modification, although it can make modification more difficult. Such anti-reverse-engineering features may also increase the difficulty of vendor maintenance of a product. Increased difficulty may be a price vendors must pay in order to have more secure software implementations.

[50]Estimates of the cost to reverse-engineer the Clipper chip nondestructively cover a wide range, from "doable in university laboratories with bright graduate students and traditions of reverse engineering" (as estimated by a number of electrical engineers in academia with extensive experience in reverse engineering) to as much as $30 million to $50 million (as estimated in informal conversations between JASON members and DOD engineers). The cost may well be lower if large numbers of chips are available for destructive inspection.

example, will have access to the chip that provides encryption and key escrow services.

The comments above refer to the feasibility of maintaining implementation secrecy. But there are issues related to its desirability as well. For example, implementation secrecy implies that only a limited number of vendors can be trusted to produce a given implementation. Thus, foreign production of Clipper/Capstone-compliant devices under classification guidelines raises problems unless foreign producers are willing to abide by U.S. security requirements.

A more important point is that implementation secrecy also demands trust between user and supplier/vendor. Users within government agencies generally trust other parts of the government to provide adequate services as a supplier. But in the private sector, such trust is not necessarily warranted. Users that are unable to determine for themselves what algorithms are embedded in computer and communications products used must trust the vendor to have provided algorithms that do what the user wants done, and the vast majority of users fall into this category. Such opacity functions as a de facto mechanism of secrecy that also impedes user knowledge about the inner workings and that is exploited by the distributors of computer viruses and worms. As a result, choosing between self-implemented source code and a prepackaged program for use in performing certain functions is in many ways analogous to choosing between unclassified and classified algorithms.

An information security manager with very high security needs must make trade-offs in assurance vs. cost. In general, the only way to be certain that the algorithms used are the ones claimed to be used is to implement them on one's own. Yet if a manager lacks the necessary knowledge and experience, a self-implementation may not be as secure or as capable as one developed by a trusted vendor. A self-implementer also carries the considerable burden of development costs that a commercial vendor can amortize over many sales.

As a result, security-conscious users of products whose inner workings are kept secret must (1) trust the vendor implicitly (based on factors such as reputation), or (2) face the possibility of various extreme scenarios. Here are two:

• The hardware of a secret device can be dynamically modified; for example, electrically erasable read-only memories can direct the operation of a processor. One possible scenario with secret hardware is that a chip that initially provides Clipper-chip functionality might be reprogrammed when it first contacts a Clipper/Capstone-compliant device to allow nonescrowed but unauthorized access to it; such a means of "infection" is common with computer viruses. In other words, the Skipjack algorithm may have been embedded in the chip when it was first shipped, but after the initial contact, the algorithm controlling the chip is no longer Skipjack.

• An algorithm that is not Skipjack is embedded by the manufacturer in chips purporting to be Clipper or Capstone chips. Since the utility of a vector test depends on the availability of an independent implementation of the algorithm, it is impossible for the user to perform this test independently if the user has no reference point. As a result, the user has no access to an independent test of the chip that is in the user's "Clipper/Capstone-compliant" device, and so any algorithm might have been embedded.[51]

Any technically trained person can invent many other such scenarios. Thus, public trust in the technical desirability of the EES and Fortezza for exceptional access depends on a high degree of trust in the government, entirely apart from any fears about compromising escrow agents wherever they are situated.

Of course, some of the same considerations go beyond the Skipjack algorithm and the Clipper/Capstone approach. In general, users need confidence that a given product with encryption capabilities indeed implements a given algorithm. Labeling a box with the letters "DES" does not ensure that the product inside really implements DES. In this case, the fact that the DES algorithm is publicly known facilitates testing to verify that the algorithm is implemented correctly.[52] If its source code is available for inspection, other security-relevant aspects of a software product can be examined to a certain extent, at least up to the limits of the expertise of the person checking the source code. But for software products without source code, and especially for hardware products that cannot easily be disassembled, and even more so for hardware products that are specifically designed to resist disassembly, confidence in the non-algorithm security aspects of the product is more a matter of trusting the vendor than of the user making an independent technical verification of

---

[51]According to Dorothy Denning, the review team for Skipjack (see footnote 5 of this chapter) compared the output from Clipper chips with output from the software version of Skipjack that the review team obtained for review to verify that the algorithm on the chips was the same as the software version (personal communication, Dorothy Denning, Georgetown University, March 1996).

[52]As described in Chapter 4, the product tester can use the product to encrypt a randomly chosen set of values with a randomly chosen key, and compare the encrypted output to the known correct result obtained through the use of a product known to implement the algorithm correctly. This is known as a vector test.

an implementation.[53]   In some sectors (e.g., banking, classified military applications), however, independent technical verification is regarded as essential.

Finally, a given product may properly implement an algorithm but still be vulnerable to attacks that target the part of the product surrounding the implementation of the algorithm.   Such vulnerabilities are most common in the initial releases of products that have not been exposed to public test and scrutiny.   For example, a security problem with the Netscape Navigator's key-generation facility could have been found had the implementation in which the key generator was embedded been available for public examination prior to its release, even though the encryption algorithm itself was properly implemented.[54]

5.11 THE HARDWARE-SOFTWARE CHOICE IN PRODUCT IMPLEMENTATION

After the Clipper initiative was announced, and as the debate over escrowed encryption broadened to include the protection of data communications and stored data, the mass market software industry emphasized that a hardware solution to cryptographic security—as exemplified by the Clipper chip—would not be satisfactory. The industry argued with some force that only a software-based approach would encourage the widespread use of encryption envisioned for the world's electronic future, making several points:

• Customers have a strong preference for using integrated cryptographic products. While stand-alone products with encryption capabilities could be made to work, in general they lack operational convenience for the applications that software and systems vendors address.

• Compared to software, hardware is expensive to manufacture. In particular, the relevant cost is not simply the cost of the hardware encryption device compared to a software encryption package,[55] but also the cost of any modifications to the hardware environment needed to accept

---

[53]Such a comment is not meant to preclude the possibility of an independent certifying authority, a kind of "Consumers' Union" for cryptography equipment and products. Such organizations have been proposed to evaluate and certify computer security, and as of this writing, three U.S. firm have received NIST approval to evaluate the conformance of products to FIPS 140-1, the FIPS for cryptography modules.

[54]This security problem is referenced in footnote 34, Chapter 2. The lack of prior vetting for Netscape Navigator is described by Kathleen Murphy, "A Second Security Breach," *Web Week*, Volume 1(6), October 1995, p. 8.

[55]In a recent contract, a vendor agreed to provide Fortezza cards at $69 per card. See Paul Constance, "After Complaining $99 Was Too Low, Fortezza Vendors Come in at $69," *Government Computer News*, October 2, 1995, p. 6.

the hardware encryption device.[56] For example, one major company noted to the committee that adoption of the Fortezza card, a card that fits into the PC-card slots available on most laptop computers, would be very expensive in its desktop computing environment, because most of its desktop computers do not have a PC-card slot and would have to be modified to accept the Fortezza card. By contrast, a software encryption product can simply be loaded via common media (e.g., a CD-ROM or a floppy disk) or downloaded via a network.

• The fact that hardware is difficult to change means that problems found subsequent to deployment are more difficult to fix. For example, most users would prefer to install a software fix by loading a CD-ROM into their computers than to open up their machines to install a new chip with a hardware fix.

• Hardware-based security products have a history of being market-unfriendly. Hardware will, in general, be used only to the extent that the required hardware (and its specific configuration) is found in user installations. Moreover, hardware requirements can be specified for software only when that hardware is widely deployed. For example, a technical approach to the software piracy problem has been known for many years; the approach requires the installation of special-purpose hardware that is available only to those who obtain the software legitimately. This "solution" has failed utterly in the marketplace, and software piracy remains a multibillion-dollar-per-year problem.

• Hardware for security consumes physical space and power in products. For example, a hardware-based encryption card that fits into an expansion slot on a computer takes up a slot permanently, unless the user is willing to install and deinstall the card for every use. It also creates an additional power demand on electronic devices where power and battery life are limited.

In general, products with encryption capabilities today use software or hardware or both to help ensure security.[57] The crux of the hardware-

---

[56] One vendor is manufacturing a circuit board for encryption that fits into a 3.5" floppy disk drive. However, this device does not employ the Capstone/Foretzza approach. See Elizabeth Sikorovsky, "Device Offers Alternative to PC Card-Based Encryption," *Federal Computer Week*, November 13, 1995, pp. 29 and 35.

[57] Note that the dividing line between hardware and software is not always clear. In particular, product designers use the term "firmware" to refer to a design approach that enters software into a special computer memory (an integrated circuit chip) that usually is subsequently unchangeable (read-only memory; ROM). Sometimes an alternate form of memory is used that does permit changes under controlled conditions (electrically programmable ROM; EPROM). Such software-controlled hardware (microprogrammed hardware) has the convenience that the functionality of the item can be updated or changed without redesign of the hardware portion.

software debate is what is good enough to ensure security. The security needed to manage electronic cash in the international banking system needs to be much stronger than the security to protect word processing files created by private individuals. Thus, software-based cryptography might work for the latter, while hardware-based cryptography might be essential for the former.

Products with encryption capabilities must be capable of resisting attack. But since such products are often embedded in operating environments that are themselves insecure, an attacker may well choose to attack the environment rather than the product itself. For example, a product with encryption capabilities may be hardware-based, but the operating environment may leave the encryption keys or the unencrypted text exposed.[58] More generally, in an insecure environment, system security may well not depend very much on whether the cryptography per se is implemented in hardware or software or whether it is weak or strong.

In the context of escrowed encryption, a second security concern arises—a user of an escrowed encryption product may wish to defeat the escrow mechanism built into the product. Thus, the escrow features of the product must be bound to the product in a way that cannot be bypassed by some reverse-engineered modification to the product. This particular problem is known as binding or, more explicitly, escrow binding; escrow binding is an essential element of any escrow scheme that is intended to provide exceptional access.

Concern over how to solve the escrow binding problem was the primary motivation for the choice of a hardware approach to the Clipper initiative. As suggested in Section 5.10, the functionality of a hardware system designed to resist change is indeed difficult to change, and so hardware implementations have undeniable advantages for solving the escrow binding problem.[59] An EES-compliant device would be a telephone without software accessible to the user, and would provide high assurance that the features for exceptional access would not be bypassed.

As the debate has progressed, ideas for software-based escrow processes have been proposed. The primary concern of the U.S. government about software implementations is that once a change has been designed and developed that can bypass the escrow features ("break the escrow binding"), such a change can be easily propagated through many different channels and installed with relatively little difficulty. In the committee's view, the important question is whether software solutions to the escrow

---

[58]Peter G. Neumann, *Can Systems Be Trustworthy with Software-Implemented Cryptography?*, SRI International, Menlo Park, Calif., October 28, 1994.

[59]A device controlled by software stored in read-only memory is for all intents and purposes the same as "pure hardware" in this context.

binding problem can provide an acceptable level of protection against reverse engineering. Whether an escrowed encryption product is implemented in software (or hardware for that matter), the critical threshold is the difficulty of breaking the escrow binding (i.e., bypassing the escrowing features) compared to the effort necessary to set up an independent unescrowed encryption system (perhaps as part of an integrated product). If it is more difficult to bypass the escrow features than to build an unescrowed system, then "rogues" who want to defeat exceptional access will simply build an unescrowed system. The bottom line is that an escrowed encryption product does not have to be perfectly resistant to breaking the escrow binding.

A possible mitigating factor is that even if a software "patch" is developed that would break the escrow binding of an escrowed encryption software product, it may not achieve wide distribution even among the criminals who would have the most to gain from such a change. Experience with widely deployed software products (e.g., operating systems) indicates that even when a software fix is made available for a problem in a product, it may not be implemented unless the anomalous or incorrect software behavior is particularly significant to an end user. If this is the case for products that are as critical as operating systems, it may well be true for products with more specialized applications. On the other side of the coin, many parties (e.g., criminals) may care a great deal about the presence of escrowing and thus be highly motivated to find "fixes" that eliminate escrowing.

5.12 RESPONSIBILITY FOR GENERATION OF UNIT KEYS

Key generation is the process by which cryptographic keys are generated. Two types of keys are relevant:

• A session key is required for each encryption of plaintext into ciphertext; this is true whether the information is to be stored or communicated. Ultimately, the intended recipients of this information (those who retrieve it from storage or those who receive it at the other end of a communications channel) must have the same session key. For maximum information security, a new session key is used with every encryption. (See footnote 7 of this chapter for more discussion.)

• A unit key is a cryptographic key associated with a particular product or device owned or controlled by a specific individual. Unit keys are often used to protect session keys from casual observation in escrowed encryption products, but precisely how they are used depends on the specifics of a given product.

In the most general case, the session key is a random number, and a different one is generated anew for each encryption. But the unit key is a cryptographic variable that typically changes on a much longer time scale than does the session key. In many escrowed encryption schemes, knowledge of the unit key enables a third party to obtain the session key associated with any given encryption.

The Clipper/Capstone approach requires that the unit key be generated by the manufacturer at the time of manufacture ("at birth") and then registered prior to sale with escrow agents in accordance with established procedures. Such an approach has one major advantage from the standpoint of those who may require exceptional access in the future—it guarantees registration of keys, because users need not take any action to ensure registration.

At the same time, since the Clipper/Capstone approach is based on a hardware-based implementation that is not user-modifiable, a given device has only one unit key for its entire lifetime, although, at some cost, the user may change the Clipper chip embedded in the device.[60] If the unit key is compromised, the user's only recourse is to change the chip. A user who does not do so violates one basic principle of information security—frequent changing of keys (or passwords).[61] In addition, the fact that all unit keys are known at the time of manufacture raises concerns that all keys could be kept (perhaps surreptitiously) in some master databank that would be accessible without going to the designated escrow agents. The implication is that the user is forced to trust several organizations and individuals involved with the manufacturing process. Such trust becomes an implicit aspect of the secrecy associated with EES-compliant devices.

One alternative to unit key generation at birth is the generation (or input) of a new unit key at user request. This approach has the advantage that the user can be confident that no one else retains a copy of the new key without his or her knowledge. The disadvantage is that escrow of that key would require explicit action on the user's part for that purpose.

An alternative that has some of the advantages of each approach is to install and register a unit key at birth, but to design the product to allow the user to change the unit key later. Thus, all products designed in this manner would have "default" unit keys installed by the manufacturer

---

[60] A Clipper chip costs about $10 when bought in large lots (personal communication, Jimmy Dolphin, Mykotronx, March 22, 1996). Even when including retail mark-up costs and labor, the cost of changing a Clipper chip is likely to be less than $100.

[61] However, since the Skipjack algorithm is classified, simple knowledge of the unit key (or the session key) would enable only those with knowledge of the algorithm to decrypt the session key (or the session).

and recorded with some escrow agent; each of these keys would be different. Users who took the trouble to install a new unit key would have to take an explicit action to escrow it, but in many cases the inconvenience and bother of changing the unit key would result in no action being taken. Thus, valid unit keys would be held by escrow agents in two cases—for products owned by users who did not change the unit key, and for products owned by users who chose to register their new keys with escrow agents.

Who is responsible for the collection of unit keys? Under the Clipper/Capstone approach, the responsible party is the U.S. government. But if nongovernment agencies were to be responsible for escrowing keys (see Section 5.8), a large market with many vendors producing many different types of encryption products in large volume could result in a large administrative burden on these vendors.

The specific implementation of EES also raises an additional point. As proposed, EES requires that unit keys be given to government authorities upon presentation of legal authorization. If these keys are still available to the authorities after the period of legal authorization has expired, the EES device is forever open to government surveillance. To guard against this possibility, Administration plans for the final Clipper key escrow system provide for automatic key deletion from the decrypting equipment upon expiration of the authorized period. Key deletion is to be implemented on the tamper-resistant device that law enforcement authorities will use to decrypt Clipper-encrypted traffic. However, by early 1996, the deployed interim key escrow system had not been upgraded to include that feature.

5.13 ISSUES RELATED TO THE ADMINISTRATION PROPOSAL TO RELAX EXPORT CONTROLS ON 64-BIT ESCROWED ENCRYPTION IN SOFTWARE

As noted in Chapter 4, the Administration has proposed to treat software products with 64-bit encryption using any algorithm as it currently treats products that are based on 40-bit RC2/RC4 algorithms, providing that products using this stronger encryption are "properly escrowed." This change is intended to make available to foreign customers of U.S. software products stronger cryptographic protection than they currently have today. This proposal has raised several issues.

5.13.1 The Definition of "Proper Escrowing"

The definition of "proper escrowing" (as the phrase is used in the Administration's proposed new export rules in Box 5.3) is that keys should be escrowed only with "escrow agent(s) certified by the U.S. Government, or certified by foreign governments with which the U.S. Government has formal agreements consistent with U.S. law enforcement and national security requirements." These agents would not necessarily be government agencies, although in principle they could be.

The obvious question is whether foreign consumers will be willing to purchase U.S. products with encryption capabilities when it is openly announced that the information security of those products could be compromised by or with the assistance of escrow agents certified by the U.S. government. While the draft definition does envision the possibility that escrow agents could be certified by foreign governments (e.g., those in the country of sale), formal agreements often take a long time to negotiate, during which time U.S. escrow agents would hold the keys, or the market for such products would fail to develop.

For some applications (e.g., U.S. companies doing business with foreign suppliers), interim U.S. control of escrow agents may prove acceptable. But it is easy to imagine other applications for which it would not, and in any case a larger question is begged: What would be the incentive for foreign users to purchase such products from U.S. vendors if comparably strong but unescrowed foreign products with encryption capabilities were available? As the discussion in Chapter 2 points out, integrated products with encryption capabilities are generally available today from U.S. vendors. However, how long the U.S. monopoly in this market will last is an open question.

The issue of who holds the keys in an international context is explored further in Appendix G.

5.13.2 The Proposed Limitation of Key Lengths to 64 Bits or Less

The most important question raised by the 64-bit limitation is this: If the keys are escrowed and available to law enforcement and national security authorities, why does it matter how long the keys are? In response to this question, senior Administration officials have said that the limitation to 64 bits is a way of hedging against the possibility of finding easily proliferated ways to break the escrow binding built into software, with the result that U.S. software products without effective key escrow would become available worldwide. Paraphrasing the remarks of a senior Administration official at the International Cryptography Institute 1995 conference, "The 64-bit limit is there because we might have a chance of dealing with a breakdown of software key escrow 10 to 15 years down the line; but if the key length implied a work factor of something like triple-DES, we would *never* [emphasis in original] be able to do it."

Two factors must be considered in this argument. One is the likelihood that software key escrow can in fact be compromised. This subject is considered in Sections 5.10.2 and 5.11. But a second point is the fact that the 64-bit limit is easily circumvented by multiple encryption under some circumstances. Specifically, consider a stand-alone security-specific product for file encryption that is based on DES and is escrowed. Such a product—in its unaltered state—meets all of the proposed draft criteria for export. But disassembly of the object code of the program (to defeat the escrow binding) may also reveal the code for DES encryption in the product. Once the source code for the DES encryption is available, it is a technically straightforward exercise to implement a package that will use the product to implement a triple-DES encryption on a file.

5.14 RECAP

Escrowed encryption is one of several approaches to providing exceptional access to encrypted information. The U.S. government has advanced a number of initiatives to support the insertion of escrow features into products with encryption capabilities that will become available in the future, including the Escrowed Encryption Standard, the Capstone/ Fortezza initiative, and a proposal to liberalize export controls on products using escrowed encryption. Its support of escrowed encryption embodies the government's belief that the benefit to law enforcement and national security from exceptional access to encrypted information outweighs the damage owing to loss of confidentiality that might occur with the failure of procedures intended to prevent unauthorized access to the escrow mechanism.

Escrowed encryption provides *more* confidentiality than leaving information unprotected (as most information is today), but *less* confidentiality than what could be provided by good implementations of unescrowed cryptography. On the other hand, escrowed encryption provides *more* capability for exceptional access under circumstances of key loss or unavailability than does unescrowed encryption. All users will have to address this trade-off between level of confidentiality and key unavailability.

The central questions with respect to escrowed encryption are the following:

• With what degree of confidence is it possible to ensure that third parties will have access to encrypted information only under lawfully authorized circumstances?

• What is the trade-off for the user between potentially lower levels of confidentiality and higher degrees of confidence that encrypted data will be available when necessary?

6

Other Dimensions of National Cryptography Policy

In addition to export controls and escrowed encryption, current national policy on cryptography is affected by government use of a large number of levers available to it, including the Communications Assistance for Law Enforcement Act, the standards-setting process, R&D funding, procurement practices, education and public jawboning, licenses and certification, and arrangements both formal and informal with various other governments (state, local, and foreign) and organizations (e.g., specific private companies). All of these are controversial because they embody judgments about how the interests of law enforcement and national security should be reconciled against the needs of the private sector. In addition, the international dimensions of cryptography are both critical (because cryptography affects communications and communications are fundamentally international) and enormously difficult (because national interests differ from government to government).

6.1 THE COMMUNICATIONS ASSISTANCE FOR LAW ENFORCEMENT ACT

The Communications Assistance for Law Enforcement Act (CALEA) was widely known as the "digital telephony" bill before its formal passage. The CALEA is not explicitly connected to national cryptography policy, but it is an important aspect of the political context in which national cryptography policy has been discussed and debated.

6.1.1 Brief Description of and Stated Rationale for the CALEA

General Description

The Communications Assistance for Law Enforcement Act (CALEA) was passed in October 1994. The act imposes on telecommunications carriers four requirements in connection with those services or facilities that allow customers to originate, terminate, or direct communications:

- To expeditiously isolate and enable the government to intercept, pursuant to court order or other lawful authorization, all wire and electronic communications in the carrier's control to or from the equipment, facilities, or services of a subscriber, in real time or at any later time acceptable to the government. Carriers are not responsible for decrypting encrypted communications that are the subject of court-ordered wiretaps, unless the carrier provided the encryption and can decrypt it. Moreover, carriers are not prohibited from deploying an encryption service for which it does not retain the ability to decrypt communications for law enforcement access.

- To expeditiously isolate and enable the government to access, pursuant to court order or other lawful authorization, reasonably available call-identifying information about the origin and destination of communications. Access must be provided in such a manner that the information may be associated with the communication to which it pertains and is provided to the government before, during, or immediately after the communication's transmission to or from the subscriber.

- To make intercepted communications and call-identifying information available to government, pursuant to court order or other lawful authorization, so that they may be transmitted over lines or facilities leased or procured by law enforcement to a location away from the carrier's premises.

- To meet these requirements with a minimum of interference with the subscriber's service and in such a way that protects the privacy of communications and call-identifying information that are not targeted by electronic surveillance orders, and that maintains the confidentiality of the government's interceptions.

The CALEA also authorizes federal money for retrofitting common carrier systems to comply with these requirements. As this report is being written, no money has yet been appropriated for this task.

The CALEA requirements apply only to those services or facilities that enable a subscriber to make, receive, or direct calls. They do not apply to information services, such as the services of electronic mail providers; on-line services such as Compuserve or America Online; or

Internet access providers; or to private networks or services whose sole purpose is to interconnect carriers. Furthermore, the CALEA requires law enforcement authorities to use carrier employees or personnel to activate a surveillance. The CALEA also provides that a warrant is needed to tap a cordless telephone; wiretaps on cellular telephones are already governed by Title III or the Foreign Intelligence Surveillance Act.

The Stated Rationale for the CALEA

Historically, telecommunications service providers have cooperated with law enforcement officials in allowing access to communications upon legal authorization. New telecommunications services (e.g., call forwarding, paging, cellular calls) and others expected in the future have diminished the ability of law enforcement agencies to carry out legally authorized electronic surveillance. The primary rationale for the CALEA is to ensure that within 4 years, telecommunications service providers will still be able to provide the assistance necessary to law enforcement officials to conduct surveillance of wire and electronic communications (both content and call-identifying information) controlled by the carrier, regardless of the nature of the particular services being offered.

6.1.2 Reducing Resource Requirements for Wiretaps

Once a surveillance order has been approved judicially, it must be implemented. In practice, the implementation of a surveillance order requires the presence of at least two agents around the clock. Such a presence is required if real-time minimization requirements are to be met.[1] As a result, personnel requirements are the most expensive aspect of electronic surveillance. The average cost of a wiretap order is $57,000 (Appendix D), or approximately one-half of a full-time-equivalent agent-year. Such costs are not incurred lightly by law enforcement agencies.

---

[1]Minimization refers to the practice, required by Title III, of monitoring only those portions of a conversation that are relevant to the crime under investigation. If a subject discusses matters that are strictly personal, such discussions are not subject to monitoring. In practice, a team of agents operate a tape recorder on the wiretapped line. Minimization requires agents to turn off the tape recorder and to cease monitoring the conversation for a short period of time if they overhear nonrelevant discussions. At the end of that time period, they are permitted to resume monitoring. For obvious reasons, this practice is conducted in real time. When agents encounter a foreign language with which they are unfamiliar, they are allowed to record the entire conversation; the tape is then "minimized" after the fact of wiretapping. Additional discussion of the requirements imposed on wiretapping by Title III is contained in Appendix D.

Under these circumstances, procedures and/or technologies that could reduce the labor required to conduct wiretaps pose a potential problem for individuals concerned about excessive use of wiretaps. Specifically, these individuals are concerned that the ability to route wiretapped calls to a central location would enable a single team of agents to monitor multiple conversations.[2] Such time sharing among monitoring teams could lower wiretap costs significantly. From the standpoint of law enforcement, these savings could be used for other law enforcement purposes, and they would have the additional effect of eliminating an operational constraint on the frequency with which wiretap authority is sought today.

Technologies that would enable minimization without human assistance are in their infancy today. For example, the technology of speech recognition for the most part cannot cope with speech that is speaker-independent and continuous, and artificial intelligence programs today and for the foreseeable future will be unable to distinguish between the criminally relevant and nonrelevant parts of a conversation. Human agents are an essential component of a wiretap, and law enforcement officials have made three key points in response to the concern raised above:

• Most importantly, today's wiretaps are performed generally with law enforcement agencies paying telecommunications service providers for delivering the intercepted communications to a point of law enforcement's choosing.

• From an operational standpoint, the real-time minimization of wiretapped conversations requires agents who are personally familiar with the details of the case under investigation, so that they know when the subjects are engaged in conversations related to the case—agents exceed their authority if they monitor unrelated conversations.

• Procedural rules require that all evidence be maintained through a proper chain of custody and in a manner such that the authenticity of evidence can be established. Law enforcement officials believe that the

---

[2]For example, such a concern was raised at the Fifth Conference on Computers, Freedom, and Privacy held in San Francisco in March 1995. The argument goes as follows. While the CALEA authorizes $500 million to pay for existing in-place telephone switch conversions to implement the capabilities desired by law enforcement, this amount is intended as a one-time cost; upgrades of switching systems are expected to implement these capabilities without government subsidy. The point is that additional wiretap orders would not pose an additional incremental cost (though the original cost of $57,000 would still obtain), and the barrier of incremental cost would not impede more wiretap orders. In short, critics argue that it would make good economic sense to make additional use of resources if such use can "piggyback" on an already-made investment.

use of one team to monitor different conversations could call into question the ability to establish a clear chain of custody.

6.1.3 Obtaining Access to Digital Streams in the Future

In the conduct of any wiretap, the first technical problem is simply gaining access to the relevant traffic itself, whether encrypted or not. For law enforcement, products with encryption capabilities and features that allow exceptional access are useless without access to the traffic in question. The CALEA was an initiative spearheaded by law enforcement to deal with the access problem created by new telecommunications services.

The problems addressed by the CALEA will inevitably resurface as newer communications services are developed and deployed for use by common carriers and private entities (e.g., corporations) alike. It is axiomatic that the complexity of interactions among communications systems will continually increase, both as a result of increased functionality and the need to make more efficient use of available bandwidth. Consequently, isolation of the digital streams associated with the party or parties targeted by law enforcement will become increasingly difficult if the cooperation of the service provider is not forthcoming, for all of the reasons described in Chapter 2. (It is for this reason that the CALEA applies to parties that are not common carriers today upon appropriate designation by the Federal Communications Commission (FCC).)

Moreover, even when access to the digital stream of an application is assured, the structure of the digital stream may be so complex that it would be extremely costly to determine all of the information present without the assistance of the application developer. Tools designed to isolate the relevant portions of a given digital stream transmitted on open systems will generally be less expensive than tools for proprietary systems, but since both open and proprietary systems will be present in any future telecommunications environment, law enforcement authorities will need tools for both. The development of such tools will require considerable technical skill, skill that is most likely possessed by the application developers; cooperation with product developers may decrease the cost of developing these tools.

Finally, as the telecommunications system becomes more and more heterogeneous, even the term "common carrier" will become harder to define or apply. The routing of an individual data communication through the "network" will be dynamic and may take any one of a number of paths, decisions about which are not under the user's control. While only one link in a given route need be a common carrier for CALEA purposes, identifying that common carrier in practice may be quite difficult.

6.1.4 The CALEA Exemption of Information Service Providers and Distinctions Between Voice and Data Services

At present, users of data communications services access networks such as the Internet either through private networks (e.g., via their employers) or through Internet service providers that provide connections for a variety of individuals and organizations. Both typically make use of lines owned and operated by telecommunications service providers. In the former case, law enforcement access to the digital stream is more or less the same problem as it is for the employer (and law enforcement has access through the legal process to the employer). In the latter case, the CALEA requires the telephone service provider to provide to law enforcement authorities a copy of the digital stream being transported.

The CALEA exempts on-line information service providers such as America Online and Compuserve from its requirements. In the future, other CALEA issues may arise as the capabilities provided by advanced information technologies grow more sophisticated. For example, the technological capability exists to use Internet-based services to supply real-time voice communications.[3] Even today, a number of Internet and network service providers are capable of supporting (or are planning to support) real-time "push-to-talk" voice communications. The CALEA provides that a party providing communications services that in the judgment of the FCC are "a replacement for a substantial portion of the local telephone exchange service" may be deemed a carrier subject to the requirements of the CALEA. Thus, one possible path along which telecommunications services may evolve could lead to the imposition of CALEA requirements on information service providers, even though they were exempted as an essential element of a legislative compromise that enabled the CALEA to pass in the first place.

These possibilities are indicative of a more general problem: the fact that lines between "voice" and "data" services are being increasingly blurred. This issue is addressed in greater detail in Chapter 7.

6.2 OTHER LEVERS USED IN NATIONAL CRYPTOGRAPHY POLICY

The government has a number of tools to influence the possession and use of cryptography domestically and abroad. How the government uses these tools in the context of national cryptography policy reflects the government's view of how to balance the interests of the various stakeholders affected by cryptography.

---

[3]Fred Hapgood, "IPHONE," *Wired*, October 1995, p. 140; and Lawrence M. Fisher, "Long-Distance Phone Calls in the Internet," *New York Times*, March 14, 1995, p. D6.

6.2.1 Federal Information Processing Standards

Federal Information Processing Standards (FIPSs) are an important element of national cryptography policy, and all federal agencies are encouraged to cite FIPSs in their procurement specifications. (Box 6.1 contains a brief description of all FIPSs related to cryptography.) The National Institute of Standards and Technology (NIST) is responsible for issuing FIPSs.

FIPSs can have enormous significance to the private sector as well, despite the face that the existence of a FIPS does not legally compel a private party to adopt it. One reason is that to the extent that a FIPS is based on existing private sector standards (which it often is), it codifies standards of existing practice and contributes to a planning environment of greater certainty. A second reason is that a FIPS is often taken as a government endorsement of the procedures, practices, and algorithms contained therein, and thus a FIPS may set a de facto "best practices" standard for the private sector. A third reason is related to procurements that are FIPS-compliant as discussed in the next section.

NIST has traditionally relied on private sector standards-setting processes when developing FIPSs. Such practice reflects NIST's recognition of the fact that the standards it sets will be more likely to succeed—in terms of reducing procurement costs, raising quality, and influencing the direction of information technology market development—if they are supported by private producers and users.[4]

The existence of widely accepted standards is often an enormous boon to interoperability of computers and communication devices, and the converse is generally true as well: the absence of widely accepted standards often impedes the growth of a market.

In the domain of cryptography, FIPSs have had a mixed result. The promulgation of FIPS 46-1, the Data Encryption Standard (DES) algorithm for encrypting data, was a boon to cryptography and vendors of cryptographic products. On the other hand, the two cryptography-related FIPSs most recently produced by NIST (FIPS 185, the Escrowed Encryption Standard (EES), and FIPS 186, the Digital Signature Standard (DSS)) have met with a less favorable response. Neither was consistent with existing de facto industry standards or practice, and both met with significant negative response from private industry and users.[5]

---

[4]Carl F. Cargill, *Information Technology Standardization*, Digital Press, Bedford, Mass., 1989, p. 213.

[5]The story of resistance to the EES is provided in Susan Landau et al., *Codes, Keys, and Conflicts*, Association for Computing Machinery Inc., Washington, D.C., June 1994, p. 48; to DSS, in Landau et al., *Codes, Keys, and Conflicts*, 1994, pp. 41-43. In the case of DSS, a de facto industry standard had already emerged based on RSA Data Security Inc.'s public-key algorithm.

BOX 6.1
Cryptography-related Federal Information Processing Standards

- *FIPS 46, 46-1 and 46-2:* Data Encryption Standard (DES). Specification of DES algorithm and rules for implementing DES in hardware. FIPS 46-1 recertifies DES and extends it for software implementation. FIPS 46-2 reaffirms the Data Encryption Standard algorithm until 1998 and allows for its implementation in software, firmware or hardware. Several other FIPSs address interoperability and security requirements for using DES in the physical layer of data communications (FIPS 139) and in fax machines (FIPS 141), guidelines for implementing and using DES (FIPS 74), modes of operation of DES (FIPS 81), and use of DES for authentication purposes (FIPS 113).

- *FIPS 180-1:* Secure Hash Standard. This standard specifies a Secure Hash Algorithm (SHA) that can be used to generate a condensed representation of a message called a message digest. The SHA is required for use with the Digital Signature Algorithm (DSA) as specified in the Digital Signature Standard (DSS) and whenever a secure hash algorithm is required for federal applications. The SHA is used by both the transmitter and intended receiver of a message in computing and verifying a digital signature.

- *FIPS 186:* Digital Signature Standard. This standard specifies a Digital Signature Algorithm (DSA) appropriate for applications requiring a digital rather than a written signature. The DSA digital signature is a pair of large numbers represented in a computer as strings of binary digits. The digital signature is computed using a set of rules (i.e., the DSA) and a set of parameters such that the identity of the signatory and integrity of the data can be verified. The DSA provides the capability to generate and verify signatures.

- *FIPS 140-1:* Security Requirements for Cryptographic Modules. This standard provides specifications for cryptographic modules which can be used within computer and telecommunications systems to protect unclassified information in a variety of different applications.

- *FIPS 185:* Escrowed Encryption Standard (see main text).

- *FIPS 171:* Key Management Using ANSI X9.17. This standard specifies a selection of options for the automated distribution of keying material by the federal government when using the protocols of ANSI X9.17. The standard defines procedures for the manual and automated management of keying materials and contains a number of options. The selected options will allow the development of cost-effective systems that will increase the likelihood of interoperability.

Other FIPSs that address matters related more generally to computer security include the following:

- *FIPS 48:* Guidelines on Evaluation of Techniques for Automated Personal Identification,
- *FIPS 83:* Guidelines on User Authentication Techniques for Computer Network Access Control,
- *FIPS 112:* Password Usage,
- *FIPS 113:* Computer Data Authentication, and
- *FIPS 73:* Guidelines for Security of Computer Applications.

The promulgation of the EES and the DSS, as well as current Administration plans to promulgate a modification of the EES to accommodate escrowed encryption for data storage and communications and another FIPS for key escrow to performance requirements for escrow agents and for escrowed encryption products, has generated a mixed market reaction. Some companies see the promulgation of these standards as a market opportunity, while others see these standards as creating yet more confusion and uncertainty in pushing escrowed encryption on a resistant market.

Appendix M contains a general discussion of FIPSs and the standards-setting process.

6.2.2 The Government Procurement Process

Government procurement occurs in two domains. One domain is special-purpose equipment and products, for which government is the only consumer. Such products are generally classified in certain ways; weapons and military-grade cryptography are two examples. The other domain is procurement of products that are useful in both the private and public sectors.

Where equipment and products serve both government and private sector needs, in some instances the ability of the government to buy in bulk guarantees vendors a large enough market to take advantage of mass production, thereby driving down for all consumers the unit costs of a product that the government is buying in bulk. Through its market power, government has some ability to affect the price of products that are offered for sale on the open market. Furthermore, acceptance by the government is often taken as a "seal of approval" for a given product that reassures potential buyers in the private sector.

History offers examples with variable success in promoting the widespread public use of specific information technologies through the use of government standards.

• The DES was highly successful. DES was first adopted as a cryptographic standard for federal use in 1975. Since then, its use has become commonplace in cryptographic applications around the world, and many implementations of DES now exist worldwide.

• A less successful standard is GOSIP, the Government OSI Profile, FIPS 146.[6] The GOSIP was intended to specify the details of an OSI configuration for use in the government so that interoperable OSI net-

---

[6]OSI refers to Open Systems Interconnect, a standardized suite of international networking protocols developed and promulgated in the early 1980s.

work products could be procured from commercial vendors and to encourage the market development of products. GOSIP has largely failed in this effort, and network products based on the TCP/IP protocols now dominate the market.[7]

In the case of the EES, the government chose not to seek legislation outlawing cryptography without features for exceptional access, but chose instead to use the EES to influence the marketplace for cryptography. This point was acknowledged by Administration officials to the committee on a number of occasions. Specifically, the government hoped that the adoption of the EES to ensure secure communications within the government and for communications of other parties with the federal government would lead to a significant demand for EES-compliant devices, thus making possible production in larger quantities and thereby driving unit costs down and making EES-compliant devices more attractive to other users. A secondary effect would be the fact that two nongovernmental parties wishing to engage in secure communications would be most likely to use EES-compliant devices if they already own them rather than purchase other devices. As part of this strategy to influence the market, the government persuaded AT&T in 1992 to base a secure telephone on the EES.

In the case of the Fortezza card, the large government procurement for use with the Defense Messaging System may well lower unit costs sufficiently that vendors of products intended solely for the commercial nondefense market will build support for the Fortezza card into their products.[8] Given the wide availability of PC-Card slots on essentially all notebook and laptop computers, it is not inconceivable that the security advantages offered by hardware-based authentication would find a wide commercial market. At the same time, the disadvantages of hardware-based cryptographic functionality discussed in Chapter 5 would remain as well.

6.2.3 Implementation of Policy: Fear, Uncertainty, Doubt, Delay, Complexity

The implementation of policy contributes to how those affected by policy will respond to it. This important element is often unstated, and it refers to the role of government in creating a climate of predictability. A

---

[7]See Computer Science and Telecommunications Board, National Research Council, *Realizing the Information Future: The Internet and Beyond*, National Academy Press, Washington, D.C., 1994, Chapter 6.

[8]In a recent contract, a vendor agreed to provide Fortezza cards at $69 per card. See Paul Constance, "After Complaining $99 Was Too Low, Fortezza Vendors Come in at $69," *Government Computer News*, October 2, 1995, p. 6.

government that speaks with multiple voices on a question of policy, or one that articulates isolated elements of policy in a piecemeal fashion, or one that leaves the stakeholders uncertain about what is or is not permissible, creates an environment of fear, uncertainty, and doubt that can inhibit action. Such an environment can result from a deliberate choice on the part of policy makers, or it can be inadvertent, resulting from overlapping and/or multiple sources of authority that may have at least partial responsibility for the policy area in question. Decisions made behind closed doors and protected by government security classifications tend to reinforce the concerns of those who believe that fear, uncertainty, and doubt are created deliberately rather than inadvertently.

The committee observes that cryptography policy has indeed been shrouded in secrecy for many years and that many agencies have partial responsibility in this area. It also believes that fear, uncertainty, and doubt are common in the marketplace. For example, the introduction of nonmarket-driven standards such as the DSS and the EES may have created market uncertainty that impeded the rapid proliferation of high-quality products with encryption capabilities both internationally and domestically. Uncertainty over whether or not the federal government would recertify the DES as a FIPS has plagued the marketplace in recent years, because withdrawal of the DES as a FIPS could cause considerable consternation among some potential buyers that might suddenly be using products based on a decertified standard, although in fact the government has recertified the DES in each case. On the other hand, the DES is also a standard of the American National Standards Institute and the American Banking Association, and if these organizations continue to endorse it, the DES will arguably represent a viable algorithm for a wide range of products.

Many parties in industry believe that the complexity and opacity of the decision-making process with respect to cryptography are major contributors to this air of uncertainty. Of course, the creation of uncertainty may be desirable from the perspective of policy makers if their goal is to retard action in a given area. Impeding the spread of high-quality products with encryption capabilities internationally is the stated and explicit goal of export controls; on the domestic front, impeding the spread of high-quality products with encryption capabilities has been a desirable outcome from the standpoint of senior officials in the law enforcement community.

A very good example of the impact of fear, uncertainty, and doubt on the marketplace for cryptography can be found in the impact of government action (or more precisely, inaction) with respect to authentication. As noted in Chapter 2, cryptography supports digital signatures, a technology that provides high assurance for both data integrity and user authentication. However, federal actions in this area have led to considerable controversy. One example is that the federal government failed to adopt what was (and still is) the de facto commercial standard algorithm on digital signatures, namely the RSA algorithm. Government sources told the committee that the fact that the RSA algorithm is capable of providing strong confidentiality as well as digital signatures was one reason that the government deemed it inappropriate for promulgation as a FIPS.[9] Further, the government's adoption of the Digital Signature Standard[10] in 1993 occurred despite widespread opposition from industry to the specifics of that standard.

6.2.4 R&D Funding

An agency that supports research (and/or conducts such research on its own in-house) in a given area of technology is often able to shape the future options from which the private sector and policy makers will choose. For example, an agency that wishes to maintain a monopoly of expertise in a given area may not fund promising research proposals that originate from outside. Multiple agencies active in funding a given area may thus yield a broader range of options for future policy makers.

In the context of cryptography and computer and communications security, it is relevant that the National Security Agency (NSA) has been the main supporter and performer of R&D in this area.[11] The NSA's R&D

---

[9]The specific concern was that widespread adoption of RSA as a signature standard would result in an infrastructure that could support the easy and convenient distribution of DES keys. The two other reasons for the government's rejection of RSA were the desire to promulgate an approach to digital signatures that would be royalty-free (RSA is a patented algorithm) and the desire to reduce overall system costs for digital signatures. For a discussion of the intellectual issues involved in the rejection of the RSA algorithm and the concern over confidentiality, see Office of Technology Assessment, *Information Security and Privacy in Network Environments*, OTA-TCT-606, U.S. Government Printing Office, Washington, D.C., September 1994, pp. 167-168 and pp. 217-222.

[10]The DSS is based on an unclassified algorithm known as the Digital Signature Algorithm that does not explicitly support confidentiality. However, the DSS and its supporting documentation do amount to U.S. government endorsement of a particular one-way hash function, and document in detail how to generate the appropriate number-theoretic constants needed to implement it. Given this standard, it is possible to design a confidentiality standard that is as secure as the DSS. In other words, the DSS is a road map to a confidentiality standard, although it is not such a standard explicitly. Whether an ersatz confidentiality standard would pass muster in the commercial market remains to be seen.

[11]It is important to distinguish between R&D undertaken internally and externally to NSA. Internal R&D work can be controlled and kept private to NSA; by contrast, it is much more difficult to control the extent to which external R&D work is disseminated. Thus, decisions regarding specific external cryptography-related R&D projects could promote or inhibit public knowledge of cryptography.

orientation has been, quite properly, on technologies that would help it to perform more effectively and efficiently its two basic missions: (1) defending national security by designing and deploying strong cryptography to protect classified information and (2) performing signals intelligence against potential foreign adversaries. In the information security side of the operation, NSA-developed technology has extraordinary strengths that have proven well suited to the protection of classified information relevant to defense or foreign policy needs.

How useful such technologies will prove for corporate information security remains to be seen. Increasing needs for information security in the private sector suggest that NSA technology may have much to offer, especially if such technology can be made available to the private sector without limitation. At the same time, the environment in which private sector information security needs are manifested may be different enough from the defense and foreign policy worlds that these technologies may not be particularly relevant in practice to the private sector. Furthermore, the rapid pace of commercial developments in information technology may make it difficult for the private sector to use technologies developed for national security purposes in a less rapidly changing environment.

These observations suggest that commercial needs for cryptographic technology may be able to draw on NSA technologies for certain applications, and most certainly will draw on nonclassified R&D work in cryptography (both in the United States and abroad); even the latter will have a high degree of sophistication. Precisely how the private sector will draw on these two sources of technology will depend on policy decisions to be made in the future. Finally, it is worth noting that nonclassified research on cryptography appearing in the open literature has been one of the most important factors leading to the dilemma that policy makers face today with respect to cryptography.

6.2.5 Patents and Intellectual Property

A number of patents involving cryptography have been issued. Patents affect cryptography because patent protection can be used by both vendors and governments to keep various patented approaches to cryptography out of broad use in the public domain.[12]

The DES, first issued in 1977, is an open standard, and the algorithm it uses is widely known. According to NIST, devices implementing the DES may be covered by U.S. and foreign patents issued to IBM (although the original patents have by now expired).[13] However, IBM granted

---

[12]See footnote 9.

[13]National Institute of Standards and Technology, "FIPS 46-2: Announcing the Data Encryption Standard," NIST, Gaithersburg, Md., December 30, 1993.

nonexclusive, royalty-free licenses under the patents to make, use, and sell apparatus that complies with the standard.

RSA Data Security Inc. (RSA) holds the licensing rights to RC2, RC4, and RC5, which are variable-key-length ciphers developed by Ronald Rivest.[14] RC2 and RC4 are not patented, but rather are protected as trade secrets (although both algorithms have been published on the Internet without RSA's approval). RSA has applied for a patent for RC5 and has proposed it as a security standard for the Internet. Another alternative for data encryption is IDEA, a block cipher developed by James Massey and Xueija Lai of the Swiss Federal Institute of Technology (ETH), Zurich. The patent rights to IDEA are held by Ascom Systec AG, a Swiss firm. IDEA is implemented in the software application PGP.

In addition to the above patents, which address symmetric-key encryption technologies, there are several important patent issues related to public-key cryptography. The concept of public-key cryptography, as well as some specific implementing methods, is covered by U.S. Patents 4,200,770 (M. Hellman, W. Diffie, and R. Merkle, 1980) and 4,218,582 (M. Hellman and R. Merkle, 1980), both of which are owned by Stanford University. The basic patent for the RSA public-key crypto-system, U.S. Patent 4,405,829 (R. Rivest, A. Shamir, and L. Adelman, 1983), is owned by the Massachusetts Institute of Technology. The 4,218,582 patent has counterparts in several other countries. These basic public-key patents and related ones have been licensed to many vendors worldwide. With the breakup of the partnership that administered the licensing of Stanford University's and MIT's patents, the validity of the various patents has become the subject of current litigation. In any event, the terms will expire in 1997 for the first two of the above patents and in 2000 for the third.[15]

In 1994, NIST issued the Digital Signature Standard, FIPS 186. The DSS uses the NIST-developed Digital Signature Algorithm, which according to NIST is available for use without a license. However, during the DSS's development, concern arose about whether the DSS might infringe on the public-key patents cited above, as well as a patent related to signature verification held by Claus Schnorr of Goethe University in Frankfurt, Germany.[16] NIST asserts that the DSS does not infringe on any of these

---

[14]See RSA Data Security Inc. home page at http://www.rsa.com.

[15]In 1994, Congress changed patent terms from 17 years after issuance to 20 years from the date of filing the patent application; however, applications for these patents were filed in or before 1977, and so they will not be affected.

[16]See Office of Technology Assessment, *Information Security and Privacy in Network Environments,* 1994, p. 220.

patents.[17] At the least, U.S. government users have the right to use public-key cryptography without paying a license fee for the Stanford and MIT patents because the concepts were developed at these universities with federal research support. However, there remains some disagreement about whether commercial uses of the DSS (e.g., in a public-key infrastructure) will require a license from one or more of the various patent holders.

A potential patent dispute regarding the key-escrow features of the EES may have been headed off by NIST's negotiation of a nonexclusive licensing agreement with Silvio Micali in 1994.[18] Micali has patents that are relevant to dividing a key into components that can be separately safeguarded (e.g., by escrow agents) and later combined to recover the original key.

A provision of the U.S. Code (Title 35, U.S.C., Section 181) allows the Patent and Trademark Office (PTO) to withhold a patent and order that the invention be kept secret if publication of the patent is detrimental to national security. Relevant to cryptography is the fact that a patent application for the Skipjack encryption algorithm was filed on February 7, 1994. This application was examined and all of the claims allowed, and notification of the algorithm's patentability was issued on March 28, 1995. Based on a determination by NSA, the Armed Services Patent Advisory Board issued a secrecy order for the Skipjack patent application; the effect of the secrecy order is that even though Skipjack can be patented, a patent will not be issued until the secrecy order is rescinded. Since applications are kept in confidence until a patent is issued, no uninvolved party can find out any information concerning the application. In this way, the patentability of the algorithm has been established without having to disclose the detailed information publicly.[19] Since 35 U.S.C. 181 also provides that the PTO can rescind the secrecy order upon notification that publication is no longer detrimental to national security, compromise and subsequent public revelation of the Skipjack algorithm (e.g., through reverse engineering of a Clipper chip) might well cause a patent to be issued for Skipjack that would give the U.S. government control over its subsequent use in products.

---

[17]National Institute of Standards and Technology, "Digital Signature Standard," Computer Systems Laboratory (CSL) Bulletin, NIST, Gaithersburg, Md., November 1994. Available on-line at http://csrc.ncsl.nist.gov/nistbul/csl94-11.txt.

[18]National Institute of Standards and Technology press release, "Patent Agreement Removes Perceived Barrier to Telecommunications Security System," NIST, Gaithersburg, Md., July 11, 1994. Available on-line at gopher://rigel.nist.gov:7346/0/.docs/.releases/N94-28.REL.

[19]Clinton C. Brooks, National Security Agency, provided this information to the committee in an e-mail message dated May 23, 1995.

6.2.6 Formal and Informal Arrangements with Various Other Governments and Organizations

International agreements can be an important part of national policy. For example, for many years the Coordinating Committee (CoCom) nations cooperated in establishing a common export control policy on militarily significant items with civilian purposes, including cryptography (Appendix G has more details).

International agreements can take a variety of different forms. The most formal type of agreement is a treaty between (or among) nations that specifies the permissible, required, and prohibited actions of the various nations. Treaties require ratification by the relevant national political bodies as well as signature before entry into force. In the United States treaties must be approved by the U.S. Senate by a two-thirds vote. Sometimes treaties are self-executing, but often they need to be followed by implementing legislation enacted by the Congress in the normal manner for legislation.

Another type of agreement is an executive agreement. In the United States, executive agreements are, as the name implies, entered into by the executive branch. Unlike the treaty, no Senate ratification is involved, but the executive branch has frequently sought approval by a majority of both houses of the Congress. For all practical purposes executive agreements with other countries bind the United States in international law just as firmly as treaties do, although a treaty may carry greater weight internally due to the concurrence by a two-thirds vote of the Senate. Executive agreements can also be changed with much greater flexibility than treaties.

Finally, nations can agree to cooperate through diplomacy. Even though cooperation is not legally required under such arrangements, informal understandings can work very effectively so long as relationships remain good and the countries involved continue to have common goals. In fact, informal understanding is the main product of much diplomacy and is the form that most of the world's business between governments takes. For example, although the United States maintains formal mutual legal assistance treaties with a number of nations, U.S. law enforcement agencies cooperate (sometimes extensively) with foreign counterparts in a much larger number of nations. Indeed, in some instances, such cooperation is stronger, more reliable, and more extensive than is the case with nations that are a party to a formal mutual legal assistance treaty with the United States.

Note that the more formal the agreement, the more public is the substance of the agreement; such publicity often leads to attention that may compromise important and very sensitive matters, such as the extent to which a nation supports a given policy position or the scope and nature of a nation's capabilities. When informal arrangements are negotiated and entered into force, they may not be known by all citizens or even by all parts of the governments involved. Because they are less public, informal arrangements also allow more latitude for governments to make decisions on a case-by-case basis. In conducting negotiations that may involve sensitive matters or agreements that may require considerable flexibility, governments are often inclined to pursue more informal avenues of approach.

6.2.7 Certification and Evaluation

Analogous to *Good Housekeeping* seals of approval or "check ratings" for products reviewed in *Consumer Reports*, independent testing and certification of products can provide assurance in the commercial marketplace that a product can indeed deliver the services and functionality that it purports to deliver. For example, the results of government crash tests of automobiles are widely circulated as data relevant to consumer purchases of automobiles. Government certification that a commercial airplane is safe to fly provides significant reassurance to the public about flight safety. At the same time, while evaluation and certification would in principle help users to avoid products that implement a sound algorithm in a way that undermines the security offered by the algorithm, the actual behavior of users demonstrates that certification of a product is not necessarily a selling point. Many of the DES products in the United States have never been evaluated relative to FS 1027 or FIPS 140-1, and yet such products are used by many parties.

The government track record in the cryptography and computer security domain is mixed. For example, a number of DES products were evaluated with respect to FS 1027 (the precursor to FIPS 140-1) over several years and a number of products were certified by NSA. For a time, government agencies purchased DES hardware only if it met FS 1027, or FIPS 140. Commercial clients often required compliance because it provided the only assurance that a product embodying DES was secure in a broader sense. In this case, the alignment between government and commercial security requirements seems to have been reasonably good, and thus this program had some success. Two problems with this evaluation program were that it addressed only hardware and that it lagged in allowing use of public-key management technology in products (in the absence of suitable standards).

A second attempt to provide product evaluation was represented by the National Computer Security Center (NCSC), which was established by the Department of Defense (DOD) for the purpose of certifying various computer systems for security. The theory underlying the center was that the government needed secure systems but could not afford to build them. The quid pro quo was that industry would design and implement secure operating systems that the government would test and evaluate at no cost to industry; systems meeting government requirements would receive a seal of approval.

Although the NCSC still exists, the security evaluation program it sponsors, the Trusted Product Evaluation Program (TPEP), has more or less lapsed into disuse. In the judgment of many, the TPEP was a relative failure because of an underlying premise that the information security problems of the government and the private sector were identical to those of the defense establishment. In fact, the private sector has for the most part found that a military approach to computer security is inadequate for its needs. A second major problem was that the time scale of the evaluation process was much longer than the private sector could tolerate, and products that depended on NCSC evaluation would reach market already on the road to obsolescence, perhaps superseded by a new version to which a given evaluation would not necessarily apply. In late 1995, articles in the trade press reported that the DOD was attempting to revive the evaluation program in a way that would involve private contractors.[20]

A recent attempt to provide certification services is the Cryptographic Module Validation Program (CMVP) to test products for conformance to FIPS 140-1, *Security Requirements for Cryptographic Modules.*[21] FIPS 140-1 provides a broad framework for all NIST cryptographic standards, specifying design, function, and documentation requirements for cryptographic modules—including hardware, software, "firmware," and combinations thereof—used to protect sensitive, unclassified information in computer and telecommunication systems.[22] The CMVP was established in July 1995 by NIST and the Communications Security Establishment of the government of Canada.

The validation program is currently optional: agencies may purchase products based on a vendor's written assurance of compliance with the standard. However, beginning in 1997, U.S. federal procurement will require cryptographic products to be validated by an independent, third

---

[20]See, for example, Paul Constance, "Secure Products List Gets CPR," *Government Computing News,* November 13, 1995, p. 40.

[21]National Institute of Standards and Technology press release, "Cryptographic Module Validation Program Announced," NIST, Gaithersburg, Md., July 17, 1995.

[22]National Institute of Standards and Technology, *Federal Information Processing Standards Publication 140-1: Security Requirements for Cryptographic Modules,* NIST, Gaithersburg, Md., January 11, 1994.

party. Under the program, vendors will submit their products for testing by an independent, NIST-accredited laboratory.[23]

Such a laboratory evaluates both the product and its associated documentation against the requirements in FIPS 140-1. NIST has also specified test procedures for all aspects of the standard. Examples include attempting to penetrate tamper-resistant coatings and casings, inspecting software source code and documentation, attempting to bypass protection of stored secret keys, and statistically verifying the performance of random number generators.[24] The vendor sends the results of independent tests to NIST, which determines whether these results show that the tested product complies with the standard and then issues validation certificates for products that do. Time will tell whether the CMVP will prove more successful than the NCSC.

6.2.8 Nonstatutory Influence

By virtue of its size and role in society, government has considerable ability to influence public opinion and to build support for policies. In many cases, this ability is not based on specific legislative authority, but rather on the use of the "bully pulpit." For example, the government can act in a convening role to bring focus and to stimulate the private sector to work on a problem.[25] The bully pulpit can be used to convey a sense of urgency that is tremendously important in how the private sector reacts, especially large companies that try to be good corporate citizens and responsive to informal persuasion by senior government officials. Both vendors and users can be influenced by such authority.[26]

---

[23]As of September 1995, the National Institute of Standards and Technology's National Voluntary Laboratory Accreditation Program had accredited three U.S. companies as competent to perform the necessary procedures: CygnaCom Solutions Laboratory (McLean, Va.), DOMUS Software Limited (Ottawa, Canada), and InfoGard Laboratories (San Luis Obispo, Calif.). A current list of these companies is available on-line at http://csrc.ncsl.nist.gov/fips/1401labs.txt.

[24]National Institute of Standards and Technology, *Derived Test Requirements for FIPS Publication 140-1*, NIST, Gaithersburg, Md., March 1995.

[25]One advantage of government's acting in this way is that it may provide some assurance to the private sector that any coordinated action taken in response to government calls for action will be less likely to be interpreted by government as a violation of antitrust provisions.

[26]For example, in responding favorably to a request by President Clinton for a particular action in a labor dispute, the chairman of American Airlines noted, "He [President Clinton] is the elected leader of the country. For any citizen or any company or any union to say 'No, I won't do that' to the President requires an awfully good reason." See Gwen Ifill, "Strike at American Airlines; Airline Strike Ends as Clinton Steps In," *New York Times*, November 23, 1993, p. 1.

In the security domain, the Clinton Administration has sponsored several widely publicized public meetings to address security dimensions of the national information infrastructure (NII). These meetings were meetings of the NII Security Issues Forum, held in 1994 and 1995.[27] They were announced in the *Federal Register* and were intended to provide a forum in which members of the interested public could air their concerns about security.

In the cryptography domain, the U.S. government has used its convening authority to seek comments on various proposed cryptographic standards and to hold a number of workshops related to key escrow (discussed in Chapter 5). Many in the affected communities believe that these attempts at outreach were too few and too late to influence anything more than the details of a policy outline on which the government had already decided. A second example demonstrating the government's nonstatutory influence was the successful government request to AT&T to base the 3600 Secure Telephone Unit on the Clipper chip instead of an unescrowed DES chip (as described in Appendix E).

6.2.9 Interagency Agreements Within the Executive Branch

Given that one government agency may have expertise or personnel that would assist another agency in doing its job better, government agencies often conclude agreements between them that specify the terms and nature of their cooperative efforts. In the domain of cryptography policy, NSA's technical expertise in the field has led to memorandums of understanding with NIST and with the FBI (Appendix N).

The memorandum of understanding (MOU) between NIST and NSA outlines several areas of cooperation between the two agencies that are intended to implement the Computer Security Act of 1987; joint NIST-NSA activities are described in Box 6.2. This MOU has been the subject of some controversy, with critics believing that the MOU and its implementation cede too much authority to NSA and defenders believing that the

---

[27]Office of Management and Budget press release, "National Information Infrastructure Security Issues Forum Releases 'NII Security: The Federal Role,'" Washington, D.C., June 14, 1995. The subjects of these meetings were "Commercial Security on the NII," which focused on the need for intellectual property rights protection in the entertainment, software, and computer industries; "Security of Insurance and Financial Information"; "Security of Health and Education Information"; "Security of the Electronic Delivery of Government Services and Information"; "Security for Intelligent Transportation Systems and Trade Information"; and "The NII: Will It Be There When You Need It?," addressing the availability and reliability of the Internet, the public switched telecommunicatins network, and cable, wireless, and satellite communications services. Available on-line at gopher://ntiant1.ntia.doc.gov:70/00/iitf/security/files/fedworld.txt.

BOX 6.2
Overview of Joint NIST-NSA Activities

The National Security Agency provides technical advice and assistance to the National Institute of Standards and Technology in accordance with Public Law 100-235, the Computer Security Act of 1987. An overview of NIST-NSA activities follows.

National conference. NIST and NSA jointly sponsor, organize, and chair the prestigious National Computer Security Conference, held yearly for the past 16 years. The conference is attended by over 2,000 people from government and private industry.

Common criteria. NSA is providing technical assistance to NIST for the development of computer security criteria that would be used by both the civilian and defense sides of the government. Representatives from Canada and Europe are joining the United States in the development of the criteria.

Product evaluations. NIST and NSA are working together to perform evaluations of computer security products. In the Trusted Technology Assessment Program, evaluations of some computer security products will be performed by NIST and its laboratories, while others will be performed by NSA. NIST and NSA engineers routinely exchange information and experiences to ensure uniformity of evaluations.

Standards development. NSA supports NIST in the development of standards that promote interoperability among security products. Sample standards include security protocol standards, digital signature standards, key management standards, and encryption algorithm standards (e.g., the DES, Skipjack).

Research and development. Under the Joint R&D Technology Exchange Program, NIST and NSA hold periodic technical exchanges to share information on new and ongoing programs. Research and development are performed in areas such as security architectures, labeling standards, privilege management, and identification and authentication. Test-bed activities are conducted in areas related to electronic mail, certificate exchange and management, protocol conformity, and encryption technologies.

SOURCE: National Security Agency, April 1994 (as reprinted in Office of Technology Assessment, *Information Security and Privacy in Network Environments*, OTA-TCT-606, U.S. Government Printing Office, Washington D.C., September 1994, Box 4-8, p. 165).

MOU is faithful to both the spirit and letter of the Computer Security Act of 1987.[28]

The MOU between the FBI and NSA, declassified for the National Research Council, states that the NSA will provide assistance to the FBI upon request, when the assistance is consistent with NSA policy (includ-

---

[28]For more discussion of these critical perspectives, see Office of Technology Assessment, *Information Security and Privacy in Network Environments*, 1994, Box 4-8, pp. 164-171.

ing protection of sources and methods), and in accordance with certain administrative requirements. Furthermore, if the assistance requested is for the support of an activity that may be conducted only pursuant to a court order or with the authorization of the Attorney General, the FBI request to the NSA must include a copy of that order or authorization.

In 1995, the National Security Agency, the Advanced Research Projects Agency, and the Defense Information Systems Agency (DISA) signed a memorandum of agreement (MOA) to coordinate research and development efforts in system security. This MOA provides for the establishment of the Information Systems Security Research-Joint Technology Office (ISSR-JTO). The role of the ISSR-JTO is "to optimize use of the limited research funds available, and strengthen the responsiveness of the programs to DISA, expediting delivery of technologies that meet DISA's requirements to safeguard the confidentiality, integrity, authenticity, and availability of data in DOD information systems, provide a robust first line of defense for defensive information warfare, and permit electronic commerce between the DOD and its contractors."[29]

6.3 ORGANIZATION OF THE FEDERAL GOVERNMENT WITH RESPECT TO INFORMATION SECURITY

6.3.1 Role of National Security vis-à-vis Civilian Information Infrastructures

The extent to which the traditional national security model is appropriate for an information infrastructure supporting both civilian and military applications is a major point of contention in the public debate. There are two schools of thought on this subject:

• The traditional national security model should be applied to the national information infrastructure, because protecting those networks also protects services that are essential to the military, and the role of the defense establishment is indeed to protect important components of the national infrastructure that private citizens and businesses depend upon.[30]

---

[29]See "Memorandum of Agreement Between the Advanced Research Projects Agency, the Defense Information Systems Agency, and the National Security Agency Concerning the Information Systems Security Research-Joint Technology Office"; MOA effective April 2, 1995. The full text of the MOA is available in Appendix N and on-line at http://www.ito.darpa.mil/ResearchAreas/Information_Survivability/MOA.html.

[30]For example, the Joint Security Commission recommended that "policy formulation for information systems security be consolidated under a joint DoD/DCI security executive committee, and that the committee oversee development of a coherent network-oriented information systems security policy for the DoD and the Intelligence Community that could also serve the entire government." See Joint Security Commission, *Redefining Security*, Washington, D.C., February 28, 1994, p. 107.

• The traditional national security model should not be applied to the national information infrastructure, because the needs of civilian activities are so different from those of the military, and the imposition of a national security model would impose an unacceptable burden on the civilian sector. Proponents of this view argue that the traditional national security model of information security—a top-down approach to information security management—would be very difficult to scale up to a highly heterogeneous private sector involving hundreds of millions of people and tens of millions of computers in the United States alone.

There is essential unanimity that the world of classified information (both military and nonmilitary) is properly a domain in which the DOD and NSA can and should exercise considerable influence. But moving outside this domain raises many questions that have a high profile in the public debate—specifically, what the DOD and NSA role should be in dealing with the following categories of information:

1. Unclassified government information that is military in nature,
2. Unclassified government information that is nonmilitary in nature, and
3. Nongovernment information.

To date, policy decisions have been made that give the DOD jurisdiction in information security policy for category 1. For categories 2 and 3, the debate continues. It is clear that the security needs for business and for national security purposes are both similar (Box 6.3) and different (Box 6.4). In category 2, the argument is made that DOD and NSA have a great deal of expertise in protecting information, and that the government should draw on an enormous historical investment in NSA expertise to protect all government information. At the same time, NIST has the responsibility for protecting such information under the Computer Security Act of 1987, with NSA's role being one of providing technical assistance. Some commentators believe that NIST has not received resources adequate to support its role in this area.[31]

---

[31]For example, the Office of Technology Assessment stated that "the current state of government security practice for unclassified information has been depressed by the chronic shortage of resources for NIST's computer security activities in fulfillment of its government-wide responsibilities under the Computer Security Act of 1987. Since enactment of the Computer Security Act, there has been no serious (i.e., adequately funded and properly staffed), sustained effort to establish a center of information-security expertise and leadership outside the defense/intelligence communities." See Office of Technology Assessment, *Issue Update on Information Security and Privacy in Network Environments*, OTA-BP-ITC-147, U.S. Government Printing Office, Washington, D.C., June 1995, p. 42. A similar conclusion

> **BOX 6.3**
> **Similarities in Commercial Security Needs and National Security Needs**
>
> • Strong aversion to public discussion of security breaches. Information about threats is regarded as highly sensitive. Such a classification makes it very difficult to conduct effective user education, because security awareness depends on an understanding of the true scope and nature of a threat.
> • Need to make cost-benefit trade-offs in using security technology. Neither party can afford the resources to protect against an arbitrary threat model.
> • Strong preference for self-reliance (government relying on government, industry relying on industry) to meet security needs.
> • Strong need for high security. Both government and industry need strong cryptography with no limitations for certain applications. However, the best technology and tools are often reserved for government and military use because commercial deployment cannot be adequately controlled, resulting in opportunities for adversaries to obtain and examine the systems so that they can plan how to exploit them.
> • Increasing reliance on commercial products in many domains (business, Third World nations).
> • Increasing scale and sophistication of the security threat for businesses, which is now approaching that posed by foreign intelligence services and foreign governments.
> • Possibility that exceptional access to encrypted information and data may become important to commercial entities.

In category 3, the same argument is made with respect to non-government information on the grounds that the proper role of government is to serve the needs of the entire nation. A second argument is made that the military depends critically on nongovernment information infrastructures (e.g., the public switched telecommunications network) and that it is essential to protect those networks not just for civilian use but also for military purposes. (Note that NSA does not have broad authority to assist private industry with information security, although it does conduct for industry, upon request, unclassified briefings related to foreign information security threats; NSD 42 (text provided in Appendix N) also gives NSA

---

was reached by the Board on Assessment of NIST Programs of the National Research Council, which wrote that "the Computer Security Division is severely understaffed and underfunded given its statutory security responsibilities, the growing national recognition of the need to protect unclassified but sensitive information, and the unique role the division can play in fostering security in commercial architectures, hardware, and software." See Board on Assessment of NIST Programs, National Research Council, *An Assessment of the National Institute of Standards and Technology, Fiscal Year 1993*, National Academy Press, Washington, D.C., 1994, p. 228.

BOX 6.4
**Differences in Commercial Security Needs and
National Security Needs**

• Business wants market-driven cryptographic technology; government is apprehensive about such technology. For example, standards are a critical element of market-driven cryptography. Market forces and the need to respond to rapidly evolving dynamic new markets demand an approach to establishing cryptographic standards; businesses want standards for interoperability, and they want to create market critical mass in order to lower the cost of cryptography.

• By its nature, the environment of business must include potential adversaries within its security perimeter. Commercial enterprises now realize that electronic delivery of their products and services to their customers will increase. They must design systems and processes explicitly so that customers can enter into transactions with considerable ease. Business strategies of today empower the customer through software and technology. Enterprise networks have value in allowing the maximum number of people to be attached to the network. Customers will choose which enterprise to enter in order to engage in electronic commerce, and making it difficult for the customer will result in loss of business. But adversaries masquerading as customers (or who indeed may be customers themselves) can enter as well. By contrast, the traditional national security model keeps potential adversaries outside the security perimeter, allowing access only to those with a real need. However, to the extent that U.S. military forces work in collaboration with forces of other nations, the security perimeter for the military may also become similarly blurred.

• Business paradigms value teamwork, openness, trust, empowerment, and speed. Such values are often difficult to sustain in the national security establishment. The cultures of the two worlds are different and are reflected in, for example, the unwillingness of business to use multilevel security systems designed for military use. Such systems failed the market test, although they met Defense Department criteria for security.

• National security resources (personnel with cryptographic expertise, funding) are much larger than the resources in nondefense government sectors and in private industry and universities. As a result, a great deal of cryptographic knowledge resides within the world of national security. Industry wants access to this knowledge to ensure appropriate use of protocols and strong algorithms, as well as development of innovative new products and services.

• National security places considerable emphasis on confidentiality as well as on authentication and integrity. Today's commercial enterprises stress authentication of users and data integrity much more than they stress confidentiality (although this balance may shift in the future). For example, improperly denying a junior military officer access to a computer facility may not be particularly important in a military context, whereas improperly denying a customer access to his bank account because of a faulty authentication can pose enormous problems for the bank.

• While both businesses and national security authorities have an interest in safeguarding secrets, the tools available to businesses to discourage individuals from disclosing secrets (generally civil suits) are less stringent than those available to national security authorities (criminal prosecution).

the authority to work with private industry when such work involves national security information systems used by private industry.)

6.3.2 Other Government Entities with Influence on Information Security

As noted above, NSA has primary responsibility for information security in the classified domain, while NIST has primary responsibility for information security in the unclassified domain, but for government information only. No organization or entity within the federal government has the responsibility for promoting information security in the private sector.[32]

The Security Policy Board (SPB) does have a coordination function. Specifically, the charge of the SPB is to consider, coordinate, and recommend for implementation to the President policy directives for U.S. security policies, procedures, and practices, including those related to security for both classified and unclassified government information. The SPB is intended to be the principal mechanism for reviewing and proposing legislation and executive orders pertaining to security policy, procedures, and practices. The Security Policy Advisory Board provides a nongovernmental perspective on security policy initiatives to the SPB and independent input on such matters to the President. The SPB does not have operational responsibilities.

Other entities supported by the federal government have some influence over information security, though little actual policy-making authority. These include:

- *The Computer Emergency Response Team (CERT).* CERT was formed by the Defense Advanced Research Projects Agency (DARPA) in November 1988 in response to the needs exhibited during the Internet worm incident. CERT's charge is to work with the Internet community to facilitate its response to computer security events involving Internet hosts, to take proactive steps to raise the community's awareness of computer security issues, and to conduct research targeted at improving the security of existing systems.[33] CERT offers around-the-clock technical assistance for responding to computer security incidents, educates users regarding product vulnerability

---

[32]This observation was also made in Computer Science and Telecommunications Board, National Research Council, *Computers at Risk: Safe Computing in the Information Age*, National Academy Press, Washington, D.C., 1991, a report that proposed an Information Security Foundation as the most plausible type of organization to promote information security in the private sector.

[33]Available on-line at http://www.sei.cmu.edu/technology/cert.faqintro.html.

through technical documents and seminars, and provides tools for users to undertake their own vulnerability analyses.

• *The Information Infrastructure Task Force's (IITF) National Information Infrastructure Security Issues Forum.* The forum is charged with addressing institutional, legal, and technical issues surrounding security in the NII. A draft report issued by the forum proposes federal actions to address these issues.[34] The intent of the report, and of the Security Issues Forum more generally, is to stimulate a dialogue on how the federal government should cooperate with other levels of government and the private sector to ensure that participants can trust the NII. The draft report proposes a number of security guidelines (proposed NII security tenets), the adoption of Organization of Economic Cooperation and Development security principles for use on the NII, and a number of federal actions to promote security.

• *The Computer System Security and Privacy Advisory Board (CSSPAB).* CSSPAB was created by the Computer Security Act of 1987 as a statutory federal public advisory committee. The law provides that the board shall identify emerging managerial, technical, administrative, and physical safeguard issues relative to computer systems security and privacy; advise the National Institute of Standards and Technology and the secretary of commerce on security and privacy issues pertaining to federal computer systems; and report its findings to the secretary of commerce, the directors of the Office of Management and Budget and the National Security Agency, and the appropriate committees of the Congress. The board's scope is limited to federal computer systems or those operated by a contractor on behalf of the federal government and which process sensitive but unclassified information. The board's authority does not extend to private sector systems, systems that process classified information, or DOD unclassified systems related to military or intelligence missions as covered by the Warner Amendment (10 U.S.C. 2315). The activities of the board bring it into contact with a broad cross section of the nondefense agencies and departments; consequently, it often deals with latent policy considerations and societal consequences of information technology.

• *The National Counterintelligence Center (NACIC).* Established in 1994 by Presidential Decision Directive NSC-24, NACIC is primarily responsible for coordinating national-level counterintelligence activities, and it reports to the National Security Council. Operationally, the NACIC works

---

[34]Office of Management and Budget press release, "National Information Infrastructure Security Issues Forum Releases 'NII Security: The Federal Role,'" Washington, D.C., June 14, 1995. Available on-line at gopher://ntiant1.ntia.doc.gov:70/00/iitf/security/files/fedworld.txt.

with private industry through an industry council (consisting of senior security officials or other senior officials of major U.S. corporations) and sponsors counterintelligence training and awareness programs, seminars, and conferences for private industry. NACIC also produces coordinated national-level, all-source, foreign intelligence threat assessments to support private sector entities having responsibility for the protection of classified, sensitive, or proprietary information, as well as such assessments for government use.[35]

In addition, a number of private organizations (e.g., trade or professional groups) are active in information security.

6.4 INTERNATIONAL DIMENSIONS OF CRYPTOGRAPHY POLICY

The cryptography policy of the United States must take into account a number of international dimensions. Most importantly, the United States does not have the unquestioned dominance in the economic, financial, technological, and political affairs of the world as it might have had at the end of World War II. Indeed, the U.S. economy is increasingly intertwined with that of other nations. To the extent that these economically significant links are based on communications that must be secure, cryptography is one aspect of ensuring such security. Differing national policies on cryptography that lead to difficulties in communicating internationally work against overall national policies that are aimed at opening markets and reducing commercial and trade barriers.

Other nations have the option to maintain some form of export controls on cryptography, as well as controls on imports and use of cryptography; such controls form part of the context in which U.S. cryptography policy must be formulated. Specifically, foreign export control regimes more liberal than that of the United States have the potential to undercut U.S. export control efforts to limit the spread of cryptography. On the other hand, foreign controls on imports and use of cryptography could vitiate relaxation of U.S. export control laws; indeed, relaxation of U.S. export controls laws might well prompt a larger number of nations to impose additional barriers on the import and use of cryptography within their borders. Finally, a number of other nations have no explicit laws regarding the use of cryptography, but nevertheless have tools at their

---

[35]National Counterintelligence Center (NACIC), *Counterintelligence News and Developments*, Issue No. 1, NACIC, Washington, D.C. This newsletter is available on-line at http://www. oss.net/oss.

disposal to discourage its use; such tools include laws related to the postal, telephone, and telegraph (PTT) system, laws related to content carried by electronic media, laws related to the protection of domestic industries that discourage the entry of foreign products, laws related to classification of patents, and informal arrangements related to licensing of businesses.

As a first step in harmonizing cryptography policies across national boundaries, the Organization for Economic Cooperation and Development (OECD) held a December 1995 meeting in France among member nations to discuss how these nations were planning to cope with the public policy problems posed by cryptography. What the Paris meeting made clear is that many OECD member nations are starting to come to grips with the public policy problems posed by encryption, but that the dialogue on harmonizing policies across national borders has not yet matured. Moreover, national policies are quite fluid at this time, with various nations considering different types of regulation regarding the use, export, and import of cryptography.

Appendix G contains more discussion of international issues relevant to national cryptography policy.

6.5 RECAP

While export controls and escrowed encryption are fundamental pillars of current national cryptography policy, many other aspects of government action also have some bearing on it. The Communications Assistance for Law Enforcement (Digital Telephony) Act calls attention to the relationship between access to a communications stream and government access to the plaintext associated with that digital stream. The former problem must be solved (and was solved, by the CALEA, for telephone communications) before the latter problem is relevant.

The government can influence the deployment and use of cryptography in many ways. Federal Information Processing Standards often set a "best practice" standard for the private sector, even though they have no official standing outside government use. By assuring large-volume sales when a product is new, government procurement practices can reduce the cost of preferred cryptography products to the private sector, giving these products a price advantage over possible competitors. Policy itself can be implemented in ways that instill action-inhibiting uncertainty in the private sector. Government R&D funding and patents on cryptographic algorithms can narrow technical options to some degree. Formal and informal arrangements with various other governments and organizations can promote various policies or types of cooperation. Product certification can be used to provide the information necessary for a flourishing free market in products with encryption capabilities. Convening authority can help to establish the importance of a topic or approach to policy.

In some ways, the debate over national cryptography policy reflects a tension in the role of the national security establishment with respect to information infrastructures that are increasingly important to civilian use. In particular, the use of cryptography has been the domain of national security and foreign policy for most of its history, a history that has led to a national cryptography policy that today has the effect of discouraging the use of cryptography in the private sector.

PART III

Policy Options, Findings, and Recommendations

PART III CONSISTS OF TWO CHAPTERS. *Chapter 7 considers diverse policy options ranging in scope and scale from large to small. Not every item described in Chapter 7 has been deemed worthy of adoption by the committee, but the committee hopes to broaden the public's understanding of crytography policy by discussing ideas that at least have the support of respectable and responsible elements of the various stakeholding communities.*

Chapter 8 is a synthesizing chapter that brings together threads of the previous seven chapters and presents the committee's findings and recommendations.

7

Policy Options for the Future

Current national cryptography policy defines only one point in the space of possible policy options. A major difficulty in the public debate over cryptography policy has been incomplete explanation of why the government has rejected certain policy options. Chapter 7 explores a number of possible alternatives to current national cryptography policy, selected by the committee either because they address an important dimension of national cryptography policy or because they have been raised by a particular set of stakeholders. Although in the committee's judgment these alternatives deserve analysis, it does not follow that they necessarily deserve consideration for adoption. The committee's judgments about appropriate policy options are discussed in Chapter 8.

7.1 EXPORT CONTROL OPTIONS FOR CRYPTOGRAPHY

7.1.1 Dimensions of Choice for Controlling the Export of Cryptography

An export control regime—a set of laws and regulations governing what may or may not be exported under any specified set of circumstances—has many dimensions that can be considered independently. These dimensions include:

- *The type of export license granted.* Three types of export licenses are available:

—A general license, under which export of an item does not in general require prior government approval but nonetheless is tracked under an export declaration;

—A special license, under which prior government approval is required but which allows multiple and continuing transactions under one license validation; and

—An individual license, under which prior government approval is required for each and every transaction.

As a general rule, only individual licenses are granted for the export of items on the U.S. Munitions List, which includes "strong" cryptography.[1]

• *The strength of a product's cryptographic capabilities.* Current policy recognizes the difference between RC2/RC4 algorithms using 40-bit keys and other types of cryptography, and places fewer and less severe restrictions on the former.

• *The default encryption settings on the delivered product.* Encryption can be tacitly discouraged, but not forbidden, by the use of appropriate settings.[2]

• *The type of product.* Many different types of products can incorporate encryption capabilities. Products can be distinguished by medium (e.g., hardware vs. software) and/or intended function (e.g., computer vs. communications).

• *The extent and nature of features that allow exceptional access.* The Administration has suggested that it would permit the export of encryption software with key lengths of 64 bits or less if the keys were "properly escrowed."[3] Thus, inclusion in a product of a feature for exceptional access could be made one condition for allowing the export of that product. In addition, the existence of specific institutional arrangements (e.g., which specific parties would hold the information needed to implement exceptional access) might be made a condition for the export of these products.

• *The ultimate destination or intended use of the delivered product.* U.S.

---

[1]However, as noted in Chapter 4, the current export control regime for cryptography involves a number of categorical exemptions as well as some uncodified "in-practice" exemptions.

[2]Software, and even software-driven devices, commonly have operational parameters that can be selected or set by a user. An example is the fax machine that allows many user choices to be selected by keyboard actions. The parameters chosen by a manufacturer before it ships a product are referred to as the "defaults" or "default condition." Users are generally able to alter such parameters at will.

[3]At the time of this writing, the precise definition of "properly escrowed" is under debate and review in the Administration. The most recent language on this definition as of December 1995 is provided in Chapter 5.

export controls have long distinguished between exports to "friendly" and "hostile" nations. In addition, licenses have been granted for the sale of certain controlled products only when a particular benign use (e.g., financial transactions) could be certified. A related consideration is the extent to which nations cooperate with respect to re-export of a controlled product and/or export of their own products. For example, CoCom member nations[4] in principle agreed to joint controls on the export of certain products to the Eastern bloc; as a result, certain products could be exported to CoCom member nations much more easily than to other nations.

At present, there are few clear guidelines that enable vendors to design a product that will have a high degree of assurance of being exportable (Chapters 4 and 6). Table 7.1 describes various mechanisms that might be used to manage the export of products with encryption capabilities.

This remainder of Section 7.1 describes a number of options for controlling the export of cryptography, ranging from the sweeping to the detailed.

7.1.2 Complete Elimination of Export Controls on Cryptography

The complete elimination of export controls (both the USML and the Commerce Control List controls) on cryptography is a proposal that goes beyond most made to date, although certainly such a position has advocates. If export controls on cryptography were completely eliminated, it is possible that within a short time most information technology products exported from the United States would have encryption capabilities. It would be difficult for the U.S. government to influence the capabilities of these products, or even to monitor their deployment and use worldwide, because numerous vendors would most probably be involved.

Note, however, that the simple elimination of U.S. export controls on cryptography does not address the fact that other nations may have import controls and/or restrictions on the use of cryptography internally. Furthermore, it takes time to incorporate products into existing infrastructures, and slow market growth may encourage some vendors to take their time in developing new products. Thus, simply eliminating U.S. export controls on cryptography would not ensure markets abroad for U.S. products with encryption capabilities; indeed, the elimination of U.S.

---

[4]CoCom refers to the Coordinating Committee, a group of Western nations (and Japan) that agreed to a common set of export control practices during the Cold War to control the export of militarily useful technologies to Eastern bloc nations. CoCom was disbanded in March 1994, and a successor regime known as the New Forum is being negotiated as this report is being written.

TABLE 7.1 Mechanisms of Export Management

Type	Description	When Appropriate
Total embargo	All or most exports of cryptography to target country prohibited (this would be more restrictive than today's regime). Hypothetical example: no products with encryption capabilities can be exported to Vietnam, Libya, Iraq, Iran.	Appropriate during wartime or other acute national emergency or when imposed pursuant to United Nations or other broad international effort.
Selective export prohibitions	Certain products with encryption capabilities barred for export to target country. Hypothetical example: nothing cryptographically stronger than 40-bit RC4 can be exported to South Africa.	Appropriate when supplier countries agree on items for denial and cooperate on restrictions.
Selective activity prohibitions	Exports of cryptography for use in particular activities in target country prohibited. Hypothetical example: PGP allowed for export to pro-democracy groups in People's Republic of China but not for government use.	Appropriate when supplier countries identify proscribed operations and agree to cooperate on restrictions.
Transactional licensing	Products with encryption capabilities require government agency licensing for export to a particular country or country group. Hypothetical example: State Department individual validated license for a DES encryption product. Licensing actions may be conditioned on end-use verification or postexport verification.	Appropriate when product is inherently sensitive for export to any destination, or when items have both acceptable and undesired potential applications. Also requires an effective multilateral control regime.

Bulk licensing	Exporter obtains government authority to export categories of products with encryption capabilities to particular consignees for a specified time period. Hypothetical examples: Commerce Department distribution license, ITAR foreign manufacturing license. Note that categories can be determined with considerable freedom. Enforcement may rely on after-the-fact audits.	Same as preceding circumstances, but when specific transaction facts are not critical to effective export control.
Preexport notification	Exporter must prenotify shipment; government agency may prohibit, impose conditions, or exercise persuasion. Hypothetical example: requirement imposed on vendors of products with encryption capabilities to notify the U.S. government prior to shipping product overseas.	Generally regarded as an inappropriate export control measure because exporter cannot accept last-minute uncertainty.
Conditions on general authority or right to export	Exporter not required to obtain government agency license but must meet regulatory conditions that preclude high-risk exports. (In general, 40-bit RC2/RC4 encryption falls into this category once the Commodity Jurisdiction procedure has determined that a particular product with encryption capabilities may be governed by the CCL. Hypothetical example: Commerce Department general licenses.	Appropriate when risk of diversion or undesired use is low.
Postexport recordkeeping	While no license may be necessary, exporter must keep records of particulars of exports for specified period and submit or make available to government agency. Hypothetical example: vendor is required to keep records of foreign sales of 40-bit RC2/RC4 encryption products under a Shippers Export Declaration.	Appropriate when it is possible to monitor exports of weak cryptography for possible diversion.

SOURCE: Adapted from National Research Council, *Finding Common Ground: U.S. Export Controls in a Changed Global Environment*, National Academy Press, Washington, D.C., 1990, p. 109.

export controls could in itself stimulate foreign nations to impose import controls more stringently. Appendix G contains more discussion of these issues.

The worldwide removal of all controls on the export, import, and use of products with encryption capabilities would likely result in greater standardization of encryption techniques. Standardization brought about in this manner would result in:

- Higher degrees of international interoperability of these products;
- Broader use, or at least more rapid spread, of encryption capabilities as the result of the strong distribution capabilities of U.S. firms;
- Higher levels of confidentiality, as a result of greater ease in adopting more powerful algorithms and longer keys as standards; and
- Greater use of cryptography by hostile, criminal, and unfriendly parties as they, too, begin to use commercial products with strong encryption capabilities.

On the other hand, rapid, large-scale standardization would be unlikely unless a few integrated software products with encryption capabilities were able to achieve worldwide usage very quickly. Consider, for example, that although there are no restrictions on domestic use of cryptography in the United States, interoperability is still difficult, in many cases owing to variability in the systems in which the cryptography is embedded. Likewise, many algorithms stronger than DES are well known, and there are no restrictions in place on the domestic use of such algorithms, and yet only DES even remotely approaches common usage (and not all DES-based applications are interoperable).

For reasons well articulated by the national security and law enforcement communities (see Chapter 3) and accepted by the committee, the complete elimination of export controls on products with encryption capabilities does not seem reasonable in the short term. Whether export controls will remain feasible and efficacious in the long term has yet to be seen, although clearly, maintaining even their current level of effectiveness will become increasingly difficult.

7.1.3 Transfer of All Cryptography Products to the Commerce Control List

As discussed in Chapter 4, the Commerce Control List (CCL) complements the U.S. Munitions List (USML) in controlling the export of cryptography. (Box 4.2 in Chapter 4 describes the primary difference between the USML and the CCL.) In 1994, Representative Maria Cantwell (D-Washington) introduced legislation to transfer all mass-market software products involving cryptographic functions to the CCL. Although this legislation never passed, it resulted in the promise and subsequent delivery of an executive branch report on the international market for computer software with encryption.[5]

The Cantwell bill was strongly supported by the software industry because of the liberal consideration afforded products controlled for export by the CCL. Many of the bill's advocates believed that a transfer of jurisdiction to the Commerce Department would reflect an explicit recognition of cryptography as a commercial technology that should be administered under a dual-use export control regime. Compared to the USML, they argued that the CCL is a more balanced regime that still has considerable effectiveness in limiting exports to target destinations and end users.

On the other hand, national security officials regard the broad authorities of the Arms Export Control Act (AECA) as essential to the effective control of encryption exports. The AECA provides authority for case-by-case regulation of exports of cryptography to all destinations, based on national security considerations. In particular, licensing decisions are not governed by factors such as the country of destination, end users, end uses, or the existence of bilateral or multilateral agreements that often limit the range of discretionary action possible in controlling exports pursuant to the Export Administration Act. Further, the national security provisions of the AECA provide a basis for classifying the specific rationale for any particular export licensing decision made under its authority, thus protecting what may be very sensitive information about the particular circumstances surrounding that decision.

Although sympathetic to the Cantwell bill's underlying rationale, the committee believes that the bill does not address the basic dilemma of cryptography policy. As acknowledged by some of the bill's supporters, transfer of a product's jurisdiction to the CCL does not mean automatic decontrol of the product, and national security authorities could still have considerable input into how exports are actually licensed. In general, the committee believes that the idea of split jurisdiction, in which some types of cryptography are controlled under the CCL and others under the USML, makes considerable sense given the various national security implications of widespread use of encryption. However, where the split should be made is a matter of discussion; the committee expresses its own judgments on this point in Chapter 8.

---

[5]Department of Commerce and National Security Agency, *A Study of the International Market for Computer Software with Encryption,* prepared for the Interagency Working Group on Encryption and Telecommunications Policy, Office of the Secretary of Commerce, released January 11, 1996.

7.1.4 End-use Certification

Explicitly exempted under the current International Traffic in Arms Regulations (ITAR) is the export of cryptography for ensuring the confidentiality of financial transactions, specifically for cryptographic equipment and software that are "specially designed, developed or modified for use in machines for banking or money transactions, and restricted to use only in such transactions."[6] In addition, according to senior National Security Agency (NSA) officials, cryptographic systems, equipment, and software are in general freely exportable for use by U.S.-controlled foreign companies and to banking and financial institutions for purposes other than financial transactions, although NSA regards these approvals as part of the case-by-case review associated with equipment and products that do not enjoy an explicit exemption in the ITAR.

In principle, the ITAR could explicitly exempt products with encryption capabilities for use by foreign subsidiaries of U.S. companies, foreign companies that are U.S.-controlled, and banking and financial institutions. Explicit "vertical" exemptions for these categories could do much to alleviate confusion among users, many of whom are currently uncertain about what cryptographic protection they may be able to use in their international communications, and could enable vendors to make better informed judgments about the size of a given market.

Specific vertical exemptions could also be made for different industries (e.g., health care or manufacturing) and perhaps for large foreign-owned companies that would be both the largest potential customers and the parties most likely to be responsible corporate citizens. Inhibiting the diversion to other uses of products with encryption capabilities sold to these companies could be the focus of explicit contractual language binding the recipient to abide by certain terms that would be required of any vendor as a condition of sale to a foreign company, as it is today under USML procedures under the ITAR. Enforcement of end-use restrictions is discussed in Chapter 4.

7.1.5 Nation-by-Nation Relaxation of Controls and Harmonization of U.S. Export Control Policy on Cryptography with Export/Import Policies of Other Nations

The United States could give liberal export consideration to products with encryption capabilities intended for sale to recipients in a select set of nations;[7] exports to nations outside this set would be restricted. Na-

---

[6]International Traffic in Arms Regulations, Section 121.1, Category XIII (b)(1)(ii).

[7]For example, products with encryption capabilities can be exported freely to Canada without the need of a USML export license if intended for domestic Canadian use.

tions in the select set would be expected to have a more or less uniform set of regulations to control the export of cryptography, resulting in a more level playing field for U.S. vendors. In addition, agreements would be needed to control the re-export of products with encryption capabilities outside this set of nations.

Nation-by-nation relaxation of controls is consistent with the fact that different countries generally receive different treatment under the U.S. export control regime for military hardware. For example, exports of U.S. military hardware have been forbidden to some countries because they were terrorist nations, and to others because they failed to sign the nuclear nonproliferation treaty. A harmonization of export control regimes for cryptography would more closely resemble the former CoCom approach to control dual-use items than the approach reflected in the unilateral controls on exports imposed by the USML.

From the standpoint of U.S. national security and foreign policy, a serious problem with harmonization is the fact that the relationship between the United States and almost all other nations has elements of both competition and cooperation that may change over time. The widespread use of U.S. products with strong encryption capabilities under some circumstances could compromise U.S. positions with respect to these competitive elements, although many of these nations are unlikely to use U.S. products with encryption capabilities for their most sensitive communications.

Finally, as is true for other proposals to liberalize U.S. export controls on cryptography, greater liberalization may well cause some other nations to impose import controls where they do not otherwise exist. Such an outcome would shift the onus for impeding vendor interests away from the U.S. government; however, depending on the nature of the resulting import controls, U.S. vendors of information technology products with encryption capabilities might be faced with the need to conform to a multiplicity of import control regimes established by different nations.

7.1.6 Liberal Export for Strong Cryptography with Weak Defaults

An export control regime could grant liberal export consideration to products with encryption capabilities designed in such a way that the defaults for usage result in weak or nonexistent encryption (Box 7.1), but also so that users could invoke options for stronger encryption through an affirmative action.

For example, such a product might be a telephone designed for end-to-end security. The default mode of operation could be set in two different ways. One way would be for the telephone to establish a secure connection if the called party has a comparable unit. The second way

---

BOX 7.1
Possible Examples of Weak Encryption Defaults

• The product does not specify a minimum password length. Many users will generate short, and thus poor or weak, passwords.

• The product does not perform link encryption automatically. The user on either side of the communication link must select an option explicitly to encrypt the communications before encryption happens.

• The product requires user key generation rather than simple passwords and retains a user key or generates a record of one. Users might well accidentally compromise it and make it available, even if they had the option to delete it.

• The product generates a key and instructs the user to register it.

• E-mail encryption is not automatic. The sender must explicitly select an encryption option to encrypt messages.

---

would be for the telephone always to establish an insecure connection; establishing a secure connection would require an explicit action by the user. All experience suggests that the second way would result in far fewer secure calls than the first way.[8]

An export policy favoring the export of encryption products with weak defaults benefits the information-gathering needs of law enforcement and signals intelligence efforts because of user psychology. Many people, criminals and foreign government workers included, often make mistakes by using products "out of the box" without any particular attempt to configure them properly. Such a policy could also take advantage of the distribution mechanisms of the U.S. software industry to spread weaker defaults.

Experience to date suggests that good implementations of cryptography for confidentiality are transparent and automatic and thus do not require positive user action. Such implementations are likely to be chosen by organizations that are most concerned about confidentiality and that have a staff dedicated to ensuring confidentiality (e.g., by resetting weak vendor-supplied defaults). End users that obtain their products with encryption capabilities on the retail store market are the most likely to be affected by this proposal, but such users constitute a relatively small part of the overall market.

---

[8]Of course, other techniques can be used to further discourage the use of secure modes. For example, the telephone could be designed to force the user to wait several seconds for establishment of the secure mode.

7.1.7 Liberal Export for Cryptographic Applications Programming Interfaces

A cryptographic applications programming interface (CAPI; see Appendix K) is a well-defined boundary between a baseline product (such as an operating system, a database management program, or a word processing program) and a cryptography module that provides a secure set of cryptographic services such as authentication, digital signature generation, random number generation, and stream or block mode encryption. The use of a CAPI allows vendors to support cryptographic functions in their products without actually providing them at distribution.

Even though such products have no cryptographic functionality per se and are therefore not specifically included in Category XIII of the ITAR (see Appendix N), license applications for the export of products incorporating CAPIs have in general been denied. The reason is that strong cryptographic capabilities could be deployed on a vast scale if U.S. vendors exported applications supporting a common CAPI and a foreign vendor then marketed an add-in module with strong encryption capabilities.[9]

To meet the goals of less restrictive export controls, liberal export consideration could be given to products that incorporate a CAPI designed so that only "certified" cryptographic modules could be incorporated into and used by the application. That is, the application with the CAPI would have to ensure that the CAPI would work only with certified cryptographic modules. This could be accomplished by incorporating into the application a check for a digital signature whose presence would indicate that the add-on cryptographic module was indeed certified; if and only if such a signature were detected by the CAPI would the product allow use of the module.

One instantiation of a CAPI is the CAPI built into applications that use the Fortezza card (discussed in Chapter 5). CAPI software for Fortezza is available for a variety of operating systems and PC-card reader types; such software incorporates a check to ensure that the device being used is itself a Fortezza card. The Fortezza card contains a private Digital Signature Standard (DSS) key that can be used to sign a challenge from the workstation. The corresponding DSS public key is made available in the

---

[9]This discussion refers only to "documented" or "open" CAPIs, i.e., CAPIs that are accessible to the end user. Another kind of CAPI is "undocumented" and "closed"; that is, it is inaccessible to the end user, though it is used by system developers for their own convenience. While a history of export licensing decisions and practices supports the conclusion that most products implementing "open" CAPIs will not receive export licenses, history provides no consistent guidance with respect to products implementing CAPIs that are inaccessible to the end user.

BOX 7.2
The Microsoft CryptoAPI

In June 1995, Microsoft received commodity jurisdiction (CJ) to the Commerce Control List (CCL) for Windows NT with CryptoAPI (a Microsoft trademark) plus a "base" crypto-module that qualifies for CCL jurisdiction under present regulations (i.e., it uses a 40-bit RC4 algorithm for confidentiality); a similar CJ application for Windows '95 is pending. The "base" crypto-module can be supplemented by a crypto-module provided by some other vendor of cryptography, but the cryptographic applications programming interface within the operating system will function only with crypto-modules that have been digitally signed by Microsoft, which will provide a digital signature for a crypto-module only if the crypto-module vendor certifies that it (the module vendor) will comply with all relevant U.S. export control regulations. (In the case of a crypto-module for sale in the United States only, Microsoft will provide a digital signature upon the module vendor's statement to that effect.)

Responsibility for complying with export control regulations on cryptography is as follows:

• Windows NT (and Windows '95, should the pending application be successful) qualify for CCL jurisdiction on the basis of a State Department export licensing decision.

• Individual crypto-modules are subject to a case-by-case licensing analysis, and the cryptography vendor is responsible for compliance.

• Applications that use Windows NT or Windows '95 for cryptographic services should not be subject to export control regulations on cryptography. At the time of this writing, Microsoft is seeking an advisory opinion to this effect so that applications vendors do not need to submit a request for a CJ cryptography licensing decision.

CAPI, and thus the CAPI is able to verify the authenticity of the Fortezza card.

A second approach to the use of a CAPI has been proposed by Microsoft and is now eligible for liberal export consideration by the State Department (Box 7.2). The Microsoft approach involves three components: an operating system with a CAPI embedded within it, modules providing cryptographic services through the CAPI, and applications that can call on the modules through the CAPI provided by the operating system. In principle, each of these components is the responsibility of different parties: Microsoft is responsible for the operating system, cryptography vendors are responsible for the modules, and independent applications vendors are responsible for the applications that run on the operating system.

From the standpoint of national security authorities, the effectiveness of an approach based on the use of a certified CAPI/module combination depends on a number of factors. For example, the product incorporating the CAPI should be known to be implemented in a manner that enforces the appropriate constraints on crypto-modules that it calls; furthermore, the code that provides such enforcement should not be trivially bypassed. The party certifying the crypto-module should protect the private signature key used to sign it. Vendors would still be required to support domestic and exportable versions of an application if the domestic version was allowed to use any module while the export version was restricted in the set of modules that would be accepted, although the amount of effort required to develop these two different versions would be quite small.

The use of CAPIs that check for appropriate digital signatures would shift the burden for export control from the applications or systems vendors to the vendors of the cryptographic modules. This shift could benefit both the government and vendors because of the potential to reduce the number of players engaged in the process. For example, all of the hundreds of e-mail applications on the market could quickly support encrypted e-mail by supporting a CAPI developed by a handful of software and/or hardware cryptography vendors. The cryptography vendors would be responsible for dealing with the export and import controls of various countries, leaving e-mail application vendors to export freely anywhere in the world. Capabilities such as escrowed encryption could be supported within the cryptography module itself, freeing the applications or system vendor from most technical, operational, and political issues related to export control.

A trustworthy CAPI would also help to support cryptography policies that might differ among nations. In particular, a given nation might specify certain performance requirements for all cryptography modules used or purchased within its borders.[10] International interoperability

---

[10]An approach to this effect is the thrust of a proposal from Hewlett-Packard. The Hewlett-Packard International Cryptography Framework (ICF) proposal includes a stamp size "policy card" (smart card) that would be inserted into a cryptographic unit that is a part of a host system. Cryptographic functions provided within the cryptographic unit could be executed only with the presence of a valid policy card. The policy card could be configured to enable only those cryptographic functions that are consistent with government export and local policies. The "policy card" allows for managing the use of the integrated cryptography down to the application-specific level. By obtaining a new policy card, customers could be upgraded to take advantage of varying cryptographic capabilities as government policies or organizational needs change. As part of an ICF solution, a network security server could be implemented to provide a range of different security services, including verification of the other three service elements (the card, the host system, the cryptographic unit). Sources: Carl Snyder, Hewlett-Packard, testimony to the NRC committee in February 1995; Hewlett-Packard, *International Cryptography Framework White Paper*, February 1994.

problems resulting from conflicting national cryptography policies would still remain.

7.1.8 Liberal Export for Escrowable Products with Encryption Capabilities

As discussed in Chapter 5, the Administration's proposal of August 17, 1995, would allow liberal export consideration for software products with encryption capabilities whose keys are "properly escrowed." In other words, strong cryptography would be enabled for these products only when the keys were escrowed with appropriate escrow agents.

An escrowed encryption product differs from what might be called an "escrowable" product. Specifically, an escrowed encryption product is one whose key *must be* escrowed with a registered, approved agent before the use of (strong) cryptography can be enabled, whereas an escrowable product is one that provides full cryptographic functionality that includes optional escrow features for the user. The user of an escrowable product can choose whether or not to escrow the relevant keys, but regardless of the choice, the product still provides its full suite of encryption capabilities.[11]

Liberal export consideration for escrowable products could be granted and incentives promulgated to encourage the use of escrow features. While the short-term disadvantage of this approach from the standpoint of U.S. national security is that it allows encryption stronger than the current 40-bit RC2/RC4 encryption allowed under present regulations to diffuse into foreign hands, it has the long-term advantage of providing foreign governments with a tool for influencing or regulating the use of cryptography as they see fit. Currently, most products with encryption capabilities do not have built-in features to support escrow built into them. However, if products were designed and exported with such features, governments would have a hook for exercising some influence. Some governments might choose to require the escrowing of keys, while others might simply provide incentives to encourage escrowing. In any event, the diffusion of escrowable products abroad would raise the awareness of foreign governments, businesses, and individuals about encryption and thus lay a foundation for international cooperation on the formulation of national cryptography policies.

---

[11]For example, an escrowable product would not enable the user to encrypt files with passwords. Rather, the installation of the product would require the user to create a key or set of named keys, and these keys would be used when encrypting files. The installation would also generate a protected "safe copy" of the keys with instructions to users that they should register the key "somewhere." It would be up to the users to decide where or whether to register the keys.

7.1.9 Alternatives to Government Certification of Escrow Agents Abroad

As discussed in Chapter 5, the Administration's August 1995 proposal focuses on an implementation of escrowed encryption that involves the use of "escrow agents certified by the U.S. government or by foreign governments with which the U.S. government has formal agreements consistent with U.S. law enforcement and national security requirements."[12] This approach requires foreign customers of U.S. escrowed encryption products to use U.S. escrow agents until formal agreements can be negotiated that specify the responsibilities of foreign escrow agents to the United States for law enforcement and national security purposes.

Skeptics ask what incentives the U.S. government would have to conclude the formal agreements described in the August 1995 proposal if U.S. escrow agents would, by default, be the escrow agents for foreign consumers. They believe that the most likely result of adopting the Administration's proposal would be U.S. foot-dragging and inordinate delays in the consummation of formal agreements for certifying foreign escrow agents. Appendix G describes some of the U.S. government efforts to date to promote a dialogue on such agreements.

The approaches described below address problems raised by certifying foreign escrow agents:

• *Informal arrangements for cooperation.* One alternative is based on the fact that the United States enjoys strong cooperative law enforcement relationships with many nations with which it does not have formal agreements regarding cooperation. Negotiation of a formal agreement between the United States and another nation could be replaced by presidential certification that strong cooperative law enforcement relationships exist between the United States and that nation. Subsequent cooperation would be undertaken on the same basis that cooperation is offered today.

• *Contractual key escrow.* A second alternative is based on the idea that formal agreements between nations governing exchange of escrowed key information might be replaced by private contractual arrangements.[13] A user that escrows key information with an escrow agent, wherever that agent is located, would agree contractually that the U.S. government would have access to that information under a certain set of carefully specified circumstances. A suitably designed exportable product would provide strong encryption only upon receipt of affirmative confirmation that the relevant key information had been deposited with escrow agents requiring such contracts with users. Alternatively, as a condition of sale,

---

[12]See Box 5.3, Chapter 5.

[13]Henry Perritt, "Transnational Key Escrow," paper presented at the International Cryptography Institute 1995 conference, Washington, D.C., September 22, 1995.

end users could be required to deposit keys with escrow agents subject to such a contractual requirement.

7.1.10 Use of Differential Work Factors in Cryptography

Differential work factor cryptography is an approach to cryptography that presents different work factors to different parties attempting to cryptanalyze a given piece of encrypted information.[14] Iris Associates, the creator of Notes, proposed such an approach for Lotus Notes Version 4 to facilitate its export, and the U.S. government has accepted it. Specifically, the international edition of Lotus Notes Version 4 is designed to present a 40-bit work factor to the U.S. government and a 64-bit work factor to all other parties. It implements this differential work factor by encrypting 24 bits of the 64-bit key with the public-key portion of an RSA key pair held by the U.S. government. Because the U.S. government can easily decrypt these 24 bits, it faces only a 40-bit work factor when it needs access to a communications stream overseas encrypted by the international edition. All other parties attempting to cryptanalyze a message face a 64-bit work factor.

Differential work factor cryptography is similar to partial key escrow (described in Chapter 5) in that both provide very strong protection against most attackers but are vulnerable to attack by some specifically chosen authority. However, they are different in that differential work factor cryptography does not require user interaction with an escrow agent, and so it can offer strong cryptography "out of the box." Partial key escrow offers all of the strengths and weaknesses of escrowed encryption, including the requirement that the enabling of strong cryptography does require interaction with an escrow agent.

7.1.11 Separation of Cryptography from Other Items on the U.S. Munitions List

As noted in Chapter 4, the inclusion of products with encryption capabilities on the USML puts them on a par with products intended for strictly military purposes (e.g., tanks, missiles). An export control regime that authorized the U.S. government to separate cryptography—a true dual-use technology—from strictly military items would provide much needed flexibility in dealing with nations on which the United States wishes to place sanctions.

---

[14]Recall from Chapter 2 that a work factor is a measure of the amount of work that it takes to undertake a brute-force exhaustive cryptanalytic search.

7.2 ALTERNATIVES FOR PROVIDING GOVERNMENT EXCEPTIONAL ACCESS TO ENCRYPTED DATA

Providing government exceptional access to encrypted data is an issue with a number of dimensions, only some of which relate directly to encryption.

7.2.1 A Prohibition on the Use and Sale of Cryptography Lacking Features for Exceptional Access

One obvious approach to ensuring government exceptional access to encrypted information is to pass legislation that forbids the use of cryptography lacking features for such access, presumably with criminal penalties attached for violation. (Given that escrowed cryptography appears to be the most plausible approach to providing government exceptional access, the term "unescrowed cryptography" is used here as a synonym for cryptography without features for exceptional access.) Indeed, opponents of the Escrowed Encryption Standard (EES) and the Clipper chip have argued repeatedly that the EES approach would succeed only if alternatives were banned.[15] Many concerns have been raised about the prospect of a mandatory prohibition on the use of unescrowed cryptography.

From a law enforcement standpoint, a legislative prohibition on the use of unescrowed encryption would have clear advantages. Its primary impact would be to eliminate the commercial supply of unescrowed products with encryption capabilities—vendors without a market would most likely not produce or distribute such products, thus limiting access of criminals to unescrowed encryption and increasing the inconvenience of evading a prohibition on the use of unescrowed encryption. At the same time, such a prohibition would leave law-abiding users with strong concerns about the confidentiality of their information being subject to procedures beyond their control.

A legislative prohibition on the use of unescrowed encryption also raises specific technical, economic, and legal issues.

Concerns About Personal Freedom

The Clinton Administration has stated that it has no intention of outlawing unescrowed cryptography, and it has repeatedly and explicitly disavowed any intent to regulate the domestic use of cryptography. How-

---

[15]For example, see Electronic Privacy Information Center, press release, August 16, 1995, available on-line at http://www.epic.org.

ever, no administration can bind future administrations (a fact freely acknowledged by administration officials). Thus, some critics of the Administration position believe that the dynamics of the encryption problem may well drive the government—sooner or later—to prohibit the use of encryption without government access.[16] The result is that the Administration is simply not believed when it forswears any intent to regulate cryptography used in the United States. Two related concerns are raised:

- *The "slippery slope."* Many skeptics fear that current cryptography policy is the first step down a slippery slope toward a more restrictive policy regime under which government may not continue to respect limits in place at the outset. An oft-cited example is current use of the Social Security Number, which was not originally intended to serve as a universal identifier when the Social Security Act was passed in 1935 but has, over the last 50 years, come to serve exactly that role by default, simply because it was there to be exploited for purposes not originally intended by the enabling legislation.

- *Misuse of deployed infrastructure for cryptography.* Many skeptics are concerned that a widely deployed infrastructure for cryptography could be used by a future administration or Congress to promulgate and/or enforce restrictive policies regarding the use of cryptography. With such an infrastructure in place, critics argue that a simple policy change might be able to transform a comparatively benign deployment of technology into an oppressive one. For example, critics of the Clipper proposal were concerned about the possibility that a secure telephone system with government exceptional access capabilities could, under a strictly voluntary program to encourage its purchase and use, achieve moderate market penetration. Such market penetration could then facilitate legislation outlawing all other cryptographically secure telephones.[17]

------

[16]For example, Senator Charles Grassley (R-Iowa) introduced legislation (The Anti-Electronic Racketeering Act of 1995) on June 27, 1995, to "prohibit certain acts involving the use of computers in the furtherance of crimes." The proposed legislation makes it unlawful "to distribute computer software that encodes or encrypts electronic or digital communications to computer networks that the person distributing the software knows or reasonably should know, is accessible to foreign nationals and foreign governments, regardless of whether such software has been designated as nonexportable," except for software that uses "a universal decoding device or program that was provided to the Department of Justice prior to the distribution."

[17]By contrast, a deployed infrastructure could have characteristics that would make it quite difficult to implement policy changes on a short time scale. For example, it would be very difficult to implement a policy change that would change the nature of the way in which people use today's telephone system. Not surprisingly, policy makers would prefer to work with infrastructures that are quickly responsive to their policy preferences.

BOX 7.3
Bobby Inman on the Classification of Cryptologic Research

In 1982, then-Deputy Director of the Central Intelligence Agency Bobby R. Inman wrote that

[a] . . . source of tension arises when scientists, completely separate from the federal government, conduct research in areas where the federal government has an obvious and preeminent role for society as a whole. One example is the design of advanced weapons, especially nuclear ones. Another is cryptography. While nuclear weapons and cryptography are heavily dependent on theoretical mathematics, there is no public business market for nuclear weapons. Such a market, however, does exist for cryptographic concepts and gear to protect certain types of business communications.

[However], . . . cryptologic research in the business and academic arenas, no matter how useful, remains redundant to the necessary efforts of the federal government to protect its own communications. I still am concerned that indiscriminate publication of the results of that research will come to the attention of foreign governments and entities and, thereby, could cause irreversible and unnecessary harm to U.S. national security interests. . . . [While] key features of science—unfettered research, and the publication of the results for validation by others and for use by all mankind—are essential to the growth and development of science, . . . nowhere in the scientific ethos is there any requirement that restrictions cannot or should not, when necessary, be placed on science. Scientists do not immunize themselves from social responsibility simply because they are engaged in a scientific pursuit. Society has recognized over time that certain kinds of scientific inquiry can endanger society as a whole and has applied either directly, or through scientific/ethical constraints, restrictions on the kind and amount of research that can be done in those areas.

For the original text of Inman's article, see "Classifying Science: A Government Proposal . . . ," *Aviation Week and Space Technology*, February 8, 1982.

Adding to these concerns are suggestions such as those made by a responsible and senior government official that even research in cryptography conducted in the civilian sector should be controlled in a legal regime similar to that which governs research with relevance to nuclear weapons design (Box 7.3). Ironically, former NSA Director Bobby Inman's comments on scientific research appeared in an article that called for greater cooperation between academic scientists and national security authorities and used as a model of cooperation an arrangement, recommended by the Public Cryptography Study Group, that has worked generally well in balancing the needs of academic science and those of national security.[18] Nevertheless, Inman's words are often cited as reflecting a national security mind-set that could lead to a serious loss of intellectual freedom and discourse. More recently, FBI Director Louis Freeh stated to the committee that "other approaches may be necessary" if technology vendors do not adopt escrowed encryption on their own. Moreover, the current Administration has explicitly rejected the premise that "every American, as a matter of right, is entitled to an unbreakable encryption product."[19]

Given concerns about possible compromises of personal and civil liberties, many skeptics of government in this area believe that the safest approach is for government to stay out of cryptography policy entirely. They argue that any steps in this area, no matter how well intentioned or plausible or reasonable, must be resisted strongly, because such steps will inevitably be the first poking of the camel's nose under the tent.

Technical Issues

Even if a legislative prohibition on the use of unescrowed encryption were enacted, it would be technically easy for parties with special needs for security to circumvent such a ban. In some cases, circumvention would be explicitly illegal, while in others it might well be entirely legal. For example:

• Software for unescrowed encryption can be downloaded from the Internet; such software is available even today. Even if posting such software in the United States were to be illegal under a prohibition, it would nonetheless be impossible to prevent U.S. Internet users from downloading software that had been posted on sites abroad.

---

[18]The arrangement recommended by the Public Cryptography Study Group called for voluntary prepublication review of all cryptography research undertaken in the private sector. For more discussion of this arrangement, see Public Cryptography Study Group, *Report of the Public Cryptography Study Group*, American Council on Education, Washington, D.C., February, 1981. A history leading to the formation of the Public Cryptography Study Group can be found in National Research Council, "Voluntary Restraints on Research with National Security Implications: The Case of Cryptography, 1972-1982," in *Scientific Communication and National Security*, National Academy Press, Washington, D.C., 1982, Appendix E, pp. 120-125. The ACM study on cryptography policy concluded that this prepublication arrangement has not resulted in any chilling effects in the long term (see Susan Landau et al., *Codes, Keys and Conflicts: Issues in U.S. Crypto Policy*, Association for Computing Machinery Inc., New York, 1994, p. 39.)

[19]"Questions and Answers About the Clinton Administration's Telecommunications Initiative," undated document released on April 16, 1993, with "Statement by the Press Secretary on the Clipper Chip." See *The Third CPSR Cryptography and Privacy Conference Source Book*, Computer Professionals for Social Responsibility, Washington, D.C., June 7, 1993, Part III.

• Superencryption can be used. Superencryption (sometimes also known as double encryption) is encryption of traffic before it is given to an escrowed encryption device or system. For technical reasons, superencryption is impossible to detect without monitoring and attempting to decrypt all escrow-encrypted traffic, and such large-scale monitoring would be seriously at odds with the selected and limited nature of wiretaps today.

An additional difficulty with superencryption is that it is not technically possible to obtain escrow information for all layers simultaneously, because the fact of double and triple encryption cannot be known in advance. Even if the second (or third or fourth) layers of encryption were escrowed, law enforcement authorities would have to approach separately and sequentially the escrow agents holding key information for those layers.

• Talent for hire is easy to obtain. A criminal party could easily hire a knowledgable person to develop needed software. For example, an out-of-work or underemployed scientist or mathematician from the former Soviet Union would find a retainer fee of $500 per month to be a king's ransom.[20]

• Information can be stored remotely. An obvious noncryptographic circumvention is to store data on a remote computer whose Internet address is known only to the user. Such a computer could be physically located anywhere in the world (and might even automatically encrypt files that were stored there). But even if it were not encrypted, data stored on a remote computer would be impossible for law enforcement officials to access without the cooperation of the data's owner. Such remote storage could occur quite legally even with a ban on the use of unescrowed encryption.

• Demonstrating that a given communication or data file is "encrypted" is fraught with ambiguities arising from the many different possibilities for sending information:

—An individual might use an obscure data format. For example, while ASCII is the most common representation of alphanumeric characters today, Unicode (a proposed 16-bit representation) and EBCDIC (a more-or-less obsolete 8-bit representation) are equally good for sending plain English text.

---

[20] Alan Cooperman and Kyrill Belianinov, "Moonlighting by Modem in Russia," *U.S. News & World Report*, April 17, 1995, pp. 45-48. In addition, many high-technology jobs are moving overseas in general, not just to the former Soviet Union. See, for example, Keith Bradsher, "Skilled Workers Watch Their Jobs Migrate Overseas," *New York Times*, August 28, 1995, p. 1.

—An individual talking to another individual might speak in a language such as Navajo.

—An individual talking to another individual might speak in code phrases.

—An individual might send compressed digital data that could easily be confused with encrypted data despite having no purpose related to encryption. If, for example, an individual develops his own good compression algorithm and does not share it with anyone, that compressed bit stream may prove as difficult to decipher as an encrypted bit stream.[21]

—An individual might deposit fragments of a text or image that he wished to conceal or protect in a number of different Internet-accessible computers. The plaintext (i.e., the reassembled version) would be reassembled into a coherent whole only when downloaded into the computer of the user.[22]

—An individual might use steganography.[23]

None of these alternative coding schemes provides confidentiality as strong as would be provided by good cryptography, but their extensive use could well complicate attempts by government to obtain plaintext information.

Given so many different ways to subvert a ban on the use of unescrowed cryptography, emergence of a dedicated subculture is likely in which the nonconformists would use coding schemes or unescrowed cryptography impenetrable to all outsiders.

---

[21]A discussion of using text compression for confidentiality purposes can be found in Ian Whitten and John Cleary, "On the Privacy Afforded by Adaptive Text Compression," *Computers and Security*, July 1988, Volume 7(4), pp. 397-408. One problem in using compression schemes as a technique for ensuring confidentiality is that almost any practical compression scheme has the characteristic that closely similar plaintexts would generate similar ciphertexts, thereby providing a cryptanalyst with a valuable advantage not available if a strong encryption algorithm is used.

[22]Jaron Lanier, "Unmuzzling the Internet: How to Evade the Censors and Make a Statement, Too," Op-Ed, *New York Times*, January 2, 1996, p. A15.

[23]Steganography is the name given to techniques for hiding a message within another message. For example, the first letter of each word in a sentence or a paragraph can be used to spell out a message, or a photograph can be constructed so as to conceal information. Specifically, most black-and-white pictures rendered in digital form use at most 2^{16} (65,536) shades of gray, because the human eye is incapable of distinguishing any more shades. Each element of a digitized black-and-white photo would then be associated with 16 bits of information about what shade of gray should be used. If a picture were digitized with 24 bits of gray scale, the last 8 bits could be used to convey a concealed message that would never appear except for someone who knew to look for it. The digital size of the picture would be 50% larger than it would ordinarily be, but no one but the creator of the image would know.

Economic Concerns

An important economic issue that would arise with a legislative prohibition on the use of unescrowed cryptography would involve the political difficulty of mandating abandonment of existing user investments in products with encryption capabilities. These investments, considerable even today, are growing rapidly, and the expense to users of immediately having to replace unescrowed encryption products with escrowed ones could be enormous;[24] a further expense would be the labor cost involved in decrypting existing encrypted archives and reencrypting them using escrowed encryption products. One potential mitigating factor for cost is the short product cycle of information technology products. Whether users would abandon nonconforming products in favor of new products with escrowing features—knowing that they were specifically designed to facilitate exceptional access—is open to question.

Legal and Constitutional Issues

Even apart from the issues described above, which in the committee's view are quite significant, a legislative ban on the domestic use of unescrowed encryption would raise constitutional issues. Insofar as a prohibition on unescrowed encryption were treated for constitutional purposes as a limitation on the content of communications, the government would have to come forward with a compelling state interest to justify the ban. To some, a prohibition on the use of unescrowed encryption would be the equivalent of a law proscribing use of a language (e.g., Spanish), which would almost certainly be unconstitutional. On the other hand, if such a ban were regarded as tantamount to eliminating a method of communication (i.e., were regarded as content-neutral), then the courts would employ a simple balancing test to determine its constitutionality. The government would have to show that the public interests were jeopardized by a world of unrestrained availability of encryption, and these interests would have to be weighed against the free speech interests sacrificed by the ban. It would also be significant to know what alternative

---

[24]Existing unescrowed encryption products could be kept in place if end users could be made to comply with a prohibition on the use of such products. In some cases, a small technical fix might suffice to disable the cryptography features of a system; such fixes would be most relevant in a computing environment in which the software used by end users is centrally administered (as in the case of many corporations) and provides system administrators with the capability for turning off encryption. In other cases, users—typically individual users who had purchased their products from retail store outlets—would have to be trusted to refrain from using encryption.

forms of methods of anonymous communication would remain available with a ban and how freedom of speech would be affected by the specific system of escrow chosen by the government. These various considerations are difficult, and in some cases impossible, to estimate in advance of particular legislation and a particular case, but the First Amendment issues likely to arise with a total prohibition on the use of unescrowed encryption are not trivial.[25]

A step likely to raise fewer constitutional problems, but not eliminate them, is one that would impose restrictions on the commercial sale of unescrowed products with encryption capabilities.[26] Under such a regime, products with encryption capabilities eligible for sale would have to conform to certain restrictions intended to ensure public safety, in much the same way that other products such as drugs, automobiles, and meat must satisfy particular government regulations. "Freeware" or home-grown products with encryption capabilities would be exempt from such regulations as long as they were used privately. The problem of already-deployed products would remain, but in a different form: new products would either interoperate or not interoperate with existing already-deployed products. If noninteroperability were required, users attempting to maintain and use two noninteroperating systems would be faced with enormous expenses. If interoperability were allowed, the intent of the ban would be thwarted.

Finally, any national policy whose stated purpose is to prevent the use of unescrowed encryption preempts decision making that the committee believes properly belongs to users. As noted in Chapter 5, escrowed encryption reduces the level of assured confidentiality in exchange for allowing controlled exceptional access to parties that may need to retrieve encrypted data. Only in a policy regime of voluntary compliance can users decide how to make that trade-off. A legislative prohibition on the use or sale of unescrowed encryption would be a clear statement that law enforcement needs for exceptional access to information clearly outweigh user interests in having maximum possible protection

---

[25]For a view arguing that relevant Fourth and Fifth Amendment issues would be resolved against a constitutionality of such a prohibition, see Michael Froomkin, "The Metaphor Is the Key: Cryptography, The Clipper Chip and the Constitution," *University of Pennsylvania Law Review*, Volume 143(3), January 1995, pp. 709-897. The committee takes no position on these Fourth and Fifth Amendment issues.

[26]Such a scheme has been suggested by Dorothy Denning in "The Future of Cryptography," *Internet Security Monthly*, October 1995, p. 10. (Also available on-line at http://www.cosc.georgetown.edu/~denning/crypto.) Denning's paper does not suggest that "freeware" be exempt, although her proposal would provide an exemption for personally developed software used to encrypt personal files.

for their information, a position that has yet to be defended or even publicly argued by any player in the debate.

7.2.2 Criminalization of the Use of Cryptography in the Commission of a Crime

Proposals to criminalize the use of cryptography in the commission of a crime have the advantage that they focus the weight of the criminal justice system on the "bad guy" without placing restrictions on the use of cryptography by "good guys." Further, deliberate use of cryptography in the commission of a crime could result in considerable damage, either to society as a whole or to particular individuals, in circumstances suggesting premeditated wrongdoing, an act that society tends to view as worthy of greater punishment than a crime committed in the heat of the moment.

Two approaches could be taken to criminalize the use of cryptography in the commission of a crime:

• Construct a specific list of crimes in which the use of cryptography would subject the criminal to additional penalties. For example, using a deadly weapon in committing a robbery or causing the death of someone during the commission of a crime are themselves crimes that lead to additional penalties.

• Develop a blanket provision stating that the use of cryptography for illegal purposes (or for purposes contrary to law) is itself a felony.

In either event, additional penalties for the use of cryptography could be triggered by a conviction for a primary crime, or they could be imposed independently of such a conviction. Precedents include the laws criminalizing mail fraud (fraud is a crime, generally a state crime, but mail fraud—use of the mails to commit fraud—is an additional federal crime) and the use of a gun during the commission of a felony.

Intentional use of cryptography in the concealment of a crime could also be criminalized. Since the use of cryptography is a prima facie act of concealment, such an expansion would reduce the burden of proof on law enforcement officials, who would have to prove only that cryptography was used *intentionally* to conceal a crime. Providers of cryptography would be criminally liable only if they had knowingly provided cryptography for use in criminal activity. On the other hand, a law of more expansive scope might well impose additional burdens on businesses and raise civil liberties concerns.

In considering legal penalties for misuse of cryptography, the question of what it means to "use" cryptography must be addressed. For example, if and when encryption capabilities are integrated seamlessly into applications and are invoked automatically without effort on the part of a user, should the use of these applications for criminal purposes lead to additional penalties or to a charge for an additional offense? Answering yes to this question provides another avenue for prosecuting a criminal (recall that Al Capone was convicted for income tax evasion rather than bank robbery). Answering no leaves open the possibility of prosecutorial abuse. A second question is what counts as "cryptography." As noted above in the discussion of prohibiting unescrowed encryption, a number of mathematical coding schemes can serve to obscure the meaning of plaintext even if they are not encryption schemes in the technical sense of the word. These and related questions must be addressed in any serious consideration of the option for criminalizing the use of cryptography in the commission of a crime.

7.2.3 Technical Nonescrow Approaches for Obtaining Access to Information

Escrowed encryption is not the only means by which law enforcement can gain access to encrypted data. For example, as advised by Department of Justice guidelines for searching and seizing computers, law enforcement officials can approach the software vendor or the Justice Department computer crime laboratory for assistance in cryptanalyzing encrypted files. These guidelines also advise that "clues to the password [may be found] in the other evidence seized—stray notes on hardware or desks; scribble in the margins of manuals or on the jackets of disks. Agents should consider whether the suspect or someone else will provide the password if requested."[27] Moreover, product designs intended to facilitate exceptional access can include alternatives with different strengths and weaknesses such as link encryption, weak encryption, hidden back doors, and translucent cryptography.

Link Encryption

With link encryption, which applies only to communications and stands in contrast to end-to-end encryption (Box 7.4), a plaintext message enters a communications link, is encrypted for transmission through the link, and is decrypted upon exiting the link. In a communication that may involve many links, sensitive information can be found in plaintext form at the ends of each link (but not during transit). Thus, for purposes of protecting sensitive information on an open network accessible to anyone (the Internet is a good example), link encryption is more vulnerable than

---

[27]Criminal Division, U.S. Department of Justice, *Federal Guidelines for Searching and Seizing Computers*, Washington, D.C., July 1994, p. 55.

BOX 7.4
Link vs. End-to-End Encryption of Communications

End-to-end encryption involves a stream of data traffic (in one or both directions) that is encrypted by the end users involved before it is fed into the communications link; traffic in between the end users is never seen in plaintext, and the traffic is decrypted only upon receipt by an end user. Link encryption is encryption performed on data traffic after it leaves one of the end users; the traffic enters one end of the link, is encrypted and transmitted, and then is decrypted upon exit from that link.

TABLE 7.2 Comparison of End-to-End and Link Encryption

	End-to-End Encryption	Link Encryption
Controlling party	User	Link provider
Suitable traffic	Most suitable for encryption of individual messages	Facilitates bulk encryption of data
Potential leaks of plaintext	Only at transmitting and receiving stations	At either end of the link, which may not be within the user's security perimeter
Point of responsibility	User must take responsibility	Link provider takes responsibility

end-to-end encryption, which protects sensitive information from the moment it leaves party A to the moment it arrives at party B. However, from the standpoint of law enforcement, link encryption facilitates legally authorized intercepts, because the traffic of interest can always be obtained from one of the nodes in which the traffic is unencrypted.

On a relatively closed network or one that is used to transmit data securely and without direct user action, link encryption may be cost-effective and desirable. A good example would be encryption of the wireless radio link between a cellular telephone and its ground station; the cellular handset encrypts the voice signal and transmits it to the ground station, at which point it is decrypted and fed into the land-based network. Thus, the land-based network carries only unencrypted voice traffic, even though it was transmitted by an encrypted cellular telephone. A second example is the "bulk" encryption of multiple channels—each individually unencrypted—over a multiplexed fiber-optic link. In both of these instances of link encryption, only those with access to carrier facilities—presumably law enforcement officials acting under proper legal authorization—would have the opportunity to tap such traffic.

Weak Encryption

Weak encryption allowing exceptional access would have to be strong enough to resist brute-force attack by unauthorized parties (e.g., business competitors) but weak enough to be cracked by authorized parties (e.g., law enforcement agencies). However, "weak" encryption is a moving target. The difference between cracking strong and weak encryption by brute-force attack is the level of computational resources that can be brought to such an attack, and those resources are ever increasing. In fact, the cost of brute-force attacks on cryptography drops exponentially over time, in accordance with Moore's law.[28]

Widely available technologies now enable multiple distributed workstations to work collectively on a computational problem at the behest of only a few people; Box 4.6 in Chapter 4 discusses the brute-force cryptanalysis of messages encrypted with the 40-bit RC4 algorithm, and it is not clear that the computational resources of unauthorized parties can be limited in any meaningful way. In today's environment, unauthorized parties will almost always be able to assemble the resources needed to mount successful brute-force attacks against weak cryptography, to the detriment of those using such cryptography. Thus, any technical dividing line between authorized and unauthorized decryption would change rather quickly.

Hidden Back Doors

A "back door" is an entry point to an application that permits access or use by other than the normal or usual means. Obviously, a back door known to government can be used to obtain exceptional access. Back doors may be open or hidden. An open back door is one whose existence is announced publicly; an example is an escrowed encryption system, which everyone knows is designed to allow exceptional access.[29] By its

---

[28]Moore's law is an empirical observation that the cost of computation drops by a factor of two approximately every 18 months.

[29]Of course, the fact that a particular product is escrowed may not necessarily be known to any given user. Many users learn about the features of a product through reading advertisments and operating manuals for the product; if these printed materials do not mention the escrowing features, and no one tells the user, he or she may well remain ignorant of them, even though the fact of escrow is "public knowledge."

nature, an open back door is explicit; it must be deliberately and intentionally created by a designer or implementer.

A hidden back door is one whose existence is not widely known, at least upon initial deployment. It can be created deliberately (e.g., by a designer who insists on retaining access to a system that he may have created) or accidentally (e.g., as the result of a design flaw). Often, a user wishing access through a deliberately created hidden back door must pass through special system-provided authorization services. Almost by definition, an accidentally created hidden back door requires no special authorization for its exploitation, although finding it may require special knowledge. In either case, the existence of hidden back doors may or may not be documented; frequently, it is not.

Particularly harmful hidden back doors can appear when "secure" applications are implemented using insecure operating systems; more generally, "secure" applications layered on top of insecure systems may not be secure in practice. Cryptographic algorithms implemented on weak operating systems present another large class of back doors that can be used to undermine the integrity and the confidentiality that cryptographic implementations are intended to provide. For example, a database application that provides strong access control and requires authorization for access to its data files but is implemented on an operating system that allows users to view those files without going through the database application does not provide strong confidentiality. Such an application may well have its data files encrypted for confidentiality.

The existence of back doors can pose high-level risks. The shutdown or malfunction of life-critical systems, loss of financial stability in electronic commerce, and compromise of private information in database systems can all have serious consequences. Even if back doors are undocumented, they can be discovered and misused by insiders or outsiders. Reliance on "security by obscurity" is always dangerous, because trying to suppress knowledge of a design fault is generally very difficult. If a back door exists, it will eventually be discovered, and its discoverer can post that knowledge worldwide. If systems containing a discovered back door were on the Internet or were accessible by modem, massive exploitation could occur almost instantaneously, worldwide. If back doors lack a capability for adequate authentication and accountability, then it can be very difficult to detect exploitation and to identify the culprit.

Translucent Cryptography

Translucent cryptography has been proposed by Ronald Rivest as an alternative to escrowed encryption.[30] The proposed technical scheme, which involves no escrow of unit keys, would ensure that any given message or file could be decrypted by the government with probability p; the value of p $(0 < p < 1)$ would be determined by the U.S. Congress. In other words, on average, the government would be able to decrypt a fraction p of all messages or files to which it was given legal access. Today (without encryption), $p = 1$. In a world of strong (unescrowed) encryption, $p = 0$. A large value of p favors law enforcement, while a small value of p favors libertarian privacy. Rivest proposes that some value of p balances the interests on both sides.

It is not necessary that the value of p be fixed for all time or be made uniform for all devices. p could be set differently for cellular telephones and for e-mail, or it could be raised or lowered as circumstances dictated. The value of p would be built into any given encryption device or program.

Note that in contrast to escrowed encryption, translucent cryptography requires no permanent escrowing of unit keys, although it renders access indeterminate and probabilistic.

7.2.4 Network-based Encryption

Security for Voice Communications

In principle, secure telephony can be made the responsibility of telephone service providers. Under the current regulatory regime (changing even as this report is being written), tariffs often distinguish between data and voice. Circuits designated as carrying ordinary voice (also to include fax and modem traffic) could be protected by encryption supplied by the service provider, perhaps as an extra security option that users could purchase. Common carriers (service providers in this context) that provide encryption services are required by the Communications Assistance for Law Enforcement Act to decrypt for law enforcement authorities upon legal request. (The "trusted third party" (TTP) concept discussed in Europe[31] is similar in the sense that TTPs are responsible for providing key management services for secure communications. In particular, TTPs provide session keys over secure channels to end users that they can then

---

[30]Ronald Rivest, "Translucent Cryptography: An Alternative to Key Escrow," paper presented at the Crypto 1995 Rump Session, August 29, 1995.

[31]See, for example, Nigel Jefferies, Chris Mitchell, and Michael Walker, *A Proposed Architecture for Trusted Third Party Services*, Royal Holloway, University of London, 1995.

use to encrypt communications with parties of interest; these keys are made available to law enforcement officials upon authorized request.)

The simplest version of network-based encryption would provide for link encryption (e.g., encrypting the voice traffic only between switches). Link encryption would leave the user vulnerable to eavesdropping at a point between the end-user device and the first switching office. In principle, a secure end-user device could be used to secure this "last mile" link.[32]

Whether telecommunications service providers will move ahead on their own with network-based encryption for voice traffic is uncertain for a number of reasons. Because most people today either believe that their calls are reasonably secure or are not particularly concerned about the security of their calls, the extent of demand for such a service within the United States is highly uncertain. Furthermore, by moving ahead in a public manner with voice encryption, telephone companies would be admitting that calls carried on their network are today not as secure as they could be; such an acknowledgment might undermine their other business interests. Finally, making network-based encryption work internationally would remain a problem, although any scheme for ensuring secure international communications will have drawbacks.

More narrowly focused network-based encryption could be used with that part of the network traffic that is widely acknowledged to be vulnerable to interception—namely, wireless voice communications. Wireless communications can be tapped "in the ether" on an entirely passive basis, without the knowledge of either the sending or receiving party. Of particular interest is the cellular telephone network; all of the current standards make some provisions for encryption. Encryption of the wireless link is also provided by the Global System for Mobile Communications (GSM), a European standard for mobile communications. In general, communication is encrypted from the mobile handset to the cell, but not end to end. Structured in this manner, encryption would not block the ability of law enforcement to obtain the contents of a call, because access could always be obtained by tapping the ground station.

At present, transmission of most wireless communications is analog. Unless special measures are taken to prevent surveillance, analog transmissions are relatively easy to intercept. However, it is widely expected

---

[32]The "last mile" is a term describing that part of a local telephone network between the premises of an individual subscriber and the central-office switch from which service is received. The vulnerability of the "last mile" is increased because it is easier to obtain access to the physical connections and because the volume of traffic is small enough to permit the relevant traffic to be isolated easily. On the other hand, the vulnerability of the switch is increased because it is often accessible remotely through dial-in ports.

that wireless communications will become increasingly digital in the future, with two salutary benefits for security. One is that compared to analog signals, even unencrypted digital communications are difficult for the casual eavesdropper to decipher or interpret, simply because they are transmitted in digital form. The second is that digital communications are relatively easy to encrypt.

Security for Data Communications

The body responsible for determining technical standards for Internet communications, the Internet Engineering Task Force, has developed standards for the Internet Protocol (version 6, also known as IPv6) that require conforming implementations to have the ability to encrypt data packets, with the default method of encryption being DES.[33] However, IPv6 standards are silent with respect to key management, and so leave open the possibility that escrow features might or might not be included at the vendor's option.

If the proposed standards are finalized, vendors may well face a Hobson's choice: to export Internet routing products that do not conform to the IPv6 standard (to obtain favorable treatment under the current ITAR, which do not allow exceptions for encryption stronger than 40-bit with RC2 or RC4), or to develop products that are fully compliant with IPv6 (a strong selling point), but only for the domestic market. Still,

---

[33]The Network Working Group has described protocols that define standards for encryption, authentication, and integrity in the Internet Protocol. These protocols are described in the following documents, issued by the Network Working Group as Requests for Comments (RFCs) in August 1995:

RFC   *Title*

1825   Security Architecture for the Internet Protocol (IP); describes the security mechanisms for IP version 4 (IPv4) and IP version 6 (IPv6).

1826   IP Authentication Header (AH); describes a mechanism for providing cryptographic authentication for IPv4 and IPv6 datagrams.

1827   IP Encapsulating Security Payload (ESP); describes a mechanism that works in both IPv4 and IPv6 for providing integrity and confidentiality to IP datagrams.

1828   IP Authentication using Keyed MD5; describes the use of a particular authentication technique with IP-AH.

1829   The ESP DES-CBC Transform; describes the use of a particular encryption technique with the IP Encapsulating Security Payload.

These documents are available from ftp://ds.internic.net/rfc/rfcNNNN.txt, where NNNN is the RFC number.

escrowed implementations of IPv6 would be consistent with the proposed standard and might be granted commodities jurisdiction to the Commerce Control List under regulations proposed by the Administration for escrowed encryption products.

7.2.5 Distinguishing Between Encrypted Voice and Data Communications Services for Exceptional Access

For purposes of allowing exceptional access, it may be possible to distinguish between encrypted voice and data communications, at least in the short run. Specifically, a proposal by the JASON study group suggests that efforts to install features for exceptional access should focus on secure voice communications, while leaving to market forces the evolution of secure data communications and storage.[34] This proposal rests on the following propositions:

• Telephony, as it is experienced by the end user, is a relatively mature and stable technology, compared to data communications services that evolve much more rapidly. Many people—perhaps the majority of the population—will continue to use devices that closely resemble the telephones of today, and many more people are familiar with telephones than are familiar with computers or the Internet.

An important corollary is that regulation of rapidly changing technologies is fraught with more danger than is the regulation of mature technologies, simply because regulatory regimes are inherently slow to react and may well pose significant barriers to the development of new technologies. This is especially true in a field moving as rapidly as information technology.

• Telephony has a long-standing regulatory and technical infrastructure associated with it, backed by considerable historical precedent, such as that for law enforcement officials obtaining wiretaps on telephonic communications under court order. By contrast, data communications services are comparatively unregulated (Box 7.5).

• In remarks to the committee, FBI Director Louis Freeh pointed out that it was voice communications that drove the FBI's desire for passage of the Communications Assistance for Law Enforcement Act (CALEA); he acknowledged that other mechanisms for communication might be relevant to law enforcement investigations but has undertaken nonlegislative approaches to deal with those mechanisms.

---

[34]JASON Program Office, *JASON Encryption/Privacy Study*, Report JSR-93-520 (unpublished), MITRE Corporation, McLean, Va., 1993.

BOX 7.5
Two Primary Rate and Service Models for
Telecommunications Today

Regulated Common Carrier Telephony Services

Regulated common carrier telephony services are usually associated with voice telephony, including fax and low-speed modem data communications. If a "common carrier" provision applies to a given service provider, the provider must provide service to anyone who asks at a rate that is determined by a public utilities commission. Common carriers often own their own transport facilities (e.g., fiber-optic cables, telephone wires, and so on), and thus the service provider exerts considerable control over the routing of a particular communication. Pricing of service for the end user is often determined on the basis of actual usage. The carrier also provides value-added services (e.g., call waiting) to enhance the value of the basic service to the customer. Administratively, the carrier is usually highly centralized.

Bulk Data Transport

Bulk services are usually associated with data transport (e.g., data sent from one computer to another) or with "private" telephony (e.g., a privately owned or operated branch exchange for telephone service within a company). Pricing for bulk services is usually a matter of negotiation between provider and customer and may be based on statistical usage, actual usage, reliability of transport, regional coverage, or other considerations. Policy for use is set by the party that pays for the bulk service, and thus, taken over the multitude of organizations that use bulk services, is administratively decentralized. In general, the customer provides value-added services. Routing paths are often not known in advance, but instead may be determined dynamically.

- Demand for secure telephone communications, at least domestically, is relatively small, if only because most users consider today's telephone system to be relatively secure. A similar perception of Internet security does *not* obtain today, and thus the demand for highly secure data communications is likely to be relatively greater and should not be the subject of government interference.

Under the JASON proposal, attempts to influence the inclusion of escrow features could affect only the hardware devices that characterize telephony today (e.g., a dedicated fax device, an ordinary telephone). In general, these devices do now allow user programming or additions and, in particular, lack the capability enabling the user to provide encryption easily.

The JASON study also recognized that technical trends in telecommunications are such that telephony will be increasingly indistinguishable from data communications. One reason is that communications are becoming increasingly digital. A bit is a bit, whether it was originally part of a voice communication or part of a data communication, and the purpose of a communications infrastructure is to transport bits from Point A to Point B, regardless of the underlying information content; reconstituting the transported bits into their original form will be a task left to the parties at Point A and Point B. Increasingly, digitized signals for voice, data, images, and video will be transported in similar ways over the same network facilities, and often they will be combined into single multiplexed streams of bits as they are carried along.[35]

For example, a voice-generated analog sound wave that enters a telephone may be transmitted to a central switching office, at which point it generally is converted into a digital bit stream and merged with other digital traffic that may originally have been voices, television signals, and high-speed streams of data from a computer. The network transports all of this traffic across the country by a fiber-optic cable and converts the bits representing voice back into an analog signal only when it reaches the switching office that serves the telephone of the called party. To a contemporary user of the telephone, the conversation proceeds just as it might have done 30 years ago (although probably with greater fidelity), but the technology used to handle the call is entirely different.

Alternatively, a computer connected to a data network can be converted into the functional equivalent of a telephone.[36] Some on-line service providers will be offering voice communications capability in the near future, and the Internet itself can be used today to transport real-time voice and even video communications, albeit with relatively low fidelity and reliability but also at very low cost.[37] Before these modalities

---

[35]Note, however, that the difficulty of *searching* for a given piece of information does depend on whether it is voice or text. It is quite straightforward to search a given digital stream for a sequence of bits that represents a particular word as text, but quite difficult to search a digital stream for a sequence of bits that represents that particular word as voice.

[36]For example, an IBM catalogue offers for general purchase a "DSP Modem and Audio Card" with "Telephony Enhancement" that provides a full-duplex speaker telephone for $254. The card is advertised as being able to make the purchaser's PC into "a telephone communications center with telephone voice mail, caller ID, and full duplex speakerphone capability (for true simultaneous, two-way communications)." See *The IBMPC Direct Source Book*, Fall 1994, p. 43. An article in the *Hewlett-Packard Journal* describes the ease with which a telephone option card was developed for a workstation; see S. Paul Tucker, "HP TeleShare: Integrating Telephone Capabilities on a Computer Workstation," *Hewlett-Packard Journal*, April 1995, pp. 69-74.

[37]In January 1996, it was estimated that approximately 20,000 people worldwide are users of Internet telephone service. See Mike Mills, "It's the Net's Best Thing to Being There," *Washington Post*, January 23, 1996, p. C1.

become acceptable for mainstream purposes, the Internet (or its successor) will have to implement on a wide scale new protocols and switching services to eliminate current constraints that involve time delays and bandwidth limitations.

A second influence that will blur the distinction between voice and data is that the owners of the devices and lines that transport bits today are typically the common carriers—firms originally formed to carry long-distance telephone calls and today subject to all of the legal requirements imposed on common carriers (see Box 7.5). But these firms sell transport capacity to parties connecting data networks, and much of today's bulk data traffic is carried over communications links that are owned by the common carriers. The Telecommunications Reform Act of 1996 will further blur the lines among service providers.

The lack of a technical boundary between telephony and data communications results from the way today's networks are constructed. Networks are built on a protocol "stack" that embodies protocols at different layers of abstraction. At the very bottom are the protocols for the physical layer that define the voltages and other physical parameters that represent ones and zeros. On top of the physical layer are other protocols that provide higher-level services by making use of the physical layer. Because the bulk of network traffic is carried over a physical infrastructure designed for voice communications (i.e., the public switched telecommunications network), interactions at the physical layer can be quite naturally regarded as being in the domain of "voice." But interactions at higher layers in the stack are more commonly associated with "data."

Acknowledging these difficulties, the JASON study concluded that limiting efforts to promote escrowed encryption products to those associated with voice communications had two important virtues. First, it would help to preserve law enforcement needs for access to a communications mode—namely telephony—that is widely regarded as important to law enforcement. Second, it would avoid premature government regulation in the data services area (an area that is less important historically to criminal investigation and prosecution than is telephony), thus avoiding the damage that could be done to a strong and rapidly evolving U.S. information technology industry. It would take—several years to a decade—for the technical "loopholes" described above to become significant, thus giving law enforcement time to adapt to a new technical reality.

7.2.6 A Centralized Decryption Facility
for Government Exceptional Access

Proposed procedures to implement the retrieval of keys escrowed under the Clipper initiative call for the escrowed key to be released by the escrow agencies to the requesting law enforcement authorities upon presentation of proper legal authorization, such as a court order. Critics have objected to this arrangement because it potentially compromises keys for all time—that is, once the key to a specific telephone has been divulged, it is in principle possible to eavesdrop forever on conversations using that telephone, despite the fact that court-ordered wiretaps must have a finite duration.

To counter this criticism, Administration officials have designed a plan that calls for keys to be transmitted electronically to EES decryption devices in such a way that the decryption device will erase the key at the time specified in the court order. However, acceptance of this plan relies on assurances that the decryption device would indeed work in this manner. In addition, this proposal is relevant only to the final plan—the interim procedures specify manual key handling.

Another way to counter the objection to potential long-lasting compromise of keys involves the use of a centralized government-operated decryption facility. Such a facility would receive EES-encrypted traffic forwarded by law enforcement authorities and accompanied by appropriate legal authorization. Keys would be made available by the escrow agents to the facility rather than to the law enforcement authorities themselves, and the plaintext would be returned to the requesting authorities. Thus, keys could never be kept in the hands of the requesting authorities, and concern about illicit retention of keys by law enforcement authorities could be reduced. Of course, concerns about retention by the decryption facility would remain, but since the number of decryption facilities would be small compared to the number of possible requesting law enforcement authorities, the problem would be more manageable. Since the decryption facilities would likely be under centralized control as well, it would be easier to promulgate and enforce policies intended to prevent abuse.[38]

---

[38]The committee suspects that the likelihood of abusive exercise of wiretap authority is greater for parties that are farther removed from higher levels of government, although the consequences may well be more severe when parties closer to the top levels of government are involved. A single "bad apple" near the top of government can set a corrupt and abusive tone for an entire government, but at least "bad apples" tend to be politically accountable. By contrast, the number of parties tends to increase as those parties are farther and farther removed from the top, and the likelihood that at least some of these parties will be abusive seems higher. (Put differently, the committee believes that state/local authorities are more likely to be abusive in their exercise of wiretapping authority simply because they do the majority of the wiretaps. Note that while Title III calls for a report to be filed on every federal and state wiretap order, the majority of missing reports are mostly from state wiretap orders rather than federal orders. (See Administrative Office of the United States Courts, *Wiretap Report*, AOUSC, Washington, D.C., April 1995, Table 2.)

One important aspect of this proposal is that the particular number of facilities constructed and the capacity of each could limit the number of simultaneous wiretaps possible at any given time. Such a constraint would force law enforcement authorities to exercise great care in choosing targets for interception, just as they must when they are faced with constraints on resources in prosecuting cases. A result could be greater public confidence that only wiretaps were being used only in important cases. On the other hand, a limit on the number of simultaneous wiretaps possible is also a potential disadvantage from the standpoint of the law enforcement official, who may not wish to make resource-driven choices about how and whom to prosecute or investigate. Making encryption keys directly available to law enforcement authorities allows them to conduct wiretaps unconstrained by financial and personnel limitations.

A centralized decryption facility would also present problems of its own. For example, many people would regard it as more threatening to give a centralized entity the capability to acquire and decrypt all traffic than to have such capabilities distributed among local law enforcement agencies. In addition, centralizing all wiretaps and getting the communications out into the field in real time could require a complex infrastructure. The failure of a centralized facility would have more far-reaching effects than a local failure, crippling a much larger number of wiretaps at once.

7.3 LOOMING ISSUES

Two looming issues have direct significance for national cryptography policy: determining the level of encryption needed to protect against high-quality attacks, and organizing the U.S. government for a society that will need better information security. Appendix M describes two other issues that relate but are not central to the current debate over cryptography policy: digital cash and the use of cryptography to protect intellectual property.

7.3.1 The Adequacy of Various Levels of Encryption Against High-Quality Attack

What level of encryption strength is needed to protect information against high-quality attack? For purposes of analysis, this discussion considers only perfect implementations of cryptography for confidentiality (i.e., implementations without hidden "trap doors," installed on secure operating systems, and so on). Thus, the only issue of significance for this discussion is the size of the key and the algorithm used to encrypt the original plaintext.

Any cryptanalysis problem can be solved by brute force given enough computers and time; the question is whether it is possible to assemble enough computational resources to allow a brute-force cryptanalysis on a time scale and cost reasonable for practical purposes.

As noted in Chapter 4, a message encoded with a 40-bit RC4 algorithm was recently broken in 8 days by a brute-force search through the use of a single workstation optimized for speed in graphics processing.

Even so, such a key size is adequate for many purposes (e.g., credit card purchases). It is also sufficient to deny access to parties with few technical skills, or to those with access to limited computing resources. But if the data being protected is valuable (e.g., if it refers to critical proprietary information), 40-bit keys are inadequate from an information security perspective. The reason is that for logistical and administrative reasons, it does not make sense to require a user to decide what information is or is not critical—the simplest approach is to protect both critical and noncritical information alike at the level required for protecting critical information. If this approach is adopted, the user does not run the risk of inadequately protecting sensitive information. Furthermore, the compromise of a single piece of information can be catastrophic, and since it is generally impossible to know if a particular piece of information has been compromised, those with a high degree of concern for the confidentiality of information must be concerned about protecting all information at a level higher than the thresholds offered by the 8-day cryptanalysis time described above.

From an interceptor's point of view, the cryptanalysis times provided by such demonstrations are quite daunting, because they refer to the time needed to cryptanalyze a single message. A specific encrypted message cryptanalyzed in this time may be useful when it is known with high probability to be useful; however, such times are highly burdensome when many messages must be collected and processed to yield one useful message. An eavesdropper could well have considerable difficulty in *finding* the ciphertext corresponding to critical information, but the information security manager cannot take the chance that a critical piece of information might be compromised anyway.[39]

A larger key size increases the difficulty of a brute-force search. For

---

[39]In general, information security managers must develop a model of the threat and respond to that threat, rather than simply assuming the worst (for which the only possible response would be to do "everything"). However, in the case of encryption and in the absence of governmental controls on technology, strong encryption costs about the same as weak encryption. Under such circumstances, it makes no sense at all for the information security manager to choose weak encryption.

symmetric algorithms, a 56-bit key entails a work factor that is 2^{16} (65,536) times larger than that of a 40-bit key, and implies a search time of about 1,430 years to accomplish (assuming that the algorithm using that key would take about the same time to execute as the RC4 algorithm). Using more computers could decrease the time proportionally. (A discussion of key lengths for asymmetric algorithms is contained in Chapter 2.)

Large speed-up factors for search time would be possible through the use of special-purpose hardware, which can be optimized to perform specific tasks. Estimates have been made regarding the amount of money and time needed to conduct an exhaustive key search against a message encrypted using the DES algorithm. Recent work by Wiener in 1993,[40] Dally in 1994,[41] and Diffie et al. in 1996[42] suggest the feasibility of using special-purpose processors costing a few million dollars working in parallel or in a distributed fashion to enable a brute-force solution of a single 56-bit DES cipher on a time scale of hours. When the costs of design, operation, and maintenance are included (and these costs are generally much larger than the cost of the hardware itself), the economic burden of building and using such a machine would be significant for most individuals and organizations. Criminal organizations would have to support an infrastructure for cracking DES through brute-force search clandestinely, to avoid being targeted and infiltrated by law enforcement officials. As a result, developing and sustaining such an infrastructure would be even more difficult for criminals attempting to take that approach.

Such estimates suggest that brute-force attack against 56-bit algorithms such as DES would require the significant effort of a well-funded adversary with access to considerable resources. Such attacks would be far more likely from foreign intelligence services or organized criminal cartels with access to considerable resources and expertise, for whom the plaintext information sought would have considerable value, than from the casual snoop or hacker who is merely curious or nosy.

Thus, for routine information of relatively low or moderate sensitivity or value, 56-bit protection probably suffices at this time. But for information of high value, especially information that would be valuable to

---

[40]M.J. Wiener, "Efficient DES Key Search," TR-244, May 1994, School of Computer Science, Carleton University, Ottawa, Canada; presented at the Rump Session of Crypto '93.

[41]William P. Dally, Professor of Electrical Engineering, Massachusetts Institute of Technology, private communication to the committee, September 1995.

[42]Matt Blaze, Whitfield Diffie, Ronald L. Rivest, Bruce Schneier, Tsutomu Shimomura, Eric Thompson, and Michael Wiener, "Minimal Key Lengths for Symmetric Ciphers to Provide Adequate Commercial Security: A Report by an Ad Hoc Group of Cryptographers and Computer Scientists," January 1996. Available on-line at http://www.bsa.org.

foreign intelligence services or major competitors, the adequacy in a decade of 56-bit encryption against a determined and rich attacker is open to question.

7.3.2 Organizing the U.S. Government
for Better Information Security on a National Basis

As noted in Chapter 6, no organization or entity within the federal government has the responsibility for promoting information security in the private sector or for coordinating information security efforts between government and nongovernment parties. NIST is responsible for setting Federal Information Processing Standards, and from time to time the private sector adopts these standards, but NIST has authority for information security only in unclassified government information systems. Given the growing importance of the private nongovernment sector technologically and the dependence of government on the private information infrastructure, security practices of the private information infrastructure may have a profound effect on government activities, both civilian and military.

How can coordination be pursued? Coherent policy regarding information assurance, information security, and the operation of the information infrastructure itself is needed. Business interests and the private sector need to be represented at the policy-making table, and a forum for resolving policy issues is needed. And, since the details of implementation are often critical to the success of any given policy, policy implementation and policy formulation must go hand in hand.

Information security functions that may call for coordinated national action vary in scale from large to small:

• Assisting individual companies in key commercial sectors at their own request to secure their corporate information infrastructures by providing advice, techniques, and analysis that can be adopted at the judgment and discretion of the company involved. In some key sectors (e.g., banking and telecommunications), conduits and connections for such assistance already exist as the result of government regulation of firms in those sectors. At present, the U.S. government will provide advice regarding information security threats, vulnerabilities, and solutions only to government contractors (and federal agencies).[43]

• Educating users both inside and outside government about vari-

---

[43]This responsibility belongs to the NSA, as specified in the NSA-NIST Memorandum of Understanding of March 24, 1989 (reprinted in Office of Technology Assessment, *Information Security and Privacy in Network Environments*, OTA-TCT-606, U.S. Government Printing Office, Washington, D.C., September 1994, and in Appendix N).

ous aspects of better information security. For example, many product vendors and potential users are unaware of the fact that there are no legal barriers to the use of cryptography domestically. Outreach efforts could also help in publicizing the information security threat.

• Certifying appropriate entities that perform some cryptographic service. For example, a public-key infrastructure for authentication requires trusted certification authorities (Appendix H). Validating the bona fides of these authorities (e.g., through a licensing procedure) will be an essential aspect of such an infrastructure. In the event that private escrow agents become part of an infrastructure for the wide use of cryptography, such agents will need to be approved or certified to give the public confidence in using them.

• Setting de jure standards for information security. As noted above, the NIST charter prevents it from giving much weight to commercial or private sector needs in the formulation of Federal Information Processing Standards if those needs conflict with those of the federal government, even when such standards affect practice in the private sector. Standards of technology and of practice that guide the private sector should be based on private sector needs, both to promote "best practices" for information security and to provide a legitimate defense in liability cases involving breaches of information security.

How such functions should be implemented is another major question. The committee does not wish to suggest that the creation of a new organization is the only possible mechanism for performing these functions; some existing organization or entity could well be retooled to service these purposes. But it is clear that whatever entity assumes these functions must be highly insulated from political pressure (arguing for a high degree of independence from the executive branch), broadly representative (arguing for the involvement of individuals who have genuine policy-making authority drawn from a broad range of constituencies, not just government), and fully capable of hearing and evaluating classified arguments if necessary (arguing the need for security clearances).[44]

One proposal that has been discussed for assuming these responsibilities is based on the Federal Reserve Board. The Federal Reserve Board oversees the Federal Reserve System (FRS), the nation's central bank. The

---

[44]As noted in the preface to this report, the committee concluded that the broad outlines of national cryptography policy can be argued on an unclassified basis. Nevertheless, it is a reality of decision making in the U.S. government on these matters that classified information may nevertheless be invoked in such discussions and uncleared participants asked to leave the room. To preclude this possibility, participating members should have the clearances necessary to engage as full participants in order to promote an effective interchange of views and perspectives.

FRS is responsible for setting monetary policy (e.g., setting the discount rate), the supervision of banking organizations and open market operations, and providing services to financial institutions. The Board of Governors is the FRS's central coordinating body. Its seven members are appointed by the President of the United States and confirmed by the Senate for 14-year terms. These terms are staggered to insulate the governors from day-to-day political pressure. Its primary function is the formulation of monetary policy, but the Board of Governors also has supervisory and regulatory responsibilities over the activities of banking organizations and the Federal Reserve Banks.

A second proposal has been made by the Cross-Industry Working Team (XIWT) of the Corporation for National Research Initiatives for the U.S. government to establish a new Joint Security Technology Policy Board as an independent agency of the government.[45] Under this proposal, the board would be an authoritative agency and coordination body officially chartered by statute or executive order "responsible and answerable" for federal performance across all of its agencies, and for promotion of secure information technology environments for the public. In addition, the board would solicit input, analysis, and recommendations about security technology policy concerns from private sector groups and government agencies, represent these groups and agencies within the board, disseminate requests and inquiries and information back to these groups and agencies, review draft legislation in cognizant areas and make recommendations about the legislation, and represent the U.S. government in international forums and other activities in the domain of international security technology policy. The board would be chaired by the Vice President of the United States and would include an equal number of members appointed from the private sector and the federal government.

A third proposal, perhaps more in keeping with the objective of minimal government, could be to utilize existing agencies and organizational structures. The key element of the proposal would be to create an explicit function in the government, that of *domestic information security*. Because information policy intersects with the interests and responsibilities of several agencies and cabinet departments, the policy role should arguably reside in the Executive Office of the President. Placing the policy function there would also give it the importance and visibility it requires. It might also be desirable to give specific responsibility for the initiation and coordination of policy to a Counselor to the President for Domestic Informa-

---

[45]Cross-Industry Working Team, *A Process for Information Security Technology: An XIWT Report on Industry-Government Cooperation for Effective Public Policy*, March 1995. Available from Corporation for National Research Initiatives, Reston, Va., or on-line at http://www.cnri.reston.va.us.

tion Security (DIS). This individual could chair an interagency committee consisting of agencies and departments with a direct interest in and responsibilities for information security matters, including the operating agency, economic policy agencies (Departments of Treasury and Commerce), law enforcement agencies (FBI; Drug Enforcement Administration; Bureau of Alcohol, Tobaccco, and Firearms), and international affairs and intelligence agencies (Departments of State and Defense, CIA).

Operationally, a single agency could have responsibility for standards setting, certification of escrow agents, approval of certificate holders for authentication purposes, public education on information security, definition of "best practices," management of cryptography on the Commerce Control List, and so on. The operating agency could be one with an economic policy orientation, such as the Department of Commerce. An alternative point of responsibility might be the Treasury Department, although its law enforcement responsibilities could detract from the objective of raising the economic policy profile of the information security function.

The public advisory committee, which is an essential element of this structure, could be made up of representatives of the computing, telecommunications, and banking industries, as well as "public" members from academia, law, and so on. This committee could be organized along the lines of the President's Foreign Intelligence Advisory Board and could report to the Counselor for DIS.

7.4 RECAP

This chapter describes a number of possible policy options but does not attempt to pull together how these options might fit together in a coherent policy framework. That is the function of Chapter 8.

8

Synthesis, Findings, and Recommendations

8.1 SYNTHESIS AND FINDINGS

In an age of explosive worldwide growth of electronic data storage and communications, many vital national interests require the effective protection of information. Especially when used in coordination with other tools for information security, cryptography in all of its applications, including data confidentiality, data integrity, and user authentication, is a most powerful tool for protecting information.

8.1.1 The Problem of Information Vulnerability

Because digital representations of large volumes of information are increasingly pervasive, both the benefits and the risks of digital representation have increased. The benefits are generally apparent to users of information technology—larger amounts of information, used more effectively and acquired more quickly, can increase the efficiency with which businesses operate, open up entirely new business opportunities, and play an important role in the quality of life for individuals.

The risks are far less obvious. As discussed in Chapter 1, one of the most significant risks of a digital information age is the potential vulnerability of important information as it is communicated and stored. When information is transmitted in computer-readable form, it is highly vulnerable to unauthorized disclosure or alteration:

• Many communications are carried over channels (e.g., satellites, cellular telephones, and local area networks) that are easily tapped. Tapping wireless channels is almost impossible to detect and to stop, and tapping local area networks may be very hard to detect or stop as well. Other electronic communications are conducted through data networks that can be easily penetrated (e.g., the Internet).

• Approximately 10 billion words of information in computer-readable form can be scanned for $1 today (as discussed in Chapter 1), allowing intruders, the malicious, or spies to separate the wheat from the chaff very inexpensively. For example, a skilled person with criminal intentions can easily develop a program that recognizes and records all credit card numbers in a stream of unencrypted data traffic.[1] The decreasing cost of computation will reduce even further the costs involved in such searches.

• Many users do not know about their vulnerabilities to the theft or compromise of information; in some instances, they are ignorant of or even complacent about them. Indeed, the insecurity of computer networks today is much more the result of poor operational practices on the part of users and poor implementations of technology on the part of product developers than of an inadequate technology base or a poor scientific understanding.

In the early days of computing, the problems caused by information vulnerability were primarily the result of relatively innocent trespasses of amateur computer hackers who were motivated mostly by technical curiosity. But this is no longer true, and has not been true for some time. The fact that the nation is moving into an information age on a large scale means that a much larger number of people are likely to have strong financial, political, or economic motivations to exploit information vulnerabilities that still exist. For example, electronic interceptions and other technical operations account for the largest portion of economic and industrial information lost by U.S. corporations to foreign parties, as noted in Chapter 1.

Today, the consequences of large-scale information vulnerability are potentially quite serious:

• U.S. business, governmental, and individual communications are

---

[1]The feasibility of designing a program to recognize text strings that represent credit card numbers has been demonstrated most recently by the First Virtual Corporation. See press release of February 7, 1996, "First Virtual Holdings Identifies Major Flaw in Software-Based Encryption of Credit Cards; Numbers Easily Captured by Automated Program," First Virtual Corporation, San Diego, Calif. Available on-line at http://www.fv.com/gabletxt/release2_7_96.html.

targets or potential targets for intelligence organizations of foreign governments, competitors, vandals, suppliers, customers, and organized crime. Businesses send through electronic channels considerable amounts of confidential information, including items such as project and merger proposals, trade secrets, bidding information, corporate strategies for expansion in critical markets, research and development information relevant to cost reduction or new products, product specifications, and expected delivery dates. Most importantly, U.S. businesses must compete on a worldwide basis. International exposure increases the vulnerability to compromise of sensitive information. Helping to defend U.S. business interests against such compromises of information is an important function of law enforcement.

• American values such as personal rights to privacy are at stake. Private citizens may conduct sensitive financial transactions electronically or by telephone. Data on their medical histories, including mental illnesses, addictions, sexually transmitted diseases, and personal health habits, are compiled in the course of providing medical care. Driving records, spending patterns, credit histories, and other financial information are available from multiple sources. All such information warrants protection.

• The ability of private citizens to function in an information economy is at risk. Even today, individuals suffer as criminals take over their identities and run up huge credit card bills in their names. Toll fraud on cellular telephones is so large that some cellular providers have simply terminated international connections in the areas that they serve. Inaccuracies as the result of incorrectly posted information ruin the credit records of some individuals. Protecting individuals against such problems warrants public concern and is again an area in which law enforcement and other government authorities have a role to play.

• The federal government has an important stake in assuring that its important and sensitive political, economic, law enforcement, and military information, both classified and unclassified, is protected from misuse by foreign governments or other parties whose interests are hostile to those of the United States.

• Elements of the U.S. civilian infrastructure such as the banking system, the electric power grid, the public switched telecommunications network, and the air traffic control system are central to so many dimensions of modern life that protecting these elements must have a high priority. Defending these assets against information warfare and crimes of theft, misappropriation, and misuse potentially conducted by hostile nations, terrorists, criminals, and electronic vandals is a matter of national security and will require high levels of information protection and strong security safeguards.

8.1.2 Cryptographic Solutions to Information Vulnerabilities

Cryptography does not solve all problems of information security; for example, cryptography cannot prevent a party authorized to view information from improperly disclosing that information. Although it is not a "silver bullet" that can stand by itself, cryptography is a powerful tool that can be used to protect information stored and communicated in digital form: cryptography can help to assure confidentiality of data, to detect unauthorized alterations in data and thereby help to maintain its integrity, and to authenticate the asserted identity of an individual or a computer system (Chapter 2). Used in conjunction with other information security measures, cryptography has considerable value in helping law-abiding citizens, businesses, and the nation as a whole defend their legitimate interests against information crimes and threats such as fraud, electronic vandalism, the improper disclosure of national security information, or information warfare.

Modern cryptographic techniques used for confidentiality make it possible to develop and implement ciphers that are for all practical purposes impossible for unauthorized parties to penetrate but that still make good economic sense to use.

- Strong encryption is economically feasible today. For example, many integrated circuit chips that would be used in a computer or communications device can inexpensively accommodate the extra elements needed to implement the Data Encryption Standard (DES) encryption algorithm. If implemented in software, the cost is equally low, or even lower.

- Public-key cryptography can help to eliminate the expense of using couriers, registered mail, or other secure means for exchanging keys. Compared to a physical infrastructure for key exchange, an electronic infrastructure based on public-key cryptography to exchange keys will be faster and more able to facilitate secure communications between parties that have never interacted directly with each other prior to the first communication. Public-key cryptography also enables the implementation of the digital equivalent of a written signature, enabling safer electronic commerce.

- Encryption can be integrated by vendors into end-user applications and hardware for the benefit of the large majority of users who do not have the technical skill to perform their own integration. Encryption can also be made automatic and transparent in ways that require no extra action on the part of the user, thus ensuring that cryptographic protection will be present regardless of user complacency or ignorance.

8.1.3 The Policy Dilemma Posed by Cryptography

The confidentiality of information that cryptography can provide is useful not only for the legitimate purposes of preventing information crimes (e.g., the theft of trade secrets or unauthorized disclosure of sensitive medical records) but also for illegitimate purposes (e.g., shielding from law enforcement officials a conversation between two terrorists planning to bomb a building). Although strong automatic encryption implemented as an integral part of data processing and communications provides confidentiality for "good guys" against "bad guys" (e.g., U.S. business protecting information against economic intelligence efforts of foreign nations), it unfortunately also protects "bad guys" against "good guys" (e.g., terrorists evading law enforcement agencies). Under appropriate legal authorization such as a court order, law enforcement authorities may gain access to "bad guy" information for the purpose of investigating and prosecuting criminal activity. Similarly, intelligence gathering for national security and foreign policy purposes depends on having access to information of foreign governments and other foreign entities. (See Chapter 3.) Because such activities benefit our society as a whole (e.g., by limiting organized crime and terrorist activities), "bad guy" use of cryptography used for confidentiality poses a problem for society as a whole, not just for law enforcement and national security personnel.

Considered in these terms, it is clear that the development and widespread deployment of cryptography that can be used to deny government access to information represents a challenge to the balance of power between the government and the individual. Historically, all governments, under circumstances that further the common good, have asserted the right to compromise the privacy of individuals (e.g., through opening mail, tapping telephone calls, inspecting bank records); unbreakable cryptography for confidentiality provides the individual with the ability to frustrate assertions of that right.

The confidentiality that cryptography can provide thus creates conflicts. Nevertheless, all of the stakes described above—privacy for individuals, protection of sensitive or proprietary information for businesses and other organizations in the prevention of information crimes, ensuring the continuing reliability and integrity of nationally critical information systems and networks, law enforcement access to stored and communicated information for purposes of investigating and prosecuting crime, and national security access to information stored or communicated by foreign powers or other entities and organizations whose interests and intentions are relevant to the national security and the foreign policy interests of the United States—are legitimate. Informed public discussion of the issues must begin by acknowledging the legitimacy of both information security for law-abiding individuals and businesses and information gathering for law enforcement and national security purposes.

A major difficulty clouding the public policy debate regarding cryptography has been that certain elements have been removed from public view due to security classification. However, for reasons noted in the preface, the cleared members of the committee (13 of its 16 members) concluded that **the debate over national cryptography policy can be carried out in a reasonable manner on an unclassified basis.** Although many of the details relevant to policy makers are necessarily classified, these details are not central to making policy arguments one way or the other. Classified material, while important to operational matters in specific cases, is not essential to the big picture of why policy has the shape and texture that it does today nor to the general outline of how technology will, and policy should, evolve in the future.

To manage the policy dilemma created by cryptography, the United States has used a number of tools to balance the interests described above. For many years, concern over foreign threats to national security has been the primary driver of a national cryptography policy that has sought to maximize the protection of U.S. military and diplomatic communications while denying the confidentiality benefits of cryptography to foreign adversaries through the use of controls on the export of cryptographic technologies, products, and related technical information (Chapter 4). More recently, the U.S. government has aggressively promoted escrowed encryption as the technical foundation for national cryptography policy, both to serve domestic interests in providing strong protection for legitimate uses while enabling legally authorized access by law enforcement officials when warranted and also as the basis for more liberal export controls on cryptography (Chapter 5).

Both escrowed encryption and export controls have generated considerable controversy. Escrowed encryption has been controversial because its promotion by the U.S. government appears to some important constituencies to assert the primacy of information access needs of law enforcement and national security over the information security needs of businesses and individuals. Export controls on cryptography have been controversial because they pit the interests of U.S. vendors and some U.S multinational corporations against some of the needs of national security.

8.1.4 National Cryptography Policy for the Information Age

In a world of ubiquitous computing and communications, a concerted effort to protect the information assets of the United States is critical. While cryptography is only one element of a comprehensive approach to information security, it is nevertheless an essential element. Given the committee's basic charge to focus on national cryptography policy rather than national policy for information security, the essence of the committee's basic conclusion about policy is summarized by the following principle:

Basic Principle: U.S. national policy should be changed to support the broad use of cryptography in ways that take into account competing U.S. needs and desires for individual privacy, international economic competitiveness, law enforcement, national security, and world leadership.

In practice, this principle suggests three basic objectives for national cryptography policy:

1. **Broad availability of cryptography to all legitimate elements of U.S. society.** Cryptography supports the confidentiality and integrity of digitally represented information (e.g., computer data, software, video) and the authentication of individuals and computer systems communicating with other computer systems; these capabilities are important in varying degrees to protecting the information security interests of many different private and public stakeholders, including law enforcement and national security. Furthermore, cryptography can help to support law enforcement objectives in preventing information crimes such as economic espionage.

2. **Continued economic growth and leadership of key U.S. industries and businesses in an increasingly global economy, including but not limited to U.S. computer, software, and communications companies.** Such leadership is an integral element of national security. U.S. companies in information technology today have undeniable strengths in foreign markets, but current national cryptography policy threatens to erode these advantages. The largest economic opportunities for U.S. firms in all industries lie in using cryptography to support their critical domestic and international business activities, including international intrafirm and interfirm communications with strategic partners, cooperative efforts with foreign collaborators and researchers in joint business ventures, and real-time connections to suppliers and customers, rather than in selling information technology (Chapter 4).

3. **Public safety and protection against foreign and domestic threats.** Insofar as possible, communications and stored information of foreign parties whose interests are hostile to those of the United States should be accessible to U.S. intelligence agencies. Similarly, the communications and stored information of criminal elements that are a part of U.S. and global society should be available to law enforcement authorities as authorized by law (Chapter 3).

Objectives 1 and 2 argue for a policy that actively promotes the use of strong cryptography on a broad front and that places few restrictions on the use of cryptography. Objective 3 argues that some kind of government role in the deployment and use of cryptography may continue to be necessary for public safety and national security reasons. The committee believes that these three objectives can be met within a framework recognizing that **on balance, the advantages of more widespread use of cryptography outweigh the disadvantages**.

The committee concluded that cryptography is one important tool for protecting information and that it is very difficult for governments to control; it thus believes that the widespread nongovernment use of cryptography in the United States and abroad is inevitable in the long run. Cryptography is important because when it is combined with other measures to enhance information security, it gives end users significant control over their information destinies. Even though export controls have had a nontrivial impact on the worldwide spread of cryptography in previous years, over the long term cryptography is difficult to control because the relevant technology diffuses readily through national boundaries; export controls can inhibit the diffusion of products with encryption capabilities but cannot contain the diffusion of knowledge (Chapter 4). The spread of cryptography is inevitable because in the information age the security of information will be as important in all countries as other attributes valued today, such as the reliability and ubiquity of information.

Given the inevitability that cryptography will become widely available, policy that manages how cryptography becomes available can help to mitigate the deleterious consequences of such availability. Indeed, governments often impose regulations on various types of technology that have an impact on the public safety and welfare, and cryptography may well fall into this category. National policy can have an important effect on the rate and nature of the transition from today's world to that of the long-term future. Still, given the importance of cryptography to a more secure information future and its consequent importance to various dimensions of economic prosperity, policy actions that inhibit the use of cryptography should be scrutinized with special care.

The committee's policy recommendations are intended to facilitate a judicious transition between today's world of high information vulnerability and a future world of greater information security, while to the extent possible meeting government's legitimate needs for information gathering for law enforcement, national security, and foreign policy purposes. National cryptography policy should be expected to evolve over time in response to events driven by an era of rapid political, technological, and economic change.

The committee recognizes that national cryptography policy is intended to address only certain aspects of a much larger information security problem faced by citizens, businesses, and government. Nevertheless, the committee found that **current national policy is not adequate to support the information security requirements of an information society.** Cryptography is an important dimension of information security, but current policy discourages the use of this important tool in both intentional and unintentional ways, as described in Chapters 4 and 6. For example, through the use of export controls, national policy has explicitly sought to limit the use of encryption abroad but has also had the effect of reducing the domestic availability of products with strong encryption capabilities to businesses and other users. Furthermore, government action that discourages the use of cryptography contrasts sharply with national policy and technological and commercial trends in other aspects of information technology. Amidst enormous changes in the technological environment in the past 20 years, today the federal government actively pursues its vision of a national information infrastructure, and the use of computer and communications technology by private parties is growing rapidly.

The committee believes that a mismatch between the speed at which the policy process moves and the speed with which new products develop has had a profound impact on the development of the consensus necessary with respect to cryptography policy (Chapters 4 and 6). This mismatch has a negative impact on both users and vendors. For example, both are affected by an export control regime that sometimes requires many months or even years to make case-by-case decisions on export licensing, while high-value sales to these users involving integrated products with encryption capabilities can be negotiated and consummated on a time scale of days or weeks. Since the basic knowledge underlying cryptography is well known, cryptographic functionality can be implemented into new products on the time scale of new releases of products (several months to a year). Both users and vendors are affected by the fact that significant changes in the export control regulations governing cryptography have not occurred for 4 years (since 1992) at a time when needs for information security are growing, a period that could have accommodated several product cycles. Promulgation of cryptographic standards not based on commercial acceptability (e.g., the Escrowed Encryption Standard (FIPS 185), the Digital Signature Standard (FIPS 180-1)) raised significant industry opposition (from both vendors and users) and led to controversy and significant delays in or outright resistance to commercial adoption of these standards.

These examples suggest that the time scales on which cryptography policy is made and is operationally implemented are incompatible with the time scales of the marketplace. A more rapid and market-responsive decision-making process would leverage the strengths of U.S. businesses in the international marketplace before significant foreign competition develops. As is illustrated by the shift in market position from IBM to Microsoft in the 1980s, the time scale on which significant competition can arise is short indeed.

Attempts to promote a policy regime that runs against prevailing commercial needs, practice, and preference may ultimately result in a degree of harm to law enforcement and national security interests far greater than what would have occurred if a more moderate regime had been promoted in the first place. The reason is that proposed policy regimes that attempt to impose market-unfriendly solutions will inevitably lead to resistance and delay; whether desirable or not, this is a political reality. Responsible domestic businesses, vendors, and end users are willing to make some accommodations to U.S. national interests in law enforcement and national security, but cannot be expected to do so willingly when those accommodations are far out of line with the needs of the market. Such vendors and users are likely to try to move ahead on their own—and quickly so—if they believe that government requirements are not reasonable. Moreover, foreign vendors may well attempt to step into the vacuum. The bottom line is that the U.S. government may have only a relatively small window of time in which to influence the deployment of cryptography worldwide.

The committee also notes that the public debate has tended to draw lines that divide the policy issues in an overly simplistic manner, i.e., setting the privacy of individuals and businesses against the needs of national security and law enforcement. As observed above, such a dichotomy does have a kernel of truth. But viewed in the large, the dichotomy as posed is misleading. If cryptography can protect the trade secrets and proprietary information of businesses and thereby reduce economic espionage (which it can), it also supports in a most important manner the job of law enforcement. If cryptography can help protect nationally critical information systems and networks against unauthorized penetration (which it can), it also supports the national security of the United States. Framing national cryptography policy in this larger context would help to reduce some of the polarization among the relevant stakeholders.

Finally, the national cryptography policy of the United States is situated in an international context, and the formulation and implementation of U.S. policy must take into account international dimensions of the problem if U.S. policy is to be successful. These international dimensions, discussed in Chapter 6 and Appendix G, include the international scope of business today; the possibility of significant foreign competition in information technology; an array of foreign controls on the export, import, and use of cryptography; important similarities in the interests of the United States and other nations in areas such as law enforcement and antiterrorist activities; and important differences in other areas such as the relationship between the government and the governed.

8.2 RECOMMENDATIONS

The recommendations below address several critical policy areas. Each recommendation is cast in broad terms, with specifically actionable items identified for each when appropriate. In accordance with the committee's finding that the broad picture of cryptography policy can be understood on an unclassified basis, no findings or recommendations were held back on the basis of classification, and this report is unclassified in its entirety.

Recommendation 1: No law should bar the manufacture, sale, or use of any form of encryption within the United States.

This recommendation is consistent with the position of the Clinton Administration that legal prohibitions on the domestic use of any kind of cryptography are inappropriate,[2] and the committee endorses this aspect of the Administration's policy position without reservation.

For technical reasons described in Chapter 7, the committee believes that a legislative ban on the use of unescrowed encryption would be largely unenforceable. Products using unescrowed encryption are in use today by millions of users, and such products are available from many difficult-to-censor Internet sites abroad. Users could pre-encrypt their data, using whatever means were available, before their data were accepted by an escrowed encryption device or system. Users could store their data on remote computers, accessible through the click of a mouse but otherwise unknown to anyone but the data owner; such practices could occur quite legally even with a ban on the use of unescrowed encryption. Knowledge of strong encryption techniques is available from official U.S. government publications and other sources worldwide, and experts understanding how to use such knowledge might well be in high demand from criminal elements. Even demonstrating that a given communication or data file is "encrypted" may be difficult to prove, as algo-

---

[2]For example, see "Questions and Answers About the Clinton Administration's Encryption Policy," February 4, 1994. Reprinted in David Banisar (ed.), *1994 Cryptography and Privacy Sourcebook*, Electronic Privacy Information Center, Washington, D.C., 1994.

rithms for data compression illustrate. Such potential technical circumventions suggest that even with a legislative ban on the use of unescrowed cryptography, determined users could easily evade the enforcement of such a law.

In addition, a number of constitutional issues, especially those related to free speech, would be almost certain to arise. Insofar as a ban on the use of unescrowed encryption would be treated (for constitutional purposes) as a limitation on the "content" of communications, the government would have to come forward with a compelling state interest to justify the ban. These various considerations are difficult, and in some cases impossible, to estimate in advance of particular legislation as applied to a specific case, but the First Amendment issues likely to arise with a ban on the use of unescrowed encryption are not trivial. In addition, many people believe with considerable passion that government restrictions on the domestic use of cryptography would threaten basic American values such as the right to privacy and free speech. Even if the constitutional issues could be resolved in favor of some type of ban on the use of unescrowed encryption, these passions would surely result in a political controversy that could divide the nation and at the very least impede progress on the way to the full use of the nation's information infrastructure.

Finally, a ban on the use of any form of encryption would directly challenge the principle that users should be responsible for assessing and determining their own approaches to meeting their security needs. This principle is explored in greater detail in Recommendation 3.

Recommendation 2: National cryptography policy should be developed by the executive and legislative branches on the basis of open public discussion and governed by the rule of law.

In policy areas that have a direct impact on large segments of the population, history demonstrates that the invocation of official government secrecy often leads to public distrust and resistance. Such a result is even more likely where many members of society are deeply skeptical about government.

Cryptography policy set in the current social climate is a case in point. When cryptography was relevant mostly to government interests in diplomacy and national security, government secrecy was both necessary and appropriate. But in an era in which cryptography plays an important role in protecting information in all walks of life, public consensus and government secrecy related to information security in the private sector are largely incompatible. If a broadly acceptable social consensus that satisfies the interests of all legitimate stakeholders is to be found regarding the nation's cryptographic future, a national discussion of the issue must occur.

The nation's best forum for considering multiple views across the entire spectrum is the U.S. Congress, and only comprehensive congressional deliberation and discussion conducted in the open can generate the public acceptance that is necessary for policy in this area to succeed. In turn, a consensus derived from such deliberations, backed by explicit legislation when necessary, will lead to greater degrees of public acceptance and trust, a more certain planning environment, and better connections between policy makers and the private sector on which the nation's economy and social fabric rest. For these reasons, congressional involvement in the debate over cryptography policy is an asset rather than a liability. Moreover, some aspects of cryptography policy will require legislation if they are to be properly implemented (as discussed under Recommendation 5.3).

This argument does not suggest that there are no legitimate secrets in this area. However, in accordance with the committee's conclusion that the broad outlines of national cryptography policy can be analyzed on an unclassified basis, the committee believes that the U.S. Congress can also debate the fundamental issues in the open. Nor is the committee arguing that *all* aspects of policy should be handled in Congress. The executive branch is necessarily an important player in the formulation of national cryptography policy, and of course it must *implement* policy. Moreover, while working with the Congress, the executive branch must develop a coherent voice on the matter of cryptography policy—one that it does not currently have—and establish a process that is efficient, comprehensive, and decisive in bringing together and rationalizing many disparate agency views and interests.

Instances in which legislation may be needed are found in Recommendations 4, 5, and 6.

Recommendation 3: National cryptography policy affecting the development and use of commercial cryptography should be more closely aligned with market forces.

As cryptography has assumed greater importance to nongovernment interests, national cryptography policy has become increasingly disconnected from market reality and the needs of parties in the private sector. As in many other areas, national policy on cryptography that runs counter to user needs and against market forces is unlikely to be successful over the long term. User needs will determine the large-scale demand for information security, and policy should seek to exploit the advantages of market forces whenever and wherever possible. Indeed, many decades of experience with technology deployment suggest that reliance on user choices and market forces is generally the most rapid and effective way to promote the widespread utilization of any new and useful technology. Since the committee believes that the widespread deployment and use of cryptography will be in the national interest, it believes that national cryptography policy should align itself with user needs and market forces to the maximum feasible extent.

The committee recognizes that considerations of public safety and national security make it undesirable to maintain an entirely laissez-faire approach to national cryptography policy. But it believes that government intervention in the market should be carefully tailored to specific circumstances. The committee describes a set of appropriate government interventions in Recommendations 4, 5, and 6.

A national cryptography policy that is aligned with market forces would emphasize the freedom of domestic users to determine cryptographic functionality, protection, and implementations according to their security needs as they see fit. Innovation in technologies such as escrowed encryption would be examined by customers for their business fitness of purpose. Diverse user needs would be accommodated; some users will find it useful to adopt some form of escrowed encryption to ensure their access to encrypted data, while others will find that the risks of escrowed encryption (e.g., the dangers of compromising sensitive information through a failure of the escrowing system) are not worth the benefits (e.g., the ability to access encrypted data the keys to which have been lost or corrupted). Since no single cryptographic solution or approach will fit the business needs of all users, users will be free to make their own assessments and judgments about the products they wish to use. Such a policy would permit, indeed encourage, vendors to implement and customers to use products that have been developed within an already-existing framework of generally accepted encryption methods and to choose key sizes and management techniques without restriction.

Standards are another dimension of national cryptography policy with a significant impact on commercial cryptography and the market (Chapter 6). Cryptographic standards that are inconsistent with prevailing or emerging industry practice are likely to encounter significant market resistance. Thus, to the maximum extent possible, national cryptography policy that is more closely aligned with market forces should encourage adoption by the federal government and private parties of cryptographic standards that are consistent with prevailing industry practice.

Finally, users in the private sector need confidence that products with cryptographic functionality will indeed perform as advertised. To the maximum degree possible, national cryptography policy should support the use of algorithms, product designs, and product implementations that are open to public scrutiny. Information security mechanisms for widespread use that depend on a secret algorithm or a secret implementation invite a loss of public confidence, because they do not allow open testing of the security, they increase the cost of hardware implementations, and they may prevent the use of software implementations as described below. Technical work in cryptography conducted in the open can expose flaws through peer review and assure the private sector user community about the quality and integrity of the work underlying its cryptographic protection (Chapter 5).

Government classification of algorithms and product implementations clearly inhibits public scrutiny, and for the nongovernment sector, government classification in cryptography is incompatible with most commercial and business interests in information security. Moreover, the use of classified algorithms largely precludes the use of software solutions, since it is impossible to prevent a determined and technically sophisticated opponent from reverse-engineering an algorithm implemented in software. A similar argument applies to unclassified company-proprietary algorithms and product designs, although the concerns that arise with classified algorithms and implementations are mitigated somewhat by the fact that it is often easier for individuals to enter into the nondisclosure agreements necessary to inspect proprietary algorithms and product designs than to obtain U.S. government security clearances. Legally mandated security requirements to protect classified information also add to costs in a way that protection of company-proprietary information does not.

Recommendation 4: **Export controls on cryptography should be progressively relaxed but not eliminated.**

For many years, the United States has controlled the export of cryptographic technologies, products, and related technical information as munitions (on the U.S. Munitions List (USML) administered by the State Department). These controls have been used to deny potential adversaries access to U.S. encryption technology that might reveal important characteristics of U.S. information security products and/or be used to thwart U.S. attempts at collecting signals intelligence information. To date, these controls have been reasonably effective in containing the export of U.S. hardware-based products with encryption capabilities (Chapter 4). However, software-based products with encryption capabilities and cryptographic algorithms present a more difficult challenge because they can more easily bypass controls and be transmitted across national borders. In the long term, as the use of encryption grows worldwide, it is probable that national capability to conduct traditional signals intelligence against foreign parties will be diminished (as discussed in Chapter 3).

The current export control regime on strong cryptography is an increasing impediment to the information security efforts of U.S. firms competing and operating in world markets, developing strategic alliances internationally, and forming closer ties with foreign customers and suppliers. Some businesses rely on global networks to tie together branch offices and service centers across international boundaries. Other businesses are moving from a concept of operations that relies on high degrees of vertical integration to one that relies on the "outsourcing" of many business functions and activities. Consistent with rising emphasis on the international dimensions of business (for both business operations and markets), many U.S. companies must exchange important and sensitive information with an often-changing array of foreign partners, customers, and suppliers. Under such circumstances, the stronger level of cryptographic protection available in the United States is not meaningful when an adversary can simply attack the protected information through foreign channels.

Export controls also have had the effect of reducing the domestic availability of products with strong encryption capabilities. As noted in Chapter 4, the need for U.S. vendors (especially software vendors) to market their products to an international audience leads many of them to weaken the encryption capabilities of products available to the domestic market, even though no statutory restrictions are imposed on that market. Thus, domestic users face a more limited range of options for strong encryption than they would in the absence of export controls.

Looking to the future, both U.S. and foreign companies have the technical capability to integrate high-quality cryptographic features into their products and services. As demand for products with encryption capabilities grows worldwide, foreign competition could emerge at a level significant enough to damage the present U.S. world leadership in this critical industry. Today, U.S. information technology products are widely used in foreign markets because foreign customers find the package of features offered by those products to be superior to packages available from other, non-U.S. vendors, even though the encryption capabilities of U.S. products sold abroad are known to be relatively weak. However, for growing numbers of foreign customers with high security needs, the incremental advantage of superior nonencryption features offered by U.S. products may not be adequate to offset perceived deficiencies in encryption capability. Under such circumstances, foreign customers may well turn to non-U.S. sources that offer significantly better encryption capabilities in their products.

Overly restrictive export controls thus increase the likelihood that significant foreign competition will step into a vacuum left by the inability of U.S. vendors to fill a demand for stronger encryption capabilities integrated into general-purpose products. The emergence of significant foreign competition for the U.S. information technology industry has a number of possible long-term negative effects on U.S. national and economic security that policy makers would have to weigh against the contribution these controls have made to date in facilitating the collection of signals intelligence in support of U.S. national security interests (a contribution that will probably decline over time). Stimulating the growth of important foreign competitors would undermine a number of important national interests:

• *The national economic interest,* which is supported by continuing and even expanding U.S. world leadership in information technology supports. Today, U.S. information technology vendors have a window of opportunity to set important standards and deploy an installed base of technology worldwide, an opportunity that should be exploited to the maximum degree possible. Conversely, strong foreign competition would not be in the U.S. economic self-interest.

• *Traditional national security interests,* which are supported by leadership by U.S. vendors in supplying products with encryption capabilities to the world market. For example, it is desirable for the U.S. government to keep abreast of the current state of commercially deployed encryption technology, a task that is much more difficult to accomplish when the primary suppliers of such technology are foreign vendors rather than U.S. vendors.

• *U.S. business needs for trustworthy information protection,* which are supported by U.S. encryption products. Foreign vendors could be influenced by their governments to offer for sale to U.S. firms products with weak or poorly implemented cryptography. If these vendors were to gain significant market share, the information security of U.S. firms could be adversely affected.

• *Influence over the deployment of cryptography abroad,* which is supported by the significant impact of U.S. export controls on cryptography as the result of the strength of the U.S. information technology industry abroad. To the extent that the products of foreign competitors are available on the world market, the United States loses influence over cryptography deployments worldwide.

The committee believes that the importance of the U.S. information technology industry to U.S. economic interests and national security is large enough that some prudent risks can be taken to hedge against the potential damage to that industry, and some relaxation of export controls on cryptography is warranted. In the long term, U.S. signals intelligence capability is likely to decrease in any case. Consequently, the committee believes that the benefits of relaxation—namely helping to promote better information security for U.S. companies operating internationally and to extend U.S. leadership in this critical industry—are worth the short-term risk that the greater availability of U.S. products with stronger encryption capabilities will further impede U.S. signals intelligence capability.

Relaxation of export controls on cryptography is consistent with the basic principle of encouraging the use of cryptography in an information society for several reasons. First, relaxation would encourage the use of cryptography by creating an environment in which U.S. and multinational firms and users are able to use the same security products in the United States and abroad and thus to help promote better information security for U.S. firms operating internationally. Second, it would increase the availability of good cryptography products in the United States. Third, it would expand U.S. business opportunities overseas for information technology sales incorporating stronger cryptography for confidentiality by allowing U.S. vendors to compete with foreign vendors on a more equal footing, thereby helping to maintain U.S. leadership in fields critical to national security and economic competitiveness (as described in Chapter 4).

Some of these thoughts are not new. For example, in referring to a decision to relax export controls on computer exports, then-Deputy Secretary of Defense William Perry said that "however much we want to control [computers] that are likely to be available on retail mass markets, it will be impractical to control them," and that "we have to recognize we don't have any ability to control computers which are available on the mass retail market from non-CoCom countries."[3] He further noted that the U.S. government can no longer "set the standards and specifications of computers. They're going to be set in the commercial industry, and our job is to adapt to those if we want to stay current in the latest computer technology." The committee believes that exports of information technology products with encryption capabilities are not qualitatively different.

At the same time, cryptography is inherently dual-use in character (more so than most other items on the USML), with important applications to both civilian and military purposes. While this fact suggests to some that the export of all cryptography should be regulated under the Commerce Control List (CCL), the fact remains that cryptography is a particularly critical military application for which few technical alternatives are available. The USML is designed to regulate technologies with such applications for reasons of national security (as described in Chapters 3 and 4), and thus the committee concluded that the current export control regime on

---

[3]William J. Perry, Deputy Secretary of Defense, "Breakfast with Reporters, Friday, October 15, 1993, on Computer Exports," transcript of an on-the-record briefing.

cryptography should be relaxed but not eliminated. The committee believes that this action would have two major consequences:

- Relaxation will achieve a better balance between U.S. economic needs and the needs of law enforcement and national security.
- Retention of some controls will mitigate the loss to U.S. national security interests in the short term, allow the United States to evaluate the impact of relaxation on national security interests before making further changes, and "buy time" for U.S. national security authorities to adjust to a new technical reality.

Consistent with Recommendation 3, the committee believes that the export control regime for cryptography should be better aligned with technological and market trends worldwide. Recommendations 4.1 and 4.2 below reflect the committee's judgments about how the present export control regime should be relaxed expeditiously. However, it should be noted that some explicit relaxations in the export control regime have occurred over the last 15 years (see Chapter 4), although not to an extent that has fully satisfied vendor interests in liberalization. For example, under current export rules, the USML governs the export of software applications without cryptographic capabilities per se if they are designed with "hooks" that would, among other things, make it easy to interface a foreign-supplied, stand-alone cryptography module to the application (turning it into an integrated product with encryption capability so far as the user is concerned). However, the U.S. government set a precedent in 1995 by placing on the CCL the software product of a major vendor that incorporates a cryptographic applications programming interface (CAPI; as described in Chapter 7 and Appendix K).

Recommendation 4.3 is intended to provide for other important changes in the export control regime that would help to close the profound gap described in Chapter 4 regarding the perceptions of national security authorities vis-à-vis those of the private sector, including both technology vendors and users of cryptography; such changes would reduce uncertainty about the export control licensing process and eliminate unnecessary friction between the export control regime and those affected by it.

Recommendations 4.1 and 4.2 describe changes to the current export control regime, and unless stated explicitly, leave current regulations and proposals in place. However, the committee believes that certain features of the current regime are sufficiently desirable to warrant special attention here. Specifically,

- Certain products with encryption capabilities are subject to a more liberal export control regime by virtue of being placed on the CCL rather than the USML; these products include those providing cryptographic confidentiality that are specially designed, developed, or modified for use in machines for banking or money transactions and are restricted to use only in such transactions; and products that are limited in cryptographic functionality to providing capabilities for user authentication, access control, and data integrity without capabilities for confidentiality. Any change to the export control regime for cryptography should maintain at least this current treatment for these types of products.

• Since items on the CCL by definition have potential military uses, they are subject to trade embargoes against rogue nations. Thus, even products with encryption capabilities that are on the CCL require individual licenses and specific U.S. government approval if they are intended for use by a rogue destination. Furthermore, U.S. vendors are prohibited from exporting such products even to friendly nations if they know that those products will be re-exported to rogue nations. Maintaining the embargo of products with encryption capabilities against rogue nations supports the U.S. national interest and should not be relaxed now or in the future.

Finally, the committee notes that relaxation of export controls is only the first step on the road to greater use of cryptography around the world. As described in Chapter 6 and Appendix G, foreign nations are sovereign entities with the power and authority to apply import controls on products with encryption capabilities. It is thus reasonable to consider that a relaxation of U.S. export controls on cryptography may well prompt other nations to consider import controls; in such a case, U.S. vendors may be faced with the need to develop products with encryption capabilities on a nation-by-nation basis. Anticipating such eventualities as well as potential markets for escrowed encryption in both the United States and abroad, vendors may wish to develop families of "escrowable" products (as discussed in Chapter 7) that could easily be adapted to the requirements of various nations regarding key escrow; however, none of the three recommendations below, 4.1 through 4.3, is conditioned on such development.

Recommendation 4.1—Products providing confidentiality at a level that meets most general commercial requirements should be easily exportable.[4] Today, products with encryption capabilities that incorporate the 56-bit DES algorithm provide this level of confidentiality and should be easily exportable.

---

[4]For purposes of Recommendation 4.1, a product that is "easily exportable" will automatically qualify for treatment and consideration (i.e., commodity jurisdiction, or CJ) under the CCL. Automatic qualification refers to the same procedure under which software products using RC2 or RC4 algorithms for confidentiality with 40-bit key sizes currently qualify for the CCL.

A collateral requirement for products covered under Recommendation 4.1 is that a product would have to be designed so as to preclude its repeated use to increase confidentiality beyond the acceptable level (i.e., today, it would be designed to prevent the use of triple-DES). However, Recommendation 4.1 is intended to allow product implementations of layered encryption (i.e., further encryption of already-encrypted data, as might occur when a product encrypted a message for transmission on an always-encrypted communications link).

For secret keys used in products covered by Recommendation 4.1, public-key protection should be allowed that is at least as strong as the cryptographic protection of message or file text provided by those products, with appropriate safety margins that protect against possible attacks on these public-key algorithms.[5] In addition, to accommodate vendors and users who may wish to use proprietary algorithms to provide encryption capabilities, the committee believes that products incorporating any combination of algorithm and key size whose cryptographic characteristics for confidentiality are substantially equivalent to the level allowed under Recommendation 4.1 (today, 56-bit DES) should be granted commodity jurisdiction (CJ) to the CCL on a case-by-case basis.

An important collateral condition for products covered under Recommendation 4.1 (and 4.2 below) is that steps should be taken to mitigate the potential harm to U.S. intelligence-collection efforts that may result from the wider use of such products. Thus, the U.S. government should require that vendors of products with cryptographically provided confidentiality features exported under the relaxed export control regime of Recommendation 4.1 (and 4.2 below) must provide to the U.S. government under strict nondisclosure agreements (a) full technical specifications of their product, including source code and wiring schematics if necessary, and (b) reasonable technical assistance upon request in order to assist the U.S. government in understanding the product's internal operations. These requirements are consistent with those that govern export licenses granted under the case-by-case review procedure for CJ decisions today, and the nondisclosure agreements would protect proprietary vendor interests.

These requirements have two purposes. First, they would enable the U.S. government to validate that the product complies with all of the conditions required for export jurisdiction under the CCL. Second, they

---

[5]For example, the committee believes that a Rivest-Shamir-Adelman (RSA) or Diffie-Hellman key on the order of 1,024 bits would be appropriate for the protection of a 56-bit DES key. The RSA and Diffie-Hellman algorithms are asymmetric. Chapter 2 discusses why key sizes differ for asymmetric and symmetric algorithms.

would allow more cost-effective use of intelligence budgets for understanding the design of exported cryptographic systems.

Note that these requirements do not reduce the security provided by well-designed cryptographic systems. The reason is that a well-designed cryptographic system is designed on the principle that all security afforded by the system must reside in the secrecy of an easily changed, user-provided key, rather than in the secrecy of the system design or implementation. Because the disclosure of internal design and implementation information does not entail the disclosure of cryptographic keys, the security afforded by a well-designed cryptographic system is not reduced by these requirements.

Finally, the level of cryptographic strength that determines the threshold of easy exportability should be set at a level that promotes the broad use of cryptography and should be adjusted upward periodically as technology evolves.

The committee believes that today, products that incorporate 56-bit DES for confidentiality meet most general commercial requirements and thus should be easily exportable. The ability to use 56-bit DES abroad will significantly enhance the confidentiality available to U.S. multinational corporations conducting business overseas with foreign partners, suppliers, and customers and will improve the choice of products with encryption capabilities available to domestic users, as argued in Chapter 4.

Relaxation of export controls in the manner described in Recommendation 4.1 will help the United States to maintain its worldwide market leadership in products with encryption capabilities. The committee believes that many foreign customers unwilling to overlook the perceived weaknesses of 40-bit RC2/RC4 encryption, despite superior noncryptography features in U.S. information technology products, are likely to accept DES-based encryption as being adequate. Global market acceptance of U.S. products incorporating DES-based encryption is more conducive to U.S. national security interests in intelligence collection than is market acceptance of foreign products incorporating even stronger algorithm and key size combinations that may emerge to fill the vacuum if U.S. export controls are not relaxed.

Why DES? The Data Encryption Standard was promulgated by the National Bureau of Standards in 1975 as the result of an open solicitation by the U.S. government to develop an open encryption standard suitable for nonclassified purposes. Over the last 20 years, DES has gained widespread acceptance as a standard for secret-key cryptography and is currently being used by a wide range of users, both within the United States and throughout the world. This acceptance has come from a number of very important aspects that make DES a unique cryptographic solution. Specifically, DES provides the following major benefits:

- DES provides a significantly higher level of confidentiality protection than does 40-bit RC2 or RC4, the key-size and algorithm combination currently granted automatic commodity jurisdiction to the CCL. In the committee's judgment, DES provides a level of confidentiality adequate to promote broader uses of cryptography, whereas the public perception that 40-bit RC2/RC4 is "weak" does not provide such a level (even though the wide use of 40-bit RC2/RC4 would have significant benefits for information security in practice).[6]

- Since its inception, DES has been certified by the U.S. government as a high-quality solution for nonclassified security problems. Although future certification cannot be assured, its historical status has made it a popular choice for private sector purposes. Indeed, a large part of the global financial infrastructure is safeguarded by products and capabilities based on DES. Moreover, the U.S. government has developed a process by which specific DES implementations can be certified to function properly, increasing consumer confidence in implementations so certified.

- The analysis of DES has been conducted in open forums over a relatively long period of time (20 years). DES is one of a handful of encryption algorithms that has had such public scrutiny, and no flaws have been discovered that significantly reduce the work factor needed to break it; no practical shortcuts to exhaustive search for cryptanalytic attacks on DES have been found.

- DES can be incorporated into any product without a licensing agreement or fees. This means that any product vendor can include DES in its products with no legal or economic impact on its product lines.

- DES has nearly universal name recognition among both product vendors and users. Users are more likely to purchase DES-based products because they recognize the name.

- Since many foreign products are marketed as incorporating DES, U.S. products incorporating DES will not suffer a competitive market disadvantage with respect to encryption features.

These major benefits of DES are the result of the open approach taken in its development and its long-standing presence in the industry. The brute-force decryption of a single message encrypted with a 40-bit RC4 algorithm has demonstrated to information security managers around

---

[6]In other words, the market reality is that a side-by-side comparison of two products identical except for their domestic vs. exportable encryption capabilities always results in a market assessment of the stronger product as providing a "baseline" level of security and the weaker one as being inferior, rather than the weaker product providing the baseline and the stronger one being seen as superior.

the world that such a level of protection may be inadequate for sensitive information, as described in Chapter 4. A message encrypted with a 56-bit key would require about 2^{16} (65,536) times as long to break, and since a 40-bit decryption has been demonstrated using a single workstation for about a week, it is reasonable to expect that a major concerted effort, including the cost of design, operation, and maintenance (generally significantly larger than the cost of the hardware itself), would be required for effective and efficient exhaustive-search decryption with the larger 56-bit key (as described in Chapter 7).

As described in Chapter 7, the economics of DES make it an attractive choice for providing protection within mass-market products and applications intended to meet general commercial needs. When integrated into an application, the cost of using DES in practice is relatively small, whereas the cost of cracking DES is significantly higher. Since most information security threats come from individuals within an enterprise or individuals or small organizations outside the enterprise, the use of DES to protect information will be sufficient to prevent most problems. That is, DES is "good enough" for most information security applications and is likely to be good enough for the next decade because only the most highly motivated and well-funded organizations will be capable of sustaining brute-force attacks on DES during that time.

Some would argue that DES is already obsolete and that what is needed is a completely new standard that is practically impossible to break for the foreseeable future. Since computer processing speeds double every 1.5 years (for the same component costs), an exhaustive search for cryptographic keys becomes roughly 1,000 times easier every 15 years or so. Over time, any algorithm based on a fixed key length (DES uses a 56-bit key) becomes easier to attack. While the committee agrees that a successor to DES will be needed in the not-so-distant future, only DES has today the record of public scrutiny and practical experience that is necessary to engender public confidence. Developing a replacement for DES, complete with such a record, will take years by itself, and waiting for such a replacement will leave many of today's information vulnerabilities without a viable remedy. Adopting DES as today's standard will do much to relieve pressures on the export control regime stemming from commercial users needing to improve security, and will give the United States and other nations time to formulate a long-term global solution, which may or may not include provisions to facilitate authorized government access to encrypted data, based on the knowledge gained from emerging escrow techniques, digital commerce applications, and certificate authentication systems, which are all in their infancy today.

Given that a replacement for DES will eventually be necessary, product designers and users would be well advised to anticipate the need to upgrade their products in the future. For example, designers may need to design into the products of today the ability to negotiate cryptographic protocols with the products of tomorrow. Without this ability, a transition to a new cryptographic standard in the future might well be very expensive and difficult to achieve.

The committee recognizes that the adoption of Recommendation 4.1 may have a negative impact on the collection of signals intelligence. Much of the general intelligence produced today depends heavily on the ability to monitor and select items of interest from the large volumes of communications sent in the clear. If most of this traffic were encrypted, even at the levels allowed for liberal export today, the selection process would become vastly more difficult. Increasing the threshold of liberal exportability from 40-bit RC2/RC4 to 56-bit DES will not, in itself, add substantially to the difficulties of message selection. Foreign users of selected channels of high-interest communications would, in many cases, not be expected to purchase and use U.S. encryption products under any circumstances and thus in these cases would not be affected by a change in the U.S. export control regime. However, it is likely that the general use of 56-bit DES abroad will make it less likely that potentially significant messages can be successfully decrypted.

The overwhelming acceptance of DES makes it the most natural candidate for widespread use, thereby significantly increasing the security of most systems and applications. The committee believes that such an increase in the "floor" of information security outweighs the additional problems caused to national security agencies when collecting information. Since DES has been in use for 20 years, those agencies will at least be facing a problem that has well-known and well-understood characteristics. Recommendation 5 addresses measures that should help national security authorities to develop the capabilities necessary to deal with these problems.

Recommendation 4.2—Products providing stronger confidentiality should be exportable on an expedited basis to a list of approved companies if the proposed product user is willing to provide access to decrypted information upon legally authorized request.

Recommendation 4.1 addresses the needs of most general commercial users. However, some users for some purposes will require encryption capabilities at a level higher than that provided by 56-bit DES. The Administration's proposal to give liberal export consideration to software products with 64-bit encryption provided that those products are escrowed with a qualified escrow agent is a recognition that some users may need encryption capabilities stronger than those available to the general commercial market.

The philosophy behind the Administration's proposal is that the wide foreign availability of strong encryption will not significantly damage U.S. intelligence-gathering and law enforcement efforts if the United States can be assured of access to plaintext when necessary. Recommendation 4.2 builds on this philosophy to permit liberal export consideration of products with encryption capabilities stronger than that provided by 56-bit DES to users that are likely to be "trustworthy," i.e., willing to cooperate in providing access to plaintext for U.S. law enforcement authorities when a legally authorized request is made to those companies. (How firms are designated as approved companies is described below.) These approved firms will determine for themselves how to ensure access to plaintext, and many of them may well choose to use escrowed encryption products. A firm that chooses to use escrowed encryption would be free to escrow the relevant keys with any agent or agents of its own choosing, including those situated within the firm itself.

Note that while Recommendation 4.2 builds on the philosophy underlying the Administration's current software encryption proposal, it stands apart from it. In other words, Recommendation 4.2 should not be regarded as a criticism of, as a substitute for, or in contrast to the Administration's proposal.

From the standpoint of U.S. law enforcement interests, continued inclusion on the list of approved firms is a powerful incentive for a company to abide by its agreement to provide access to plaintext under the proper circumstances. While Recommendation 4.2 does not stipulate that companies must periodically requalify for the list, a refusal or inability to cooperate when required might well result in a company being dropped from the list and publicly identified as a noncooperating company, and subject the parties involved to the full range of sanctions that are available today to enforce compliance of product recipients with end-use restrictions (as described in Chapter 4).

Recommendation 4.2 also provides a tool with which the United States can promote escrowed encryption in foreign nations. Specifically, the presence of escrowed encryption products that are in fact user-escrowed would help to deploy a base of products on which the governments of the relevant nations could build policy regimes supporting escrowed encryption. It has the further advantage that it would speed the deployment of escrowed encryption in other countries because shipment of escrowed encryption products would not have to wait for the completion of formal agreements to share escrowed keys across international boundaries, a delay that would occur under the current U.S. proposal on escrowed encryption software products.

U.S. vendors benefit from Recommendation 4.2 because the foreign customers on the list of approved companies need not wait for the successful negotiation of formal agreements. Moreover, since Recommendation 4.2 allows approved companies to establish and control their own escrow agents, it eliminates the presence or absence of escrowing features as a competitive disadvantage. A final benefit for the U.S. vendor community is that Recommendation 4.2 reduces many bureaucratic impediments to sales to approved companies on the list, a benefit particularly valuable to smaller vendors that lack the legal expertise to negotiate the export control regime.

Customers choosing products covered under Recommendation 4.2 benefit because they retain the choice about how they will provide access to decrypted information. Potential customers objecting to Administration proposals on the export of escrowed encryption because their cryptographic keys might be compromised can be reassured that keys to products covered by Recommendation 4.2 could remain within their full control. If these customers choose to use escrowed encryption products to meet the need for access, they may use escrow agents of their own choosing, which may be the U.S. government, a commercial escrow agent as envisioned by the Administration's proposal, or an organization internal to the customer company.

Recommendation 4.2 is silent on how much stronger the encryption capabilities of covered products would be as compared to the capabilities of the products covered by Recommendation 4.1. The Administration has argued that the 64-bit limit on its current proposal is necessary because foreign parties with access to covered products might find a way to bypass the escrowing features. However, Recommendation 4.2 covers products that would be used by approved firms that, by assumption, would not be expected to tamper with products in a way that would prevent access to plaintext when necessary or would bypass the escrowing features of an escrowed encryption product. (The risks inherent in this assumption are addressed below in Requirements 1 through 3 for approved companies.) In addition, the committee observes that providing *much* stronger cryptographic confidentiality (e.g., 80 or 128 bits of key size rather than 56 or 64) would provide greater incentives for prospective users to adopt these products.

What firms constitute the list of approved companies? Under current practice, it is generally the case that a U.S.-controlled firm (i.e., a U.S. firm operating abroad, a U.S.-controlled foreign firm, or a foreign subsidiary of a U.S. firm) will be granted a USML license to acquire and export for its own use products with encryption capabilities stronger than that provided by 40-bit RC2/RC4 encryption. Banks and financial institutions (including stock brokerages and insurance companies), whether U.S.-controlled/owned or foreign-owned, are also generally granted USML licenses for stronger cryptography for use in internal communications and communications with other banks even if these communications are not limited strictly to banking or money transactions. Such licenses are granted on the basis of an individual review rather than through a categorical exemption from the USML.

Building on this practice, the committee believes that this category should be expanded so that a U.S.-controlled firm is able to acquire and export products covered under Recommendation 4.2 to its foreign suppliers and customers for the purpose of regular communications with the U.S.-controlled firm. A number of USML licenses for cryptography have implemented just such an arrangement, but the purpose of Recommendation 4.2 is to make these arrangements far more systematic and routine.

In addition, foreign firms specifically determined by U.S. authorities to be major and trustworthy firms should qualify for the list of approved companies. To minimize delay for U.S. information technology vendors and to help assure their competitiveness with foreign vendors, a list of the firms eligible to purchase U.S. products with encryption capabilities and/or the criteria for inclusion on the list should be made available upon request. Over time, it would be expected that the criteria would grow to be more inclusive so that more companies would qualify.

All firms on this list of approved companies would agree to certain requirements:

• *Requirement 1*—The firm will provide an end-user certification that the exported products will be used only for intrafirm business or by foreign parties in regular communications with the U.S. or approved foreign firm involved.
• *Requirement 2*—The firm will take specific measures to prevent the transfer of the exported products to other parties.
• *Requirement 3*—The firm agrees to provide the U.S. government with plaintext of encrypted information when presented with a properly authorized law enforcement request and to prove, if necessary, that the provided plaintext does indeed correspond to the encrypted information of interest. The use of escrowed encryption products would not be required, although many companies may find such products an appropriate technical way to meet this requirement.

The firms on the list of approved companies are likely to have needs for information security products of the highest strength possible for the environment in which they operate, because they are more likely to be the targets of the major concerted cryptanalytic effort described in Recommendation 4.1. On the other hand, some risks of diversion to unintended purposes do remain, and a firm's obligation to abide by Requirements 1 through 3 is a reasonable precaution that protects against such risks. Note also that the approved companies are defined in such a way as to increase the likelihood that they will be responsible corporate citizens, and as such responsive to relevant legal processes that may be invoked if access to plaintext data is sought. Further, they are likely to have assets in the United States that could be the target of appropriate U.S. legal action should they not comply with any of the three requirements above.

Recommendation 4.3—The U.S. government should streamline and increase the transparency of the export licensing process for cryptography.

As discussed in Chapters 4 and 6, the committee found a great deal of uncertainty regarding rules, time lines, and the criteria used in making decisions about the exportability of particular products. To reduce such uncertainty, as well as to promote the use of cryptography by legitimate users, the following changes in the export licensing process should occur.

a. For cryptography submitted to the State Department for export licensing, the presumptive decision should be for approval rather than disapproval. Licensing decisions involving cryptography should be presumed to be approvable unless there is a good reason to deny the license. The committee understands that foreign policy considerations may affect the granting of export licenses to particular nations, but once national security concerns have been satisfied with respect to a particular export, cryptography should not be regarded for export control purposes as differing from any other item on the CCL. Thus, if telephone switches were to be embargoed to a particular nation for foreign policy reasons, cryptography should be embargoed as well. But if telephone switches are allowed for export, cryptography should be allowed if national security concerns have been satisfied, even if other items on the USML are embargoed.

b. The State Department's licensing process for cryptography exports should be streamlined to provide more expeditious decision making. A streamlined process would build on procedural reforms already achieved and might further include the imposition of specific deadlines (e.g., if a license approved by the National Security Agency (NSA) is not denied by the State Department within 14 days, the license is automatically approved) or the establishment of a special desk within the State Department specifically with the expertise for dealing with cryptography; such a desk would consult with country or regional desks but would not be bound by their decisions or schedules for action. Such streamlining would greatly reduce the friction caused by exports determined to be consistent with U.S. national security interests but denied or delayed for reasons unrelated to national security.

c. The U.S. government should take steps to increase vendor and user understanding of the export control regime with the intent of bridging the profound gap in the perceptions of national security authorities and the private sector, including both technology vendors and users of cryptography. These steps would build on the efforts already undertaken over the last several years in this area. Possible additional steps that might be taken to reduce this gap include:

• Sponsorship of an annual briefing regarding the rules and regulations governing the export of cryptography. While established information technology vendors have learned through experience about most of the rules and regulations and informal guidelines that channel decision making regarding export licenses, newer firms lack a comparable base of experience. The U.S. government should seek a higher degree of clarity regarding what exporting vendors must do to satisfy national security concerns.

• Clarification of the rules regarding export of technical data. For example, foreign students attending U.S. universities can be exposed to any cryptographic source code without consequence, whereas U.S. vendors violate the law in developing products with encryption capabilities if they hire non-U.S. citizens to work as designers or implementors. For very complex products, it is very difficult if not impossible to "partition" the projects so that the non-U.S. citizen is unable to gain access to the cryptographic code. Such apparent inconsistencies should be reconciled, keeping in mind practicality and enforceability.

Recommendation 5: The U.S. government should take steps to assist law enforcement and national security to adjust to new technical realities of the information age.

For both law enforcement and national security, cryptography is a two-edged sword. In the realm of national security, the use of cryptography by adversaries impedes the collection of signals intelligence. Managing the damage to the collection of signals intelligence is the focus of export controls, as discussed in Chapter 4 and in the text accompanying Recommendation 4. At the same time, cryptography can help to defend vital information assets of the United States; the use of cryptography in this role is discussed in Recommendations 5.1 and 5.2 below.

From the standpoint of law enforcement, cryptography provides tools that help to prevent crime, e.g., by helping law-abiding businesses and individuals defend themselves against information crimes, such as the theft of proprietary information and the impersonation of legitimate parties by illegitimate ones. Crime prevention is an important dimension of law enforcement, especially when the crimes prevented are difficult to detect. Nevertheless, the public debate to date has focused primarily on the impact of cryptography on criminal prosecutions and investigations.

The committee accepts that the onset of an information age is likely to create many new challenges for public safety, among them the greater use of cryptography by criminal elements of society. If law enforcement authorities are unable to gain access to the encrypted communications and stored information of criminals, some criminal prosecutions will be significantly impaired, as described in Chapter 3.

The Administration's response to this law enforcement problem has been the aggressive promotion of escrowed encryption as a pillar of the technical foundation for national cryptography policy. The committee understands the Administration's rationale for promoting escrowed encryption but believes that escrowed encryption should be only one part of an overall strategy for dealing with the problems that encryption poses for law enforcement and national security.

In the context of an overall strategy, it is important to examine the specific problems that escrowed encryption might solve. For example, Administration advocates of escrowed encryption have argued that the private sector needs techniques for recovering the plaintext of stored encrypted data for which the relevant keys have been lost. To the extent that this is true, the law enforcement need for access to encrypted records could be substantially met by the exercise of the government's compulsory process authority (including search warrants and subpoenas) for information relevant to the investigation and prosecution of criminal activity against both the encrypted records and any relevant cryptographic keys, whether held by outside escrow agents or by the targets of the compulsory process. In this way, law enforcement needs for access to encrypted files, records, and stored communications such as e-mail are likely to be met by mechanisms established to serve private sector needs.

Communications (i.e., digital information in transit) pose a different problem from that of data storage. Neither private individuals nor businesses have substantial needs for exceptional access to the plaintext of encrypted communications. Thus, it is unlikely that users would voluntarily adopt on a large scale measures intended to ensure exceptional access to such communications. Law enforcement authorities are understandably concerned that they will be denied information vital for the investigation and prosecution of criminal activity. At the same time, it is not clear that encrypted digital communications will in fact be the most important problem for law enforcement authorities seeking to gain access to digital information.

In the short term, voice communications are almost certainly more important to law enforcement than are data communications, a problem addressed through Recommendation 5.2. Over the longer term, the challenges to law enforcement authorities from data communications are likely to grow as data communications become more ubiquitous and as the technical distinction between voice and data blurs. The committee believes that advanced information technologies are likely to lead to explosive increases in the amount of electronic information being transmitted (e.g., e-mail); given the likelihood that the spread of encryption capabilities will be much slower than the rate at which the volume of electronic communications increases, the opportunities for authorized law enforcement exploitation of larger amounts of unprotected computer-readable information may well increase in the short run. Nevertheless, when encrypted data communications do become ubiquitous, law enforcement may well face a serious challenge. For this reason, Recommendation 5.3, dealing with an exploration of escrowed encryption, sets into motion a prudent "hedge" strategy against this eventuality; Recommendation 5.4 begins the process of seeking to discourage criminal use of cryptography; and Recommendation 5.5 addresses the development of new technical capabilities to meet the challenge of encryption.

Against this backdrop, Recommendation 5.3 is only one part of an overall strategy for dealing with the problems that encryption poses for law enforcement and national security.

Recommendation 5.1—The U.S. government should actively encourage the use of cryptography in nonconfidentiality applications such as user authentication and integrity checks.

The nonconfidentiality applications of cryptography (e.g., digital signatures, authentication and access controls, nonrepudiation, secure time/date stamps, integrity checks) do not directly threaten law enforcement or national security interests and do not in general pose the same policy dilemma as confidentiality does. Since the deployment of infrastructures for the nonconfidentiality uses of cryptography is a necessary (though not sufficient) condition for the use of cryptography for confidentiality, the nation may take large steps in this area without having to resolve the policy dilemmas over confidentiality, confident that those steps will be beneficial to the nation in their own right. Policy can and should promote nonconfidentiality applications of cryptography in all relevant areas.

One of the most important of these areas concerns protection against systemic national vulnerabilities. Indeed, in areas in which confidence in and availability of a national information network are most critical, non-confidentiality uses of cryptography are even more important than are capabilities for confidentiality. For example, ensuring the integrity of data that circulates in the air traffic control system is almost certainly more important than ensuring its confidentiality; ensuring the integrity (accuracy) of data in the banking system is often more important than ensuring its confidentiality.[7]

Nonconfidentiality applications of cryptography support reliable user authentication. Authentication of users is an important crime-fighting measure, because authentication is the antithesis of anonymity. Criminals in general seek to conceal their identities; reliable authentication capabilities can help to prevent unauthorized access and to audit improper accesses that do occur. Nonconfidentiality applications of cryptography support reliable integrity checks on data; used properly, they can help to reduce crimes that result from the alteration of data (such as changing the payable amount on a check).

To date, national cryptography policy has not fully supported these nonconfidentiality uses. Some actions have been taken in this area, but these actions have run afoul of government concerns about confidentiality. For example, the government issued a Federal Information Processing Standard (FIPS) for the Digital Signature Standard in 1993, based on an unclassified algorithm known as the Digital Signature Algorithm. This FIPS was strongly criticized by industry and the public, largely because it did not conform to the de facto standard already in use at the time, namely one based on the Rivest-Shamir-Adelman (RSA) algorithm. Government sources told the committee that one reason the government deemed the RSA algorithm inappropriate for promulgation as a FIPS was that it is capable of providing strong confidentiality (and thus is not freely exportable) as well as digital signature capability. The two other reasons were the desire to promulgate an approach to digital signatures that would be royalty-free (RSA is a patented algorithm) and the desire to reduce overall system costs for digital signatures.[8] Export controls on cryptography for confidentiality have also had some spillover effect in affecting the foreign

---

[7]This is not to say that confidentiality plays no role in protecting national information systems from unauthorized penetration. As noted in Chapter 2, cryptographically provided confidentiality can be one important (though secondary) dimension of protecting information systems from unauthorized penetration.

[8]For a discussion of the patent issues involved in the decision regarding the Digital Signature Standard and the concern over confidentiality, see Office of Technology Assessment, *Information Security and Privacy in Network Environments*, OTA-TCT-606, U.S. Government Printing Office, Washington, D.C., 1994, pp. 167-168 and pp. 217-222.

availability of cryptography for authentication purposes, as described in Chapter 4.

The government has expressed considerably more concern in the public debate regarding the deleterious impact of widespread cryptography used for confidentiality than over the deleterious impact of not deploying cryptographic capabilities for user authentication and data integrity. The government has not fully exercised the regulatory influence it does have over certain sectors (e.g., telecommunications, air traffic control) to promote higher degrees of information security that would be met through the deployment of nonconfidentiality applications of cryptography. Finally, the committee believes that since today's trend among vendors and users is to build and use products that integrate multiple cryptographic capabilities (for confidentiality and for authentication and integrity) with general-purpose functionality, government actions that discourage capabilities for confidentiality also tend to discourage the development and use of products with authentication and integrity capabilities even if there is no direct prohibition or restriction on products with only capabilities for the latter (Chapter 4).

What specific actions can the government take to promote nonconfidentiality applications of cryptography? For illustrative purposes only, the committee notes that the government could support and foster technical standards and/or standards for business practices that encourage nonconfidentiality uses based on de facto commercial standards. One example would be the promulgation of a business requirement that all data electronically provided to the government be certified with an integrity check and a digital signature. A second example would be enactment of legislation and associated regulations setting standards to which all commercial certification authorities should conform; greater clarity regarding the liabilities, obligations, and responsibilities for certificate authorities would undoubtedly help to promote applications based on certification authorities. A third example is that the U.S. government has a great deal of expertise in the use of cryptography and other technologies for authentication purposes; an aggressive technology transfer effort in this domain would also help to promote the use of reliable authentication methods.

A final dimension of this issue is that keys used in nonconfidentiality applications of cryptography, especially ones that support established and essential business practices or legal constructs (e.g., digital signatures, authentication, integrity checks), must be controlled solely by the immediate and intended parties to those applications. Without such assurances, outside access to such keys could undermine the legal basis and threaten the integrity of these practices carried out in the electronic domain. Whatever benefits might accrue to government authorities acting in the interests of public safety or national security from being able to forge digital signatures or alter digital data clandestinely would pale by comparison to the loss of trust in such mechanisms that would result from even a hint that such activities were possible.

Recommendation 5.2—The U.S. government should promote the security of the telecommunications networks more actively. At a minimum, the U.S. government should promote the link encryption of cellular communications[9] and the improvement of security at telephone switches.

As described in Chapter 1, the public switched telecommunications network (PSTN) is both critical to many sectors of the national economy and is undergoing rapid evolution. While the U.S. government has taken some steps to improve the security of the PSTN, much more could be done based on the regulatory authority that the U.S. government has in this area.

The encryption of wireless voice communications would prevent eavesdropping that is all too easy in today's largely analog cellular telephone market. As wireless communications shift from analog to digital modes of transport, encryption will become easier even as the traffic itself becomes harder to understand. A requirement to encrypt wireless communications may also accelerate the shift to wireless modes of digital transport. However, because of the cost of retrofitting existing cellular services, this recommendation is intended to apply only to the deployment of future cellular services.

Security in telephone switches could be improved in many ways. For example, a requirement for adequate authentication to access such switches would prevent unauthorized access from maintenance ports; such ports often provide remote access to all switch functions, a level of access equal to what could be obtained by an individual standing in the control center. Yet such ports are often protected with nothing more than a single password. Telecommunications service providers could also provide services for link encryption of traffic on wired landlines (Chapter 7).

By addressing through the telecommunications service providers the public's demands for greater security in voice communications (especially

---

[9]"Link encryption" refers to the practice of encrypting information being communicated in such a way that it is encrypted only in between the node from which it is sent and the node where it is received; while the information is at the nodes themselves, it is unencrypted. In the context of link encryption for cellular communications, a cellular call would be encrypted between the mobile handset and the ground station. When carried on the landlines of the telephone network, the call would be unencrypted.

those such as cellular telephone traffic) that are widely known to be nonsecure, government would maintain law enforcement access for lawfully authorized wiretaps through the requirements imposed on carriers today to cooperate with law enforcement in such matters. For example, a cellular telephone connects to the PSTN through a ground station; since in general, the cellular telephone service provider must feed its traffic to the PSTN in unencrypted form, encrypted cellular telephone traffic from the mobile handset would be decrypted at the ground station, at which point law enforcement could gain authorized access. Thus, legitimate law enforcement access would not, in general, be impeded by link encryption of cellular traffic until communications systems that bypass the PSTN entirely become common.

Recommendation 5.2 is an instance of a general philosophy that link (or node) security provided by a service provider offers more opportunities for providing law enforcement with legally authorized access than does security provided by the end user. In the case of voice communications, improved security over the telecommunications network used for voice communications and provided by the owners and operators of that network—a good thing in its own right and consistent with the basic principle of this report—would also reduce the demand for (and thus the availability of) devices used to provide end-to-end encryption of voice communications. Without a ready supply of such devices, a criminal user would have to go to considerable trouble to obtain a device that could thwart a lawfully authorized wiretap.

Recommendation 5.2 focuses on voice communications, given that for the foreseeable future, voice is likely to be the most common form of communication used by the general public (and hence by criminals as well). The committee recognizes that data communications will pose certain problems for law enforcement, and this is the focus of Recommendation 5.3.

Recommendation 5.3—To better understand how escrowed encryption might operate, the U.S. government should explore escrowed encryption for its own uses. To address the critical international dimensions of escrowed communications, the U.S. government should work with other nations on this topic.

As described in Chapter 5, escrowed encryption (as a generic concept, not limited to the Clipper/Capstone initiatives of the U.S. government) has both benefits and risks from a public policy standpoint. The purpose of encryption is to provide users with high degrees of assurance that their sensitive information will remain secure. The primary benefit of *escrowed* encryption for law enforcement and national security is that when properly implemented and widely deployed, it provides such assurance but nevertheless enables law enforcement and national security authorities to obtain access to escrow-encrypted data in specific instances when authorized by law. Escrowed encryption also enables businesses and individuals to recover encrypted stored data to which access has been inadvertently lost, and businesses to exercise a greater degree of control over their encrypted communications. Finally, by meeting demands for better information security emanating from legitimate business and private interests, escrowed encryption may dampen the market for unescrowed encryption products that would provide similar security but without features for government exceptional access that law enforcement and national security authorities could use for legitimate and lawfully authorized purposes.

The risks of escrowed encryption are also considerable. Escrowed encryption provides a potentially lower degree of confidentiality than does properly implemented unescrowed encryption, because escrowed encryption is specifically designed to permit external access and then relies on procedures and technical controls implemented and executed by human beings to prevent unauthorized use of that access. While policy makers have confidence that procedures can be established and implemented without a significant reduction of information security, skeptics place little faith in such procedural safeguards. Maintaining system security is difficult enough without the deliberate introduction of a potential security hole, and the introduction of another route of attack on procedures simply complicates the job of the information defender. In addition, the widespread adoption of escrowed encryption, even on a voluntary basis, would lay into place mechanisms, procedures, and organizations that could be used to promulgate and/or enforce more restrictive cryptography policies. With such elements in place, some critics of escrowed encryption fear that procedural safeguards against government abuse that are administrative in nature, or that rest on the personal assurances of government officials, could be eviscerated by a future administration or Congress.

The committee believes that many policy benefits can be gained by an operational exploration of escrowed encryption by the U.S. government, but also that aggressive promotion of the concept is not appropriate at this time for four reasons.

First, not enough is yet known about how best to implement escrowed encryption on a large scale. The operational complexities of a large-scale infrastructure are significant (especially in an international context of cross-border communications), and approaches proposed today for dealing with those complexities are not based on real experience. A more prudent approach to setting policy would be to develop a base of experience that would guide policy decisions on how escrowed encryption might work on a large scale in practice.

Second, because of the ease with which escrowed encryption can be circumvented technically, it is not at all clear that escrowed encryption will be a real solution to the most serious problems that law enforcement authorities will face. Administration officials freely acknowledge that their various initiatives promoting escrowed encryption are not intended to address all criminal uses of encryption, but in fact those most likely to have information to conceal will be motivated to circumvent escrowed encryption products.

Third, information services and technologies are undergoing rapid evolution and change today, and nearly all technology transitions are characterized by vendors creating new devices and services. Imposing a particular solution to the encryption dilemma at this time is likely to have a significant negative impact on the natural market development of applications made possible by new information services and technologies. While the nation may choose to bear these costs in the future, it is particularly unwise to bear them in anticipation of a large-scale need that may not arise and in light of the nation's collective ignorance about how escrowed encryption would work on a large scale.

Fourth and most importantly, not enough is yet known about how the market will respond to the capabilities provided by escrowed encryption, nor how it will prefer the concept to be implemented, if at all. Given the importance of market forces to the long-term success of national cryptography policy, a more prudent approach to policy would be to learn more about how in fact the market will respond before advocating a specific solution driven by the needs of government.

For these reasons, the committee believes that a policy of deliberate exploration of the concept of escrowed encryption is better suited to the circumstances of today than is the current policy of aggressive promotion. The most appropriate vehicle for such an exploration is, quite naturally, government applications. Such exploration would enable the U.S. government to develop and document the base of experience on which to build a more aggressive promotion of escrowed encryption should circumstances develop in such a way that encrypted communications come to pose a significant problem for law enforcement. This base would include significant operating experience, a secure but responsive infrastructure for escrowing keys, and devices and products for escrowed encryption whose unit costs have been lowered as the result of large government purchases.

In the future, when experience has been developed, the U.S. government, by legislation and associated regulation, will have to clearly specify the responsibilities, obligations, and liabilities of escrow agents (Chapter 5). Such issues include financial liability for the unauthorized release or negligent compromise of keys, criminal penalties for the deliberate and knowing release of keys to an unauthorized party, statutory immunization of users of escrowed encryption against claims of liability that might result from the use of such encryption, and the need for explicit legal authorization for key release. Such legislation (and regulations issued pursuant to such legislation) should allow for and, when appropriate, distinguish among different types of escrow agents, including organizations internal to a user company, private commercial firms for those firms unwilling or unable to support internal organizations for key holding, and government agencies.

Such government action is a necessary (but not sufficient) condition for the growth and spread of escrowed encryption in the private sector. Parties whose needs may call for the use of escrowed encryption will need confidence in the supporting infrastructure before they will entrust encryption keys to the safekeeping of others. Moreover, if the government is to actively *promote* the voluntary use of escrowed encryption in the future, it will need to convince users that it has taken into account their concerns about compromise and abuse of escrowed information. The best way to convince users that these agents will be able to live up to their responsibilities is to point to a body of experience that demonstrates their ability to do so. In a market-driven system, this body of experience will begin to accrue in small steps—some in small companies, some in bigger ones—rather than springing up fully formed across the country in every state and every city. As this body of experience grows, government will have the ability to make wise decisions about the appropriate standards that should govern escrow agents.

In addition, the U.S. government should pursue discussions with other nations on how escrowed encryption might operate internationally (Appendix G). The scope of business and law enforcement today crosses national borders, and a successful U.S. policy on cryptography will have to be coordinated with policies of other nations. Given that the developed nations of the world have a number of common interests (e.g., in preserving authorized law enforcement access to communications, in protecting the information assets of their domestic businesses), the process begun at the Organization for Economic Cooperation and Development in December 1995 is a promising forum in which these nations can bring together representatives from business, law enforcement, and national security to discuss matters related to cryptography policy over national borders. Fruitful topics of discussion might well include how to expand the network of Mutual Law Enforcement Assistance Treaties that bind the United States and other nations to cooperate on law enforcement matters. Broader cooperation should contribute to the sharing of information regarding matters that involve the criminal use of encryption; national policies that encourage the development and export of "escrowable" encryption products; understanding of how to develop a significant base of actual experience in operating a system of escrowed encryption for communications across national borders; and the negotiation of sector-specific arrangements (e.g., a specific set of arrangements for banks) that cross international boundaries.

Recommendation 5.4—Congress should seriously consider legislation that would impose criminal penalties on the use of encrypted communications in interstate commerce with the intent to commit a federal crime.

The purpose of such a statute would be to discourage the use of cryptography for illegitimate purposes. Criminalizing the use of cryptography in this manner would provide sanctions analogous to the existing mail fraud statutes, which add penalties to perpetrators of fraud who use the mail to commit their criminal acts. Such a law would focus the weight of the criminal justice system on individuals who were in fact guilty of criminal activity, whereas a mandatory prohibition on the use of cryptography would have an impact on law-abiding citizens and criminals alike.

A concern raised about the imposition of penalties based on a peripheral aspect of a criminal act is that it may be used to secure a conviction even when the underlying criminal act has not been accomplished. The statute proposed for consideration in Recommendation 5.4 is *not* intended for this purpose, although the committee understands that it is largely the integrity of the judicial and criminal justice process that will be the ultimate check on preventing its use for such purposes.

As suggested in Chapter 7, any statute that criminalizes the use of encryption in the manner described in Recommendation 5.4 should be drawn narrowly. The limitation of Recommendation 5.4 to federal crimes restricts its applicability to major crimes that are specifically designated as such; it does not extend to the much broader class of crimes that are based on common law. Under Recommendation 5.4, federal jurisdiction arises from the limitation regarding the use of communications in interstate commerce. The focus of Recommendation 5.4 on encrypted *communications* recognizes that private sector parties have significant incentives to escrow keys used for encrypting stored data, as described in Recommendation 5.3. A statute based on Recommendation 5.4 should also make clear that speaking in foreign languages unknown to many people would not fall within its reach. Finally, the use of "encrypted" communications should be limited to communications encrypted for confidentiality purposes, not for user authentication or data integrity purposes. The drafters of the statute would also have to anticipate other potential sources of ambiguity such as the use of data compression techniques that also obscure the true content of a communication and the lack of a common understanding of what it means to "*use* encrypted communications" when encryption may be a ubiquitous and automatic feature in a communications product.

Finally, the committee recognizes the existence of debate over the effectiveness of laws targeted against the use of certain mechanisms (e.g., mail, guns) to commit crimes. Such a debate should be part of a serious consideration of a law such as that described in Recommendation 5.4. However, the committee is not qualified to resolve this debate, and the committee takes no position on this particular issue.

A second aspect of a statutory approach to controlling the socially harmful uses of encryption could be to expand its scope to include the criminalization of the intentional use of cryptography in the concealment of a crime. With such an expanded scope, the use of cryptography would constitute a prima facie act of concealment, and thus law enforcement officials would have to prove only that cryptography was used *intentionally* to conceal a crime. On the other hand, its more expansive scope might well impose additional burdens on businesses and raise other concerns, and so the committee takes no stand on the desirability of such an expansion of scope.

The committee notes the fundamental difference between Recommendation 5.4 and Recommendation 1. Recommendation 1 says that the use of *any type of encryption* within the United States should be legal, but *not that any use of encryption* should be legal. Recommendation 5.4 says that the nation should consider legislation that would make illegal *a specific use* of encryption (of whatever type), namely the use of encrypted communications in interstate commerce with the intent of committing a federal crime.

Recommendation 5.5—High priority should be given to research, development, and deployment of additional technical capabilities for law enforcement and national security for use in coping with new technological challenges.

Over the past 50 years, both law enforcement and national security authorities have had to cope with a variety of changing technological circumstances. For the most part, they have coped with these changes quite well. This record of adaptability provides considerable confidence that they can adapt to a future of digital communications and stored data as well, and they should be strongly supported in their efforts to develop new technical capabilities.

Moreover, while the committee's basic thrust is toward a wider use of cryptography throughout society, considerable time can be expected to elapse before cryptography is truly ubiquitous. For example, Recommendation 4.1 is likely to accelerate the widespread use of DES, but market forces will still have the dominant effect on its spread. Even if export controls were removed tomorrow, vendors would still take time to decide how best to proceed, and the use of DES across the breadth of society will take even longer. Thus, law enforcement and national security authorities have a window in which to develop new capabilities for addressing future challenges. Such development should be supported, because effective new capabilities are almost certain to have a greater impact on their future information collection efforts than will aggressive attempts to promote escrowed encryption to a resistant market.

An example of such support would be the establishment of a technical center for helping federal, state, and local law enforcement authorities with technical problems associated with new information technologies.[10] Such a center would of course address the use by individuals of unescrowed encryption in the commission of criminal acts, because capabilities to deal with this problem will be necessary whether or not escrowed encryption is widely deployed. Moreover, for reasons of accessibility and specific tailoring of expertise to domestic criminal matters, it is important for domestic law enforcement to develop a source of expertise on the matter. A second problem of concern to law enforcement authorities is obtaining the digital stream carrying the targeted communications. The task of isolating the proper digital stream amidst multiple applications and multiplexed channels will grow more complex as the sophistication of applications and technology increases, and law enforcement authorities will need to have (or procure) considerable technical skill to extract useful information out of the digital streams involved. These skills will need to be at least as good as those possessed by product vendors.

Compared to the use of NSA expertise, a technical center for law enforcement would have a major advantage in being dedicated to serving law enforcement needs, and hence its activities and expertise relevant to prosecution would be informed and guided by the need to discuss analytical methods in open court without concern for classification. Moreover, such a center could be quite useful to state and local law enforcement authorities who currently lack the level of access to NSA expertise accorded the Federal Bureau of Investigation (FBI).

---

[10]This example is consistent with the FBI proposal for a Technical Support Center (TSC) to serve as a central national law enforcement resource to address problems related to encryption and to technological problems with an impact on access to electronic communications and stored information. The FBI proposes that a TSC would provide law enforcement with capabilities in signals analysis (e.g., protocol recognition), mass media analysis (e.g., analysis of seized computer media), and cryptanalysis on encrypted data communications or files.

National security authorities recognize quite clearly that future capabilities to undertake traditional signals intelligence will be severely challenged by the spread of encryption and the introduction of new communications media. In the absence of improved cryptanalytic methods, cooperative arrangements with foreign governments, and new ways of approaching the information collection problem, losses in traditional signals intelligence capability would likely result in a diminished effectiveness of the U.S. intelligence community. To help ensure the continuing availability of strategic and tactical intelligence, efforts to develop alternatives to traditional signals intelligence collection techniques should be given high priority in the allocation of financial and personnel resources before products covered by Recommendation 4.1 become widely used.

Recommendation 6: The U.S. government should develop a mechanism to promote information security in the private sector.

Although the committee was asked to address national cryptography policy, any such policy is necessarily only one component of a national information security policy. Without a forward-looking and comprehensive national information security policy, changes in national cryptography policy may have little operational impact on U.S. information security. Thus, the committee believes it cannot leave unaddressed the question of a national information security policy, although it recognizes that it was not specifically chartered with such a broad issue in mind.

The committee makes Recommendation 6 based on the observation that the U.S. government itself is not well organized to meet the challenges posed by an information society. Indeed, no government agency has the responsibility to promote information security in the private sector. The information security interests of most of the private sector have no formal place at the policy-making table: the National Security Agency represents the classified government community, while the charter of the National Institute of Standards and Technology directs it to focus on the unclassified needs of the government (and its budget is inadequate to do more than that). Other organizations such as the Information Infrastructure Task Force and the Office of Management and Budget have broad influence but few operational responsibilities. As a result, business and individual stakeholders do not have adequate representation in the development of information security standards and export regimes.

For these reasons, the nation requires a mechanism that will provide accountability and focus for efforts to promote information security in the private sector. The need for information security cuts across many dimensions of the economy and the national interest, suggesting that absent a coordinated approach to promoting information security, the needs of many stakeholders may well be given inadequate attention and notice.

The importance of close cooperation with the private sector cannot be overemphasized. While the U.S. government has played an important role in promoting information security in the past (e.g., in its efforts to promulgate DES, its stimulation of a market for information security products through the government procurement process, its outreach to increase the level of information security awareness regarding Soviet collection attempts, and the stimulation of national debate on this critical subject), information security needs in the private sector in the information age will be larger than ever before (as argued in Recommendation 3). Thus, close consultations between government and the private sector are needed before policy decisions are made that affect how those needs can be addressed. Indeed, many stakeholders outside government have criticized what they believe to be an inadequate representation of the private sector at the decision-making table. While recognizing that some part of such criticism simply reflects the fact that these stakeholders did not get all that they wanted from policy makers, the committee believes that the policy-making process requires better ways for representing broadly both government and nongovernment interests in cryptography policy. Those who are pursuing enhanced information security and those who have a need for legal access to stored or communicated information must both be included in a robust process for managing the often-competing issues and interests that will inevitably arise over time.

How might the policy-making process include better representation of nongovernment interests? Experiences in trade policy suggest the feasibility of private sector advisors, who are often needed when policy cuts across many functional and organizational boundaries and interests both inside and outside government. National policy on information security certainly falls into this cross-cutting category, and thus it might make sense for the government to appoint parties from the private sector to participate in government policy discussions relevant to export control decisions and/or decisions that affect the information security interests of the private sector. Despite the committee's conclusion that the broad outlines of national cryptography policy can be argued on an unclassified basis, classified information may nevertheless be invoked in such discussions and uncleared participants asked to leave the room. To preclude this possibility, these individuals should have the clearances necessary to engage as full participants in order to promote an effective interchange of views and perspectives. While these individuals would inevitably reflect the interests of the organizations from which they were drawn, their essential role would be to present to the government their best technical and policy advice, based on their expertise and judgment, on how government policy would best serve the national interest.

How and in what areas should the U.S. government be involved in promoting information security? One obvious category of involvement is those areas in which the secure operation of information systems is critical to the nation's welfare—information systems that are invested with the public trust, such as those of the banking and financial system, the public switched telecommunications network, the air traffic control system, and extensively automated utilities such as the electric power grid. Indeed, the U.S. government is already involved to some extent in promoting the security of these systems, and these efforts should continue and even grow.

In other sectors of the economy, the committee sees no particular reason for government involvement in areas in which businesses are knowledgeable (e.g., their own operational practices, their own risk-benefit assessments), and the role of the U.S. government is most properly focused on providing information and expertise that are not easily available to the private sector. Specifically, the government should build on existing private-public partnerships and private sector efforts in disseminating information (e.g., the Forums of Incident Response and Security Teams (FIRST), the Computer Emergency Response Team (CERT), the I-4 group, the National Counterintelligence Center) to take a vigorous and proactive role in collecting and disseminating information to promote awareness of the information security threat. For illustrative purposes only, some examples follow. The government might:

- Establish mechanisms in which the sharing of sanitized security-related information (especially information related to security breaches) could be undertaken without disadvantaging the companies that reveal such information. Such efforts might well build on efforts in the private sector to do the same thing.
- Undertake a program to brief senior management in industry on the information security threat in greater detail than is usually possible in open forums but without formal security clearances being required for those individuals. Such briefings would mean that specific threat information might have to be declassified or treated on a "for official use only" basis.
- Expand the NIST program that accredits firms to test products involving cryptography for conformance to various Federal Information Processing Standards. As of this writing, three private companies today have been accredited to evaluate and certify compliance of products claiming to conform to FIPS 140-1, the FIPS for cryptographic modules; both

the range of FIPSs subject to such evaluation and the number of certifying companies could be increased.

• Help industry to develop common understandings regarding cryptography and information security standards that would constitute fair defenses against damages. These common understandings would help to reduce uncertainty over liability and "responsible practice."

• Undertake technology transfer efforts that would help the private sector to use powerful and capable authentication technologies developed by government. As noted elsewhere in this section, authentication is an application of cryptography that poses a minimal public policy dilemma, and so the use of such government-developed technology should not be particularly controversial.

Finally, in describing the need for a mechanism to promote information security in the private sector, the committee does not make a recommendation on its specific form because its charter did not call for it to address the question of government organization. As discussed in Chapter 7, such a mechanism could be a new coordinating office for information security in the Executive Office of the President. It could be one or more existing agencies or organizations with a new charter or set of responsibilities. It could be a new government agency or organization, although in the current political climate such an agency would demand the most compelling justification. It could be a quasi-governmental body or a governmentally chartered private organization, examples of which are described in Chapter 6. Because of NSA's role within the defense and intelligence communities and its consequent concern about defense and intelligence threats and systems, the committee believes the NSA is not the proper agency to assume primary responsibility for a mission that is primarily oriented toward the needs of the private sector. At the same time, experts from all parts of the U.S. government should be encouraged to assist in analyzing vulnerabilities; if such assistance requires new legislative authority, such authority should be sought from Congress.

8.3 ADDITIONAL WORK NEEDED

The committee recognizes that a number of important areas were outside the scope of this study. Two of these areas are described below:

• As noted in Chapter 2, the creation of an infrastructure (or infrastructures) to support user authentication is a central aspect of any widespread use of various forms of cryptography. The nature of these infrastructures is a matter of public policy; however, since the committee was concerned primarily with addressing issues related to cryptographic confidentiality, it did not address infrastructure issues in the depth that would be necessary to provide detailed advice to federal decision makers.

• As noted in Chapter 7 and discussed in Appendix L, digital cash and electronic money pose many issues for public policy. These issues considerably transcend what could be examined within the scope of the current study.

Although the committee realized that these areas were important, an in-depth study in each would require a committee with a different membership, a different charge, and a different time line. Problems in these areas will become relevant in the near future, and policy makers may wish to anticipate them by commissioning additional examination.

8.4 CONCLUSION

The committee believes that its recommendations will lead to enhanced confidentiality and protection of information for individuals and companies, thereby reducing economic and financial crimes and economic espionage from both domestic and foreign sources. While the recommendations will to that extent contribute to the prevention of crime and enhance national security, the committee recognizes that the spread of cryptography will increase the burden of those in government charged with carrying out certain specific law enforcement and intelligence activities. It believes that widespread commercial and private use of cryptography in the United States and abroad is inevitable in the long run and that its advantages, on balance, outweigh its disadvantages. The committee concluded that the overall interests of the government and the nation would best be served by a policy that fosters a judicious transition toward the broad use of cryptography.

APPENDIXES

A

Contributors to the NRC Project on National Cryptography Policy

A.1 COMMITTEE MEMBERS

Kenneth W. Dam, *Chair*, is the Max Pam Professor of American and Foreign Law at the University of Chicago Law School, where he is also director of the John M. Olin Program in Law and Economics. Mr. Dam received his bachelor's degree from the University of Kansas and completed his graduate work at the University of Chicago Law School. During the period from 1985 to 1992, he held the post of corporate vice president for law and external relations at IBM. Mr. Dam served as deputy secretary of state (1982-1985) and as provost of the University of Chicago (1980-1982). Mr. Dam currently serves on the board of Alcoa and on the boards of a number of nonprofit institutions, including the Brookings Institution and the Council on Foreign Relations. He is also co-chairman (with Senator Sam Nunn) of the Aspen Strategy Group. He has written books on the General Agreement on Tariffs and Trade, the international monetary system, U.S. economic policy, and the development of oil resources, as well as many articles on economic policy and antitrust law.

W.Y. Smith, *Vice Chair*, is president emeritus and a trustee of the Institute for Defense Analyses; he was its president from 1985 to 1991. Prior to that he was a fellow at the Woodrow Wilson International Center for Scholars at the Smithsonian Institution, 1983 to 1984. His military posts include deputy commander in chief of the European Command in Germany, 1981 to 1983; chief of staff of SHAPE, Belgium, 1979 to 1981; assistant to the chairman of the Joint Chiefs of Staff, 1975 to 1979; and director of Policy Plans and National Security Affairs at the Office of the Assistant Secretary for International Security Affairs. He has a BS from the U.S. Military Academy, 1948, and an MPA and a PhD from Harvard University, 1961. He is director and treasurer of the Atlantic Council of the United States and a member of the executive committee of the National Security Archives Board of Directors.

Lee Bollinger has been provost of Dartmouth College since July 1994. Previously, he was a professor at the University of Michigan Law School from 1973 and served as dean of the law school from 1987 to 1994. In 1983 he was a visiting associate at Clare Hall, Cambridge University. Mr. Bollinger received his bachelor's degree from the University of Oregon and a law degree from Columbia University School of Law. In 1972-1973, he served as a law clerk to Supreme Court Justice Warren E. Burger. His books include *Images of a Free Press* (University of Chicago Press, 1991) and *The Tolerant Society: Freedom of Speech and Extremist Speech in America* (Oxford University Press, 1987). He has published numerous articles on freedom of the press and free speech, including "The First Amendment and National Security" and "The First Amendment and New Communications Technologies." He was co-author of the National Research Council publication "Constitutional Issues in Regulating Televised Presentations of Violence" in 1982. Mr. Bollinger is a fellow of the American Academy of Arts and Sciences.

Ann Caracristi was appointed a member of President Clinton's Foreign Intelligence Advisory Board in September 1993. She was deputy director of the National Security Agency from January 1980 to August 1982. Ms. Caracristi holds a BA from Russell Sage College and is a graduate of the Federal Executive Institute. She has received the Department of Defense Distinguished Civilian Service Award, the National Intelligence Distinguished Service Medal, and the United States National Security Award. Currently she is a consultant to the NSA Scientific Advisory Board and a member of the Board of Visitors of the Defense Language Institute Foreign Language Center. She served as a member of the Chief of Naval Operations Executive Panel from October 1982 to September 1991. She was a two-term president of the Association of Former Intelligence Officers from 1989 to 1991. Most recently she was a member of the Commission on the Roles and Capabilities of the U.S. Intelligence Community.

Benjamin R. Civiletti has been in private law practice with Venable, Baetjer, Howard & Civiletti in Baltimore and Washington, D.C., since

1981. He is chairman of that firm. Prior to 1981, he was U.S. attorney general from 1979 to 1981, deputy U.S. attorney general from 1978 to 1979, and assistant attorney general for the Criminal Division of the Department of Justice, 1977 and 1978. He has an AB from Johns Hopkins University, 1957, and an LLB from the University of Maryland, 1961. He is chairman of the board of directors of Maryland Healthcorp; a director of MBNA Corporation, MBNA International, Wackenhut Corrections Corporation, and the Bethlehem Steel Corporation; a trustee of Johns Hopkins University; former chairman of Maryland Legal Services Corporation; and a chairman of the Governors Task Force for Funding of Public Education.

Colin Crook is the senior technology officer of Citicorp. He has governance and oversight responsibility for technology at Citicorp, including operational management of the global information network. Mr. Crook is a graduate of the United Kingdom's Liverpool Polytechnic, where he earned his degrees (electrical engineering) while working as a computer designer for the Plessey Company. Mr. Crook has held various positions in top management for the Motorola Corporation in the United States and Europe, as well as positions with Rank Precision Industries, Zynar, Ltd., and British Telecom. He also was senior vice president with Data General (USA). Mr. Crook has been a key speaker at international industry conferences, has published in scholarly and professional journals, and has been the subject of numerous interviews. He is a member of the Association for Computing Machinery, the Institute of Electrical and Electronics Engineers, and the Institution of Electrical Engineers (United Kingdom). In 1981, Mr. Crook was elected to the United Kingdom's Royal Academy of Engineering, the youngest person to be so honored at the time.

Samuel H. Fuller is currently a vice president and the chief scientist of Digital Equipment Corporation. Prior to joining Digital in 1978, Dr. Fuller was an associate professor of computer science and electrical engineering at Carnegie Mellon University (CMU). While at CMU, he was involved in the performance evaluation and design of several experimental multiprocessor computer systems. His fields of interest include computer science and electrical engineering. Dr. Fuller received his BS from the University of Michigan (1968) and his MS (1969) and PhD (1972) in electrical engineering and computer science from Stanford University. He is a member of the National Academy of Engineering, Institute of Electrical and Electronics Engineers, and Association for Computing Machinery. Dr. Fuller was a founding member of the Computer Science and Telecommunications Board (1986-1992) and served on the steering committee for the Competitiveness Colloquium Follow-up Workshop on Systems Integration (1989-1991). Dr. Fuller is on the board of directors of Analog Device Inc. and INSO Corporation.

Leslie H. Gelb has been president of the Council on Foreign Relations since 1993. He is a trustee of the Carnegie Endowment for International Peace and of Tufts University, a board member of Columbia University's School of International and Public Affairs, and an advisory board member for the Center on Press, Politics and Public Policy at Harvard University's John F. Kennedy School of Government. He is a member of the International Institute for Strategic Studies and a fellow of the American Academy of Arts and Sciences. In 1985, Mr. Gelb shared in the winning of the Pulitzer Prize for explanatory journalism. He was a senior associate for the Carnegie Endowment for International Peace from 1980 to 1981, and from 1977 to 1979, he served as director of the Bureau of Politico-Military Affairs, where he received the Distinguished Honor Award. He was a senior fellow at the Brookings Institution from 1969 to 1973 and also a visiting professor at Georgetown University. He was director of Policy Planning and Arms Control for International Security Affairs at the Department of Defense from 1967 to 1969, where he also served as director of the Pentagon Papers Project. While at the Defense Department, Mr. Gelb won the Pentagon's Distinguished Service Award. Mr. Gelb was executive assistant to U.S. Senator Jacob K. Javits from 1966 to 1967 and an assistant professor at Wesleyan University from 1964 to 1966. Mr. Gelb received a BA from Tufts University in 1959, and his MA in 1961 and PhD in 1964 from Harvard University. He is an author and a co-author of several foreign policy studies.

Ronald Graham is director of Information Sciences Research at AT&T Laboratories, which he joined in 1962, and has also been a professor at Rutgers University since 1987. Concurrently, he has been a Regents' Professor of Mathematics at the University of California, Los Angeles, and a frequent visiting professor of computer science at Stanford University and Princeton University. He was a Fairchild Distinguished Scholar at the California Institute of Technology in 1982. Dr. Graham's research is in combinatorics, number theory, graph theory, algorithms, and combinatorial geometry. He has a BS in physics from the University of Alaska, 1958, and an MA and a PhD in mathematics from the University of California, Berkeley, 1962. Dr. Graham was awarded the Polya Prize in combinatorics in 1972 and the Euler Medal in combinatorics in 1994. He is a member of the National Academy of Sciences and a past president of the American Mathematical Society, and he is a fellow of the American Academy of Arts and Sciences, the New York Academy of Sciences, and the American Association for the Advancement of Science.

Martin Hellman is a professor of electrical engineering at Stanford University, where he has been since 1971. Previously, he was an assistant professor at the Massachusetts Institute of Technology from 1969 to 1971 and a staff member at the IBM T.J. Watson Research Center from 1968 to 1969. Dr. Hellman's specialties are information and communication theory, cryptography and data security, and international security. His BE is from New York University and his MS and PhD in electrical engineering are from Stanford University. He is a fellow of the Institute of Electrical and Electronics Engineers and the Institute of Mathematical Statistics.

Ambassador Julius Katz is president of Hills & Company, International Consultants. The firm provides clients with strategic advice and risk analysis on trade and investment interests abroad. Ambassador Katz held the position of deputy U.S. trade representative from 1989 to 1993. During this period, he was the U.S chief negotiator for the North American Free Trade Agreement. He also had senior management responsibility for bilateral and regional negotiations with Europe and the Western Hemisphere and for the multilateral trade negotiations known as the Uruguay Round. Ambassador Katz previously worked as a public policy consultant and from 1987 to 1989 was chairman of the Government Research Corporation in Washington, D.C. From 1980 to 1985, he worked in the financial services industry, where he was chairman of Donaldson, Lufkin & Jenrette Futures Inc. Ambassador Katz joined the U.S. Department of State in 1950 and on his retirement from the State Department after 30 years of service held the position of assistant secretary of state for economic and business affairs. While at the State Department, Ambassador Katz led numerous U.S. delegations in negotiations on trade, commodity, and transport matters.

Peter G. Neumann is principal scientist in the Computer Science Laboratory at SRI, where he has worked since 1971. His projects have involved computer systems security, high assurance, human safety, and reliability. He was a member of the Air Force Studies Board database security study and of the National Research Council's System Security Study Committee that produced the report *Computers at Risk* (National Academy Press, 1991). He also served on an expert panel for the U.S. House Judiciary Committee's Subcommittee on Civil and Constitutional Rights. Dr. Neumann received his AB, SM, and PhD from Harvard University in 1954, 1955, and 1961, respectively. In 1960 he received a Dr. rerum naturarum from the Technische Hochschule, Darmstadt, Germany, where he was a Fulbright scholar for 2 years. From 1976 to 1994, he was editor of SIGSOFT Software Engineering Notes for the Association for Computing Machinery (ACM), and since 1985 he has been chairman of the ACM Committee on Computers and Public Policy. Dr. Neumann was awarded an ACM Outstanding Contribution Award in 1992 and the first SRI Exceptional Performance Award for Leadership in Community Service, also in 1992. He is a fellow of the Institute of Electrical and Electronics Engineers, the ACM, and the American Association for the Advancement of Science.

Raymond Ozzie is the founder and president of Iris Associates, the developer of Lotus Notes. Iris, which began operations in 1984, is a wholly owned subsidiary of Lotus Development Corporation and IBM Corporation. Before founding Iris, Mr. Ozzie worked at Lotus, where he was the lead architect and developer of Lotus' Symphony product. Prior to Lotus, he was an engineering manager at Software Arts, the developer of the first electronic spreadsheet, VisiCalc. Mr. Ozzie received his degree in computer science in 1978 from the University of Illinois in Urbana-Champaign, where he did research in distributed computing and was a systems programmer for PLATO, a pioneering distributed computer-based education and collaboration system connecting students and researchers at hundreds of locations worldwide.

Edward C. Schmults was senior vice president of external affairs and general counsel of GTE Corporation from 1984 to 1995. Previously he served as a deputy attorney general of the United States from 1981 to 1984, deputy counsel to the President from 1975 to 1976, and undersecretary of the Treasury Department from 1974 to 1975. Mr. Schmults was a partner of the New York law firm of White & Case from 1965 to 1973 and from 1977 to 1981. He sits on the board of directors of the GreenPoint Bank, the Germany Fund, and the Central European Equity Fund and is chairman of the board of trustees of the Refugee Policy Group. He served with the U.S. Marine Corps from 1953 to 1955. Mr. Schmults has a BS from Yale University and a JD from Harvard University, 1958.

Elliot M. Stone has been executive director of the Massachusetts Health Data Consortium since it was established in 1978 as a private, nonprofit corporation and a nonpartisan setting for the collection and analysis of the state's large health care databases. The consortium publishes annual reports and sets data standards for a broad constituency of health care organizations and business coalitions. Previously, Mr. Stone served as director of the state's Center for Health Statistics in the Massachusetts Department of Public Health. Mr. Stone has been an advisor to the

Agency for Health Care Policy & Research, the National Center for Health-care Statistics, the Health Care Financing Administration, and the Robert Wood Johnson Foundation. He is an active member of the National Association of Health Data Organizations and the Association for Health Services Research. Mr. Stone received his BA and MS degrees from Boston University. He was a member of the Institute of Medicine study that produced the report *Health Data in the Information Age: Use, Disclosure, and Privacy* (National Academy Press, 1994).

Willis H. Ware is a member (emeritus) of the Corporate Research Staff at the RAND Corporation. His career has spanned all aspects of computer science—hardware, software, architecture, software development, federal agency and military applications, real-time systems, networks, management of computer-intensive projects, and public policy. In the late 1960s he developed a research interest in the security of computer systems and networks, and shortly thereafter, a corresponding interest in the personal privacy consequences of record-keeping systems. He has written extensively on both topics. He was the first chairman of the American Federation of Information Processing Societies (AFIPS) and in the early 1970s chaired the Secretary's Advisory Committee on Automated Personal Data Systems of the Department of Health, Education, and Welfare. Its report was the foundation for the Federal Privacy Act of 1974. Subsequently, he was appointed to the Privacy Protection Study Commission by President Ford and served as both commissioner and vice chairman. Its report remains the most extensive examination of private sector record-keeping practices. He currently chairs the statutory Computer System Security and Privacy Advisory Board. Dr. Ware received his BS from the University of Pennsylvania, an SM from the Massachusetts Institute of Technology, and a PhD from Princeton University—all in electrical engineering. He is a fellow of the Institute of Electrical and Electronics Engineers, the Association for Computing Machinery, and the American Association for the Advancement of Science, and he was elected to the National Academy of Engineering in 1985.

A.2 ADDITIONAL CONTRIBUTORS TO THE PROJECT

The following individuals provided the committee with briefings, discussion, position papers, personal views, and background materials. They are listed alphabetically. Individuals who explicitly requested complete anonymity are not listed.

Edward Allen, Federal Bureau of Investigation; Edward J. Appel, National Security Council; John A. Armstrong, IBM (retired); Wendell Bailey,

National Cable Television Association; Stewart Baker, Steptoe and Johnson; Richard C. Barth, Motorola; Bill Bauriedel; David C. Bedard; Sheldon R. Bentley, Boeing Computer Services; Jerry Berman, Center for Democracy and Technology; Tom Berson, Anagram Laboratories; Rose Biancinello, Department of State; Robert Blandford; Matt Blaze; Eric Blossom; William Earl Boebert, Sandia National Laboratories; Barry Briggs, Lotus Development Corporation; David Brin; Ken Bronstein, Hewlett-Packard; Clinton Brooks, National Security Agency; Melinda Brown, Lotus Development Corporation; Robert E. Bruccoleri, Bristol-Myers Squibb Pharmaceutical Research Institute; James Carr, U.S. District Court of Toledo; Vinton G. Cerf, MCI Telecommunications Corporation; Jesse Choper, University of California, Berkeley; Anthony Clark, House Science Committee; Judi Clark; Floyd I. Clarke, MacAndrews & Forbes; David Cohen, Central Intelligence Agency; Leroy L. Cook, MITRE Corporation; Daniel Corcoran, Electronic Data Systems; Aaron W. Cross, IBM; William Crowell, National Security Agency; Walter Curtis, National Semiconductor Corporation; David Decker, GTE Laboratories; Philippe Dejean, Service Central de la Sécurité des Systèmes d'Information, Service du Premier Ministre (France); James X. Dempsey, Center for National Security Studies; Dorothy Denning, Georgetown University;

Whitfield Diffie, Sun Microsystems; M. Nanette DiTosto, U.S. Council for International Business; Esther Dyson, EDventure Holdings Inc.; Robert I. Eachus; Carl Ellison, CyberCash Inc.; Glenn Everhart; Lincoln D. Faurer, National Security Agency (retired); C. William Ferguson, Semaphore Corporation; Robert Fielding, National Security Agency; Hal Finney; Clifford S. Fishman, Catholic University of America; William Flanagan, Lotus Development Corporation; Martin L. Fogelman; Greg Frazier, House Intelligence Committee; Paul Freedenberg, Baker and Botts; Louis Freeh, Federal Bureau of Investigation; Roger E. French, Digital Equipment Corporation; A. Michael Froomkin, University of Miami Law School; Robert Gallagher, Department of Commerce; Roby Gamboa; Richard Garwin, IBM T.J. Watson Research Center; Toby Gati, Department of State; Jeffrey Gaynor, Department of Defense; Kenneth Geide, Federal Bureau of Investigation; Thomas A. Gilbert, Network Systems Corporation; Louis Giles, National Security Agency; John Gilmore, Cygnus Support; Ronald Goldstock, Kroll Associates; Jamie S. Gorelick, Department of Justice; Rebecca Gould, Business Software Alliance; Graham Greenleaf, University of New South Wales; William F. Hagerty IV, Management Advisory Group; Keith Hall, Department of Defense; Bruce Hamilton; Martha Harris, Department of State; Matthew D. Healy, Yale Center for Medical Informatics; Bruce Heiman, Business Software Alliance; David A. Hendon, Department of Trade and Industry (United Kingdom); David Henry, National Security Agency;

Richard Hertling, Senate Judiciary Committee; R.S. (Bob) Heuman; Mack Hicks, Bank of America;

Richard Hill; K. Mignon Hoffman, Boeing Computer Services; Lance Hoffman, George Washington University; Robert Hood, Congressman Newt Gingrich's Office; Eric Hughes; Deborah Hurley, Organization for Economic Cooperation and Development; Rick Jinelsky, Hewlett-Packard; Michael Paul Johnson; Thomas Kalil, National Economic Council; Raymond Kammer, National Institute of Standards and Technology; Phil Karn; Sally Katzen, Office of Management and Budget; Elizabeth Kaufman, Citibank; Stephen T. Kent, BBN Communications; Gordon Kettler, General Motors; Raymond Khan, General Motors; Joseph Kielman, Federal Bureau of Investigation; Steve Killion, Federal Bureau of Investigation; Julie Krueger, Atmel Corporation; Susan Landau, University of Massachusetts, Amherst; P.E. (Pat) Lanthier, Pacific Bell; Tony Lauck; Joshua Lederberg, Rockefeller University; Ronald Lee, National Security Agency; James Leinweber, University of Wisconsin, Madison; Blaise Liffick, Computer Professionals for Social Responsibility; Steven B. Lipner, MITRE Corporation; Myles Losch; Robert Lucky, Bell Communications Research; Deborah Malamud, University of Michigan Law School; Noel Matchett, Information Security Inc.; Timothy May; Bruce McConnell, Office of Management and Budget; Kirk McConnell, Senate Armed Services Committee; Kate McGee, Oracle Corporation; F. Lynn McNulty, McNulty and Associates;

Catherine Medich, CommerceNet; Ken Mendelson, House Judiciary Committee; Douglas Miller, Software Publishers Association; John Millis, House Select Committee on Intelligence; William Mockler, Drug Enforcement Administration; Vera A. Murray, IBM; Michael Nelson, Office of Science and Technology Policy; Robert Nieves, Drug Enforcement Administration; Edward O'Malley, OSO Group; Christopher Padilla, AT&T Government Affairs; Donn Parker, SRI International Inc.; Kumar Patel, University of California, Los Angeles; Bill Patterson; Nick Patterson, Renaissance Technologies; Craig Paul, University of Kansas; Paul J.J. Payack, Network Systems Corporation; Mona Peglow, Novell; David Pensak, DuPont Corporation; Henry H. Perritt, Jr., Villanova University; John Pescatore, International Data Corporation Government; Charles C. Philipp, Department of Energy; John Pignataro, New York City Police Department; John Podesta, The White House; Carl Pomerance, University of Georgia; William Poulos, Electronic Data Systems; William Press, Harvard College; Robert Prestel, National Security Agency (retired); Todd Quinto, Tufts University; Jim Ray; Alfred Reifman, Congressional Research Service; Robert Rich, National Security Agency (retired); Ed Roback, National Institute of

Standards and Technology; Bruce Roberts, Unisys; Cesare Rosati, Department of State;

Sholom Rosen, Citibank; Howard Rosenblum, National Security Agency (retired); Marc Rotenberg, Electronic Privacy Information Center; Lee D. Rothstein, VeriTech; Ira Rubenstein, Microsoft Corporation; Clint Sare; John Scheibel, House Foreign Affairs Committee; Roger Schell, Novell; Jeff Schiller, Massachusetts Institute of Technology; James Schindler, Hewlett-Packard; Kurt Schneckenburger; William Richard Scruggs, Department of Justice; Raymond R. Semko, Department of Energy; William S. Sessions, Sessions & Sessions, L.C.; Edward Sheehan, Electronic Data Systems; Alan Shipman, Enterprise Integration Technology, CommerceNet; Gursharan Sidhu, Apple Computer; Cheryl Simmons, Computer and Communications Industry Association; Lori S. Sinton, National Semiconductor Corporation; Landgrave T. Smith, Jr., Institute for Defense Analyses; Peter Smith, member of Parliament, United Kingdom; Teresa Smith, Central Intelligence Agency; Oliver Smoot, Information Technology Industry Council; Carl Snyder, Hewlett-Packard; Bill Sommerfeld; George Spix, Microsoft Corporation; Edward Springer, Office of Management and Budget; Ross Stapleton-Gray, TeleDiplomacy Inc.;

Vicki Stearn, Discovery Communications Inc.; Shari Steele, Electronic Frontier Foundation; John D. Steinbruner, Brookings Institution; Barry Steinhardt, American Civil Liberties Union; Ivan Sutherland, Sun Microsystems Laboratories; Raymond Tate, National Security Agency (retired); Duane Thompson; George B. Trubow, John Marshall Law School; Roger Ulbrich, Chevron Corporation; Paul Walker, House Armed Services Committee; Stephen Walker, Trusted Information Systems Inc.; Lester Waters, Microsoft Corporation; Daniel Weitzner, Center for Democracy and Technology; William Whitehurst, IBM; Daniel Whiteman, General Motors; Randy Whiting, Hewlett-Packard; Philip Wilcox, Department of State; Janice Williams, Central Intelligence Agency; Charity Wilson, Senate Judiciary Committee; Joan D. Winston, Office of Technology Assessment; R. James Woolsey, Shey & Gardner.

B

Glossary

ACCESS (to a system, to data, to a software process)—(n.) in general, the right to enter or make use of. In a computer context, entry granted to a software path that establishes the right to use a system and its resources; to read, write, modify, or delete data; and/or to use software processes with various capabilities. (v.) to achieve the status of having access.

ACCESS CONTROL—the granting or denying to a subject of certain permissions to access a resource (e.g., to view a certain file, to run a certain program).

ALGORITHM AND KEY LENGTH—the combination of cryptographic algorithm and its key length(s) often used to establish the strength of an encryption process.

ASSURANCE—confidence that a system design meets its requirements, or that its implementation meets its specification, or that some specific property is satisfied.

ASYMMETRIC CRYPTOGRAPHY (also public-key cryptography)—cryptography based on algorithms that enable the use of one key (a public key) to encrypt a message and a second, different, but mathematically related, key (a private key) to decrypt a message. Asymmetric cryptography can also be used to perform digital signatures and key exchange.

AUDITING—the process of making and keeping the records necessary to support accountability. See *audit trail*.

AUDIT TRAIL—the results of monitoring each operation of subjects on objects; for example, an audit trail might be a record of all actions taken on a particularly sensitive file or a record of all users who viewed that file.

AUTHENTICATION (OF IDENTITY)—an adjunct step to identification that confirms an asserted identity with a specified, or understood, level of confidence. Authentication can be used to provide high assurance that the purported identity is, in fact, the correct identity associated with the entity that provides it. The authentication mechanism can be based on something that the entity knows, has, or is (e.g., a password, a smart card that uses some encryption or random number for a challenge-response scheme, or a fingerprint).

AUTHENTICATION OF A MESSAGE (OR A FILE)—the process of adding one or more additional data elements to communications traffic (or files) to ensure the integrity of the traffic (or files). Such additional elements are often called "message authenticator(s)" and would be an example of an integrity lock.

AUTHENTICITY—a security service that provides a user with a means of verifying the identity of the sender of a message, a file, a computer system, a software process, or even a database or individual software component.

AUTHORIZATION—determining whether a subject (a user or system) is trusted to act for a given purpose, for example, allowed to read a particular file.

AVAILABILITY—the property that a given resource will be usable during a given time period, for example, that an encrypted file can be decrypted when necessary.

BACK DOOR—an aspect of a system's mechanism that can be exploited to circumvent the system's security.

BINARY DIGIT—one of the two symbols (0 and 1) that are commonly used to represent numerical entries in the binary number system.

BIT—a contraction of the term "binary digit."

BIT STREAM (also digital stream)—the running stream of binary symbols representing digitized information; the term is commonly used to refer to digital communications.

CAPSTONE CHIP—an integrated circuit chip that implements the Skipjack algorithm and also includes the Digital Signature Algorithm, the Secure Hash Standard, the classified Key Exchange Algorithm, circuitry for efficient exponentiation of large numbers, and a random number generator using a pure noise source.

CAPSTONE/FORTEZZA INITIATIVE—a government initiative to promote and support escrowed encryption for data storage and communications.

CERTIFICATE AUTHORITY—synonym for certification authority.

CERTIFICATE MANAGEMENT—the overall process of issuing, storing, verifying, and generally accepting responsibility for the accuracy of certifications and their secure delivery to appropriate consumers.

CERTIFICATION—the administrative act of approving a computer system or component for use in a particular application.

CERTIFICATION AUTHORITY—a specially established trusted organization or part of a larger organization that accepts the responsibilities of managing the certificate process by issuing, distributing, and verifying certificates.

CIPHERTEXT—literally, text material that has been encrypted; also used in a generic sense for the output of any encryption process, no matter what the original digitized input might have been (e.g., text, computer files, computer programs, or digitized graphical images).

CLEARTEXT (also plaintext)—the material entering into an encryption process or emerging from a decryption process. "Text" is used categorically for any digitized material.

CLIPPER CHIP—an escrowed encryption chip that implements the Skipjack algorithm to encrypt communications conducted over the public switched network (e.g., between telephones, modems, or facsimile equipment).

CLIPPER INITIATIVE —a voluntary program to improve the security of telephone communications while meeting the legitimate needs of law enforcement.

CoCom—Coordinating Committee for Multilateral Export Controls, began operations in 1950 to control export of strategic materials and technology to communist countries; participants include Australia, Belgium, Canada, Denmark, France, Germany, Greece, Italy, Japan, Luxembourg, the Netherlands, Norway, Portugal, Spain, Turkey, the United Kingdom, and the United States.

COLLATERAL CRYPTOGRAPHY—a collective term used in this report to include uses of encryption for other than confidentiality; it includes such services as authentication, integrity checks, authoritative date/time stamping, and digital signatures.

COMPETITIVE ACCESS PROVIDERS—telephone carriers that compete with local monopoly carriers.

CONFIDENTIALITY (communications)—the protection of communications traffic against interception or receipt by unauthorized third parties.

CONFIDENTIALITY (data)—an assertion about a body of data that is sensitive and must be protected against loss, misuse, destruction, unintended change, and unauthorized access or dissemination.

COUNTERMEASURE—a mechanism that reduces vulnerability to a threat.

CRYPTANALYSIS—the study and practice of various methods to penetrate ciphertext and deduce the contents of the original cleartext message.

CRYPTOGRAPHIC ALGORITHM—a mathematical procedure, used in conjunction with a closely guarded secret key, that transforms original input into a form that is unintelligible without special knowledge of the secret information and the algorithm. Such algorithms are also the basis for digital signatures and key exchange.

CRYPTOGRAPHY—originally, the science and technology of keeping information secret from unauthorized parties by using a code or a cipher. Today, cryptography can be used for many applications that do not involve confidentiality.

DATA ENCRYPTION STANDARD (DES)—a U.S. government standard (FIPS 46-1) describing a cryptographic algorithm to be used in a symmetric cryptographic application.

DATE/TIME STAMP—the date and time a transaction or document is initiated or submitted to a computer system, or the time at which a transaction is logged or archived. Often it is important that the stamp be certified by some authority to establish legal or other special status. Such a service can be provided by a cryptographic procedure.

DECOMPILING—a process through which *object code* consisting of ones and zeros can be converted into source code in a high-level computer language such as C or Pascal.

DECRYPTION—the cryptographic procedure of transforming ciphertext into the original message cleartext.

DENIAL OF SERVICE—reducing the availability of an object below the level needed to support critical processing or communication, as can happen, for example, in a system crash.

DIGEST—a much condensed version of a message produced by processing the message by a hash algorithm. Commonly, the digest has a fixed length and is not dependent on the length of the original message.

DIGITAL SIGNATURE—a digitized analog of a written signature, produced by a cryptographic procedure acting (commonly) on a digest of the message to be signed.

DIGITAL SIGNATURE STANDARD (DSS)—a U.S. government standard (FIPS 186) describing a cryptographic algorithm for producing a digital signature.

DIGITAL TELEPHONY ACT OF 1995—a law requiring that the telephone industry make such technical changes to its installed equipment as are needed to comply with court-authorized wiretap orders.

DISASSEMBLY—a process through which *object code* consisting of ones and zeros can be converted into its low-level assembly language representation.

DISCLOSURE (of data)—the act of making available; the instance of revealing.

DUAL-USE SYSTEM—a system with both military and civilian applications.

ESCROWED ENCRYPTION STANDARD (EES)—a voluntary U.S. government standard for key-escrowed encryption of voice, fax, or computer data transmitted over circuit-switched telephone systems.

EVALUATION—(1) the process of examining a computer product or system with respect to certain criteria; (2) the results of that process.

EXCEPTIONAL ACCESS—access to encrypted data granted to a recipient other than the originally intended recipient.

FEDERAL INFORMATION PROCESSING STANDARD (FIPS)—a categorical term for U.S. government standards applying to computer-based systems.

FIRMWARE—the programmable information used to control the low-level operations of hardware. Firmware is commonly stored in read only memory (ROM), which is initially installed in the factory and may be replaced in the field to fix mistakes or to improve system capabilities.

FIRST PARTY—the originator of a transaction (e.g., an electronic message or telephone call).

FUNCTIONALITY—the functional behavior of a system. Functionality requirements include, for example, confidentiality, integrity, availability, authentication, and safety.

IDENTIFICATION—the assertion by a person, process, or system wishing to communicate with another person, process, or system of the name by which it is known within the process(es) or system(s) in question.

IDENTIFICATION KEY—a key registered or issued to a specific user.

IMPLEMENTATION—the mechanism that (supposedly) realizes the specified design.

INTEGRATED PRODUCT—a product designed to provide the user a capability useful in its own right (e.g., word processing) and integrated with encryption capabilities that a user may or may not employ; a product in which the cryptographic capability is fully integrated with the other capabilities of the product.

INTEGRITY—the property that an object meets an a priori established set of expectations. One example of integrity is that changes must be accomplished in a specified and authorized manner. Data integrity, program integrity, system integrity, and network integrity are all relevant to consideration of computer and system security.

INTEGRITY CHECK—a quantity derived algorithmically from the running digital stream of a message and appended to it for transmission, or from the entire contents of a stored data file and appended to it. Some integrity checks are not cryptographically based (e.g., cyclic redundancy checks), but others are.

INTERCEPTOR—a party eavesdropping on communications.

ITAR—International Traffic in Arms Regulations.

KEY—a sequence of easily changed symbols that, used with a cryptographic algorithm, provides a cryptographic process.

KEY DISTRIBUTION—a secure method for two distant parties to exchange keys or to receive keys from a central authoritative source.

KEY ESCROW ENCRYPTION (also escrowed encryption)—an encryption system that enables exceptional access to encrypted data through special data recovery keys held by a trusted party.

KEY MANAGEMENT—the overall process of generating and distributing cryptographic keys to authorized recipients in a secure manner.

MONITORING—recording of relevant information about each operation by a subject on an object, maintained in an audit trail for subsequent analysis.

NODE—a computer system that is connected to a communications network and participates in the routing of messages within that network. Networks are usually described as a collection of nodes that are connected by communications links.

NONREPUDIATION (of a signed digital message, data, or software)— the status achieved by employing a digital-signature procedure to affirm the identity of the signer of a digital message with extremely high confidence and, hence, to protect against a subsequent attempt to deny authenticity, whether or not there had been an initial authentication.

OBJECT CODE—the "executable" code of ones and zeros that provides a computer with instructions on what steps to perform. Contrast with *source code*.

OBJECT LINKING AND EMBEDDING (OLE)—Microsoft's object-oriented software technology.

ONE-WAY HASH FUNCTION—a function that produces a message digest that cannot be reversed to obtain the original.

OPERATING SYSTEM—a program that runs on a computer whose purpose is to provide basic services that can be used by applications running on that computer. Such functions might include screen displays, file handling, and encryption. MS-DOS and Windows '95 are examples of operating systems that run on Intel microprocessors.

PASSWORD—a sequence of characters or words that a subject presents to a system for purposes of validation or verification. See *authentication*.

PCMCIA CARD—the industry-standard Personal Computer Memory Card Industry Association card and associated electrical interface for various computer components (e.g., memory, hard disks, and cryptographic processes). Also known as a PC card.

PEN REGISTER—a device that records numbers dialed from a telephone.

PIN (personal identification number)—a (generally numeric) quantity that has to be keyed into some device or process to authenticate an individual. A common example is the 4-digit PIN associated with the use of automated teller machines; another, the 4-digit PIN associated with a telephone calling card.

PLAINTEXT—a synonym for cleartext.

PRIVATE KEY—the private (secret) key associated with a given person's public key for a public-key cryptographic system.

PUBLIC KEY—the publicly known key associated with a given person's use of a public-key cryptographic system.

PUBLIC-KEY CERTIFICATE—a statement, possibly on paper but more often transmitted electronically over an information network, that establishes the relationship between a named individual (or organization) and a specified public key. In principle, it could (but need not) include collateral information such as mailing address, organizational affiliation, and telephone number.

RC2/RC4 ALGORITHMS—two variable-key-length cryptographic algorithms designed by Ronald Rivest of the Massachusetts Institute of Technology. Both are symmetric algorithms.

RELIABILITY—the ability of a computer or an information or telecommunications system to perform consistently and precisely according to its specifications and design requirements and to do so with high confidence.

REMAILER—a computer-based process that automatically redistributes electronic mail, often to multiple recipients. Remailers can be anonymous (i.e., they can be configured to strip off information identifying the sender of a message, while still enabling a return "path" so that recipients can reply to messages).

REVERSE ENGINEERING—the generic name for methods by which parties attempt to uncover technical details of a microelectronic chip or of software.

RISK—the likelihood that a vulnerability may be exploited, or that a threat may become harmful.

RSA ALGORITHM—the Rivest-Shamir-Adelman public-key encryption algorithm.

SAFETY—the property indicating that a computer system or software, when embedded in its operational environment, does not cause any actions or events that create unintended potentially or actually dangerous situations for itself or for the environment in which it is embedded.

SECOND PARTY—the recipient of a transaction (e.g., an electronic message or telephone call).

SECRET-KEY CRYPTOSYSTEM—a symmetric cryptographic process that uses the same secret key (which both parties have and keep secret) to encrypt and decrypt messages.

SECURE HASH FUNCTION—a one-way hash function for which the likelihood that two messages will yield the same digest is satisfactorily small.

SECURE HASH STANDARD—a U.S. government standard (FIPS 180-1) for a secure hash function.

SECURITY—the collection of safeguards that ensures the confidentiality of information, protects the system(s) or network(s) used to process it, and controls access to it. Hence, security safeguards impose appropriate access rules for computer information.

SECURITY-SPECIFIC (*OR* STAND-ALONE) CRYPTOGRAPHY PRODUCT—an add-on product specifically designed to provide cryptographic capabilities for one or more other software or hardware capabilities.

SHAREWARE—software offered publicly and shared rather than sold.

SKIPJACK—a classified symmetric key encryption algorithm that uses 80-bit keys; developed by the National Security Agency.

SOURCE CODE—the textual form in which a program is entered into a computer (e.g., Pascal).

SPECIFICATION—a technical description of the desired behavior of a system, as derived from its requirements. A specification is used to develop and test an implementation of a system.

SPOOFING—illicitly masquerading as a legitimate company, party, or individual.

STU-III—a U.S. government secure telephone system using end-to-end encryption.

SYMMETRIC CRYPTOGRAPHY, CRYPTOSYSTEM—a cryptographic system that uses the same key to encrypt and decrypt messages.

SYSTEM—an interdependent collection of components that can be considered as a unified whole; for example, a networked collection of computer systems, a distributed system, an editor, a memory unit, and so on.

THIRD-PARTY ACCESS—eavesdropping on or entry to data communications, telephony, or stored computer data by an unauthorized party. See *exceptional access.*

THREAT—the potential for exploitation of a vulnerability.

TOKEN—when used in the context of authentication, a (usually) physical device necessary for user identification.

TRAP AND TRACE—a device that identifies the telephone numbers from which calls have been placed to a target telephone number.

TROJAN HORSE—a computer program whose execution would result in undesired side effects, generally unanticipated by the user. A Trojan horse program may otherwise give the appearance of providing normal functionality.

TRUST—the concept that a system will provide its intended functionality with a stated level of confidence. The term is also used for other entities, e.g., trusted software, trusted network, trusted individual. Sometimes the confidence—also called the assurance—can be measured, but sometimes it is inferred on the basis of testing and other information.

TRUSTWORTHINESS—assurance that a system deserves to be trusted.

VULNERABILITY—a weakness in a system that can be exploited to violate the system's intended behavior. There may be vulnerabilities in security, integrity, availability, and other aspects. The act of exploiting a vulnerability represents a threat, which has an associated risk of being exploited.

WORK FACTOR—a measure of the difficulty of undertaking a brute-force test of all possible keys against a given ciphertext and known algorithm.

C

A Brief Primer on Cryptography

This appendix provides a brief primer on cryptography, but it is necessary to understand from the start that cryptography is not a "silver bullet" for information security. For example, a network may be insecure in the sense that it is easy for an adversary to obtain information that is flowing on the network. End users may use very strong cryptography to protect this information. But if sufficiently motivated and skilled, adversaries may well attempt to penetrate the systems attached to the network, where they can obtain the information in the clear. Or they may be able to bribe a system operator to obtain it for them. Nevertheless cryptography still has value under these circumstances, because it forces the adversary to alter his or her attack and expend greater effort to obtain information; furthermore, the use of cryptography will foil some adversaries who are not motivated or skilled enough to develop alternative attacks.

C.1 A VERY SHORT HISTORY OF CRYPTOGRAPHY

For most of its history, cryptography was more an art than a science and was devoted primarily to keeping messages and records secret. To be sure, mathematical techniques for cryptanalysis and engineering skills for building devices for encryption and decryption played important roles, but cryptography itself did not rest on a firm mathematical foundation.

The scientific basis for modern cryptography was established in 1949 with the development of information theory by Claude Shannon, who determined for the first time a mathematically rigorous basis for defining

364

a "perfect" encryption system that could be made impenetrable, even in principle, to an adversary with unlimited resources. Based on this work, secret-key cryptography (defined below) blossomed, with the most public work in this area being the Data Encryption Standard promulgated in 1975 by the National Bureau of Standards (now the National Institute of Standards and Technology). The second major revolution occurred in 1976 with the first discussion in the open literature of asymmetric cryptography, inspired by a landmark paper of Whitfield Diffie and Martin Hellman.[1]

C.2 CAPABILITIES ENABLED BY CRYPTOGRAPHY

Cryptography can help to ensure the integrity of data (i.e., that data retrieved or received are identical to data originally stored or sent), to authenticate specific parties (i.e., that the purported sender or author of a message is indeed its real sender or author), to facilitate nonrepudiation, and to preserve the confidentiality of information that may have come improperly into the possession of unauthorized parties.

To understand how cryptographic methods span a range of communication and storage needs, consider the general problem of sending a private message from Party A to Party B. Centuries ago, such a process was accomplished by Party A writing a letter containing his or her signature (authentication). The letter was sealed inside a container to prevent accidental disclosure (confidential transmission). If Party B received the container with a broken seal, it meant that the letter had been disclosed or altered and Party B would take appropriate actions (data integrity). Otherwise, Party B would verify Party A's signature and read the message. In the information era, each of the steps remains essentially the same, except that automated tools perform most of the work and are explained below.

C.2.1 Ensuring the Integrity of Data

Digital information is transmitted (or stored) so that it can be received (or retrieved). For two reasons, it is possible that the information received or retrieved might differ from the original information transmitted or stored:

1. A technical problem may inadvertently alter one or more of the bits of information in question. No digital transmission-receiving or stor-

---

[1]Whitfield Diffie and Martin Hellman, "New Directions in Cryptography," *IEEE Transactions on Information Theory,* Volume IT-22, IEEE Press, New York, 1976, pp. 644-654.

age and retrieval system is perfect—every now and then, with a frequency depending on the particular characteristics of the technology used in the system and the environment in which it operates, a "1" will be received or retrieved when a "0" is sent or stored and vice versa.

2. A third party may deliberately alter one or more of the bits of information in question. For example, a proposal by Vendor A to a buyer may offer to undertake a task for $100,000. Vendor B, competing for the same contract but wishing to charge $150,000, may intercept the digital transmission of Vendor A's proposal and deliberately alter the $100,000 to $300,000. Thus, the buyer would be presented with information that falsely understated the cost-effectiveness of Vendor A and would award the contract to Vendor B.

In some cases, the alteration of one or even many bits may not render the information received or retrieved useless (e.g., if the bits constitute a digital representation of a photograph). However, for other purposes (e.g., the transmission of a software program), even a one-bit difference between what was received and what was transmitted could make all the difference in the world.

It is therefore desirable to ensure that any alterations, whether inadvertent or deliberate, can be detected if they occur. An integrity lock or integrity check is a quantity derived algorithmically from the bits that constitute the information being transmitted or stored and appended to it for the purpose of ensuring that the information received or retrieved is identical to the information being transmitted or stored.

Cryptography is relevant to integrity checks that are intended to detect deliberate alterations. In such cases, the integrity check (also known as a message authenticator) must use a process that involves information unknown to potential penetrators; that is, it has parts that are secret and known only to the communicating parties (usually a secret key).[2]

In the example of Party A sending a message to Party B, Party A attaches a number called a cryptographic checksum that is generated

---

[2]Protecting against inadvertent alterations is the job of error-correcting codes (e.g., cyclic redundancy checks, Reed-Solomon codes, parity checks). However, for error correction, the process and techniques in question will be known commonly to all users. Thus, if a message is protected only by error-correcting codes, a person could use this knowledge to construct revised error checks that would conceal deliberate alterations. The use of error-correcting codes does not ensure integrity against intended subversions of the transmission.

Note: Although under some circumstances (e.g., for limited numbers of presumably random and inadvertent alterations), an error-correcting code can correct bits that have been changed.

Generally, a cryptography-based approach is much more sensitive to changes in the message than usual error-correction schemes; that is, cryptography provides assurances both of confidentiality and of message integrity.

BOX C.1
Checksums and Hashes

Checksums were originally used to detect errors in stored or transmitted data. The simplest checksum is a single bit that is the XOR of all message bits. This can detect single errors, but not double errors. Most error-detecting codes add more complex checksums (often called CRCs, for cyclic redundancy checks) to detect much larger numbers of errors.

For nonmalicious errors owing to physical error phenomena, such checksums are fine. But when an opponent might try to corrupt data, a cryptographically secure checksum is needed—one that will detect random errors and prevent malicious errors. For example, one of the federal standards relating to DES describes a message authentication code (MAC), which is formed by enciphering the message under a secret key known only to authorized parties and adding the last 64 bits (or less if that suffices) of ciphertext as a MAC. Clearly, another authorized user can validate the MAC by enciphering the message (which is sent in the clear—not enciphered—since only authentication is needed in this application) and comparing the computed MAC with the received MAC. An opponent who does not know the secret key has as much trouble computing a modified MAC to go with a corrupted version of the data as in breaking DES. (If enciphering and deciphering are mathematically equivalent, it is just as hard to encipher without the key as to decipher without the key.)

A hash function is a pseudorandom function that is shorter than its input. Originally used in searching and sorting algorithms, where it did not need any cryptographic properties, a one-way hash function is useful for digital signatures because the hash can be signed by the public-key cryptographic system, rather than the much longer message. "One-way" means that it is easy to compute H (message) but computationally infeasible to compute any inverse image of a given value H—or if one inverse image is known (e.g., if a spoof who has intercepted a message knows the message and H (message)), it is computationally infeasible to find another inverse image. (There are many inverse images since H is a compressive function.) The one-way property is needed because the signature is valid not only for the message signed, but also for any other message with the same hash value.

In short, a cryptographic checksum depends on a secret key known to the authorized transmitter and receiver, whereas a one-way hash value can be computed by anyone. The hash value is then acted on by the secret key in an asymmetric cryptographic system to produce a digital signature.

---

algorithmically from specific characteristics of the message (e.g., the letters and numbers in the message; see Box C.1. Party B can use the same algorithm to compute the checksum of the message received and compare it to the checksum sent, and if they match, Party B can be confident of the message's data integrity.

C.2.2 Authentication of Users

In many communications systems, it is quite important to establish the clear and unquestionable identity of the communicating parties; the process of establishing and verifying the identity of a party is referred to as *authentication*.[3]

Authentication is based on something that the proper party would know, would have, or would be. For example, a specially designed electronic ring might be owned or worn only by individuals authorized to wear it.[4] A secret password might be regarded as being known only to a certain party. Another approach based on secret knowledge involves one party challenging another party to answer certain questions that could be answered correctly only by one with the proper identity. In banking circles, a customer's mother's maiden name is often an authenticator, since it is assumed that such a fact would not be readily known to an impersonator (but contemporary dossier-quality databases of personal information significantly weaken the assurance). In telephony, humans frequently authenticate each other merely by the recognized sound of a voice or simply by the fact that a certain individual answers the telephone when the number alleged to be that individual's number is dialed. Vendors accepting credit cards use handwritten signatures to authenticate identities on the assumption that only the proper holder of a credit card can sign the credit card charge slip in a way that matches the signature on the card. Stronger authentication methods often involve hardware—a tangible object or artifact—that must be associated with authorized users and that is not easily duplicated. (The ultimate "hardware" involved might

---

[3]Authentication is almost always a requirement for authorized access (to use a system; to read, write, modify, or destroy data; to run a software process; to make use of computer or communications resources). Access rights have qualifications that are often called privileges (e.g., access to data might include some or all of the privileges of read, write, modify, destroy). Similarly, not all users of a system will be accorded free run of all the software in the system (i.e., their privileges will be restricted). A system electronically accessing another without human intervention typically will not be entitled to all of the latter's data and/or software privileges. For example, one system might be authorized, or privileged, to ask for only a certain kind of data (e.g., only the cash value of point-of-sale information will be exchanged with bankcard authorization systems).

For some security requirements, authentication by itself may be sufficient. For example, the "security" of the credit card industry is based primarily on authentication mechanisms, not secrecy mechanisms. People routinely recite their credit card numbers to anyone and everyone who wants to be paid for services or products. Some degree of security is provided by using other information, such as the expiration date or mother's maiden name, to authenticate the person using that number. Such authentication is performed only when the risk of fraud is above a given level (e.g., the purchase of an expensive item or too much credit card activity in a given period of time). Secrecy mechanisms are used, for the most part, to prevent eavesdroppers from getting one's card number, but most fraud is conducted without eavesdropping. For example, cards are stolen, numbers are stolen from vendor databases, and merchant employees copy numbers.

Authentication and confidentiality are complementary tools for supporting information security, as the discussion above and that in Box C.2 make clear.

[4]"Dick Tracy Eat Your Heart Out," *New York Times*, September 4, 1995, p. 38.

well be biometric in nature: a person's handprint, a fingerprint, or a retinal pattern.) Of course, except in the case of biometric identifiers, all authentication systems can be compromised if the secret or the hardware token belonging only to the proper party is passed on to unauthorized parties.[5]

Even though such mechanisms are not perfect, they are routinely used to conduct personal and business interactions, and most of those communications use nonprivate channels. As we move toward an electronic economy, conducted over wide-scale communication networks, it becomes increasingly important to develop stronger authentication mechanisms that prevent wrongdoers of all types from being able to access remote resources without proper authorization. The reason is that electronic commerce disconnects consumers and suppliers from the physical mechanisms that help curb fraud. For example, vendors accepting credit cards for face-to-face transactions check the signature on the card (or else accept liability for not performing the check). Mail-order and telephone vendors use the mailing address of a customer to help authenticate a purchase; large orders are generally not sent to an address different from the credit card billing address, unless extra steps are taken to ensure authenticity. However, when such mechanisms are not available, electronic commerce will require strong cryptography-based mechanisms that will help to establish the identity of the consumer.

Thus, it is the goal of most communications system designers to provide strong authenticity of the communicating parties. It should be noted, however, that in some cases (such as telephone Caller ID services), the communicating party may wish to be anonymous (or pseudonymous) for good reason and system designers must take this into account.

Cryptography-based authentication could also help to deal with the problem of controlling the secondary use of data collected from individuals (described in Chapter 1). For example, a requirement to include the source of personal data (e.g., the original party to which an individual discloses personal data) with the person-identified information at the time of disclosure would help the individual keep track of how such information is subsequently used. Such a requirement could be enforced through the use of a digital signature belonging to the data source being bound to the personal information before it is disseminated.[6]

---

[5]For this reason, very strong authentication requires hardware components that can be in the possession of only one person at a time. Nevertheless, software-based authentication has many advantages (such as ease of deployment and perhaps lower costs) that may prove decisive against the lower levels of confidence that are possible with such methods. Software-based authentication is better than nothing, and the decisions regarding medium will be made on the basis of business needs for differing levels of confidence.

[6]Personal communication, Marc Rotenberg, Electronic Privacy Information Center, Washington, D.C., March 10, 1995.

Finally, good authentication mechanisms can facilitate the generation of reliable audit trails that allow the investigation of possible wrong-doing. Such mechanisms have high value when many individuals are in a position to compromise the same sensitive data.

C.2.3 Nonrepudiation

The authentication of a user and the integrity of a message sent by a user are two different concepts. For example, being assured of a message's integrity does not in itself assure the receiver that its purported sender did in fact send it.

Nonrepudiation is a cryptographic capability that combines techniques for ensuring user authentication and message integrity in such a way that the signer of a message cannot plausibly deny that it was he who created it or claim that the message received was not in fact the message sent. In other words, nonrepudiation protects against impersonation and denial of creation.

Digital signatures typically are used to provide nonrepudiation. A digital signature is a piece of information derived from both information known only to the sender (Party A) and the exact text of the message sent.[7] On the basis of information freely available to the sender (Party A), the receiver (Party B), and any evildoer, Party B can check the digital signature of the message allegedly sent by Party A against the message actually received. If nothing improper has occurred,

- Party B can be assured that Party A was in fact the sender;
- Party B can be assured that the message received was actually the one Party A sent; and
- If Party A ever denies having sent the message, Party B can prove that Party A did.[8]

Again, if the secrets on which authentication is based are compromised, a valid signature does not mean that a message was actually sent

---

[7]Although the entire message could be run through an encryption process and some part of the result used as the digital signature, in normal practice only a digest of the message is subject to this process to conserve both time and computer resources. The digest is created by an algorithm (usually known as a secure hash algorithm) that shortens a message of any length into a result that is of fixed and known length. This result (the digest or hash) is constructed in such a way that the likelihood that different original data items will produce identical digests is very small.

[8]Strictly speaking, this is true only if an asymmetric authentication system is used. An authentication system based on symmetric cryptography and secret keys can protect only against third-party forgeries, but not against the case in which Party B forges a message, claiming it to be from Party A. The reason is that Party A and Party B (but not a third party) both know a common secret key.

by the person who would normally be associated with that signature. If Party A gives his or her secret to Party C (e.g., a secretary) and Party C uses Party A's secret to send a message, that message is indistinguishable from one actually sent by Party A. Moreover, anyone receiving a message signed by Party A has a right to expect that Party A sent it and to take action on that basis. For example, if Party A completes an electronic message to buy certain items, that party will digitally sign the message in preparation for sending it. However, if Party A's attention is diverted during this time, Party C might actually send the message to a different supplier. This different supplier can verify that the message was signed by an authorized individual (Party A) and has every right to conclude that a valid purchase order has been received.

Finally, nonrepudiation often includes a time element; for example, one must be able to prove not only that he or she directed a stockbroker to buy 1,000 shares of Company XYZ at $30 per share, but also when the order was placed. Note that if the date and time are part of the message being signed, then the sender also cannot repudiate that date and time at which he or she signed the message. A greater degree of confidence that the date and time are in fact correct can be provided by secure date/time stamps.[9]

C.2.4 Preservation of Confidentiality[10]

It is inherent and assumed in most communications system design that communications between parties should be controlled in such a way that unintended access by others is prohibited. There are three common

---

[9]Secure date/time stamping is a technique involving a trusted third party to certify the creation of a document at a given time. Conceptually, a digital document is mailed to this trusted third party, who provides a date/time stamp and a digital signature of the document-stamp combination. If the date/time stamp is inserted correctly by the third party, the digital signature of that party ensures that the document did indeed exist at the time and date in the document. More discussion of this concept can be found in Barry Cipra, "Electronic Time-Stamping: The Notary Public Goes Digital," *Science*, Volume 261(5118), July 9, 1993, pp. 162-163, and on-line at http://www.surety.com.

[10]Note that in this section (and throughout this report unless otherwise stated explicitly), the term "confidentiality" (or, synonymously, secrecy) applies to data in a technical sense. There is another sense in which the term "confidentiality" is often used that refers to a policy context—the assertion that data are sensitive and must be protected from unauthorized parties. In a policy sense, confidentiality can be accomplished by techniques based entirely on access control and authorization—individuals without proper authorization are not permitted to view confidential data.

Thus, the distinction can be made between data that *are* confidential (i.e., on policy grounds, a person's AIDS/HIV status may be confidential data; the law recognizes the confidentiality of communications between lawyer and client, husband and wife, priest and parishioner) and data that are *made* confidential by the technical means described in this section.

methods of gaining confidentiality of communications: physical security, obfuscation, and encryption.

In the case of physical security, the communicator relies on the fact that the attacker will have a very difficult time physically penetrating the communications media or devices, or that it will be too costly for an attacker to do so. An example of this is an optical fiber, a medium that is inherently difficult to tap into without being intrusive to the communication.

In the case of obfuscation, the communicator relies upon the fact that communicated information is so well hidden in some surrounding container that it will be difficult for an attacker to recognize and thus retrieve it. An example of this is steganography, in which data can be hidden in things such as photographs.[11]

Finally, with encryption, one communicating party encodes information by using an agreed-upon coding method; the information is transmitted to its destination; then the other communicating party decodes the information. In this case, the communicator is relying on the fact that for someone other than the intended recipient, it will be very difficult to break the code or discover a secret that the code depends on, such as a key.

When used for preserving confidentiality, cryptography enables the system designer to separate the security of a message from the security of the medium used to transmit that message. Since some of the most useful and least expensive media in use today are insecure (e.g., wireless communications), such separation has obvious advantages. Even the most sophisticated cryptography today requires some keeping of secrets, but a properly implemented cryptography system reduces the problem of keeping messages secret to the problem of keeping secret a much smaller key, thereby simplifying the security problem.

Note that confidentiality and authentication are tied closely together, as discussed in Box C.2. Furthermore, systems that provide strong authentication capabilities and those that provide strong confidentiality can serve a similar purpose under some circumstances. For example, confidentiality provided by cryptography can keep hackers from learning a credit card number that is sent over the Internet, while authentication provided by cryptography can keep hackers from using that credit card number once they get it.[12]

---

[11]A simple example: most black-and-white pictures rendered in digital form use at most 2^{16} (65,536) shades of gray, because the human eye is incapable of distinguishing any more shades. Each element of a digitized black-and-white photo would then be associated with 16 bits of information about what shade of gray should be used. If a picture were digitized with 24 bits of gray scale, the last 8 bits could be used to convey a concealed message that would never appear except for someone who knew to look for it. The digital size of the picture would be 50% larger than it would have to be, but no one but the creator of the image would know.

[12]Of course, the problem is that, in practice, many uses of credit card numbers do not

BOX C.2
Dependence of Confidentiality on Authentication

Confidentiality in electronic communications is not possible without authentication. Suppose that Party A and Party B want to communicate in such a way that Party C cannot eavesdrop, but that no authentication is performed. One might conjecture a system that selects a random session key, without telling Party A and Party B, and then encrypts everything communicated between them. Unfortunately, such a system is not confidential because Party C could place himself between Party A and Party B, relaying all information between both parties (or only the information Party C wanted to pass). This is possible because it was assumed that no authentication existed. That is, by assumption the system cannot distinguish among Party A, Party B, or Party C, and neither can any of the parties involved.

In practice, there are numerous mechanisms that seemingly provide a sufficient level of authentication for business or personal communications. For example, people routinely "authenticate" the person on the other end of a telephone call by recognizing the voice. Unfortunately, this still does not provide the necessary foundation for a secure telephone system. For example, Party C can simply listen to the conversation that he or she is relaying between Party A and Party B, without participating. (This scenario illustrates an illicit form of call forwarding; Party C rigs the telephone system to be called when Party A dials Party B's number, and Party C automatically dials Party B when a call from Party A is received.) Since the telephone system has no authentication, by assumption, Party C's scheme cannot be prevented even if Party A recognizes Party B's voice (which is a very strong end-to-end authentication mechanism).

Similarly, one might assume that the telephone system itself does not allow the type of tampering that Party C needs to place himself between Party A and Party B. In other words, the telephone system is designed in such a way that when Party A dials Party B's number, the call is routed directly to Party B's telephone. This arrangement is characteristic of most telephone systems today. However, its success depends on the ability of the telephone system to authenticate the maintainers of the system. Although the population of valid system users is smaller than the population of telephone users, the former is still relatively large (more than a few people), and history has shown that wide-ranging networks are difficult, if not impossible, to secure without strong authentication mechanisms.

For a communications system to be confidential, the system itself must authenticate the end users. Only then can it exchange the secret information needed to establish a confidential connection between those users. Authentication is a necessary, but not sufficient, condition for confidentiality.

---

require strong authentication (e.g., telephone orders), even if security procedures are intended to minimize the incidence of fraud in such orders (e.g., not shipping an order to an address other than the billing address on the credit card). If *every* use of a credit card required cryptographic authentication, revealing a credit card number to the world would not have much significance.

C.3 BASIC CONSTRUCTS OF CRYPTOGRAPHY

Cryptography began the science of keeping information secret from those not authorized to see it. In this classical application (called encryption in this report), cryptography has been used for thousands of years. Today, cryptographic methods help solve critical information-age problems, including those of data confidentiality (keeping data private), data integrity (ensuring that data retrieved or received are identical to data originally stored or sent), and subject authentication (ensuring that the purported sender or author of a message is indeed its real sender or author). Box C.3 contains some additional applications of cryptography.

In general, cryptographic systems involve the following:

• *The message to be sent* (usually known as the plaintext); for example, a sentence written in English. The plaintext is the message that Party A composes for reading by Party B. All plaintext messages can be represented as numbers (e.g., by using 00 for A, 01 for B, and so on, with 26 for space, 27 for comma, 28 for period, 29 for semicolon, and 30 for question mark).

• *The ciphertext* (the gibberish that results from encryption) that anyone can see without compromising the plaintext message.

• *An encryption algorithm* (a series of mathematical steps) that Party A uses, in combination with an encryption key, to generate the ciphertext.

• *A decryption algorithm* that Party B uses, in combination with a decryption key, to retrieve the plaintext from the ciphertext.

One of the simplest encryption schemes is the following: for every letter in the plaintext message (represented by a number), add 1 to obtain the corresponding ciphertext message letter. The encryption algorithm is simple addition, with an encryption key of 1.[13] The same encryption algorithm could be employed using a different encryption key (i.e., a number other than 1). The corresponding decryption algorithm is subtraction, with a decryption key of 1.

One of the fundamental goals of cryptographic research is to develop algorithms that can be used effectively within a specific system and that are difficult to "crack." (A more precise definition of "difficult" is presented in the next section.) A second goal, pursued under the label of

---

[13]In general, such schemes "wrap" at the end of the alphabet, so that 30 (originally question mark) is mapped back to the start of the alphabet (in this case A). Thus, the complete cipher is A becomes B, B becomes C, . . . Y becomes Z, Z becomes space, space becomes comma, comma becomes period, period becomes semicolon, semicolon becomes question mark, and question mark becomes A. If, as in our example, the alphabet has 31 characters, this wrap would be known as "mod 31."

BOX C.3
Additional Capabilities Enabled by Cryptography

Cryptographic techniques allow a wide variety of other capabilities, including the following:

- *Secret sharing.* Cryptography enables the division of a secret among *m* people in a way that any k people can reconstruct the secret (for *k* less than or equal to *m*), but also in such a way that any combinations of fewer than *k* people have no information at all about the secret.
- *Verifiable secret sharing.* A stronger form of secret sharing enables any of the *k* people to verify that he or she has indeed received a real part of the secret.
- *Secure function evaluation.* Cryptography enables a function to be evaluated publicly with multiple arguments in such a way that none of the holders of each argument has any knowledge about what the others are holding. One application is electronic voting in such a way that the winner of a vote can be known without forcing any individual to reveal how he or she voted.

These capabilities are less commonly discussed than the fundamental capabilities of enabling confidentiality, signature, and authentication. However, other applications in the future may well rest on them.

---

cryptanalytic research, is to develop methods and techniques for trying to read messages that have been encrypted by algorithms that may or may not be known to the cryptanalyst.

In symmetric cryptography (or, equivalently, secret-key or private-key cryptography), the encryption key is the same as the decryption key; thus, message privacy depends on the key being kept secret. A major problem faced by Party A is how to inform Party B of the key that is being used. The Data Encryption Standard (DES) is an example of a secret-key cryptographic system.

In one-time pad cryptographic systems, a key is used once and then discarded; the key must be as long as the message. Because an eavesdropper is faced with a constantly changing key pattern that is impossible to break even with exhaustive search, a one-time pad is provably unbreakable provided the key is secure. However, one-time pad systems are difficult to use, and keeping the key secure poses a big problem for key management.

In asymmetric (or, equivalently, public-key) cryptographic systems, the encryption key is different from the decryption key. Message privacy depends only on the decryption key being kept secret. The encryption key can even be published and disseminated widely, so that anyone can encrypt messages. Only the recipient Party B needs the decryption key (which is specific to that party), and Party B never needs to share it with anyone (since only he or she should be able to read messages encrypted for transmission to Party B). The RSA algorithm is a very popular algorithm at the heart of many asymmetric cryptographic systems. (Box C.4 provides more details on the mathematics of asymmetric cryptography.)

In a key-escrow cryptographic system, the decryption key is made available to parties not directly involved in a given communication—but only under certain circumstances (e.g., under judicial warrant). However, without a complete decryption key, these other parties should be unable to decipher protected communications. The Clipper initiative is a key-escrow proposal for secure telephone communications advanced by the Clinton Administration and described in Chapter 5.

Key management is an integral aspect of all cryptographic systems, which entails (1) the generation of appropriate keys and (2) the distribution of such keys only to the proper parties. Proper and efficient key management is quite complex and is needed to ensure the confidentiality, integrity, and authenticity of the keys used for encryption and decryption. For example, in a symmetric cryptographic system, each user must establish his or her own secret key to use with every other party with whom communication is desired. Thus, for a system of N users who wish to be able to communicate securely with each other, the number of secret keys that the parties (taken all together) must manage and keep secret is $N(N-1)/2$ (i.e., the number of pairs possible with N parties). When N is small, the key exchange problem can be handled by personal meetings,

---

BOX C.4
The Mathematics of Asymmetric Cryptography

Asymmetric cryptography is based on the putative existence of one-way functions: mathematical functions that are easy to compute but hard to undo. There is no mathematical proof that such functions exist, but there are functions that to date have resisted all attempts to make them easy to undo. One such function is multiplication (its inverse—factoring). It is computationally easy to multiply two prime integers, but in general it is computationally difficult to factor the product. (Computational ease and difficulty refer to the computational resources that are required to perform the task.)

An asymmetric cryptographic system based on factoring would regard the product of the two prime integers as the public key and the two prime integers as the private key. The public key can be made known—once it is known, all of the information about the private key is known in principle too, but it would simply take too long to attempt to compute it.

What does "too long" mean? If the public-key and private-key pair is well chosen, and if in fact multiplication does represent a true one-way function, it means that under no foreseeable circumstances could enough computational power be assembled to perform the factoring in a time shorter than the age of the universe.

Alas, factoring is not provably "hard," and a variety of techniques have been used in the last decade to drive down the time needed to perform factoring.

but when N is large, face-to-face meetings as a method for key exchange are impractical.

In many ways, the key management problem is conceptually the same as the cryptographic problem of keeping messages secure, although in practice the key management system usually handles a smaller volume of data, and therefore different methods can be used.[14] Asymmetric cryptographic systems greatly reduce, but do not eliminate, the problem of key distribution. For example, people using an asymmetric cryptographic system can (in principle) publish their public keys in the equivalent of a telephone book that can be distributed freely. Each user must keep track of only $N - 1$ keys (and can even keep them in a public place with no security), and he or she needs to keep secret only one piece of information—the user's own private key. Note also that the need for face-to-face meetings is eliminated.

Another approach to managing cryptographic keys that does not use asymmetric cryptography is the use of a key distribution center (KDC). A KDC is a trusted agent that knows each user's master key. This master key is employed to exchange session keys for use by users in direct communication. The advantages over link encryption are that only one node is vulnerable to attack (the KDC) and that the users can converse directly (after the initial connection protocol in which both must communicate with the KDC to set up the exchange of session keys).

Note that key management for data communications is very different than for data storage. When encrypted data are communicated, parties have incentives to keep the relevant key only for the duration of the transmission and to eliminate it permanently once the transmission is complete (typically measured in seconds or minutes). When encrypted data are stored, the storing party has a great deal of incentive to retain the key as long as the data may be important (perhaps years or decades).[15]

---

[14]The primary exception to this rule is that keys in a one-time pad are as large as the message itself; thus, the key management system for a one-time pad must be as efficient as the cryptographic system itself.

[15]One practical qualifier is important. Another constraint on data storage entirely apart from encryption is the fact that archived data must in general be copied periodically and rewritten in order to ensure that the then-current generation of technology will be able to access it. For example, in the early days of desktop computing (10 years ago), many computers used 8-inch floppy disks. Today, it is difficult to find an 8-inch floppy disk drive, and data stored on an 8-inch floppy disk would be inaccessible without such a drive. The careful archivist would have to copy the data from the 8-inch floppies to newer media, such as 5 1/4-inch floppies or CD-ROMs. When storage technologies become more capable and widespread (leading to the obsolescence of today's CD-ROM drives), the same copying and rewriting procedure will have to be followed.

Footnote continues on next page.

C.4 ATTACKS ON CRYPTOGRAPHIC SYSTEMS

A cryptographic system involves an encryption algorithm, a decryption algorithm, and keys for encryption and decryption. Although the precise boundaries between algorithm and key are fuzzy, for practical purposes the algorithm can be regarded as whatever in the mathematics is difficult to change, whereas the key is whatever is easy to change.

A basic assumption of cryptographic security is that an eavesdropper knows the relevant decryption algorithm. The algorithm may (or may not) be a public one, but the history of all information secrecy suggests that the best-kept secrets eventually leak. The use of an easily changed key thus enables the continued use of an algorithm that is known to an eavesdropper. (Any added security that results from the fact that an eavesdropper may not in fact know the algorithm is simply a bonus.) Put differently, the security of a cryptographic system should be judged by the security provided by the key alone, even if one attempts to keep the algorithm secret.

To compromise a message, an eavesdropper has two alternatives: to obtain the message in plaintext before it has been encrypted (or after it has been decrypted) or to obtain the ciphertext and decipher it without knowing all that the recipient knows about the decryption algorithm and key. (For the purposes of this appendix, the term "compromise" refers to an eavesdropper intercepting and being able to read the secret message; other types of compromise such as preventing Party B from receiving the message or deliberately garbling it so that even Party B cannot read it are not addressed here.) Although cryptography and cryptanalysis are concerned primarily with the latter, an eavesdropper does not particularly care what methods may be used to obtain the plaintext of a message. Thus, Party A and Party B must ensure that all elements of their commu-

---

Given that periodic rewriting is necessary (e.g., every 10 years), it is natural to ask if it should be the originally encrypted data or the unencrypted-and-then-reencrypted data that should be rewritten. There are advantages and disadvantages to both. Rewriting the originally encrypted data means that it does not need to be decrypted, thus improving possible losses of confidentiality. On the other hand, it also means that the key management system contemporaneous with the originally encrypted data must be preserved for future use. (Specifically, the key management system is responsible for maintaining a record of the key used to encrypt the data so that it can be decrypted later.) Preserving the key management system has many of the same problems associated with it that preserving the older storage media poses. If the choice is made to rewrite unencrypted-and-then-reencrypted data, then the originally encrypted data must be decrypted, which opens another channel for loss of confidentiality.

Different institutions will make this trade-off in different ways, but if the choice is made to rewrite the unencrypted-and-then-reencrypted data, then the time that the original key must be preserved is the time between data rewritings, which may be much shorter than the time the data is of interest.

nications system are secure; if Party A uses a secretary to encrypt the message and the secretary sells the message to an enemy agent, the best encryption scheme in the world does not matter. Similarly, if the eavesdropper is able to intercept the decryption key (e.g., because it was transmitted on an insecure channel or because it too was sold by the secretary), secret messages transmitted with the lost key are vulnerable to compromise. (The fact that Party B must have the decryption key to decrypt the message and that somehow the information identifying the decryption key must be transmitted from Party A to Party B is at the heart of the key interception problem.)

Still, it is often the case that the only real alternative for an eavesdropper is to try to decipher an intercepted ciphertext. How difficult is it for an eavesdropper to accomplish such a task?

The difficulty of cryptanalysis depends on two factors: the size of the key and the mathematical structure of the algorithm itself. Key size determines how long it would take to cryptanalyze the ciphertext by brute force—trying all possible keys with a given decryption algorithm until the (meaningful) plaintext appears.[16] With a sufficiently long key, even

---

[16]Strictly speaking, this statement is true for symmetric cryptography involving algorithms such as DES with a larger key and a few other minor modifications to make it stronger. With asymmetric cryptography, the difficulty of the problem rests in knowing the computational effort needed to invert certain functions (e.g, factoring). For more discussion, see Section C.5. For these reasons, the comment of Edgar Allen Poe (Edgar Allen Poe, *The Gold-Bug*, Creative Education Inc., Mankato, Minn., 1990, p. 63) that "it may well be doubted whether human ingenuity can construct an enigma of the kind which human ingenuity may not, by proper application, resolve" is exactly wrong—there is every reason to believe that it *is* possible to devise an impenetrable cipher. (The one-time pad is such an example.)

Quantitatively, the effort to encipher and decipher (i.e., with knowledge of the key) in conventional systems is almost independent of the key size (and sublinear in any event). For example, both RC2 and RC4 have key initialization routines that take the variable-length key and expand it into a larger "expanded key" used in the encryption and decryption process. Since the key initialization is done only once per key, it adds a fixed overhead, which is negligible in most applications because the expanded key is used to encrypt large amounts of data before the key is changed. Cryptanalysis, on the other hand, appears to be exponential in the key size (2^b, where b is the number of bits).

The bottom line is that cryptanalysis grows exponentially in b, while enciphering and deciphering grow at worst linearly in b—a very nice work factor for the cryptographer, but an awful situation for the cryptanalyst.

Asymmetric cryptographic systems are more complex. The best-known algorithms provide cryptanalytic attacks that grow as $\exp[c \cdot b^{1/3} \cdot \ln(b)^{2/3}]$ (where c is a constant equal to approximately 1.7) while enciphering and deciphering grow as b^3.

Finally, one important operational caveat for both asymmetric and symmetric systems is that one must be able to recognize the output as meaningful before one can know that the key just tested was indeed correct. When the plaintext is an English sentence, it is possible to look at the resulting sentence and recognize it for what it is. However, if the "plaintext" is in fact a computer program or an image file, it may be much more difficult to recognize the output as being correct.

an eavesdropper with very extensive computing resources would have to take a very long time (longer than the age of the universe) to test all possible combinations. On the other hand, practical considerations related to implementation issues may force a trade-off between overall security (of which key size is one element) and cost.[17]

---

[17]A relevant issue is that computers can be expected to grow more powerful over time, although there are fundamental limits on computational capability imposed by the structure of the universe (e.g., nothing travels faster than light in vacuum, and the number of atoms in the universe available to build computers is large but finite). Thus, the minimum key size needed to protect a message against a very powerful opponent will grow as computers become more powerful, although it is certainly possible to choose a key size that will be adequate for protecting against exhaustive search for all time.

Thus, although it is true that dramatic reductions in the cost of computing (or equivalently, increases in computational power) have occurred in the past four decades, it does not follow that such reductions in cost or increases in power can continue indefinitely. The commonplace belief or instinct that they can continue indefinitely is simply wrong.

What is true is that fundamental limits to computation have not yet been reached and will not be reached for a long time, but this is a result of the fact that early computational devices were so far from the fundamental limits of computation that many orders of magnitude improvement have been possible. Two illustrative calculations demonstrate the fact that there are practical limits:

1. *A limit based on the energy output of the sun.* All real computations consume energy. On the basis of standard thermodynamics and statistical mechanics, the energy cost of an irreversible computation must be on the order of kT, where T is the ambient temperature (on an absolute Kelvin scale) and k is Boltzmann's constant (equal to 1.4×10^{-23} joules per degree Kelvin). The sun's power output is approximately 3.86×10^{26} watts; thus, its total energy output over its expected lifetime of 10 billion years (3×10^{17} seconds) is about 10^{44} joules. Assume an ambient temperature of $T = 10^{-6}$ degrees, which will then impose an energy cost per operation of 1.4×10^{-29} joules per operation. Thus, the number of computational operations possible using the entire energy output of the sun is given by energy output divided by the energy cost per operation, or about 10^{73} operations. If only one operation were necessary to test a key (in practice, hundreds are necessary), then it would take 10^{73} operations to test a key of 73 decimal digits (which is equivalent to about 250 binary bits). For reference, the number of atoms in the solar system is about 10^{60}.

2. *A limit based on the mass of Earth.* The mass of Earth is about 6×10^{24} kg. A proton mass is 1.6×10^{-27} kg, so that Earth contains about 4×10^{51} protons. Assume one proton per computer, and that each computer can perform one operation in the time that it takes light to cross its diameter (i.e., 10^{-15} meters divided by 3×10^{10} meters per second, or $1/3 \times 10^{-25}$ seconds). Each computer can thus perform 3×10^{25} operations per second. If all of these computers work in parallel, they can perform $4 \times 10^{51} \times 3 \times 10^{25}$ operations per second, or 10^{77} operations per second. The age of the universe is on the order of 10 billion years, or 3×10^{17} seconds. Thus, an earthful of proton-sized computers can perform 3×10^{94} operations in the age of the universe. With the assumptions made before, this corresponds to a key size of 95 decimal digits, or about 320 bits.

Both of these calculations demonstrate that it is clearly possible to specify a key size large enough to guarantee that an attack based on exhaustive search will *never* be feasible, regardless of advances in conventional computational hardware or algorithms. (The qualification to "conventional" computing is for quantum computing, discussed in Section C.6.6.)

Nevertheless, because the cost of brute-force cryptanalysis doubles for every bit that is added to the length of a key, there is a broad consensus among cryptographers that it is possible today to encrypt data very inexpensively in a way that would be unbreakable through brute force in the foreseeable future, regardless of advances in computing technology that could be used for cryptanalysis. Put differently, for some sufficiently long key length, the possibility of brute-force cryptanalysis can be ruled out categorically for all time. In practice, "sufficiently long" may turn out to be a key length as short as 168 bits. (Of course, this analysis does not address those operational situations, encountered from time to time, in which the time required to encrypt plaintext must be kept to a minimum; in such situations, the operational performance requirements of a system may preclude the use of such a long key. Nevertheless, in many situations, the operational requirements are not quite so critical, and the system implementer can use very long key lengths without an impact on performance.)

The algorithm itself may provide an alternative to exhaustive search: a weakness in the algorithm, if exploited by an opponent, may categorically rule out certain keys, thereby reducing the number of keys that need to be tested. Such weaknesses may be introduced deliberately (resulting in a "trapdoor" that allows someone with such knowledge to decipher a message secretly) or may be accidental (perhaps as the result of insufficient analysis).

Several attack scenarios are possible for the eavesdropper:

- *Ciphertext only.* If the eavesdropper has only the intercepted ciphertext and nothing else, it may well be impossible to recover the plaintext. This is the least advantageous for the eavesdropper; however, judgments about the security of a system should not be made on the basis of this assumption since Party A and Party B may not know that this condition obtains.
- *Known plaintext.* The eavesdropper may have the intercepted ciphertext (call it C1) *and* some other ciphertext (C2), as well as the plaintext (P2) corresponding to C2. (For example, C2 may be known to be an encrypted press release that is then published by Party A the day after interception.) If the eavesdropper has reason to believe that C1 (the ciphertext of the message of interest) has been produced by the same algorithm and key, he or she may be able to derive the decryption key with much less work than by exhaustive search or the case in which only C1 is available (i.e., the ciphertext-only case).
- *Chosen plaintext.* A variant of the known plaintext attack is the *chosen plaintext* attack, in which the eavesdropper has been able to insert words of his or her own into P2. (An attack of this sort characterized U.S.

Navy intelligence just before the Battle of Midway in World War II.[18]) By controlling the plaintext, the work of the eavesdropper is eased significantly (because test cases can be generated easily, among other things).

Once the eavesdropper learns the decryption key, he or she can decipher easily any subsequent message that uses that key.

Note that much of the public debate about the ease or difficulty of breaking an encryption scheme is carried out in terms of an "ideal" implementation of a given algorithm. However, in actual practice, cryptanalysts (those trying to break encryption schemes) exploit weaknesses in the way an algorithm is implemented in practice. For example, the protection afforded by algorithm X may require the use of random numbers. However, it may turn out that the way in which system A implements algorithm X does not use true random numbers but rather numbers with a predictable sequence (e.g., consecutive numbers, or even worse, a fixed number such as zero or one).[19] A cryptanalyst who suspects that this might be true about someone who uses system A to protect communications may be able to exploit it and therefore reduce by orders of magnitude the effort required to decipher those communications. Put differently, any cryptographic system that relies on keys has a built-in vulnerability with respect to the key. The encryption may be virtually invulnerable, but the key is always vulnerable. Even if the key is ultimately divided between multiple parties, the place at which the key is generated is always a potential vulnerability.

Strong cryptography refers to cryptographic systems that are very difficult to break. Eavesdroppers with large amounts of time, money, and computing expertise (e.g., national governments) are in a much better position to break cryptographic systems of a given strength than are those with more limited resources (e.g., individuals or corporations). Organized crime may also be in a good position to obtain cryptanalytic intelli-

---

[18]To confirm a cryptanalytic solution, U.S. codebreakers asked the American garrison at Midway to report over an open and unsecured channel a shortage of fresh water. The Japanese, monitoring this channel, reported two days later that "AF" was experiencing a shortage of fresh water, thus confirming that "AF" was indeed the Japanese code designation for Midway. See David Kahn, *The Codebreakers: The Story of Secret Writing*, MacMillan, New York, 1967, p. 569.

[19]An analogy will illustrate. Computer users must often "sign on" to their computers using a secret password that cannot be guessed easily. However, it is quite common to find computer users who use passwords such as their name or some easily remembered (and therefore easily guessed) word. A person (or a computer) trying to guess passwords is obviously in a much better position if the search can be limited to all eight-character words in the dictionary and all proper names (analogous to numbers with a predictable sequence), rather than all possible combinations of eight characters (analogous to random numbers).

gence because it is able to bring large sums of money to bear on the problem if the results are worth even more.

An interesting technical question is the extent to which it is possible to build very strong cryptographic systems with no algorithmic weaknesses whose decryption keys are sufficiently large to preclude exhaustive search as an effective method of decryption. If such systems are possible, a user of such systems can, by definition, be assured that no eavesdropper can break that encryption system.

Finally, the role of operational errors in the penetration of even well-designed cryptographic systems should not be underestimated. Penetration is often possible because the user of the cryptographic system has made a mistake that compromises its security. One example that has recently come to light is the successful decryption of certain messages sent by Soviet agents in the United States regarding nuclear weapons and the U.S. nuclear program at the end of World War II. Soviet agents used a one-time pad; when used properly, a one-time pad is known with mathematical certainty to be impenetrable (as described above). However, a one-time pad is based on the idea that a certain sequence of random numbers serving as the encryption key to a message will never be used more than once. For some time, Soviet agents used a particular one-time pad to encode messages, and American analysts were unable to decipher them. However, the time came when Soviet agents began to *reuse* numbers from the one-time pad, and American cryptanalysts were able to make substantial headway in deciphering them.[20]

C.5 ELEMENTS OF CRYPTOGRAPHIC SECURITY

To keep eavesdroppers from compromising secret messages, security experts may take several approaches. By far the most common approach is to change the key frequently, although in practice the problem of key distribution may complicate matters considerably if a private-key system is used. A less frequent (though still common) technique is to encrypt a message multiple times through the same algorithm with different keys; an approach based on multiple encryption using DES has been proposed as an alternative to the Skipjack encryption-decryption algorithm. (Skipjack is the name of the algorithm on which the Clipper chip is based.)

Security experts may also attempt to keep the algorithm secret. Keeping algorithms secret has advantages and disadvantages. The advantage is that when an algorithm is kept secret, fewer people have the opportu-

---

[20]George Johnson, "The Spies' Code and How It Broke," *New York Times*, Week in Review, July 16, 1995, p. 16.

nity to learn its potential weaknesses; thus, information about its weaknesses can be less widespread should any have been overlooked. In addition, keeping algorithms secret is a way to keep out of the public domain information on what constitutes a good algorithm. The disadvantage is the flip side to the same coin—when fewer people can learn its weaknesses, an algorithm may have vulnerabilities that go undetected by its users and, thus, may be vulnerable to clandestine compromise.

Finally, in principle, it is possible to vary the algorithm as well. However, it is very difficult to develop a trusted algorithm, with the result that algorithms are changed rarely, and the number of useful algorithms is much smaller than the number of keys possible when even a small key is used.

To summarize, the fundamental question in evaluating cryptographic systems is how long the system as a whole takes to become obsolete or whether it will defy obsolescence. The algorithms and techniques for key generation and management are important, but it is a mistake to focus exclusively on these matters. A cryptographic system may well become obsolete in a given environment even though its mathematical foundations remain sound. Extending the time to obsolescence may be desirable and necessary, but no system can be extended indefinitely. The continual evolution of cryptographic techniques and the use of redundant systems are as important to security as the mathematical correctness of an algorithm and the size of an encryption key.

C.6 EXPECTED LIFETIMES OF CRYPTOGRAPHIC SYSTEMS

Because of the rapidly decreasing cost of computation, cryptographic systems that cost $1 billion to break in 1945 can be broken for approximately $10 today. In the same way, today's cryptographic systems should have large safety margins to protect against future advances in technology.

The need for safety margins varies, depending on the data entrusted to the cryptographic system. Press releases, encrypted during transmission for later release, typically need at most a few days of secrecy. Medical records, on the other hand, can have privacy time constants on the order of 50 years. Because a company or governmental agency typically uses a single cryptographic system to protect all of its data, ideally the system should have a safety margin commensurate with the longest privacy time constant encountered.[21]

Symmetric cryptographic systems allow large safety margins at low

---

[21]See also footnote 15.

cost. Asymmetric cryptographic systems have a more pronounced relationship between cost and safety margin, so that it is harder to achieve large safety margins with asymmetric systems. Even with conventional systems, where 50-year safety margins appear possible and cost-effective, national security and related "export considerations may prevent their use.

C.6.1 Background

The need for safety margins stems from two general categories of technological advances: those due to improvements in computation and those due to breakthroughs in cryptanalytic attacks.

Safety margins needed to protect against improvements in computation are easier to predict because there is a steady trend, manifest since the 1930s, that is expected to continue for the next few decades and probably beyond, in which the cost of computation has decreased by an order of magnitude (i.e., a factor of 10) every 5 to 7 years (e.g., Moore's law predicts, so far fairly accurately, that microprocessor speed doubles every 18 months, equivalent to a factor of 10 every 5 years). Consequently, a computation that costs $1 billion today may cost only $10 in 50 years.[22] Since some of the information entrusted to cryptographic systems has a privacy time constant of 50 years and more (e.g., medical records should be private for at least the duration of the patient's life), it is seen that a significant safety margin is needed.

Advances of the second type, breakthroughs in cryptanalysis and related techniques, are much harder to predict. In the case of symmetric cryptographic systems, there is little public literature to use as a guide, but asymmetric cryptographic systems offer some data points, and so they are treated first.

C.6.2 Asymmetric Cryptographic Systems

The asymmetric cryptographic systems in primary use today base their security on the difficulty of two related computational problems: factoring integers and finding discrete logarithms.[23] Factoring is used as

---

[22]This assumes that Moore's law will continue to hold. Today, the technology of silicon electronics does not run up against fundamental physical constraints, but whether the Moore's law trend will continue to hold for 50 years is open to debate. Most experts suggest that for a decade or two, it will probably remain valid.

[23]Although it is not needed to understand what follows, these two problems can be explained easily. In factoring, one is given an integer, for example 493, and asked to find all prime factors. Since $493 = 17 \times 29$, the answer here is "17 and 29." In discrete logarithms, one is given a, n, and y in the equation "a^x modulo $n = y$" and asked to find x. For example, a solution to "2^x modulo $11 = 10$" is $x = 5$. To see this, note that $2^5 = 32$ and 32 modulo $11 = 10$.

the example in what follows because it is the more studied of these two problems.

For many years, the progress of factoring was measured by the progress in factoring what are known as the Fermat numbers, denoted by F_n, the nth Fermat number. The nth Fermat number is $2^{\wedge}(2^n) + 1$ (where $\wedge$ denotes exponentiation). Hence, $F_2 = 2^4 + 1 = 17$, $F_3 = 2^8 + 1 = 257$, etc. In general, F_n is an $n + 1$ bit number. Increasing n by 1 doubles the size of the number to be factored, when measured in bits. In recent history, F_7 was factored in 1970, F_8 in 1980, F_9 in 1990, and F_{10} in 1995.

It is interesting to note that F_9 was factored by an algorithm that is much faster for "special" numbers such as $2^{\wedge}(2^n) + 1$ than for "general" numbers used in asymmetric cryptographic systems. This was not true of earlier factoring methods. Hence, although the history of the Fermat numbers can be used to illustrate the history of factoring as applied to asymmetric cryptographic systems, the future does not allow that correspondence. (More precisely, F_8 was factored with a method that is not applicable to breaking asymmetric cryptographic systems. However, another factoring method that is applicable to breaking asymmetric cryptographic systems was being tested at about the time and would have been successful in factoring F_8 in either 1980 or the next year.) Also, the factoring of F_9 involved a large network of workstations, connected over the Internet and using idle time. This networking reduced by several orders of magnitude the time needed to undertake the relevant computations. Table C.1 provides a historical record of the factoring of "nonspecial" numbers.

Some of the advances in factoring Fermat numbers were due to the decreasing cost of computation, which fell by approximately a factor of 100 in each 10-year period. However, most of the improvement was due to breakthroughs in factoring algorithms. For example, the continued fraction method, used successfully to factor F_7 in 1970, would have taken approximately a million times as much effort to factor F_8, or 10,000 times as long in 1980, given the factor-of-100 speedup in computers. In contrast,

TABLE C.1 A History of Factoring

Year	Size of Number Factored
1964	20 decimal digits (66 bits)
1974	45 decimal digits (149 bits)
1984	71 decimal digits (236 bits)
1994	129 decimal digits (429 bits)

SOURCE: Andrew Odlyzko, "The Future of Integer Factorization," *Cryptobytes*, RSA Laboratories, Redwood City, Calif., Volume 1(2), Summer 1995, p. 5.

the quadratic sieve, developed in the late 1970s, cut the required computation by a factor of roughly 100,000 when compared to continued fractions. Qualitatively similar numbers apply to the improvements that allowed F_9 to be factored in 1990.

The data points from the factoring of Fermat numbers give an estimate that key size (the size of the number to be factored) must double every 10 years to keep up with improvements in factoring. This, in turn, implies that key size must have a safety factor of 32 to be secure over 50 years (five periods of 10 years, resulting in a key size increase of $2^5 = 32$). This estimate is very approximate, and probably conservative, because the development of asymmetric cryptography gave a tremendous impetus to the study of factoring. Mathematicians working in what had been one of the purest of pure areas of mathematics, with little attendant funding, could suddenly point to immense commercial benefits from their work. Also, F_7 and F_8 were factored on single-processor machines, whereas the factorization of F_9 made use of the idle time on a network of approximately 700 workstations scattered around the world, and such an advance in computational power can come only once. A less conservative estimate would therefore be to assume at least one, and probably two, additional breakthroughs that double the size of the numbers that can be factored.

The above discussion points to a need for a safety factor of 2 to 32 in the length of the key for asymmetric cryptographic systems, an admittedly large range of uncertainty. This ambiguity is sometimes eliminated by real-world considerations. If, for example, there are significant idle computational resources available for public-key computations and they can be done in background mode without delaying current communications, then a safety margin of a factor of 32 in key size is entirely reasonable and should be used. On the other hand, if the computation to use a factor-of-four margin in key size results in unacceptable delay, one might use a factor-of-two margin, or no safety margin at all, particularly if the data has low value and a short privacy time constant. Export considerations also might limit key size, but in these latter cases users need to be aware of the danger to their communications, so that they do not trust valuable data to a system with an inappropriately low safety margin.

Today, factoring 512-bit numbers is extremely difficult, while factoring 1,024-bit numbers is computationally impossible. By using 512 bits as a reasonable security level for asymmetric cryptographic systems whose data must be secret only in the immediate future, a safety margin of 2 (the minimal indicated) would dictate the use of 1,024-bit numbers, while a safety margin of 32 (a much more conservative and safer value) would lead to roughly 16-kilobit numbers. The public-key algorithms in use today have a cost of computation that grows with b^3, where b is the number of bits. Hence, a safety margin of a factor of 32 in key size requires an increase in cost of 32^3 (more than 30,000), an uneconomic situation in most applications. At the larger bit sizes, more efficient arithmetic methods can be used that might reduce the growth curve to approximately b^2, but even $32^2 = 1,024$ is a larger cost penalty than most users will be willing to pay.

C.6.3 Conventional Cryptographic Systems

DES is the most widely studied conventional cryptographic system, and so it is used here for illustrative purposes in assessing the security levels needed in such systems. The best known *practical* method for breaking DES is exhaustive search of all 2^{56} possible keys. The correct key can be recognized because it deciphers intercepted ciphertext into meaningful plaintext. In 1977 Diffie and Hellman estimated the cost of exhaustive search at $10,000 per key.[24] Their estimate would scale to a cost of at most $100 per solution in 1994, 14 years (two periods of 7 years) later.

This figure of $100 per solution is also supported by recent work of Wiener.[25] Using commonly available components, Wiener estimated that he could build exhaustive search machines for $1 million each, which could produce a DES key every 3.5 hours. Amortizing machine cost over 5 years results in a cost of $80 per solution. Although this estimate neglects costs such as interest, design, maintenance, electricity, etc., these additional costs do not affect the estimated cost because it is only a "ballpark" estimate, accurate to at best a factor of two. More accurate estimates are not needed because of the rapidly decreasing cost of computation: an error by a factor of two is erased in 1 to 2 years. These numbers might make it seem that DES reached the end of its useful life some time ago. That is partly true and partly false for the reasons explained below.

The approximately $100 cost per solution assumes an opponent is willing to invest several million dollars in the design and production of exhaustive search cryptanalytic machines. Exhaustive search on general-purpose computers is much more expensive, costing on the order of $10 million per solution. Hence, DES is insecure against opponents who can afford to build special-purpose cryptanalytic machines, have enough problems to keep them fully loaded (idle time increases the cost per solution), and have access to modern integrated circuit technology. National intelligence organizations within the developed world meet all of these

---

[24]Whitfield Diffie and Martin Hellman, "Exhaustive Cryptanalysis of the NBS Data Encryption Standard," *Computer*, June 1977, pp. 74-84.

[25]M.J. Wiener, "Efficient DES Key Search," TR-244, School of Computer Science, Carleton University, Ottawa, Canada, May 1994; presented at the Rump Session of Crypto '93.

criteria. National intelligence organizations in less developed nations and organized crime possess the budget, but export restrictions and other government controls on cryptographic technology raise the question of whether they could purchase the required technology. Large corporations also pose a potential threat to DES, but the difficulty of hiding a several million dollar budget plus government controls make them less likely threats. Hence, DES is relatively secure today against industrial espionage, extremely insecure against major foreign powers, and questionable against lesser foreign powers and organized crime (which has no qualms about hiding budgets or conspiracies). DES's useful lifetime against commercial adversaries is on the order of 15 years, which could bring the $10 million per solution on general-purpose hardware down to $10,000 per solution, an amount that many individuals could afford.

Advances in cryptanalysis could speed the obsolescence of DES, but there are few historical data on which to base such an estimate. Prudence would dictate doubling the key size over what is indicated by current algorithms, especially since exhaustive search has been assumed in the above analysis. The frequently proposed triple-DES, which uses three DES devices in series with three different keys, more than meets this requirement and does not require any new standards. It does, however, meet with real-world problems since even single-DES is subject to U.S. Munitions List controls.

Unlike asymmetric cryptographic systems, the cost of increasing the key size of DES, or of most other conventional cryptographic systems, is minimal. Again, for illustrative purposes, DES has a 56-bit key that is expanded into a 768-bit pseudokey for use by the algorithm. Aside from the increased storage required, a 768-bit key could be used with a minimal penalty in the speed of computation. Since storing the 56-bit key consumes less than 10% of DES's required storage, doubling the key size results in at most a 10% increase in encryption-decryption cost.[26]

---

[26]In fact, a small increase in encryption time would occur, because if the DES algorithm is adapted to use a larger key size, it would also be advisable to increase the number of rounds (iterations), thus increasing the encryption-decryption time. For example, obtaining the full benefit of a 128-bit DES key would require approximately doubling the number of rounds, with an attendant doubling of computational time. Although this increase in time would be a problem in some applications, in many others it would not (e.g., telephone line communications where speeds are relatively slow). In any event, the rate of increase of computational time (as security is increased) is much slower in symmetric systems such as DES than in asymmetric systems.

C.6.4 Timing Attacks

A different type of attack against a number of cryptographic systems has been developed by Paul C. Kocher, an independent consultant.[27] Kocher's attack differs from traditional cryptanalysis in that it needs additional information on the time required by each encryption, decryption, or signing. However, it often works even when only known ciphertext is available. Although such an attack is harder to mount than a ciphertext-only attack (see definitions above), in most applications it appears comparable in difficulty to obtaining known plaintext and in most applications is no harder than mounting a chosen text attack. While the attack can thus be mounted in only a small fraction of cases, good cryptographic practice requires treating such attacks seriously. Good business practice also dictates this approach because it takes only one large loss to result in a loss of confidence or money.

Kocher's attack makes use of his insightful observation that the computation time of many systems depends in a predictable manner on the first bit of the secret key. By computing the two running times (when that bit is 0 and when it is 1) for a large number of observed computations and correlating them with the observed computation time, the attacker can make a good guess on the first bit of the secret key. If this guess is correct, the computation time depends in a predictable manner on the second bit of the secret key, which can be attacked in like manner, etc. Any errors in early decisions result in poor correlations that signal the error and invite revisiting the decision.

Although his results are very recent and therefore somewhat preliminary, Kocher has estimated that on the order of 1,000 computation times are sufficient to attack many software implementations of DES, RC5, RSA, Diffie-Hellman, and the Digital Storage Standard (DSS). He is investigating the applicability to other systems as well.

One obvious fix to this problem is to implement fixed-time-length encryptions to conceal variations in the encryption times. Of course, such a fix would also run counter to the often-present desire to minimize computational delay.

---

[27]See Paul Kocher, *Cryptanalysis of Diffie-Hellman, RSA, DSS, and Other Systems Using Timing Attacks*, Stanford, Calif., December 7, 1995; available on-line at http://www.cryptography.com/timingattack.html. A popular account of this attack is found in John Markoff, "Secure Digital Transactions Just Got a Little Less Secure," *New York Times*, December 11, 1995, p. A1.

C.6.5 Skipjack/Clipper/EES

The Skipjack encryption algorithm used in the Escrow Encryption Standard (EES; "Clipper") has an 80-bit key size. Since the algorithm itself is classified and made available only in silicon, exhaustive search cannot be contemplated by other than the U.S. government until the algorithm is reverse-engineered. Many deem that likely to happen within 5 to 10 years, perhaps even sooner at foreign national intelligence organizations. Alternatively, the algorithm may have to be divulged to such organizations if EES is to become international in scope—a prerequisite to its being widely used in this country since so much business is international in nature. For all these reasons, in what follows, the prudent assumption is made that the algorithm is known to an adversary.

Since Skipjack has a key size that is 24 bits larger than DES, exhaustive search takes 2^{24} (16 million) times as long and costs 16 million times as much. The $100-per-solution cost of DES thus scales to approximately $1 billion per solution. (Although 16 million times $100 equals $1.6 billion, the use of more than an order-of-magnitude estimate would give a misleading impression of the accuracy of these estimates.) Skipjack is thus immune to exhaustive search for some time to come. If a cost of $1 million per solution is used as ending the utility of a system, Skipjack's key size has a safety factor of 1,000, which will be erased in 15 to 21 years because of the decreasing cost of computation (three periods of 5 to 7 years).

If Skipjack is considered usable even at $1,000 per solution, that adds another 15 to 20 years to its useful life, for a total of 30 to 40 years. The figure of $1 million per solution is appropriate since some data will be worth that much to an opponent. Again, any cryptanalytic improvements over exhaustive search would decrease the lifetime of Skipjack. In summary, Skipjack's key size possesses a larger margin of safety than single-encryption DES, but that margin is smaller than would be dictated by purely economic and technical considerations. (As with DES, increasing the key size of Skipjack does not greatly increase the computation cost.)

C.6.6 A Warning

When issues related to potential weaknesses are raised, the argument is often made that when a system becomes weak, it can be replaced by a stronger one. The implied question is, Why use more security now than is needed? Although this argument makes sense for some cryptographic applications, in many cases it is wrong, given that a standard is intended for universal use.

The argument is correct for applications—such as tactical military or commercial plans—in which an opponent gains value only by cryptanalyzing the system soon after the data have been encrypted. But strategic plans, as well as medical records and many other forms of individual and corporate data, have long privacy time constants. When the old cryptographic system for such data is in danger of compromise, it does not help to reencrypt the data in a new, stronger cryptographic system: an opponent who has recorded and stored the data encrypted in the old system can attack the old, weaker cryptographic system used to encrypt the stored data.

C.6.7 Quantum and DNA Computing[28]

Two recent computing proposals may fundamentally alter the above analysis. Shor has proposed using quantum computing to factor integers.[29] Although such computing requires technology far beyond that available today, if it could be implemented, it would reduce factoring and discrete logs to easy problems and kill the currently most popular public-key cryptographic systems. Quantum computing is still embryonic, and it is not clear whether it will be practical.

Quantum computing is computing that is based on the properties of quantum mechanical systems. In classical computing, a bit is either 0 or 1. However, a fundamental property of quantum mechanical systems (such as single quantum particles) is that they can exist in a "superposition" of states, fractionally both 0 *and* 1. A properly coupled set of L quantum bits (or "qubits") can hold not just one value out of the total $N = 2^L$ possible values, but can in principle contain *all* such values simultaneously. If logical operations are now performed—and the laws of quantum mechanics do allow such operations—then computations can be performed simultaneously and in parallel on all the represented numbers.

Using these concepts, Shor was able to find a quantum algorithm that can, in principle, find the prime factors of a number N in a time propor-

---

[28]Material in this section is based on two JASON reports, one on quantum computing called *Boundaries of Computing*, and the second called *DNA Computing* (A. Despain et al., *Boundaries of Computing*, JASON Study Report JSR-95-115, MITRE Corporation, McLean, Va., September 19, 1995; N. Lewis and P. Weinberger, *DNA Computing*, JASON Study Report JSR-95-116, MITRE Corporation, McLean, Va., September 12, 1995). A lay exposition of quantum computing is contained in Seth Lloyd, "Quantum-Mechanical Computers," *Scientific American*, October 1995, pp. 140-145.

[29]Peter Shor, "Algorithms for Quantum Computation: Discrete Logarithms and Factoring," in Shafi Goldwasser (ed.), *35th Annual Symposium on Foundations of Computer Science: Proceedings*, IEEE Computer Press, New York, 1994.

tional to L, the number of bits of that number, raised to some power (i.e., in polynomial time). No factoring algorithm implementable on a classical computer is known that can factor a number with so few steps; all known classical factoring algorithms are at best barely subexponential in the number of bits. Quantitatively, given the number N and $L = \log_2 N$, the quantum algorithm can factor N in a time proportional to L^k, where k is some number; all known classical algorithms give times that are worse than this time.

It must be emphasized that it is not known today how to build a quantum computer that could execute a quantum algorithm. Indeed, while individual qubits have been created and manipulated in the laboratory, no basic circuit has yet been constructed for a quantum computation, let alone a full-up computer.[30] It has been estimated that a quantum computer that could solve cryptographically interesting problems would have a minimum of about 10^{11} quantum logic gates.

Nor is it known how broad is the class of number-theoretic problems that can be speeded up with a quantum computer. Shor's factoring algorithm makes a very special use of the fast Fourier transform as a key step. It is possible that some other computationally difficult problems on which cryptographic systems could be based are not susceptible to this trick and are equally hard for quantum computers. This is a fascinating and lively area of current research.

DNA computing is another recently described paradigm for massively parallel computation. The basic idea is that DNA strands in a test tube can be used to encode all possible answers to a given problem, such as a cryptanalytic solution to a given piece of ciphertext encoded with a known algorithm. Biochemical techniques are known for sorting out different strands of DNA; these techniques are logically equivalent to the execution of an algorithm to obtain only the strands of DNA that represent the correct answer(s) to the problem. The power of DNA computing lies in the ability to prepare and sort through a compilation of all possible answers to problems of a given computational complexity.

A small computational problem has indeed been solved by the use of a DNA computer.[31] This successful demonstration puts DNA computing on a much firmer foundation than quantum computing. However, DNA computing does not fundamentally change the hard nature of cryptanalytic problems, such as factoring or breaking DES; it merely changes the cost of the computation. At this time, it is not clear if DNA computing for

---

[30]See David DiVicenzo, "Quantum Computation," *Science*, Volume 270(5234), October 13, 1995, pp. 255-261.

[31]Leonard Adelman, "Molecular Computation of Solutions to Combinatorial Problems," *Science*, Volume 266, November 11, 1994, pp. 1021-1024.

cryptanalysis will be more or less expensive than electronic computing. If DNA cryptanalytic machines can be built more cheaply than electronic ones, they will require those concerned with information security to adopt larger safety margins in their encryption schemes (e.g., larger keys) than they previously envisioned.

An approach has been described for using DNA computing to break DES that would require about 4 months of reaction time and 1 gram of DNA to succeed.[32] Since current laboratory techniques use only micrograms, or at most milligrams, of DNA, actually implementing this approach today would probably be a multimillion dollar project, and it would reveal only a single DES key.

More relevant to the future is the fact that the amount of DNA required is exponential in the size of the problem. That is, attempting the decryption problem on a message encoded with a 57-bit key would require twice the amount of DNA required for the comparable decryption problem with a 56-bit key. An 80-bit decryption (required for Skipjack) would require 16 million grams (16 tons) of DNA. Thus, over the long run, it does not appear that even the massively parallel nature of DNA computing will be able to overcome the ease with which key sizes can be increased.

C.6.8 Elliptic Curve Cryptographic Systems

Variants of the RSA and Diffie-Hellman asymmetric cryptographic systems have been proposed that use elliptic curves instead of modular multiplication as the fundamental group operation. Today the elliptic curve variants have the advantage that the best-known algorithms for cryptanalyzing them have computational requirements that grow exponentially in the size of the modulus, as opposed to subexponential behavior for RSA and Diffie-Hellman. If this exponential behavior continues to hold, asymmetric cryptographic systems can have significant safety margins, comparable to those obtainable with conventional cryptographic systems, without undue economic or time cost to legitimate users. Caution is warranted, however, since the elliptic curve systems are fairly recent and therefore not nearly as well studied as RSA and Diffie-Hellman.

C.6.9 Quantum Cryptography

Certain techniques based on fundamental quantum mechanical properties of physical systems can be used to perform key exchange between two parties that have never met, who share no a priori secret information,

---

[32]See Dan Boneh, Christopher Dunworth, and Richard J. Lipton, *Breaking DES Using a Molecular Computer*, Technical Report CS-TR-489-95, Princeton University, Princeton, N.J., 1995.

to enable them to communicate in absolute privacy.[33] In particular, the laws of quantum mechanics allow two particles (such as photons of light in a fiber-optic cable) to be put in a state of "entangled" information. In such a state, any measurement of one of the particles necessarily disturbs the entanglement. Thus, eavesdropping on a quantum channel used to communicate a key will inevitably be detected by the intended recipient of the key, at which point a new key can be transmitted.

A working quantum cryptography apparatus has been developed, although the sending and receiving mechanisms are only 30 centimeters apart. The creators of this apparatus[34] believe that nothing in principle limits the technique from being used over much greater distances. At the same time, they note that quantum key distribution must compete with classical techniques for key exchange, which are much cheaper over long distances.

---

[33]The description in this subsection is taken from Charles Bennett et al., "Quantum Cryptography," *Scientific American*, Volume 267(4), October 1992, pp. 50-57.
[34]Bennett et al., "Quantum Cryptography," 1992.

D

An Overview of Electronic Surveillance: History and Current Status

D.1 THE LEGAL FRAMEWORK FOR DOMESTIC LAW ENFORCEMENT SURVEILLANCE

D.1.1 The General Prohibition on Electronic Surveillance

The U.S. Code, in Section 2511 of Title 18 and Sections 1809-1810 of Title 50, provides specific criminal and civil penalties for individuals (law enforcement officials and private citizens alike) who conduct electronic or wire surveillance of communications (defined below) in a manner that is not legally authorized.[1] Legal authorization for such surveillance is provided for specific circumstances in law enforcement and foreign intelligence collection as described below.

D.1.2 Title III of the Omnibus Crime Control and Safe Streets Act of 1968 and the Electronic Communications Privacy Act of 1986[2]

Congress established the statutory authority for law enforcement in-

---

[1] 18 U.S.C. Section 2511(4), (5); 50 U.S.C. Section 1809(c); and 50 U.S.C. Section 1810.

[2] The discussion in this subsection summarizes the relevant provisions. A more detailed treatment is given in Clifford S. Fishman, *Wiretapping and Eavesdropping*, The Lawyers Cooperative Publishing Co., Rochester, N.Y., 1978; and Clifford S. Fishman, *Wiretapping and Eavesdropping: Cumulative Supplement*, Clark Boardman Callaghan, Deerfield, Ill., November 1994. See also Donald P. Delaney, Dorothy E. Denning, John Kaye, and Alan R. McDonald, "Wiretap Laws and Procedures: What Happens When the U.S. Government Taps a Line," September 1993, available on-line at http://snyside.sunnyside.com/cpsr/privacy/communications/wiretap/denning_wiretap_procedure_paper.txt and other sites.

terception of communications in Title III of the Omnibus Crime Control and Safe Streets Act of 1968 (Title III). In 1986, the Electronic Communications Privacy Act (ECPA) made significant additions and amendments. Title III, as amended by ECPA, defines three categories of communications—oral, wire, and electronic—and provides varying degrees of legal protection against their unauthorized interception. Oral communications are spoken words carried by sound waves through the air. Electronic surveillance of oral communications is performed with listening devices, known as bugs. Wire communications are human speech carried over a wire or wire-like cable, including optical fiber. They may be intercepted with a wiretap. (Interception of one end of a conversation by bugging the room in which a telephone is placed is a case of oral interception.) Electronic communications are defined—with minor exceptions such as tone-only pagers—as every other form of electronically transmitted communication, including various forms of data, text, audio, and video. The legislative history of ECPA specifically mentions electronic mail, paging systems, bulletin board systems, and computer-to-computer communications, among other technologies the act was intended to address.[3]

ECPA defines radio communications, including voice conversations, as electronic, with the exception that voice conversations carried in part over radio and in part through wires or switches (such as cellular telephone calls) are treated as wire communications.[4] Some radio communications may be intercepted without penalty. Courts have found, and ECPA affirms, that if a radio transmission is readily accessible to anyone with an appropriate receiver, it does not meet the Fourth Amendment test of a "reasonable expectation of privacy" and is therefore unprotected.[5] However, ECPA specifies several forms of radio communication that are not "readily accessible" and therefore are protected from interception. These include, among others, encrypted or scrambled transmissions (digital modulation alone does not meet this standard, unless the protocols have been deliberately concealed from the public to maintain privacy); common-carrier paging services (except tone-only services); and private microwave services. In practice, unprotected radio transmissions generally relate to radio broadcasting, dispatching, public-safety radio (police, fire, etc.), amateur radio, citizens band, and similar services. In the radio

---

[3]Fishman, *Cumulative Supplement*, 1994, sections 7.31-7.49.

[4]Fishman, *Cumulative Supplement*, 1994, sections 7.4, 7.5, 7.21-7.28. See also James G. Carr, *The Law of Electronic Surveillance*, Clark Boardman Callaghan, Deerfield, Ill., September 1994, section 3.2.

[5]By similar reasoning, messages are unprotected if posted in electronic bulletin board systems that are configured to make such messages readily accessible to the general public. Fishman, *Cumulative Supplement*, 1994, section 7.67.

arena and others, the advance of communications technology, including encryption and decryption, and the development of new services will inevitably create the need for further interpretation of Title III and the ECPA by the courts and/or revision of the federal statutes.[6]

Like all searches and seizures in circumstances where a person normally has a reasonable expectation of privacy, electronic surveillance requires a warrant granted by a judge.[7] To obtain a physical search warrant (e.g., to search a person's home), officials must provide certain information. This includes a statement of facts demonstrating probable cause to believe a crime has been or will be committed; the identity of the person or place to be searched; and a particular description of the object of the search. Evidence obtained in violation of these requirements may be challenged by the defendant in a trial and may be subject to suppression. Violations leading to suppression may include errors or omissions in the application for a warrant; warrants that should not have been issued, for example, for lack of probable cause; and failure to execute the search in accordance with the terms of the warrant.[8]

In Title III, Congress added significant, new requirements specific to the electronic interception of oral and wire communications. These additional requirements, which are discussed below, set a higher standard than the physical search and seizure standard of the Fourth Amendment. They are enforced by criminal and civil penalties, as well as by a statutory exclusionary rule, which states that violations of these requirements may lead to suppression of evidence in a later trial. This suppression may throw out evidence from electronic surveillance that would ordinarily meet a Fourth Amendment test.[9]

By law, only certain, serious felonies may be investigated with Title III surveillance of oral and wire communications. These include murder, kidnapping, child molestation, organized crime, narcotics offenses, and crimes against national security, among others.[10] Before performing electronic surveillance, investigators must obtain a special type of warrant

---

[6]Clifford Fishman, personal communication, January 23, 1995. This process can be seen, for example, in the Law Enforcement Communications Act of 1994's extension to cordless telephones of the same Title III protection that applies to cellular telephones.

[7]Surveillance with the consent of one of the parties to a communication (e.g., an informant wearing a hidden microphone) does not require an intercept order (*On Lee v. United States*, 343 U.S. 747 (1952)). See Wayne R. LaFave and Jerold H. Israel, *Criminal Procedure*, 2nd ed., West Publishing, St. Paul, Minn., 1992, pp. 248, 254-255, 258-259.

[8]Stephen Patrick O'Meara, "On Getting Wired: Considerations Regarding Obtaining and Maintaining Wiretaps and 'Bugs'," *Creighton Law Review*, Volume 26, 1993, pp. 729-749.

[9]See LaFave and Israel, *Criminal Procedure*, 1992, pp. 248-256, for a discussion of Title III and the Fourth Amendment.

[10]18 U.S.C. Section 2516(1); and Carr, *The Law of Electronic Surveillance*, 1994, section 4.2.

called an "intercept order."[11] To obtain an intercept order, an applicant must show that other investigative methods, such as informants or visual surveillance, have been tried unsuccessfully or would be dangerous or unlikely to obtain the desired evidence. The applicant must also provide specific information, such as the identity of the requesting officer; facts of the case showing probable cause; period of time that surveillance will be in effect (up to 30 days, with extensions requiring another application); surveillance procedures to be followed, including plans for keeping the interception of irrelevant communications to a minimum; history of previous intercept applications concerning the same person or location; and results of the ongoing interception, if the application is for an extension of an order.[12] These requirements are somewhat flexible; not every impropriety in a surveillance results in suppression of all the evidence gathered. Numerous court decisions have found, for example, that incriminating conversations involving persons or crimes other than those identified in the warrant are admissible in a trial, as long as the warrant was valid for the purpose originally intended.[13]

Title III requires that intercept orders be requested and granted by higher-ranking officers and judges than warrants for physical searches. In federal investigations, applications must be authorized by a Department of Justice official at or above the level of Deputy Assistant Attorney General. Only federal district courts and courts of appeals may issue orders (in contrast to search warrants, which may also be issued by federal magistrates). State electronic surveillance laws must designate responsible state officials and courts of comparable stature. In addition to the Title III provisions, the Federal Bureau of Investigation (FBI) and most state enforcement agencies have detailed, internal approval procedures that officers must follow before they (or rather, a U.S. attorney acting on their behalf) may approach a court with an intercept request.[14]

---

[11]Requirements are detailed in 18 U.S.C. Section 2518. Emergency intercepts may be performed without first obtaining a warrant in certain circumstances, such as physical danger to a person or conspiracy against the national security. An application for a warrant must subsequently be made within 48 hours. There has been virtually no use of the emergency provision, and its constitutionality has not been tested in court. See LaFave and Israel, *Criminal Procedure*, 1992, p. 254.

[12]For a concise description of the application procedure, see Delaney et al., "Wiretap Laws and Procedures," 1993.

[13]In general, the Supreme Court has significantly diminished the strictness of the statutory identification provisions. Potential telephone users may be listed in the application as "others, as yet unknown." Evidence obtained in a valid wiretap about crimes other than the one specified in the application is also admissible. See Fishman, *Cumulative Supplement*, 1994, sections 49-50, 55-56.

[14]Ronald Goldstock and Clifford Fishman, briefings before the Committee to Study National Cryptography Policy, Irvine, Calif., February 10, 1995. For a description of FBI and New York State Police procedures, see Delaney et al., "Wiretap Laws and Procedures," 1993, section 2.1.

Upon receipt of a court order, communications service providers are required by law to assist law enforcement officials. The service provider must furnish information, facilities, and technical assistance necessary to accomplish the interception "unobtrusively and with a minimum of interference" with the subject's services.[15] The provider is entitled to reimbursement of expenses and is immune from any civil or criminal penalties for assisting in court-ordered surveillance.

One of the more intrusive aspects of electronic surveillance, in comparison to physical search and seizure, is the fact that the invasion of privacy continues over a period of time and is likely to intercept many communications that are irrelevant to the investigation. To restrict this invasion of privacy, Title III requires law enforcement officials to perform a procedure known as *minimization*. In the context of a wiretap or bug, minimization requires real-time monitoring of the surveillance device. When conversations are intercepted concerning irrelevant subjects, such as family gossip, monitoring officers must turn off the device. At intervals thereafter, they must turn on the device to spot-check for relevant communications, which may then be recorded. Minimization procedures must be described in the application for the intercept order. Failure to minimize properly may result in suppression of evidence.[16]

In certain cases, minimization may be postponed. Foreign-language conversations may be recorded in their entirety and minimized later, when a translator is available.[17] Similar guidelines would presumably apply to encrypted communications—they would be minimized after decryption. ECPA established that electronic communications, like oral and wire communications, are subject to minimization requirements; however, some differences in the procedures apply. For example, a text communication such as an electronic mail message clearly cannot be "turned off and on" during interception, since it is read on a full computer screen. Minimization in this

---

[15]18 U.S.C. Section 2518(4). See Fishman, *Cumulative Supplement*, 1994, section 118. See also Chapter 6 of this report for a discussion of how the Communications Assistance to Law Enforcement Act codifies specific obligations for carriers to assist authorized surveillance.

[16]The Supreme Court has interpreted minimization criteria to permit some interception of irrelevant communications. For example, monitoring of a high percentage of all calls early in the surveillance operation is permissible, provided that officers observe emerging patterns of conversations with innocent parties and adjust accordingly. See O'Meara, "On Getting Wired," 1993, p. 743. In addition, judges rarely respond to minimization failures by suppressing the entire body of evidence gathered throughout the surveillance. More typically, they suppress only the specific conversations or other interceptions that should have been minimized and were not. Clifford Fishman, briefing to the Committee to Study National Cryptography Policy, Irvine, Calif., February 10, 1995.

[17]Carr, *The Law of Electronic Surveillance*, 1994, section 5.7(c).

case would consist of deleting irrelevant sections of text and retaining only the relevant portions for further use.[18]

Following the completion of an interception, the minimized tapes of the surveillance must be sealed and delivered to the custody of the court. This provision of Title III is intended to ensure that evidence used in a subsequent trial is authentic and has not been altered. After the intercept order terminates, the issuing judge must notify the persons named in the order within 90 days that they have been subject to surveillance, unless good cause is shown for postponement.[19] For evidence to be used in a trial, the defendant must receive an inventory listing the date of the intercept order, period of surveillance, and whether any communications were intercepted. The defendant may move to receive transcripts of the interceptions, as well as the underlying application and court order. Failure to provide notice and inventory may serve as a basis for suppression of evidence if the defendant can demonstrate prejudice having been shown as a result.[20]

The procedures discussed above apply to oral and wire intercepts (bugs and wiretaps). ECPA applied most of the same procedures and restrictions to surveillance of electronic communications. It also extended Title III criminal and civil penalties for unlawful interception to electronic communications.[21] However, it did not set the same standard of protection for these communications. For example, any federal felony may be investigated through electronic interception, and a federal attorney of any rank may request an electronic communications intercept order.[22]

In addition, the statutory exclusionary rule of Title III for oral and wire communications does not apply to electronic communications. Evidence may be subject to suppression according to Fourth Amendment standards (such as probable cause), but ECPA expressly omits electronic communications from the provision that evidence obtained outside Title III procedures is suppressible in court.[23] As in the case of oral and wire surveillance, however, state statutes must apply protection at least as stringent as the federal statute. The states of Florida and Kansas impose the same requirements on electronic communications intercepts as on oral and wire intercepts.[24]

---

[18]See Fishman, *Cumulative Supplement*, 1994, sections 151-159.

[19]Delaney et al., "Wiretap Laws and Procedures," 1993, sections 2.4-2.5.

[20]Fishman, *Wiretapping and Eavesdropping*, 1978, section 203; and Fishman, *Cumulative Supplement*, 1994, section 211.

[21]Fishman, *Cumulative Supplement*, 1994, section 7.58.

[22]Fishman, *Cumulative Supplement*, 1994, sections 7.32, 42.1, 53.1.

[23]LaFave and Israel, *Criminal Procedure*, 1992, pp. 256-257.

[24]Fishman, *Cumulative Supplement*, 1994, section 42.1.

Title III, when first enacted, regulated only the interception of contents of communications. However, ECPA added new regulations on traffic analysis—the use of devices to collect information about origins and destinations of communications (particularly, telephone calls) without intercepting their contents.[25] Traffic analysis is performed with the aid of pen registers, which record the numbers dialed from a target telephone, and trap-and-trace devices, which identify telephone numbers from which calls are placed to the target telephone.[26] ECPA provides that use of these devices is a criminal offense except when performed by a law enforcement official with a court order, by a communication service provider for specified business purposes, or with the consent of the service user.

With respect to law enforcement, ECPA codified the existing judicial record on traffic analysis. Because the Supreme Court has ruled that traffic analysis information is not protected by the Fourth Amendment, evidence obtained improperly or without a warrant is not suppressible in a trial.[27] Under ECPA, a pen register or trap-and-trace order may be requested by any federal attorney and granted by any federal district judge or magistrate. States may designate comparable authorities for requesting and approving orders. If the request meets the statutory requirements, the court must grant the order. (By contrast, interception orders are subject to the judge's discretion.) The application need not present a statement of facts showing probable cause, but merely the applicant's certification that probable cause exists. In practice, one purpose of obtaining an order is to compel the cooperation of communications service providers and to protect those providers from civil and criminal liability.[28]

ECPA also governs access to stored wire and electronic communications, such as backup copies of voice mail and electronic mail messages.[29] ECPA provides criminal and civil penalties for accessing and obtaining or altering stored communications without permission of the communications service provider or subscriber. With a search warrant (for which the requirements are much less stringent than for a Title III intercept order),

---

[25]Fishman, *Cumulative Supplement*, 1994, sections 28-29.

[26]Dialed number recorders combine the functions of pen registers and trap-and-trace devices.

[27]In *Smith v. Maryland*, 442 U.S. 735 (1979), the Supreme Court ruled that a person placing a call has no "reasonable expectation of privacy" that the telephone company will not reveal the fact of the call to third parties; therefore, no warrant was required. See Fishman, *Cumulative Supplement*, 1994, section 28.

[28]Fishman, *Cumulative Supplement*, 1994, section 28.2.

[29]See Fishman, *Cumulative Supplement*, 1994, sections 7.27, 7.39, and 7.46. Definitions, procedures, and penalties related to accessing stored oral, wire, and electronic communications are given at 18 U.S.C. Sections 2701-2710.

law enforcement authorities may require a service provider to divulge stored communications without prior notice to the service subscriber or customer. The details of ECPA's applicability to electronic mail and similar communications are somewhat controversial and have yet to be tested extensively in court.[30]   For example, ECPA may make it possible for investigators to obtain, with a search warrant, electronic mail messages in temporary storage at an on-line service that the customer has not yet downloaded or deleted at the time of the investigation. However, requiring the service provider to copy and divulge all of the electronic mail addressed to a subscriber over a period of time likely involves a Title III intercept order.[31]

Tables D.1 and D.2 provide quantitative data on the scope and scale of electronic surveillance in the United States in recent years.

D.1.3 The Foreign Intelligence Surveillance Act

In the mid-1970s, Congress undertook several public investigations of controversial domestic surveillance activities by U.S. intelligence agencies, such as the Central Intelligence Agency.[32]   Title III explicitly recognized presidential authority to take measures to protect national security, and in a 1972 case, *United States v. United States District Court* (often called the Keith case), the Supreme Court ruled that it is reasonable and necessary in some circumstances to weigh Fourth Amendment rights against the constitutional responsibility of the executive branch to maintain national security.[33]   In order to achieve a balance among these conflicting demands, Congress passed the Foreign Intelligence Surveillance Act of 1978 (FISA). FISA concerns surveillance for gathering foreign intelligence

---

[30]The most significant court decision yet made on the subject, itself open to various interpretations, is *Steve Jackson Games v. United States Secret Service* (1993, W.D. Tex.), 816 F. Supp. 432, 442. On appeal, the U.S. Court of Appeals, Fifth Circuit (36 F. 3d 457), examined the question of whether "seizure of a computer used to operate an electronic bulletin board system, and containing private electronic mail which had been sent . . . but not read (retrieved) by the intended recipients, constituted an unlawful intercept under [ECPA]" and affirmed the lower court's decision that it did not.

[31]The *Wall Street Journal* reported that one of the first publicized instances of law enforcement use of a Title III intercept order to monitor a suspect's electronic mail occurred in December 1995, when a CompuServe Information Services customer was the subject of surveillance during a criminal investigation. See *Wall Street Journal*, January 2, 1996, p. B16.

[32]For a brief history of the Foreign Intelligence Surveillance Act's origins, see James E. Meason, "The Foreign Intelligence Surveillance Act: Time for Reappraisal," *International Lawyer*, Volume 24(4), Winter 1990, pp. 1043-1058.

[33]407 U.S. 297 (1972). See Allan N. Kornblum and Lubomyr M. Jachnycky, "America's Secret Court: Listening in on Espionage and Terrorism," *The Judge's Journal*, Summer 1985, pp. 15-19.

TABLE D.1 Court-ordered Electronic Surveillance Authorized Under
Title III, 1994

	Total	Federal	States
No. of orders authorized[a]	1,154	554	600
No. of orders denied[a]	0	0	0
No. of intercepts installed[b]	1,100	549	551
No. of extensions authorized[a]	861	458	403
Average duration of orders (days)[a]			
Original authorization	29	30	na[c]
Extensions	29	30	na[c]
Total days in operation[b]	44,500	25,148	19,352
Main offense specified in order[a]			
Narcotics	876	435	441
Racketeering	88	68	20
Gambling	86	8	78
Homicide and assault	19	4	15
Other	85	39	46
Type of intercept[b]			
Telephone wiretap	768	397	371
Microphone eavesdrop	52	42	10
Electronic	208	71	137
Combination	72	39	33
Average no., per installed order, intercepted:[b]			
Persons	84	112	56
Conversations	2,139	2,257	2,021
Incriminating conversations	373	374	372
Average cost per order[b]	$49,478	$66,783	$32,236
No. of arrests[b,d]	2,852	1,601	1,251
No. of convictions[b,d]	772	325	447

[a]As reported by federal and state judges issuing surveillance orders.
[b]As reported by prosecuting officials for orders actually installed.
[c]Not available.
[d]Additional arrests and convictions associated with surveillance authorized in 1994 can be expected to occur in 1995 and later years. For more complete arrest and conviction results from past years, see Table D.3.

SOURCE: Administrative Office of the U.S. Courts, *Wiretap Report for the Period January 1, 1994 to December 31, 1994,* U.S. Government Printing Office, Washington, D.C., 1995.

information, as opposed to law enforcement. Nevertheless, many of its procedures parallel those of Title III, and evidence gathered properly through FISA surveillance may, in some circumstances, be used in a trial.

Like Title III, FISA provides statutory procedures for authorizing electronic surveillance within the United States. Executive Order 12333 specifically states that no foreign intelligence collection may be undertaken for the purpose of acquiring information concerning the domestic activities of U.S. persons,[34,35] and FISA surveillance may be performed only against foreign powers or their agents. FISA regulates signals intelligence collection conducted in the United States and signals intelligence collection directed at a known U.S. person located in the United States; Executive Order 12333 regulates signals intelligence collection directed at a known U.S. person located outside the United States.[36] (See Table D.3 for a description of what approvals are required for electronic surveillance of communications in various circumstances.) To conduct surveillance of a U.S. person within the United States, the executive branch must demonstrate to a special court, the Foreign Intelligence Surveillance Court (discussed below), probable cause to conclude that the U.S. person is an "agent of a foreign power." The phrase includes persons who engage in, or aid or abet individuals who engage in, espionage, terrorism, or sabotage.[37] Each FISA warrant application is signed, under oath, by the applicant, certified by the Secretary of Defense or Deputy Secretary of Defense that it is directed against a bona fide "foreign power" or "agent of a foreign power," reviewed by the Department of Justice and endorsed by the Attorney General, and approved by a judge of the Foreign Intelligence Surveillance Court.[38] The warrant application must also identify the type of foreign intelligence information sought; communication media, facilities, and persons to be monitored; devices and procedures to be used, including those for minimization; duration of the order, up to 90 days (or 1 year if the target is a foreign power); review of previous surveillance

---

[34]Executive Order 12333, Section 2.3(b).

[35]"U.S. persons" are defined by FISA and by Executive Order 12333 to include U.S. citizens, permanent resident aliens, corporations incorporated in the United States, and unincorporated associations substantially composed of U.S. citizens or U.S. persons. See 50 U.S.C. Section 1801(i) and E.O. 12333, Section 3.4(i).

[36]Interception of communications taking place entirely outside the United States, whether or not the participants include U.S. persons, is not governed by FISA, Title III, or any other statute. Executive Order 12333 requires that the Attorney General approve the use for intelligence purposes, against a U.S. person located abroad, of any technique for which a warrant would be required if undertaken for law enforcement purposes. In each case, the Attorney General must find probable cause to conclude that the individual is an agent of a foreign power before collection may begin.

[37]50 U.S.C. Section 1801(b).

[38]Surveillance may take place without a court order for up to 1 year if the Attorney General certifies that there is very little likelihood of intercepting communications involving U.S. persons and the effort will target facilities used exclusively by foreign powers. Under limited circumstances, emergency surveillance may be performed before a warrant is obtained (Fishman, *Cumulative Supplement*, 1994, sections 361, 366).

For a discussion of FISA's applicability in various circumstances, see Fishman, *Cumulative Supplement*, 1994, sections 348-358.

TABLE D.2 Court-ordered Electronic Surveillance, 1984 to 1994

	1984	1985	1986	1987	1988	1989	1990	1991	1992	1993	1994
No. of orders authorized[a]	802	786	756	673	740	763	872	856	919	976	1,154
Federal (%)	36	31	33	35	40	41	37	42	37	46	48
State (%)	64	69	67	65	60	59	63	58	63	54	52
No. of orders denied[a]	1	2	2	0	2	0	0	0	0	0	0
No. of intercepts installed[b]	773	722	676	634	678	720	812	802	846	938	1,100
Total days in operation[b] (thousands)	20.9	22.1	20.8	19.8	26.4	27.8	28.8	30.0	32.4	39.8	44.5
Main offense (%)[a]											
Narcotics	60	55	46	56	59	62	60	63	69	70	76
Racketeering	7	8	13	9	11	12	10	13	10	10	8
Gambling	23	26	25	20	17	15	13	11	7	10	7
Homicide and assault	4	3	5	3	2	3	2	2	4	3	2
Other	6	8	11	12	11	8	15	11	10	7	7

Average no., per order, intercepted:[b]											
Persons	102	105	119	104	129	178	131	121	117	100	84
Conversations	1,209	1,320	1,328	1,299	1,251	1,656	1,487	1,584	1,861	1,801	2,139
Incriminating conversations	298	275	253	230	316	337	321	290	347	364	373
Average cost per order[b] ($ thousands)	45.0	36.5	35.6	36.9	49.3	53.1	45.1	45.0	46.5	57.3	49.5
No. arrests[b,c]	3,719	4,178	3,830	3,244	3,859	4,222	3,250	2,459	3,668	2,428	2,428
No. convictions[b,c]	2,429	2,617	2,449	1,983	2,469	2,368	1,580	2,564	1,952	1,325	772
Conviction rate (%)	65	63	64	61	64	56	48	98	49	39	27

[a]As reported by federal and state judges issuing surveillance orders.

[b]As reported by prosecuting officials for orders actually installed.

[c]Entry for each year shows arrests and convictions arising both during and after that year from surveillance authorized during that year. The large majority of arrests and convictions occur within 4 years of the surveillance. Thus, the relatively low numbers in 1993-1994 can be expected to increase over time.

SOURCE: Administrative Office of the U.S. Courts, *Wiretap Report for the Period January 1, 1993 to December 31, 1993*, U.S. Government Printing Office, Washington, D.C., 1994.

TABLE D.3 Approval Requirements for Foreign Intelligence Surveillance of Various Parties Variously Located (Under FISA in the United States and Executive Order 12333 Outside the United States)

Party	In the United States	Outside the United States
U.S. person may be targeted for wire intercepts	Only if known to be an agent of a foreign power and a FISA warrant is approved	Only with the approval of the Attorney General
Non-U.S. person may be targeted for wire intercepts	Only if a FISA warrant is approved	Without restriction

related to the same target; and certification that the information cannot be obtained through normal investigative methods.[39]

Electronic surveillance governed by FISA includes interception of wire, radio, and other electronic communications. Interception of these communications is regulated only if they take place under conditions of a reasonable expectation of privacy, in which a warrant would be required for law enforcement surveillance. It addresses only communications occurring at least partly within the United States (wholly, in the case of radio communications), although listening stations used by investigating officers may be located elsewhere. FISA also covers the use of pen registers and trap-and-trace devices.

The purpose of FISA surveillance is to obtain foreign intelligence information. FISA defines this in terms of U.S. national security, including defense against attack, sabotage, terrorism, and clandestine intelligence activities, among others. The targeted communications need not relate to any crime, although surveillance for counterespionage and counterterrorism purposes clearly has the potential to yield evidence for criminal prosecution. FISA surveillance actions are implemented operationally by the FBI—sometimes on behalf of other intelligence agencies of the U.S. government.

FISA established a special court with sole authority to review applications and grant intercept orders. The Foreign Intelligence Surveillance Court (FISA court) consists of seven U.S. district court judges appointed by the Chief Justice of the Supreme Court. The FISA court meets in secret

---

[39]50 U.S.C. Section 1805. See Delaney et al., "Wiretap Laws and Procedures," 1993, section 3.1. Some of this information may be omitted if the target is a foreign power.

twice yearly in Washington, D.C., although the court acts through a single judge who is always available.[40] One of the seven judges has always been a judge in the Washington, D.C., area to ensure local availability, and the other six judges rotate through Washington, D.C. FISA also provides for an appeals court. However, the FISA court has never denied a request for an order, and the appeals court has never met. One interpretation of this history is that the FISA court is a rubber stamp for government requests for foreign intelligence surveillance. A second interpretation is that the authorities who request such surveillance do so only when surveillance is truly necessary and prepare their cases with such thoroughness that the FISA court has never found sufficient fault with a request to deny it. Without a detailed independent review of all requests (a task beyond the scope of the committee), it is impossible to choose definitively between these two interpretations. Members of the committee having personal experience with the FISA process prefer the second interpretation. Since 1979, there has been an average of more than 500 FISA orders per year. In 1994, 576 were issued. Other information about FISA intercepts is classified.[41]

Unlike Title III, FISA does not require that the target of surveillance ever be notified that communications have been intercepted. Evidence gathered under a FISA order may be used in a trial, with the approval of the Attorney General. A defendant whose communications were intercepted then receives a transcript and may move to suppress such evidence if it was gathered unlawfully. However, the defendant is denied access to the application and FISA court order if the Attorney General certifies that national security would be harmed by release of these documents. In this case, the appropriate federal district court reviews and rules on the legality of the warrant ex parte, in camera (without adversarial representation, in secret). This may severely restrict the defendant's ability to obtain suppression.[42]

Finally, signals intelligence activities may incidentally generate information to, from, or about U.S. persons even when they are directed at foreign individuals. Information so derived is regulated by one of two sets of minimization procedures. One set is statutorily mandated by FISA.

---

[40]See Kornblum and Jachnycky, "America's Secret Court," 1985, for a description of the Foreign Intelligence Surveillance Court, a list of its members, and a review of the judicial record on the constitutionality of the court and its procedures.

[41]Benjamin Wittes, "Inside America's Most Secretive Court," *Legal Times*, February 19, 1996, p. 1.

[42]LaFave and Israel, *Criminal Procedure*, 1992, pp. 260-261.

Every FISA surveillance approval is subject to those minimization procedures. The procedures prescribe how information about U.S. persons acquired during the course of a FISA surveillance may be processed, retained, and disseminated.[43] The other set is mandated by Executive Order 12333 and regulates all other signals intelligence collection, processing, retention, and dissemination involving information on U.S. persons. This set is approved by the Secretary of Defense and the Attorney General. Copies are provided to the Senate and House Intelligence committees prior to implementation.

D.2 HISTORICAL OVERVIEW OF ELECTRONIC SURVEILLANCE

The right to privacy of communications from electronic surveillance (such as bugging and wiretapping) is protected by several federal and state statutes and by the Fourth Amendment to the Constitution. This was not always the case. Electronic surveillance of communications first came before the U.S. Supreme Court in 1927. In *Olmstead v. United States*,[44] the Court ruled by a 5-4 vote that interception of telephone conversations by federal law enforcement officials using a wiretap did not constitute a search or seizure, because nothing tangible was seized and no premises were entered and searched. The Court concluded that wiretapping was not subject to Fourth Amendment protection against unreasonable search and seizure.

New legislation, however, soon removed the wiretap from the repertoire of evidence-gathering tools. The Communications Act of 1934 made it a crime for anyone, including law enforcement officials, to intercept and subsequently divulge telephone, telegraph, or radio communications without the consent of the sender. The statute did not state specifically that evidence obtained through wiretaps was inadmissible in a trial. Subsequent court rulings held, however, that wiretap evidence gained without consent could not be used because to divulge it in court would be against the law.[45] Federal officials continued to conduct warrantless wiretaps, mainly against suspected foreign agents under the President's constitutional authority to protect national security.[46] (These activities were

---

[43]50 U.S.C. Section 1801(h).

[44]277 U.S. 438 (1928). Much of the following discussion of the evolution of electronic surveillance law is based on the work of LaFave and Israel, *Criminal Procedure*, 1992, pp. 246-256.

[45]For example, *Nardone v. United States*, 308 U.S. 338 (1939). The court also excluded evidence obtained as a result of information gained in a wiretap. See LaFave and Israel, *Criminal Procedure*, 1992, p. 246.

[46]See LaFave and Israel, *Criminal Procedure*, 1992, pp. 259-260.

later regulated with the passage of FISA in 1978.) State law enforcement agencies also continued to wiretap, where permitted by state laws and not associated with federally regulated interstate commerce.

Technological advances led to the development of other means of electronic surveillance that continued, for a time, to be accepted by the courts. In particular, electronic bugs were not restricted by the Fourth Amendment, by the same principle that applied in *Olmstead*—they seized nothing tangible. Nor were they subject to the Communications Act prohibition on divulgence of intercepted communications because they intercepted only sound waves, not wire or radio signals. In *Goldman v. United States*,[47] the Supreme Court found that federal officers could legally use a listening device placed against the wall of a room adjoining the one occupied by the target of an investigation. As long as no physical trespass took place, the Fourth Amendment did not apply and no search warrant was needed. In other cases, the Court also supported the practice of "wiring" a consenting party to the communication—such as an undercover agent or informant—with a device to record or transmit conversations in the hearing of the person wearing the wire.[48]

Over time, however, a series of decisions eroded the legal framework for bugging. In *Silverman v. United States*,[49] for example, the Court rejected agents' use of a "spike mike" driven through an adjacent wall into the heating ducts of a target's house as a Fourth Amendment violation, even though agents did not physically enter the premises. Finally, in the 1967 case of *Katz v. United States*,[50] the Court found that federal agents' bugging of a public telephone booth known to be used regularly by a particular suspect was a search and seizure protected by the Fourth Amendment. A person using a phone booth was found to have a reasonable expectation of privacy, which may not be infringed without a valid warrant based on probable cause to believe that a crime has been or will be committed. In this ruling, the Court explicitly overturned *Olmstead* and *Goldman* and determined that Fourth Amendment protection applies to persons, not merely to places that can be entered and searched.

With the *Katz* decision, law enforcement officials were left with neither bugs nor wiretaps as viable tools for gathering evidence. Their absence was significant, particularly since these tools were thought to have great potential usefulness for investigating and prosecuting conspirato-

---

[47]316 U.S. 129 (1942). See discussion in LaFave and Israel, *Criminal Procedure*, 1992, p. 248.

[48]*On Lee v. United States*, 343 U.S. 747 (1952). See LaFave and Israel, *Criminal Procedure*, 1992, pp. 248, 258-259.

[49]365 U.S. 505 (1961). See LaFave and Israel, *Criminal Procedure*, 1992, p. 248.

[50]389 U.S. 347 (1967). See LaFave and Israel, *Criminal Procedure*, 1992, p. 248.

rial activities such as organized crime, a high-profile social and political issue in the late 1960s. The judicial record made it clear that electronic surveillance with a court order would not be prohibited by the Constitution, but new legislation was needed to define and regulate court-ordered surveillance.[51] At the same time, existing statutes such as the Communications Act inadequately protected communications from malicious interception and use by private citizens acting outside a law enforcement capacity.[52]

Congress took action in 1968 to give law enforcement the tools of electronic surveillance, subject to constitutional and statutory controls, and to outlaw electronic interception of communications in most other circumstances. Title III of the Omnibus Crime Control and Safe Streets Act of 1968 created the first specific legal framework for electronic surveillance of oral and wire (telephone) communications. It made an exception to the Communications Act's divulgence prohibition for law enforcement officers with a court-issued warrant, thus bringing wiretapping back into legal use. To guard against abuse of these politically charged, highly intrusive techniques, Congress imposed special procedures for obtaining a warrant and other restrictions beyond those required under the Fourth Amendment. These are discussed in detail in Section D.1.2. Title III also specified civil and criminal penalties for anyone intercepting private communications outside these approved circumstances. In addition, it required state statutes to be at least as restrictive as Title III.[53] Currently, 37 states and the District of Columbia have electronic surveillance statutes.[54]

At the time the Omnibus Crime Control and Safe Streets Act was passed in 1968, President Johnson strongly objected to Title III, warning that it could lead to governmental abuses of civil liberties.[55] However, after an initial flurry of court challenges, a rough consensus has emerged in the nation that wiretapping under the jurisdiction of Title III represents a reasonable compromise between the rights of individuals and the law enforcement needs of the state.

In 1986, Congress passed the Electronic Communications Privacy Act. One of the act's main purposes was to update Title III. The advance of

---

[51]See Carr, *The Law of Electronic Surveillance*, 1994, section 2.3(d).

[52]LaFave and Israel, *Criminal Procedure*, 1992, p. 248.

[53]Fishman, *Wiretapping and Eavesdropping*, 1978, section 5; and Fishman, *Wiretapping and Eavesdropping: Cumulative Supplement*, 1994, section 5.

[54]Administrative Office of the United States Courts, *Wiretap Report for the Period January 1, 1994 to December 31, 1994*, U.S. Government Printing Office, Washington, D.C., 1995, p. 3.

[55]*Congressional Quarterly Almanac*, Congressional Quarterly Inc., Washington, D.C., 1968, p. 225.

technology after 1968 brought new forms of communication into common use. Many of these stretched the framework of Title III. Electronic mail, data interchange, medical records, and fund transfers are examples of potentially confidential communications that did not fit within the original Title III definitions of oral and wire communications. With respect to personal (as opposed to broadcast) radio communications, which grew rapidly with the advent of cellular and other mobile telephone services, neither Title III nor the Communications Act provided guidance for law enforcement surveillance. Treatment of video images associated with teleconferencing was also unclear.[56]

ECPA added a new category, electronic communications, to Title III's protection of oral and wire communications. In general, electronic communications are communications carried by wire (including optical fiber) or radio that do not involve the human voice; rather, they convey information such as text, images, and numerical data. Many of these communications were protected by ECPA for the first time, with both criminal and civil penalties defined for infringing on their privacy. As discussed in Section D.1.2, however, the privacy of electronic communications with respect to law enforcement was set at the Fourth Amendment standard of protection, rather than the additional level of protection given by Title III to oral and wire communications. This reflected a political compromise among several factors, including the interests of law enforcement, the telecommunications industry, and civil liberties; judicial precedent; and the judgment of Congress that bugging and telephone wiretapping are inherently more sensitive than interception of electronic communications.[57] As discussed in Section D.1.2, ECPA also created new regulations for traffic analysis and for retrieval of stored communications.

---

[56]For a detailed analysis of ECPA's additions to electronic surveillance law, see Fishman, *Cumulative Supplement*, 1994, sections 7.21-7.28, 7.32.

[57]Fishman, *Cumulative Supplement*, 1994, section 5.1; and Computer Science and Telecommunications Board staff communication with Clifford Fishman, January 23, 1995.

E

A Brief History of Cryptography Policy

In the United States cryptography policy and information about cryptography were largely the province of the National Security Agency (NSA) until the 1970s. Although a small market existed for unclassified commercial cryptography, the most advanced cryptographic techniques were classified and were limited largely to military, diplomatic, and intelligence use.[1]

E.1 EXPORT CONTROLS

One policy mechanism for controlling the diffusion of cryptography is control of exports. The earliest U.S. use of export controls was in the Trading with the Enemy Act, passed in 1917 during World War I, which empowered the President to restrict economic activities with enemy countries.[2] U.S. peacetime export control activities grew to a significant degree following World War II. The Export Control Act of 1949 gave the executive branch broad authority to determine what products or technical data are subject to export licensing, to run the licensing system, and to penalize violations. It also largely exempted the rule-making process, including

---

[1]Office of Technology Assessment, *Information Security and Privacy in Network Environments*, OTA-TCT-606, U.S. Government Printing Office, Washington, D.C., 1994, p. 115.

[2]Mitchell B. Wallerstein and William B. Snyder, Jr., "The Evolution of U.S. Export Control Policy: 1949-1989," in National Research Council, *Finding Common Ground*, National Academy Press, Washington, D.C., 1991, p. 308.

determination of what items should appear on the controlled list, from public comment and judicial review.[3]

The Export Administration Act of 1969 changed the name of the legislation and introduced the first attempt by Congress to balance control of technology for national security reasons with the goal of expanding U.S. exports. For example, Congress recommended for the first time that foreign availability of controlled items be taken into account in the licensing process. Under the Export Administration Act, the Department of Commerce is responsible for administering the Export Administration Regulations (EAR), including maintaining the Commerce Control List.

Cryptography is covered on this list. However, cryptographic products and data are also subject to licensing on the U.S. Munitions List, along with other items that are "inherently military in character." The U.S. Munitions List is administered by the Department of State under the Arms Export Controls Act, which provides the basis for the International Traffic in Arms Regulations (ITAR). There is significant overlap between the ITAR and EAR with respect to cryptography. At present, however, most software and hardware for cryptographic systems (such as those with key lengths of more than 40 bits) remain on the Munitions List unless the State Department grants jurisdiction to the Commerce Department. As discussed in Chapter 4, the National Security Agency plays a strong advisory role to the Departments of State and Commerce in deciding issues of licensing cryptographic products for export.

E.2 ACADEMIC RESEARCH AND THE CONTROL OF INFORMATION ABOUT CRYPTOGRAPHY

By the 1970s, interest in cryptography was growing not only in commercial but also in academic circles. This created conflicts due to government controls on the dissemination of information about cryptography, including at open scientific meetings. Legal basis for government control of scientific information exists in several sources. One of the first pieces of legislation addressing cryptography was a law, passed in the 1920s and still in effect, that prohibits publication of information about diplomatic codes and ciphers. This was a prior restraint on free speech that was considered justified on national security grounds.[4]

The Atomic Energy Act of 1946 created a category of information known as Restricted Data, which encompassed data on the manufacture

---

[3]Wallerstein and Snyder, "The Evolution of U.S. Export Control Policy," 1991, p. 310.
[4]James Bamford, *The Puzzle Palace: A Report on America's Most Secret Agency*, Houghton Mifflin, Boston, 1982.

or use of atomic weapons or special nuclear material. Restricted Data is essentially "born classified," subject to secrecy from its creation even if created by a private person such as an academic scientist not involved in any federal research program. Applying these rules, a court issued a preliminary injunction against *The Progressive*'s publishing an article on the working of hydrogen bombs, even though it was based on information from publicly available sources.[5] (The injunction was later lifted when a newspaper published similar information.)

The EAR and ITAR prohibit not only the export of listed items without a license, but also the distribution of technical data about items that are subject to export controls. The restriction on technical data has been applied to restrict dissemination of academic research, for example, at open scientific meetings within the United States, because the accessibility of such data to foreign persons implies the possibility of "export" of the data.[6]

Prepublication review clauses in contracts and grants for government sponsored university research, the restricted contact between cryptographers and foreign visitors, and NSA review of material to be presented at open meetings have all provoked conflict between the academic and government cryptography communities. One result of such conflicts (not only in the area of cryptography) was a National Academy of Sciences review of scientific communication and national security, which concluded that policies of "security through secrecy" would chill scientific activity and ultimately weaken U.S. technological capabilities to the point of adversely affecting U.S. security.[7] (The report, published in 1982, recommended limits on the use of contract clauses to control scientific information.)

In the late 1970s, academic research in cryptography achieved several major advances, prompting responses from NSA. For example, an NSA employee unofficially informed the Institute for Electrical and Electronics Engineers that a conference presentation by Stanford University researchers (including Martin Hellman) of work related to public-key cryptography could violate export control laws. After consultation with university counsel, the presentation went forward.[8] NSA also imposed a secrecy order on a patent application filed by University of Wisconsin professor

---

[5]Office of Technology Assessment (OTA), *Defending Secrets, Sharing Data*, U.S. Government Printing Office, Washington, D.C., 1987, pp. 141-142.

[6]OTA, *Defending Secrets*, 1987, p. 142.

[7]National Academy of Sciences, *Scientific Communication and National Security: A Report*, National Academy Press, Washington, D.C., 1982.

[8]Susan Landau et al., *Codes, Keys, and Conflicts: Issues in U.S. Crypto Policy*, Association for Computing Machinery Inc., New York, June 1994, pp. 37-38; and Martin Hellman, communication with Computer Science and Telecommunications Board staff, December 1995.

George Davida; the order was later lifted. However, at NSA's request, the American Council on Education formed a study group that recommended a 2-year experiment in which cryptography research would be submitted to NSA for review, on a voluntary basis, before publication. This procedure began in 1980 and remains in effect. Over this time, NSA has made only a few requests for changes, and there appear to have been no long-term chilling effects on academic research.[9]

Funding of academic cryptography has also been influenced by secrecy concerns. In 1980, Leonard Adleman (another of the RSA algorithm's authors) submitted a grant proposal for research, including work on cryptography, to the National Science Foundation (NSF). NSA offered to assume all responsibility for funding unclassified cryptographic research, in place of NSF; this would give NSA the opportunity to subject all research proposals to secrecy review. Interpretations vary about the extent to which this proposal reflected a power struggle between NSA and NSF; ultimately, a decision at the White House level determined that both agencies would continue to fund cryptographic research.[10]

E.3 COMMERCIAL CRYPTOGRAPHY

Growing interest and technical capabilities in cryptography within commercial communities brought cryptography policy into public debate in the 1970s.[11] The spark that began much of this debate was the National Bureau of Standards (NBS) 1975 proposal for a new cryptographic technology standard required for government use—and recommended for commercial use—outside classified (military and intelligence) applications. This was the Data Encryption Standard (DES).

NBS proposed the DES under its authority, in the Brooks Act of 1965, to recommend uniform data processing standards for federal government purchasing.[12] The proposed DES was based on an IBM-developed technology. NSA's role in recommending changes to IBM's original algorithm raised questions of whether the agency had weakened the standard. The reduction in key length from 128 bits in IBM's original version to 56 bits clearly weakened the algorithm considerably, all else being equal.[13] Public debate also addressed whether the revised algorithm con-

---

[9]Landau et al., *Codes, Keys, and Conflicts,* 1994, p. 38.

[10]Landau et al., *Codes, Keys, and Conflicts,* 1994, p. 38; and OTA, *Defending Secrets,* 1987, pp. 144-145.

[11]Landau et al., *Codes, Keys, and Conflicts,* 1994, pp. 37-38.

[12]OTA, *Information Security and Privacy in Network Environments,* 1994, pp. 134-136.

[13]Horst Feistel, "Cryptography and Computer Privacy," *Scientific American,* Volume 228(5), May 1973, pp. 15-23.

tained a trapdoor or other vulnerabilities. A review led by Representative Jack Brooks, however, concluded that changes had been made freely by IBM. Apart from the key length reduction, some changes that NSA suggested appear to have strengthened the algorithm against a form of attack, differential cryptanalysis, that was not widely known at the time.[14]

In 1977, the DES was issued as a Federal Information Processing Standard (FIPS). Its promulgation as a stable, certified technology stimulated its widespread use in commercial applications. It has been reviewed every 5 years for continued suitability in the face of advances in computing power and techniques available to attackers. NSA subsequently has played an important role in testing and certifying products for conformity to the DES. By 1986, NSA had certified more than 400 voice, data, and file encryption products using the DES.

In the mid-1980s, however, NSA announced it would stop endorsing DES products after 1988, instead focusing on a set of classified, hardware-based standards for modular products that were incompatible with the DES. (This approach is reflected, for example, in the Fortezza card-based systems that NSA is now promoting.) These plans raised immediate concern about the cost of switching over to new equipment in industries such as banking that relied heavily on products incorporating the DES.

This controversy was one factor that motivated passage of the 1987 Computer Security Act, which placed responsibility for standards development and product evaluation for nonclassified applications in the National Institute of Standards and Technology (NIST), the renamed NBS. As an agency of the Department of Commerce, NIST has a mandate to support U.S. commercial interests. In cryptography policy making, therefore, NIST could be expected to take commercial factors into account more wholeheartedly than NSA. NIST recertified the DES in 1988, and NIST became responsible for assessing product conformity to the standard. (The DES was most recently recertified in 1993 and, according to NIST, may or may not be recertified in 1998.[15]) NIST also developed other cryptographic FIPSs, including standards for algorithms (such as the Digital Signature Standard) and for implementation of cryptographic systems.

Another factor leading to the Computer Security Act was the need to resolve conflicts in agency responsibilities among the Brooks Act, various

---

[14]OTA, *Information Security and Privacy in Network Environments*, 1994, p. 123.

[15]The announcement of the most recent recertification of the DES states, "At the next review (1998), the algorithm specified in this standard will be over twenty years old. NIST will consider alternatives which offer a higher level of security. One of these alternatives may be proposed as a replacement standard at the 1998 review." See NIST, *Announcing the Data Encryption Standard*, FIPS Publication 46-2, December 30, 1993; available on-line at http://csrc.ncsl.nist.gov/fips.

Office of Management and Budget directives, and the 1984 National Security Decision Directive 145 (NSDD-145), which created a new process for setting standards for federal systems to protect "sensitive but not classified" national security information. NSDD-145 also made the director of NSA responsible for evaluating vulnerabilities and reviewing and approving security standards and systems for government information and telecommunication systems.[16]

NIST and NSA signed a memorandum of understanding (MOU) in 1989 delineating the agencies' roles under the Computer Security Act with respect to cryptography and other issues. Under the MOU, NIST is responsible for, among other activities, developing standards and procedures for the protection of sensitive (but not classified) information in federal computer systems, drawing on computer security guidelines of NSA where appropriate, and for coordinating with NSA and other agencies to ensure that these standards are consistent with those for protection of classified information. NSA provides NIST and other agencies with technical assistance related to cryptographic algorithms and techniques and to endorse products for application to secure systems. The two agencies also agreed to establish a technical working group to review issues of mutual interest related to protecting unclassified information.[17]

E.4 RECENT DEVELOPMENTS

NSA played a strong role in the development of the Escrowed Encryption Standard (EES), through the process outlined in the MOU.[18] The standard was in part an effort to forestall a mass market for telephone encryption devices that would obstruct authorized wiretaps. In 1992, AT&T announced plans to produce the first encrypted telephone backed by the marketing strength of a major corporation, the Model 3600 Telephone Security Device, which used the DES for encryption.[19] On April

---

[16]OTA, *Information Security and Privacy in Network Environments*, 1994, p. 143.

[17]*Memorandum of Understanding Between the Director of the National Institute of Standards and Technology and the Director of the National Security Agency Concerning the Implementation of Public Law 100-235*; reprinted in OTA, *Information Security and Privacy in Network Environments*, 1994, p. 197; reprinted also in Appendix N.

[18]It has been a matter of debate whether NSA's influence over NIST in the development of the EES was so great as to exceed NSA's advisory role authorized in the Computer Security Act. OTA concluded that "interagency discussions and negotiations by agency staffs under the MOU can result in delay, modification, or abandonment of proposed NIST standards activities, without notice or the benefit of oversight that is required by law." OTA also noted that NIST and NSA officials disagreed with this conclusion. See OTA, *Information Security and Privacy in Network Environments*, 1994, p. 168.

[19]Landau et al., *Codes, Keys, and Conflicts*, 1994, p. 45.

16, 1993, the White House announced an effort to develop a new standard for encryption of digitized voice communications that would allow law enforcement access by recovering an "escrowed" decryption key. The standard would be based on a classified algorithm made available by NSA—Skipjack—implemented in a hardware device, the Clipper chip. (See Chapter 5 for technical details of Clipper, the Skipjack algorithm, and key escrow.)

In February 1994, following a formal comment period in which virtually all written comments received by NIST were opposed to the proposed standard, NIST announced the adoption of FIPS 185, the EES.[20] As a voluntary standard, EES is available for federal agencies (and private firms that so desire) to cite in procurement specifications for encrypted voice products, in lieu of the DES. AT&T incorporated Clipper into its encrypted voice product, now called the Surity Telephone Device 3600. A second initiative led to standards for data encryption devices using a smart-card design called Fortezza. The Fortezza card includes a Capstone chip, which uses Skipjack for confidentiality and several other algorithms for integrity and key exchange. In 1995, Fortezza was specified in a large procurement (750,000 units) of data encryption products for the Defense Messaging System.[21]

Recent federal initiatives have sought to promote broader use of escrowed encryption technologies. On September 6-7, 1995, NIST sponsored a workshop to discuss draft criteria under which software products with escrow features for authorized third-party access to keys could receive expedited export licensing review on the Commerce Control List, as opposed to the U.S. Munitions List. One criterion allows export of escrowed key systems with key lengths up to 64 bits. On September 15, 1995, another NIST workshop sought comments from private industry on the development of a new FIPS that would allow for both hardware and software implementations of escrowed key cryptosystems. In both of these areas, additional workshops and discussions are expected to continue.[22]

────────────

[20]Landau et al., *Codes, Keys, and Conflicts*, 1994, p. 48; NIST, *Escrowed Encryption Standard*, FIPS Publication 185, February 9, 1994, available from NIST via the Internet at http://csrc.ncsl.nist.gov/fips.

[21]Kevin Power, *Government Computer News*, July 31, 1995, p. 1.

[22]NIST, "Media Advisory: U.S. Government Seeks Public Comment on Draft Export Criteria for Key Escrow Encryption," November 6, 1995, available on-line at http://csrc.ncsl.nist.gov/keyescrow; and committee and staff attendance at workshops.

F

A Brief Primer on Intelligence

Intelligence gathering takes place for both tactical and strategic purposes. Tactical intelligence is primarily the domain of agencies within the military services. Tactical intelligence provides advantages on the battlefield against hostile military forces (or in support of counterterrorist operations) through direct support to operational commanders in areas such as reconnaissance, mapping, and early warning of enemy force movements. Intelligence for strategic purposes (national intelligence) serves foreign policy, national security, and national economic objectives. National intelligence focuses on foreign political and economic events and trends; strategic military concerns such as plans, doctrine, scientific and technical resources; weapons system capabilities; and nuclear program development.[1]

Signals intelligence (SIGINT) is one key source of intelligence, important to both tactical and national intelligence. Strictly speaking, SIGINT encompasses two different forms of intelligence—communications intel-

---

NOTE: Some material in this appendix, including the organizational makeup of the intelligence community and the stages of the intelligence cycle, is adapted from the Central Intelligence Agency, "Factbook on Intelligence," September 1995, available on-line at http://www.odci.gov/cia/publications.

[1]As a result of operational successes in the Persian Gulf War, however, increased demand by field commanders for real-time access to national intelligence resources, such as satellite reconnaissance, is blurring the boundary between these areas. See, for example, Desmond Ball, *Signals Intelligence in the Post-Cold War Era: Developments in the Asia-Pacific Region*, Institute of Southeast Asian Studies, Singapore, 1993.

ligence (COMINT) and electronic intelligence (ELINT). ELINT refers to the capture and analysis of electromagnetic signals from emitters such as radars; in general, these signals do not carry information in the communications sense of the term. In this report, and because it conforms to conventions that have been established by the public debate to date, SIGINT is used to refer to communications intelligence—the capture and analysis of signals (from whatever source) that carry communications information.

It is difficult or impossible to identify a single source that is more critical or important than all others because the essence of intelligence is the synthesis of information from all available sources ("all-source" synthesis). No single source is necessarily critical, although any one might be in any given instance, and it is a matter of judgment as to whether a certain source should be accorded a higher priority than another. Many important sources are open and public, but others are secret or clandestine. Clandestine information gathering, directed toward foreign and domestic military, political, economic, criminal, and other sources to which open, public access is denied, is a core element of national intelligence activities.

The community responsible for all-source synthesis is the intelligence community, which consists of a number of civilian and military agencies. The Director of Central Intelligence (DCI) is both the coordinator of this community and the director of the Central Intelligence Agency (CIA). Under the National Security Act of 1947, the CIA is the coordinating agency for foreign intelligence analysis and dissemination. The CIA produces finished (refined) intelligence for the President and the National Security Council, and it is engaged in many aspects of information collection. The Defense Intelligence Agency and the Bureau of Intelligence and Research of the Department of State also analyze and produce finished intelligence, primarily for the Secretaries of Defense and State, respectively. The National Security Agency (NSA) is responsible for collecting signals intelligence—monitoring, decrypting, and translating foreign communications—and for developing cryptographic and other techniques to protect U.S. communications and computer security. Other parts of the community include intelligence agencies of each of the military services; the National Reconnaissance Office (NRO), through which the Air Force and CIA jointly manage space-based (satellite) data collection; the Central Imagery Office, for processing photographic intelligence; and elements of the Departments of Treasury and Energy, among others.

Intelligence (and counterintelligence[2]) have foreign and domestic com-

---

[2]Protecting secrets from disclosure to others is the focus of counterintelligence, a closely related activity involving many of the same processes as intelligence.

ponents, including infiltration of human agents into organizations operating abroad and in the United States and electronic and photographic surveillance. The Federal Bureau of Investigation (FBI) is responsible for conducting these activities in the United States. By law, foreign intelligence agencies such as the CIA and NSA are barred from domestic surveillance. Transgressions in this area have occurred, however, providing part of the rationale for creation in the 1970s of the Senate and House Select Committees on Intelligence. These committees provide legislative oversight as well as budget authorization.

Finally, it is important to note that intelligence is pursued largely on a level-of-effort basis, rather than in response to some set of specific needs that must be met at all costs. Thus, its importance is more a judgment question than one based on any analytical argument. This means, for example, that it is very hard to exclude or include missions or capabilities on the basis of a "must-have" list.

F.1 THE INTELLIGENCE MISSION

The mission of national intelligence is defined by the National Security Act and by relevant presidential directives, of which the most recent is Executive Order 12333, signed by President Reagan on December 4, 1981. Executive Order 12333 authorizes the DCI to develop and implement a National Foreign Intelligence Program to provide "[t]imely and accurate information about the activities, capabilities, plans, and intentions of foreign powers, organizations, and persons and their agents."[3] Its primary purpose is to provide the President and designated officials, such as the National Security Council, with decision support—information on which to base decisions on foreign, defense, and economic policy and the protection of U.S. national security interests.

In the post-Cold War environment, the definition of national security interests goes far beyond a focus on a single rival such as the Soviet Union, and the United States is now concerned with threats throughout the world.[4] Many of these threats are lower in intensity, but in some ways more complex and difficult to address, than those of the former Soviet Union. They include not only conventional military threats, but also issues such as the proliferation of nuclear, biological, and chemical weapons of mass destruction; terrorism; and political and economic instability,

---

[3]Ronald Reagan, *United States Intelligence Activities*, Executive Order 12333, The White House, Washington, D.C., December 4, 1981; reprinted in Appendix N.

[4]S. Turner, "Intelligence for a New World Order," *Foreign Affairs*, Volume 70(4), 1991, pp. 150-166.

which often leads to demands for U.S. or United Nations military or humanitarian intervention.

Counterterrorism efforts are on the rise. For example, public reports indicate that SIGINT was responsible for determining Libyan involvement in the terrorist bombing of Pan Am flight 103 in 1988.[5] During the Persian Gulf War, intercepted communications enabled identification and forestallment of Iraqi terrorist teams.[6] Evidence from wiretaps formed an important part of the case against Sheik Omar Abdel Rahman in the case of an alleged conspiracy by Islamic fundamentalists to blow up the United Nations, the Hudson River tunnels, and the federal building in Manhattan.[7]

National security is also increasingly recognized as including broader, nonmilitary areas. Monitoring and countering the international drug trade is a relatively new priority for the U.S. intelligence community. Economic strength, industrial technology development, and environmental protection contribute to national security, creating demand among policy makers for collection and analysis of information in areas traditionally unfamiliar to the intelligence community.

The net result is that the number and range of tasks being assigned to the intelligence community are growing rapidly. Intelligence efforts have expanded to include the support of activities in the following areas:

• *Counterproliferation.* The United States has a policy to discourage the proliferation of weapons of mass destruction (nuclear, chemical, biological) and the capabilities of other countries to acquire such weapons. (Ballistic missiles are also subject to significant counter-proliferation efforts.) Since the United States is not the only possible supplier of components for these weapons, it must rely on the cooperation of other possible supplier nations to discourage proliferation. Thus, intelligence efforts are directed toward identifying potential suppliers and purchasers, and the information derived from these efforts is passed to policy makers who can undertake appropriate actions in response.

• *Sanctions enforcement.* The United States is a supporter of many sanctions around the world. For example, the United Nations may decide to impose—and the United States decide to support—economic sanctions on a nation such that only humanitarian supplies may enter it. Intelligence efforts are needed to identify potential sources of leakages (e.g., sanctioned shipments masquerading as humanitarian supplies).

---

[5]"There Are Some Secrets the NSA Doesn't Want Kept," Newsday, August 21, 1989, p. 54.
[6]Ball, *Signals Intelligence in the Post-Cold War Era,* 1993.
[7]See Joseph P. Fried, "Sheik's Tapped Calls Entered in Terrorism Trial," *New York Times,* April 23, 1995, p. 45.

• *Economic and trade relations.* U.S. trade relations with the rest of the world are increasingly important in a globally interdependent economy. Two key dimensions of such relations are the following:

—*Trade treaties.* U.S. negotiators meet with their foreign counterparts to secure treaty arrangements that are fair, are equitable, and advance U.S. interests. Public sources assert that intelligence efforts sometimes support the positions of U.S. negotiators.[8]

—*Trade practices.* U.S. companies often compete against foreign companies for international contracts. Although the U.S. intelligence community does *not* provide support to individual U.S. companies, it does play a role in identifying unfair trade practices (e.g., illegal activities undertaken by foreign governments on behalf of their constituents) and providing information to U.S. policy makers who might be responsible for remedial actions.

One result of the expanding plate of activities is that the parts of the national intelligence community that traditionally focus on strategic issues are spending a larger percentage of their time on activities that provide real-time operational support. Whereas in the past the intelligence community concentrated primarily on strategic intelligence (large-scale trends and the like) that was actionable by policy makers on a scale of years, the community today must also provide products that are actionable in the time scale of hours, days, or weeks. Such time pressures obviously place greater demands on the intelligence cycle, and in such an environment real-time information is at a premium.

F.2 THE INTELLIGENCE CYCLE

Historically, the process of intelligence production has been cyclical. Planning, which entails the prioritization of information demands and the allocation of resources, represents both the first and the last stage. Information is collected from a variety of sources, processed into useful form, analyzed, by drawing upon all available sources to generate balanced conclusions, and disseminated to the consumers of intelligence—the President, national security officials, and others in the executive and legislative branches of government with a need for information to support national

---

[8]For example, public sources reported that the U.S. intelligence community was active in supporting U.S. negotiators on the General Agreement on Tariffs and Trade. See Craig Whitney, "France Accuses 5 Americans of Spying; Asks They Leave," *New York Times,* February 23, 1995, p. A1; Tim Weiner, "C.I.A. Faces Issue of Economic Spying," *New York Times,* February 23, 1995, p. A1.

security decisions. Dissemination of finished intelligence products may stimulate demand for new requests for intelligence information.

F.2.1 Planning

National intelligence planning, management, prioritization, and resource allocation are overseen by the DCI, as well as the Deputy Director of Central Intelligence. The DCI chairs the National Foreign Intelligence Board, which includes officials of the Department of Defense, NSA, FBI, and other agencies and advises DCI on both analytical and administrative issues. The National Intelligence Council, comprised of senior intelligence experts inside and outside the government, produces National Intelligence Estimates, assesses the quality of analyses, and identifies critical gaps requiring new collection priorities. Among others with senior planning roles are the Executive Director for Intelligence Community Affairs; the Executive Director and Deputy Director of the CIA and deputy directors of its Intelligence, Operations, Administration, and Science and Technology branches; and officials of other intelligence agencies.

In the context of the intelligence cycle, planning entails the identification of collection priorities in response to requests from intelligence consumers. An example of the planning stage is the determination of how many surveillance satellites the United States needs, the corresponding allocation of financial resources made available by Congress, and the continual process of selecting targets at which the satellites' cameras and antennas should be aimed.

Planning of collection efforts is an essential element of the intelligence cycle because the United States does not have unlimited intelligence collection assets. A central authority is needed to weigh competing demands for collection and decide which collection assets should be assigned to which tasks. Far more requests for collection are submitted by various users than are actually approved.

F.2.2 Collection

Collection of foreign intelligence relies heavily on technical means. The bulk of the intelligence budget is for acquisition and operation of technical systems, most of which are related to collection.[9] Technical collection assets include various satellites; ground-based monitoring stations; and airborne, ocean surface, and underwater platforms.

---

[9]H. Nelson, "The U.S. Intelligence Budget in the 1990s," *International Journal of Intelligence and Counterintelligence*, Volume 6(1), 1993, pp. 195-203.

Technical collection methods are categorized broadly as image intelligence (IMINT; e.g., overhead photographs) and SIGINT. IMINT is collected from aircraft, such as the U-2 and the SR-71 Blackbird, and satellites.

The NSA is the lead agency for SIGINT, the monitoring of electronic signals. These include intercepted radio, microwave, satellite, and telephone communications; telemetry, such as data streams transmitted during ballistic missile tests; and radar emissions. Some signals are intercepted through the antenna arrays of ground stations around the world, which monitor broadcast, satellite-linked, and other radio communications. Space-based SIGINT collection comes from a variety of satellites.

Historically, technical collection means have been critical in the verification of arms control agreements, through monitoring of missile tests, radiation and seismic detection, and direct observation of nuclear production facilities and weapons sites.[10]

Nontechnical intelligence collection can be open or covert. Although there is substantial debate over the extent to which the intelligence community (particularly the CIA) has made effective use of open-source intelligence,[11] it is widely recognized that a great deal of relevant information about foreign political, economic, military, and other issues is publicly available. Other potential open sources of material for intelligence analysis include foreign broadcasts and newspapers; academic, scientific, and trade journals; books; scientific conference reports; diplomatic contacts (e.g., foreign attachés); and debriefings of U.S. scientists and businesspeople who attend international meetings.[12]

Clandestine nontechnical intelligence collection is the concern of human intelligence, or HUMINT. Case officers, usually operating under cover as U.S. officials in foreign posts, are the backbone of this effort. Through their political, economic, and social contacts, case officers recruit local agents to provide information unavailable through technical means. Placement of agents under nonofficial "deep" cover may facilitate entry into particularly difficult to penetrate organizations such as drug cartels; however, deep cover involves potentially greater risk to the agent.[13]

---

[10] J.A. Adam, G. Zorpette, S.M. Meyer, and J. Horgan, "Peacekeeping by Technical Means: Special Report/Verification," *IEEE Spectrum*, Volume 23(July), 1986, pp. 42-80.

[11] R.D. Steele, "A Critical Evaluation of U.S. National Intelligence Capabilities," *International Journal of Intelligence and Counterintelligence*, Volume 6(2), 1993, pp. 173-193.

[12] R. Godson (ed.), *Intelligence Requirements for the 1990s: Collection, Analysis, Counterintelligence, and Covert Action*, Lexington Books, Lexington, Mass., 1989.

[13] Godson, *Intelligence Requirements for the 1990s*, 1989.

F.2.3 Processing

The information collected by intelligence assets—particularly, technical means—must be converted to a usable form before it can be analyzed. Encrypted communications have to be decrypted for maximum utility (although full decryption may not be necessary for traffic analysis, which itself provides some useful information); language experts translate SIGINT into English; IMINT is processed electronically to assist in interpretation of imagery.

F.2.4 Analysis

As noted earlier, all-source analysis is the basis of the intelligence production effort. All-source analysis converts collected information from multiple sources into finished intelligence products that are useful to intelligence consumers. At the simplest level, clearly, extensive editing and prioritizing are necessary to reduce and simplify the voluminous stream of collected data. The practice of analysis, however, involves more than editing. In the traditional view of the intelligence community, all-source analysis is both science and art. It includes integration and evaluation of all available data, finding patterns among fragmentary or contradictory sources, and drawing inferences from incomplete evidence. Whereas all-source analysis can add significant value to raw information, it is subject to potential pitfalls that can lead to major errors. These include, for example, a lack of awareness of other cultures, leading to "mirror imaging"—the assumption that foreign policy makers will behave as Americans would. Overreliance on clandestine or technical sources, simply because they are uniquely available to intelligence analysts, is another risk.[14]

Analysts, who are typically regional or subject matter specialists, prepare a variety of products for intelligence consumers. These include, among others, (1) current intelligence on political and other events; (2) encyclopedic intelligence—compilations of data for future use, such as maps or economic statistics; and (3) estimative intelligence—predictions of trends and events, with a focus on potential threats to U.S. security. The traditional view of analysis, developed in the CIA's early history and incorporated into its training for many years, held that analysis should be conducted at arm's length from intelligence consumers. This distance would enable analysts to avoid being biased by domestic political concerns.[15] More recently, a competing view has emerged within the intelli-

---

[14]Victor Marchetti and John D. Marks, *The CIA and the Cult of Intelligence*, Alfred A. Knopf, New York, 1974.

[15]Godson, *Intelligence Requirements for the 1990s*, 1989.

gence community that analysts should actively seek to meet the specific needs of policy makers, for example, by identifying opportunities for proactive measures that advance U.S. policies.

F.2.5 Dissemination

The final step of the cycle is dissemination of the finished product to consumers. Finished intelligence prepared under the DCI's direction is hand-carried daily to the President and key national security advisers. Other selected intelligence products, such as classified papers and encrypted electronic documents, are distributed to national security planners and policy makers on the basis of their need to know, as determined, in most cases, by the intelligence community. Broader, longer-range products prepared under the National Intelligence Council's direction are disseminated as National Intelligence Estimates. As these dissemination efforts lead to new requirements for information, the intelligence cycle begins again.

G

The International Scope of
Cryptography Policy

G.1 INTERNATIONAL DIMENSIONS OF
CRYPTOGRAPHY POLICY

Any U.S. cryptography policy must take into account a number of international dimensions, the most important of which is the fact that the United States today does not have unquestioned dominance in the economic, financial, technological, and political affairs of the world as it might have had at the end of World War II. Thus, the United States is not in a position to dictate how the rest of the world should regard cryptographic technology as it becomes more relevant to nonmilitary and nondiplomatic matters.

A second critical consideration is the international scope of business, as described in Chapter 1. Increasingly, firms need to be able to communicate with their subsidiaries or affiliates across national boundaries, as well as with nonaffiliated partners in joint ventures or in strategic alliances. Whether multinational or not, U.S. firms will need to communicate with customers and suppliers on a worldwide basis. Foreign customers need to be able to pay U.S. vendors, and vice versa, in a way that respects different monetary systems; thus, financial transactions occur increasingly over international boundaries, resulting in a truly global banking and financial system. To the extent that these various types of communications must be secure, cryptography provides a very important tool for ensuring such security.[1] Thus, differing national policies on cryptography that lead to difficulties in international communications work against overall national policies that are aimed at opening markets and reducing commercial and trade barriers.

Related is the fact that U.S. companies, including the high-technology companies that manufacture information technology products with worldwide acceptance and popularity, face the potential of significant foreign competition, as discussed in Chapter 4. To the extent that these companies constitute major U.S. national assets, policy actions that affect their international competitiveness must be considered very carefully.

A final international dimension is that other nations also have the option to maintain some form of export controls on cryptography, as well as controls on the import and use of cryptography. Such controls form part of the context in which U.S. cryptography policy must be formulated.

G.2 SIMILARITIES IN AND DIFFERENCES BETWEEN THE UNITED STATES AND OTHER NATIONS WITH RESPECT TO CRYPTOGRAPHY

Despite the international scope of cryptography policy, the international scene is dominated by national governments. All national governments have certain basic goals in common:

- To maintain national sovereignty,
- To protect public safety and domestic order,
- To look after their nation's economic interests, and
- To advance their national interests internationally.

These common goals translate into policy and interests that are sometimes similar and sometimes different between nations. Perhaps the most important point of similarity is that national governments are likely to take actions to mitigate the threat that the use of cryptography may pose to their ability to achieve the goals listed above.[2] A corollary is that foreign national governments are likely to resist unilateral U.S. decisions

---

[1]In the international arena, as elsewhere, not all aspects of cryptography are necessarily equally critical to all problems of security. For example, to some extent, the security of international electronic payments and other financial transactions can be enhanced through collateral (nonconfidentiality) uses of cryptography, as discussed in Chapter 2.

[2]Experience in other Internet-related matters suggests that many governments are willing to wield their influence in areas that they believe affect the public safety and welfare. For example:

- The CompuServe on-line service suspended access worldwide to approximately 200 Internet "newsgroups" at the request of the German government. These newsgroups were

that affect the use of cryptographic technologies within their borders (e.g., by threatening their control over cryptography). For example, they will likely oppose the use of cryptographic communications systems within their borders for which the keys are escrowed solely in the United States.

The existence of a range of limited, shared interests among nations nevertheless suggests at least the possibility of international cooperation and formal agreements on cryptography policy. For example, law enforcement is a concern that constitutes a generally shared interest. The reason is that many nations have a more or less equivalent sense of actions that should subject an individual to the sanction of law, at least in certain domains—murder and kidnapping are examples of actions that are crimes in almost every nation.[3] Some aspects of law enforcement have explicitly international dimensions, such as global organized crime and terrorism.[4] A second area of shared interest is in maintaining the integrity

---

suspected of carrying child pornography. See John Markoff, "On-Line Service Blocks Access to Topics Called Pornographic," *New York Times*, December 29, 1995, p. A1.

• The People's Republic of China declared its intent to supervise the content of all financial news reports that collect information in China. Specifically, it announced that "foreign economic information providers will be punished in accordance with the law if their released information to Chinese users contains anything forbidden by Chinese laws and regulations, or slanders or jeopardizes the national interests of China." See Seth Faison, "Citing Security, China Will Curb Foreign Financial News Agencies," *New York Times*, January 17, 1996, p. A1. China is also attempting to develop Internet-compatible technology that will enable a strong degree of government control over the content that is accessible to Chinese residents. See "Chinese Firewall: Beijing Seeks to Build Version of the Internet That Can Be Censored," *Wall Street Journal*, January 31, 1996, p. 1.

• Singapore announced that it would hold providers of access to the Internet and content providers responsible for preventing information deemed to be pornographic or politically objectionable from reaching Internet users in Singapore. See Darren McDermott, "Singapore Unveils Sweeping Measures to Control Words, Images on Internet," *Wall Street Journal*, March 6, 1996, p. B6.

[3]At the same time, differences of national law in certain other important areas should not be overlooked. Specifically, the crimes for which an individual may be extradited vary from nation to nation (e.g., some nations will not extradite a person for financial fraud); in addition, some nations may criminalize certain activity related to computers and/or electronic communications that other nations do not. Enforcement of laws is often difficult over national boundaries, even if relevant laws in another nation do criminalize particular acts. The reason is that if Nation A suffers the brunt of actions taken by a citizen resident of Nation B, Nation B may have little incentive to prosecute those actions even if its laws criminalize them, since it does not particularly suffer from those actions. Both of these factors complicate the feasibility of achieving international agreements. Some discussion of different international perspectives on computer crime can be found in the *United Nations Manual on the Prevention and Control of Computer-Related Crime*, available on-line at http://www.ifs.univie.ac.at/~pr2gq1/rev4344.html.

[4]See, for example, Phil Williams, "Transnational Criminal Organizations and International Security," *Survival*, Volume 36(1), Spring 1994, pp. 96-113.

of the financial systems of each nation, because failures in one part of an interconnected financial system may well ripple through the entire system. Individual privacy is another common interest; in some nations, for example, the notion of widespread government surveillance of communications in society causes public and political concern, as it would in the United States.[5]

On the other hand, there are many national differences that potentially obstruct the achievement of agreements:

- *Differing expectations regarding citizens' rights* (e.g., rights to privacy, rights to trial, rights to express dissent freely, the relative balance of personal versus societal rights) *and methods by which such rights can be enforced.* For example, the United States has a tendency to enforce privacy rights through market mechanisms, whereas many European governments generally take a more active policy role in protecting such rights. Moreover, the United States has a rich tradition of public debate and argument, and dissenting discourse is far more the rule than the exception compared to most foreign nations, whose publics tend to exhibit a greater willingness to grant certain powers to the state, a less adversarial relationship toward the government, and more trust in the ability of government to do what is in the national interest. (Indeed, at a public meeting a representative of the National Security Agency noted complaints from foreign intelligence services that the U.S. policy debate had raised public visibility of the cryptography issue within their countries.)
- *Business-government relationships.* In some nations, it is the expectation that national intelligence services will cooperate with and assist businesses that in the United States would be regarded as entirely separate from government. Indeed, many foreign nations operate with fewer and more blurred lines between government and "private" businesses than is true in the United States. In areas such as standards setting that are relevant to businesses, the United States tends to rely on market forces rather than government much more than other nations do.
- *What constitutes "fair" business practices.* In principle, many nations give lip service to the idea of confidentiality in commercial transactions and the notion of fair competition, but the actual practices of nations are often at variance with these statements.
- *Status.* As a global power, the U.S. scope of activities for monitoring external traffic (i.e., traffic between two other nations) is greater than that of other nations, which are concerned mostly about communications

---

[5]For example, a disclosure that a Spanish military secret service intercepted hundreds of mobile telephone conversations caused considerable public uproar. See "Spaniards Stunned by Military Eavesdropping," *New York Times,* June 16, 1995, p. A5.

into and out of their borders. The status of the United States as a global power also makes its citizens and facilities high-profile targets for terrorist attacks throughout the world.

• *Access to technology.* On average, U.S. citizens tend to have a higher degree of access to and familiarity with information technology than do citizens of other nations. Furthermore, the information technology deployed internationally has tended to be less sophisticated than that deployed in the United States; with some exceptions, this lack of sophistication is reflected generally as well in the level of deployed technology that supports security.[6] Thus, the body politic in the United States arguably has more at stake than that in other nations.

Finally, the foreign governments relevant to the policy issues of cryptography range from very friendly to very hostile.

• Some nations are very closely aligned with the United States, and the United States has no real need to target their communications (nor they ours).

• Some nations are allies in some domains and competitors in others, and the circumstances of the moment determine U.S. needs for access to their communications.

• Some nations are pariah or rogue nations, and as a general rule, the United States would be highly interested in the substance of their communications.

G.3 FOREIGN EXPORT CONTROL REGIMES

The United States is not the only nation that imposes export control restrictions on cryptography. Many other nations, especially former members of the Coordinating Committee (CoCom—see below), control the export of cryptography to some extent.[7] CoCom nations included Australia, Belgium, Canada, Denmark, France, Germany, Greece, Italy, Japan, Luxembourg, the Netherlands, Norway, Portugal, Spain, Turkey, the United Kingdom, and the United States.[8]

---

[6]For example, 37% of U.S. households have personal computers, compared with 21% in Spain, 9% in Britain, 19% in Germany, 14% in Italy, 15% in France (excluding Minitel), and 15% in other European nations. See John Tagliabue, "Europeans Buy Home PC's at Record Pace," *New York Times*, December 11, 1995, p. D1.

[7]The most authoritative study on the laws of other nations regarding controls on the export, import, and use of cryptography is a study produced by the Department of Commerce and the National Security Agency. See Department of Commerce and National Security Agency, *A Study of the International Market for Computer Software with Encryption*, Washington, D.C., released January 11, 1996.

[8]National Research Council (NRC), *Finding Common Ground*, National Academy Press, Washington, D.C., 1991, p. 62 (footnote).

CoCom was a Western response to the threat of the Soviet Union in the days of the Cold War.[9] Under the CoCom export control regime, member nations agreed to abide by regulations governing the export of many militarily useful items, including cryptography, to nations that were potential adversaries of the West (generally Eastern bloc nations and rogue nations).

The regime was more successful in those instances in which the technology in question was U.S. source, and thus what was needed from other CoCom members was control over re-export, or in which there was strong cooperation based on political agreement that the technology should be kept away from controlled destinations, despite its general availability in other CoCom nations. CoCom controls did not work perfectly, but they had some nontrivial impact. For example, export controls did not prevent the Soviets from obtaining certain types of computers, but they probably had fewer of those computers than if there had been no export controls. This had some advantages for the West: the Soviets were locked into old first-generation computers in many cases; also, they did not have many and, thus, had to use them only on their highest-priority projects.

On the other hand, CoCom controls were less successful when

- Non-CoCom countries (e.g., Taiwan and Korea) developed indigenous capabilities to produce CoCom-controlled technologies and a willingness to sell them;
- CoCom member nations disagreed among themselves about the danger of exporting certain products to Eastern bloc nations; and
- The items in question were dual-use items.

All of these conditions currently or potentially obtain with respect to cryptography,[10] although they should not be taken to mean that cooperative, multinational CoCom-like controls on cryptography would be hopeless. Also, it is important to note that the intent of the CoCom export control regime was to prevent militarily significant technologies (including cryptography) from falling into the hands of the Eastern bloc, rather than to inhibit mutually advantageous sharing of military technology among the member states.

History demonstrates that the United States has always applied tighter export controls for security and foreign policy reasons than any agreement with other nations might otherwise mandate.[11] For example,

---

[9]For detailed discussion of the CoCom regime, see NRC, *Finding Common Ground*, 1991, and NRC, *Balancing the National Interest*, National Academy Press, Washington, D.C., 1987.

[10]For example, most countries have not yet attained the degree of success in producing shrink-wrapped software applications incorporating cryptography that the United States has; potentially, they could do so and become significant suppliers of such applications.

[11]For example, see NRC, *Finding Common Ground*, 1991, pp. 99-100.

since cryptography is in general controlled by the United States as a munitions item, the same export controls on cryptography apply to products destined for England (a CoCom member) and Saudi Arabia (a non-CoCom member), though the decision-making process might well generate different answers depending on the receiving nation. A staff study by the U.S. International Trade Commission found that the export controls on encryption maintained by many other nations apply for the most part to certain proscribed (or "rogue") nations. Thus, there are in general more restrictions on the export of products with encryption capability from the United States than from these other nations, even though all of the nations in question maintain export controls on encryption.[12]

G.4 FOREIGN IMPORT AND USE CONTROL REGIMES

A number of nations discourage cryptography within their jurisdictions through a combination of import controls and use controls. Import controls refer to restrictions on products with encryption capability that may be taken into a given nation; use controls refer to restriction on the use of such products within their jurisdictions.

At the time of this writing (early 1996), Finland, France, Israel, Russia, and South Africa assert the authority, through an explicit law or decree, to exercise some degree of explicit legal control over the use and/or import of cryptography within their borders;[13] a number of other nations are reported to be investigating the possibilities of legal restrictions. On the other hand, the fact that a law regulating the use of cryptography is on the books of a nation does not mean that the law is consistently enforced. For example, at the International Cryptography Institute 1995 conference,[14] speakers from France and Russia both noted the existence of such laws in their nations and observed that for the most part those laws generally were not enforced and thus did not inhibit the widespread use of cryptography in those nations.[15]

---

[12]Office of Industries, U.S. International Trade Commission, *Global Competitiveness of the U.S. Computer Software and Service Industries*, Staff Research Study #21, Washington, D.C., June 1995, Chapter 3.

[13]Department of Commerce and National Security Agency, *A Study of the International Market for Computer Software with Encryption*, 1996, Part II.

[14]International Cryptography Institute (ICI) 1995, George Washington University, Sept. 22.

[15]Still, the mere existence of such laws—whether or not enforced—serves as an obstacle to large vendors who wish to sell products with encryption capabilities or to provide encryption services, thereby reducing their availability to the average consumer. In addition, such nations may well practice selective enforcement of such laws. For example, a representative of a major computer company with a French subsidiary observed at the ICI 1995 conference that although French laws forbidding the use of unregistered encryption were not regularly enforced against private users, they did inhibit this company from marketing products with encryption capabilities in France.

The flip side of unenforced laws is the case of a nation that applies informal controls: a nation without explicit laws forbidding the use of secure communications devices may nonetheless discourage their import.[16] In addition, nations have a variety of mechanisms for influencing the use of cryptography within the country:

- *Laws related to the public telephone system.* In most nations the government has the legal authority to regulate equipment that is connected to the public telephone network (e.g., in homologation laws). In the event that a nation wishes to discourage the use of encrypted telephonic communications, it may choose to use existing homologation laws as a pretext to prevent users from connecting to the network with secure telephones.

- *Laws related to content carried by electronic media.* In some nations, the transmission of certain types of content (e.g., sexually explicit material) is prohibited. Thus, a nation could argue that it must be able to read encrypted transmissions in order to ensure that such content is indeed not being transmitted.

- *Trade laws or other practices related to the protection of domestic industries.* Many nations have trade policies intended to discourage the purchase of foreign products and/or to promote the purchase of domestic products; examples in the United States include "buy American" laws. Such policies could be used selectively to prevent the import of products with encryption capabilities that might pose a threat to the law enforcement or national security interests of such a nation. In other nations, laws may be explicitly neutral with respect to local or foreign purchases, but long-standing practices of buying locally may prove to be formidable barriers to the import of foreign products.

- *Licensing arrangements.* A company (especially a foreign one) seeking to do business under the jurisdiction of a particular cryptography-unfriendly government may have to obtain a number of licenses to do so. Many governments use their discretionary authority to impose "unofficial" requirements as conditions for doing business or granting the licenses necessary to operate (e.g., the need to bribe various government

---

[16]The feasibility of such practices is documented in a 1992 report by the U.S. Department of Commerce, which describes foreign governments' assistance to their domestic industries. This report found that foreign governments assist their industries by creating barriers to the domestic market (e.g., through tariffs or quotas, testing regulations, investment restrictions, and product and service standards), by devising incentives for domestic production (e.g., tax policies and legal regimes for intellectual property that favor domestic industries), and by aiding in market development (e.g., guaranteeing a certain minimum level of sales through government purchase, providing foreign aid to buy domestic goods, applying political pressure to potential customers). See U.S. Department of Commerce, *Foreign Government Assistance to Domestic Industry*, U.S. Government Printing Office, Washington, D.C., September 1992, p. iii.

individuals or informal "understandings" that the company will refrain from using cryptography).

Many anecdotal examples of active government discouragement of cryptography circulate in the business community. For example, a businessperson traveling in a foreign nation brought a secure telephone for use in her hotel room; a few hours after using it, she was asked by a hotel manager to discontinue use of that phone. A press report in the Karachi daily *Dawn* reported on February 26, 1995, that the government of Pakistan shut down a cellular network run by Mobilink, a joint venture between Motorola and Pakistani SAIF Telecom, because it was unable to intercept traffic.[17]

Nevertheless, it is possible (or will be in the near future) to circumvent local restrictions through technical means even if attempts are made to enforce them. For example, direct satellite uplinks can carry communications without ever passing that information through the telecommunications network of the host nation.[18] If available, superencryption (i.e., encrypting information before it is entered into an approved encryption device) can defeat an eavesdropper armed with the key to only the outer layer of encryption; the use of superencryption cannot even be detected unless a portion of the encrypted communication is decrypted and analyzed. (See also the discussion in Chapter 7 on prohibiting the use of unescrowed encryption.)

To summarize, in some cases, a U.S. vendor that receives an export license from U.S. authorities to sell in a given foreign market may well encounter additional complications due to the import and use controls of the target nation. Indeed, a number of other nations rely on U.S. export controls to keep strong encryption products out of the market in their countries.

G.5 THE STATE OF INTERNATIONAL AFFAIRS TODAY

Today, international communications are conducted with no universally adopted information or communications privacy and security standards or policies. This is not surprising; the communications systems in

---

[17]According to the article, the company was unable to provide interception services to Pakistani intelligence agencies. According to a Mobilink official, "There are no commercial products . . . that enable over-the-air monitoring of calls." However, it remains unclear why agencies would require monitoring of wireless mobile-to-base traffic, instead of intercepting at the base station. Although the Global System for Mobile Communication's digitally encrypted wireless traffic may be hard to tap in real time, it is decrypted at the base station.

[18]There are several systems in preparation that use low-Earth-orbit satellites to provide direct communications links, including Iridium and Odyssey.

use worldwide are highly heterogeneous, are made by many different manufacturers, and embody many different standards; under these circumstances, security-specific aspects of these systems cannot be expected to be either standardized or government certified. In the absence of common understanding, ensuring information privacy or security is an ad hoc affair. Cryptographic equipment is freely available, and standards to ensure interoperability and compatibility emerge, in many cases, through a market process with no intervention on the part of any national government. Cryptographic equipment on the market is not always tested or certified by national authorities or any organization with the responsibility for undertaking such testing.

Some of the future consequences of this current are likely to include the following:

• Interoperability of communications equipment involving cryptography will be difficult.[19]

• Some companies and businesses will be able to implement very high quality security, while others fall victim to the purveyors of shoddy security products.

• National governments will be unable to use wiretapping as a tool for enforcing criminal laws and pursuing national security interests in many cases.

Needless to say, these consequences are undesirable for reasons related to business and commerce, national security, and law enforcement. How governments have responded to these undesirable consequences is discussed in Section G.7.

G.6 OBTAINING INTERNATIONAL COOPERATION ON POLICY REGARDING SECURE COMMUNICATIONS

If the use of the global information infrastructure (GII) is to grow with the blessings of governments, common arrangements among governments are needed. To the extent that U.S. national cryptography policy affects communications and information transfer across national boundaries, it has international implications.

One approach is that the United States will set a standard on secure communications that accommodates the needs of various national governments around the world. This approach is based on the assumption that the United States is the dominant player with respect to international communications and information transfer, and that actions taken by the

---

[19]Indeed, in the absence of standards, interoperability is often a problem even when cryptography is not involved.

United States to promote a future global information infrastructure set at least a de facto standard to which all other parties to the GII will have to adhere. The result would be that U.S. national policy becomes the de facto international policy.

The committee does not believe that this approach is feasible today. Rather, the committee proceeds from the belief that the United States will be an important but not the controlling international player with respect to international communications and information transfer. Thus, the United States cannot operate unilaterally and will have to reach accommodation with other national governments.

By taking as given the fact that nation-states will continue to try to exert sovereignty over activities within their borders, including the pursuit of law enforcement and national security activities, the following statements seem warranted:

1. Common and cooperative policies are possible if and only if national governments agree to them.

2. National governments will allow policies to be set in place if these policies are consistent in some overall sense with the equities they seek to maintain.

3. A national government will not base its policies on the assumption that it will abuse the rights of its citizens (as it defines them).

By assumption, cryptography threatens the ability of national governments to monitor the communications of others. Thus, according to statement 2, controls on the use of cryptography are a plausible governmental policy option as discussed above. At the same time and despite this threat, some foreign governments could be willing to allow secure international communications on a case-by-case basis, where the scope and nature of use are clearly delimited (i.e., relatively small-scale use, clearly specified use). Of course, the United States places no restrictions at all on the use of secure communications domestically at this time.

Over the next 10 years, some of those countries will surely change their minds about encryption, though in what direction is as yet not clear. Other nations are beginning to pay attention to these issues related to interception of communications and wiretapping and have many of the same concerns that the U.S. government has. Indeed, as international partnerships between U.S. and foreign telecommunications companies increase, it is likely that foreign intelligence agencies' awareness of these issues will increase. Such concerns in principle suggest that an international agreement might be possible with respect to these issues.

At the same time, the United States has a stronger tradition of individual liberties than many other nations, and it is conceivable that the United States might be the "odd man out" internationally. For example, the official U.S. view that it will not impose legal restrictions on the use of cryptography within its borders may run contrary to the positions taken by other nations. An international agreement that accommodates such differing degrees of legal restriction is hard to imagine.

A global information infrastructure allows conceptually for two different policy structures regarding international communication and data transmission:

1. Common policies shared and implemented by many nations cooperatively, or
2. Individual policies implemented by each nation on its own.

Of course, it may be that some group of nations can agree to a set of common policies, while other nations will operate individually.

By definition, individual policies of nations may conflict at national borders.[20] For nations whose policies on cryptography do not agree, international interconnection will be possible only through national gateways and interfaces that handle all international traffic.[21] For example, Nations A and B might require users to deposit all cryptographic keys with the national government but otherwise leave the choice of cryptographic equipment up to the relevant users. An A national communicating with a B national might see his or her traffic routed to a switch that would decrypt A's transmission into plaintext and re-encrypt it with the B national's key for ultimate transmission to the B national.[22]

---

[20]Although the notion of a global information infrastructure is based to a large degree on the idea that national boundaries are porous to information, nations can and do exert some influence over what information may cross their borders. For example, while traffic may traverse many countries between Nation A and Nation B, it is not inconceivable that an intermediate nation might attempt to establish a policy on cryptography that any incoming traffic had to be sent in the clear. Enforcing such a policy would be technically difficult for individual nations to accomplish in today's networking environment, but a different architecture might make it easier.

[21]An additional challenge is the emergence of national or commercial parties that will provide communications that are independent of any physical infrastructure under the control of any given nation. For example, a person in Japan might use a portable device to communicate with someone in Peru, connecting directly through a future American communications satellite. Such a channel might bypass entirely the Japanese and Peruvian national authorities. Even more complicated might be the use of a communications satellite bought from an American manufacturer by Indonesia and launched into orbit by the French. (However, satellite communications are subject to a degree of control over services offered, in the form of international agreements in the International Telecommunication Union on the uses of electromagnetic frequency spectrum.)

[22]Policies regarding cryptography are complicated further by policies on data. For example, a number of European nations will not permit the transport of personal data (e.g., on employees) out of their countries for privacy reasons, even though a multinational firm might like to be able to process such data in one central location. To ensure that such data are not transported, those nations may demand the ability to inspect all transborder data flows outward. *Footnote continues on next page.*

This hypothetical arrangement is insecure in the sense that text can be found in the clear at the border interface points. It is therefore clumsy and arguably unworkable on a practical scale. Thus, the problem of obtaining international cooperation on policy regarding secure communication is addressed here.

In the export control domain, attempts are under way to establish an organization known as the New Forum to achieve some common policy regarding exports. The mandate of the New Forum is to "prevent desta-bilizing buildups of weapons and technologies in regions of tension, such as South Asia and the Middle East, by establishing a formal process of transparency, consultation, and multilateral restraint [in the export of critical technologies]."[23] The New Forum is expected to include the CoCom nations, as well as Hungary, Poland, and the Czech Republic and a number of cooperating states. The New Forum is similar in many ways to CoCom, but one critical difference is that unlike CoCom, New Forum members do not have veto power over individual exports involving member nations; member states retain the right to decide how to apply the New Forum export control regime to specific instances.[24]

In the domain of policy regarding the use of encryption, serious attempts at international discussion are beginning as of this writing (early 1996). For example, in December 1995, the Organization for Economic Cooperation and Development (OECD) held a meeting in Paris, France, among member nations to discuss how these nations were planning to cope with the public policy problems posed by cryptography.

In order to stimulate thought about alternative ways of approaching an international regime for cryptography (with respect to both export control and use), it is useful to consider how international regimes in other areas of policy are constructed. This is to a certain extent a taxo-

---

Controlling inbound data may pose problems. For example, a dictatorial government may assert the right to monitor data flowing into its nation, perhaps to combat subversive agitation. Even democratic governments may wish for the ability to monitor certain incoming data to prevent money laundering.

Laws governing privacy can conflict with laws on cryptography. For example, a law on data privacy may require that certain sensitive data associated with an individual be protected, while a law on cryptography may forbid the use of cryptography. Such laws would obviously conflict if a situation arose in which cryptography were the only feasible tool for protecting such data.

In short, policies regarding data export, import, and privacy are an additional dimension of resolving policy with respect to cryptography.

[23]U.S. State Department, "Press Release: New Multilateral Export Control Arrangement," Office of the Spokesman, Washington, D.C., January 23, 1996.

[24]See Sarah Walking, "Russia Ready to Join New Post-CoCom Organization," *Arms Control Today*, September 1995, pp. 31-33.

nomic exercise, but it has the virtue that it opens wider perspectives than if we limit ourselves to prior arrangements in the law enforcement and intelligence fields. Moreover, it permits an analysis to profit from experience in other fields of foreign policy. That said, most successful international efforts are built on precedents from the past, and therefore it may be a mistake to start out too ambitiously.

Two dimensions should be kept separate, one organizational and the other substantive. Is there to be an international organization; a treaty; something less, such as an international agreement; parallel bilateral agreements; or, at the least ambitious end, merely a coordination of policy between the U.S. executive branch and other governments?

With respect to international agreement on the substantive dimension, four different approaches reflect varying levels of ambition:

- *Unification of law in the cooperating countries involved.* Unification means simply that the law of each cooperating country would be the same.
- *Harmonization.* Harmonization refers to a general similarity of law among national laws, with purely local differences or relatively unimportant differences remaining. These differences would be slight enough to preclude major distortions of trade or serious policy disagreements among nations. Harmonization of law is particularly common in Europe.
- *Mutual recognition.* Under mutual recognition, when one government approves a product manufactured within its borders as being consistent with an agreed-upon standard, another government will allow that product to be imported and used within its territory. In a world with a variety of cryptographic options, the options then would have to be certified by the home government before they could be imported and used in the territories of cooperating countries. For example, perhaps mutual recognition would require that any escrow holder certified by one government would be acceptable to other governments.
- *Interoperability.* Cooperating nations would work, perhaps in part through telephone companies and PTTs, to ensure that encrypted communications across national borders would remain encrypted but also conform to national laws. Interoperability would require some agreement among cooperating nations that limited the kinds of encryption acceptable domestically and provided for exchange of keys. (For example, a foreign government might require an interface for international communications at a border through which traffic would have to be passed in the clear or encrypted in a way that it could read.) Technical approaches to interoperability would probably require translation facilities that reconcile policies at national borders, automatic recognition of protocols being used, and automatic engagement of the necessary technology.

The feasibility of a cooperative regime on secure international communications is likely to require the consensus of a core group of nations. Such a consensus would then set standards that other nations would have to follow if they wanted to share the benefits of interacting with those core nations; nations that refuse to accept the arrangement would by implication be cut off from applications that demand cryptographic protection (although they would still be able to transact and communicate in the clear). For obvious reasons, this suggests that the core group of nations would have considerable aggregate economic power and influence. (Note that a division of the world into core and noncore nations might require the fractionation of a multinational company's information network into those inside and outside the core group.)

G.7 THE FUNDAMENTAL QUESTIONS OF INTERNATIONAL CRYPTOGRAPHY POLICY

If the assumption is made that escrowed encryption is the underpinning of national governments' attempting to manage cryptography, three basic questions arise regarding cryptography policy internationally.

G.7.1 Who Holds the Keys?

Any of the agents described in Chapter 5 are candidates for key holders: these include government agencies, private for-profit organizations that make a business out of holding keys, vendors of escrowed encryption products, and customers themselves (perhaps the end user, perhaps an organization within the corporation making the purchase). The various pros and cons of different types of escrow agents described in Chapter 5 apply equally in an international context.

G.7.2 Under What Circumstances Does the Key Holder Release the Keys to Other Parties?

From the standpoint of U.S. policy, one essential question is which nation's or nations' laws control the actions of escrow agents vis-à-vis the release of keys. Conceptually, three possibilities exist:

1. The U.S. government (or escrow agents subject to U.S. law) holds all keys for all escrowed encryption products used by U.S. persons or sold

by U.S. vendors, regardless of whether these products are used domestically or abroad.[25]

2. The U.S. government (or escrow agents subject to U.S. law) holds all keys for all escrowed encryption products used by U.S. persons, and foreign governments (or escrow agents subject to the laws of those foreign governments) hold all keys for escrowed encryption products used by nationals of those governments.[26]

3. Both the U.S. government and Nation X have access to all keys for escrowed encryption products that are used in Nation X, and either the United States or Nation X can obtain the necessary keys.

Products used in Nation X would most likely be purchased in Nation X, but this is not a requirement. Note also that a wide variety of escrowing schemes exist, many of which are described in Chapter 5.

For the most part, options 1 and 3 compromise the sovereignty of foreign nations, and it is hard to imagine that a strong U.S. ally would publicly announce that its citizens and industries were vulnerable to U.S. spying without their approval. Early in this study (late 1994), the committee took testimony from senior Administration officials to the effect that option 1 was likely feasible, but the Administration appears to have backed off from this position in its most recent statements (late 1995).

Only option 2 is symmetric: the United States holds keys for escrowed encryption products used by U.S. persons or sold in the United States, and foreign nations do the same for their persons and products. Option 2 could meet the international law enforcement concern in much the same way that the law enforcement agencies of various nations cooperate today on other matters. Such cooperation might be the focus of explicit bilateral agreements between the United States and other nations; such agreements might well build on existing cooperative arrangements for law enforcement (Box G.1), and they are most likely to be concluded successfully if they are arranged informally, on a case-by-case basis in which the scope and nature of use are clearly delimited (i.e., relatively small-scale and

---

[25]Under the Clipper initiative, U.S. policy is that the two escrow agents in the United States have Clipper/Capstone keys because they are available and put into escrow at the time they are programmed at the U.S. factory. Since there is no formal policy governing what should be done if a foreign nation purchases Clipper-compliant devices, the current policy obtains by default.

[26]An important operational question is the following: If the keys are generated in the United States, on what basis could any foreign user be confident that the United States did not retain a copy of the keys that were issued to him or her? Such a question arises most strongly in a hardware-based escrow encryption product with a U.S.-classified design in which the United States is the designated key generator for reasons of classification.

BOX G.1
On Mutual Assistance Agreements for Law Enforcement

The United States has mutual assistance agreements for law enforcement with many other nations. These agreements, managed by the Criminal Division of the Department of Justice with a State Department liaison, provide for mutual cooperation for the prevention, investigation, and prosecution of crime, to the extent permitted by the laws of each nation, in many areas. In general, these agreements discuss cooperation in certain listed areas as illustrative, but they usually have a "catchall" category. Some of the listed areas include:

- Assistance in obtaining documents;
- Release of interviews and statements of witnesses;
- Arrangement of depositions;
- Assistance in securing compulsory process (e.g., subpoenas);
- Cooperation in obtaining extradition consistent with existing extradition treaties; and
- Cooperation in obtaining forensic information (e.g., laboratory results and fingerprints).

These agreements are meant to enhance the collection of information and evidence in foreign nations when a crime is being committed or planned. Thus, they could serve as the vehicle for cooperative action with respect to sharing cryptographic keys available to the government (pursuant to its law enforcement objectives) of a given nation for specific law enforcement purposes; keys given by Nation A to Nation B would be obtained in accordance with the laws of Nation A and the mutual assistance agreement between Nations A and B. These agreements do not make new law; unlike treaties, they simply facilitate cooperation with respect to existing law.

To adapt these agreements to cover sharing of cryptographic information, the nations involved could use the catchall category or explicitly negotiate agreements covering this area; the first could suffice until the second was implemented.

In general, these agreements have worked well. Nevertheless, some problems exist. For example, they may not work fast enough to provide time-urgent responses to pressing law enforcement needs. In addition, some nations that are party to a mutual assistance agreement may not be trustworthy with respect to certain areas (e.g., the Colombian government with respect to drugs, the Mexican government with respect to immigration matters and smuggling of aliens).

---

clearly specified use). Alternatively, access might be requested on an ad hoc basis as the occasion arises, as is the case for other types of informally arranged law enforcement cooperation.

Option 2 alone will not satisfy U.S. needs for intelligence gathering from the foreign nations involved, because by assumption it requires the involvement (and hence the knowledge) of an escrow agent that is subject to another nation's jurisdiction. Further, it is inconceivable that the United States is a party to any formal or informal agreement to obtain keys from nations that are most likely to be the targets of interest to U.S. decision makers (e.g., rogue nations). On the other hand, options 1 and 3 also pose problems for U.S. intelligence gathering, because even with the ability to obtain keys individually, the United States loses the ability to conduct good bulk intercepts. On the assumption that there is no large-scale "master key," individual keys would still have to be obtained. This would inevitably be a time-consuming process and could diminish the flow of signals intelligence information, since obtaining individual keys is a much more time- and labor-intensive activity than listening to unencrypted traffic.

The Administration's position on foreign escrow agents is stated in one of its proposed criteria for liberalized export consideration for escrowed encryption software. Specifically, it proposes that the relevant keys be escrowed with "escrow agent(s) certified by the U.S. Government, or . . . by foreign governments with which the U.S. Government has formal agreements consistent with U.S. law enforcement and national security requirements."[27]

Note that all of the issues discussed in Chapter 5 with respect to liability for unauthorized disclosure of keys necessarily apply in an international context.[28]

G.7.3 How Will Nations Reach Consensus on International Cryptography Policy Regarding Exports and Use?

Harmonized Export Policies

Agreement on the following points would be necessary to develop a common export control policy that would help to preserve law enforcement and intelligence-gathering capabilities by retarding the spread of cryptography worldwide:

- Rough concurrence among nations exporting cryptography about the nations whose access to encryption capabilities should be kept to a minimum and what policy toward those nations should be;
- Willingness to allow relatively free trade in products with encryption capabilities among member nations;
- Willingness to abide by prohibitions on re-export to rogue nations; and
- Agreement among member nations about the types of encryption capabilities that would constitute a threat if widely deployed.

---

[27]National Institute of Standards and Technology, *Draft Software Key Escrow Encryption Export Criteria*, November 6, 1995; see Box 5.3, Chapter 5.

[28]Some agreements establish the extent and nature of liability in other contexts (e.g., the Warsaw Convention and airline travel), thus suggesting that the international dimensions of liability for unauthorized release of keys are not necessarily insurmountable.

The extent to which agreement on these points can be reached is an open question, although there are precedents to some degree in the U.S. bilateral arrangements with various other nations for cooperation in law enforcement matters. A high degree of concurrence among these nations (a "crypto-CoCom") would help to retard the spread of encryption capabilities to rogue nations, with all of the attendant benefits for law enforcement and national security.

Many problems stand in the way of achieving a plausible crypto-CoCom regime. These include the following:

• *The scope of a crypto-CoCom.* Given that the basic algorithms for cryptography are known worldwide, it is not clear that the developed nations of the world have a true monopoly on the technology. Many of the traditional lesser developed countries in Asia and Latin America are demonstrating significant interest in modernizing their communications infrastructures, and they will almost certainly be driven to an interest in secure communications as well.

• *The absence of a pervasive threat.* With the demise of the Soviet Union, it has proven much more difficult for the United States to take the lead in matters requiring international cooperation.

• *The implied connection between third-party decryption for governments and export-import controls.* International arrangements will have to satisfy the needs of participating nations for third-party decryption before they will agree to relax import and use controls.

Harmonized Policies Regarding Use

As noted above, the Organization for Economic Cooperation and Development held a December 1995 meeting in Paris among member nations to discuss how these nations were planning to cope with the public policy problems posed by cryptography.[29] What this meeting made clear is that many OECD member nations are starting to come to grips with the public policy problems posed by encryption, but that the dialogue on harmonizing policies across national borders has not yet matured. Moreover, national policies are quite fluid at this time, with various nations considering different types of regulation regarding the use, export, and import of cryptography.

---

[29]Additional information on this meeting can be found in Stewart Baker, *Summary Report on the OECD Ad Hoc Meeting of Experts on Cryptography,* Steptoe and Johnson, Washington, D.C., undated. Available on-line at sbaker@steptoe.com or check http://www.us.net/~steptoe/276908.html.

The majority view of the assembled nations was that national policies had to balance the needs of corporate users, technology vendors, individuals, law enforcement, and national security. A number of participants appeared to favor a "trusted third-party" approach that would rely on nongovernment entities (the trusted third party) to serve as the generators of cryptographic keys for confidentiality for use by the public as well as escrow agents holding these keys and responding to legally authorized requests for encryption keys for law enforcement purposes.[30] However, the needs of national security were not mentioned for the most part.[31,32]

---

[30]See, for example, Nigel Jefferies, Chris Mitchell, and Michael Walker, *A Proposed Architecture for Trusted Third Party Services,* Royal Holloway, University of London, 1995.

[31]For additional industry-oriented views on international policies concerning the use of cryptography, see U.S. Council for International Business, *Business Requirements for Encryption*, New York, October 10, 1994; INFOSEC Business Advisory Group, *Commercial Use of Cryptography*, statement presented at the ICC-BIAC-OECD Business-Government Forum, Paris, France, December 1995; European Association of Manufacturers of Business Machines and Information Technology Industry (EUROBIT), Information Technology Association of Canada (ITAC), Information Technology Industry Council (ITIC), and Japan Electronic Industry Development Association (JEIDA), *Principles of Global Cryptographic Policy*, statement presented at the ICC-BIAC-OECD Business-Government Forum, Paris, France, December 19, 1995. The statements from the Paris meeting are available on-line at http://www.cosc.georgetown.edu/~denning/crypto/#ici.

[32]Intelligence needs may conflict directly with needs for business information security. For example, U.S. and foreign companies sometimes form consortia that work cooperatively to make money; national intelligence agencies often funnel information to individual companies to develop competitive advantage. One major reason that U.S. companies operating internationally want to have encrypted communications is to protect themselves against the threat of national intelligence agencies. Thus, they would require that any escrow arrangements at a minimum include audit trails to ensure that their communications were being monitored in accordance with laws governing criminal investigations and the like (in the United States, this might be a court order) to ensure that data from wiretaps were not being funneled to foreign competitors. However, it is very hard to imagine that a foreign intelligence agency would be willing to provide such assurances or to live with such audit restrictions. Ultimately, the trade-off might be the willingness of an international corporation to bargain with the host nation about the ability to have secure communications, using its willingness to invest in the host nation as its ultimate bargaining chip to force the host nation to acquiesce.

H

Summary of Important Requirements for a Public-Key Infrastructure

Based on information from a National Institute of Standards and Technology (NIST) document on public-key infrastructure,[1] this appendix briefly summarizes the user, technical, and legal requirements of a federal public-key infrastructure, as well as other observations obtained through interviews and the analysis of pertinent standards.

- *Ease of Use.* Certificate infrastructures should not make applications utilizing digital signature capabilities more difficult to use. To support ease of use, the infrastructure must provide a uniform way to obtain certificates in spite of the possible differences in certificate management policies employed by different segments of the infrastructure.

- *User Authentication.* To ensure proper linkage of a public key with a specific user, the identity of that user must be authenticated. User authentication is usually conducted by the certification authority (CA) during the key certification process.

- *Certification Policies.* If the existence of different certification policies is allowed, certification policies for both individual users and organizational users must be clearly articulated. In addition, mechanisms must

---

[1]Shimshon Berkovits et al. (MITRE Corporation), *Public Key Infrastructure Study: Final Report*, National Institute of Standards and Technology, Gaithersburg, Md., April 1994.

be provided to enable each user to be aware of the policies governing any certificate that he may encounter. In particular, a user should be able to establish how carefully and thoroughly the CA authenticated owner identity of the public key before certifying the association between the user and the key.

- *Trusted Certificate Authority.* Digital signatures are used to ensure sender authentication, nonrepudiation, and message integrity. To trust these security services, the user needs to be assured that the public key used to verify a signature is actually the key of the person who signed the transaction. To ensure that certificates are generated by and obtained from trusted sources, mechanisms are needed to prevent any user from creating false certificates that are signed with the user's regular private key. Even though a signature can be verified by employing the user's properly certified public key, the false certificates must not be accepted as legitimate. Then a pretender cannot create signatures that will be accepted because they are verified using keys obtained from the false certificates. Since the CA performs user authentication at key certification time and is responsible for keeping the user's name and public key associated, each CA must be a trusted entity, at least to the extent defined in the pertinent PCA policies. This implies the provision of some security protection for each CA, specifically the private key of the CA, so that the CA cannot be modified or impersonated. Certification policies can specify the security measures that a particular CA undertakes. Users must determine whether the CA is sufficiently trustworthy for their applications. The basic trust rests in the certification policies and security mechanisms established for the infrastructure.

- *User Affiliation.* To have a CA certify a public key, a user must provide a unique name in addition to the public key that is to be certified. That name usually contains the user's organizational affiliation. It is possible, however, that some private citizens may wish to have their keys certified independently of any organization. Therefore, provisions for certifying private citizens must also be made.

- *Privacy of User's Identity.* Some users may wish to remain anonymous but still register with a CA. This may require the establishment of certification agencies that would register users requesting nondisclosure of their identification information. Alternatively, policy choices in different segments of the infrastructure could include or exclude anonymous certificates.

• *Multiple Certificates.* In some instances a user may have several certificates, each issued by a different CA. This situation may occur if a user belongs to more than one organization and needs a certificate from each organization or if a user has a certificate as an employee and another certificate as a residential user. If the naming convention includes a user's organizational affiliation in the person's unique name, then a user can have several unique names with a different certificate associated with each. Multiple certificates assigned to a single unique name may be used to simplify recovery from CA private-key compromise. The infrastructure may have to handle multiple certificates for a single user.

• *Certification Revocation Lists.* When a private key is known to be compromised or even when its compromise is only suspected, it must be replaced immediately. The certificate containing the associated public key must be revoked immediately. To inform users of such a compromised key, thus allowing them to identify and reject possibly fraudulent transactions, the certificate is placed on a Certificate Revocation List (CRL). Placing a certificate on a CRL can also be used to announce the severing of a relationship between a signer and the organization with which he or she was once associated.

• *Services of CA.* CAs will need to certify public keys, create certificates, distribute certificates, generate CRLs, and distribute CRLs. Distribution of certificates and of CRLs will be accomplished by depositing them with a generally available directory service.

• *Security and Legal Efficacy.* There is an inherent linkage between security and legal efficacy. The security of electronic messages and records is not only a business requirement, but also an underlying legal requirement. This linkage determines what is sufficiently secure by considering what presumptions apply to the particular message's or document's purpose(s) and by considering the risks it confronts. Legal requirements should clarify reasonable security procedures without sacrificing needed flexibility. The question is not whether to have or not to have security, but rather whether the implemented security mechanisms provide the degree of security offered by the digital signatures. The answer rests squarely on the strength of the infrastructure's security mechanisms.

• *Liability.* The extent of the infrastructure's liability must be founded on a balance between the interest of the government, which would limit it, and of the private sector, which would expand it. Bringing suit must be allowable, but there must also be a reasonable limit on the extent of the infrastructure's liability. Different levels of liability limitations can be offered. For a price, users might even be allowed to tailor the extent of protection to their needs.

In committee discussions, it was noted that the liability of those providing authentication services is a critical issue. When the provider of authentication services is a business with which one is interacting for other purposes (e.g., to buy something), that business will generally have to accept liability for the interaction. Thus, if it wrongly certifies that Joe is Jack, and if Joe then steals money out of Jack's account, the bank that authenticated the transaction is liable. Likewise, third-party authentication services whose job it is to provide authentication services, but nothing more, would or should accept liability. Appropriate insurance requirements and a legislative framework might be necessary to regulate such services to ensure that they adhere to good practice.

As an agency of the federal government, the infrastructure may be considered to have sovereign immunity. Such immunity would imply that the infrastructure and its managers cannot be sued for any losses resulting from their actions or from their inaction. Although such a status may be attractive, it undermines the usefulness of the certification infrastructure. Without reasonable assurances that potential losses due to malfeasance will be recoverable, a typical nongovernment user will shy away from relying on the public-key infrastructure. Any set of laws and regulations must strike a balance between protection of the government from excessive claims and blocking users from any chance of reimbursement. The following items summarize what may be considered reasonable limits on the extent of liability to which a CA at any level and ultimately the public-key infrastructure as a whole should be exposed.

—A CA has no liability associated with the loss of the private keys of its clients or with their generating weak private keys.

—A key-generation facility has no liability associated with the compromise of the private keys it produces unless it can be proved that the documented policies and procedures relevant to the facility were not followed during the key-generation process, resulting in a weak private key that is more susceptible to compromise or the actual revelation of a private key.

—A key-generation facility has limited liability for the compromise of a private key during the key distribution process if the documented policies and procedures relevant to the facility are not followed, resulting in the revelation of the private key.

—A CA has no liability associated with forged signatures unless the forgery results because the documented policies and procedures relevant to the CA were not followed.

—A CA has no liability associated with the wrongful binding of an individual's identity with an associated public key unless it can be proved that the documented policies and procedures for identification and authentication relevant to the CA were not followed.

—A CA has limited liability for not revoking certificates according to its revocation policy.

—A CA has limited liability for revoking a certificate for a reason not specified in its revocation policy.

—A CA has limited liability if, despite its having followed published policies and procedures, a certificate in the database is modified or deleted.

- *Liability Policy.* The extent of liability in the above situations is conceivably a part of the policy under which a CA or key-generation facility operates. The policy must distinguish between direct liability on the one hand and indirect and consequential damages on the other.

I

Industry-Specific Dimensions
of Security

The discussion in Chapter 1 is couched in terms that are relatively independent of the specific industry or business involved. However, industries differ in the specifics of the information they wish to protect and in the operational questions they ask about security. What follows is an indicative—not exhaustive—discussion of security issues as they relate to specific types of business.[1] As discussed in Chapters 1 and 2, cryptography is only part of an overall approach to dealing with information security concerns; other factors also matter, such as administrative and technical procedures for controlling access to sensitive information and the trustworthiness of computer operating systems and applications software, among others. However, cryptographic technologies for authentication, integrity, and confidentiality can strengthen an organization's overall information security in many ways.

I.1 BANKING AND FINANCIAL SERVICES

Banking and financial services are a good example of how communications underpin the economy. The flow of currency is largely digital. Funds are transferred from account to account, from customer to vendor,

---

[1]These industry-specific comments should not be read as being mutually exclusive—concerns raised in the discussion of one industry may apply to other industries as well. Nevertheless, as presented, they do reflect concerns raised in discussions with representatives from the industries indicated.

from bank to bank—all without the trade of tangible property. As evidenced recently by the economic crisis in Mexico, the rapid transfer of investments has the ability to make or break an economy, much as the weather affected economies during the agricultural era. Network-enabled communications speed back-office (check and accounts) processing, as well as mortgage and loan application processing, and indeed interlink financial services, banking, and investment systems worldwide. Wholly new securities (e.g., derivatives and indexes) and services are created by the effective use of information communicated in a prompt and timely fashion.

Banks and financial service institutions have had a long history of being a target of nefarious elements in society and thus traditionally have been willing to spend money on security measures (e.g., safes). This history, coupled with their dependence on information technology and their capability for networked communication among themselves, has led to a relatively high degree of concern within the banking and financial services sector for information security. Given the importance of U.S. banks in the world economy, large U.S. banks with multinational connections have needs for security that are quite stringent.

In the matter of managing electronic transfers of financial transaction information, banks are much more concerned with authentication than with data confidentiality, although concerns about the latter are growing as the result of regulation and increasingly common business practices. The reason is that false authentication may lead to an unrecoverable loss of financial assets, an event regarded as more disastrous than the loss of privacy. Nonetheless, confidentiality is important as well,[2] not so much because personal financial transactions need to be kept private (they do, but the ramifications of divulging one person's transactions are generally limited to that person), but because an adversary's understanding of the data flows within the banking system can itself lead to security breakdowns. (For example, with access to confidential information, an adversary may learn how to bypass certain access controls.)

Banking is extensively international today and will become more so in the future. Moreover, it has moved relatively quickly to bring customers (both individual and institutional) on line in an attempt to reduce costs. (For example, some banks with South American customers call the United States and are answered in Spanish or Portuguese from processing and customer service centers in Europe.) For these reasons, the banking industry may represent the leading edge of information security needs

---

[2]Note that banks, as part of a highly regulated industry, are relatively less concerned about government monitoring of their financial transactions, since governments usually have extensive authority to monitor any aspect of bank transactions in any event.

as far as other increasingly internationalized and electronically interconnected industries are concerned. (Box I.1 describes some of the issues that arise when retail customers might apply for a loan through an electronic connection.)

To date, losses due to electronic penetration of banking systems have been a relatively small fraction of the billions of dollars written off every year in bad loans, unrepayable debt, and the like.[3] Yet the fact that any penetrations at all have occurred raise the specter of much larger losses (billions rather than millions of dollars) as the result of similar but more sophisticated actions. In addition, given the central importance of banking systems in the U.S. economy, a major disruption of service in these systems could have cataclysmic consequences for the world economy. Finally, customer and patron trust is at the heart of modern financial systems around the world, and such trust, once lost, is difficult to regain. Even small bank losses—if made widely known—could adversely affect customer trust in banks, and the result could be a significant and widespread loss of trust leading to enormous financial disruption and chaos.

I.2 MEDICAL CONSULTATIONS AND HEALTH CARE

Many health care professionals believe that computer-based health care information systems, both within individual institutions and networked over a national information infrastructure, hold great potential for improving the quality of health care, reducing administrative and clinical costs, increasing access (e.g., through telemedicine in rural areas), and enabling data aggregation in support of research on the cost and effectiveness of alternative treatments. Computer storage, retrieval, and network accessibility of health care information, such as medical records and diagnostic test data, can sharply increase the efficiency with which patients, care providers, and others (such as payers, researchers, and public health officials) use that information.[4]

At the same time, the digitization and transmission of such information raises concerns about the heightened vulnerability of personal infor-

---

[3]For example, losses on credit cards issued to consumers are considerable, but the amount lost due to outright fraud is small compared to the debts that consumers are simply unable or unwilling to pay.

[4]See, for example, Institute of Medicine, *The Computer-Based Patient Record: An Essential Technology for Health Care*, R.S. Dick and E.B. Steen (eds.), National Academy Press, Washington, D.C., 1991; and Information Infrastructure Task Force Committee on Applications and Technology, *Putting the Information Infrastructure to Work*, NIST Special Publication 857, U.S. Department of Commerce, National Institute of Standards and Technology, Gaithersburg, Md., 1994.

BOX I.1
Loans by Network

Loans are an essential part of many large transactions such as the purchase of houses and automobiles. Consumers provide information in loan applications which the loan provider uses as the basis of a loan approval. The formal approval commits the lender to a specific interest rate and, when it is accepted, the user to a specific repayment schedule. Since only information is exchanged, an application in principle could be conducted entirely without face-to-face interaction between consumer and provider, thus freeing the consumer to search the Internet for a provider offering the best rate.[1]

In practice, however, the prospect of an Internet loan application raises many questions:

• How is the personal data transmitted from the consumer to the provider to be protected as it crosses the Internet? In a face-to-face interaction, the information is provided at the bank, and so there is no difficulty in protecting the information in transit.

• How does the consumer know that she or he is sending the data to the proper bank? In a face-to-face interaction, the consumer can look at the sign on the front of the building to verify that it is indeed a branch of First Citibank of Washington, for example. (People have been known to send faxes to the wrong fax number.)

• How does the consumer know that the institution with which he or she is interacting is a trustworthy one (e.g., an organization chartered and regulated by the Federal Deposit Insurance Corporation)? In a face-to-face interaction, the consumer can look for the Federal Deposit Insurance Corporation seal at the front of the building and have some confidence that the seal is indeed associated with the offices inside the building.

• How do the parties ensure the integrity of a quoted interest rate? In a face-to-face interaction (or over the telephone), the parties can simultaneously view a piece of paper on which a certain interest rate is typed.

• In many loans, the interest rate is tied in an algorithmic fashion to a market index of some sort (e.g., 3 percentage points over the prime interest rate). In a face-to-face interaction, the lender can pull out a copy of the *Wall Street Journal* and point to p. B4.

• How does the lender verify the consumer's identity? In a face-to-face interaction, the consumer can present two photo identification cards and a recent tax return.

• How can the lender as a commercial entity protect itself against cyber-anarchists who believe that commercial transactions have no place on the Internet? In offering services to consumers on a face-to-face basis, police and security guards protect the bank against robbers.

---

[1] Indeed, laws and regulations governing the granting of credit explicitly or implicitly forbid the inclusion of factors such as race or "character" that might be ascertained in a face-to-face interaction.

mation in a profession with a tradition of maintaining the confidentiality of patient records that goes back to the days of Hippocrates.[5] Indeed, patient records may contain a great deal of sensitive information, photographs and other images, physicians' observations, clinical tests, diagnoses and treatments, life-style information (e.g., tobacco and alcohol use and sexual behavior), family medical history, and genetic conditions. If divulged to parties outside the patient-caregiver relationship, such information carries the risk of causing great personal anguish and/or financial harm (e.g., loss of insurance, employment).

Trends in health care today suggest an increasing aggregation of clinical, demographic, and utilization information into a single, patient-based record[6] or the development and deployment of systems for virtually linking these sources of information.[7] As a result, the number of access points to the information contained in computer-based patient records is increasing, thereby increasing its potential vulnerability. In addition, as the practice of telemedicine spreads, patient information and conferences among geographically separated medical professionals treating a single patient, which are transmitted across communications networks may be susceptible to interception.

Data aggregation presents another concern. For example, databases without personal identifiers may be assembled for purposes of research or public health planning.[8] Despite the fact that it may not be necessary to know the identities of individual patients, it may be possible to cross-index these databases with others (such as employment histories, insurance records, and credit reports), enabling the determination of personal identities.[9] This might be done, for example, in order to generate a list of names and addresses for direct marketing of a pharmaceutical product or a health service. Box I.2 describes one cryptographic method that can be used to reduce the risk of improper data aggregation.

The risks of improper disclosure of patient information come from

---

[5]It is interesting to note that for health care professionals, "confidentiality" refers to keeping certain information out of the hands of unauthorized individuals by whatever mechanisms are necessary, whereas for information security providers the term refers to a specific property of encrypted information.

[6]L.O. Gostin, J. Turek-Brezina, M. Powers, R. Kozloff, R. Faden, and D.D. Steinauer, "Privacy and Security of Personal Information in a New Health Care System," *Journal of the American Medical Association,* Volume 270(20), 1993, pp. 2487-2493.

[7]Personal communication, E.H. Shortliffe, Stanford University School of Medicine, November 5, 1994.

[8]Institute of Medicine, *Health Data in the Information Age: Use, Disclosure, and Privacy,* M.S. Donaldson and K.N. Lohr (eds.), National Academy Press, Washington, D.C., 1994.

[9]E. Meux, "Encrypting Personal Identifiers," *Health Services Research,* Volume 29(2), 1994, pp. 247-256.

BOX I.2
Preventing the Unauthorized Aggregation of
Health Care Information

Use of the Social Security Number as a de facto universal identifier gives rise to concerns on the part of privacy advocates regarding the unauthorized aggregation of data about individuals collected from many different institutions that have been individually authorized to release specific data. Peter Szolovits and Isaac Kohane have proposed a mechanism based on public-key cryptography that would generate a unique identifier tied to the individual and a specific institution under which that individual's information could be stored by that institution. With such a mechanism in place, a positive user action would be required to create an identifier, and the individual would gain control over the parties who could aggregate personal data because he or she could refuse to create an identifier for any given institution requesting particular data.

In essence, the scheme relies on the individual's performing a public-key digital signature on the institution's name. The result of this operation is a piece of data, usable as an identifier, that only the individual could have created, but that anyone can verify the individual has created. More specifically, the individual "decrypts" the plaintext that gives the name of the institution using his or her private key. Only the individual could have created the result, because only the individual knows the private key. However, anyone can encrypt the identifier using the individual's public key. If the result of this encryption is the name of the institution, it can be known with confidence that indeed the individual generated the identifier.

Of course, policy would be needed to support this mechanism as well. For example, it might be necessary to conduct random data audits of various institutions that would check to see if a given institution was indeed properly authorized by the individual to receive given data.

SOURCE: P. Szolovits and I. Kohane, "Against Universal Health-care Identifiers," *Journal of the American Medical Informatics Association*, Volume 1, 1994, pp. 316-319.

two sources: disclosure through actions taken by unauthorized "outside" parties (e.g., eavesdroppers, hackers, visitors wandering through a hospital unchallenged, individuals posing over the telephone as physicians and convincing medical personnel to divulge sensitive information or grant remote access to an information system) or disclosure through actions taken by authorized "inside" parties who abuse their authorization (e.g., a hospital staff member snooping out of curiosity into the records of relatives, friends, or celebrities or a medical records clerk motivated by financial, political, or other concerns who gives or sells lists of women with appointments for abortions to an antiabortion political group.[10])

---

[10]Personal communication, E.H. Shortliffe, Stanford University School of Medicine, November 5, 1994.

Health care organizations tend to be much more concerned about the "insider" than the "outsider" threat. Information systems for health care organizations are no longer freestanding "islands of information"; instead, because they are increasingly networked beyond their walls, the number of "inside" authorized users is expanding to include other primary and specialty health care providers, health insurers, employers or purchasers, government agencies, and the patient or consumer.

A final category of concern related to health care information security is the need to ensure the integrity and the authenticity of data associated with a patient. Thus, computer-based patient records must be secure against improper alteration or deletion of data (data integrity) and known with high confidence to be associated with the particular individual with whom they are claimed to be associated (data and user authenticity).

This categorization of risks suggests that, within health care organizations, the need for authentication of users and access controls (for both insiders and outsiders) may well be more important than encryption for confidentiality (in the information security sense of the term). The reason is that good authentication and access controls enable to a very high degree the creation of audit trails that can help document who has accessed what information and for what reason. However, the need for interorganizational transmission of data is encouraging many health care administrators to re-evaluate their strategic risk analysis and consider cryptography for data confidentiality.

Some informal discussions with health care leaders reveal that security issues are generally delegated to their chief information officers and are not a standing top-priority item in their overall strategic planning. However, many of the country's foremost health care organizations continuously conduct risk analysis and generally have decided that serving the needs of authorized patient caregivers for rapid access to clinical information is their paramount priority. Any technical or policy approach to implementing cryptography for confidentiality will always be measured against this patient care priority.

I.3 MANUFACTURING

Large manufacturing companies are increasingly multinational. For example, General Motors (GM), the world's largest full-line vehicle manufacturer of cars, trucks, and automotive systems, has units worldwide that support all dimensions of its production. Its divisions range from those that build mechanical subsystems and components for automobiles and electronic systems for automotive electronics, telecommunications, and space and defense electronics to those that provide financing and insurance for dealers and end customers. GM has about 600,000 employees in 170 countries worldwide.

Manufacturers are placing more emphasis on product variety.[11] Variation inevitably increases costs (e.g., each variant requires considerable engineering; thus, the engineering costs per variant rise). To amortize these fixed costs, manufacturers necessarily seek larger markets for these variants, and the result is often a global market. For example, a market for a certain product in a particular foreign nation may exist, and a variant of a product originally intended for a U.S. market with local content added in that foreign nation may prove quite successful. To manage sales globally, companies may well need to establish company offices in foreign countries that remain in frequent communication with company headquarters in the United States.

Manufacturing operations must be managed globally as well. For example, a problem in a manufacturing plant in Brazil may require an engineering change order to be generated at an engineering design center in Germany and synchronized with tooling supplied by Japan and parts manufactured in Mexico. A second incentive for global operations is that labor costs are often lower abroad as well, for both white-collar and blue-collar workers.

The network of vendors and suppliers that serve large manufacturing operations is also global. The day is long since gone when it makes economic sense for a manufacturer to take responsibility for fabricating every component under its own direct control—outsourcing such fabrication is often much more efficient. In some cases, foreign suppliers of parts are used because foreign purchase of parts is an additional incentive for a foreign nation to buy the finished U.S. product. However, to obtain the right mix of price, quality, volume, and timeliness, manufacturers increasingly search globally for subcontractors, and these subcontractors must be integrated into the manufacturer's information network. At the same time, it may not be desirable for subcontractors to share the same level of access as the primary company, especially if these subcontractors are competitors. Unauthorized disclosure of information between such parties constitutes a threat by endangering and presenting a risk to important communications links between the company and the customers and suppliers (reducing business trust). The same is true for manufacturers and customers: a manufacturer of capital-intensive products may well wish to share product information with potential customers. Yet since potential customers may be competitors among themselves (e.g., an airplane manufacturer may have several airlines among its customers)

---

[11]For more discussion, see Computer Science and Telecommunications Board, National Research Council, *Information Technology for Manufacturing: A Research Agenda*, National Academy Press, Washington, D.C., 1995.

and information regarding customer-desired product configurations may have competitive significance, the manufacturer has an important requirement to keep information about one customer private to that customer.

The information flows associated with such activities are enormously valuable to manufacturing firms. These flows contain sensitive and proprietary information related to:

- Product design and research and development;
- Marketing, sales, and bidding;
- Plant operations, capabilities, and efficiencies;
- Costs and prices of parts or services being purchased and products being sold;
- Strategic plans;
- Profits and losses;
- Orders to and from suppliers;
- Product readiness and repair; and
- Product problems and incident investigations.

These information flows need not necessarily be electronic; many companies still use people on airplanes with briefcases locked to their wrists. In electronic form, however, they can be transmitted instantly via electronic mail, telephone, fax, and videoconference, and action can be taken on a much shorter time scale. Specialized communications infrastructures can make all the difference in the world—one manufacturer reported that before a specialized network was installed, engineers in the United States were cutting large engineering drawings into $8 \frac{1}{2} \times 11$ sheets and faxing them to their counterparts in another country.

At the same time, the compromise of communications can be significant in manufacturing. Theft of product design data can result in the loss of competitive advantage in products; if the products in question have military significance, such data may well be classified and the compromise of data may lead to a national security threat to the United States. Premature release of financial information can affect stock prices. Knowledge of specific problems in a given plant can give competitors unwarranted leverage. Unauthorized changes to engineering orders can result in chaos on the assembly line or in operational disaster. Destruction or alteration of key data by insiders or outsiders could be as significant as physical sabotage, and subtle changes to digital designs or software may be undetectable for an indefinite time with possible consequences such as product recall.

I.4 THE PETROLEUM INDUSTRY

The petroleum industry is inherently international; a typical multinational oil company may operate in dozens of nations. Moreover, the scale of oil exploration and production requires substantial collaborative efforts, even among potential competitors. Thus, this industry highlights the need for protecting sensitive proprietary information that must be shared worldwide, potentially across telecommunication networks. Sensitive information of particular significance to the petroleum industry includes the following:

- *Personnel information.* Top executives of large multinational oil companies are often placed at substantial physical risk by threats of kidnapping, extortion, and other criminal activity. Thus, the whereabouts of such individuals are often confidential.
- *Personal information.* Midlevel employees who work and live in politically unstable areas are often concerned about maintaining their personal safety. Since they may engage routinely in communications between home and office that could disclose their whereabouts, compromise of these communications could subject them to personal attack.
- *Seismic and other data indicating the whereabouts of oil and natural gas underground.* Such data are particularly sensitive because the competitive advantage of a given oil company may well be in the data it has been able to collect on a given field. The use of such data, coupled with advanced computing capabilities, has saved hundreds of millions of dollars by helping drillers to avoid "dry" wells.[12]
- *Information related to bidding.* Oil companies often bid for rights to drill or to explore in certain locations, and premature disclosure or disclosure to inappropriate parties of such information could seriously compromise bidding negotiations.
- *Conferences among technical experts.* With worldwide operations, it may be necessary, for example, for experts at a potential drilling site to consult with experts located halfway around the world to make a reasoned decision about drilling. These experts display the same seismic data on their computer screens (data that is confidential as described above), but the in-house expertise needed to interpret such data (as expressed in their communications) can be an additional competitive advantage that cannot be compromised.

A significant amplifier of the information security threat relevant to U.S. multinational oil companies is the fact that the oil companies of other nations are often state owned and operated. The close integration between such foreign oil companies and their governments, combined with

---

[12]Written testimony of Jack L. Brock to the Subcommittee on Science, Technology and Space of the Senate Commerce Committee, March 5, 1991, p. 4.

the large economic stakes involved, raises significant concerns in U.S. oil companies that all of the resources of those foreign governments may be brought to bear against them, including foreign intelligence services.

I.5 THE PHARMACEUTICAL AND CHEMICAL INDUSTRIES

The pharmaceutical and chemical industries are also global, since foreign nations often possess both the intellectual expertise and the natural resources needed to be successful in these industries.[13] The critical dimensions of these industries in which information must be protected involve not products per se but rather other areas:

• *The scientific and technical expertise that allows companies to conceptualize new molecules or adapt previously known molecules to new functionality.* Research and development of new drugs and chemicals is the lifeblood of these industries, and information or data in which the creativity of their chemists is reflected is critical.

• *The regime of intellectual property protection.* Intellectual property rights are one primary mechanism on which the pharmaceutical and chemical industries depend to protect their large investments in research and development. However, intellectual property rights are generally granted to the parties that are first with a discovery or invention.[14] Thus, the speed with which discoveries can be made or a patent application filed becomes a parameter of critical importance; nonrepudiable (i.e., irrefutable) proof of the integrity of data from clinical trials and of the dates of patentable discoveries can be useful to strengthen patent claims. In addition, given the public nature of much of the science underlying these discoveries, small intellectual advances that save time may be the only advantage that a company has in the race to be first. Premature disclosure of information associated with the protection of intellectual property rights can lead to patent challenges or even loss of protection and thus may be extraordinarily damaging.

• *The processes by which drugs and chemicals are manufactured.* In general, drugs and chemicals are at the end of a long processing chain in which raw materials are transformed into the desired substances. Even

---

[13]For example, in August 1995, Upjohn announced a merger with a Swedish competitor (Pharmacia AB) that would result in the ninth-largest drug company in the world, with 34,500 employees worldwide. See Associated Press, "Upjohn, Rival Drug Firm Plan Merger," *Washington Post*, August 21, 1995, p. A6.

[14]In some regimes, "first" means first to discover or invent. In others, first means first to file for patent protection. For purposes of this discussion, the distinction is irrelevant.

small process improvements that reduce the volume of raw materials necessary, problems of quality control, or the dangers or complexity of the overall manufacturing process can be reflected in large savings of time and money. Such improvements may be protected by intellectual property rights, but enforcement may be difficult if it is not known that a competitor is using a stolen process improvement. In other instances (e.g., safety), widespread publicity of information taken out of context may cause a company many public relations difficulties.

I.6 THE ENTERTAINMENT INDUSTRY

The product of the entertainment industry is information, information that is increasingly migrating to digital form. The dominant concern of the entertainment industry is how to protect digitized music, movies, games, and the like from unauthorized mass distribution without proper payment of royalties and fees. A secondary, though still important, concern is how the integrity of such products can be ensured. For example, an unprotected digitized movie could be altered unmaliciously (with the intent of enhancing its appeal, e.g., by colorizing an original black-and-white movie) or maliciously (e.g., by changing a scene for purposes of embarrassing the producing company).

I.7 GOVERNMENT

The U.S. government is, and will continue to be, a major user of cryptography, both for internal purposes and in its exchanges with citizens. As more and more government services are implemented using electronic methods, it becomes increasingly important to identify and authenticate individuals and to verify the accuracy of data. To the extent that people wish to use electronic means to communicate personal information to the government, the need to maintain confidentiality also increases. Cryptography supports all of these goals in an electronic world. Several of the many examples of how cryptography will be used in the federal government are described here.

The Internal Revenue Service (IRS) is responsible for collecting the taxes that fuel all government programs. Every year, citizens and corporations transmit financial data to the IRS and interact with the agency to resolve any problems. The agency processes approximately 100 million individual tax returns and more than 1 billion supporting documents (e.g., W-2 forms, 1099 forms) annually. The primary goal of the IRS's Tax Systems Modernization (TSM) effort is to facilitate this process by increasing its use of electronic processing and electronic interchange of information.[15]

The TSM effort will allow the IRS to process 100% of all tax return data on line and will significantly increase the amounts of data that are submitted electronically. It is this latter capability that requires the use of cryptography, primarily in the form of digital signatures, to ensure that tax returns are submitted in a proper manner. Currently, the IRS is required to store the handwritten signature of the person(s) for each and every tax return, including those submitted electronically. The use of digital signatures will allow the IRS to eliminate handwritten signatures without loss of authentication, which will streamline the data-gathering process. The IRS will be supporting the Digital Signature Standard, as well as other signature standards that become de facto commercial standards.[16] While most electronic filing of income tax returns is currently carried out by authorized tax preparers, the IRS is working on creating a secure system using cryptography that would enable taxpayers to file directly from their home computers.

Similar to the IRS, the Social Security Administration (SSA) also collects data from citizens and corporations on a regular basis. Furthermore, the SSA is responsible for disbursing funds for old-age and survivors' insurance, disability insurance, and supplemental security income programs. The effective and efficient management of these programs increasingly relies on automated data processing and electronic exchanges among the SSA, citizens, and corporations. The agency is also involved in the deployment of digital signatures to streamline its operations. Digital signatures will allow citizens with home computers to check the status of their benefits 24 hours a day, rather than waiting for a telephone service representative to provide the needed information. Without digital signatures, such a service cannot be provided electronically because of concerns about protecting the security of the private information involved in such an exchange.

The wide-scale government use of cryptography will require an extensive infrastructure for maintaining public keys for all citizens, corporations, and organizations. The Security Infrastructure Program Management Office at the General Services Administration is planning pilot

---

[15]Computer Science and Telecommunications Board, National Research Council, *Review of the Tax Systems Modernization of the Internal Revenue Service*, National Academy Press, Washington, D.C., 1992; and CSTB, *Continued Review of the Tax Systems Modernization of the Internal Revenue Service*, 1994.

[16]"IRS, SSA to Let Public Try Digital Signatures," *Government Computer News*, November 13, 1995, p. 1.

projects to test the use of cryptography in electronic communications between agencies and citizens. Agencies such as SSA, IRS, and the Department of Education will participate. Citizens participating in the pilot tests will use a personal computer or government kiosk and the Internet to access Social Security information, file income tax forms, or—in time—apply for a student loan.

In the pilot studies, the U.S. Postal Service (USPS) will be responsible for issuing the digital signatures that will identify users through the use of tokens. It will develop an infrastructure for assigning and maintaining the critical "certificates" that are needed for proper authentication.[17] Many believe that the USPS is a natural candidate for such a responsibility because of its vast network of postal offices and operations that are aimed specifically at providing individual and business services. Furthermore, the USPS is a "trusted" organization that has the backing of legislation to perform its duties, as well as a mature oversight framework.

In addition to the citizen-to-government interactions described above, there is a complete spectrum of cryptographic methods used throughout the government for internal communication and processing purposes. The Treasury Department has long used cryptographic methods for the authentication, integrity, and confidentiality of financial transactions. The Department of Energy has also been a long-time user and developer of cryptographic methods, which are employed to safeguard nuclear control systems, among other things. A number of nondefense agencies have begun to adopt Fortezza PCMCIA cards (described in Chapter 5), including the Departments of Commerce, Justice, Energy, State, and Treasury, as well as the National Aeronautics and Space Administration, the IRS, and the Coast Guard. The broad-based use of this system among civilian agencies is as yet uncertain.[18]

The effort to make the federal government more efficient often increases the need for and difficulty of protecting copyrighted, private, and proprietary information. For example, improving federal services to citizens by providing them electronically requires more sharing of information and resources among agencies and between federal agencies and state or local agencies. Increased sharing of information requires interagency coordination of privacy and security policies to ensure uniformly adequate protection. During a time of tight federal budgets, information security managers in federal agencies increasingly must compete for resources and support to implement the needed safeguards properly. Agencies must look for the least expensive way to ensure security, and the cost of some encryption systems currently is prohibitive for some civilian agencies.

---

[17]*Government Computer News*, November 13, 1995.
[18]"Fortezza Faces Uncertain Future," *Federal Computer Week*, November 13, 1995, p. 12.

J

Examples of Risks Posed by Unprotected Information

The following cases in which commercial, national security, and other sensitive information was compromised illustrate the variety and seriousness of threats to personal assets and privacy, business interests, and public well-being, among others. No claim is made that cryptography alone could have prevented these violations, but in the instances cited, cryptography might have had some role in protecting information against misappropriation and misuse. As discussed in Chapters 1 and 2, cryptographic technologies are part of an overall strategy to reduce information vulnerability.

J.1 RISKS ADDRESSED BY CRYPTOGRAPHY FOR AUTHENTICATION

- A pair of reporters wrote a controversial book about the hacking activities of a particular group. They subsequently found that their telephone had been "call forwarded" without their permission to another location where callers were greeted with obscenities, and that their Internet mailboxes had been filled with junk e-mail.[1] Cryptography for authentication might have reduced the likelihood that the hackers would be able to penetrate the telephone switch servicing the reporters' homes.
- Secret documents belonging to General Motors (GM) containing

---

[1]Philip Elmer-Dewitt, "Terror on the Internet," *Time*, December 12, 1994, p. 73.

information about a new GM vehicle to be sold in Europe and a top-secret experimental car were seized at an apartment used by a former GM executive who had since joined Volkswagen.[2] Cryptography for authentication that created an audit trail might have helped to identify the former executive sooner.

• Insiders at the First National Bank of Chicago transferred $70 million in bogus transactions out of client accounts. One transaction exceeded permissible limits, but the insiders managed to intercept the telephone request for manual authorization.[3] Cryptography for authentication might have helped to deny access of the insiders to the telephone request for authorization.

• A Dutch bank employee made two bogus computer-based transfers to a Swiss account, for $8.4 million and $6.7 million, in 1987. Each transfer required the password of two different people for authorization; however, the employee knew someone else's password as well as his own.[4] Cryptography for authentication might have hindered the ability of a single individual to pretend that he was the second employee.

• The First Interstate Bank of California received a bogus request to transfer $70 million over the automated clearinghouse network. The request came via computer tape, accompanied by phony authorization forms, and was detected and canceled only because it overdrew the debited account.[5] Cryptography for authentication might have demonstrated that the authorization was invalid.

• Forty-five Los Angeles police officers were cited from 1989 to 1992 for using department computers to run background checks for personal reasons.[6] Cryptography for authentication might have been part of an audit trail that would have reduced the likelihood of abusing the department's computer system.

J.2 RISKS ADDRESSED BY CRYPTOGRAPHY FOR CONFIDENTIALITY

• According to unclassified sources, a foreign intelligence service conducted signal intelligence (SIGINT) operations against a major U.S. airplane manufacturer, intercepting telemetry data transmitted from an airplane under development during a particular set of flight tests and a

---

[2]See Frank Swoboda and Rick Atkinson, "Lopez Said to Order GM Papers; Volkswagen Denies Receiving Documents," *Washington Post*, July 23, 1993.

[3]See Peter G. Neumann, *Computer-Related Risks*, Addison-Wesley, Reading, Mass., 1995, p. 166.

[4]Neumann, *Computer-Related Risks*, 1995, p. 168.

[5]Neumann, *Computer-Related Risks*, 1995, p. 167.

[6]Neumann, *Computer-Related Risks*, 1995, p. 184.

video teleconference held among company engineers located at various sites.[7] Encryption of the telemetry data and the video conference might have kept sensitive information away from the foreign intelligence service.

- A bounty of $80,000 was reportedly posted on the Internet in 1994 for a notebook computer belonging to any Fortune 100 executive.[8] Encryption of the files on the laptop might have helped to keep sensitive information confidential).

- A Green Bay Packer football player was overheard calling a male escort service and making explicit requests.[9] A 23-minute conversation allegedly between Princess Diana and a man who called her "my darling Squidge" was taped by a retired bank manager in Oxford and transcribed in *The Sun*.[10] The transcript of that conversation has now been circulated widely. Encryption of these communications would have prevented the disclosure of the information in question.

- In one instance relayed to the committee, a large multinational manufacturer dispatched a salesperson to engage in negotiations with a foreign nation. A laptop computer that carried a great deal of sensitive information relevant to those negotiations was seized by the border authorities and returned to the salesperson three days later. As the negotiations proceeded, it became clear to the salesperson that his opposites had all of the information carried on his laptop. In another instance, a major multinational company with customer support offices in China experienced a break-in in which Chinese nationals apparently copied paper documents and unencrypted computer files. Encryption of the stored files might have reduced the likelihood that the data contained therein would have been compromised.

J.3 RISKS ADDRESSED BY CRYPTOGRAPHY FOR BOTH AUTHENTICATION AND CONFIDENTIALITY

In the following instances, both authentication and confidentiality might have had a useful role to play. Authentication could have been useful to keep intruders out of the computer systems in question, while confidentiality could have helped frustrate their attempt to view or obtain

---

[7]Peter Schweizer, *Friendly Spies*, Atlantic Monthly Press, New York, 1993, pp. 122-124.

[8]Dan Costa, "Not-So-Soft Security," *Mobile Office*, August 1995, p. 75.

[9]John Flinn, *San Francisco Examiner*, November 1, 1992; see also Neumann, *Computer-Related Risks*, 1995, p. 186.

[10]Flinn, *San Francisco Examiner*, 1992; see also Neumann, *Computer-Related Risks*, 1995, p. 186.

plaintext of information stored on those systems. However, in any individual example, it is not known if cryptographic authentication or encryption was or was not a part of the computer systems or networks that were penetrated.

- A reporter for *Newsweek* who wrote an article on malicious hacking activities was subjected to an electronic bulletin board trial and pronounced guilty. Subsequently, someone accessed a TRW credit database to obtain and post the reporter's credit card numbers. As a result, $1,100 in merchandise was charged to him, and his home computer was crashed remotely via his unlisted telephone number.[11]
- An employee of Disney World gained illegal access to Disney computer systems in 1994, reading confidential data files on employees and deleting information from the systems.[12]
- A major multinational chemical manufacturer headquartered in the United States has deployed an on-line videotext system that contains considerable amounts of proprietary information about processes used by that company. This manufacturer has disconnected one of its plants, located in the Far East, from the videotext network because of evidence that the government of the nation in which the plant is located is both willing and able to tap into this network to obtain valuable information that could be passed on to the manufacturer's foreign competitors.
- The domestic security service of a major Western European nation found information belonging to a major multinational manufacturer headquartered in the United States in the private homes of individuals with no connection to the manufacturer. This information was found marked for sale to a competitor of the manufacturer in question and was apparently obtained through the computer hacking efforts of these individuals.

J.4 RISKS ADDRESED BY CRYPTOGRAPHY FOR DATA INTEGRITY

- A convicted forger serving a 33-year term was released from jail after a forged fax had been received ordering his release. A legitimate fax had been altered to bear his name.[13] Cryptography to ensure data integrity might have helped to detect the forgery.

---

[11]Neumann, *Computer-Related Risks*, 1995, p. 137.

[12]Richard Burnett, "More Hackers Speak in Code; Rise in Peeping Toms Alarms Central Florida Businesses," *The Orlando Sentinel*, July 4, 1994, p. 10.

[13]See "Fraudulent Fax Gets Forger Freed," *San Francisco Chronicle*, December 18, 1991, p. A3.

- A prison inmate gained access to the on-line prison information system and managed to alter his release date. The alteration was detected by a suspicious deputy comparing the on-line entry with manual records, after the inmate had bragged about how he was going to get out early.[14] Cryptography to ensure data integrity might have helped to detect the alteration of the files.

---

[14]*San Jose Mercury News*, December 14, 1984.

K

Cryptographic Applications Programming Interfaces

Modern software systems are built using various techniques that provide flexibility and reliability. One of the most important techniques centers on the use of an applications programming interface.

An applications programming interface (API) is a well-defined boundary between two system components that isolates a specific process or set of services. For example, it is quite common now for an application to interact with an electronic mail (e-mail) server through an e-mail API, such as MAPI (Microsoft), VIM (Lotus), or AOCE (Apple), to name a few. In such cases, the API defines a set of services that allow an application to retrieve or submit mail messages from or to the mail server. APIs can be implemented by using hardware, software, or some combination. Furthermore, software APIs can be implemented by using dynamically linked libraries, statically linked libraries, remote procedure calls, or any combination.

APIs have evolved as the result of both technical and business pressures. Technically, software developers have moved increasingly to "open," client-server systems. An open system is one in which interoperable products from different vendors are used to provide the functionality required by the users. Such systems depend heavily on commercial standards and APIs are often used to support those standards. For example, e-mail exchange using the X.400 standard is now supported by the CMC API. An API allows multiple vendors to develop interoperable products, even though individual product versions are continually changing.

Although APIs are used to support open standards, a large number of proprietary APIs are also used by vendors to safeguard their technical investments. Even within these closed environments, APIs provide a major technical and business benefit for those vendors licensed to develop products using that API. For example, Novell was one of the first network operating system vendors to make extensive use of an API to support a wide range of add-on products. Under its approach, a "netware" loadable module (NLM) can be developed by a third-party developer and incorporated into an operational system by the user. The use of a proprietary API allows vendors to maintain the quality of third party products, to provide a basis for the development of niche products, and to maintain a competitive advantage. In Novell's case, the development of NLMs for major database products has boosted its sales in that competitive server market.

Perhaps the most common API today is Microsoft's object linking and embedding (OLE) software technology, which provides general-purpose sockets for modules that can undertake many different functions. For example, an OLE socket can provide the user with the capability to insert a module for file encryption or for file compression. Thus, although it might be possible to use government regulations to prevent the widespread use of sockets for encryption, it would be difficult to dampen the spread of a general-purpose socket that has many uses. OLE interfaces could plausibly support some level of encryption capability; however, since OLE interfaces are not specifically designed for security, they may have weaknesses that render them unsuitable for security-specific applications.

A cryptographic applications programming interface (CAPI) is an API specifically designed to support the introduction of cryptographic functions into products. It is not necessary to actually provide the cryptographic functions when the system is initially sold. Users would then be able to incorporate the cryptographic add-ons of their choice. Technically, a CAPI would provide an interface to a set of cryptographic services; it would usually include authentication, digital signature generation, random number generation, and stream or block mode encryption. Although there are some technical problems specific to CAPIs, most notably those associated with ensuring the integrity of the security processing, they exhibit, for the most part, the same advantages as any other API. That is, there are strong technical and business reasons for incorporating a CAPI into open systems.

CAPIs would enable applications developers to take for granted the existence of cryptographic functionality and not have to provide for such functionality themselves. Moreover, by separating the cryptography from the baseline product, major system vendors will be able to make changes to the baseline product driven by market considerations without waiting for an export license review that would be necessary for a product with built-in cryptographic functionality.

Cryptographic APIs are likely to have a profound effect on the rapidity with which cryptography will diffuse into various information technology applications. If implemented properly (not a trivial task), they can enhance the security of stored data and communications. When effective CAPI technologies are embedded into the operating systems upon which IT applications build, the result will likely be encrypted files and communications galore. Operating systems will be shipped with default cryptographic modules that are active "out of the box," and users will have the option of replacing default modules with more capable modules procured from other vendors.

The notion of a CAPI is not new. However, in general, export licenses for products incorporating CAPIs have been denied, even though such products, with no cryptographic capabilities built into them, have no cryptographic functionality and are therefore not specifically included in Category XIII of the International Traffic in Arms Regulations (see Appendix N). The reason for such denial has been that strong cryptographic capabilities could be deployed on a vast scale if U.S. vendors exported applications supporting a common CAPI and a foreign vendor marketed (or some party made available over the Internet) an add-on module with strong cryptography, which foreign users could then plug into the baseline U.S. product.

L

Other Looming Issues Related to Cryptography Policy

L.1 DIGITAL CASH[1]

National economies are based on money. The most basic form of money is cash. Coins, originally made of valuable metals, had intrinsic value and came to be more or less universally acceptable. Paper money (bills) came to substitute for coins as the value of transactions increased and it became physically impractical to carry ever-larger volumes of coins. However, paper money was originally backed by stores of precious metals (gold and silver). In 1971, the United States abandoned its last effective link to the gold standard, and paper money—with no intrinsic value—came to represent value that was backed by the integrity and solvency of the (increasingly international) banking system. Other mediums of exchange have come to supplement cash, including paper checks written by consumers; bank-to-bank financial interactions that are electronically mediated; nonretail business transactions conducted through electronic data interchange among customers, vendors, and suppliers; and credit and debit cards used to make retail purchases.

Today, interest in so-called digital cash is increasing. Digital cash is similar to paper cash in the sense that neither the paper on which paper

---

[1]This section draws heavily on Cross Industry Working Team, *Electronic Cash, Tokens, and Payments in the National Information Infrastructure,* Corporation for National Research Initiatives, 1895 Preston White Drive, Suite 100, Reston, Va., 1994; available on-line at info-xiwt@cnri.reston.va.us.

BOX L.1
Characteristics of Digital Cash Tokens

• *Monetary value.* Electronic tokens must have a monetary value; they must represent either cash (currency), a bank-authorized credit, or a bank-certified electronic check.

• *Exchangeability.* Electronic tokens must be exchangeable as payment for other electronic tokens, paper cash, goods or services, lines of credit, deposits in banking accounts, bank notes or obligations, electronic benefits transfers, and the like.

• *Storability and retrievability.* Electronic tokens must be able to be stored and retrieved. Remote storage and retrieval (e.g., from a telephone or personal communications device) would allow users to exchange electronic tokens (e.g., withdraw from and deposit into banking accounts) from home or office or while traveling. The tokens could be stored in any appropriate electronic device that might serve as an electronic "wallet."

• *Tamper-resistance.* Electronic tokens should be tamper-proof and be difficult to copy or forge. This characteristic prevents or detects duplication and double spending. Counterfeiting poses a particular problem, since a counterfeiter may, in network applications, be anywhere in the world and consequently be difficult to catch without appropriate international agreements. Detection is essential to determine whether preventive measures are working.

SOURCE: Adapted from Cross Industry Working Team, *Electronic Cash, Tokens, and Payments in the National Information Infrastructure*, Corporation for National Research Initiatives, Reston, Va., 1994.

money is printed nor the string of bits that represents digital cash has intrinsic value; value is conferred on a piece of paper or a particular string of bits if, and only if, an institution is willing to accept responsibility for them. The basic characteristics of digital cash are described in Box L.1.

Public interest in digital cash is driven largely by pressures for electronic commerce. For example, cash is usually the medium of choice in conducting low-value transactions; present mechanisms for conducting transactions at a distance make economic sense only when the value is relatively high (the average credit card transaction is several tens of dollars). In addition, these mechanisms generally require a preexisting arrangement between vendors and credit card companies: completely spontaneous transactions between parties without such arrangements are not possible with credit cards as they are with cash. Instant settlement when conducting financial transactions at a distance and reducing the cost of managing physical cash are still other advantages.

Both cryptography and information technology, including computer hardware and software, underlie the feasibility of digital cash. Strong cryptographic technologies and secure network architectures are necessary to give users of a digital cash system confidence in its security and integrity, while the exponentially improving price-performance ratio of computer hardware is needed for the extensive computation required for strong cryptography in a mobile environment. Moreover, important advances in making electronics tamper-proof—another feature needed to ensure confidence—may be in the hands of any number of users. Box L.2 describes the properties that a digital cash system must have.

Digital cash raises many basic questions. For example, if electronic cash is legal tender, who should be authorized to issue it and how should the public be assured that a particular issuing authority is legitimate? How does a digital U.S. dollar affect the U.S. position in the world economy? How will the money supply be controlled or even measured with digital cash

---

BOX L.2
Essential Properties of a Digital Cash System

It is widely accepted that a digital cash system must have the following properties:

• *Authentication.* Users must be assured that digital cash tokens cannot be easily forged or altered and that, if they are altered, evidence of this tampering will be apparent immediately.

• *Nonrefutable.* Users must also be able to verify that exchanges have taken place between the intended parties, despite any complications that may result from delivery of services over long periods of time, interruptions in service, or differences in billing and collection policies of various service providers. ("Nonrepudiable" is the term used in traditional computer and network security work.)

• *Accessible and reliable.* Users must find the exchange process to be accessible, easy to effect, quick, and available when necessary, regardless of component failures in other parts of the system.

• *Private.* Users must be assured that knowledge of transactions will be confidential within the limits of policy decisions made about features of the overall system. Privacy must be maintained against unauthorized parties.

• *Protected.* Users must be assured that they cannot be easily duped or swindled, or be falsely implicated in a fraudulent transaction. Users must be protected against eavesdroppers, impostors, and counterfeiters. For many types of transactions, trusted third-party agents will be needed to serve this purpose.

All of these features depend on cryptography and secure hardware in varying degrees.

SOURCE: Cross Industry Working Team, *Electronic Cash, Tokens, and Payments in the National Information Infrastructure*, Corporation for National Research Initiatives, Reston, Va., 1994.

in circulation? Apart from such questions, digital cash also raises policy issues that are part of cryptography policy writ large. Based largely on the reference in footnote 1, the discussion below sketches some of the main issues.

L.1.1 Anonymity and Criminal Activity

The technology of digital cash will support essentially any degree of anonymity desired. Digital cash can be designed so that it is as closely associated with the user as electronic funds transfer is today (i.e., highly nonanonymous) or in a way that disassociates it entirely from the user (i.e., more anonymous than physical cash is today). Intermediate levels of anonymity are technically possible as well: for example, transactions could be anonymous except when a court order or warrant compelled disclosure of the identities of parties involved in a transaction. Furthermore, the various parties—payer, payee, and bank—could be identified or not, depending on policy choices.

Many privacy advocates support digital cash because such a system can provide high levels of anonymity for electronic transactions comparable to the anonymity of face-to-face transactions made with physical cash. Such anonymity is not generally possible for other types of electronic payment vehicles. On the other hand, anonymous perpetrators of crimes cannot be identified and apprehended. To the extent that digital cash facilitates the commission of anonymous crimes, it raises important social issues. Box L.3 describes what might be considered a "perfect crime" possible with anonymous digital cash. Fraud, embezzlement, and transportation of stolen property and information products are other crimes of direct concern. Highly anonymous digital cash may also facilitate money laundering, a key element of many different types of criminal activity. Law enforcement officials consider financial audit trails an essential crime-fighting tool; a digital cash system designed to support the highest levels of anonymity may put such tools at risk.

The important policy issue for digital cash is the extent to which the anonymity possible with physical cash in face-to-face transactions should also be associated with electronic transactions. Note that the question of the appropriate degree of anonymity for a digital cash system replays to a considerable degree the debate over the conditions, if any, under which law enforcement officials should have access to encrypted communications.

L.1.2 Public Trust

Public confidence in the monetary system is a prerequisite for its success. Most members of the public have sufficient confidence in the

---

BOX L.3
A Perfect Crime Using Digital Cash

Anonymous digital cash provides the user with anonymity and untraceability, attributes that could be used, in theory, to commit a "perfect crime"—that is, a crime in which the financial trail is untraceable and therefore useless in identifying and capturing the criminal.

A famous kidnapping case in Tokyo in the early 1970s serves to illustrate the concept. A man opened a bank account under the false name Kobayashi and obtained a credit card drawing on the account. He kidnapped the baby of a famous actor and demanded that a 5 million yen ransom be deposited in the account. The police monitored automated teller machines (ATMs) drawing on Kobayashi's bank, and when Kobayashi later tried to withdraw the ransom money using his card, they arrested him.

Kobayashi's use of a physical token, the credit card, unambiguously linked him to the account. Anonymous digital cash presents the opportunity to eliminate this link. Creation of anonymous cash involves a set of calculations performed in turn by the user who requests the cash and a bank. The user's calculations involve a blinding factor, chosen and known only by him or her. These procedures yield digital cash that the merchant and bank can verify is valid when it is presented for a purchase, while simultaneously making it impossible to trace the cash to the user who originally requested it from the bank.

Ordinarily, the procedures by which digital cash is created occur in a real-time transaction between the user's and the bank's computers. However, a criminal such as the kidnapper Kobayashi could choose a set of blinding factors, perform the subsequent calculations, and mail the results to the bank along with the ransom demand. Kobayashi could insist that the bank perform its portion of the calculations and publish the results in a newspaper. He could then complete the procedures on his own computer. This would give Kobayashi valid, untraceable cash, without the need for any direct link to the bank (such as a visit to an ATM or a dial-in computer connection) that could reveal him to waiting authorities.

SOURCE: Adapted from Sebastiaan von Solms and David Naccache, "On Blind Signatures and Perfect Crimes," *Building in Big Brother*, Lance J. Hoffman (ed.), Springer-Verlag, New York, 1995, pp. 449-452.

---

exchange of physical cash and checks and of credit or debit cards to make the system work. However, the logic underlying these mediums of exchange is straightforward by comparison to the mathematics of digital cash, which are quite complex; a public understanding of how digital cash works may be essential to the success of any such system and to the infrastructure needed to support it.

A second major trust issue relates to the counterfeiting of digital cash. With paper money, the liability for a counterfeit bill belongs to the one who last accepted it because that person could have taken steps to check its legitimacy (e.g., check for a watermark) and thus may not disclaim liability by asserting that it was accepted in good faith. No such protection is available with counterfeit digital cash. An individual can rely only upon the cryptographic protection built into the digital cash system. A forged digital bank note that gets into circulation has by definition broken through that protection; thus, it is the bank that purportedly issued the note that must hold the liability.

L.1.3 Taxation

If a digital cash system is designed to support the highest levels of anonymity so that financial transactions are effectively untraceable, the collection of taxes may become problematic. Most taxes bear some relationship to a financial quantity that must be determined, such as the income collected in a year or the amount of a sales transaction. When money flows only between two parties, how will the government determine how much money has changed hands or even know that a transaction has occurred at all?

L.1.4 Cross-Border Movements of Funds

Governments find it desirable as an instrument of policy to be able to track money flows across their borders. Today, the "cross-border" movement of funds does not really transfer cash. Instead, messages direct actions in, for example, two banks in the United States and two banks in the United Kingdom to complete a transaction involving dollars-to-pounds conversion. Moving cash outside national borders has effects on the economy, and governments will have to come to terms with these effects.

L.2 CRYPTOGRAPHY FOR PROTECTING INTELLECTUAL PROPERTY

Much of the interest in a global information infrastructure comes from the prospect of transporting digitized information objects over communications lines without the need for transport of physical matter. At the same time, concerns are raised about the fact that digital information objects can be retransmitted in the same way by the receiving party. Thus, for example, the entertainment industry looks forward to the possibility of large-scale distribution of its products electronically but is concerned about how to ensure receipt of appropriate compensation for them. Even today, cable television vendors encrypt their transmissions domestically for that very reason. The software industry is concerned about the theft that occurs when a person buys one copy of a software package and duplicates it for resale. Thus, a global information infrastructure raises many questions about how best to compensate authors and producers of intellectual property for each use, as well as how to prevent piracy of intellectual property.[2]

One approach to protecting digital representations of intellectual property involves the use of cryptography to scramble a digital information object.[3] Without the appropriate decryption key, the encrypted object is worthless. The basic notion is that vendors can distribute large digital objects in an encrypted form to users, who would then pay the vendor for the decryption key. Since the decryption key is in general much smaller than the digital object, the cost of transmitting the decryption key is much lower and, for example, could be performed over the telephone upon submission of a credit card number.

The Administration's Working Group on Intellectual Property Rights concluded the following:

> Development of an optimal NII [national information infrastructure] and GII [global information infrastructure] requires strong security as well as strong intellectual property rights. Copyright owners will not use the NII or GII unless they can be assured of strict security to protect against piracy. Encryption technology is vital because it gives copyright owners an additional degree of protection against misappropriation.[4]

Using cryptography to protect intellectual property raises questions related to the strength of algorithms used to encrypt and decrypt digital objects. Specifically, the use of weak cryptography to protect exported digital objects could well result in considerable financial damage to the original creators of intellectual property.[5] If it proves reasonable to protect intellectual property through encryption, pressures may well grow to allow stronger cryptography to be deployed worldwide so that creators of intellectual property can market their products safely and without fear of significant financial loss.

---

[2]See Information Infrastructure Task Force (IITF), Working Group on Intellectual Property Rights, *Intellectual Property and the National Information Infrastructure*, U.S. Government Printing Office, Washington, D.C., 1995.

[3]For example, see Carl Weinschenk, "Cablevision to Test Anti-Theft System," *Cable World*, February 6, 1995, p. 22.

[4]IITF, *Intellectual Property and the National Information Infrastructure*, 1995.

[5]For example, an article in the *Wall Street Journal* reports that pirates of direct digital satellite television broadcasts are able to obtain decoders that are capable of decrypting encrypted signals that are received, thus allowing these individuals to avoid the monthly fee for authorized service. See Jeffrey Trachtenberg and Mark Robichaux, "Crooks Crack Digital Codes of Satellite TV," *Wall Street Journal*, January 12, 1996, p. B1.

Cryptography may also support the embedding of digital "watermarks" into specific pieces of intellectual property to facilitate tracing the theft to an original copy. Such a scheme would insert information that would not affect the use of the object but could be subsequently identified should ownership of that work be called into question. For example, a digital watermark might embed information into a digital representation of a photograph in such a way that it did not affect the visual presentation of the photograph; nevertheless, if the photograph were copied and distributed, all subsequent copies would have that hidden information in them.

M

Federal Information Processing Standards

Agencies at all levels of government set regulatory standards for products and processes in order to protect health, safety, and the environment. They also produce specifications for public procurement of goods and services. The *Federal Register* regularly publishes requests for comments on standards proposed by federal agencies. Some of these are developed by agencies, while others originate as voluntary standards set in the private sector and are adopted by reference within the text of regulations and specifications.

In 1965 the Brooks Act gave responsibility for federal information technology procurement standards to the National Bureau of Standards, now the National Institute of Standards and Technology (NIST).[1] To meet this requirement, NIST produces Federal Information Processing Standards (FIPSs). All federal agencies are encouraged to cite FIPSs in their procurement specifications.

NIST has traditionally relied on private sector standards-setting processes when developing FIPSs.[2] Many standards-setting bodies follow

---

[1] Carl Cargill, *Information Technology Standardization*, Digital Press, Bedford, Mass., 1989, pp. 212-213.

[2] Many standards related to information used in private industry are developed through voluntary consensus processes. Among the most active information technology standards developers are the Institute of Electrical and Electronics Engineers (IEEE), a professional society; the Information Technology Industry Coalition (ITIC), which administers information processing standards development in Committee X3; and the Alliance for Telecommu-

consensus standards development procedures promulgated by the American National Standards Institute (ANSI). These include open participation of volunteer technical experts in standards-writing committees; consensus among committee members in support of any proposed standard; and elements of administrative due process, such as opportunities for comment and voting by affected parties. These procedures increase the likelihood of achieving a broad-based consensus and enhancing the acceptance of the resulting standard.[3]

NIST personnel are frequent participants in consensus standards committees, and FIPSs generally cite or draw on consensus and de facto industry standards.[4] This practice is consistent with government-wide policy; Office of Management and Budget Circular A-119 requires that all federal agencies cite existing consensus standards in regulation and procurement wherever possible, rather than develop government-unique

---

nications Industry Solutions (ATIS), coordinator of Committee T1 for telecommunication standards. The American Banking Association sponsors Committee X9, which is currently developing a cryptographic standard for interbank transactions based on the triple-DES algorithm. The Internet Engineering Task Force determines the protocols that are used (in varying degrees of compliance) to communicate between Internet sites.

Other private sector standards result from competition in the commercial marketplace. When one firm's product becomes so widespread that its specifications guide the decisions of other market participants, those specifications become a de facto industry standard. Firms may promote their technologies as de facto standards in pursuit of goals such as gaining economies of scale, protecting or increasing market share, and obtaining revenues from licensing intellectual property, among others. The IBM-compatible personal computer architecture is an example of a de facto industry standard. See Michael Hergert, "Technical Standards and Competition in the Microcomputer Industry," in H. Landis Gabel (ed.), *Product Standardization and Competitive Strategy*, Elsevier Science Publishers B.V., Amsterdam, 1987.

In recent years, some firms in the information technology industry have tried to establish de facto standards by promoting them through industry consortia. The Open Software Foundation's efforts to set a de facto UNIX operating system standard are an example. See Carl Cargill and Martin Weiss, "Consortia in the Standards Development Process," *Journal of the American Society for Information Science*, Volume 43(8), 1992, pp. 559-565.

The decentralized nature of standard setting in the United States can be confusing and inefficient in specific circumstances. A recent National Research Council study of standards and international trade in many industry sectors concluded, however, that the existence of multiple standard-setting processes generally serves the national interest well, for reasons that include flexibility in responding to changing technological and market forces and competitive pressures placed on rival standards developers. See National Research Council, *Standards, Conformity Assessment, and Trade*, National Academy Press, Washington, D.C., 1995, pp. 60-61.

[3]Ross Cheit, *Setting Safety Standards: Regulation in the Public and Private Sectors*, University of California Press, Berkeley, 1990, p. 15.

[4]Cargill, *Information Technology Standardization*, 1989, pp. 213-214.

standards.[5] NIST's participation also reflects its recognition of the fact that the standards it sets will be more likely to succeed—in terms of reducing procurement costs, raising quality, and influencing the direction of information technology market development—if they are supported by private producers and users.[6]

There is an additional benefit to government reliance on industry standards that is especially relevant to information technology. Recent economic analysis and ample experience demonstrate that standards governing the interoperability of information technology products pose special challenges. Such standards control the ability of separate users, devices, software, and services to work with each other. Examples include computer operating systems and cryptographic algorithms used for communication or data exchange.

Reliance on de facto industry standards may involve problems as well. For example, the establishment of a formal standard based on de facto informal industry standards may freeze technology prematurely. User commitments to the use of that standard and a hard-to-change infrastructure can then restrict the development and deployment of new and more useful technologies. Moreover, a standard that is popular in the marketplace may not necessarily be the most appropriate for all end-user applications.

One vexing problem with industry standards relates to the competitive nature of the marketplace. The setting of a formal standard that has the effect of favoring any individual company or set of companies could be viewed as unfair and anticompetitive if it has the effect of suppressing other, equally useful technologies. Further problems arise if the payment of royalties is necessary to use a particular formal standard, and many standards-setting bodies do not adopt patented technology unless the patent holders agree to certain terms with regard to licensing those who wish to implement the standards.

The issuance of a FIPS can have enormous significance to the private sector as well, despite the face that the existence of a FIPS does not legally compel a private party to adopt it. One reason has already been stated—

---

[5]Office of Management and Budget, Circular No. A-119, Revised, *Federal Register*, October 26, 1993, p. 57644. The Department of Defense, among others, has experienced dramatic reductions in procurement costs by taking advantage of the economies of scale inherent in large-volume commercial production relative to production solely for the government market. Purchasing commercial products also reduces significant cost burdens on suppliers of meeting separate commercial and military-unique standards. For further discussion of government use of private standards, see National Research Council, *Standards, Conformity Assessment, and Trade*, 1995, pp. 54-57.

[6]Cargill, *Information Technology Standardization*, 1989, p. 213.

to the extent that a FIPS is based on existing private sector standards, it codifies standards of existing practice with all of the benefits (and costs) described above. A second reason is that a FIPS is often taken as a government endorsement of the procedures, practices, and algorithms contained therein and thus sets a de facto "best-practices" standard for the private sector. A third reason is related to procurements that are FIPS-compliant as discussed in Chapter 6.

Products such as computers and communication devices that are intended to interoperate with other equipment are of little value if they are based on a standard few others use—there is no one to communicate with. For this reason, interoperability standards often foster a sudden acceleration in market share growth—a bandwagon effect—in which users afraid of being left out rush to adopt a standard once it appears clear that most other users will adopt that standard. The flip side of this phenomenon is the potential for significant delay in development of a market prior to this takeoff point: users put off purchasing products and services that might become "orphaned" in the future. During a period in which more than one competing standard exists, the entire market's growth may be adversely affected. The failure of a consumer market for AM stereo receivers, for example, was largely due to the lack of a dominant standard.[7]

Competing standards developed in the private and public sectors could be slowing the spread of cryptographic products and services. The two cryptography-related FIPSs most recently produced by NIST were not consistent with existing de facto industry standards. As discussed previously, the Escrowed Encryption Standard was adopted as FIPS 185 despite the overwhelmingly negative response from private industry and users to the public notice in the *Federal Register*.[8] The Digital Signature Standard was also adopted despite both negative public comments and the apparent emergence of a de facto industry based on RSA's public-key algorithm.[9]

---

[7]For further discussion of the interactions between interoperability standards and development of markets for goods and services, see Stanley Besen and Joseph Farrell, "Choosing How to Compete: Strategies and Tactics in Standardization," *Journal of Economic Perspectives*, Volume 8(2), Spring 1994, pp. 1-15; and Joseph Farrell and Garth Saloner, "Competition, Compatibility and Standards," *Product Standardization and Competitive Strategy*, H. Landis Gabel, ed. Elsevier Science Publishers B.V., Amsterdam, 1987.

[8]Susan Landau et al., *Codes, Keys, and Conflicts: Issues in U.S. Crypto Policy*, Association for Computing Machinery Inc., New York, 1994, p. 48.

[9]Landau et al., *Codes, Keys, and Conflicts*, 1994, pp. 41-43.

N

Laws, Documents, and Regulations, Relevant to Cryptography

N.1 STATUTES

N.1.1 Wire and Electronic Communications Interception and Interception of Oral Communications (U.S. Code, Title 18, Chapter 119)

Sec. 2510. Definitions.

As used in this chapter:

(1) 'wire communication' means any aural transfer made in whole or in part through the use of facilities for the transmission of communications by the aid of wire, cable, or other like connection between the point of origin and the point of reception (including the use of such connection in a switching station) furnished or operated by any person engaged in providing or operating such facilities for the transmission of interstate or foreign communications or communications affecting interstate or foreign commerce and such term includes any electronic storage of such communication;

NOTE: The material presented in this appendix has been reprinted from electronic files available on the Internet and is intended for use as a general reference, and not for legal research or other work requiring authenticated primary sources.

(2) 'oral communication' means any oral communication uttered by a person exhibiting an expectation that such communication is not subject to interception under circumstances justifying such expectation, but such term does not include any electronic communication;

(3) 'State' means any State of the United States, the District of Columbia, the Commonwealth of Puerto Rico, and any territory or possession of the United States;

(4) 'intercept' means the aural or other acquisition of the contents of any wire, electronic, or oral communication through the use of any electronic, mechanical, or other device;

(5) 'electronic, mechanical, or other device' means any device or apparatus which can be used to intercept a wire, oral, or electronic communication other than—
(a) any telephone or telegraph instrument, equipment or facility, or any component thereof, (i) furnished to the subscriber or user by a provider of wire or electronic communication service in the ordinary course of its business and being used by the subscriber or user in the ordinary course of its business or furnished by such subscriber or user for connection to the facilities of such service and used in the ordinary course of its business; or (ii) being used by a provider of wire or electronic communication service in the ordinary course of its business, or by an investigative or law enforcement officer in the ordinary course of his duties;
(b) a hearing aid or similar device being used to correct subnormal hearing to not better than normal;

(6) 'person' means any employee, or agent of the United States or any State or political subdivision thereof, and any individual, partnership, association, joint stock company, trust, or corporation;

(7) 'Investigative or law enforcement officer' means any officer of the United States or of a State or political subdivision thereof, who is empowered by law to conduct investigations of or to make arrests for offenses enumerated in this chapter, and any attorney authorized by law to prosecute or participate in the prosecution of such offenses;

(8) 'contents', when used with respect to any wire, oral, or electronic communication, includes any information concerning the substance, purport, or meaning of that communication;

(9) 'Judge of competent jurisdiction' means—
(a) a judge of a United States district court or a United States court of appeals; and
(b) a judge of any court of general criminal jurisdiction of a State who is authorized by a statute of that State to enter orders authorizing interceptions of wire, oral, or electronic communications;

(10) 'communication common carrier' shall have the same meaning which is given the term 'common carrier' by section 153(h) of title 47 of the United States Code;

(11) 'aggrieved person' means a person who was a party to any intercepted wire, oral, or electronic communication or a person against whom the interception was directed;

(12) 'electronic communication' means any transfer of signs, signals, writing, images, sounds, data, or intelligence of any nature transmitted in whole or in part by a wire, radio, electromagnetic, photoelectronic or photooptical system that affects interstate or foreign commerce, but does not include—
(a)   any wire or oral communication;
(b)   any communication made through a tone-only paging device; or
(c)   any communication from a tracking device (as defined in section 3117 of this title);

(13) 'user' means any person or entity who—
(a)   uses an electronic communication service; and
(b)   is duly authorized by the provider of such service to engage in such use;

(14) 'electronic communications system' means any wire, radio, electromagnetic, photooptical or photoelectronic facilities for the transmission of electronic communications, and any computer facilities or related electronic equipment for the electronic storage of such communications;

(15) 'electronic communication service' means any service which provides to users thereof the ability to send or receive wire or electronic communications;

(16) 'readily accessible to the general public' means, with respect to a radio communication, that such communication is not—
(a)   scrambled or encrypted;
(b)   transmitted using modulation techniques whose essential parameters have been withheld from the public with the intention of preserving the privacy of such communication;
(c)   carried on a subcarrier or other signal subsidiary to a radio transmission;
(d)   transmitted over a communication system provided by a common carrier, unless the communication is a tone only paging system communication;
(e)   transmitted on frequencies allocated under part 25, subpart D, E, or F of part 74, or part 94 of the Rules of the Federal Communications Commission, unless, in the case of a communication transmitted on a frequency allocated under part 74 that is not exclusively allocated to broadcast auxiliary services, the communication is a two-way voice communication by radio; or
(f)   an electronic communication;

(17) 'electronic storage' means—
(a)   any temporary, intermediate storage of a wire or electronic communication incidental to the electronic transmission thereof; and

(b)   any storage of such communication by an electronic communication service for purposes of backup protection of such communication; and

(18)   'aural transfer' means a transfer containing the human voice at any point between and including the point of origin and the point of reception.

Sec. 2511.   Interception and disclosure of wire, oral, or electronic communications prohibited.

(1)   Except as otherwise specifically provided in this chapter any person who—

(a)   intentionally intercepts, endeavors to intercept, or procures any other person to intercept or endeavor to intercept, any wire, oral, or electronic communication;
(b)   intentionally uses, endeavors to use, or procures any other person to use or endeavor to use any electronic, mechanical, or other device to intercept any oral communication when—
(i)   such device is affixed to, or otherwise transmits a signal through, a wire, cable, or other like connection used in wire communication; or
(ii)   such device transmits communications by radio, or interferes with the transmission of such communication; or
(iii)   such person knows, or has reason to know, that such device or any component thereof has been sent through the mail or transported in interstate or foreign commerce; or
(iv)   such use or endeavor to use
(A)   takes place on the premises of any business or other commercial establishment the operations of which affect interstate or foreign commerce; or
(B)   obtains or is for the purpose of obtaining information relating to the operations of any business or other commercial establishment the operations of which affect interstate or foreign commerce; or
(v)   such person acts in the District of Columbia, the Commonwealth of Puerto Rico, or any territory or possession of the United States; and
(A)   intentionally discloses, or endeavors to disclose, to any other person the contents of any wire, oral, or electronic communication, knowing or having reason to know that the information was obtained through the interception of a wire, oral, or electronic communication in violation of this subsection; or
(B)   intentionally uses, or endeavors to use, the contents of any wire, oral, or electronic communication, knowing or having reason to know that the information was obtained through the interception of a wire, oral, or electronic communication in violation of this subsection;

shall be punished as provided in subsection (4) or shall be subject to suit as provided in subsection (5).

(2)(a)(i)   It shall not be unlawful under this chapter for an operator of a switchboard, or an officer, employee, or agent of a provider of wire or electronic communication service, whose facilities are used in the transmission of a wire or electronic communication, to intercept, disclose, or use that communication in the normal course of his employment while engaged in any activity which is a necessary incident to the rendition of his service or to the protection of the rights or property of the provider of that service, except that a provider of wire communication service to the public shall not utilize service observing or random monitoring except for mechanical or service quality control checks.

(ii)　Notwithstanding any other law, providers of wire or electronic communication service, their officers, employees, and agents, landlords, custodians, or other persons, are authorized to provide information, facilities, or technical assistance to persons authorized by law to intercept wire, oral, or electronic communications or to conduct electronic surveillance, as defined in section 101 of the Foreign Intelligence Surveillance Act of 1978, if such provider, its officers, employees, or agents, landlord, custodian, or other specified person, has been provided with—

(A)　a court order directing such assistance signed by the authorizing judge, or

(B)　a certification in writing by a person specified in section 2518(7) of this title or the Attorney General of the United States that no warrant or court order is required by law, that all statutory requirements have been met, and that the specified assistance is required, setting forth the period of time during which the provision of the information, facilities, or technical assistance is authorized and specifying the information, facilities, or technical assistance required. No provider of wire or electronic communication service, officer, employee, or agent thereof, or landlord, custodian, or other specified person shall disclose the existence of any interception or surveillance or the device used to accomplish the interception or surveillance with respect to which the person has been furnished a court order or certification under this chapter, except as may otherwise be required by legal process and then only after prior notification to the Attorney General or to the principal prosecuting attorney of a State or any political subdivision of a State, as may be appropriate. Any such disclosure, shall render such person liable for the civil damages provided for in section 2520. No cause of action shall lie in any court against any provider of wire or electronic communication service, its officers, employees, or agents, landlord, custodian, or other specified person for providing information, facilities, or assistance in accordance with the terms of a court order or certification under this chapter.

(b)　It shall not be unlawful under this chapter for an officer, employee, or agent of the Federal Communications Commission, in the normal course of his employment and in discharge of the monitoring responsibilities exercised by the Commission in the enforcement of chapter 5 of title 47 of the United States Code, to intercept a wire or electronic communication, or oral communication transmitted by radio, or to disclose or use the information thereby obtained.

(c)　It shall not be unlawful under this chapter for a person acting under color of law to intercept a wire, oral, or electronic communication, where such person is a party to the communication or one of the parties to the communication has given prior consent to such interception.

(d)　It shall not be unlawful under this chapter for a person not acting under color of law to intercept a wire, oral, or electronic communication where such person is a party to the communication or where one of the parties to the communication has given prior consent to such interception unless such communication is intercepted for the purpose of committing any criminal or tortious act in violation of the Constitution or laws of the United States or of any State.

(e)   Notwithstanding any other provision of this title or section 705 or 706 of the Communications Act of 1934, it shall not be unlawful for an officer, employee, or agent of the United States in the normal course of his official duty to conduct electronic surveillance, as defined in section 101 of the Foreign Intelligence Surveillance Act of 1978, as authorized by that Act.

(f)   Nothing contained in this chapter or chapter 121, or section 705 of the Communications Act of 1934, shall be deemed to affect the acquisition by the United States Government of foreign intelligence information from international or foreign communications, or foreign intelligence activities conducted in accordance with otherwise applicable Federal law involving a foreign electronic communications system, utilizing a means other than electronic surveillance as defined in section 101 of the Foreign Intelligence Surveillance Act of 1978, and procedures in this chapter or chapter 121 and the Foreign Intelligence Surveillance Act of 1978 shall be the exclusive means by which electronic surveillance, as defined in section 101 of such Act, and the interception of domestic wire and oral communications may be conducted.

(g)   It shall not be unlawful under this chapter or chapter 121 of this title for any person—

(i)   to intercept or access an electronic communication made through an electronic communication system that is configured so that such electronic communication is readily accessible to the general public;

(ii)   to intercept any radio communication which is transmitted—

(I)   by any station for the use of the general public, or that relates to ships, aircraft, vehicles, or persons in distress;

(II)   by any governmental, law enforcement, civil defense, private land mobile, or public safety communications system, including police and fire, readily accessible to the general public;

(III)   by a station operating on an authorized frequency within the bands allocated to the amateur, citizens band, or general mobile radio services; or

(IV)   by any marine or aeronautical communications system;

(iii)   to engage in any conduct which—

(I)   is prohibited by section 633 of the Communications Act of 1934; or

(II)   is excepted from the application of section 705(a) of the Communications Act of 1934 by section 705(b) of that Act;

(iv)   to intercept any wire or electronic communication the transmission of which is causing harmful interference to any lawfully operating station or consumer electronic equipment, to the extent necessary to identify the source of such interference; or

(v)   for other users of the same frequency to intercept any radio communication made through a system that utilizes frequencies monitored by individuals engaged in the provision or the use of such system, if such communication is not scrambled or encrypted.

(h)   It shall not be unlawful under this chapter—

(i)   to use a pen register or a trap and trace device (as those terms are defined for the purposes of chapter 206 (relating to pen registers and trap and trace devices) of this title); or

(ii) for a provider of electronic communication service to record the fact that a wire or electronic communication was initiated or completed in order to protect such provider, another provider furnishing service toward the completion of the wire or electronic communication, or a user of that service, from fraudulent, unlawful or abusive use of such service.

(3)(a) Except as provided in paragraph (b) of this subsection, a person or entity providing an electronic communication service to the public shall not intentionally divulge the contents of any communication (other than one to such person or entity, or an agent thereof) while in transmission on that service to any person or entity other than an addressee or intended recipient of such communication or an agent of such addressee or intended recipient.

(b) A person or entity providing electronic communication service to the public may divulge the contents of any such communication—

(i) as otherwise authorized in section 2511(2)(a) or 2517 of this title;

(ii) with the lawful consent of the originator or any addressee or intended recipient of such communication;

(iii) to a person employed or authorized, or whose facilities are used, to forward such communication to its destination; or

(iv) which were inadvertently obtained by the service provider and which appear to pertain to the commission of a crime, if such divulgence is made to a law enforcement agency.

(4)(a) Except as provided in paragraph (b) of this subsection or in subsection (5), whoever violates subsection (1) of this section shall be fined under this title or imprisoned not more than five years, or both.

(b) If the offense is a first offense under paragraph (a) of this subsection and is not for a tortious or illegal purpose or for purposes of direct or indirect commercial advantage or private commercial gain, and the wire or electronic communication with respect to which the offense under paragraph (a) is a radio communication that is not scrambled, encrypted, or transmitted using modulation techniques the essential parameters of which have been withheld from the public with the intention of preserving the privacy of such communication, then

(i) if the communication is not the radio portion of a cellular telephone communication, a cordless telephone communication that is transmitted between the cordless telephone handset and the base unit, a public land mobile radio service communication or a paging service communication, and the conduct is not that described in subsection (5), the offender shall be fined under this title or imprisoned not more than one year, or both; and

(ii) if the communication is the radio portion of a cellular telephone communication, a cordless telephone communication that is transmitted between the cordless telephone handset and the base unit, a public land mobile radio service communication or a paging service communication, the offender shall be fined not more than $500.

(c) Conduct otherwise an offense under this subsection that consists of or relates to the interception of a satellite transmission that is not encrypted or scrambled and that is transmitted—

(i)   to a broadcasting station for purposes of retransmission to the general public; or
(ii)   as an audio subcarrier intended for redistribution to facilities open to the public, but not including data transmissions or telephone calls,

is not an offense under this subsection unless the conduct is for the purposes of direct or indirect commercial advantage or private financial gain.

(5)(a)(i)   If the communication is—

(A)   a private satellite video communication that is not scrambled or encrypted and the conduct in violation of this chapter is the private viewing of that communication and is not for a tortious or illegal purpose or for purposes of direct or indirect commercial advantage or private commercial gain; or
(B)   a radio communication that is transmitted on frequencies allocated under subpart D of part 74 of the rules of the Federal Communications Commission that is not scrambled or encrypted and the conduct in violation of this chapter is not for a tortious or illegal purpose or for purposes of direct or indirect commercial advantage or private commercial gain,

then the person who engages in such conduct shall be subject to suit by the Federal Government in a court of competent jurisdiction.
(ii)   In an action under this subsection—
(A)   if the violation of this chapter is a first offense for the person under paragraph (a) of subsection (4) and such person has not been found liable in a civil action under section 2520 of this title, the Federal Government shall be entitled to appropriate injunctive relief; and
(B)   if the violation of this chapter is a second or subsequent offense under paragraph (a) of subsection (4) or such person has been found liable in any prior civil action under section 2520, the person shall be subject to a mandatory $500 civil fine.
(b)   The court may use any means within its authority to enforce an injunction issued under paragraph (ii)(A), and shall impose a civil fine of not less than $500 for each violation of such an injunction.

Sec. 2512.   Manufacture, distribution, possession, and advertising of wire, oral, or electronic communication intercepting devices prohibited.

(1)   Except as otherwise specifically provided in this chapter, any person who intentionally—

(a)   sends through the mail, or sends or carries in interstate or foreign commerce, any electronic, mechanical, or other device, knowing or having reason to know that the design of such device renders it primarily useful for the purpose of the surreptitious interception of wire, oral, or electronic communications;
(b)   manufactures, assembles, possesses, or sells any electronic, mechanical, or other device, knowing or having reason to know that the design of such device renders it primarily useful for the purpose of the surreptitious interception of wire, oral, or electronic communications, and that such device or any component

thereof has been or will be sent through the mail or transported in interstate or foreign commerce; or

(c) places in any newspaper, magazine, handbill, or other publication any advertisement of—

(i) any electronic, mechanical, or other device knowing or having reason to know that the design of such device renders it primarily useful for the purpose of the surreptitious interception of wire, oral, or electronic communications; or

(ii) any other electronic, mechanical, or other device, where such advertisement promotes the use of such device for the purpose of the surreptitious interception of wire, oral, or electronic communications, knowing or having reason to know that such advertisement will be sent through the mail or transported in interstate or foreign commerce,

shall be fined not more than $10,000 or imprisoned not more than five years, or both.

(2) It shall not be unlawful under this section for—

(a) a provider of wire or electronic communication service or an officer, agent, or employee of, or a person under contract with, such a provider, in the normal course of the business of providing that wire or electronic communication service; or

(b) an officer, agent, or employee of, or a person under contract with, the United States, a State, or a political subdivision thereof, in the normal course of the activities of the United States, a State, or a political subdivision thereof,

to send through the mail, send or carry in interstate or foreign commerce, or manufacture, assemble, possess, or sell any electronic, mechanical, or other device knowing or having reason to know that the design of such device renders it primarily useful for the purpose of the surreptitious interception of wire, oral, or electronic communications.

Sec. 2513. Confiscation of wire, oral, or electronic communication intercepting devices.

Any electronic, mechanical, or other device used, sent, carried, manufactured, assembled, possessed, sold, or advertised in violation of section 2511 or section 2512 of this chapter may be seized and forfeited to the United States. All provisions of law relating to (1) the seizure, summary and judicial forfeiture, and condemnation of vessels, vehicles, merchandise, and baggage for violations of the customs laws contained in title 19 of the United States Code, (2) the disposition of such vessels, vehicles, merchandise, and baggage or the proceeds from the sale thereof, (3) the remission or mitigation of such forfeiture, (4) the compromise of claims, and (5) the award of compensation to informers in respect of such forfeitures, shall apply to seizures and forfeitures incurred, or alleged to have been incurred, under the provisions of this section, insofar as applicable and not inconsistent with the provisions of this section; except that such duties as are imposed upon the collector of customs or any other person with respect to the seizure and forfeiture of vessels, vehicles, merchandise, and baggage under the provisions of the customs laws contained in title 19 of the United States Code shall be performed with respect to seizure and forfeiture of electronic, mechanical, or other intercepting devices under this section by such officers, agents, or other persons as may be authorized or designated for that purpose by the Attorney General.

Sec. 2514.   Repealed.

Sec. 2515.   Prohibition of use as evidence of intercepted wire or oral communications.

Whenever any wire or oral communication has been intercepted, no part of the contents of such communication and no evidence derived therefrom may be received in evidence in any trial, hearing, or other proceeding in or before any court, grand jury, department, officer, agency, regulatory body, legislative committee, or other authority of the United States, a State, or a political subdivision thereof if the disclosure of that information would be in violation of this chapter.

Sec. 2516.   Authorization for interception of wire, oral, or electronic communications.

(1)   The Attorney General, Deputy Attorney General, Associate Attorney General,[1] or any Assistant Attorney General, any acting Assistant Attorney General, or any Deputy Assistant Attorney General or acting Deputy Assistant Attorney General in the Criminal Division specially designated by the Attorney General, may authorize an application to a Federal judge of competent jurisdiction for, and such judge may grant in conformity with section 2518 of this chapter an order authorizing or approving the interception of wire or oral communications by the Federal Bureau of Investigation, or a Federal agency having responsibility for the investigation of the offense as to which the application is made, when such interception may provide or has provided evidence of—
(a)   any offense punishable by death or by imprisonment for more than one year under sections 2274 through 2277 of title 42 of the United States Code (relating to the enforcement of the Atomic Energy Act of 1954), section 2284 of title 42 of the United States Code (relating to sabotage of nuclear facilities or fuel), or under the following chapters of this title: chapter 37 (relating to espionage), chapter 105 (relating to sabotage), chapter 115 (relating to treason), chapter 102 (relating to riots), chapter 65 (relating to malicious mischief), chapter 111 (relating to destruction of vessels), or chapter 81 (relating to piracy);

---

[1]See 1984 Amendment note below.

(b)   a violation of section 186 or section 501(c) of title 29, United States Code (dealing with restrictions on payments and loans to labor organizations), or any offense which involves murder, kidnapping, robbery, or extortion, and which is punishable under this title;

(c)   any offense which is punishable under the following sections of this title: section 201 (bribery of public officials and witnesses), section 215 (relating to bribery of bank officials), section 224 (bribery in sporting contests), subsection (d), (e), (f), (g), (h), or (i) of section 844 (unlawful use of explosives), section 1032 (relating to concealment of assets), section 1084 (transmission of wagering information), section 751 (relating to escape), section 1014 (relating to loans and credit applications generally; renewals and discounts), sections 1503, 1512, and 1513 (influencing or injuring an officer, juror, or witness generally), section 1510 (obstruction of criminal investigations), section 1511 (obstruction of State or local law enforcement), section 1751 (Presidential and Presidential staff assassination, kidnaping, and assault), section 1951 (interference with commerce by threats or violence), section 1952 (interstate and foreign travel or transportation in aid of racketeering enterprises), section 1958 (relating to use of interstate commerce facilities in the commission of murder for hire), section 1959 (relating to violent crimes in aid of racketeering activity), section 1954 (offer, acceptance, or solicitation to influence operations of employee benefit plan), section 1955 (prohibition of business enterprises of gambling), section 1956 (laundering of monetary instruments), section 1957 (relating to engaging in monetary transactions in property derived from specified unlawful activity), section 659 (theft from interstate shipment), section 664 (embezzlement from pension and welfare funds), section 1343 (fraud by wire, radio, or television), section 1344 (relating to bank fraud), sections 2251 and 2252 (sexual exploitation of children), sections 2312, 2313, 2314, and 2315 (interstate transportation of stolen property), section 2321 (relating to trafficking in certain motor vehicles or motor vehicle parts), section 1203 (relating to hostage taking), section 1029 (relating to fraud and related activity in connection with access devices), section 3146 (relating to penalty for failure to appear), section 3521(b)(3) (relating to witness relocation and assistance), section 32 (relating to destruction of aircraft or aircraft facilities), section 1963 (violations with respect to racketeer influenced and corrupt organizations), section 115 (relating to threatening or retaliating against a Federal official), and section 1341 (relating to mail fraud), section 351 (violations with respect to congressional, Cabinet, or Supreme Court assassinations, kidnaping, and assault), section 831 (relating to prohibited transactions involving nuclear materials), section 33 (relating to destruction of motor vehicles or motor vehicle facilities), section 175 (relating to biological weapons), or section 1992 (relating to wrecking trains);

(d)   any offense involving counterfeiting punishable under section 471, 472, or 473 of this title;

(e)   any offense involving fraud connected with a case under title 11 or the manufacture, importation, receiving, concealment, buying, selling, or otherwise dealing in narcotic drugs, marihuana, or other dangerous drugs, punishable under any law of the United States;

(f)   any offense including extortionate credit transactions under sections 892, 893, or 894 of this title;

(g)   a violation of section 5322 of title 31, United States Code (dealing with the reporting of currency transactions);

(h)   any felony violation of sections 2511 and 2512 (relating to interception and disclosure of certain communications and to certain intercepting devices) of this title;

(i)   any felony violation of chapter 71 (relating to obscenity) of this title;

(j)   any violation of section 11(c)(2) of the Natural Gas Pipeline Safety Act of 1968 (relating to destruction of a natural gas pipeline) or subsection (i) or (n) of section 902 of the Federal Aviation Act of 1958 (relating to aircraft piracy);

(k)   any criminal violation of section 2778 of title 22 (relating to the Arms Export Control Act);

(l)   the location of any fugitive from justice from an offense described in this section; or[2]

(m)   any felony violation of sections 922 and 924 of title 18, United States Code (relating to firearms);

(n)   any violation of section 5861 of the Internal Revenue Code of 1986 (relating to firearms); and[3]

(o)   any conspiracy to commit any offense described in any subparagraph of this paragraph.

(2)   The principal prosecuting attorney of any State, or the principal prosecuting attorney of any political subdivision thereof, if such attorney is authorized by a statute of that State to make application to a State court judge of competent jurisdiction for an order authorizing or approving the interception of wire, oral, or electronic communications, may apply to such judge for, and such judge may grant in conformity with section 2518 of this chapter and with the applicable State statute an order authorizing, or approving the interception of wire, oral, or electronic communications by investigative or law enforcement officers having responsibility for the investigation of the offense as to which the application is made, when such interception may provide or has provided evidence of the commission of the offense of murder, kidnapping, gambling, robbery, bribery, extortion, or dealing in narcotic drugs, marihuana or other dangerous drugs, or other crime dangerous to life, limb, or property, and punishable by imprisonment for more than one year, designated in any applicable State statute authorizing such interception, or any conspiracy to commit any of the foregoing offenses.

(3)   Any attorney for the Government (as such term is defined for the purposes of the Federal Rules of Criminal Procedure) may authorize an application to a Federal judge of competent jurisdiction for, and such judge may grant, in conformity with section 2518 of this title, an order authorizing or approving the interception of electronic communications by an investigative or law enforcement officer having responsibility for the investigation of the offense as to which the application is made, when such interception may provide or has provided evidence of any Federal felony.

---

[2]So in original. The word 'or' probably should not appear.

[3]So in original. Probably should be 'or'.

Sec. 2517. Authorization for disclosure and use of intercepted wire, oral, or electronic communications.

(1) Any investigative or law enforcement officer who, by any means authorized by this chapter, has obtained knowledge of the contents of any wire, oral, or electronic communication, or evidence derived therefrom, may disclose such contents to another investigative or law enforcement officer to the extent that such disclosure is appropriate to the proper performance of the official duties of the officer making or receiving the disclosure.

(2) Any investigative or law enforcement officer who, by any means authorized by this chapter, has obtained knowledge of the contents of any wire, oral, or electronic communication or evidence derived therefrom may use such contents to the extent such use is appropriate to the proper performance of his official duties.

(3) Any person who has received, by any means authorized by this chapter, any information concerning a wire, oral, or electronic communication, or evidence derived therefrom intercepted in accordance with the provisions of this chapter may disclose the contents of that communication or such derivative evidence while giving testimony under oath or affirmation in any proceeding held under the authority of the United States or of any State or political subdivision thereof.

(4) No otherwise privileged wire, oral, or electronic communication intercepted in accordance with, or in violation of, the provisions of this chapter shall lose its privileged character.

(5) When an investigative or law enforcement officer, while engaged in intercepting wire, oral, or electronic communications in the manner authorized herein, intercepts wire, oral, or electronic communications relating to offenses other than those specified in the order of authorization or approval, the contents thereof, and evidence derived therefrom, may be disclosed or used as provided in subsections (1) and (2) of this section. Such contents and any evidence derived therefrom may be used under subsection (3) of this section when authorized or approved by a judge of competent jurisdiction where such judge finds on subsequent application that the contents were otherwise intercepted in accordance with the provisions of this chapter. Such application shall be made as soon as practicable.

Sec. 2518. Procedure for interception of wire, oral, or electronic communications.

(1) Each application for an order authorizing or approving the interception of a wire, oral, or electronic communication under this chapter shall be made in writing upon oath or affirmation to a judge of competent jurisdiction and shall

state the applicant's authority to make such application. Each application shall include the following information:

(a)   the identity of the investigative or law enforcement officer making the application, and the officer authorizing the application;

(b)   a full and complete statement of the facts and circumstances relied upon by the applicant, to justify his belief that an order should be issued, including (i) details as to the particular offense that has been, is being, or is about to be committed, (ii) except as provided in subsection (11), a particular description of the nature and location of the facilities from which or the place where the communication is to be intercepted, (iii) a particular description of the type of communications sought to be intercepted, (iv) the identity of the person, if known, committing the offense and whose communications are to be intercepted;

(c)   a full and complete statement as to whether or not other investigative procedures have been tried and failed or why they reasonably appear to be unlikely to succeed if tried or to be too dangerous;

(d)   a statement of the period of time for which the interception is required to be maintained. If the nature of the investigation is such that the authorization for interception should not automatically terminate when the described type of communication has been first obtained, a particular description of facts establishing probable cause to believe that additional communications of the same type will occur thereafter;

(e)   a full and complete statement of the facts concerning all previous applications known to the individual authorizing and making the application, made to any judge for authorization to intercept, or for approval of interceptions of, wire, oral, or electronic communications involving any of the same persons, facilities or places specified in the application, and the action taken by the judge on each such application; and

(f)   where the application is for the extension of an order, a statement setting forth the results thus far obtained from the interception, or a reasonable explanation of the failure to obtain such results.

(2)   The judge may require the applicant to furnish additional testimony or documentary evidence in support of the application.

(3)   Upon such application the judge may enter an ex parte order, as requested or as modified, authorizing or approving interception of wire, oral, or electronic communications within the territorial jurisdiction of the court in which the judge is sitting (and outside that jurisdiction but within the United States in the case of a mobile interception device authorized by a Federal court within such jurisdiction), if the judge determines on the basis of the facts submitted by the applicant that—

(a)   there is probable cause for belief that an individual is committing, has committed, or is about to commit a particular offense enumerated in section 2516 of this chapter;

(b)   there is probable cause for belief that particular communications concerning that offense will be obtained through such interception;

(c) normal investigative procedures have been tried and have failed or reasonably appear to be unlikely to succeed if tried or to be too dangerous;

(d) except as provided in subsection (11), there is probable cause for belief that the facilities from which, or the place where, the wire, oral, or electronic communications are to be intercepted are being used, or are about to be used, in connection with the commission of such offense, or are leased to, listed in the name of, or commonly used by such person.

(4) Each order authorizing or approving the interception of any wire, oral, or electronic communication under this chapter shall specify—

(a) the identity of the person, if known, whose communications are to be intercepted;

(b) the nature and location of the communications facilities as to which, or the place where, authority to intercept is granted;

(c) a particular description of the type of communication sought to be intercepted, and a statement of the particular offense to which it relates;

(d) the identity of the agency authorized to intercept the communications, and of the person authorizing the application; and

(e) the period of time during which such interception is authorized, including a statement as to whether or not the interception shall automatically terminate when the described communication has been first obtained. An order authorizing the interception of a wire, oral, or electronic communication under this chapter shall, upon request of the applicant, direct that a provider of wire or electronic communication service, landlord, custodian or other person shall furnish the applicant forthwith all information, facilities, and technical assistance necessary to accomplish the interception unobtrusively and with a minimum of interference with the services that such service provider, landlord, custodian, or person is according the person whose communications are to be intercepted. Any provider of wire or electronic communication service, landlord, custodian or other person furnishing such facilities or technical assistance shall be compensated therefor by the applicant for reasonable expenses incurred in providing such facilities or assistance.

Pursuant to section 2522 of this chapter, an order may also be issued to enforce the assistance capability and capacity requirements under the Communications Assistance for Law Enforcement Act.

(5) No order entered under this section may authorize or approve the interception of any wire, oral, or electronic communication for any period longer than is necessary to achieve the objective of the authorization, nor in any event longer than thirty days. Such thirty-day period begins on the earlier of the day on which the investigative or law enforcement officer first begins to conduct an interception under the order or ten days after the order is entered. Extensions of an order may be granted, but only upon application for an extension made in accordance with subsection (1) of this section and the court making the findings required by subsection (3) of this section. The period of extension shall be no longer than the authorizing judge deems necessary to achieve the purposes for

which it was granted and in no event for longer than thirty days. Every order and extension thereof shall contain a provision that the authorization to intercept shall be executed as soon as practicable, shall be conducted in such a way as to minimize the interception of communications not otherwise subject to interception under this chapter, and must terminate upon attainment of the authorized objective, or in any event in thirty days. In the event the intercepted communication is in a code or foreign language, and an expert in that foreign language or code is not reasonably available during the interception period, minimization may be accomplished as soon as practicable after such interception. An interception under this chapter may be conducted in whole or in part by Government personnel, or by an individual operating under a contract with the Government, acting under the supervision of an investigative or law enforcement officer authorized to conduct the interception.

(6)   Whenever an order authorizing interception is entered pursuant to this chapter, the order may require reports to be made to the judge who issued the order showing what progress has been made toward achievement of the authorized objective and the need for continued interception. Such reports shall be made at such intervals as the judge may require.

(7)   Notwithstanding any other provision of this chapter, any investigative or law enforcement officer, specially designated by the Attorney General, the Deputy Attorney General, the Associate Attorney General, or by the principal prosecuting attorney of any State or subdivision thereof acting pursuant to a statute of that State, who reasonably determines that—

(a)   an emergency situation exists that involves—
(i)   immediate danger of death or serious physical injury to any person,
(ii)   conspiratorial activities threatening the national security interest, or
(iii)   conspiratorial activities characteristic of organized crime, that requires a wire, oral, or electronic communication to be intercepted before an order authorizing such interception can, with due diligence, be obtained, and
(b)   there are grounds upon which an order could be entered under this chapter to authorize such interception,

may intercept such wire, oral, or electronic communication if an application for an order approving the interception is made in accordance with this section within forty-eight hours after the interception has occurred, or begins to occur. In the absence of an order, such interception shall immediately terminate when the communication sought is obtained or when the application for the order is denied, whichever is earlier. In the event such application for approval is denied, or in any other case where the interception is terminated without an order having been issued, the contents of any wire, oral, or electronic communication intercepted shall be treated as having been obtained in violation of this chapter, and an inventory shall be served as provided for in subsection (d) of this section on the person named in the application.

(8)(a) The contents of any wire, oral, or electronic communication intercepted by any means authorized by this chapter shall, if possible, be recorded on tape or wire or other comparable device. The recording of the contents of any wire, oral, or electronic communication under this subsection shall be done in such a way as will protect the recording from editing or other alterations. Immediately upon the expiration of the period of the order, or extensions thereof, such recordings shall be made available to the judge issuing such order and sealed under his directions. Custody of the recordings shall be wherever the judge orders. They shall not be destroyed except upon an order of the issuing or denying judge and in any event shall be kept for ten years. Duplicate recordings may be made for use or disclosure pursuant to the provisions of subsections (1) and (2) of section 2517 of this chapter for investigations. The presence of the seal provided for by this subsection, or a satisfactory explanation for the absence thereof, shall be a prerequisite for the use or disclosure of the contents of any wire, oral, or electronic communication or evidence derived therefrom under subsection (3) of section 2517.

(b) Applications made and orders granted under this chapter shall be sealed by the judge. Custody of the applications and orders shall be wherever the judge directs. Such applications and orders shall be disclosed only upon a showing of good cause before a judge of competent jurisdiction and shall not be destroyed except on order of the issuing or denying judge, and in any event shall be kept for ten years.

(c) Any violation of the provisions of this subsection may be punished as contempt of the issuing or denying judge.

(d) Within a reasonable time but not later than ninety days after the filing of an application for an order of approval under section 2518(7)(b) which is denied or the termination of the period of an order or extensions thereof, the issuing or denying judge shall cause to be served, on the persons named in the order or the application, and such other parties to intercepted communications as the judge may determine in his discretion that is in the interest of justice, an inventory which shall include notice of—

(1) the fact of the entry of the order or the application;
(2) the date of the entry and the period of authorized, approved or disapproved interception, or the denial of the application; and
(3) the fact that during the period wire, oral, or electronic communications were or were not intercepted.

The judge, upon the filing of a motion, may in his discretion make available to such person or his counsel for inspection such portions of the intercepted communications, applications and orders as the judge determines to be in the interest of justice. On an ex parte showing of good cause to a judge of competent jurisdiction the serving of the inventory required by this subsection may be postponed.

(9) The contents of any wire, oral, or electronic communication intercepted pursuant to this chapter or evidence derived therefrom shall not be received in evidence or otherwise disclosed in any trial, hearing, or other proceeding in a Federal or State court unless each party, not less than ten days before the trial,

hearing, or proceeding, has been furnished with a copy of the court order, and accompanying application, under which the interception was authorized or approved. This ten-day period may be waived by the judge if he finds that it was not possible to furnish the party with the above information ten days before the trial, hearing, or proceeding and that the party will not be prejudiced by the delay in receiving such information.

(10)(a)   Any aggrieved person in any trial, hearing, or proceeding in or before any court, department, officer, agency, regulatory body, or other authority of the United States, a State, or a political subdivision thereof, may move to suppress the contents of any wire or oral communication intercepted pursuant to this chapter, or evidence derived therefrom, on the grounds that—
(i)   the communication was unlawfully intercepted;
(ii)   the order of authorization or approval under which it was intercepted is insufficient on its face; or
(iii)   the interception was not made in conformity with the order of authorization or approval.

Such motion shall be made before the trial, hearing, or proceeding unless there was no opportunity to make such motion or the person was not aware of the grounds of the motion. If the motion is granted, the contents of the intercepted wire or oral communication, or evidence derived therefrom, shall be treated as having been obtained in violation of this chapter. The judge, upon the filing of such motion by the aggrieved person, may in his discretion make available to the aggrieved person or his counsel for inspection such portions of the intercepted communication or evidence derived therefrom as the judge determines to be in the interests of justice.
(b)   In addition to any other right to appeal, the United States shall have the right to appeal from an order granting a motion to suppress made under paragraph (a) of this subsection, or the denial of an application for an order of approval, if the United States attorney shall certify to the judge or other official granting such motion or denying such application that the appeal is not taken for purposes of delay. Such appeal shall be taken within thirty days after the date the order was entered and shall be diligently prosecuted.
(c)   The remedies and sanctions described in this chapter with respect to the interception of electronic communications are the only judicial remedies and sanctions for nonconstitutional violations of this chapter involving such communications.

(11)   The requirements of subsections (1)(b)(ii) and (3)(d) of this section relating to the specification of the facilities from which, or the place where, the communication is to be intercepted do not apply if—
(a)   in the case of an application with respect to the interception of an oral communication—
(i)   the application is by a Federal investigative or law enforcement officer and is approved by the Attorney General, the Deputy Attorney General, the Associate

Attorney General, an Assistant Attorney General, or an acting Assistant Attorney General;

(ii)   the application contains a full and complete statement as to why such specification is not practical and identifies the person committing the offense and whose communications are to be intercepted; and

(iii)   the judge finds that such specification is not practical; and

(b)   in the case of an application with respect to a wire or electronic communication—

(i)   the application is by a Federal investigative or law enforcement officer and is approved by the Attorney General, the Deputy Attorney General, the Associate Attorney General, an Assistant Attorney General, or an acting Assistant Attorney General;

(ii)   the application identifies the person believed to be committing the offense and whose communications are to be intercepted and the applicant makes a showing of a purpose, on the part of that person, to thwart interception by changing facilities; and

(iii)   the judge finds that such purpose has been adequately shown.

(12)   An interception of a communication under an order with respect to which the requirements of subsections (1)(b)(ii) and (3)(d) of this section do not apply by reason of subsection (11) shall not begin until the facilities from which, or the place where, the communication is to be intercepted is ascertained by the person implementing the interception order. A provider of wire or electronic communications service that has received an order as provided for in subsection (11)(b) may move the court to modify or quash the order on the ground that its assistance with respect to the interception cannot be performed in a timely or reasonable fashion. The court, upon notice to the government, shall decide such a motion expeditiously.

Sec. 2519.   Reports concerning intercepted wire, oral, or electronic communications.

(1)   Within thirty days after the expiration of an order (or each extension thereof) entered under section 2518, or the denial of an order approving an interception, the issuing or denying judge shall report to the Administrative Office of the United States Courts—

(a)   the fact that an order or extension was applied for;

(b)   the kind of order or extension applied for (including whether or not the order was an order with respect to which the requirements of sections 2518(1)(b)(ii) and 2518(3)(d) of this title did not apply by reason of section 2518(11) of this title);

(c)   the fact that the order or extension was granted as applied for, was modified, or was denied;

(d)   the period of interceptions authorized by the order, and the number and duration of any extensions of the order;

(e)   the offense specified in the order or application, or extension of an order;

(f)   the identity of the applying investigative or law enforcement officer and agency making the application and the person authorizing the application; and
(g)   the nature of the facilities from which or the place where communications were to be intercepted.

(2)   In January of each year the Attorney General, an Assistant Attorney General specially designated by the Attorney General, or the principal prosecuting attorney of a State, or the principal prosecuting attorney for any political subdivision of a State, shall report to the Administrative Office of the United States Courts—
(a)   the information required by paragraphs (a) through (g) of subsection (1) of this section with respect to each application for an order or extension made during the preceding calendar year;
(b)   a general description of the interceptions made under such order or extension, including (i) the approximate nature and frequency of incriminating communications intercepted, (ii) the approximate nature and frequency of other communications intercepted, (iii) the approximate number of persons whose communications were intercepted, and (iv) the approximate nature, amount, and cost of the manpower and other resources used in the interceptions;
(c)   the number of arrests resulting from interceptions made under such order or extension, and the offenses for which arrests were made;
(d)   the number of trials resulting from such interceptions;
(e)   the number of motions to suppress made with respect to such interceptions, and the number granted or denied;
(f)   the number of convictions resulting from such interceptions and the offenses for which the convictions were obtained and a general assessment of the importance of the interceptions; and
(g)   the information required by paragraphs (b) through (f) of this subsection with respect to orders or extensions obtained in a preceding calendar year.

(3)   In April of each year the Director of the Administrative Office of the United States Courts shall transmit to the Congress a full and complete report concerning the number of applications for orders authorizing or approving the interception of wire, oral, or electronic communications pursuant to this chapter and the number of orders and extensions granted or denied pursuant to this chapter during the preceding calendar year. Such report shall include a summary and analysis of the data required to be filed with the Administrative Office by subsections (1) and (2) of this section. The Director of the Administrative Office of the United States Courts is authorized to issue binding regulations dealing with the content and form of the reports required to be filed by subsections (1) and (2) of this section.

Sec. 2520.   Recovery of civil damages authorized.

(a)   In General.—Except as provided in section 2511(2)(a)(ii), any person whose wire, oral, or electronic communication is intercepted, disclosed, or intentionally used in violation of this chapter may in a civil action recover from the person or entity which engaged in that violation such relief as may be appropriate.

(b) Relief.—In an action under this section, appropriate relief includes—
(1) such preliminary and other equitable or declaratory relief as may be appropriate;
(2) damages under subsection (c) and punitive damages in appropriate cases; and
(3) a reasonable attorney's fee and other litigation costs reasonably incurred.

(c) Computation of Damages.—(1) In an action under this section, if the conduct in violation of this chapter is the private viewing of a private satellite video communication that is not scrambled or encrypted or if the communication is a radio communication that is transmitted on frequencies allocated under subpart D of part 74 of the rules of the Federal Communications Commission that is not scrambled or encrypted and the conduct is not for a tortious or illegal purpose or for purposes of direct or indirect commercial advantage or private commercial gain, then the court shall assess damages as follows:
(A) If the person who engaged in that conduct has not previously been enjoined under section 2511(5) and has not been found liable in a prior civil action under this section, the court shall assess the greater of the sum of actual damages suffered by the plaintiff, or statutory damages of not less than $50 and not more than $500.
(B) If, on one prior occasion, the person who engaged in that conduct has been enjoined under section 2511(5) or has been found liable in a civil action under this section, the court shall assess the greater of the sum of actual damages suffered by the plaintiff, or statutory damages of not less than $100 and not more than $1000.
(2) In any other action under this section, the court may assess as damages whichever is the greater of—
(A) the sum of the actual damages suffered by the plaintiff and any profits made by the violator as a result of the violation; or
(B) statutory damages of whichever is the greater of $100 a day for each day of violation or $10,000.

(d) Defense.—A good faith reliance on—

(1) a court warrant or order, a grand jury subpoena, a legislative authorization, or a statutory authorization;
(2) a request of an investigative or law enforcement officer under section 2518(7) of this title; or
(3) a good faith determination that section 2511(3) of this title permitted the conduct complained of;

is a complete defense against any civil or criminal action brought under this chapter or any other law.

(e) Limitation.—A civil action under this section may not be commenced later than two years after the date upon which the claimant first has a reasonable opportunity to discover the violation.

Sec. 2521.   Injunction against illegal interception.

Whenever it shall appear that any person is engaged or is about to engage in any act which constitutes or will constitute a felony violation of this chapter, the Attorney General may initiate a civil action in a district court of the United States to enjoin such violation. The court shall proceed as soon as practicable to the hearing and determination of such an action, and may, at any time before final determination, enter such a restraining order or prohibition, or take such other action, as is warranted to prevent a continuing and substantial injury to the United States or to any person or class of persons for whose protection the action is brought. A proceeding under this section is governed by the Federal Rules of Civil Procedure, except that, if an indictment has been returned against the respondent, discovery is governed by the Federal Rules of Criminal Procedure.

Sec. 2522.   Enforcement of the Communications Assistance for Law Enforcement Act.

(a)   Enforcement by Court Issuing Surveillance Order.—If a court authorizing an interception under this chapter, a State statute, or the Foreign Intelligence Surveillance Act of 1978 (50 U.S.C. 1801 et seq.) or authorizing use of a pen register or a trap and trace device under chapter 206 or a State statute finds that a telecommunications carrier has failed to comply with the requirements of the Communications Assistance for Law Enforcement Act, the court may, in accordance with section 108 of such Act, direct that the carrier comply forthwith and may direct that a provider of support services to the carrier or the manufacturer of the carrier's transmission or switching equipment furnish forthwith modifications necessary for the carrier to comply.

(b)   Enforcement Upon Application by Attorney General.—The Attorney General may, in a civil action in the appropriate United States district court, obtain an order, in accordance with section 108 of the Communications Assistance for Law Enforcement Act, directing that a telecommunications carrier, a manufacturer of telecommunications transmission or switching equipment, or a provider of telecommunications support services comply with such Act.

(c)   Civil Penalty.—
(1)   In General.—A court issuing an order under this section against a telecommunications carrier, a manufacturer of telecommunications transmission or switching equipment, or a provider of telecommunications support services may

impose a civil penalty of up to $10,000 per day for each day in violation after the issuance of the order or after such future date as the court may specify.

(2) Considerations.—In determining whether to impose a civil penalty and in determining its amount, the court shall take into account—

(A) the nature, circumstances, and extent of the violation;

(B) the violator's ability to pay, the violator's good faith efforts to comply in a timely manner, any effect on the violator's ability to continue to do business, the degree of culpability, and the length of any delay in undertaking efforts to comply; and

(C) such other matters as justice may require.

(d) Definitions.—As used in this section, the terms defined in section 102 of the Communications Assistance for Law Enforcement Act have the meanings provided, respectively, in such section.

N.1.2 Foreign Intelligence Surveillance (U.S. Code, Title 50, Chapter 36)

Sec. 1801. Definitions.

As used in this chapter:

(a) 'Foreign power' means—

(1) a foreign government or any component thereof, whether or not recognized by the United States;

(2) a faction of a foreign nation or nations, not substantially composed of United States persons;

(3) an entity that is openly acknowledged by a foreign government or governments to be directed and controlled by such foreign government or governments;

(4) a group engaged in international terrorism or activities in preparation therefor;

(5) a foreign-based political organization, not substantially composed of United States persons; or

(6) an entity that is directed and controlled by a foreign government or governments.

(b) 'Agent of a foreign power' means—

(1) any person other than a United States person, who—

(A) acts in the United States as an officer or employee of a foreign power, or as a member of a foreign power as defined in subsection (a)(4) of this section;

(B) acts for or on behalf of a foreign power which engages in clandestine intelligence activities in the United States contrary to the interests of the United States, when the circumstances of such person's presence in the United States indicate that such person may engage in such activities in the United States, or when such person knowingly aids or abets any person in the conduct of such activities or knowingly conspires with any person to engage in such activities; or

(2) any person who—

(A)   knowingly engages in clandestine intelligence gathering activities for or on behalf of a foreign power, which activities involve or may involve a violation of the criminal statutes of the United States;

(B)   pursuant to the direction of an intelligence service or network of a foreign power, knowingly engages in any other clandestine intelligence activities for or on behalf of such foreign power, which activities involve or are about to involve a violation of the criminal statutes of the United States;

(C)   knowingly engages in sabotage or international terrorism, or activities that are in preparation therefor, for or on behalf of a foreign power; or

(D)   knowingly aids or abets any person in the conduct of activities described in subparagraph (A), (B), or (C) or knowingly conspires with any person to engage in activities described in subparagraph (A), (B), or (C).

(c)   'International terrorism' means activities that—

(1)   involve violent acts or acts dangerous to human life that are a violation of the criminal laws of the United States or of any State, or that would be a criminal violation if committed within the jurisdiction of the United States or any State;

(2)   appear to be intended—

(A)   to intimidate or coerce a civilian population;

(B)   to influence the policy of a government by intimidation or coercion; or

(C)   to affect the conduct of a government by assassination or kidnapping; and

(3)   occur totally outside the United States, or transcend national boundaries in terms of the means by which they are accomplished, the persons they appear intended to coerce or intimidate, or the locale in which their perpetrators operate or seek asylum.

(d)   'Sabotage' means activities that involve a violation of chapter 105 of title 18, or that would involve such a violation if committed against the United States.

(e)   'Foreign intelligence information' means—

(1)   information that relates to, and if concerning a United States person is necessary to, the ability of the United States to protect against—

(A)   actual or potential attack or other grave hostile acts of a foreign power or an agent of a foreign power;

(B)   sabotage or international terrorism by a foreign power or an agent of a foreign power; or

(C)   clandestine intelligence activities by an intelligence service or network of a foreign power or by an agent of a foreign power; or

(2)   information with respect to a foreign power or foreign territory that relates to, and if concerning a United States person is necessary to—

(A)   the national defense or the security of the United States; or

(B)   the conduct of the foreign affairs of the United States.

(f)   'Electronic surveillance' means—

(1)   the acquisition by an electronic, mechanical, or other surveillance device of the contents of any wire or radio communication sent by or intended to be re-

ceived by a particular, known United States person who is in the United States, if the contents are acquired by intentionally targeting that United States person, under circumstances in which a person has a reasonable expectation of privacy and a warrant would be required for law enforcement purposes;

(2) the acquisition by an electronic, mechanical, or other surveillance device of the contents of any wire communication to or from a person in the United States, without the consent of any party thereto, if such acquisition occurs in the United States;

(3) the intentional acquisition by an electronic, mechanical, or other surveillance device of the contents of any radio communication, under circumstances in which a person has a reasonable expectation of privacy and a warrant would be required for law enforcement purposes, and if both the sender and all intended recipients are located within the United States; or

(4) the installation or use of an electronic, mechanical, or other surveillance device in the United States for monitoring to acquire information, other than from a wire or radio communication, under circumstances in which a person has a reasonable expectation of privacy and a warrant would be required for law enforcement purposes.

(g) 'Attorney General' means the Attorney General of the United States (or Acting Attorney General) or the Deputy Attorney General.

(h) 'Minimization procedures', with respect to electronic surveillance, means—

(1) specific procedures, which shall be adopted by the Attorney General, that are reasonably designed in light of the purpose and technique of the particular surveillance, to minimize the acquisition and retention, and prohibit the dissemination, of nonpublicly available information concerning unconsenting United States persons consistent with the need of the United States to obtain, produce, and disseminate foreign intelligence information;

(2) procedures that require that nonpublicly available information, which is not foreign intelligence information, as defined in subsection (e)(1) of this section, shall not be disseminated in a manner that identifies any United States person, without such person's consent, unless such person's identity is necessary to understand foreign intelligence information or assess its importance;

(3) notwithstanding paragraphs (1) and (2), procedures that allow for the retention and dissemination of information that is evidence of a crime which has been, is being, or is about to be committed and that is to be retained or disseminated for law enforcement purposes; and

(4) notwithstanding paragraphs (1), (2), and (3), with respect to any electronic surveillance approved pursuant to section 1802(a) of this title, procedures that require that no contents of any communication to which a United States person is a party shall be disclosed, disseminated, or used for any purpose or retained for longer than twenty-four hours unless a court order under section 1805 of this title is obtained or unless the Attorney General determines that the information indicates a threat of death or serious bodily harm to any person.

(i) 'United States person' means a citizen of the United States, an alien lawfully admitted for permanent residence (as defined in section 1101(a)(20) of title 8), an unincorporated association a substantial number of members of which are citizens of the United States or aliens lawfully admitted for permanent residence, or a corporation which is incorporated in the United States, but does not include a corporation or an association which is a foreign power, as defined in subsection (a)(1), (2), or (3) of this section.

(j) 'United States', when used in a geographic sense, means all areas under the territorial sovereignty of the United States and the Trust Territory of the Pacific Islands.

(k) 'Aggrieved person' means a person who is the target of an electronic surveillance or any other person whose communications or activities were subject to electronic surveillance.

(l) 'Wire communication' means any communication while it is being carried by a wire, cable, or other like connection furnished or operated by any person engaged as a common carrier in providing or operating such facilities for the transmission of interstate or foreign communications.

(m) 'Person' means any individual, including any officer or employee of the Federal Government, or any group, entity, association, corporation, or foreign power.

(n) 'Contents', when used with respect to a communication, includes any information concerning the identity of the parties to such communication or the existence, substance, purport, or meaning of that communication.

(o) 'State' means any State of the United States, the District of Columbia, the Commonwealth of Puerto Rico, the Trust Territory of the Pacific Islands, and any territory or possession of the United States.

Sec. 1802. Electronic surveillance authorization without court order; certification by Attorney General; reports to Congressional committees; transmittal under seal; duties and compensation of communication common carrier; applications; jurisdiction of court.

(a)(1) Notwithstanding any other law, the President, through the Attorney General, may authorize electronic surveillance without a court order under this chapter to acquire foreign intelligence information for periods of up to one year if the Attorney General certifies in writing under oath that—

(A) the electronic surveillance is solely directed at—
(i) the acquisition of the contents of communications transmitted by means of communications used exclusively between or among foreign powers, as defined in section 1801(a)(1), (2), or (3) of this title; or
(ii) the acquisition of technical intelligence, other than the spoken communica-

tions of individuals, from property or premises under the open and exclusive control of a foreign power, as defined in section 1801(a)(1), (2), or (3) of this title;

(B) there is no substantial likelihood that the surveillance will acquire the contents of any communication to which a United States person is a party; and

(C) the proposed minimization procedures with respect to such surveillance meet the definition of minimization procedures under section 1801(h) of this title;

and if the Attorney General reports such minimization procedures and any changes thereto to the House Permanent Select Committee on Intelligence and the Senate Select Committee on Intelligence at least thirty days prior to their effective date, unless the Attorney General determines immediate action is required and notifies the committees immediately of such minimization procedures and the reason for their becoming effective immediately.

(a)(2) An electronic surveillance authorized by this subsection may be conducted only in accordance with the Attorney General's certification and the minimization procedures adopted by him. The Attorney General shall assess compliance with such procedures and shall report such assessments to the House Permanent Select Committee on Intelligence and the Senate Select Committee on Intelligence under the provisions of section 1808(a) of this title.

(a)(3) The Attorney General shall immediately transmit under seal to the court established under section 1803(a) of this title a copy of his certification. Such certification shall be maintained under security measures established by the Chief Justice with the concurrence of the Attorney General, in consultation with the Director of Central Intelligence, and shall remain sealed unless—

(A) an application for a court order with respect to the surveillance is made under sections 1801(h)(4) and 1804 of this title; or

(B) the certification is necessary to determine the legality of the surveillance under section 1806(f) of this title.

(a)(4) With respect to electronic surveillance authorized by this subsection, the Attorney General may direct a specified communication common carrier to—

(A) furnish all information, facilities, or technical assistance necessary to accomplish the electronic surveillance in such a manner as will protect its secrecy and produce a minimum of interference with the services that such carrier is providing its customers; and

(B) maintain under security procedures approved by the Attorney General and the Director of Central Intelligence any records concerning the surveillance or the aid furnished which such carrier wishes to retain. The Government shall compensate, at the prevailing rate, such carrier for furnishing such aid.

(b) Applications for a court order under this chapter are authorized if the President has, by written authorization, empowered the Attorney General to approve applications to the court having jurisdiction under section 1803 of this title, and a judge to whom an application is made may, notwithstanding any other law, grant an order, in conformity with section 1805 of this title, approving electronic surveillance of a foreign power or an agent of a foreign power for the purpose of obtaining foreign intelligence information, except that the court shall not have jurisdiction to grant any order approving electronic surveillance directed solely as described in paragraph (1)(A) of subsection (a) of this section unless such surveillance may involve the acquisition of communications of any United States person.

Sec. 1803.   Designation of judges.

(a)   Court to hear applications and grant orders; record of denial; transmittal to court of review.—The Chief Justice of the United States shall publicly designate seven district court judges from seven of the United States judicial circuits who shall constitute a court which shall have jurisdiction to hear applications for and grant orders approving electronic surveillance anywhere within the United States under the procedures set forth in this Act, except that no judge designated under this subsection shall hear the same application for electronic surveillance under this Act which has been denied previously by another judge designated under this subsection. If any judge so designated denies an application for an order authorizing electronic surveillance under this Act, such judge shall provide immediately for the record a written statement of each reason of his decision and, on motion of the United States, the record shall be transmitted, under seal, to the court of review established in subsection (b) of this section.

(b)   Court of review; record, transmittal to Supreme Court;—The Chief Justice shall publicly designate three judges, one of whom shall be publicly designated as the presiding judge, from the United States district courts or courts of appeals who together shall comprise a court of review which shall have jurisdiction to review the denial of any application made under this Act. If such court determines that the application was properly denied, the court shall immediately provide for the record a written statement of each reason for its decision and, on petition of the United States for a writ of certiorari, the record shall be transmitted under seal to the Supreme Court, which shall have jurisdiction to review such decision.

(c)   Expeditious conduct of proceedings; security measures for maintenance of records.—Proceedings under this Act shall be conducted as expeditiously as possible. The record of proceedings under this Act, including applications made and orders granted, shall be maintained under security measures established by the Chief Justice in consultation with the Attorney General and the Director of Central Intelligence.

(d)   Tenure;—Each judge designated under this section shall so serve for a maximum of seven years and shall not be eligible for redesignation, except that the judges first designated under subsection (a) of this section shall be designated for terms of from one to seven years so that one term expires each year, and that judges first designated under subsection (b) of this section shall be designated for terms of three, five, and seven years.

Sec. 1804.   Applications for court orders.

(a)   Submission by Federal officer; approval of Attorney General; contents.—Each application for an order approving electronic surveillance under this chapter shall be made by a Federal officer in writing upon oath or affirmation to a judge having jurisdiction under section 1803 of this title. Each application shall require the approval of the Attorney General based upon his finding that it satisfies the criteria and requirements of such application as set forth in this chapter. It shall include—

(1)   the identity of the Federal officer making the application;

(2)   the authority conferred on the Attorney General by the President of the United States and the approval of the Attorney General to make the application;

(3)   the identity, if known, or a description of the target of the electronic surveillance;

(4)   a statement of the facts and circumstances relied upon by the applicant to justify his belief that—

(A)   the target of the electronic surveillance is a foreign power or an agent of a foreign power; and

(B)   each of the facilities or places at which the electronic surveillance is directed is being used, or is about to be used, by a foreign power or an agent of a foreign power;

(5)   a statement of the proposed minimization procedures;

(6)   a detailed description of the nature of the information sought and the type of communications or activities to be subjected to the surveillance;

(7)   a certification or certifications by the Assistant to the President for National Security Affairs or an executive branch official or officials designated by the President from among those executive officers employed in the area of national security or defense and appointed by the President with the advice and consent of the Senate—

(A)   that the certifying official deems the information sought to be foreign intelligence information;

(B)   that the purpose of the surveillance is to obtain foreign intelligence information;

(C)   that such information cannot reasonably be obtained by normal investigative techniques;

(D)   that designates the type of foreign intelligence information being sought according to the categories described in section 1801(e) of this title; and

(E)   including a statement of the basis for the certification that—

(i)   the information sought is the type of foreign intelligence information designated; and

(ii)   such information cannot reasonably be obtained by normal investigative techniques;

(8)   a statement of the means by which the surveillance will be effected and a statement whether physical entry is required to effect the surveillance;

(9)   a statement of the facts concerning all previous applications that have been made to any judge under this chapter involving any of the persons, facilities, or places specified in the application, and the action taken on each previous application;

(10)   a statement of the period of time for which the electronic surveillance is required to be maintained, and if the nature of the intelligence gathering is such that the approval of the use of electronic surveillance under this chapter should

not automatically terminate when the described type of information has first been obtained, a description of facts supporting the belief that additional information of the same type will be obtained thereafter; and

(11)   whenever more than one electronic, mechanical or other surveillance device is to be used with respect to a particular proposed electronic surveillance, the coverage of the devices involved and what minimization procedures apply to information acquired by each device.

(b)   Exclusion of certain information respecting foreign power targets.— Whenever the target of the electronic surveillance is a foreign power, as defined in section 1801(a)(1), (2), or (3) of this title, and each of the facilities or places at which the surveillance is directed is owned, leased, or exclusively used by that foreign power, the application need not contain the information required by paragraphs (6), (7)(E), (8), and (11) of subsection (a) of this section, but shall state whether physical entry is required to effect the surveillance and shall contain such information about the surveillance techniques and communications or other information concerning United States persons likely to be obtained as may be necessary to assess the proposed minimization procedures.

(c)   Additional affidavits or certifications.—The Attorney General may require any other affidavit or certification from any other officer in connection with the application.

(d)   Additional information.—The judge may require the applicant to furnish such other information as may be necessary to make the determinations required by section 1805 of this title.

Sec. 1805.   Issuance of order.

(a)   Necessary findings.—Upon an application made pursuant to section 1804 of this title, the judge shall enter an ex parte order as requested or as modified approving the electronic surveillance if he finds that—

(1)   the President has authorized the Attorney General to approve applications for electronic surveillance for foreign intelligence information;

(2)   the application has been made by a Federal officer and approved by the Attorney General;

(3)   on the basis of the facts submitted by the applicant there is probable cause to believe that—

(A)   the target of the electronic surveillance is a foreign power or an agent of a foreign power: Provided, That no United States person may be considered a foreign power or an agent of a foreign power solely upon the basis of activities protected by the first amendment to the Constitution of the United States; and

(B)   each of the facilities or places at which the electronic surveillance is directed is being used, or is about to be used, by a foreign power or an agent of a foreign power;

(4) the proposed minimization procedures meet the definition of minimization procedures under section 1804(h) of this title; and

(5) the application which has been filed contains all statements and certifications required by section 1804 of this title and, if the target is a United States person, the certification or certifications are not clearly erroneous on the basis of the statement made under section 1804(a)(7)(E) of this title and any other information furnished under section 1804(d) of this title.

(b) Specifications and directions of orders.—An order approving an electronic surveillance under this section shall—

(1) specify—

(A) the identity, if known, or a description of the target of the electronic surveillance;

(B) the nature and location of each of the facilities or places at which the electronic surveillance will be directed;

(C) the type of information sought to be acquired and the type of communications or activities to be subjected to the surveillance;

(D) the means by which the electronic surveillance will be effected and whether physical entry will be used to effect the surveillance;

(E) the period of time during which the electronic surveillance is approved; and

(F) whenever more than one electronic, mechanical, or other surveillance device is to be used under the order, the authorized coverage of the devices involved and what minimization procedures shall apply to information subject to acquisition by each device; and

(2) direct—

(A) that the minimization procedures be followed;

(B) that, upon the request of the applicant, a specified communication or other common carrier, landlord, custodian, or other specified person furnish the applicant forthwith all information, facilities, or technical assistance necessary to accomplish the electronic surveillance in such a manner as will protect its secrecy and produce a minimum of interference with the services that such carrier, landlord, custodian, or other person is providing that target of electronic surveillance;

(C) that such carrier, landlord, custodian, or other person maintain under security procedures approved by the Attorney General and the Director of Central Intelligence any records concerning the surveillance or the aid furnished that such person wishes to retain; and

(D) that the applicant compensate, at the prevailing rate, such carrier, landlord, custodian, or other person for furnishing such aid.

(c) Exclusion of certain information respecting foreign power targets.— Whenever the target of the electronic surveillance is a foreign power, as defined in section 1801(a)(1), (2), or (3) of this title, and each of the facilities or places at which the surveillance is directed is owned, leased, or exclusively used by that foreign power, the order need not contain the information required by subparagraphs (C), (D), and (F) of subsection (b)(1) of this section, but shall generally describe the information sought, the communications or activities to be subjected to the surveillance, and the type of electronic surveillance involved, including whether physical entry is required.

(d) Duration of order; extensions; review of circumstances under which information was acquired, retained or disseminated.

(1) An order issued under this section may approve an electronic surveillance for the period necessary to achieve its purpose, or for ninety days, whichever is less, except that an order under this section shall approve an electronic surveillance targeted against a foreign power, as defined in section 1801(a)(1), (2), or (3) of this title, for the period specified in the application or for one year, whichever is less.

(2) Extensions of an order issued under this chapter may be granted on the same basis as an original order upon an application for an extension and new findings made in the same manner as required for an original order, except that an extension of an order under this Act for a surveillance targeted against a foreign power, as defined in section 1801(a)(5) or (6) of this title, or against a foreign power as defined in section 1801(a)(4) of this title that is not a United States person, may be for a period not to exceed one year if the judge finds probable cause to believe that no communication of any individual United States person will be acquired during the period.

(3) At or before the end of the period of time for which electronic surveillance is approved by an order or an extension, the judge may assess compliance with the minimization procedures by reviewing the circumstances under which information concerning United States persons was acquired, retained, or disseminated.

(e) Emergency orders.—Notwithstanding any other provision of this chapter, when the Attorney General reasonably determines that—

(1) an emergency situation exists with respect to the employment of electronic surveillance to obtain foreign intelligence information before an order authorizing such surveillance can with due diligence be obtained; and

(2) the factual basis for issuance of an order under this chapter to approve such surveillance exists;

he may authorize the emergency employment of electronic surveillance if a judge having jurisdiction under section 1803 of this title is informed by the Attorney General or his designee at the time of such authorization that the decision has been made to employ emergency electronic surveillance and if an application in accordance with this chapter is made to that judge as soon as practicable, but not more than twenty-four hours after the Attorney General authorizes such surveillance. If the Attorney General authorizes such emergency employment of electronic surveillance, he shall require that the minimization procedures required by this chapter for the issuance of a judicial order be followed. In the absence of a judicial order approving such electronic surveillance, the surveillance shall terminate when the information sought is obtained, when the application for the order is denied, or after the expiration of twenty-four hours from the time of authorization by the Attorney General, whichever is earliest. In the event that such application for approval is denied, or in any other case where the electronic surveillance is terminated and no order is issued approving the surveillance, no information obtained or evidence derived from such surveillance shall be received in evidence or otherwise disclosed in any trial, hearing, or other proceeding in or before any court, grand jury, department, office, agency, regulatory body, legislative committee, or other authority of the United States, a State, or political subdivision thereof, and no information concerning any United States person acquired from such surveillance shall subsequently be used or disclosed in any other manner by Federal officers or employees without the consent of such person, except with the approval of the Attorney General if the information indicates a threat of death or serious bodily harm to any person. A denial of the application made under this subsection may be reviewed as provided in section 1803 of this title.

(f) Testing of electronic equipment; discovering unauthorized electronic surveillance; training of intelligence personnel.—Notwithstanding any other provision of this chapter, officers, employees, or agents of the United States are authorized in the normal course of their official duties to conduct electronic surveillance not targeted against the communications of any particular person or persons, under procedures approved by the Attorney General, solely to—

(1)   test the capability of electronic equipment, if—

(A)   it is not reasonable to obtain the consent of the persons incidentally subjected to the surveillance;

(B)   the test is limited in extent and duration to that necessary to determine the capability of the equipment;

(C)   the contents of any communication acquired are retained and used only for the purpose of determining the capability of the equipment, are disclosed only to test personnel, and are destroyed before or immediately upon completion of the test; and:

(D)   Provided, That the test may exceed ninety days only with the prior approval of the Attorney General;

(2)   determine the existence and capability of electronic surveillance equipment being used by persons not authorized to conduct electronic surveillance, if—

(A)   it is not reasonable to obtain the consent of persons incidentally subjected to the surveillance;

(B)   such electronic surveillance is limited in extent and duration to that necessary to determine the existence and capability of such equipment; and

(C)   any information acquired by such surveillance is used only to enforce chapter 119 of title 18, or section 605 of title 47, or to protect information from unauthorized surveillance; or

(3)   train intelligence personnel in the use of electronic surveillance equipment, if—

(A)   it is not reasonable to—

(i)   obtain the consent of the persons incidentally subjected to the surveillance;

(ii)   train persons in the course of surveillances otherwise authorized by this chapter; or

(iii)   train persons in the use of such equipment without engaging in electronic surveillance;

(B)   such electronic surveillance is limited in extent and duration to that necessary to train the personnel in the use of the equipment; and

(C)   no contents of any communication acquired are retained or disseminated for any purpose, but are destroyed as soon as reasonably possible.

(g) Retention of certifications, applications and orders.—Certifications made by the Attorney General pursuant to section 1802(a) of this title and applications made and orders granted under this chapter shall be retained for a period of at least ten years from the date of the certification or application.

Sec. 1806. Use of information.

(a) Compliance with minimization procedures; privileged communications; lawful purposes.—Information acquired from an electronic surveillance conducted pursuant to this chapter concerning any United States person may be used and disclosed by Federal officers and employees without the consent of the United States person only in accordance with the minimization procedures required by this chapter. No otherwise privileged communication obtained in accordance with, or in violation of, the provisions of this chapter shall lose its privileged character. No information acquired from an electronic surveillance pursuant to this chapter may be used or disclosed by Federal officers or employees except for lawful purposes.

(b) Statement for disclosure.—No information acquired pursuant to this chapter shall be disclosed for law enforcement purposes unless such disclosure is accompanied by a statement that such information, or any information derived therefrom, may only be used in a criminal proceeding with the advance authorization of the Attorney General.

(c) Notification by United States.—Whenever the Government intends to enter into evidence or otherwise use or disclose in any trial, hearing, or other proceeding in or before any court, department, officer, agency, regulatory body, or other authority of the United States, against an aggrieved person, any information obtained or derived from an electronic surveillance of that aggrieved person pursuant to the authority of this chapter, the Government shall, prior to the trial, hearing, or other proceeding or at a reasonable time prior to an effort to so disclose or so use that information or submit it in evidence, notify the aggrieved person and the court or other authority in which the information is to be disclosed or used that the Government intends to so disclose or so use such information.

(d) Notification by States or political subdivisions.—Whenever any State or political subdivision thereof intends to enter into evidence or otherwise use or disclose in any trial, hearing, or other proceeding in or before any court, department, officer, agency, regulatory body, or other authority of a State or a political subdivision thereof, against an aggrieved person any information obtained or derived from an electronic surveillance of that aggrieved person pursuant to the authority of this chapter, the State or political subdivision thereof shall notify the aggrieved person, the court or other authority in which the information is to be disclosed or used, and the Attorney General that the State or political subdivision thereof intends to so disclose or so use such information.

(e)   Motion to suppress.—Any person against whom evidence obtained or derived from an electronic surveillance to which he is an aggrieved person is to be, or has been, introduced or otherwise used or disclosed in any trial, hearing, or other proceeding in or before any court, department, officer, agency, regulatory body, or other authority of the United States, a State, or a political subdivision thereof, may move to suppress the evidence obtained or derived from such electronic surveillance on the grounds that—

(1)   the information was unlawfully acquired; or
(2)   the surveillance was not made in conformity with an order of authorization or approval.

Such a motion shall be made before the trial, hearing, or other proceeding unless there was no opportunity to make such a motion or the person was not aware of the grounds of the motion.

(f)   In camera and ex parte review by district court.—Whenever a court or other authority is notified pursuant to subsection (c) or (d) of this section, or whenever a motion is made pursuant to subsection (e) of this section, or whenever any motion or request is made by an aggrieved person pursuant to any other statute or rule of the United States or any State before any court or other authority of the United States or any State to discover or obtain applications or orders or other materials relating to electronic surveillance or to discover, obtain, or suppress evidence or information obtained or derived from electronic surveillance under this Act, the United States district court or, where the motion is made before another authority, the United States district court in the same district as the authority, shall, notwithstanding any other law, if the Attorney General files an affidavit under oath that disclosure or an adversary hearing would harm the national security of the United States, review in camera and ex parte the application, order, and such other materials relating to the surveillance as may be necessary to determine whether the surveillance of the aggrieved person was lawfully authorized and conducted. In making this determination, the court may disclose to the aggrieved person, under appropriate security procedures and protective orders, portions of the application, order, or other materials relating to the surveillance only where such disclosure is necessary to make an accurate determination of the legality of the surveillance.

(g)   Suppression of evidence; denial of motion.—If the United States district court pursuant to subsection (f) of this section determines that the surveillance was not lawfully authorized or conducted, it shall, in accordance with the requirements of law, suppress the evidence which was unlawfully obtained or derived from electronic surveillance of the aggrieved person or otherwise grant the motion of the aggrieved person. If the court determines that the surveillance was lawfully authorized and conducted, it shall deny the motion of the aggrieved person except to the extent that due process requires discovery or disclosure.

(h)   Finality of orders.—Orders granting motions or requests under subsection (g) of this section, decisions under this section that electronic surveillance was not lawfully authorized or conducted, and orders of the United States district court requiring review or granting disclosure of applications, orders, or other materials relating to a surveillance shall be final orders and binding upon all courts of the United States and the several States except a United States court of appeals and the Supreme Court.

(i)   Destruction of unintentionally acquired information.—In circumstances involving the unintentional acquisition by an electronic, mechanical, or other surveillance device of the contents of any radio communication, under circumstances in which a person has a reasonable expectation of privacy and a warrant would be required for law enforcement purposes, and if both the sender and all intended recipients are located within the United States, such contents shall be destroyed upon recognition, unless the Attorney General determines that the contents indicate a threat of death or serious bodily harm to any person.

(j)   Notification of emergency employment of electronic surveillance; contents; postponement, suspension or elimination.—If an emergency employment of electronic surveillance is authorized under section 1805(e) of this title and a subsequent order approving the surveillance is not obtained, the judge shall cause to be served on any United States person named in the application and on such other United States persons subject to electronic surveillance as the judge may determine in his discretion it is in the interest of justice to serve, notice of—

(1)   the fact of the application;
(2)   the period of the surveillance; and
(3)   the fact that during the period information was or was not obtained.

On an ex parte showing of good cause to the judge the serving of the notice required by this subsection may be postponed or suspended for a period not to exceed ninety days. Thereafter, on a further ex parte showing of good cause, the court shall forego ordering the serving of the notice required under this subsection.

Sec. 1807.   Report to Administrative Office of the United States Court and to Congress.

In April of each year, the Attorney General shall transmit to the Administrative Office of the United States Court and to Congress a report setting forth with respect to the preceding calendar year—

(a)   the total number of applications made for orders and extensions of orders approving electronic surveillance under this chapter; and

(b)   the total number of such orders and extensions either granted, modified, or denied.

Sec. 1808. Report of Attorney General to Congressional committees; limitation on authority or responsibility of information gathering activities of Congressional committees; report of Congressional committees to Congress.

(a) On a semiannual basis the Attorney General shall fully inform the House Permanent Select Committee on Intelligence and the Senate Select Committee on Intelligence concerning all electronic surveillance under this chapter. Nothing in this chapter shall be deemed to limit the authority and responsibility of the appropriate committees of each House of Congress to obtain such information as they may need to carry out their respective functions and duties.

(b) On or before one year after October 25, 1978, and on the same day each year for four years thereafter, the Permanent Select Committee on Intelligence and the Senate Select Committee on Intelligence shall report respectively to the House of Representatives and the Senate, concerning the implementation of this Act. Said reports shall include but not be limited to an analysis and recommendations concerning whether this Act should be

(1) amended,
(2) repealed, or
(3) permitted to continue in effect without amendment.

Sec. 1809. Criminal sanctions.

(a) *Prohibited activities* A person is guilty of an offense if he intentionally—

(1) engages in electronic surveillance under color of law except as authorized by statute; or
(2) discloses or uses information obtained under color of law by electronic surveillance, knowing or having reason to know that the information was obtained through electronic surveillance not authorized by statute.

(b) *Defense* It is a defense to a prosecution under subsection (a) of this section that the defendant was a law enforcement or investigative officer engaged in the course of his official duties and the electronic surveillance was authorized by and conducted pursuant to a search warrant or court order of a court of competent jurisdiction.

(c) *Penalties* An offense described in this section is punishable by a fine of not more than $10,000 or imprisonment for not more than five years, or both.

(d) *Federal jurisdiction* There is Federal jurisdiction over an offense under this section if the person committing the offense was an officer or employee of the United States at the time the offense was committed.

Sec. 1810.   Civil liability.

An aggrieved person, other than a foreign power or an agent of a foreign power, as defined in section 1801(a) or (b)(1)(A) of this title, respectively, who has been subjected to an electronic surveillance or about whom information obtained by electronic surveillance of such person has been disclosed or used in violation of section 1809 of this title shall have a cause of action against any person who committed such violation and shall be entitled to recover—
(a)   actual damages, but not less than liquidated damages of $1,000 or $100 per day for each day of violation, whichever is greater;
(b)   punitive damages; and
(c)   reasonable attorney's fees and other investigation and litigation costs reasonably incurred.

Sec. 1811.   Authorization during time of war.

Notwithstanding any other law, the President, through the Attorney General, may authorize electronic surveillance without a court order under this chapter to acquire foreign intelligence information for a period not to exceed fifteen calendar days following a declaration of war by the Congress.

N.1.3   Pen Register and Traffic Analysis (U.S. Code, Title 18, Chapters 121 and 206)

Chapter 121

Sec. 2701.   Unlawful access to stored communications.

(a)   Offense.—Except as provided in subsection (c) of this section whoever—

(1)   intentionally accesses without authorization a facility through which an electronic communication service is provided; or
(2)   intentionally exceeds an authorization to access that facility;

and thereby obtains, alters, or prevents authorized access to a wire or electronic communication while it is in electronic storage in such system shall be punished as provided in subsection (b) of this section.

(b)   Punishment.— The punishment for an offense under subsection (a) of this section is—
(1)   if the offense is committed for purposes of commercial advantage, malicious destruction or damage, or private commercial gain—
(A)   a fine of not more than $250,000 or imprisonment for not more than one year, or both, in the case of a first offense under this subparagraph; and

(B)   a fine under this title or imprisonment for not more than two years, or both, for any subsequent offense under this subparagraph; and
(2)   a fine of not more than $5,000 or imprisonment for not more than six months, or both, in any other case.

(c)   Exceptions.— Subsection (a) of this section does not apply with respect to conduct authorized—
(1)   by the person or entity providing a wire or electronic communications service;
(2)   by a user of that service with respect to a communication of or intended for that user; or
(3)   in section 2703, 2704 or 2518 of this title.

Sec. 2702.   Disclosure of contents.

(a)   Prohibitions.—Except as provided in subsection (b)—
(1)   a person or entity providing an electronic communication service to the public shall not knowingly divulge to any person or entity the contents of a communication while in electronic storage by that service; and
(2)   a person or entity providing remote computing service to the public shall not knowingly divulge to any person or entity the contents of any communication which is carried or maintained on that service—
(A)   on behalf of, and received by means of electronic transmission from (or created by means of computer processing of communications received by means of electronic transmission from), a subscriber or customer of such service; and
(B)   solely for the purpose of providing storage or computer processing services to such subscriber or customer, if the provider is not authorized to access the contents of any such communications for purposes of providing any services other than storage or computer processing.

(b)   Exceptions.—A person or entity may divulge the contents of a communication—
(1)   to an addressee or intended recipient of such communication or an agent of such addressee or intended recipient;
(2)   as otherwise authorized in section 2517, 2511(2)(a), or 2703 of this title;
(3)   with the lawful consent of the originator or an addressee or intended recipient of such communication, or the subscriber in the case of remote computing service;
(4)   to a person employed or authorized or whose facilities are used to forward such communication to its destination;
(5)   as may be necessarily incident to the rendition of the service or to the protection of the rights or property of the provider of that service; or
(6)   to a law enforcement agency, if such contents—
(A)   were inadvertently obtained by the service provider; and
(B)   appear to pertain to the commission of a crime.

Sec. 2703.   Requirements for governmental access.

(a)   Contents of Electronic Communications in Electronic Storage.—A governmental entity may require the disclosure by a provider of electronic communication service of the contents of an electronic communication, that is in electronic storage in an electronic communications system for one hundred and eighty days or less, only pursuant to a warrant issued under the Federal Rules of Criminal Procedure or equivalent State warrant. A governmental entity may require the disclosure by a provider of electronic communications services of the contents of an electronic communication that has been in electronic storage in an electronic communications system for more than one hundred and eighty days by the means available under subsection (b) of this section.

(b)   Contents of Electronic Communications in a Remote Computing Service.—
(1)   A governmental entity may require a provider of remote computing service to disclose the contents of any electronic communication to which this paragraph is made applicable by paragraph (2) of this subsection—
(A)   without required notice to the subscriber or customer, if the governmental entity obtains a warrant issued under the Federal Rules of Criminal Procedure or equivalent State warrant; or (B) with prior notice from the governmental entity to the subscriber or customer if the governmental entity—
(i)   uses an administrative subpoena authorized by a Federal or State statute or a Federal or State grand jury or trial subpoena; or
(ii)   obtains a court order for such disclosure under subsection (d) of this section; except that delayed notice may be given pursuant to section 2705 of this title.
(2)   Paragraph one is applicable with respect to any electronic communication that is held or maintained on that service—
(A)   on behalf of, and received by means of electronic transmission from (or created by means of computer processing of communications received by means of electronic transmission from), a subscriber or customer of such remote computing service; and
(B)   solely for the purpose of providing storage or computer processing services to such subscriber or customer, if the provider is not authorized to access the contents of any such communications for purposes of providing any services other than storage or computer processing.

(c)   Records Concerning Electronic Communication Service or Remote Computing Service.—
(1)(A)   Except as provided in subparagraph (B), a provider of electronic communication service or remote service may disclose a record or other information pertaining to a subscriber to or customer of such service (not including the contents of communications covered by subsection (a) or (b) of this section) to any person other than a governmental entity.
(B)   A provider of electronic communication service or remote computing service shall disclose a record or other information pertaining to a subscriber to or customer of such service (not including the contents of communications covered

by subsection (a) or (b) of this section) to a governmental entity only when the governmental entity—

(i)   obtains a warrant issued under the Federal Rules of Criminal Procedure or equivalent State warrant;

(ii)   obtains a court order for such disclosure under subsection (d) of this section; or

(iii)   has the consent of the subscriber or customer to such disclosure.

(C)   A provider of electronic communication service or remote computing service shall disclose to a governmental entity the name, address, telephone toll billing records, telephone number or other subscriber number or identity, and length of service of a subscriber to or customer of such service and the types of services the subscriber or customer utilized, when the governmental entity uses an administrative subpoena authorized by a Federal or State statute or a Federal or State grand jury or trial subpoena or any means available under subparagraph (B).

(2)   A governmental entity receiving records or information under this subsection is not required to provide notice to a subscriber or customer.

(d)   Requirements for Court Order.—A court order for disclosure under subsection (b) or (c) may be issued by any court that is a court of competent jurisdiction described in section 3126(2)(A) and shall issue only if the governmental entity offers specific and articulable facts showing that there are reasonable grounds to believe that the contents of a wire or electronic communication, or the records or other information sought, are relevant and material to an ongoing criminal investigation. In the case of a State governmental authority, such a court order shall not issue if prohibited by the law of such State. A court issuing an order pursuant to this section, on a motion made promptly by the service provider, may quash or modify such order, if the information or records requested are unusually voluminous in nature or compliance with such order otherwise would cause an undue burden on such provider.

(e)   No Cause of Action Against a Provider Disclosing Information Under This Chapter.—No cause of action shall lie in any court against any provider of wire or electronic communication service, its officers, employees, agents, or other specified persons for providing information, facilities, or assistance in accordance with the terms of a court order, warrant, subpoena, or certification under this chapter.

Sec. 2704.   Backup preservation.

(a)   Backup Preservation.—

(1)   A governmental entity acting under section 2703(b)(2) may include in its subpoena or court order a requirement that the service provider to whom the request is directed create a backup copy of the contents of the electronic communications sought in order to preserve those communications.

Without notifying the subscriber or customer of such subpoena or court order, such service provider shall create such backup copy as soon as practicable consistent with its regular business practices and shall confirm to the governmental entity that such backup copy has been made. Such backup copy shall be created within two business days after receipt by the service provider of the subpoena or court order.

(2)   Notice to the subscriber or customer shall be made by the governmental entity within three days after receipt of such confirmation, unless such notice is delayed pursuant to section 2705(a).

(3)   The service provider shall not destroy such backup copy until the later of—

(A)   the delivery of the information; or

(B)   the resolution of any proceedings (including appeals of any proceeding) concerning the government's subpoena or court order.

(4)   The service provider shall release such backup copy to the requesting governmental entity no sooner than fourteen days after the governmental entity's notice to the subscriber or customer if such service provider—

(A)   has not received notice from the subscriber or customer that the subscriber or customer has challenged the governmental entity's request; and

(B)   has not initiated proceedings to challenge the request of the governmental entity.

(5)   A governmental entity may seek to require the creation of a backup copy under subsection (a)(1) of this section if in its sole discretion such entity determines that there is reason to believe that notification under section 2703 of this title of the existence of the subpoena or court order may result in destruction of or tampering with evidence. This determination is not subject to challenge by the subscriber or customer or service provider.

(b)   Customer Challenges.—

(1)   Within fourteen days after notice by the governmental entity to the subscriber or customer under subsection (a)(2) of this section, such subscriber or customer may file a motion to quash such subpoena or vacate such court order, with copies served upon the governmental entity and with written notice of such challenge to the service provider. A motion to vacate a court order shall be filed in the court which issued such order. A motion to quash a subpoena shall be filed in the appropriate United States district court or State court. Such motion or application shall contain an affidavit or sworn statement—

(A)   stating that the applicant is a customer or subscriber to the service from which the contents of electronic communications maintained for him have been sought; and

(B)   stating the applicant's reasons for believing that the records sought are not relevant to a legitimate law enforcement inquiry or that there has not been substantial compliance with the provisions of this chapter in some other respect.

(2)   Service shall be made under this section upon a governmental entity by delivering or mailing by registered or certified mail a copy of the papers to the person, office, or department specified in the notice which the customer has received pursuant to this chapter. For the purposes of this section, the term 'delivery' has the meaning given that term in the Federal Rules of Civil Procedure.

(3)   If the court finds that the customer has complied with paragraphs (1) and (2) of this subsection, the court shall order the governmental entity to file a sworn

response, which may be filed in camera if the governmental entity includes in its response the reasons which make in camera review appropriate. If the court is unable to determine the motion or application on the basis of the parties' initial allegations and response, the court may conduct such additional proceedings as it deems appropriate. All such proceedings shall be completed and the motion or application decided as soon as practicable after the filing of the governmental entity's response.

(4)   If the court finds that the applicant is not the subscriber or customer for whom the communications sought by the governmental entity are maintained, or that there is a reason to believe that the law enforcement inquiry is legitimate and that the communications sought are relevant to that inquiry, it shall deny the motion or application and order such process enforced. If the court finds that the applicant is the subscriber or customer for whom the communications sought by the governmental entity are maintained, and that there is not a reason to believe that the communications sought are relevant to a legitimate law enforcement inquiry, or that there has not been substantial compliance with the provisions of this chapter, it shall order the process quashed.

(5)   A court order denying a motion or application under this section shall not be deemed a final order and no interlocutory appeal may be taken therefrom by the customer.

Sec. 2705.   Delayed notice.

(a)   Delay of Notification.—

(1)   A governmental entity acting under section 2703(b) of this title may—

(A)   where a court order is sought, include in the application a request, which the court shall grant, for an order delaying the notification required under section 2703(b) of this title for a period not to exceed ninety days, if the court determines that there is reason to believe that notification of the existence of the court order may have an adverse result described in paragraph (2) of this subsection; or

(B)   where an administrative subpoena authorized by a Federal or State statute or a Federal or State grand jury subpoena is obtained, delay the notification required under section 2703(b) of this title for a period not to exceed ninety days upon the execution of a written certification of a supervisory official that there is reason to believe that notification of the existence of the subpoena may have an adverse result described in paragraph (2) of this subsection.

(2)   An adverse result for the purposes of paragraph (1) of this subsection is—

(A)   endangering the life or physical safety of an individual;

(B)   flight from prosecution;

(C)   destruction of or tampering with evidence;

(D)   intimidation of potential witnesses; or

(E)   otherwise seriously jeopardizing an investigation or unduly delaying a trial.

(3)   The governmental entity shall maintain a true copy of certification under paragraph (1)(B).

(4)   Extensions of the delay of notification provided in section 2703 of up to ninety

days each may be granted by the court upon application, or by certification by a governmental entity, but only in accordance with subsection (b) of this section.

(5)   Upon expiration of the period of delay of notification under paragraph (1) or (4) of this subsection, the governmental entity shall serve upon, or deliver by registered or first-class mail to, the customer or subscriber a copy of the process or request together with notice that—

(A)   states with reasonable specificity the nature of the law enforcement inquiry; and

(B)   informs such customer or subscriber—

(i)   that information maintained for such customer or subscriber by the service provider named in such process or request was supplied to or requested by that governmental authority and the date on which the supplying or request took place;

(ii)   that notification of such customer or subscriber was delayed;

(iii)   what governmental entity or court made the certification or determination pursuant to which that delay was made; and

(iv)   which provision of this chapter allowed such delay.

(6)   As used in this subsection, the term 'supervisory official' means the investigative agent in charge or assistant investigative agent in charge or an equivalent of an investigating agency's headquarters or regional office, or the chief prosecuting attorney or the first assistant prosecuting attorney or an equivalent of a prosecuting attorney's headquarters or regional office.

(b)   Preclusion of Notice to Subject of Governmental Access.—A governmental entity acting under section 2703, when it is not required to notify the subscriber or customer under section 2703(b)(1), or to the extent that it may delay such notice pursuant to subsection (a) of this section, may apply to a court for an order commanding a provider of electronic communications service or remote computing service to whom a warrant, subpoena, or court order is directed, for such period as the court deems appropriate, not to notify any other person of the existence of the warrant, subpoena, or court order. The court shall enter such an order if it determines that there is reason to believe that notification of the existence of the warrant, subpoena, or court order will result in—

(1)   endangering the life or physical safety of an individual;

(2)   flight from prosecution;

(3)   destruction of or tampering with evidence;

(4)   intimidation of potential witnesses; or

(5)   otherwise seriously jeopardizing an investigation or unduly delaying a trial.

Sec. 2706.   Cost reimbursement.

(a)   Payment.—Except as otherwise provided in subsection (c), a governmental entity obtaining the contents of communications, records, or other information under section 2702, 2703, or 2704 of this title shall pay to the person or entity assembling or providing such information a fee for reimbursement for such costs as are reasonably necessary and which have been directly incurred in searching for, assembling, reproducing, or otherwise providing such information. Such reimbursable costs shall include any costs due to necessary disruption of normal operations of any electronic communication service or remote computing service in which such information may be stored.

(b) Amount.—The amount of the fee provided by subsection (a) shall be as mutually agreed by the governmental entity and the person or entity providing the information, or, in the absence of agreement, shall be as determined by the court which issued the order for production of such information (or the court before which a criminal prosecution relating to such information would be brought, if no court order was issued for production of the information).

(c) Exception.—The requirement of subsection (a) of this section does not apply with respect to records or other information maintained by a communications common carrier that relate to telephone toll records and telephone listings obtained under section 2703 of this title. The court may, however, order a payment as described in subsection (a) if the court determines the information required is unusually voluminous in nature or otherwise caused an undue burden on the provider.

Sec. 2707. Civil action.

(a) Cause of Action.—Except as provided in section 2703(e), any provider of electronic communication service, subscriber, or customer aggrieved by any violation of this chapter in which the conduct constituting the violation is engaged in with a knowing or intentional state of mind may, in a civil action, recover from the person or entity which engaged in that violation such relief as may be appropriate.

(b) Relief.—In a civil action under this section, appropriate relief includes—
(1) such preliminary and other equitable or declaratory relief as may be appropriate;
(2) damages under subsection (c); and
(3) a reasonable attorney's fee and other litigation costs reasonably incurred.

(c) Damages.—The court may assess as damages in a civil action under this section the sum of the actual damages suffered by the plaintiff and any profits made by the violator as a result of the violation, but in no case shall a person entitled to recover receive less than the sum of $1,000.

(d) Defense.—A good faith reliance on—
(1) a court warrant or order, a grand jury subpoena, a legislative authorization, or a statutory authorization;
(2) a request of an investigative or law enforcement officer under section 2518(7) of this title; or
(3) a good faith determination that section 2511(3) of this title permitted the

conduct complained of; is a complete defense to any civil or criminal action brought under this chapter or any other law.

(e) Limitation.—A civil action under this section may not be commenced later than two years after the date upon which the claimant first discovered or had a reasonable opportunity to discover the violation.

Sec. 2708. Exclusivity of remedies.

The remedies and sanctions described in this chapter are the only judicial remedies and sanctions for nonconstitutional violations of this chapter.

Sec. 2709. Counterintelligence access to telephone toll and transactional records.

(a) Duty to Provide.—A wire or electronic communication service provider shall comply with a request for subscriber information and toll billing records information, or electronic communication transactional records in its custody or possession made by the Director of the Federal Bureau of Investigation under subsection (b) of this section.

(b) Required Certification.—The Director of the Federal Bureau of Investigation (or an individual within the Federal Bureau of Investigation designated for this purpose by the Director) may request any such information and records if the Director (or the Director's designee) certifies in writing to the wire or electronic communication service provider to which the request is made that—
(1)   the information sought is relevant to an authorized foreign counterintelligence investigation; and
(2)   there are specific and articulable facts giving reason to believe that the person or entity to whom the information sought pertains is a foreign power or an agent of a foreign power as defined in section 101 of the Foreign Intelligence Surveillance Act of 1978 (50 U.S.C. 1801).

(c) Prohibition of Certain Disclosure.—No wire or electronic communication service provider, or officer, employee, or agent thereof, shall disclose to any person that the Federal Bureau of Investigation has sought or obtained access to information or records under this section.

(d) Dissemination by Bureau.—The Federal Bureau of Investigation may disseminate information and records obtained under this section only as provided in guidelines approved by the Attorney General for foreign intelligence collection and foreign counterintelligence investigations conducted by the Federal Bureau of Investigation, and, with respect to dissemination to an agency of the United States, only if such information is clearly relevant to the authorized responsibilities of such agency.

(e) Requirement That Certain Congressional Bodies Be Informed.—On a semiannual basis the Director of the Federal Bureau of Investigation shall fully inform the Permanent Select Committee on Intelligence of the House of Representatives and the Select Committee on Intelligence of the Senate concerning all requests made under subsection (b) of this section.

Sec. 2710. Wrongful disclosure of video tape rental or sale records. . . .

Sec. 2711. Definitions for chapter.

As used in this chapter—
(1) the terms defined in section 2510 of this title have, respectively, the definitions given such terms in that section; and
(2) the term 'remote computing service' means the provision to the public of computer storage or processing services by means of an electronic communications system.

Chapter 206

Sec. 3121. General prohibition on pen register and trap and trace device use; exception.

(a) In General.—Except as provided in this section, no person may install or use a pen register or a trap and trace device without first obtaining a court order under section 3123 of this title or under the Foreign Intelligence Surveillance Act of 1978 (50 U.S.C. 1801 et seq.).

(b) Exception.—The prohibition of subsection (a) does not apply with respect to the use of a pen register or a trap and trace device by a provider of electronic or wire communication service—
(1) relating to the operation, maintenance, and testing of a wire or electronic communication service or to the protection of the rights or property of such provider, or to the protection of users of that service from abuse of service or unlawful use of service; or
(2) to record the fact that a wire or electronic communication was initiated or completed in order to protect such provider, another provider furnishing service toward the completion of the wire communication, or a user of that service, from fraudulent, unlawful or abusive use of service; or
(3) where the consent of the user of that service has been obtained.

(c) Limitation.—A government agency authorized to install and use a pen register under this chapter or under State law shall use technology reasonably available to it that restricts the recording or decoding of electronic or other impulses to the dialing and signaling information utilized in call processing.

(d) Penalty.—Whoever knowingly violates subsection (a) shall be fined under this title or imprisoned not more than one year, or both.

Sec. 3122. Application for an order for a pen register or a trap and trace device.

(a) Application.—(1) An attorney for the Government may make application for an order or an extension of an order under section 3123 of this title authorizing or approving the installation and use of a pen register or a trap and trace device under this chapter, in writing under oath or equivalent affirmation, to a court of competent jurisdiction.

(2) Unless prohibited by State law, a State investigative or law enforcement officer may make application for an order or an extension of an order under section 3123 of this title authorizing or approving the installation and use of a pen register or a trap and trace device under this chapter, in writing under oath or equivalent affirmation, to a court of competent jurisdiction of such State.

(b) Contents of Application.—An application under subsection (a) of this section shall include—

(1) the identity of the attorney for the Government or the State law enforcement or investigative officer making the application and the identity of the law enforcement agency conducting the investigation; and

(2) a certification by the applicant that the information likely to be obtained is relevant to an ongoing criminal investigation being conducted by that agency.

Sec. 3123. Issuance of an order for a pen register or a trap and trace device.

(a) In General.—Upon an application made under section 3122 of this title, the court shall enter an ex parte order authorizing the installation and use of a pen register or a trap and trace device within the jurisdiction of the court if the court finds that the attorney for the Government or the State law enforcement or investigative officer has certified to the court that the information likely to be obtained by such installation and use is relevant to an ongoing criminal investigation.

(b) Contents of Order.—An order issued under this section—

(1) shall specify—

(A) the identity, if known, of the person to whom is leased or in whose name is listed the telephone line to which the pen register or trap and trace device is to be attached;

(B) the identity, if known, of the person who is the subject of the criminal investigation;

(C) the number and, if known, physical location of the telephone line to which the pen register or trap and trace device is to be attached and, in the case of a trap and trace device, the geographic limits of the trap and trace order; and

(D)   a statement of the offense to which the information likely to be obtained by the pen register or trap and trace device relates; and

(2)   shall direct, upon the request of the applicant, the furnishing of information, facilities, and technical assistance necessary to accomplish the installation of the pen register or trap and trace device under section 3124 of this title.

(c)   Time Period and Extensions.—

(1)   An order issued under this section shall authorize the installation and use of a pen register or a trap and trace device for a period not to exceed sixty days.

(2)   Extensions of such an order may be granted, but only upon an application for an order under section 3122 of this title and upon the judicial finding required by subsection (a) of this section. The period of extension shall be for a period not to exceed sixty days.

(d)   Nondisclosure of Existence of Pen Register or a Trap and Trace Device.—An order authorizing or approving the installation and use of a pen register or a trap and trace device shall direct that—

(1)   the order be sealed until otherwise ordered by the court; and

(2)   the person owning or leasing the line to which the pen register or a trap and trace device is attached, or who has been ordered by the court to provide assistance to the applicant, not disclose the existence of the pen register or trap and trace device or the existence of the investigation to the listed subscriber, or to any other person, unless or until otherwise ordered by the court.

Sec. 3124.   Assistance in installation and use of a pen register or a trap and trace device.

(a)   Pen Registers.—Upon the request of an attorney for the Government or an officer of a law enforcement agency authorized to install and use a pen register under this chapter, a provider of wire or electronic communication service, landlord, custodian, or other person shall furnish such investigative or law enforcement officer forthwith all information, facilities, and technical assistance necessary to accomplish the installation of the pen register unobtrusively and with a minimum of interference with the services that the person so ordered by the court accords the party with respect to whom the installation and use is to take place, if such assistance is directed by a court order as provided in section 3123(b)(2) of this title.

(b)   Trap and Trace Device.—Upon the request of an attorney for the Government or an officer of a law enforcement agency authorized to receive the results of a trap and trace device under this chapter, a provider of a wire or electronic communication service, landlord, custodian, or other person shall install such device forthwith on the appropriate line and shall furnish such investigative or law enforcement officer all additional information, facilities and technical assistance including installation and operation of the device unobtrusively and with a minimum of interference with the services that the person so ordered by the court accords the party with respect to whom the installation and use is to take place, if such installation and assistance is directed by a court order as provided in section 3123(b)(2) of this title. Unless otherwise ordered by the court, the results of the trap and trace device shall be furnished, pursuant to section 3123(b) or section 3125 of this title, to the officer of a law enforcement agency, designated in the court order, at reasonable intervals during regular business hours for the duration of the order.

(c) Compensation.—A provider of a wire or electronic communication service, landlord, custodian, or other person who furnishes facilities or technical assistance pursuant to this section shall be reasonably compensated for such reasonable expenses incurred in providing such facilities and assistance.

(d) No Cause of Action Against a Provider Disclosing Information Under This Chapter.—No cause of action shall lie in any court against any provider of a wire or electronic communication service, its officers, employees, agents, or other specified persons for providing information, facilities, or assistance in accordance with the terms of a court order under this chapter or request pursuant to section 3125 of this title.

(e) Defense.—A good faith reliance on a court order under this chapter, a request pursuant to section 3125 of this title, a legislative authorization, or a statutory authorization is a complete defense against any civil or criminal action brought under this chapter or any other law.

Sec. 3125.   Emergency pen register and trap and trace device installation.

(a) Notwithstanding any other provision of this chapter, any investigative or law enforcement officer, specially designated by the Attorney General, the Deputy Attorney General, the Associate Attorney General, any Assistant Attorney General, any acting Assistant Attorney General, or any Deputy Assistant Attorney General, or by the principal prosecuting attorney of any State or subdivision thereof acting pursuant to a statute of that State, who reasonably determines that—
(1)   an emergency situation exists that involves—

(A)   immediate danger of death or serious bodily injury to any person; or
(B)   conspiratorial activities characteristic of organized crime,

that requires the installation and use of a pen register or a trap and trace device before an order authorizing such installation and use can, with due diligence, be obtained, and
(2)   there are grounds upon which an order could be entered under this chapter to authorize such installation and use '''[1] may have installed and use a pen register

or trap and trace device if, within forty-eight hours after the installation has occurred, or begins to occur, an order approving the installation or use is issued in accordance with section 3123 of this title."[4]

(b)   In the absence of an authorizing order, such use shall immediately terminate when the information sought is obtained, when the application for the order is denied or when forty-eight hours have lapsed since the installation of the pen register or trap and trace device, whichever is earlier.

(c)   The knowing installation or use by any investigative or law enforcement officer of a pen register or trap and trace device pursuant to subsection (a) without application for the authorizing order within forty-eight hours of the installation shall constitute a violation of this chapter.

(d)   A provider for a wire or electronic service, landlord, custodian, or other person who furnished facilities or technical assistance pursuant to this section shall be reasonably compensated for such reasonable expenses incurred in providing such facilities and assistance.

Sec. 3126.   Reports concerning pen registers and trap and trace devices.

The Attorney General shall annually report to Congress on the number of pen register orders and orders for trap and trace devices applied for by law enforcement agencies of the Department of Justice.

Sec. 3127.   Definitions for chapter.

As used in this chapter—

(1)   the terms "wire communication", "electronic communication", and "electronic communication service" have the meanings set forth for such terms in section 2510 of this title;

(2)   the term "court of competent jurisdiction" means—
(A)   a district court of the United States (including a magistrate of such a court) or a United States Court of Appeals; or
(B)   a court of general criminal jurisdiction of a State authorized by the law of that State to enter orders authorizing the use of a pen register or a trap and trace device;

---

[4]So in original. A comma probably should appear after the word "use", the quotation marks probably should not appear, and the words beginning with "may" probably should appear flush left.

(3)   the term "pen register" means a device which records or decodes electronic or other impulses which identify the numbers dialed or otherwise transmitted on the telephone line to which such device is attached, but such term does not include any device used by a provider or customer of a wire or electronic communication service for billing, or recording as an incident to billing, for communications services provided by such provider or any device used by a provider or customer of a wire communication service for cost accounting or other like purposes in the ordinary course of its business;

(4)   the term "trap and trace device" means a device which captures the incoming electronic or other impulses which identify the originating number of an instrument or device from which a wire or electronic communication was transmitted;

(5)   the term "attorney for the Government" has the meaning given such term for the purposes of the Federal Rules of Criminal Procedure; and

(6)   the term "State" means a State, the District of Columbia, Puerto Rico, and any other possession or territory of the United States.

N.1.4   Communications Assistance for Law Enforcement Act of 1995

Title I—Interception of Digital and Other Communications

Sec. 101.   Short title.

This title may be cited as the "Communications Assistance for Law Enforcement Act".

Sec. 102.   Definitions.

For purposes of this title—

(1)   The terms defined in section 2510 of title 18, United States Code, have, respectively, the meanings stated in that section.

(2)   The term "call-identifying information" means dialing or signaling information that identifies the origin, direction, destination, or termination of each communication generated or received by a subscriber by means of any equipment, facility, or service of a telecommunications carrier.

(3)   The term "Commission" means the Federal Communications Commission.

(4)   The term "electronic messaging services" means software-based services that enable the sharing of data, images, sound, writing, or other information among computing devices controlled by the senders or recipients of the messages.

(5)   The term "government" means the government of the United States and any agency or instrumentality thereof, the District of Columbia, any commonwealth, territory, or possession of the United States, and any State or political subdivision thereof authorized by law to conduct electronic surveillance.

(6)   The term "information services"—
(A)   means the offering of a capability for generating, acquiring, storing, transforming, processing, retrieving, utilizing, or making available information via telecommunications; and
(B)   includes—
(i)   a service that permits a customer to retrieve stored information from, or file information for storage in, information storage facilities;
(ii)   electronic publishing; and
(iii)   electronic messaging services; but
(C)   does not include any capability for a telecommunications carrier's internal management, control, or operation of its telecommunications network.

(7)   The term "telecommunications support services" means a product, software, or service used by a telecommunications carrier for the internal signaling or switching functions of its telecommunications network.

(8)   The term "telecommunications carrier"—
(A)   means a person or entity engaged in the transmission or switching of wire or electronic communications as a common carrier for hire; and
(B)   includes—
(i)   a person or entity engaged in providing commercial mobile service (as defined in section 332(d) of the Communications Act of 1934 (47 U.S.C. 332(d))); or
(ii)   a person or entity engaged in providing wire or electronic communication switching or transmission service to the extent that the Commission finds that such service is a replacement for a substantial portion of the local telephone exchange service and that it is in the public interest to deem such a person or entity to be a telecommunications carrier for purposes of this title; but
(C)   does not include—
(i)   persons or entities insofar as they are engaged in providing information services; and
(ii)   any class or category of telecommunications carriers that the Commission exempts by rule after consultation with the Attorney General.

Sec. 103.   Assistance capability requirements.

(a)   Capability Requirements.—Except as provided in subsections (b), (c), and (d) of this section and sections 108(a) and 109(b) and (d), a telecommunications carrier shall ensure that its equipment, facilities, or services that provide a customer or subscriber with the ability to originate, terminate, or direct communications are capable of—

(1)   expeditiously isolating and enabling the government, pursuant to a court order or other lawful authorization, to intercept, to the exclusion of any other communications, all wire and electronic communications carried by the carrier within a service area to or from equipment, facilities, or services of a subscriber of such carrier concurrently with their transmission to or from the subscriber's equipment, facility, or service, or at such later time as may be acceptable to the government;

(2)   expeditiously isolating and enabling the government, pursuant to a court order or other lawful authorization, to access call-identifying information that is reasonably available to the carrier—

(A)   before, during, or immediately after the transmission of a wire or electronic communication (or at such later time as may be acceptable to the government); and

(B)   in a manner that allows it to be associated with the communication to which it pertains, except that, with regard to information acquired solely pursuant to the authority for pen registers and trap and trace devices (as defined in section 3127 of title 18, United States Code), such call-identifying information shall not include any information that may disclose the physical location of the subscriber (except to the extent that the location may be determined from the telephone number);

(3)   delivering intercepted communications and call-identifying information to the government, pursuant to a court order or other lawful authorization, in a format such that they may be transmitted by means of equipment, facilities, or services procured by the government to a location other than the premises of the carrier; and

(4)   facilitating authorized communications interceptions and access to call-identifying information unobtrusively and with a minimum of interference with any subscriber's telecommunications service and in a manner that protects—

(A)   the privacy and security of communications and call-identifying information not authorized to be intercepted; and

(B)   information regarding the government's interception of communications and access to call-identifying information.

(b)   Limitations.—

(1)   Design of features and systems configurations.—This title does not authorize any law enforcement agency or officer—

(A)   to require any specific design of equipment, facilities, services, features, or system configurations to be adopted by any provider of a wire or electronic communication service, any manufacturer of telecommunications equipment, or any provider of telecommunications support services; or

(B)   to prohibit the adoption of any equipment, facility, service, or feature by any provider of a wire or electronic communication service, any manufacturer of telecommunications equipment, or any provider of telecommunications support services.

(2)   Information services; private networks and interconnection services and facilities.—The requirements of subsection (a) do not apply to—

(A)   information services; or

(B)   equipment, facilities, or services that support the transport or switching of communications for private networks or for the sole purpose of interconnecting telecommunications carriers.

(3)   Encryption.—A telecommunications carrier shall not be responsible for decrypting, or ensuring the government's ability to decrypt, any communication encrypted by a subscriber or customer, unless the encryption was provided by the carrier and the carrier possesses the information necessary to decrypt the communication.

(c)   Emergency or Exigent Circumstances.—In emergency or exigent circumstances (including those described in sections 2518 (7) or (11)(b) and 3125 of title 18, United States Code, and section 1805(e) of title 50 of such Code), a carrier at its discretion may comply with subsection (a)(3) by allowing monitoring at its premises if that is the only means of accomplishing the interception or access.

(d)   Mobile Service Assistance Requirements.—A telecommunications carrier that is a provider of commercial mobile service (as defined in section 332(d) of the Communications Act of 1934) offering a feature or service that allows subscribers to redirect, hand off, or assign their wire or electronic communications to another service area or another service provider or to utilize facilities in another service area or of another service provider shall ensure that, when the carrier that had been providing assistance for the interception of wire or electronic communications or access to call-identifying information pursuant to a court order or lawful authorization no longer has access to the content of such communications or call-identifying information within the service area in which interception has been occurring as a result of the subscriber's use of such a feature or service, information is made available to the government (before, during, or immediately after the transfer of such communications) identifying the provider of wire or electronic communication service that has acquired access to the communications.

Sec. 104.   Notices of capacity requirements.

(a)   Notices of Maximum and Actual Capacity Requirements.—

(1)   In general.—Not later than 1 year after the date of enactment of this title, after consulting with State and local law enforcement agencies, telecommunications carriers, providers of telecommunications support services, and manufacturers of telecommunications equipment, and after notice and comment, the Attorney General shall publish in the Federal Register and provide to appropriate telecommunications industry associations and standard-setting organizations—

(A)   notice of the actual number of communication interceptions, pen registers, and trap and trace devices, representing a portion of the maximum capacity set forth under subparagraph (B), that the Attorney General estimates that government agencies authorized to conduct electronic surveillance may conduct and use simultaneously by the date that is 4 years after the date of enactment of this title; and

(B)   notice of the maximum capacity required to accommodate all of the communication interceptions, pen registers, and trap and trace devices that the Attorney General estimates that government agencies authorized to conduct electronic surveillance may conduct and use simultaneously after the date that is 4 years after the date of enactment of this title.

(2)   Basis of notices.—The notices issued under paragraph (1)—

(A)   may be based upon the type of equipment, type of service, number of subscribers, type or size or carrier, nature of service area, or any other measure; and

(B)   shall identify, to the maximum extent practicable, the capacity required at specific geographic locations.

(b)   Compliance With Capacity Notices.—

(1)   Initial capacity.—Within 3 years after the publication by the Attorney General of a notice of capacity requirements or within 4 years after the date of enactment of this title, whichever is longer, a telecommunications carrier shall, subject to subsection (e), ensure that its systems are capable of—

(A)   accommodating simultaneously the number of interceptions, pen registers, and trap and trace devices set forth in the notice under subsection (a)(1)(A); and

(B)   expanding to the maximum capacity set forth in the notice under subsection (a)(1)(B).

(2)   Expansion to maximum capacity.—After the date described in paragraph (1), a telecommunications carrier shall, subject to subsection (e), ensure that it can accommodate expeditiously any increase in the actual number of communication interceptions, pen registers, and trap and trace devices that authorized agencies may seek to conduct and use, up to the maximum capacity requirement set forth in the notice under subsection (a)(1)(B).

(c)   Notices of Increased Maximum Capacity Requirements.—

(1)   Notice.—The Attorney General shall periodically publish in the Federal Register, after notice and comment, notice of any necessary increases in the maximum capacity requirement set forth in the notice under subsection (a)(1)(B).

(2)   Compliance.—Within 3 years after notice of increased maximum capacity requirements is published under paragraph (1), or within such longer time period as the Attorney General may specify, a telecommunications carrier shall, subject to subsection (e), ensure that its systems are capable of expanding to the increased maximum capacity set forth in the notice.

(d)   Carrier Statement.—Within 180 days after the publication by the Attorney General of a notice of capacity requirements pursuant to subsection (a) or (c), a telecommunications carrier shall submit to the Attorney General a statement identifying any of its systems or services that do not have the capacity to accommodate simultaneously the number of interceptions, pen registers, and trap and trace devices set forth in the notice under such subsection.

(e) Reimbursement Required for Compliance.—The Attorney General shall review the statements submitted under subsection (d) and may, subject to the availability of appropriations, agree to reimburse a telecommunications carrier for costs directly associated with modifications to attain such capacity requirement that are determined to be reasonable in accordance with section 109(e). Until the Attorney General agrees to reimburse such carrier for such modification, such carrier shall be considered to be in compliance with the capacity notices under subsection (a) or (c).

Sec. 105. Systems security and integrity.

A telecommunications carrier shall ensure that any interception of communications or access to call-identifying information effected within its switching premises can be activated only in accordance with a court order or other lawful authorization and with the affirmative intervention of an individual officer or employee of the carrier acting in accordance with regulations prescribed by the Commission.

Sec. 106. Cooperation of equipment manufacturers and providers of telecommunications support services.

(a) Consultation.—A telecommunications carrier shall consult, as necessary, in a timely fashion with manufacturers of its telecommunications transmission and switching equipment and its providers of telecommunications support services for the purpose of ensuring that current and planned equipment, facilities, and services comply with the capability requirements of section 103 and the capacity requirements identified by the Attorney General under section 104.

(b) Cooperation.—Subject to sections 104(e), 108(a), and 109(b) and (d), a manufacturer of telecommunications transmission or switching equipment and a provider of telecommunications support services shall, on a reasonably timely basis and at a reasonable charge, make available to the telecommunications carriers using its equipment, facilities, or services such features or modifications as are necessary to permit such carriers to comply with the capability requirements of section 103 and the capacity requirements identified by the Attorney General under section 104.

Sec. 107. Technical requirements and standards; extension of compliance date.

(a) Safe Harbor.—

(1) Consultation.—To ensure the efficient and industry-wide implementation

of the assistance capability requirements under section 103, the Attorney General, in coordination with other Federal, State, and local law enforcement agencies, shall consult with appropriate associations and standard-setting organizations of the telecommunications industry, with representatives of users of telecommunications equipment, facilities, and services, and with State utility commissions.

(2)   Compliance under accepted standards.—A telecommunications carrier shall be found to be in compliance with the assistance capability requirements under section 103, and a manufacturer of telecommunications transmission or switching equipment or a provider of telecommunications support services shall be found to be in compliance with section 106, if the carrier, manufacturer, or support service provider is in compliance with publicly available technical requirements or standards adopted by an industry association or standard-setting organization, or by the Commission under subsection (b), to meet the requirements of section 103.

(3)   Absence of standards.—The absence of technical requirements or standards for implementing the assistance capability requirements of section 103 shall not—

(A)   preclude a telecommunications carrier, manufacturer, or telecommunications support services provider from deploying a technology or service; or

(B)   relieve a carrier, manufacturer, or telecommunications support services provider of the obligations imposed by section 103 or 106, as applicable.

(b)   Commission Authority.—If industry associations or standard-setting organizations fail to issue technical requirements or standards or if a government agency or any other person believes that such requirements or standards are deficient, the agency or person may petition the Commission to establish, by rule, technical requirements or standards that—

(1)   meet the assistance capability requirements of section 103 by cost-effective methods;

(2)   protect the privacy and security of communications not authorized to be intercepted;

(3)   minimize the cost of such compliance on residential ratepayers;

(4)   serve the policy of the United States to encourage the provision of new technologies and services to the public; and

(5)   provide a reasonable time and conditions for compliance with and the transition to any new standard, including defining the obligations of telecommunications carriers under section 103 during any transition period.

(c)   Extension of Compliance Date for Equipment, Facilities, and Services.—

(1)   Petition.—A telecommunications carrier proposing to install or deploy, or having installed or deployed, any equipment, facility, or service prior to the effective date of section 103 may petition the Commission for 1 or more extensions of the deadline for complying with the assistance capability requirements under section 103.

(2)   Grounds for extension.—The Commission may, after consultation with the Attorney General, grant an extension under this subsection, if the Commission determines that compliance with the assistance capability requirements under section 103 is not reasonably achievable through application of technology available within the compliance period.

(3)   Length of extension.—An extension under this subsection shall extend for no longer than the earlier of—
(A)   the date determined by the Commission as necessary for the carrier to comply with the assistance capability requirements under section 103; or
(B)   the date that is 2 years after the date on which the extension is granted.
(4)   Applicability of extension.—An extension under this subsection shall apply to only that part of the carrier's business on which the new equipment, facility, or service is used.

Sec. 108.   Enforcement orders.

(a)   Grounds for Issuance.—A court shall issue an order enforcing this title under section 2522 of title 18, United States Code, only if the court finds that—
(1)   alternative technologies or capabilities or the facilities of another carrier are not reasonably available to law enforcement for implementing the interception of communications or access to call-identifying information; and
(2)   compliance with the requirements of this title is reasonably achievable through the application of available technology to the equipment, facility, or service at issue or would have been reasonably achievable if timely action had been taken.

(b)   Time for Compliance.—Upon issuing an order enforcing this title, the court shall specify a reasonable time and conditions for complying with its order, considering the good faith efforts to comply in a timely manner, any effect on the carrier's, manufacturer's, or service provider's ability to continue to do business, the degree of culpability or delay in undertaking efforts to comply, and such other matters as justice may require.

(c)   Limitations.—An order enforcing this title may not—
(1)   require a telecommunications carrier to meet the government's demand for interception of communications and acquisition of call-identifying information to any extent in excess of the capacity for which the Attorney General has agreed to reimburse such carrier;
(2)   require any telecommunications carrier to comply with assistance capability requirement of section 103 if the Commission has determined (pursuant to section 109(b)(1)) that compliance is not reasonably achievable, unless the Attorney General has agreed (pursuant to section 109(b)(2)) to pay the costs described in section 109(b)(2)(A); or
(3)   require a telecommunications carrier to modify, for the purpose of complying with the assistance capability requirements of section 103, any equipment, facility, or service deployed on or before January 1, 1995, unless—
(A)   the Attorney General has agreed to pay the telecommunications carrier for all reasonable costs directly associated with modifications necessary to bring the equipment, facility, or service into compliance with those requirements; or
(B)   the equipment, facility, or service has been replaced or significantly upgraded or otherwise undergoes major modification.

Sec. 109. Payment of costs of telecommunications carriers to comply with capability requirements.

(a) Equipment, Facilities, and Services Deployed on or Before January 1, 1995.—The Attorney General may, subject to the availability of appropriations, agree to pay telecommunications carriers for all reasonable costs directly associated with the modifications performed by carriers in connection with equipment, facilities, and services installed or deployed on or before January 1, 1995, to establish the capabilities necessary to comply with section 103.

(b) Equipment, Facilities, and Services Deployed After January 1, 1995.—
(1) Determinations of reasonably achievable.—The Commission, on petition from a telecommunications carrier or any other interested person, and after notice to the Attorney General, shall determine whether compliance with the assistance capability requirements of section 103 is reasonably achievable with respect to any equipment, facility, or service installed or deployed after January 1, 1995. The Commission shall make such determination within 1 year after the date such petition is filed. In making such determination, the Commission shall determine whether compliance would impose significant difficulty or expense on the carrier or on the users of the carrier's systems and shall consider the following factors:
(A) The effect on public safety and national security.
(B) The effect on rates for basic residential telephone service.
(C) The need to protect the privacy and security of communications not authorized to be intercepted.
(D) The need to achieve the capability assistance requirements of section 103 by cost-effective methods.
(E) The effect on the nature and cost of the equipment, facility, or service at issue.
(F) The effect on the operation of the equipment, facility, or service at issue.
(G) The policy of the United States to encourage the provision of new technologies and services to the public.
(H) The financial resources of the telecommunications carrier.
(I) The effect on competition in the provision of telecommunications services.
(J) The extent to which the design and development of the equipment, facility, or service was initiated before January 1, 1995.
(K) Such other factors as the Commission determines are appropriate.
(2) Compensation.—If compliance with the assistance capability requirements of section 103 is not reasonably achievable with respect to equipment, facilities, or services deployed after January 1, 1995—
(A) the Attorney General, on application of a telecommunications carrier, may agree, subject to the availability of appropriations, to pay the telecommunications carrier for the additional reasonable costs of making compliance with such assistance capability requirements reasonably achievable; and
(B) if the Attorney General does not agree to pay such costs, the telecommunications carrier shall be deemed to be in compliance with such capability requirements.

(c) Allocation of Funds for Payment.—The Attorney General shall allocate funds appropriated to carry out this title in accordance with law enforcement priorities determined by the Attorney General.

(d) Failure To Make Payment With Respect To Equipment, Facilities, and Services Deployed on or Before January 1, 1995.—If a carrier has requested payment in accordance with procedures promulgated pursuant to subsection (e), and the Attorney General has not agreed to pay the telecommunications carrier for all reasonable costs directly associated with modifications necessary to bring any equipment, facility, or service deployed on or before January 1, 1995, into compliance with the assistance capability requirements of section 103, such equipment, facility, or service shall be considered to be in compliance with the assistance capability requirements of section 103 until the equipment, facility, or service is replaced or significantly upgraded or otherwise undergoes major modification.

(e) Cost Control Regulations.—
(1) In general.—The Attorney General shall, after notice and comment, establish regulations necessary to effectuate timely and cost-efficient payment to telecommunications carriers under this title, under chapters 119 and 121 of title 18, United States Code, and under the Foreign Intelligence Surveillance Act of 1978 (50 U.S.C. 1801 et seq.).
(2) Contents of regulations.—The Attorney General, after consultation with the Commission, shall prescribe regulations for purposes of determining reasonable costs under this title. Such regulations shall seek to minimize the cost to the Federal Government and shall—
(A) permit recovery from the Federal Government of—
(i) the direct costs of developing the modifications described in subsection (a), of providing the capabilities requested under subsection (b)(2), or of providing the capacities requested under section 104(e), but only to the extent that such costs have not been recovered from any other governmental or nongovernmental entity;
(ii) the costs of training personnel in the use of such capabilities or capacities; and
(iii) the direct costs of deploying or installing such capabilities or capacities;
(B) in the case of any modification that may be used for any purpose other than lawfully authorized electronic surveillance by a law enforcement agency of a government, permit recovery of only the incremental cost of making the modification suitable for such law enforcement purposes; and
(C) maintain the confidentiality of trade secrets.
(3) Submission of claims.—Such regulations shall require any telecommunications carrier that the Attorney General has agreed to pay for modifications pursuant to this section and that has installed or deployed such modification to submit to the Attorney General a claim for payment that contains or is accompanied by such information as the Attorney General may require.

Sec. 110. Authorization of appropriations.

There are authorized to be appropriated to carry out this title a total of $500,000,000 for fiscal years 1995, 1996, 1997, and 1998. Such sums are authorized to remain available until expended.

Sec. 111. Effective date.

(a) In General.—Except as provided in subsection (b), this title shall take effect on the date of enactment of this Act.

(b) Assistance Capability and Systems Security and Integrity Requirements.—Sections 103 and 105 of this title shall take effect on the date that is 4 years after the date of enactment of this Act.

Sec. 112. Reports.

(a) Reports by the Attorney General.—
(1) In general.—On or before November 30, 1995, and on or before November 30 of each year thereafter, the Attorney General shall submit to Congress and make available to the public a report on the amounts paid during the preceding fiscal year to telecommunications carriers under sections 104(e) and 109.
(2) Contents.—A report under paragraph (1) shall include—
(A) a detailed accounting of the amounts paid to each carrier and the equipment, facility, or service for which the amounts were paid; and
(B) projections of the amounts expected to be paid in the current fiscal year, the carriers to which payment is expected to be made, and the equipment, facilities, or services for which payment is expected to be made.

(b) Reports by the Comptroller General.—
(1) Payments for modifications.—On or before April 1, 1996, and every 2 years thereafter, the Comptroller General of the United States, after consultation with the Attorney General and the telecommunications industry, shall submit to the Congress a report—
(A) describing the type of equipment, facilities, and services that have been brought into compliance under this title; and
(B) reflecting its analysis of the reasonableness and cost-effectiveness of the payments made by the Attorney General to telecommunications carriers for modifications necessary to ensure compliance with this title.
(2) Compliance cost estimates.—A report under paragraph (1) shall include the findings and conclusions of the Comptroller General on the costs to be incurred by telecommunications carriers to comply with the assistance capability requirements of section 103 after the effective date of such section 103, including projections of the amounts expected to be incurred and a description of the equipment, facilities, or services for which they are expected to be incurred.

N.1.5   Computer Security Act of 1987

Sec. 1.   Short Title.

The Act may be cited as the "Computer Security Act of 1987".

Sec. 2.   Purpose.

(a)   IN GENERAL.—The Congress declares that improving the security and privacy of sensitive information in Federal computer systems is in the public interest, and hereby creates a means for establishing minimum acceptable security practices for such systems, without limiting the scope of security measures already planned or in use.

(b)   SPECIFIC PURPOSES.—The purposes of this Act are—
(1)   by amending the Act of March 3, 1901, to assign to theNational Bureau of Standards responsibility for developing standards and guidelines for Federal computer systems, including responsibility for developing standards and guidelines needed to assure the cost-effective security and privacy of sensitive information in Federal computer systems, drawing on the technical advice and assistance (including work products) of the National Security Agency, where appropriate;
(2)   to provide for promulgation of such standards and guidelines by amending section 111(d) of the Federal Property and Administrative Services Act of 1949;
(3)   to require establishment of security plans by all operators of Federal computer systems that contain sensitive information; and
(4)   to require mandatory periodic training for all persons involved in management, use, or operation of Federal computer systems that contain sensitive information.

Sec. 3.   Establishment of computer standards program.

The Act of March 3, 1901, (15 U.S.C. 271-278h), is amended—

(1)   in section 2(f), by striking out "and" at the end of paragraph (18), by striking out the period at the end of paragraph (19) and inserting in lieu thereof: "; and", and by inserting after such paragraph the following:

"(20) the study of computer systems (as that term is defined in section 20(d) of this Act) and their use to control machinery and processes.";

(2)   by redesignating section 20 as section 22, and by inserting after section 19 the following new sections:

"SEC. 20. (a) The National Bureau of Standards shall—
"(1) have the mission of developing standards, guidelines, and associated methods and techniques for computer systems;

"(2) except as described in paragraph (3) of this subsection (relating to security standards), develop uniform standards and guidelines for Federal computer systems, except those systems excluded by section 2315 of title 10, United States Code, or section 3502(2) of title 44, United States Code.

"(3) have responsibility within the Federal Government for developing technical, management, physical, and administrative standards and guidelines for the cost-effective security and privacy of sensitive information in Federal computer systems except—

"(A) those systems excluded by section 2315 of title 10, United States Code, or section 3502(2) of title 44, United States Code; and

"(B) those systems which are protected at all times by procedures established for information which has been specifically authorized under criteria established by an Executive Order or an Act of Congress to be kept secret in the interest of national defense or foreign policy, the primary purpose of which standards and guidelines shall be to control loss and unauthorized modification or disclosure of sensitive information in such systems and to prevent computer-related fraud and misuse;

"(4) submit standards and guidelines developed pursuant to paragraphs (2) and (3) of this subsection, along with recommendations as to the extent to which these should be made compulsory and binding, to the Secretary of Commerce for promulgation under section 111(d) of the Federal Property and Administrative Services Act of 1949;

"(5) develop guidelines for use by operators of Federal computer systems that contain sensitive information in training their employees in security awareness and accepted security practice, as required by section 5 of the Computer Security Act of 1987; and

"(6) develop validation procedures for, and evaluate the effectiveness of, standards and guidelines developed pursuant to paragraphs (1), (2), and (3) of this subsection through research and liaison with other government and private agencies.

"(b) In fulfilling subsection (a) of this section, the National Bureau of Standards is authorized—

"(1) to assist the private sector, upon request, in using and applying the results of the programs and activities under this section;

"(2) to make recommendations, as appropriate, to the Administrator of General Services on policies and regulations proposed pursuant to section 111(d) of the Federal Property and Administrative Services Act of 1949;

"(3) as requested, to provide to operators of Federal computer systems technical assistance in implementing the standards and guidelines promulgated pursuant to section 111(d) of the Federal Property and Administrative Services Act of 1949;

"(4) to assist, as appropriate, the Office of Personnel Management in developing regulations pertaining to training, as required by section 5 of the Computer Security Act of 1987;

"(5) to perform research and to conduct studies, as needed, to determine the nature and extent of the vulnerabilities of, and to devise techniques for the cost effective security and privacy of sensitive information in Federal computer systems; and

"(6) to coordinate closely with other agencies and offices (including, but not limited to, the Departments of Defense and Energy, the National Security Agency, the General Accounting Office, the Office of Technology Assessment, and the Office of Management and Budget)—

"(A) to assure maximum use of all existing and planned programs, materials, studies, and reports relating to computer systems security and privacy, in order to avoid unnecessary and costly duplication of effort; and

"(B) to assure, to the maximum extent feasible, that standards developed pursuant to subsection (a) (3) and (5) are consistent and compatible with standards and procedures developed for the protection of information in Federal computer systems which is authorized under criteria established by Executive order or an Act of Congress to be kept secret in the interest of national defense or foreign policy.

"(c) For the purposes of—

"(1) developing standards and guidelines for the protection of sensitive information in Federal computer systems under subsections (a)(1) and (a)(3), and

"(2) performing research and conducting studies under subsection (b)(5), the National Bureau of Standards shall draw upon computer system technical security guidelines developed by the National Security Agency to the extent that the National Bureau of Standards determines that such guidelines are consistent with the requirements for protecting sensitive information in Federal computer systems.

"(d) As used in this section—

"(1) the term 'computer system'—

"(A) means any equipment or interconnected system or subsystems of equipment that is used in the automatic acquisition, storage, manipulation, management, movement, control, display, switching, interchange, transmission, or reception, of data or information; and

"(B) includes—

"(i) computers;

"(ii) ancillary equipment;

"(iii) software, firmware, and similar procedures;

"(iv) services, including support services; and

"(v) related resources as defined by regulations issued by the Administrator for General Services pursuant to section 111 of the Federal Property and Administrative Services Act of 1949;

"(2) the term 'Federal computer system'—

"(A) means a computer system operated by a Federal agency or by a contractor of a Federal agency or other organization that processes information (using a computer system) on behalf of the Federal Government to accomplish a Federal function; and

"(B) includes automatic data processing equipment as that term is defined in section 111(a)(2) of the Federal Property and Administrative Services Act of 1949;

"(3) the term 'operator of a Federal computer system' means a Federal agency, contractor of a Federal agency, or other organization that processes information using a computer system on behalf of the Federal Government to accomplish a Federal function;

"(4) the term 'sensitive information' means any information, the loss, misuse, or unauthorized access to or modification of which could adversely affect the national interest or the conduct of Federal programs, or the privacy to which individuals are entitled under section 552a of title 5, United States Code (the Privacy Act), but which has not been specifically authorized under criteria established by an Executive order or an Act of Congress to be kept secret in the interest of national defense or foreign policy; and

"(5) the term 'Federal agency' has the meaning given such term by section 3(b) of the Federal Property and Administrative Services Act of 1949.

"SEC. 21. (a) There is hereby established a Computer System Security and Privacy Advisory Board within the Department of Commerce. The Secretary of Commerce shall appoint the chairman of the Board. The Board shall be composed of twelve additional members appointed by the Secretary of Commerce as follows:

"(1) four members from outside the Federal Government who are eminent in the computer or telecommunications industry, at least one of whom is representative of small or medium sized companies in such industries;

"(2) four members from outside the Federal Government who are eminent in the fields of computer or telecommunications technology, or related disciplines, but who are not employed by or representative of a producer of computer or telecommunications equipment; and

"(3) four members from the Federal Government who have computer systems management experience, including experience in computer systems security and privacy, at least one of whom shall be from the National Security Agency.

"(b) The duties of the Board shall be—

"(1) to identify emerging managerial, technical, administrative, and physical safeguard issues relative to computer systems security and privacy;

"(2) to advise the Bureau of Standards and the Secretary of Commerce on security and privacy issues pertaining to Federal computer systems; and

"(3) to report its findings to the Secretary of Commerce, the Director of the Office of Management and Budget, the Director of the National Security Agency, and the appropriate Committees of the Congress.

"(c) The term of office of each member of the Board shall be four years, except that—

"(1) of the initial members, three shall be appointed for terms of one year, three shall be appointed for terms of two years, three shall be appointed for terms of three years, and three shall be appointed for terms of four years; and

"(2) any member appointed to fill a vacancy in the Board shall serve for the remainder of the term for which his predecessor was appointed.

"(d) The Board shall not act in the absence of a quorum, which shall consist of seven members.

"(e) Members of the Board, other than full-time employees of the Federal Government while attending meetings of such committees or while otherwise performing duties at the request of the Board Chairman while away from their homes or a regular place of business, may be allowed travel expenses in accordance with subchapter I of chapter 57 of title 5, United States Code.

"(f) To provide the staff services necessary to assist the Board in carrying out its functions, the Board may utilize personnel from the National Bureau of Standards or any other agency of the Federal Government with the consent of the head of the agency.

"(g) As used in this section, the terms 'computer system' and 'Federal computer system' have the meanings given in section 20(d) of this Act."; and

(3) by adding at the end thereof the following new section:

"SEC. 23.   This Act may be cited as the National Bureau of Standards Act."

Sec. 4.   Amendment to Brooks Act.

Section 111(d) of the Federal Property and Administrative Services Act of 1949 (40 U.S.C. 759(d)) is amended to read as follows:

"(d)(1) The Secretary of Commerce shall, on the basis of standards and guidelines developed by the National Bureau of Standards pursuant to section 20(a) (2) and (3) of the National Bureau of Standards Act, promulgate standards and guidelines pertaining to Federal computer systems, making such standards compulsory and binding to the extent to which the Secretary determines necessary to improve the efficiency of operation or security and privacy of Federal computer systems. The President may disapprove or modify such standards and guidelines if he determines such action to be in the public interest. The President's authority to disapprove or modify such standards and guidelines may not be delegated. Notice of such disapproval or modification shall be submitted promptly to the Committee on Government Operations of the House of Representatives and the Committee on Governmental Affairs of the Senate and shall be published promptly in the Federal Register. Upon receiving notice of such disapproval or modification, the Secretary of Commerce shall immediately rescind or modify such standards or guidelines as directed by the President.

"(2) The head of a Federal agency may employ standards for the cost effective security and privacy of sensitive information in a Federal computer system within or under the supervision of that agency that are more stringent than the standards promulgated by the Secretary of Commerce, if such standards contain, at a minimum, the provisions of those applicable standards made compulsory and binding by the Secretary of Commerce.

"(3) The standards determined to be compulsory and binding may be waived by the Secretary of Commerce in writing upon a determination that compliance would adversely affect the accomplishment of the mission of an operator of a Federal computer system, or cause a major adverse financial impact on the operator which is not offset by government-wide savings. The Secretary may delegate to the head of one or more Federal agencies authority to waive such standards to the extent to which the Secretary determines such action to be necessary and desirable to allow for timely and effective implementation of Federal computer systems standards. The head of such agency may redelegate such authority only to a senior official designated pursuant to section 3506(b) of title 44, United States Code. Notice of each such waiver and delegation shall be transmitted promptly to the Committee on Government Operations of the House of Representatives and the Committee on Governmental Affairs of the Senate and shall be published promptly in the Federal Register.

"(4) The Administrator shall revise the Federal information resources management regulations (41 CFR ch. 201) to be consistent with the standards and guidelines promulgated by the Secretary of Commerce under this subsection.

"(5) As used in this subsection, the terms 'Federal computer system' and 'operator of a Federal computer system' have the meanings given in section 20(d) of the National Bureau of Standards Act.".

Sec. 5.   Federal computer system security training.

(a)   In General.—Each Federal agency shall provide for the mandatory periodic training in computer security awareness and accepted computer security practice of all employees who are involved with the management, use, or operation of each Federal computer system within or under the supervision of that agency. Such training shall be—
(1)   provided in accordance with the guidelines developed pursuant to section 20(a)(5) of the National Bureau of Standards Act (as added by section 3 of this Act), and in accordance with the regulations issued under subsection (c) of this section for Federal civilian employees; or
(2)   provided by an alternative training program approved by the head of that agency on the basis of a determination that the alternative training program is at least as effective in accomplishing the objectives of such guidelines and regulations.

(b)   Training Objectives.—Training under this section shall be started within 60 days after the issuance of the regulations described in subsection (c). Such training shall be designed—
(1)   to enhance employees' awareness of the threats to and vulnerability of computer systems; and
(2)   to encourage the use of improved computer security practices.

(c)   Regulations.—Within six months after the date of the enactment of this Act, the Director of the Office of Personnel Management shall issue regulations prescribing the procedures and scope of the training to be provided Federal civilian employees under subsection (a) and the manner in which such training is to be carried out.

Sec. 6.   Additional responsibilities for computer systems security and privacy.

(a)   Identification of systems that contain sensitive information—Within 6 months after the date of enactment of this Act, each Federal agency shall identify each Federal computer system, and system under development, which is within or under the supervision of that agency and which contains sensitive information.

(b)   Security Plan.—Within one year after the date of enactment of this Act, each such agency shall, consistent with the standards, guidelines, policies, and regulations prescribed pursuant to section 111(d) of the Federal Property and Administrative Services Act of 1949, establish a plan for the security and privacy of each Federal computer system identified by that agency pursuant to subsection (a) that is commensurate with the risk and magnitude or the harm resulting from the loss, misuse, or unauthorized access to or modification of the information contained in such system. Copies of each such plan shall be transmitted to the National Bureau of Standards and the National Security Agency for advice and comment. A summary of such plan shall be included in the agency's five-year plan required by section 3505 of title 44, United States Code. Such plan shall be subject to disapproval by the Director of the Office of Management and Budget. Such plan shall be revised annually as necessary.

Sec. 7.   Definitions.

As used in this Act, the terms "computer system", "Federal computer system", "operator of a Federal computer system", "sensitive information", and "Federal agency" have the meanings given in section 20(d) of the National Bureau of Standards Act (as added by section 3 of this Act).

Sec. 8.   Rules of construction of act.

Nothing in this Act, or in any amendment made by this Act, shallbe construed—

(1)   to constitute authority to withhold information sought pursuant to section 552 of title 5, United States Code; or

(2)   to authorize any Federal agency to limit, restrict, regulate, or control the collection, maintenance, disclosure, use, transfer, or sale of any information (regardless of the medium in which the information may be maintained) that is—
(A)   privately-owned information;
(B)   disclosable under section 552 of title 5, United States Code, orother law requiring or authorizing the public disclosure of information; or
(C)   public domain information.

N.1.6   Arms Export Control Act (U.S. Code, Title 22, Chapter 39)

Sec. 2751.   Need for international defense cooperation and military export controls; Presidential waiver; report to Congress; arms sales policy.

As declared by the Congress in the Arms Control and Disarmament Act (22 U.S.C. 2551 et seq.), an ultimate goal of the United States continues to be a world which is free from the scourge of war and the dangers and burdens of armaments; in which the use of force has been subordinated to the rule of law; and in which international adjustments to a changing world are achieved peacefully. In furtherance of that goal, it remains the policy of the United States to encourage regional arms control and disarmament agreements and to discourage arms races.

The Congress recognizes, however, that the United States and other free and independent countries continue to have valid requirements for effective and mutually beneficial defense relationships in order to maintain and foster the environment of international peace and security essential to social, economic, and political progress. Because of the growing cost and complexity of defense equipment, it is increasingly difficult and uneconomic for any country, particularly a developing country, to fill all of its legitimate defense requirements from its own design and production base. The need for international defense cooperation among the United States and those friendly countries to which it is allied by mutual defense treaties is especially important, since the effectiveness of their armed forces to act in concert to deter or defeat aggression is directly related to the operational compatibility of their defense equipment.

Accordingly, it remains the policy of the United States to facilitate the common defense by entering into international arrangements with friendly countries which further the objective of applying agreed resources of each country to programs and projects of cooperative exchange of data, research, development, production, procurement, and logistics support to achieve specific national defense requirements and objectives of mutual concern. To this end, this chapter authorizes sales by the United States Government to friendly countries having sufficient wealth to maintain and equip their own military forces at adequate strength, or to assume progressively larger shares of the costs thereof, without undue burden to their economies, in accordance with the restraints and control measures specified herein and in furtherance of the security objectives of the United States and of the purposes and principles of the United Nations Charter.

It is the sense of the Congress that all such sales be approved only when they are consistent with the foreign policy interests of the United States, the purposes of the foreign assistance program of the United States as embodied in the Foreign Assistance Act of 1961, as amended (22 U.S.C. 2151 et seq.), the extent and character of the military requirement, and the economic and financial capability of the recipient country, with particular regard being given, where appropriate, to proper balance among such sales, grant military assistance, and economic assistance as well as to the impact of the sales on programs of social and economic development and on existing or incipient arms races.

It shall be the policy of the United States to exert leadership in the world community to bring about arrangements for reducing the international trade in implements of war and to lessen the danger of outbreak of regional conflict and the burdens of armaments. United States programs for or procedures governing the export, sale, and grant of defense articles and defense services to foreign countries and international organizations shall be administered in a manner which will carry out this policy.

It is the sense of the Congress that the President should seek to initiate multilateral discussions for the purpose of reaching agreements among the principal arms suppliers and arms purchasers and other countries with respect to the control of the international trade in armaments. It is further the sense of Congress that the President should work actively with all nations to check and control the international sale and distribution of conventional weapons of death and destruction and to encourage regional arms control arrangements. In furtherance of this policy, the President should undertake a concerted effort to convene an international conference of major arms-supplying and arms-purchasing nations which shall consider measures to limit conventional arms transfers in the interest of international peace and stability.

It is the sense of the Congress that the aggregate value of defense articles and defense services—

(1)   which are sold under section 2761 or section 2762 of this title; or

(2)   which are licensed or approved for export under section 2778 of this title to, for the use, or for benefit of the armed forces, police, intelligence, or other internal security forces of a foreign country or international organization under a commercial sales contract;

in any fiscal year should not exceed current levels.

It is the sense of the Congress that the President maintain adherence to a policy of restraint in conventional arms transfers and that, in implementing this policy worldwide, a balanced approach should be taken and full regard given to the security interests of the United States in all regions of the world and that particular attention should be paid to controlling the flow of conventional arms to the nations of the developing world. To this end, the President is encouraged to continue discussions with other arms suppliers in order to restrain the flow of conventional arms to less developed countries.

Sec. 2752.   Coordination with foreign policy.

(a)   Noninfringement of powers or functions of Secretary of State. Nothing contained in this chapter shall be construed to infringe upon the powers or functions of the Secretary of State.

(b)   Responsibility for supervision and direction of sales, leases, financing, cooperative projects, and exports. Under the direction of the President, the Secretary of State (taking into account other United States activities abroad, such as military assistance, economic assistance, and the food for peace program) shall be responsible for the continuous supervision and general direction of sales, leases, financing, cooperative projects, and exports under this chapter, including, but not limited to, determining—

(1)   whether there will be a sale to or financing for a country and the amount thereof;
(2)   whether there will be a lease to a country;
(3)   whether there will be a cooperative project and the scope thereof; and
(4)   whether there will be delivery or other performance under such sale, lease, cooperative project, or export,

to the end that sales, financing, leases, cooperative projects, and exports will be integrated with other United States activities and to the end that the foreign policy of the United States would be best served thereby.

(c)   Coordination among representatives of the United States. The President shall prescribe appropriate procedures to assure coordination among representatives of the United States Government in each country, under the leadership of the Chief of the United States Diplomatic Mission. The Chief of the diplomatic mission shall make sure that recommendations of such representatives pertaining to sales are coordinated with political and economic considerations, and his comments shall accompany such recommendations if he so desires.

Sec. 2753.   Eligibility for defense services or defense articles.

(a)   Prerequisites for consent by President; report to Congress.
No defense article or defense service shall be sold or leased by the United States Government under this chapter to any country or international organization, and no agreement shall be entered into for a cooperative project (as defined in section 2767 of this title), unless—
(1)   the President finds that the furnishing of defense articles and defense services to such country or international organization will strengthen the security of the United States and promote world peace;
(2)   the country or international organization shall have agreed not to transfer title to, or possession of, any defense article or related training or other defense service so furnished to it, or produced in a cooperative project (as defined in section 2767 of this title), to anyone not an officer, employee, or agent of that country or international organization (or the North Atlantic Treaty Organization or the specified member countries (other than the United States) in the case of a cooperative project) and not to use or permit the use of such article or related training or other defense service for purposes other than those for which furnished unless the consent of the President has first been obtained:
(3)   the country or international organization shall have agreed that it will maintain the security of such article or service and will provide substantially the same degree of security protection afforded to such article or service by the United States Government; and

(4)   the country or international organization is otherwise eligible to purchase or lease defense articles or defense services.

In considering a request for approval of any transfer of any weapon, weapons system, munitions, aircraft, military boat, military vessel, or other implement of war to another country, the President shall not give his consent under paragraph (2) to the transfer unless the United States itself would transfer the defense article under consideration to that country. In addition, the President shall not give his consent under paragraph (2) to the transfer of any significant defense articles on the United States Munitions List unless the foreign country requesting consent to transfer agrees to demilitarize such defense articles prior to transfer, or the proposed recipient foreign country provides a commitment in writing to the United States Government that it will not transfer such defense articles, if not demilitarized, to any other foreign country or person without first obtaining the consent of the President. The President shall promptly submit a report to the Speaker of the House of Representatives and to the Committee on Foreign Relations of the Senate on the implementation of each agreement entered into pursuant to clause (2) of this subsection. . . .

Sec. 2754.   Purposes for which military sales or leases by the United States are authorized; report to Congress.

Defense articles and defense services shall be sold or leased by the United States Government under this chapter to friendly countries solely for internal security, for legitimate self-defense, to permit the recipient country to participate in regional or collective arrangements or measures consistent with the Charter of the United Nations, or otherwise to permit the recipient country to participate in collective measures requested by the United Nations for the purpose of maintaining or restoring international peace and security, or for the purpose of enabling foreign military forces in less developed friendly countries to construct public works and to engage in other activities helpful to the economic and social development of such friendly countries. It is the sense of the Congress that such foreign military forces should not be maintained or established solely for civic action activities and that such civic action activities not significantly detract from the capability of the military forces to perform their military missions and be coordinated with and form part of the total economic and social development effort: Provided, That none of the funds contained in this authorization shall be used to guarantee, or extend credit, or participate in an extension of credit in connection with any sale of sophisticated weapons systems, such as missile systems and jet aircraft for military purposes, to any underdeveloped country other than Greece, Turkey, Iran, Israel, the Republic of China, the Philippines and Korea unless the President determines that such financing is important to the national security of the United States and reports within thirty days each such determination to the Congress. . . .

Sec. 2770.   General authority.

(a)   Sale of defense articles and services by the President to United States companies; restriction on performance of services; reimbursement credited to selling agency. Subject to the conditions specified in subsection (b) of this section, the President may, on a negotiated contract basis, under cash terms (1) sell defense articles at not less than their estimated replacement cost (or actual cost in the case of services), or (2) procure or manufacture and sell defense articles at not less than their contract or manufacturing cost to the United States Government, to any United States company for incorporation into end items (and for concurrent or follow-on support) to be sold by such a company either (i) on a direct commercial basis to a friendly foreign country or international organization pursuant to an export license or approval under section 2778 of this title or (ii) in the case of ammunition parts subject to subsection (b) of this section, using commercial practices which restrict actual delivery directly to a friendly foreign country or international organization pursuant to approval under section 2778 of this title. The President may also sell defense services in support of such sales of defense articles, subject to the requirements of this chapter: Provided, however, That such services may be performed only in the United States. The amount of reimbursement received from such sales shall be credited to the current applicable appropriation, fund, or account of the selling agency of the United States Government.

(b)   Conditions of sale. Defense articles and defense services may be sold, procured and sold, or manufactured and sold, pursuant to subsection (a) of this section only if (1) the end item to which the articles apply is to be procured for the armed forces of a friendly country or international organization, (2) the articles would be supplied to the prime contractor as government-furnished equipment or materials if the end item were being procured for the use of the United States Armed Forces, and (3) the articles and services are available only from United States Government sources or are not available to the prime contractor directly from United States commercial sources at such times as may be required to meet the prime contractor's delivery schedule.

(c)   'Defense articles' and 'defense services' defined. For the purpose of this section, the terms 'defense articles' and 'defense services' mean defense articles and defense services as defined in section 2794(3) and (4) of this title. . . .

Sec. 2778.   Control of arms exports and imports.

(a)   Presidential control of exports and imports of defense articles and services, guidance of policy, etc.; designation of United States Munitions List; issuance of export licenses; condition for export; negotiations information.
(1)   In furtherance of world peace and the security and foreign policy of the United States, the President is authorized to control the import and the export of defense articles and defense services and to provide foreign policy guidance to persons of the United States involved in the export and import of such articles and

services. The President is authorized to designate those items which shall be considered as defense articles and defense services for the purposes of this section and to promulgate regulations for the import and export of such articles and services. The items so designated shall constitute the United States Munitions List.

(2)   Decisions on issuing export licenses under this section shall be made in coordination with the Director of the United States Arms Control and Disarmament Agency and shall take into account the Director's opinion as to whether the export of an article will contribute to an arms race, support international terrorism, increase the possibility of outbreak or escalation of conflict, or prejudice the development of bilateral or multilateral arms control arrangements.

(3)   In exercising the authorities conferred by this section, the President may require that any defense article or defense service be sold under this chapter as a condition of its eligibility for export, and may require that persons engaged in the negotiation for the export of defense articles and services keep the President fully and currently informed of the progress and future prospects of such negotiations.

(b)   Registration and licensing requirements for manufacturers, exporters, or importers of designated defense articles and defense services.

(1)(A) As prescribed in regulations issued under this section, every person (other than an officer or employee of the United States Government acting in an official capacity) who engages in the business of manufacturing, exporting, or importing any defense articles or defense services designated by the President under subsection (a)(1) of this section shall register with the United States Government agency charged with the administration of this section, and shall pay a registration fee which shall be prescribed by such regulations. Such regulations shall prohibit the return to the United States for sale in the United States (other than for the Armed Forces of the United States and its allies or for any State or local law enforcement agency) of any military firearms or ammunition of United States manufacture furnished to foreign governments by the United States under this chapter or any other foreign assistance or sales program of the United States, whether or not enhanced in value or improved in condition in a foreign country. This prohibition shall not extend to similar firearms that have been so substantially transformed as to become, in effect, articles of foreign manufacture.

(B)   The prohibition under such regulations required by the second sentence of subparagraph (A) shall not extend to any military firearms (or ammunition, components, parts, accessories, and attachments for such firearms) of United States manufacture furnished to any foreign government by the United States under this chapter or any other foreign assistance or sales program of the United States if—

(i)   such firearms are among those firearms that the Secretary of the Treasury is, or was at any time, required to authorize the importation of by reason of the provisions of section 925(e) of title 18 (including the requirement for the listing of such firearms as curios or relics under section 921(a)(13) of that title); and

(ii)   such foreign government certifies to the United States Government that such firearms are owned by such foreign government.

(C)   A copy of each registration made under this paragraph shall be transmitted to the Secretary of the Treasury for review regarding law enforcement concerns. The Secretary shall report to the President regarding such concerns as necessary. (2)   Except as otherwise specifically provided in regulations issued under subsection (a)(1) of this section, no defense articles or defense services designated by the President under subsection (a)(1) of this section may be exported or imported without a license for such export or import, issued in accordance with this chapter and regulations issued under this chapter, except that no license shall be required for exports or imports made by or for an agency of the United States Government (A)   for official use by a department or agency of the United States Government, or (B)   for carrying out any foreign assistance or sales program authorized by law and subject to the control of the President by other means. (3)(A)   For each of the fiscal years 1988 and 1989, $250,000 of registration fees collected pursuant to paragraph (1) shall be credited to a Department of State account, to be available without fiscal year limitation. Fees credited to that account shall be available only for the payment of expenses incurred for— (i)   contract personnel to assist in the evaluation of munitions control license applications, reduce processing time for license applications, and improve monitoring of compliance with the terms of licenses; and (ii)   the automation of munitions control functions and the processing of munitions control license applications, including the development, procurement, and utilization of computer equipment and related software. (B)   The authority of this paragraph may be exercised only to such extent or in such amounts as are provided in advance in appropriation Acts.

(c)   Criminal violations; punishment. Any person who willfully violates any provision of this section or section 2779 of this title, or any rule or regulation issued under either section, or who willfully, in a registration or license application or required report, makes any untrue statement of a material fact or omits to state a material fact required to be stated therein or necessary to make the statements therein not misleading, shall upon conviction be fined for each violation not more than $1,000,000 or imprisoned not more than ten years, or both.

(d)   Repealed. Pub. L. 96-70, title III, Sec. 3303(a)(4), Sept. 27, 1979, 93 Stat. 499.

(e)   Enforcement powers of President. In carrying out functions under this section with respect to the export of defense articles and defense services, the President is authorized to exercise the same powers concerning violations and enforcement which are conferred upon departments, agencies and officials by subsections (c), (d), (e), and (g) of section 11 of the Export Administration Act of 1979 (50 App. U.S.C. 2410(c), (d), (e), and (g)), and by subsections (a) and (c) of section 12 of such Act (50 App. U.S.C. 2411(a) and (c)), subject to the same terms and conditions as are applicable to such powers under such Act (50 App. U.S.C. 2401 et seq.). Nothing in this subsection shall be construed as authorizing the withholding of information from the Congress. Notwithstanding section 11(c) of the Export Administration Act of 1979, the civil penalty for each violation involving controls imposed on the export of defense articles and defense services under this section may not exceed $500,000.

(f)   Periodic review of items on Munitions List. The President shall periodically review the items on the United States Munitions List to determine what items, if any, no longer warrant export controls under this section. The results of such reviews shall be reported to the Speaker of the House of Representatives and to the Committee on Foreign Relations and the Committee on Banking, Housing, and Urban Affairs of the Senate. Such a report shall be submitted at least 30 days before any item is removed from the Munitions List and shall describe the nature of any controls to be imposed on that item under the Export Administration Act of 1979 (50 App. U.S.C. 2401 et seq.).

(g)   Identification of persons convicted or subject to indictment for violations of certain provisions.

(1)   The President shall develop appropriate mechanisms to identify, in connection with the export licensing process under this section—

(A)   persons who are the subject of an indictment for, or have been convicted of, a violation under—

(i)   this section,

(ii)   section 11 of the Export Administration Act of 1979 (50 U.S.C. App. 2410),

(iii)   section 793, 794, or 798 of title 18 (relating to espionage involving defense or classified information),

(iv)   section 16 of the Trading with the Enemy Act (50 U.S.C. App. 16),

(v)   section 206 of the International Emergency Economic Powers Act (relating to foreign assets controls; 50 U.S.C. App. 1705) (50 U.S.C. 1705),

(vi)   section 30A of the Securities Exchange Act of 1934 (15 U.S.C. 78dd-1) or section 104 of the Foreign Corrupt Practices Act (15 U.S.C. 78dd-2),

(vii)   chapter 105 of title 18 (relating to sabotage),

(viii)   section 4(b) of the Internal Security Act of 1950 (relating to communication of classified information; 50 U.S.C. 783(b)),

(ix)   section 57, 92, 101, 104, 222, 224, 225, or 226 of the Atomic Energy Act of 1954 (42 U.S.C. 2077, 2122, 2131, 2134, 2272, 2274, 2275, and 2276),

(x)   section 601 of the National Security Act of 1947 (relating to intelligence identities protection; 50 U.S.C. 421), or

(xi)   section 603(b) or (c) of the Comprehensive Anti-Apartheid Act of 1986 (22 U.S.C. 5113(b) and (c));

(B)   persons who are the subject of an indictment or have been convicted under section 371 of title 18 for conspiracy to violate any of the statutes cited in subparagraph (A); and

(C)   persons who are ineligible—

(i)   to contract with,

(ii)   to receive a license or other form of authorization to export from, or

(iii)   to receive a license or other form of authorization to import defense articles or defense services from,

any agency of the United States Government.

(2)   The President shall require that each applicant for a license to export an item on the United States Munitions List identify in the application all consignees and freight forwarders involved in the proposed export.

(3)   If the President determines—

(A)   that an applicant for a license to export under this section is the subject of an indictment for a violation of any of the statutes cited in paragraph (1),

(B)   that there is reasonable cause to believe that an applicant for a license to export under this section has violated any of the statutes cited in paragraph (1), or

(C)   that an applicant for a license to export under this section is ineligible to contract with, or to receive a license or other form of authorization to import defense articles or defense services from, any agency of the United States Government,

the President may disapprove the application. The President shall consider requests by the Secretary of the Treasury to disapprove any export license application based on these criteria.

(4)   A license to export an item on the United States Munitions List may not be issued to a person—

(A)   if that person, or any party to the export, has been convicted of violating a statute cited in paragraph (1), or

(B)   if that person, or any party to the export, is at the time of the license review ineligible to receive export licenses (or other forms of authorization to export) from any agency of the United States Government,

except as may be determined on a case-by-case basis by the President, after consultation with the Secretary of the Treasury, after a thorough review of the circumstances surrounding the conviction or ineligibility to export and a finding by the President that appropriate steps have been taken to mitigate any law enforcement concerns.

(5)   A license to export an item on the United States Munitions List may not be issued to a foreign person (other than a foreign government).

(6)   The President may require a license (or other form of authorization) before any item on the United States Munitions List is sold or otherwise transferred to the control or possession of a foreign person or a person acting on behalf of a foreign person.

(7)   The President shall, in coordination with law enforcement and national security agencies, develop standards for identifying high-risk exports for regular end-use verification. These standards shall be published in the Federal Register and the initial standards shall be published not later than October 1, 1988.

(8)   Upon request of the Secretary of State, the Secretary of Defense and the Secretary of the Treasury shall detail to the office primarily responsible for export licensing functions under this section, on a nonreimbursable basis, personnel with appropriate expertise to assist in the initial screening of applications for export licenses under this section in order to determine the need for further review of those applications for foreign policy, national security, and law enforcement concerns.

(9)   For purposes of this subsection—

(A)   the term 'foreign corporation' means a corporation that is not incorporated in the United States;

(B)   the term 'foreign government' includes any agency or subdivision of a foreign government, including an official mission of a foreign government;

(C)   the term 'foreign person' means any person who is not a citizen or national of the United States or lawfully admitted to the United States for permanent residence under the Immigration and Nationality Act (8 U.S.C. 1101 et seq.), and includes foreign corporations, international organizations, and foreign governments;

(D) the term 'party to the export' means—

(i) the president, the chief executive officer, and other senior officers of the license applicant;

(ii) the freight forwarders or designated exporting agent of the license application; and

(iii) any consignee or end user of any item to be exported; and

(E) the term 'person' means a natural person as well as a corporation, business association, partnership, society, trust, or any other entity, organization, or group, including governmental entities.

(h) Judicial review of designation of items as defense articles or services. The designation by the President (or by an official to whom the President's functions under subsection (a) of this section have been duly delegated), in regulations issued under this section, of items as defense articles or defense services for purposes of this section shall not be subject to judicial review. . . .

Sec. 2780. Transactions with countries supporting acts of international terrorism.

(a) Prohibited transactions by United States Government. The following transactions by the United States Government are prohibited:

(1) Exporting or otherwise providing (by sale, lease or loan, grant, or other means), directly or indirectly, any munitions item to a country described in subsection (d) of this section under the authority of this chapter, the Foreign Assistance Act of 1961 (22 U.S.C. 2151 et seq.), or any other law (except as provided in subsection (h) of this section). In implementing this paragraph, the United States Government—

(A) shall suspend delivery to such country of any such item pursuant to any such transaction which has not been completed at the time the Secretary of State makes the determination described in subsection (d) of this section, and

(B) shall terminate any lease or loan to such country of any such item which is in effect at the time the Secretary of State makes that determination.

(2) Providing credits, guarantees, or other financial assistance under the authority of this chapter, the Foreign Assistance Act of 1961 (22 U.S.C. 2151 et seq.), or any other law (except as provided in subsection (h) of this section), with respect to the acquisition of any munitions item by a country described in subsection (d) of this section. In implementing this paragraph, the United States Government shall suspend expenditures pursuant to any such assistance obligated before the Secretary of State makes the determination described in subsection (d) of this section. The President may authorize expenditures otherwise required to be suspended pursuant to the preceding sentence if the President has determined, and

reported to the Congress, that suspension of those expenditures causes undue financial hardship to a supplier, shipper, or similar person and allowing the expenditure will not result in any munitions item being made available for use by such country.

(3)   Consenting under section 2753(a) of this title, under section 505(a) of the Foreign Assistance Act of 1961 (22 U.S.C. 2314(a)), under the regulations issued to carry out section 2778 of this title, or under any other law (except as provided in subsection (h) of this section), to any transfer of any munitions item to a country described in subsection (d) of this section. In implementing this paragraph, the United States Government shall withdraw any such consent which is in effect at the time the Secretary of State makes the determination described in subsection (d) of this section, except that this sentence does not apply with respect to any item that has already been transferred to such country.

(4)   Providing any license or other approval under section 2778 of this title for any export or other transfer (including by means of a technical assistance agreement, manufacturing licensing agreement, or coproduction agreement) of any munitions item to a country described in subsection (d) of this section. In implementing this paragraph, the United States Government shall suspend any such license or other approval which is in effect at the time the Secretary of State makes the determination described in subsection (d) of this section, except that this sentence does not apply with respect to any item that has already been exported or otherwise transferred to such country.

(5)   Otherwise facilitating the acquisition of any munitions item by a country described in subsection (d) of this section. This paragraph applies with respect to activities undertaken—

(A)   by any department, agency, or other instrumentality of the Government,

(B)   by any officer or employee of the Government (including members of the United States Armed Forces), or

(C)   by any other person at the request or on behalf of the Government.

The Secretary of State may waive the requirements of the second sentence of paragraph (1), the second sentence of paragraph (3), and the second sentence of paragraph (4) to the extent that the Secretary determines, after consultation with the Congress, that unusual and compelling circumstances require that the United States Government not take the actions specified in that sentence.

(b)   Prohibited transactions by United States persons.

(1)   In general. A United States person may not take any of the following actions:

(A)   Exporting any munitions item to any country described in subsection (d) of this section.

(B)   Selling, leasing, loaning, granting, or otherwise providing any munitions item to any country described in subsection (d) of this section.

(C)   Selling, leasing, loaning, granting, or otherwise providing any munitions item to any recipient which is not the government of or a person in a country described in subsection (d) of this section if the United States person has reason to know that the munitions item will be made available to any country described in subsection (d) of this section.

(D)   Taking any other action which would facilitate the acquisition, directly or indirectly, of any munitions item by the government of any country described in subsection (d) of this section, or any person acting on behalf of that government, if the United States person has reason to know that that action will facilitate the acquisition of that item by such a government or person.

(2)   Liability for actions of foreign subsidiaries, etc. A United States person violates this subsection if a corporation or other person that is controlled in fact by that United States person (as determined under regulations, which the President shall issue) takes an action described in paragraph (1) outside the United States.

(3)   Applicability to actions outside the United States. Paragraph (1) applies with respect to actions described in that paragraph which are taken either within or outside the United States by a United States person described in subsection (l)(3)(A) or (B) of this section. To the extent provided in regulations issued under subsection (l)(3)(D) of this section, paragraph (1) applies with respect to actions described in that paragraph which are taken outside the United States by a person designated as a United States person in those regulations.

(c)   Transfers to governments and persons covered. This section applies with respect to—

(1)   the acquisition of munitions items by the government of a country described in subsection (d) of this section; and

(2)   the acquisition of munitions items by any individual, group, or other person within a country described in subsection (d) of this section, except to the extent that subparagraph (D) of subsection (b)(1) of this section provides otherwise.

(d)   Countries covered by prohibition. The prohibitions contained in this section apply with respect to a country if the Secretary of State determines that the government of that country has repeatedly provided support for acts of international terrorism.

(e)   Publication of determinations. Each determination of the Secretary of State under subsection (d) of this section shall be published in the Federal Register.

(f)   Rescission.

(1)   A determination made by the Secretary of State under subsection (d) of this section may not be rescinded unless the President submits to the Speaker of the House of Representatives and the chairman of the Committee on Foreign Relations of the Senate—

(A)   before the proposed rescission would take effect, a report certifying that—

(i)   there has been a fundamental change in the leadership and policies of the government of the country concerned;

(ii)   that government is not supporting acts of international terrorism; and

(iii)   that government has provided assurances that it will not support acts of international terrorism in the future; or

(B)   at least 45 days before the proposed rescission would take effect, a report justifying the rescission and certifying that—

(i)   the government concerned has not provided any support for international terrorism during the preceding 6-month period; and

(ii)   the government concerned has provided assurances that it will not support acts of international terrorism in the future.

(2)(A) No rescission under paragraph (1)(B) of a determination under subsection (d) of this section may be made if the Congress, within 45 days after receipt of a report under paragraph (1)(B), enacts a joint resolution the matter after the resolving clause of which is as follows: 'That the proposed rescission of the determination under section 40(d) of the Arms Export Control Act pursuant to the report submitted to the Congress on XXXXXXXXX is hereby prohibited.', the blank to be completed with the appropriate date.

(B)   A joint resolution described in subparagraph (A) and introduced within the appropriate 45-day period shall be considered in the Senate and the House of Representatives in accordance with paragraphs (3) through (7) of section 8066(c) of the Department of Defense Appropriations Act (as contained in Public Law 98-473), except that references in such paragraphs to the Committees on Appropriations of the House of Representatives and the Senate shall be deemed to be references to the Committee on Foreign Affairs of the House of Representatives and the Committee on Foreign Relations of the Senate, respectively.

(g)   Waiver. The President may waive the prohibitions contained in this section with respect to a specific transaction if—

(1)   the President determines that the transaction is essential to the national security interests of the United States; and

(2)   not less than 15 days prior to the proposed transaction, the President—

(A)   consults with the Committee on Foreign Affairs of the House of Representatives and the Committee on Foreign Relations of the Senate; and

(B)   submits to the Speaker of the House of Representatives and the chairman of the Committee on Foreign Relations of the Senate a report containing—

(i)   the name of any country involved in the proposed transaction, the identity of any recipient of the items to be provided pursuant to the proposed transaction, and the anticipated use of those items;

(ii)   a description of the munitions items involved in the proposed transaction (including their market value) and the actual sale price at each step in the transaction (or if the items are transferred by other than sale, the manner in which they will be provided);

(iii)   the reasons why the proposed transaction is essential to the national security interests of the United States and the justification for such proposed transaction;

(iv)   the date on which the proposed transaction is expected to occur; and

(v)   the name of every United States Government department, agency, or other entity involved in the proposed transaction, every foreign government involved in the proposed transaction, and every private party with significant participation in the proposed transaction.

To the extent possible, the information specified in subparagraph (B) of paragraph (2) shall be provided in unclassified form, with any classified information provided in an addendum to the report.

(h) Exemption for transactions subject to National Security Act reporting requirements. The prohibitions contained in this section do not apply with respect to any transaction subject to reporting requirements under title V of the National Security Act of 1947 (50 U.S.C. 413 et seq.; relating to congressional oversight of intelligence activities).

(i) Relation to other laws.
(1) In general. With regard to munitions items controlled pursuant to this chapter, the provisions of this section shall apply notwithstanding any other provision of law, other than section 614(a) of the Foreign Assistance Act of 1961 (22 U.S.C. 2364(a)).
(2) Section 614(a) waiver authority. If the authority of section 614(a) of the Foreign Assistance Act of 1961 (22 U.S.C. 2364(a)) is used to permit a transaction under that Act (22 U.S.C. 2151 et seq.) or this chapter which is otherwise prohibited by this section, the written policy justification required by that section shall include the information specified in subsection (g)(2)(B) of this section.

(j) Criminal penalty. Any person who willfully violates this section shall be fined for each violation not more than $1,000,000, imprisoned not more than 10 years, or both.

(k) Civil penalties; enforcement. In the enforcement of this section, the President is authorized to exercise the same powers concerning violations and enforcement which are conferred upon departments, agencies, and officials by sections 11(c), 11(e), 11(g), and 12(a) of the Export Administration Act of 1979 (50 App. U.S.C. 2410(c), (e), (g), 2411(a)) (subject to the same terms and conditions as are applicable to such powers under that Act (50 App. U.S.C. 2401 et seq.)), except that, notwithstanding section 11(c) of that Act, the civil penalty for each violation of this section may not exceed $500,000.

(l) Definitions. As used in this section—
(1) the term 'munitions item' means any item enumerated on the United States Munitions List (without regard to whether the item is imported into or exported from the United States);
(2) the term 'United States', when used geographically, means the several States, the District of Columbia, the Commonwealth of Puerto Rico, the Commonwealth of the Northern Mariana Islands, and any territory or possession of the United States; and
(3) the term 'United States person' means—
(A) any citizen or permanent resident alien of the United States;
(B) any sole proprietorship, partnership, company, association, or corporation having its principal place of business within the United States or organized under the laws of the United States, any State, the District of Columbia, the Common-

wealth of Puerto Rico, the Commonwealth of the Northern Mariana Islands, or any territory or possession of the United States;

(C)   any other person with respect to that person's actions while in the United States; and

(D)   to the extent provided in regulations issued by the Secretary of State, any person that is not described in subparagraph (A), (B), or (C) but—

(i)   is a foreign subsidiary or affiliate of a United States person described in subparagraph (B) and is controlled in fact by that United States person (as determined in accordance with those regulations), or

(ii)   is otherwise subject to the jurisdiction of the United States, with respect to that person's actions while outside the United States. . . .

Sec. 2794.   Definitions.

For purposes of this chapter, the term—

(1)   "excess defense article" has the meaning provided by section 2403(g) of this title;

(2)   "value" means, in the case of an excess defense article, except as otherwise provided in section 2761(a) of this title, not less than the greater of—

(A)   the gross cost incurred by the United States Government in repairing, rehabilitating, or modifying such article, plus the scrap value; or

(B)   the market value, if ascertainable;

(3)   "defense article", except as provided in paragraph (7) of this section, includes—

(A)   any weapon, weapons system, munition, aircraft, vessel, boat, or other implement of war,

(B)   any property, installation, commodity, material, equipment, supply, or goods used for the purposes of making military sales,

(C)   any machinery, facility, tool, material, supply, or other item necessary for the manufacture, production, processing, repair, servicing, storage, construction, transportation, operation, or use of any article listed in this paragraph, and

(D)   any component or part of any article listed in this paragraph,

but does not include merchant vessels or (as defined by the Atomic Energy Act of 1954 (42 U.S.C. 2011 et seq.)) source material (except uranium depleted in the isotope 235 which is incorporated in defense articles solely to take advantage of high density or pyrophoric characteristics unrelated to radioactivity), byproduct material, special nuclear material, production facilities, utilization facilities, or atomic weapons or articles involving Restricted Data;

(4)   "defense service", except as provided in paragraph (7) of this section, includes any service, test, inspection, repair, training, publication, technical or other assistance, or defense information (as defined in section 2403(e) of this title),

used for the purposes of making military sales, but does not include design and construction services under section 2769 of this title;

(5) "training" includes formal or informal instruction of foreign students in the United States or overseas by officers or employees of the United States, contract technicians, or contractors (including instruction at civilian institutions), or by correspondence courses, technical, educational, or information publications and media of all kinds, training aid, orientation, training exercise, and military advice to foreign military units and forces;

(6) "major defense equipment" means any item of significant military equipment on the United States Munitions List having a nonrecurring research and development cost of more than $50,000,000 or a total production cost of more than $200,000,000;

(7) "defense articles and defense services" means, with respect to commercial exports subject to the provisions of section 2778 of this title, those items designated by the President pursuant to subsection (a)(1) of such section; and

(8) "design and construction services" means, with respect to sales under section 2769 of this title, the design and construction of real property facilities, including necessary construction equipment and materials, engineering services, construction contract management services relating thereto, and technical advisory assistance in the operation and maintenance of real property facilities provided or performed by any department or agency of the Department of Defense or by a contractor pursuant to a contract with such department or agency.

N.2   EXECUTIVE ORDERS

N.2.1   Executive Order 12333 (U.S. Intelligence Activities)

Timely and accurate information about the activities, capabilities, plans, and intentions of foreign powers, organizations, and persons and their agents, is essential to the national security of the United States. All reasonable and lawful means must be used to ensure that the United States will receive the best intelligence available. For that purpose, by virtue of the authority vested in me by the Constitution and statutes of the United States of America, including the National Security Act of 1947, as amended, and as President of the United States of America, in order to provide for the effective conduct of United States intelligence activities and the protection of constitutional rights, it is hereby ordered as follows:

Part 1
Goals, Direction, Duties and Responsibilities With Respect to the
National Intelligence Effort

1.1   Goals. The United States intelligence effort shall provide the President
and the National Security Council with the necessary information on which to
base decisions concerning the conduct and development of foreign, defense and
economic policy, and the protection of United States national interests from foreign security threats. All departments and agencies shall cooperate fully to fulfill
this goal.

(a)   Maximum emphasis should be given to fostering analytical competition among appropriate elements of the Intelligence Community.

(b)   All means, consistent with applicable United States law and this Order, and with full consideration of the rights of United States persons, shall be
used to develop intelligence information for the President and the National Security Council. A balanced approach between technical collection efforts and other
means should be maintained and encouraged.

(c)   Special emphasis should be given to detecting and countering espionage and other threats and activities directed by foreign intelligence services
against the United States Government, or United States corporations, establishments, or persons.

(d)   To the greatest extent possible consistent with applicable United States
law and this Order, and with full consideration of the rights of United States
persons, all agencies and departments should seek to ensure full and free exchange of information in order to derive maximum benefit from the United States
intelligence effort.

1.2   The National Security Council.

(a)   Purpose. The National Security Council (NSC) was established by the
National Security Act of 1947 to advise the President with respect to the integration of domestic, foreign and military policies relating to the national security. The
NSC shall act as the highest Executive Branch entity that provides review of,
guidance for and direction to the conduct of all national foreign intelligence,
counterintelligence, and special activities, and attendant policies and programs.

(b)   Committees. The NSC shall establish such committees as may be necessary to carry out its functions and responsibilities under this Order. The NSC, or
a committee established by it, shall consider and submit to the President a policy
recommendation, including all dissents, on each special activity and shall review
proposals for other sensitive intelligence operations.

1.3   National Foreign Intelligence Advisory Groups.

(a)   Establishment and Duties. The Director of Central Intelligence shall
establish such boards, councils, or groups as required for the purpose of obtaining
advice from within the Intelligence Community concerning:

(1)   Production, review and coordination of national foreign intelligence;

(2) Priorities for the National Foreign Intelligence Program budget;

(3) Interagency exchanges of foreign intelligence information;

(4) Arrangements with foreign governments on intelligence matters;

(5) Protection of intelligence sources and methods;

(6) Activities of common concern; and

(7) Such other matters as may be referred by the Director of Central Intelligence.

(b) Membership. Advisory groups established pursuant to this section shall be chaired by the Director of Central Intelligence or his designated representative and shall consist of senior representatives from organizations within the Intelligence Community and from departments or agencies containing such organizations, as designated by the Director of Central Intelligence. Groups for consideration of substantive intelligence matters will include representatives of organizations involved in the collection, processing and analysis of intelligence. A senior representative of the Secretary of Commerce, the Attorney General, the Assistant to the President for National Security Affairs, and the Office of the Secretary of Defense shall be invited to participate in any group which deals with other than substantive intelligence matters.

1.4   The Intelligence Community. The agencies within the Intelligence Community shall, in accordance with applicable United States law and with the other provisions of this Order, conduct intelligence activities necessary for the conduct of foreign relations and the protection of the national security of the United States, including:

(a) Collection of information needed by the President, the National Security Council, the Secretaries of State and Defense, and other Executive Branch officials for the performance of their duties and responsibilities;

(b) Production and dissemination of intelligence;

(c) Collection of information concerning, and the conduct of activities to protect against, intelligence activities directed against the United States, international terrorist and international narcotics activities, and other hostile activities directed against the United States by foreign powers, organizations, persons, and their agents;

(d) Special activities;

(e) Administrative and support activities within the United States and abroad necessary for the performance of authorized activities; and

(f) Such other intelligence activities as the President may direct from time to time.

1.5   Director of Central Intelligence. In order to discharge the duties and responsibilities prescribed by law, the Director of Central Intelligence shall be responsible directly to the President and the NSC and shall:

(a) Act as the primary adviser to the President and the NSC on national foreign intelligence and provide the President and other officials in the Executive Branch with national foreign intelligence;

(b) Develop such objectives and guidance for the Intelligence Community as will enhance capabilities for responding to expected future needs for national foreign intelligence;

(c) Promote the development and maintenance of services of common concern by designated intelligence organizations on behalf of the Intelligence Community;

(d) Ensure implementation of special activities;

(e) Formulate policies concerning foreign intelligence and counterintelligence arrangements with foreign governments, coordinate foreign intelligence and counterintelligence relationships between agencies of the Intelligence Community and the intelligence or internal security services of foreign governments, and establish procedures governing the conduct of liaison by any department or agency with such services on narcotics activities;

(f) Participate in the development of procedures approved by the Attorney General governing criminal narcotics intelligence activities abroad to ensure that these activities are consistent with foreign intelligence programs;

(g) Ensure the establishment by the Intelligence Community of common security and access standards for managing and handling foreign intelligence systems, information, and products;

(h) Ensure that programs are developed which protect intelligence sources, methods, and analytical procedures;

(i) Establish uniform criteria for the determination of relative priorities for the transmission of critical national foreign intelligence, and advise the Secretary of Defense concerning the communications requirements of the Intelligence Community for the transmission of such intelligence;

(j) Establish appropriate staffs, committees, or other advisory groups to assist in the execution of the Director's responsibilities;

(k) Have full responsibility for production and dissemination of national foreign intelligence, and authority to levy analytic tasks on departmental intelligence production organizations, in consultation with those organizations, ensuring that appropriate mechanisms for competitive analysis are developed so that diverse points of view are considered fully and differences of judgment within the Intelligence Community are brought to the attention of national policymakers;

(l) Ensure the timely exploitation and dissemination of data gathered by national foreign intelligence collection means, and ensure that the resulting intelligence is disseminated immediately to appropriate government entities and military commands;

(m) Establish mechanisms which translate national foreign intelligence objectives and priorities approved by the NSC into specific guidance for the Intelligence Community, resolve conflicts in tasking priority, provide to departments and agencies having information collection capabilities that are not part of the National Foreign Intelligence Program advisory tasking concerning collection of national foreign intelligence, and provide for the development of plans and arrangements for transfer of required collection tasking authority to the Secretary of Defense when directed by the President;

(n) Develop, with the advice of the program managers and departments and agencies concerned, the consolidated National Foreign Intelligence Program budget, and present it to the President and the Congress;

(o) Review and approve all requests for reprogramming National Foreign Intelligence Program funds, in accordance with guidelines established by the Office of Management and Budget;

(p) Monitor National Foreign Intelligence Program implementation, and, as necessary, conduct program and performance audits and evaluations;

(q) Together with the Secretary of Defense, ensure that there is no unnecessary overlap between national foreign intelligence programs and Department of Defense intelligence programs consistent with the requirement to develop competitive analysis, and provide to and obtain from the Secretary of Defense all information necessary for this purpose;

(r) In accordance with law and relevant procedures approved by the Attorney General under this Order, give the heads of the departments and agencies access to all intelligence, developed by the CIA or the staff elements of the Director of Central Intelligence, relevant to the national intelligence needs of the departments and agencies; and

(s) Facilitate the use of national foreign intelligence products by Congress in a secure manner.

1.6 Duties and Responsibilities of the Heads of Executive Branch Departments and Agencies.

(a) The heads of all Executive Branch departments and agencies shall, in accordance with law and relevant procedures approved by the Attorney General under this Order, give the Director of Central Intelligence access to all information relevant to the national intelligence needs of the United States, and shall give due consideration to the requests from the Director of Central Intelligence for appropriate support for Intelligence Community activities.

(b) The heads of departments and agencies involved in the National Foreign Intelligence Program shall ensure timely development and submission to the Director of Central Intelligence by the program managers and heads of component activities of proposed national programs and budgets in the format designated by the Director of Central Intelligence, and shall also ensure that the Director of Central Intelligence is provided, in a timely and responsive manner, all information necessary to perform the Director's program and budget responsibilities.

(c) The heads of departments and agencies involved in the National Foreign Intelligence Program may appeal to the President decisions by the Director of Central Intelligence on budget or reprogramming matters of the National Foreign Intelligence Program.

1.7 Senior Officials of the Intelligence Community. The heads of departments and agencies with organizations in the Intelligence Community or the heads of such organizations, as appropriate, shall:

(a) Report to the Attorney General possible violations of federal criminal laws by employees and of specified federal criminal laws by any other person as provided in procedures agreed upon by the Attorney General and the head of the department or agency concerned, in a manner consistent with the protection of intelligence sources and methods, as specified in those procedures;

(b)   In any case involving serious or continuing breaches of security, recommend to the Attorney General that the case be referred to the FBI for further investigation;

(c)   Furnish the Director of Central Intelligence and the NSC, in accordance with applicable law and procedures approved by the Attorney General under this Order, the information required for the performance of their respective duties;

(d)   Report to the Intelligence Oversight Board, and keep the Director of Central Intelligence appropriately informed, concerning any intelligence activities of their organizations that they have reason to believe may be unlawful or contrary to Executive order or Presidential directive;

(e)   Protect intelligence and intelligence sources and methods from unauthorized disclosure consistent with guidance from the Director of Central Intelligence;

(f)   Disseminate intelligence to cooperating foreign governments under arrangements established or agreed to by the Director of Central Intelligence;

(g)   Participate in the development of procedures approved by the Attorney General governing production and dissemination of intelligence resulting from criminal narcotics intelligence activities abroad if their departments, agencies, or organizations have intelligence responsibilities for foreign or domestic narcotics production and trafficking;

(h)   Instruct their employees to cooperate fully with the Intelligence Oversight Board; and

(i)   Ensure that the Inspectors General and General Counsels for their organizations have access to any information necessary to perform their duties assigned by this Order.

1.8   The Central Intelligence Agency. All duties and responsibilities of the CIA shall be related to the intelligence functions set out below. As authorized by this Order; the National Security Act of 1947, as amended; the CIA Act of 1949, as amended; appropriate directives or other applicable law, the CIA shall:

(a)   Collect, produce and disseminate foreign intelligence and counterintelligence, including information not otherwise obtainable. The collection of foreign intelligence or counterintelligence within the United States shall be coordinated with the FBI as required by procedures agreed upon by the Director of Central Intelligence and the Attorney General;

(b)   Collect, produce and disseminate intelligence on foreign aspects of narcotics production and trafficking;

(c)   Conduct counterintelligence activities outside the United States and, without assuming or performing any internal security functions, conduct counterintelligence activities within the United States in coordination with the FBI as required by procedures agreed upon by the Director of Central Intelligence and the Attorney General;

(d)   Coordinate counterintelligence activities and the collection of information not otherwise obtainable when conducted outside the United States by other departments and agencies;

(e)   Conduct special activities approved by the President. No agency except the CIA (or the Armed Forces of the United States in time of war declared by Congress or during any period covered by a report from the President to the Congress under the War Powers Resolution (87 Stat. 855))* may conduct any special activity unless the President determines that another agency is more likely to achieve a particular objective;

(f)   Conduct services of common concern for the Intelligence Community as directed by the NSC;

(g)   Carry out or contract for research, development and procurement of technical systems and devices relating to authorized functions;

(h)   Protect the security of its installations, activities, information, property, and employees by appropriate means, including such investigations of applicants, employees, contractors, and other persons with similar associations with the CIA as are necessary; and

(i)   Conduct such administrative and technical support activities within and outside the United States as are necessary to perform the functions described in sections (a) through (h) above, including procurement and essential cover and proprietary arrangements.

1.9   The Department of State. The Secretary of State shall:

(a)   Overtly collect information relevant to United States foreign policy concerns;

(b)   Produce and disseminate foreign intelligence relating to United States foreign policy as required for the execution of the Secretary's responsibilities;

(c)   Disseminate, as appropriate, reports received from United States diplomatic and consular posts;

(d)   Transmit reporting requirements of the Intelligence Community to the Chiefs of United States Missions abroad; and

(e)   Support Chiefs of Missions in discharging their statutory responsibilities for direction and coordination of mission activities.

1.10   The Department of the Treasury. The Secretary of the Treasury shall:

(a)   Overtly collect foreign financial and monetary information;

(b)   Participate with the Department of State in the overt collection of general foreign economic information;

(c)   Produce and disseminate foreign intelligence relating to United States economic policy as required for the execution of the Secretary's responsibilities; and

(d)   Conduct, through the United States Secret Service, activities to determine the existence and capability of surveillance equipment being used against the President of the United States, the Executive Office of the President, and, as authorized by the Secretary of the Treasury or the President, other Secret Service protectees and United States officials.

No information shall be acquired intentionally through such activities except to protect against such surveillance, and those activities shall be conducted pursuant to procedures agreed upon by the Secretary of the Treasury and the Attorney General.

1.11   The Department of Defense. The Secretary of Defense shall:
  (a)   Collect national foreign intelligence and be responsive to collection tasking by the Director of Central Intelligence;
  (b)   Collect, produce and disseminate military and military-related foreign intelligence and counterintelligence as required for execution of the Secretary's responsibilities;
  (c)   Conduct programs and missions necessary to fulfill national, departmental and tactical foreign intelligence requirements;
  (d)   Conduct counterintelligence activities in support of Department of Defense components outside the United States in coordination with the CIA, and within the United States in coordination with the FBI pursuant to procedures agreed upon by the Secretary of Defense and the Attorney General;
  (e)   Conduct, as the executive agent of the United States Government, signals intelligence and communications security activities, except as otherwise directed by the NSC;
  (f)   for the timely transmission of critical intelligence, as defined by the Director of Central Intelligence, within the United States Government;
  (g)   Carry out or contract for research, development and procurement of technical systems and devices relating to authorized intelligence functions;
  (h)   Protect the security of Department of Defense installations, activities, property, information, and employees by appropriate means, including such investigations of applicants, employees, contractors, and other persons with similar associations with the Department of Defense as are necessary;
  (i)   Establish and maintain military intelligence relationships and military intelligence exchange programs with selected cooperative foreign defense establishments and international organizations, and ensure that such relationships and programs are in accordance with policies formulated by the Director of Central Intelligence;
  (j)   Direct, operate, control and provide fiscal management for the National Security Agency and for defense and military intelligence and national reconnaissance entities; and
  (k)   Conduct such administrative and technical support activities within and outside the United States as are necessary to perform the functions described in sections (a) through (j) above.

1.12   Intelligence Components Utilized by the Secretary of Defense. In carrying out the responsibilities assigned in section 1.11, the Secretary of Defense is authorized to utilize the following:
  (a)   Defense Intelligence Agency, whose responsibilities shall include;
      (1)   Collection, production, or, through tasking and coordination, provision of military and military-related intelligence for the Secretary of Defense, the Joint Chiefs of Staff, other Defense components, and, as appropriate, non-Defense agencies;
      (2)   Collection and provision of military intelligence for national foreign intelligence and counterintelligence products;
      (3)   Coordination of all Department of Defense intelligence collection requirements;

(4)   Management of the Defense Attache system; and

(5)   Provision of foreign intelligence and counterintelligence staff support as directed by the Joint Chiefs of Staff.

(b)   National Security Agency, whose responsibilities shall include:

(1)   Establishment and operation of an effective unified organization for signals intelligence activities, except for the delegation of operational control over certain operations that are conducted through other elements of the Intelligence Community. No other department or agency may engage in signals intelligence activities except pursuant to a delegation by the Secretary of Defense;

(2)   Control of signals intelligence collection and processing activities, including assignment of resources to an appropriate agent for such periods and tasks as required for the direct support of military commanders;

(3)   Collection of signals intelligence information for national foreign intelligence purposes in accordance with guidance from the Director of Central Intelligence;

(4)   Processing of signals intelligence data for national foreign intelligence purposes in accordance with guidance from the Director of Central Intelligence;

(5)   Dissemination of signals intelligence information for national foreign intelligence purposes to authorized elements of the Government, including the military services, in accordance with guidance from the Director of Central Intelligence;

(6)   Collection, processing and dissemination of signals intelligence information for counterintelligence purposes;

(7)   Provision of signals intelligence support for the conduct of military operations in accordance with tasking, priorities, and standards of timeliness assigned by the Secretary of Defense. If provision of such support requires use of national collection systems, these systems will be tasked within existing guidance from the Director of Central Intelligence;

(8)   Executing the responsibilities of the Secretary of Defense as executive agent for the communications security of the United States Government;

(9)   Conduct of research and development to meet the needs of the United States for signals intelligence and communications security;

(10)   Protection of the security of its installations, activities, property, information, and employees by appropriate means, including such investigations of applicants, employees, contractors, and other persons with similar associations with the NSA as are necessary;

(11)   Prescribing, within its field of authorized operations, security regulations covering operating practices, including the transmission, handling and distribution of signals intelligence and communications security material within and among the elements under control of the Director of the NSA, and exercising the necessary supervisory control to ensure compliance with the regulations;

(12)   Conduct of foreign cryptologic liaison relationships, with liaison for intelligence purposes conducted in accordance with policies formulated by the Director of Central Intelligence; and

(13)   Conduct of such administrative and technical support activities

within and outside the United States as are necessary to perform the functions described in sections (1) through (12) above, including procurement.

(c)   Offices for the collection of specialized intelligence through reconnaissance programs, whose responsibilities shall include:

(1)   Carrying out consolidated reconnaissance programs for specialized intelligence;

(2)   Responding to tasking in accordance with procedures established by the Director of Central Intelligence; and

(3)   Delegating authority to the various departments and agencies for research, development, procurement, and operation of designated means of collection.

(d)   The foreign intelligence and counterintelligence elements of the Army, Navy, Air Force, and Marine Corps, whose responsibilities shall include:

(1)   Collection, production and dissemination of military and military-related foreign intelligence and counterintelligence, and information on the foreign aspects of narcotics production and trafficking. When collection is conducted in response to national foreign intelligence requirements, it will be conducted in accordance with guidance from the Director of Central Intelligence. Collection of national foreign intelligence, not otherwise obtainable, outside the United States shall be coordinated with the CIA, and such collection within the United States shall be coordinated with the FBI;

(2)   Conduct of counterintelligence activities outside the United States in coordination with the CIA, and within the United States in coordination with the FBI; and

(3)   Monitoring of the development, procurement and management of tactical intelligence systems and equipment and conducting related research, development, and test and evaluation activities.

(e)   Other offices within the Department of Defense appropriate for conduct of the intelligence missions and responsibilities assigned to the Secretary of Defense. If such other offices are used for intelligence purposes, the provisions of Part 2 of this Order shall apply to those offices when used for those purposes.

1.13   The Department of Energy. The Secretary of Energy shall:

(a)   Participate with the Department of State in overtly collecting information with respect to foreign energy matters;

(b)   Produce and disseminate foreign intelligence necessary for the Secretary's responsibilities;

(c)   Participate in formulating intelligence collection and analysis requirements where the special expert capability of the Department can contribute; and

(d)   Provide expert technical, analytical and research capability to other agencies within the Intelligence Community.

1.14   The Federal Bureau of Investigation. Under the supervision of the Attorney General and pursuant to such regulations as the Attorney General may establish, the Director of the FBI shall:

(a)   Within the United States conduct counterintelligence and coordinate counterintelligence activities of other agencies within the Intelligence Community. When a counterintelligence activity of the FBI involves military or civilian personnel of the Department of Defense, the FBI shall coordinate with the Department of Defense;

(b) Conduct counterintelligence activities outside the United States in coordination with the CIA as required by procedures agreed upon by the Director of Central Intelligence and the Attorney General;

(c) Conduct within the United States, when requested by officials of the Intelligence Community designated by the President, activities undertaken to collect foreign intelligence or support foreign intelligence collection requirements of other agencies within the Intelligence Community, or, when requested by the Director of the National Security Agency, to support the communications security activities of the United States Government;

(d) Produce and disseminate foreign intelligence and counterintelligence; and

(e) Carry out or contract for research, development and procurement of technical systems and devices relating to the functions authorized above.

Part 2
Conduct of Intelligence Activities

2.1 Need. Accurate and timely information about the capabilities, intentions and activities of foreign powers, organizations, or persons and their agents is essential to informed decisionmaking in the areas of national defense and foreign relations. Collection of such information is a priority objective and will be pursued in a vigorous, innovative and responsible manner that is consistent with the Constitution and applicable law and respectful of the principles upon which the United States was founded.

2.2 Purpose. This Order is intended to enhance human and technical collection techniques, especially those undertaken abroad, and the acquisition of significant foreign intelligence, as well as the detection and countering of international terrorist activities and espionage conducted by foreign powers. Set forth below are certain general principles that, in addition to and consistent with applicable laws, are intended to achieve the proper balance between the acquisition of essential information and protection of individual interests. Nothing in this Order shall be construed to apply to or interfere with any authorized civil or criminal law enforcement responsibility of any department or agency.

2.3 Collection of Information. Agencies within the Intelligence Community are authorized to collect, retain or disseminate information concerning United States persons only in accordance with procedures established by the head of the agency concerned and approved by the Attorney General, consistent with the authorities provided by Part 1 of this Order. Those procedures shall permit collection, retention and dissemination of the following types of information:

(a)   Information that is publicly available or collected with the consent of the person concerned;

(b)   Information constituting foreign intelligence or counterintelligence, including such information concerning corporations or other commercial organizations. Collection within the United States of foreign intelligence not otherwise obtainable shall be undertaken by the FBI or, when significant foreign intelligence is sought, by other authorized agencies of the Intelligence Community, provided that no foreign intelligence collection by such agencies may be undertaken for the purpose of acquiring information concerning the domestic activities of United States persons;

(c)   Information obtained in the course of a lawful foreign intelligence, counterintelligence, international narcotics or international terrorism investigation;

(d)   Information needed to protect the safety of any persons or organizations, including those who are targets, victims or hostages of international terrorist organizations;

(e)   Information needed to protect foreign intelligence or counterintelligence sources or methods from unauthorized disclosure. Collection within the United States shall be undertaken by the FBI except that other agencies of the Intelligence Community may also collect such information concerning present or former employees, present or former intelligence agency contractors or their present or former employees, or applicants for any such employment or contracting;

(f)   Information concerning persons who are reasonably believed to be potential sources or contacts for the purpose of determining their suitability or credibility;

(g)   Information arising out of a lawful personnel, physical or communications security investigation;

(h)   Information acquired by overhead reconnaissance not directed at specific United States persons;

(i)   Incidentally obtained information that may indicate involvement in activities that may violate federal, state, local or foreign laws; and

(j)   Information necessary for administrative purposes. In addition, agencies within the Intelligence Community may disseminate information, other than information derived from signals intelligence, to each appropriate agency within the Intelligence Community for purposes of allowing the recipient agency to determine whether the information is relevant to its responsibilities and can be retained by it.

2.4   Collection Techniques.   Agencies within the Intelligence Community shall use the least intrusive collection techniques feasible within the United States or directed against United States persons abroad. Agencies are not authorized to use such techniques as electronic surveillance, unconsented physical search, mail surveillance, physical surveillance, or monitoring devices unless they are in accordance with procedures established by the head of the agency concerned and approved by the Attorney General. Such procedures shall protect constitutional and other legal rights and limit use of such information to lawful governmental purposes. These procedures shall not authorize:

(a) The CIA to engage in electronic surveillance within the United States except for the purpose of training, testing, or conducting countermeasures to hostile electronic surveillance;

(b) Unconsented physical searches in the United States by agencies other than the FBI, except for:

(1) Searches by counterintelligence elements of the military services directed against military personnel within the United States or abroad for intelligence purposes, when authorized by a military commander empowered to approve physical searches for law enforcement purposes, based upon a finding of probable cause to believe that such persons are acting as agents of foreign powers; and

(2) Searches by CIA of personal property of non-United States persons lawfully in its possession.

(c) Physical surveillance of a United States person in the United States by agencies other than the FBI, except for:

(1) Physical surveillance of present or former employees, present or former intelligence agency contractors or their present of former employees, or applicants for any such employment or contracting; and

(2) Physical surveillance of a military person employed by a nonintelligence element of a military service.

(d) Physical surveillance of a United States person abroad to collect foreign intelligence, except to obtain significant information that cannot reasonably be acquired by other means.

2.5 Attorney General Approval. The Attorney General hereby is delegated the power to approve the use for intelligence purposes, within the United States or against a United States person abroad, of any technique for which a warrant would be required if undertaken for law enforcement purposes, provided that such techniques shall not be undertaken unless the Attorney General has determined in each case that there is probable cause to believe that the technique is directed against a foreign power or an agent of a foreign power. Electronic surveillance, as defined in the Foreign Intelligence Surveillance Act of 1978, shall be conducted in accordance with that Act, as well as this Order.

2.6 Assistance to Law Enforcement Authorities. Agencies within the Intelligence Community are authorized to:

(a) Cooperate with appropriate law enforcement agencies for the purpose of protecting the employees, information, property and facilities of any agency within the Intelligence Community;

(b) Unless otherwise precluded by law or this Order, participate in law enforcement activities to investigate or prevent clandestine intelligence activities by foreign powers, or international terrorist or narcotics activities;

(c) Provide specialized equipment, technical knowledge, or assistance of expert personnel for use by any department or agency, or, when lives are endangered, to support local law enforcement agencies. Provision of assistance by expert personnel shall be approved in each case by the General Counsel of the providing agency; and

(d) Render any other assistance and cooperation to law enforcement authorities not precluded by applicable law.

2.7   Contracting.   Agencies within the Intelligence Community are authorized to enter into contracts or arrangements for the provision of goods or services with private companies or institutions in the United States and need not reveal the sponsorship of such contracts or arrangements for authorized intelligence purposes. Contracts or arrangements with academic institutions may be undertaken only with the contract of appropriate officials of the institution.

2.8   Consistency With Other Laws.   Nothing in this Order shall be construed to authorize any activity in violation of the Constitution or statutes of the United States.

2.9   Undisclosed Participation in Organizations Within the United States.   No one acting on behalf of agencies within the Intelligence Community may join or otherwise participate in any organization in the United States on behalf of any agency within the Intelligence Community without disclosing his intelligence affiliation to appropriate officials of the organization, except in accordance with procedures established by the head of the agency concerned and approved by the Attorney General. Such participation shall be authorized only if it is essential to achieving lawful purposes as determined by the agency head or designee. No such participation may be undertaken for the purpose of influencing the activity of the organization or its members except in cases where:

(a)   The participation is undertaken on behalf of the FBI in the course of a lawful investigation; or

(b)   The organization concerned is composed primarily of individuals who are not United States persons and is reasonably believed to be acting on behalf of a foreign power.

2.10   Human Experimentation.   No agency within the Intelligence Community shall sponsor, contract for or conduct research on human subjects except in accordance with guidelines issued by the Department of Health and Human Services. The subject's informed consent shall be documented as required by those guidelines.

2.11   Prohibition on Assassination.   No person employed by or acting on behalf of the United States Government shall engage in, or conspire to engage in, assassination.

2.12   Indirect Participation.   No agency of the Intelligence Community shall participate in or request any person to undertake activities forbidden by this Order.

Part 3
General Provisions

3.1 Congressional Oversight. The duties and responsibilities of the Director of Central Intelligence and the heads of other departments, agencies, and entities engaged in intelligence activities to cooperate with the Congress in the conduct of its responsibilities for oversight of intelligence activities shall be as provided in title 50, United States Code, section 413. The requirements of section 662 of the Foreign Assistance Act of 1961, as amended (22 U.S.C. 2422), and section 501 of the National Security Act of 1947, as amended (50 U.S.C. 413), shall apply to all special activities as defined in this Order.

3.2 Implementation. The NSC, the Secretary of Defense, the Attorney General, and the Director of Central Intelligence shall issue such appropriate directives and procedures as are necessary to implement this Order. Heads of agencies within the Intelligence Community shall issue appropriate supplementary directives and procedures consistent with this Order. The Attorney General shall provide a statement of reasons for not approving any procedures established by the head of an agency in the Intelligence Community other than the FBI. The National Security Council may establish procedures in instances where the agency head and the Attorney General are unable to reach agreement on other than constitutional or other legal grounds.

3.3 Procedures. Until the procedures required by this Order have been established, the activities herein authorized which require procedures shall be conducted in accordance with existing procedures or requirements established under Executive Order No. 12036. Procedures required by this Order shall be established as expeditiously as possible. All procedures promulgated pursuant to this Order shall be made available to the congressional intelligence committees.

3.4 Definitions. For the purposes of this Order, the following terms shall have these meanings:

(a) Counterintelligence means information gathered and activities conducted to protect against espionage, other intelligence activities, sabotage, or assassinations conducted for or on behalf of foreign powers, organizations or persons, or international terrorist activities, but not including personnel, physical, document or communications security programs.

(b) Electronic surveillance means acquisitions of a nonpublic communication by electronic means without the consent of a person who is a party to an electronic communication or, in the case of a nonelectronic communication, without the consent of a person who is visably present at the place of communication, but not including the use of radio direction-finding equipment solely to determine the location of a transmitter.

(c) Employee means a person employed by, assigned to or acting for an agency within the Intelligence Community.

(d) Foreign intelligence means information relating to the capabilities, intentions and activities of foreign powers, organizations or persons, but not including counterintelligence except for information on international terrorist activities.

(e) Intelligence activities means all activities that agencies within the Intelligence Community are authorized to conduct pursuant to this Order.

(f) Intelligence Community and agencies within the Intelligence Community refer to the following agencies or organizations:

(1) The Central Intelligence Agency (CIA);

(2) The National Security Agency (NSA);

(3) The Defense Intelligence Agency (DIA);

(4) The offices within the Department of Defense for the collection of specialized national foreign intelligence through reconnaissance programs;

(5) The Bureau of Intelligence and Research of the Department of State;

(6) The intelligence elements of the Army, Navy, Air Force, and Marine Corps, the Federal Bureau of Investigation (FBI), the Department of the Treasury, and the Department of Energy; and

(7) The staff elements of the Director of Central Intelligence.

(g) The National Foreign Intelligence Program includes the programs listed below, but its composition shall be subject to review by the National Security Council and modification by the President:

(1) The programs of the CIA;

(2) The Consolidated Cryptologic Program, the General Defense Intelligence Program, and the programs of the offices within the Department of Defense for the collection of specialized national foreign intelligence through reconnaissance, except such elements as the Director of Central Intelligence and the Secretary of Defense agree should be excluded;

(3) Other programs of agencies within the Intelligence Community designated jointly by the Director of Central Intelligence and the head of the department or by the President as national foreign intelligence or counterintelligence activities;

(4) Activities of the staff elements of the Director of Central Intelligence;

(5) Activities to acquire the intelligence required for the planning and conduct of tactical operations by the United States military forces are not included in the National Foreign Intelligence Program.

(h) Special activities means activities conducted in support of national foreign policy objectives abroad which are planned and executed so that the role of the United States Government is not apparent or acknowledged publicly, and functions in support of such activities, but which are not intended to influence United States political processes, public opinion, policies, or media and do not include diplomatic activities or the collection and production of intelligence or related support functions.

(i) United States person means a United States citizen, an alien known by the intelligence agency concerned to be a permanent resident alien, an unincorporated association substantially composed of United States citizens or permanent resident aliens, or a corporation incorporated in the United States, except for a corporation directed and controlled by a foreign government or governments.

3.5   Purpose and Effect.   This Order is intended to control and provide direction and guidance to the Intelligence Community. Nothing contained herein or in any procedures promulgated hereunder is intended to confer any substantive or procedural right or privilege on any person or organization.

3.6   Revocation.   Executive Order No. 12036 of January 24, 1978, as amended, entitled 'United States Intelligence Activities,' is revoked.

RONALD REAGAN, THE WHITE HOUSE, December 4, 1981.

N.2.2   Executive Order 12958 (Classified National Security Information)

This order prescribes a uniform system for classifying, safeguarding, and declassifying national security information. Our democratic principles require that the American people be informed of the activities of their Government. Also, our Nation's progress depends on the free flow of information. Nevertheless, throughout our history, the national interest has required that certain information be maintained in confidence in order to protect our citizens, our democratic institutions, and our participation within the community of nations. Protecting information critical to our Nation's security remains a priority. In recent years, however, dramatic changes have altered, although not eliminated, the national security threats that we confront. These changes provide a greater opportunity to emphasize our commitment to open Government.

NOW, THEREFORE, by the authority vested in me as President by the Constitution and the laws of the United States of America, it is hereby ordered as follows:

Part 1
Original Classification

Section 1.1. Definitions. For purposes of this order:

(a)   "National security" means the national defense or foreign relations of the United States.

(b)   "Information" means any knowledge that can be communicated or documentary material, regardless of its physical form or characteristics, that is owned by, produced by or for, or is under the control of the United States Government. "Control" means the authority of the agency that originates information, or its successor in function, to regulate access to the information.

(c)   "Classified national security information" (hereafter "classified information") means information that has been determined pursuant to this order or any predecessor order to require protection against unauthorized disclosure and is marked to indicate its classified status when in documentary form.

    (d) "Foreign Government Information" means:

        (1) information provided to the United States Government by a foreign government or governments, an international organization of governments, or any element thereof, with the expectation that the information, the source of the information, or both, are to be held in confidence;

        (2) information produced by the United States pursuant to or as a result of a joint arrangement with a foreign government or governments, or an international organization of governments, or any element thereof, requiring that the information, the arrangement, or both, are to be held in confidence; or

        (3) information received and treated as "Foreign Government Information" under the terms of a predecessor order.

    (e) "Classification" means the act or process by which information is determined to be classified information.

    (f) "Original classification" means an initial determination that information requires, in the interest of national security, protection against unauthorized disclosure.

    (g) "Original classification authority" means an individual authorized in writing, either by the President, or by agency heads or other officials designated by the President, to classify information in the first instance.

    (h) "Unauthorized disclosure" means a communication or physical transfer of classified information to an unauthorized recipient.

    (i) "Agency" means any "Executive agency," as defined in 5 U.S.C. 105, and any other entity within the executive branch that comes into the possession of classified information.

    (j) "Senior agency official" means the official designated by the agency head under section 5.6(c) of this order to direct and administer the agency's program under which information is classified, safeguarded, and declassified.

    (k) "Confidential source" means any individual or organization that has provided, or that may reasonably be expected to provide, information to the United States on matters pertaining to the national security with the expectation that the information or relationship, or both, are to be held in confidence.

    (l) "Damage to the national security" means harm to the national defense or foreign relations of the United States from the unauthorized disclosure of information, to include the sensitivity, value, and utility of that information.

Sec. 1.2. Classification Standards.

    (a) Information may be originally classified under the terms of this order only if all of the following conditions are met:

        (1) an original classification authority is classifying the information;

        (2) the information is owned by, produced by or for, or is under the control of the United States Government;

        (3) the information falls within one or more of the categories of information listed in section 1.5 of this order; and

        (4) the original classification authority determines that the unauthorized disclosure of the information reasonably could be expected to result in

damage to the national security and the original classification authority is able to identify or describe the damage.

(b)   If there is significant doubt about the need to classify information, it shall not be classified. This provision does not:

(1)   amplify or modify the substantive criteria or procedures for classification; or

(2)   create any substantive or procedural rights subject to judicial review.

(c)   Classified information shall not be declassified automatically as a result of any unauthorized disclosure of identical or similar information.

Sec. 1.3. Classification Levels.

(a)   Information may be classified at one of the following three levels:

(1)   "Top Secret" shall be applied to information, the unauthorized disclosure of which reasonably could be expected to cause exceptionally grave damage to the national security that the original classification authority is able to identify or describe.

(2)   "Secret" shall be applied to information, the unauthorized disclosure of which reasonably could be expected to cause serious damage to the national security that the original classification authority is able to identify or describe.

(3)   "Confidential" shall be applied to information, the unauthorized disclosure of which reasonably could be expected to cause damage to the national security that the original classification authority is able to identify or describe.

(b)   Except as otherwise provided by statute, no other terms shall be used to identify United States classified information.

(c)   If there is significant doubt about the appropriate level of classification, it shall be classified at the lower level.

Sec. 1.4. Classification Authority.

(a)   The authority to classify information originally may be exercised only by:

(1)   the President;

(2)   agency heads and officials designated by the President in the Federal Register; or

(3)   United States Government officials delegated this authority pursuant to paragraph (c), below.

(b)   Officials authorized to classify information at a specified level are also authorized to classify information at a lower level.

(c)   Delegation of original classification authority.

(1)   Delegations of original classification authority shall be limited to the minimum required to administer this order. Agency heads are responsible for ensuring that designated subordinate officials have a demonstrable and continuing need to exercise this authority.

(2)   "Top Secret" original classification authority may be delegated only by the President or by an agency head or official designated pursuant to paragraph (a)(2), above.

(3) "Secret" or "Confidential" original classification authority may be delegated only by the President; an agency head or official designated pursuant to paragraph (a)(2), above; or the senior agency official, provided that official has been delegated "Top Secret" original classification authority by the agency head.

(4) Each delegation of original classification authority shall be in writing and the authority shall not be redelegated except as provided in this order. Each delegation shall identify the official by name or position title.

(d) Original classification authorities must receive training in original classification as provided in this order and its implementing directives.

(e) Exceptional cases. When an employee, contractor, licensee, certificate holder, or grantee of an agency that does not have original classification authority originates information believed by that person to require classification, the information shall be protected in a manner consistent with this order and its implementing directives. The information shall be transmitted promptly as provided under this order or its implementing directives to the agency that has appropriate subject matter interest and classification authority with respect to this information. That agency shall decide within 30 days whether to classify this information. If it is not clear which agency has classification responsibility for this information, it shall be sent to the Director of the Information Security Oversight Office. The Director shall determine the agency having primary subject matter interest and forward the information, with appropriate recommendations, to that agency for a classification determination.

Sec. 1.5. Classification Categories. Information may not be considered for classification unless it concerns:

(a) military plans, weapons systems, or operations;

(b) foreign government information;

(c) intelligence activities (including special activities), intelligence sources or methods, or cryptology;

(d) foreign relations or foreign activities of the United States, including confidential sources;

(e) scientific, technological, or economic matters relating to the national security;

(f) United States Government programs for safeguarding nuclear materials or facilities; or

(g) vulnerabilities or capabilities of systems, installations, projects or plans relating to the national security.

Sec. 1.6. Duration of Classification.

(a) At the time of original classification, the original classification authority shall attempt to establish a specific date or event for declassification based upon the duration of the national security sensitivity of the information. The date or event shall not exceed the time frame in paragraph (b), below.

(b) If the original classification authority cannot determine an earlier specific date or event for declassification, information shall be marked for declassification 10 years from the date of the original decision, except as provided in paragraph (d), below.

(c)   An original classification authority may extend the duration of classification or reclassify specific information for successive periods not to exceed 10 years at a time if such action is consistent with the standards and procedures established under this order. This provision does not apply to information contained in records that are more than 25 years old and have been determined to have permanent historical value under title 44, United States Code.

(d)   At the time of original classification, the original classification authority may exempt from declassification within 10 years specific information, the unauthorized disclosure of which could reasonably be expected to cause damage to the national security for a period greater than that provided in paragraph (b), above, and the release of which could reasonably be expected to:

(1)   reveal an intelligence source, method, or activity, or a cryptologic system or activity;

(2)   reveal information that would assist in the development or use of weapons of mass destruction;

(3)   reveal information that would impair the development or use of technology within a United States weapons system;

(4)   reveal United States military plans, or national security emergency preparedness plans;

(5)   reveal foreign government information;

(6)   damage relations between the United States and a foreign government, reveal a confidential source, or seriously undermine diplomatic activities that are reasonably expected to be ongoing for a period greater than that provided in paragraph (b), above;

(7)   impair the ability of responsible United States Government officials to protect the President, the Vice President, and other individuals for whom protection services, in the interest of national security, are authorized; or

(8)   violate a statute, treaty, or international agreement.

(e)   Information marked for an indefinite duration of classification under predecessor orders, for example, "Originating Agency's Determination Required," or information classified under predecessor orders that contains no declassification instructions shall be declassified in accordance with part 3 of this order.

Sec. 1.7. Identification and Markings.

(a)   At the time of original classification, the following shall appear on the face of each classified document, or shall be applied to other classified media in an appropriate manner:

(1)   one of the three classification levels defined in section 1.3 of this order;

(2)   the identity, by name or personal identifier and position, of the original classification authority;

(3)   the agency and office of origin, if not otherwise evident;

(4)   declassification instructions, which shall indicate one of the following:

(A)   the date or event for declassification, as prescribed in section 1.6(a) or section 1.6(c); or

(B)   the date that is 10 years from the date of original classification, as prescribed in section 1.6(b); or

(C)   the exemption category from classification, as prescribed in section 1.6(d); and

(5)   a concise reason for classification which, at a minimum, cites the applicable classification categories in section 1.5 of this order.

(b)   Specific information contained in paragraph (a), above, may be excluded if it would reveal additional classified information.

(c)   Each classified document shall, by marking or other means, indicate which portions are classified, with the applicable classification level, which portions are exempt from declassification under section 1.6(d) of this order, and which portions are unclassified. In accordance with standards prescribed in directives issued under this order, the Director of the Information Security Oversight Office may grant waivers of this requirement for specified classes of documents or information. The Director shall revoke any waiver upon a finding of abuse.

(d)   Markings implementing the provisions of this order, including abbreviations and requirements to safeguard classified working papers, shall conform to the standards prescribed in implementing directives issued pursuant to this order.

(e)   Foreign government information shall retain its original classification markings or shall be assigned a U.S. classification that provides a degree of protection at least equivalent to that required by the entity that furnished the information.

(f)   Information assigned a level of classification under this or predecessor orders shall be considered as classified at that level of classification despite the omission of other required markings. Whenever such information is used in the derivative classification process or is reviewed for possible declassification, holders of such information shall coordinate with an appropriate classification authority for the application of omitted markings.

(g)   The classification authority shall, whenever practicable, use a classified addendum whenever classified information constitutes a small portion of an otherwise unclassified document.

Sec. 1.8. Classification Prohibitions and Limitations.

(a)   In no case shall information be classified in order to:

(1)   conceal violations of law, inefficiency, or administrative error;

(2)   prevent embarrassment to a person, organization, or agency;

(3)   restrain competition; or

(4)   prevent or delay the release of information that does not require protection in the interest of national security.

(b)   Basic scientific research information not clearly related to the national security may not be classified.

(c)   Information may not be reclassified after it has been declassified and released to the public under proper authority.

(d)   Information that has not previously been disclosed to the public under proper authority may be classified or reclassified after an agency has received a request for it under the Freedom of Information Act (5 U.S.C. 552) or the Privacy Act of 1974 (5 U.S.C. 552a), or the mandatory review provisions of section 3.6 of this order only if such classification meets the requirements of this order and is accomplished on a document-by-document basis with the personal participation or under the direction of the agency head, the deputy agency head, or the senior agency official designated under section 5.6 of this order. This provision does not apply to classified information contained in records that are more than 25 years old and have been determined to have permanent historical value under title 44, United States Code.

(e)   Compilations of items of information which are individually unclassified may be classified if the compiled information reveals an additional association or relationship that:

(1)   meets the standards for classification under this order; and

(2)   is not otherwise revealed in the individual items of information.

As used in this order, "compilation" means an aggregation of pre-existing unclassified items of information.

Sec. 1.9. Classification Challenges.

(a)   Authorized holders of information who, in good faith, believe that its classification status is improper are encouraged and expected to challenge the classification status of the information in accordance with agency procedures established under paragraph (b), below.

(b)   In accordance with implementing directives issued pursuant to this order, an agency head or senior agency official shall establish procedures under which authorized holders of information are encouraged and expected to challenge the classification of information that they believe is improperly classified or unclassified. These procedures shall assure that:

(1)   individuals are not subject to retribution for bringing such actions;

(2)   an opportunity is provided for review by an impartial official or panel; and

(3)   individuals are advised of their right to appeal agency decisions to the Interagency Security Classification Appeals Panel established by section 5.4 of this order.

Part 2
Derivative Classification

Sec. 2.1. Definitions. For purposes of this order:

(a)   "Derivative classification" means the incorporating, paraphrasing, restating or generating in new form information that is already classified, and marking the newly developed material consistent with the classification markings that apply to the source information. Derivative classification includes the classification of information based on classification guidance. The duplication or reproduction of existing classified information is not derivative classification.

(b)   "Classification guidance" means any instruction or source that prescribes the classification of specific information.

(c)   "Classification guide" means a documentary form of classification guidance issued by an original classification authority that identifies the elements of information regarding a specific subject that must be classified and establishes the level and duration of classification for each such element.

(d)   "Source document" means an existing document that contains classified information that is incorporated, paraphrased, restated, or generated in new form into a new document.

(e)   "Multiple sources" means two or more source documents, classification guides, or a combination of both.

Sec. 2.2. Use of Derivative Classification.

(a)   Persons who only reproduce, extract, or summarize classified information, or who only apply classification markings derived from source material or as directed by a classification guide, need not possess original classification authority.

(b)   Persons who apply derivative classification markings shall:

(1)   observe and respect original classification decisions; and

(2)   carry forward to any newly created documents the pertinent classification markings.

For information derivatively classified based on multiple sources, the derivative classifier shall carry forward:

(A)   the date or event for declassification that corresponds to the longest period of classification among the sources; and

(B)   a listing of these sources on or attached to the official file or record copy.

Sec. 2.3. Classification Guides.

(a)   Agencies with original classification authority shall prepare classification guides to facilitate the proper and uniform derivative classification of information. These guides shall conform to standards contained in directives issued under this order.

(b)   Each guide shall be approved personally and in writing by an official who:

(1)   has program or supervisory responsibility over the information or is the senior agency official; and

(2)   is authorized to classify information originally at the highest level of classification prescribed in the guide.

(c)   Agencies shall establish procedures to assure that classification guides are reviewed and updated as provided in directives issued under this order.

Part 3
Declassification and Downgrading

Sec. 3.1. Definitions. For purposes of this order:

(a)   "Declassification" means the authorized change in the status of information from classified information to unclassified information.

(b)   "Automatic declassification" means the declassification of information based solely upon:

(1)   the occurrence of a specific date or event as determined by the original classification authority; or

(2)   the expiration of a maximum time frame for duration of classification established under this order.

(c)   "Declassification authority" means:

(1)   the official who authorized the original classification, if that official is still serving in the same position;

(2)   the originator's current successor in function;

(3)   a supervisory official of either; or

(4)   officials delegated declassification authority in writing by the agency head or the senior agency official.

(d)   "Mandatory declassification review" means the review for declassification of classified information in response to a request for declassification that meets the requirements under section 3.6 of this order.

(e)   "Systematic declassification review" means the review for declassification of classified information contained in records that have been determined by the Archivist of the United States ("Archivist") to have permanent historical value in accordance with chapter 33 of title 44, United States Code.

(f)   "Declassification guide" means written instructions issued by a declassification authority that describes the elements of information regarding a specific subject that may be declassified and the elements that must remain classified.

(g)   "Downgrading" means a determination by a declassification authority that information classified and safeguarded at a specified level shall be classified and safeguarded at a lower level.

(h)   "File series" means documentary material, regardless of its physical form or characteristics, that is arranged in accordance with a filing system or maintained as a unit because it pertains to the same function or activity.

Sec. 3.2. Authority for Declassification.

(a)   Information shall be declassified as soon as it no longer meets the standards for classification under this order.

(b)   It is presumed that information that continues to meet the classification requirements under this order requires continued protection. In some exceptional cases, however, the need to protect such information may be outweighed by the public interest in disclosure of the information, and in these cases the information should be declassified. When such questions arise, they shall be referred to the agency head or the senior agency official. That official will determine, as an exercise of discretion, whether the public interest in disclosure outweighs the damage to national security that might reasonably be expected from disclosure. This provision does not:

(1)   amplify or modify the substantive criteria or procedures for classification; or

(2) create any substantive or procedural rights subject to judicial review.

(c)   If the Director of the Information Security Oversight Office determines that information is classified in violation of this order, the Director may require the information to be declassified by the agency that originated the classification. Any such decision by the Director may be appealed to the President through the Assistant to the President for National Security Affairs. The information shall remain classified pending a prompt decision on the appeal.

(d)   The provisions of this section shall also apply to agencies that, under the terms of this order, do not have original classification authority, but had such authority under predecessor orders.

Sec. 3.3. Transferred Information.

(a)   In the case of classified information transferred in conjunction with a transfer of functions, and not merely for storage purposes, the receiving agency shall be deemed to be the originating agency for purposes of this order.

(b)   In the case of classified information that is not officially transferred as described in paragraph (a), above, but that originated in an agency that has ceased to exist and for which there is no successor agency, each agency in possession of such information shall be deemed to be the originating agency for purposes of this order. Such information may be declassified or downgraded by the agency in possession after consultation with any other agency that has an interest in the subject matter of the information.

(c)   Classified information accessioned into the National Archives and Records Administration ("National Archives") as of the effective date of this order shall be declassified or downgraded by the Archivist in accordance with this order, the directives issued pursuant to this order, agency declassification guides, and any existing procedural agreement between the Archivist and the relevant agency head.

(d)   The originating agency shall take all reasonable steps to declassify classified information contained in records determined to have permanent historical value before they are accessioned into the National Archives. However, the Archivist may require that records containing classified information be accessioned into the National Archives when necessary to comply with the provisions of the Federal Records Act. This provision does not apply to information being transferred to the Archivist pursuant to section 2203 of title 44, United States Code, or information for which the National Archives and Records Administration serves as the custodian of the records of an agency or organization that goes out of existence.

(e)   To the extent practicable, agencies shall adopt a system of records management that will facilitate the public release of documents at the time such documents are declassified pursuant to the provisions for automatic declassification in sections 1.6 and 3.4 of this order.

Sec. 3.4. Automatic Declassification.

(a)   Subject to paragraph (b), below, within 5 years from the date of this order, all classified information contained in records that (1) are more than 25 years old, and (2) have been determined to have permanent historical value under title 44, United States Code, shall be automatically declassified whether or not the records have been reviewed. Subsequently, all classified information in such records shall be automatically declassified no longer than 25 years from the date of its original classification, except as provided in paragraph (b), below.

(b) An agency head may exempt from automatic declassification under paragraph (a), above, specific information, the release of which should be expected to:

(1) reveal the identity of a confidential human source, or reveal information about the application of an intelligence source or method, or reveal the identity of a human intelligence source when the unauthorized disclosure of that source would clearly and demonstrably damage the national security interests of the United States;

(2) reveal information that would assist in the development or use of weapons of mass destruction;

(3) reveal information that would impair U.S. cryptologic systems or activities;

(4) reveal information that would impair the application of state of the art technology within a U.S. weapon system;

(5) reveal actual U.S. military war plans that remain in effect;

(6) reveal information that would seriously and demonstrably impair relations between the United States and a foreign government, or seriously and demonstrably undermine ongoing diplomatic activities of the United States;

(7) reveal information that would clearly and demonstrably impair the current ability of United States Government officials to protect the President, Vice President, and other officials for whom protection services, in the interest of national security, are authorized;

(8) reveal information that would seriously and demonstrably impair current national security emergency preparedness plans; or

(9) violate a statute, treaty, or international agreement.

(c) No later than the effective date of this order, an agency head shall notify the President through the Assistant to the President for National Security Affairs of any specific file series of records for which a review or assessment has determined that the information within those file series almost invariably falls within one or more of the exemption categories listed in paragraph (b), above, and which the agency proposes to exempt from automatic declassification. The notification shall include:

(1) a description of the file series;

(2) an explanation of why the information within the file series is almost invariably exempt from automatic declassification and why the information must remain classified for a longer period of time; and

(3) except for the identity of a confidential human source or a human intelligence source, as provided in paragraph (b), above, a specific date or event for declassification of the information.

The President may direct the agency head not to exempt the file series or to declassify the information within that series at an earlier date than recommended.

(d) At least 180 days before information is automatically declassified under this section, an agency head or senior agency official shall notify the Director of the Information Security Oversight Office, serving as Executive Secretary of the Interagency Security Classification Appeals Panel, of any specific information beyond that included in a notification to the President under paragraph (c), above, that the agency proposes to exempt from automatic declassification. The notification shall include:

(1) a description of the information;

(2) an explanation of why the information is exempt from automatic declassification and must remain classified for a longer period of time; and

(3) except for the identity of a confidential human source or a human intelligence source, as provided in paragraph (b), above, a specific date or event for declassification of the information. The Panel may direct the agency not to exempt the information or to declassify it at an earlier date than recommended. The agency head may appeal such a decision to the President through the Assistant to the President for National Security Affairs. The information will remain classified while such an appeal is pending.

(e) No later than the effective date of this order, the agency head or senior agency official shall provide the Director of the Information Security Oversight Office with a plan for compliance with the requirements of this section, including the establishment of interim target dates. Each such plan shall include the requirement that the agency declassify at least 15 percent of the records affected by this section no later than 1 year from the effective date of this order, and similar commitments for subsequent years until the effective date for automatic declassification.

(f) Information exempted from automatic declassification under this section shall remain subject to the mandatory and systematic declassification review provisions of this order.

(g) The Secretary of State shall determine when the United States should commence negotiations with the appropriate officials of a foreign government or international organization of governments to modify any treaty or international agreement that requires the classification of information contained in records affected by this section for a period longer than 25 years from the date of its creation, unless the treaty or international agreement pertains to information that may otherwise remain classified beyond 25 years under this section.

Sec. 3.5. Systematic Declassification Review.

(a) Each agency that has originated classified information under this order or its predecessors shall establish and conduct a program for systematic declassification review. This program shall apply to historically valuable records exempted from automatic declassification under section 3.4 of this order. Agencies shall prioritize the systematic review of records based upon:

(1) recommendations of the Information Security Policy Advisory Council, established in section 5.5 of this order, on specific subject areas for systematic review concentration; or

(2) the degree of researcher interest and the likelihood of declassification upon review.

(b) The Archivist shall conduct a systematic declassification review program for classified information:

(1)   accessioned into the National Archives as of the effective date of this order;

(2)   information transferred to the Archivist pursuant to section 2203 of title 44, United States Code; and

(3)   information for which the National Archives and Records Administration serves as the custodian of the records of an agency or organization that has gone out of existence.

This program shall apply to pertinent records no later than 25 years from the date of their creation. The Archivist shall establish priorities for the systematic review of these records based upon the recommendations of the Information Security Policy Advisory Council; or the degree of researcher interest and the likelihood of declassification upon review. These records shall be reviewed in accordance with the standards of this order, its implementing directives, and declassification guides provided to the Archivist by each agency that originated the records. The Director of the Information Security Oversight Office shall assure that agencies provide the Archivist with adequate and current declassification guides.

(c)   After consultation with affected agencies, the Secretary of Defense may establish special procedures for systematic review for declassification of classified cryptologic information, and the Director of Central Intelligence may establish special procedures for systematic review for declassification of classified information pertaining to intelligence activities (including special activities), or intelligence sources or methods.

Sec. 3.6. Mandatory Declassification Review.

(a)   Except as provided in paragraph (b), below, all information classified under this order or predecessor orders shall be subject to a review for declassification by the originating agency if:

(1)   the request for a review describes the document or material containing the information with sufficient specificity to enable the agency to locate it with a reasonable amount of effort;

(2)   the information is not exempted from search and review under the Central Intelligence Agency Information Act; and

(3)   the information has not been reviewed for declassification within the past 2 years.

If the agency has reviewed the information within the past 2 years, or the information is the subject of pending litigation, the agency shall inform the requester of this fact and of the requester's appeal rights.

(b)   Information originated by:

(1)   the incumbent President;

(2)   the incumbent President's White House Staff;

(3)   committees, commissions, or boards appointed by the incumbent President; or

(4)   other entities within the Executive Office of the President that solely advise and assist the incumbent President is exempted from the provisions of paragraph (a), above. However, the Archivist shall have the authority to review, downgrade, and declassify information of former Presidents under the control of the Archivist pursuant to sections 2107, 2111, 2111 note, or 2203 of title 44,

United States Code. Review procedures developed by the Archivist shall provide for consultation with agencies having primary subject matter interest and shall be consistent with the provisions of applicable laws or lawful agreements that pertain to the respective Presidential papers or records. Agencies with primary subject matter interest shall be notified promptly of the Archivist's decision. Any final decision by the Archivist may be appealed by the requester or an agency to the Interagency Security Classification Appeals Panel. The information shall remain classified pending a prompt decision on the appeal.

(c)   Agencies conducting a mandatory review for declassification shall declassify information that no longer meets the standards for classification under this order. They shall release this information unless withholding is otherwise authorized and warranted under applicable law.

(d)   In accordance with directives issued pursuant to this order, agency heads shall develop procedures to process requests for the mandatory review of classified information. These procedures shall apply to information classified under this or predecessor orders. They also shall provide a means for administratively appealing a denial of a mandatory review request, and for notifying the requester of the right to appeal a final agency decision to the Interagency Security Classification Appeals Panel.

(e)   After consultation with affected agencies, the Secretary of Defense shall develop special procedures for the review of cryptologic information, the Director of Central Intelligence shall develop special procedures for the review of information pertaining to intelligence activities (including special activities), or intelligence sources or methods, and the Archivist shall develop special procedures for the review of information accessioned into the National Archives.

Sec. 3.7. Processing Requests and Reviews. In response to a request for information under the Freedom of Information Act, the Privacy Act of 1974, or the mandatory review provisions of this order, or pursuant to the automatic declassification or systematic review provisions of this order:

(a)   An agency may refuse to confirm or deny the existence or nonexistence of requested information whenever the fact of its existence or nonexistence is itself classified under this order.

(b)   When an agency receives any request for documents in its custody that contain information that was originally classified by another agency, or comes across such documents in the process of the automatic declassification or systematic review provisions of this order, it shall refer copies of any request and the pertinent documents to the originating agency for processing, and may, after consultation with the originating agency, inform any requester of the referral unless such association is itself classified under this order. In cases in which the originating agency determines in writing that a response under paragraph (a), above, is required, the referring agency shall respond to the requester in accordance with that paragraph.

Sec. 3.8. Declassification Database.

(a)   The Archivist in conjunction with the Director of the Information Security Oversight Office and those agencies that originate classified information, shall establish a Governmentwide database of information that has been declassified. The Archivist shall also explore other possible uses of technology to facilitate the declassification process.

(b)   Agency heads shall fully cooperate with the Archivist in these efforts.

(c)   Except as otherwise authorized and warranted by law, all declassified information contained within the database established under paragraph (a), above, shall be available to the public.

Part 4
Safeguarding

Sec. 4.1. Definitions. For purposes of this order:

(a)   "Safeguarding" means measures and controls that are prescribed to protect classified information.

(b)   "Access" means the ability or opportunity to gain knowledge of classified information.

(c)   "Need-to-know" means a determination made by an authorized holder of classified information that a prospective recipient requires access to specific classified information in order to perform or assist in a lawful and authorized governmental function.

(d)   "Automated information system" means an assembly of computer hardware, software, or firmware configured to collect, create, communicate, compute, disseminate, process, store, or control data or information.

(e)   "Integrity" means the state that exists when information is unchanged from its source and has not been accidentally or intentionally modified, altered, or destroyed.

(f)   "Network" means a system of two or more computers that can exchange data or information.

(g)   "Telecommunications" means the preparation, transmission, or communication of information by electronic means.

(h)   "Special access program" means a program established for a specific class of classified information that imposes safeguarding and access requirements that exceed those normally required for information at the same classification level.

Sec. 4.2. General Restrictions on Access.

(a)   A person may have access to classified information provided that:

(1)   a favorable determination of eligibility for access has been made by an agency head or the agency head's designee;

(2)   the person has signed an approved nondisclosure agreement; and

(3)   the person has a need-to-know the information.

(b)   Classified information shall remain under the control of the originating agency or its successor in function. An agency shall not disclose information originally classified by another agency without its authorization. An official or employee leaving agency service may not remove classified information from the agency's control.

(c)   Classified information may not be removed from official premises without proper authorization.

(d)   Persons authorized to disseminate classified information outside the executive branch shall assure the protection of the information in a manner equivalent to that provided within the executive branch.

(e)   Consistent with law, directives, and regulation, an agency head or senior agency official shall establish uniform procedures to ensure that automated information systems, including networks and telecommunications systems, that collect, create, communicate, compute, disseminate, process, or store classified information have controls that:

(1)   prevent access by unauthorized persons; and

(2)   ensure the integrity of the information.

(f)   Consistent with law, directives, and regulation, each agency head or senior agency official shall establish controls to ensure that classified information is used, processed, stored, reproduced, transmitted, and destroyed under conditions that provide adequate protection and prevent access by unauthorized persons.

(g)   Consistent with directives issued pursuant to this order, an agency shall safeguard foreign government information under standards that provide a degree of protection at least equivalent to that required by the government or international organization of governments that furnished the information. When adequate to achieve equivalency, these standards may be less restrictive than the safeguarding standards that ordinarily apply to United States "Confidential" information, including allowing access to individuals with a need-to-know who have not otherwise been cleared for access to classified information or executed an approved nondisclosure agreement.

(h)   Except as provided by statute or directives issued pursuant to this order, classified information originating in one agency may not be disseminated outside any other agency to which it has been made available without the consent of the originating agency. An agency head or senior agency official may waive this requirement for specific information originated within that agency. For purposes of this section, the Department of Defense shall be considered one agency.

Sec. 4.3. Distribution Controls.

(a)   Each agency shall establish controls over the distribution of classified information to assure that it is distributed only to organizations or individuals eligible for access who also have a need-to-know the information.

(b)   Each agency shall update, at least annually, the automatic, routine, or recurring distribution of classified information that they distribute. Recipients shall cooperate fully with distributors who are updating distribution lists and shall notify distributors whenever a relevant change in status occurs.

Sec. 4.4. Special Access Programs.

(a)   Establishment of special access programs. Unless otherwise authorized by the President, only the Secretaries of State, Defense and Energy, and the

Director of Central Intelligence, or the principal deputy of each, may create a special access program. For special access programs pertaining to intelligence activities (including special activities, but not including military operational, strategic and tactical programs), or intelligence sources or methods, this function will be exercised by the Director of Central Intelligence. These officials shall keep the number of these programs at an absolute minimum, and shall establish them only upon a specific finding that:

(1) the vulnerability of, or threat to, specific information is exceptional; and

(2) the normal criteria for determining eligibility for access applicable to information classified at the same level are not deemed sufficient to protect the information from unauthorized disclosure; or

(3) the program is required by statute.

(b) Requirements and Limitations.

(1) Special access programs shall be limited to programs in which the number of persons who will have access ordinarily will be reasonably small and commensurate with the objective of providing enhanced protection for the information involved.

(2) Each agency head shall establish and maintain a system of accounting for special access programs consistent with directives issued pursuant to this order.

(3) Special access programs shall be subject to the oversight program established under section 5.6(c) of this order. In addition, the Director of the Information Security Oversight Office shall be afforded access to these programs, in accordance with the security requirements of each program, in order to perform the functions assigned to the Information Security Oversight Office under this order. An agency head may limit access to a special access program to the Director and no more than one other employee of the Information Security Oversight Office; or, for special access programs that are extraordinarily sensitive and vulnerable, to the Director only.

(4) The agency head or principal deputy shall review annually each special access program to determine whether it continues to meet the requirements of this order.

(5) Upon request, an agency shall brief the Assistant to the President for National Security Affairs, or his or her designee, on any or all of the agency's special access programs.

(c) Within 180 days after the effective date of this order, each agency head or principal deputy shall review all existing special access programs under the agency's jurisdiction. These officials shall terminate any special access programs that do not clearly meet the provisions of this order. Each existing special access program that an agency head or principal deputy validates shall be treated as if it were established on the effective date of this order.

(d) Nothing in this order shall supersede any requirement made by or under 10 U.S.C. 119.

Sec. 4.5. Access by Historical Researchers and Former Presidential Appointees.

(a) The requirement in section 4.2(a)(3) of this order that access to classified information may be granted only to individuals who have a need-to-know the information may be waived for persons who:

(1) are engaged in historical research projects; or

(2) previously have occupied policy-making positions to which they were appointed by the President.

(b) Waivers under this section may be granted only if the agency head or senior agency official of the originating agency:

(1) determines in writing that access is consistent with the interest of national security;

(2) takes appropriate steps to protect classified information from unauthorized disclosure or compromise, and ensures that the information is safeguarded in a manner consistent with this order; and

(3) limits the access granted to former Presidential appointees to items that the person originated, reviewed, signed, or received while serving as a Presidential appointee.

Part 5
Implementation and Review

Sec. 5.1. Definitions. For purposes of this order:

(a) "Self-inspection" means the internal review and evaluation of individual agency activities and the agency as a whole with respect to the implementation of the program established under this order and its implementing directives.

(b) "Violation" means:

(1) any knowing, willful, or negligent action that could reasonably be expected to result in an unauthorized disclosure of classified information;

(2) any knowing, willful, or negligent action to classify or continue the classification of information contrary to the requirements of this order or its implementing directives; or

(3) any knowing, willful, or negligent action to create or continue a special access program contrary to the requirements of this order.

(c) "Infraction" means any knowing, willful, or negligent action contrary to the requirements of this order or its implementing directives that does not comprise a "violation," as defined above.

Sec. 5.2. Program Direction.

(a) The Director of the Office of Management and Budget, in consultation with the Assistant to the President for National Security Affairs and the co-chairs of the Security Policy Board, shall issue such directives as are necessary to implement this order. These directives shall be binding upon the agencies. Directives issued by the Director of the Office of Management and Budget shall establish standards for:

(1) classification and marking principles;

(2) agency security education and training programs;

(3) agency self-inspection programs; and

(4) classification and declassification guides.

(b)   The Director of the Office of Management and Budget shall delegate the implementation and monitorship functions of this program to the Director of the Information Security Oversight Office.

(c)   The Security Policy Board, established by a Presidential Decision Directive, shall make a recommendation to the President through the Assistant to the President for National Security Affairs with respect to the issuance of a Presidential directive on safeguarding classified information. The Presidential directive shall pertain to the handling, storage, distribution, transmittal, and destruction of and accounting for classified information.

Sec. 5.3. Information Security Oversight Office.

(a)   There is established within the Office of Management and Budget an Information Security Oversight Office. The Director of the Office of Management and Budget shall appoint the Director of the Information Security Oversight Office, subject to the approval of the President.

(b)   Under the direction of the Director of the Office of Management and Budget acting in consultation with the Assistant to the President for National Security Affairs, the Director of the Information Security Oversight Office shall:

(1)   develop directives for the implementation of this order;

(2)   oversee agency actions to ensure compliance with this order and its implementing directives;

(3)   review and approve agency implementing regulations and agency guides for systematic declassification review prior to their issuance by the agency;

(4)   have the authority to conduct on-site reviews of each agency's program established under this order, and to require of each agency those reports, information, and other cooperation that may be necessary to fulfill its responsibilities. If granting access to specific categories of classified information would pose an exceptional national security risk, the affected agency head or the senior agency official shall submit a written justification recommending the denial of access to the Director of the Office of Management and Budget within 60 days of the request for access. Access shall be denied pending a prompt decision by the Director of the Office of Management and Budget, who shall consult on this decision with the Assistant to the President for National Security Affairs;

(5)   review requests for original classification authority from agencies or officials not granted original classification authority and, if deemed appropriate, recommend Presidential approval through the Director of the Office of Management and Budget;

(6)   consider and take action on complaints and suggestions from persons within or outside the Government with respect to the administration of the program established under this order;

(7)   have the authority to prescribe, after consultation with affected agencies, standardization of forms or procedures that will promote the implementation of the program established under this order;

(8)   report at least annually to the President on the implementation of this order; and

(9)   convene and chair interagency meetings to discuss matters pertaining to the program established by this order.

Sec. 5.4. Interagency Security Classification Appeals Panel.
      (a)   Establishment and Administration.
      (1)   There is established an Interagency Security Classification Appeals Panel ("Panel"). The Secretaries of State and Defense, the Attorney General, the Director of Central Intelligence, the Archivist of the United States, and the Assistant to the President for National Security Affairs shall each appoint a senior level representative to serve as a member of the Panel. The President shall select the Chair of the Panel from among the Panel members.
      (2)   A vacancy on the Panel shall be filled as quickly as possible as provided in paragraph (1), above.
      (3)   The Director of the Information Security Oversight Office shall serve as the Executive Secretary. The staff of the Information Security Oversight Office shall provide program and administrative support for the Panel.
      (4)   The members and staff of the Panel shall be required to meet eligibility for access standards in order to fulfill the Panel's functions.
      (5)   The Panel shall meet at the call of the Chair. The Chair shall schedule meetings as may be necessary for the Panel to fulfill its functions in a timely manner.
      (6)   The Information Security Oversight Office shall include in its reports to the President a summary of the Panel's activities.
      (b)   Functions. The Panel shall:
      (1)   decide on appeals by persons who have filed classification challenges under section 1.9 of this order;
      (2)   approve, deny, or amend agency exemptions from automatic declassification as provided in section 3.4 of this order; and
      (3)   decide on appeals by persons or entities who have filed requests for mandatory declassification review under section 3.6 of this order.
      (c)   Rules and Procedures. The Panel shall issue bylaws, which shall be published in the Federal Register no later than 120 days from the effective date of this order. The bylaws shall establish the rules and procedures that the Panel will follow in accepting, considering, and issuing decisions on appeals. The rules and procedures of the Panel shall provide that the Panel will consider appeals only on actions in which:
      (1)   the appellant has exhausted his or her administrative remedies within th responsible agency;
      (2)   there is no current action pending on the issue within the federal courts; and
      (3)   the information has not been the subject of review by the federal courts or the Panel within the past 2 years.
      (d)   Agency heads will cooperate fully with the Panel so that it can fulfill its functions in a timely and fully informed manner. An agency head may appeal a decision of the Panel to the President through the Assistant to the President for National Security Affairs. The Panel will report to the President through the As-

sistant to the President for National Security Affairs any instance in which it believes that an agency head is not cooperating fully with the Panel.

(e) The Appeals Panel is established for the sole purpose of advising and assisting the President in the discharge of his constitutional and discretionary authority to protect the national security of the United States. Panel decisions are committed to the discretion of the Panel, unless reversed by the President.

Sec. 5.5. Information Security Policy Advisory Council.

(a) Establishment. There is established an Information Security Policy Advisory Council ("Council"). The Council shall be composed of seven members appointed by the President for staggered terms not to exceed 4 years, from among persons who have demonstrated interest and expertise in an area related to the subject matter of this order and are not otherwise employees of the Federal Government. The President shall appoint the Council Chair from among the members. The Council shall comply with the Federal Advisory Committee Act, as amended, 5 U.S.C. App. 2.

(b) Functions. The Council shall:

(1) advise the President, the Assistant to the President for National Security Affairs, the Director of the Office of Management and Budget, or such other executive branch officials as it deems appropriate, on policies established under this order or its implementing directives, including recommended changes to those policies;

(2) provide recommendations to agency heads for specific subject areas for systematic declassification review; and

(3) serve as a forum to discuss policy issues in dispute.

(c) Meetings. The Council shall meet at least twice each calendar year, and as determined by the Assistant to the President for National Security Affairs or the Director of the Office of Management and Budget.

(d) Administration.

(1) Each Council member may be compensated at a rate of pay not to exceed the daily equivalent of the annual rate of basic pay in effect for grade GS-18 of the general schedule under section 5376 of title 5, United States Code, for each day during which that member is engaged in the actual performance of the duties of the Council.

(2) While away from their homes or regular place of business in the actual performance of the duties of the Council, members may be allowed travel expenses, including per diem in lieu of subsistence, as authorized by law for persons serving intermittently in the Government service (5 U.S.C. 5703(b)).

(3) To the extent permitted by law and subject to the availability of funds, the Information Security Oversight Office shall provide the Council with administrative services, facilities, staff, and other support services necessary for the performance of its functions.

(4) Notwithstanding any other Executive order, the functions of the President under the Federal Advisory Committee Act, as amended, that are applicable to the Council, except that of reporting to the Congress, shall be performed by the Director of the Information Security Oversight Office in accordance with

the guidelines and procedures established by the General Services Administration.

Sec. 5.6. General Responsibilities. Heads of agencies that originate or handle classified information shall:

(a)   demonstrate personal commitment and commit senior management to the successful implementation of the program established under this order;

(b)   commit necessary resources to the effective implementation of the program established under this order; and

(c)   designate a senior agency official to direct and administer the program, whose responsibilities shall include:

(1)   overseeing the agency's program established under this order, provided, an agency head may designate a separate official to oversee special access programs authorized under this order. This official shall provide a full accounting of the agency's special access programs at least annually;

(2)   promulgating implementing regulations, which shall be published in the Federal Register to the extent that they affect members of the public;

(3)   establishing and maintaining security education and training programs;

(4)   establishing and maintaining an ongoing self-inspection program, which shall include the periodic review and assessment of the agency's classified product;

(5)   establishing procedures to prevent unnecessary access to classified information, including procedures that: (i) require that a need for access to classified information is established before initiating administrative clearance procedures; and (ii) ensure that the number of persons granted access to classified information is limited to the minimum consistent with operational and security requirements and needs;

(6)   developing special contingency plans for the safeguarding of classified information used in or near hostile or potentially hostile areas;

(7)   assuring that the performance contract or other system used to rate civilian or military personnel performance includes the management of classified information as a critical element or item to be evaluated in the rating of: (i) original classification authorities; (ii) security managers or security specialists; and (iii) all other personnel whose duties significantly involve the creation or handling of classified information;

(8)   accounting for the costs associated with the implementation of this order, which shall be reported to the Director of the Information Security Oversight Office for publication; and

(9)   assigning in a prompt manner agency personnel to respond to any request, appeal, challenge, complaint, or suggestion arising out of this order that pertains to classified information that originated in a component of the agency that no longer exists and for which there is no clear successor in function.

Sec. 5.7. Sanctions.

(a)   If the Director of the Information Security Oversight Office finds that a violation of this order or its implementing directives may have occurred, the

Director shall make a report to the head of the agency or to the senior agency official so that corrective steps, if appropriate, may be taken.

(b)   Officers and employees of the United States Government, and its contractors, licensees, certificate holders, and grantees shall be subject to appropriate sanctions if they knowingly, willfully, or negligently:

(1)   disclose to unauthorized persons information properly classified under this order or predecessor orders;

(2)   classify or continue the classification of information in violation of this order or any implementing directive;

(3)   create or continue a special access program contrary to the requirements of this order; or

(4)   contravene any other provision of this order or its implementing directives.

(c)   Sanctions may include reprimand, suspension without pay, removal, termination of classification authority, loss or denial of access to classified information, or other sanctions in accordance with applicable law and agency regulation.

(d)   The agency head, senior agency official, or other supervisory official shall, at a minimum, promptly remove the classification authority of any individual who demonstrates reckless disregard or a pattern of error in applying the classification standards of this order.

(e)   The agency head or senior agency official shall:

(1)   take appropriate and prompt corrective action when a violation or infraction under paragraph (b), above, occurs; and

(2)   notify the Director of the Information Security Oversight Office when a violation under paragraph (b)(1), (2) or (3), above, occurs.

Part 6
General Provisions

Sec. 6.1. General Provisions.

(a)   Nothing in this order shall supersede any requirement made by or under the Atomic Energy Act of 1954, as amended, or the National Security Act of 1947, as amended. "Restricted Data" and "Formerly Restricted Data" shall be handled, protected, classified, downgraded, and declassified in conformity with the provisions of the Atomic Energy Act of 1954, as amended, and regulations issued under that Act.

(b)   The Attorney General, upon request by the head of an agency or the Director of the Information Security Oversight Office, shall render an interpretation of this order with respect to any question arising in the course of its administration.

(c)   Nothing in this order limits the protection afforded any information by other provisions of law, including the exemptions to the Freedom of Information Act, the Privacy Act, and the National Security Act of 1947, as amended. This order is not intended, and should not be construed, to create any right or benefit, substantive or procedural, enforceable at law by a party against the United States, its agencies, its officers, or its employees. The foregoing is in addition to the specific provisos set forth in sections 1.2(b), 3.2(b) and 5.4(e) of this order.

(d)   Executive Order No. 12356 of April 6, 1982, is revoked as of the effective date of this order.

Sec. 6.2. Effective Date. This order shall become effective 180 days from the date of this order.

WILLIAM J. CLINTON, THE WHITE HOUSE, April 17, 1995.

N.2.3   Executive Order 12472 (Assignment of National Security and Emergency Preparedness Telecommunications Functions)

By the authority vested in me as President by the Constitution and laws of the United States of America, including the Communications Act of 1934, as amended (47 U.S.C. 151), the National Security Act of 1947, as amended, the Defense Production Act of 1950, as amended (50 U.S.C. App. 2061), the Federal Civil Defense Act of 1950, as amended (50 U.S.C. App. 2251), the Disaster Relief Act of 1974 (42 U.S.C. 5121), Section 5 of Reorganization Plan No. 1 of 1977 (3 C.F.R. 197, 1978 Comp.), and Section 203 of Reorganization Plan No. 3 of 1978 (3 C.F.R. 389, 1978 Comp.), and in order to provide for the consolidation of assignment and responsibility for improved execution of national security and emergency preparedness telecommunications functions, it is hereby ordered as follows:

Sec. 1. The National Communications System.

(a)   There is hereby established the National Communications System (NCS). The NCS shall consist of the telecommunications assets of the entities represented on the NCS Committee of Principals and an administrative structure consisting of the Executive Agent, the NCS Committee of Principals and the Manager. The NCS Committee of Principals shall consist of representatives from those Federal departments, agencies or entities, designated by the President, which lease or own telecommunications facilities or services of significance to national security or emergency preparedness, and, to the extent permitted by law, other Executive entities which bear policy, regulatory or enforcement responsibilities of importance to national security or emergency preparedness telecommunications capabilities.

(b)   The mission of the NCS shall be to assist the President, the National Security Council, the Director of the Office of Science and Technology Policy and the Director of the Office of Management and Budget in:

(1)   the exercise of the telecommunications functions and responsibilities set forth in Section 2 of this Order; and

(2)   the coordination of the planning for and provision of national security and emergency preparedness communications for the Federal govern-

ment under all circumstances, including crisis or emergency, attack, recovery and reconstitution.

(c)   The NCS shall seek to ensure that a national telecommunications infrastructure is developed which:

(1)   Is responsive to the national security and emergency preparedness needs of the President and the Federal departments, agencies and other entities, including telecommunications in support of national security leadership and continuity of government;

(2)   Is capable of satisfying priority telecommunications requirements under all circumstances through use of commercial, government and privately owned telecommunications resources;

(3)   Incorporates the necessary combination of hardness, redundancy, mobility, connectivity, interoperability, restorability and security to obtain, to the maximum extent practicable, the survivability of national security and emergency preparedness telecommunications in all circumstances, including conditions of crisis or emergency; and

(4)   Is consistent, to the maximum extent practicable, with other national telecommunications policies.

(d)   To assist in accomplishing its mission, the NCS shall:

(1)   serve as a focal point for joint industry-government national security and emergency preparedness telecommunications planning; and

(2)   establish a joint industry-government National Coordinating Center which is capable of assisting in the initiation, coordination, restoration and reconstitution of national security or emergency preparedness telecommunications services or facilities under all conditions of crisis or emergency.

(e)   The Secretary of Defense is designated as the Executive Agent for the NCS. The Executive Agent shall:

(1)   Designate the Manager of the NCS;

(2)   Ensure that the NCS conducts unified planning and operations, in order to coordinate the development and maintenance of an effective and responsive capability for meeting the domestic and international national security and emergency preparedness telecommunications needs of the Federal government;

(3)   Ensure that the activities of the NCS are conducted in conjunction with the emergency management activities of the Federal Emergency Management Agency;

(4)   Recommend, in consultation with the NCS Committee of Principals, to the National Security Council, the Director of the Office of Science and Technology Policy, or the Director of the Office of Management and Budget, as appropriate:

a.   The assignment of implementation or other responsibilities to NCS member entities;

b.   New initiatives to assist in the exercise of the functions specified in Section 2; and

c.   Changes in the composition or structure of the NCS;

(5)   Oversee the activities of and provide personnel and administrative support to the Manager of the NCS;

(6)   Provide staff support and technical assistance to the National Security Telecommunications Advisory Committee established by Executive Order No. 12382, as amended; and

(7)   Perform such other duties as are from time to time assigned by the President or his authorized designee.

(f)   The NCS Committee of Principals shall:

(1)   Serve as the forum in which each member of the Committee may review, evaluate, and present views, information and recommendations concerning ongoing or prospective national security or emergency preparedness telecommunications programs or activities of the NCS and the entities represented on the Committee;

(2)   Serve as the forum in which each member of the Committee shall report on and explain ongoing or prospective telecommunications plans and programs developed or designed to achieve national security or emergency preparedness telecommunications objectives;

(3)   Provide comments or recommendations, as appropriate, to the National Security Council, the Director of the Office of Science and Technology Policy, the Director of the Office of Management and Budget, the Executive Agent, or the Manager of the NCS, regarding ongoing or prospective activities of the NCS; and

(4)   Perform such other duties as are from time to time assigned by the President or his authorized designee.

(g)   The Manager of the NCS shall:

(1)   Develop for consideration by the NCS Committee of Principals and the Executive Agent:

a.   A recommended evolutionary telecommunications architecture designed to meet current and future Federal government national security and emergency preparedness telecommunications requirements;

b.   Plans and procedures for the management, allocation and use, including the establishment of priorities or preferences, of Federally owned or leased telecommunications assets under all conditions of crisis or emergency;

c.   Plans, procedures and standards for minimizing or removing technical impediments to the interoperability of government-owned and/or commercially-provided telecommunications systems;

d.   Test and exercise programs and procedures for the evaluation of the capability of the Nation's telecommunications resources to meet national security or emergency preparedness telecommunications requirements; and

e.   Alternative mechanisms for funding, through the budget review process, national security or emergency preparedness telecommunications initiatives which benefit multiple Federal departments, agencies, or entities. Those mechanisms recommended by the NCS Committee of Principals and the Executive Agent shall be submittted to the Director of the Office of Management and Budget.

(2)   Implement and administer any approved plans or programs as assigned, including any system of priorities and preferences for the provision of communications service, in consultation with the NCS Committee of Principals

and the Federal Communications Commission, to the extent practicable or otherwise required by law or regulation;

(3) Chair the NCS Committee of Principals and provide staff support and technical assistance thereto;

(4) Serve as a focal point for joint industry-government planning, including the dissemination of technical information, concerning the national security or emergency perparedness telecommunications requirements of the Federal government;

(5) Conduct technical studies or analyses, and examine research and development programs, for the purpose of identifying, for consideration by the NCS Committee of Principals and the Executive Agent, improved approaches which may assist Federal entities in fulfilling national security or emergency preparedness telecommunications objectives;

(6) Pursuant to the Federal Standardization Program of the General Services Administration, and in consultation with other appropriate entities of the Federal government including the NCS Committee of Principals, manage the Federal Telecommunications Standards Program, ensuring wherever feasible that existing or evolving industry, national, and international standards are used as the basis for Federal telecommunications standards; and

(7) Provide such reports and perform such other duties as are from time to time assigned by the President or his authorized designee, the Executive Agent, or the NCS Committee of Principals. Any such assignments of responsibility to, or reports made by, the Manager shall be transmitted through the Executive Agent.

Sec. 2. Executive Office Responsibilities.

(a) Wartime Emergency Functions.

(1) The National Security Council shall provide policy direction for the exercise of the war power functions of the President under Section 606 of the Communications Act of 1934, as amended (47 U.S.C. 606), should the President issue implementing instructions in accordance with the National Emergencies Act (50 U.S.C. 1601).

(2) The Director of the Office of Science and Technology Policy shall direct the exercise of the war power functions of the President under Section 606 (a), (c)-(e), of the Communications Act of 1934, as amended (47 U.S.C. 606), should the President issue implementing instructions in accordance with the National Emergencies Act (50 U.S.C. 1601).

(b) Non-Wartime Emergency Functions.

(1) The National Security Council shall:

a. Advise and assist the President in coordinating the development of policy, plans, programs and standards within the Federal government for the identification, allocation, and use of the Nation's telecommunications resources by the Federal government, and by State and local governments, private industry and volunteer organizations upon request, to the extent practicable and otherwise consistent with law, during those crises or emergencies in which the exercise of the President's war power functions is not required or permitted by law; and

b. Provide policy direction for the exercise of the President's non-wartime emergency telecommunications functions, should the President so instruct.

(2) The Director of the Office of Science and Technology Policy shall provide information, advice, guidance and assistance, as appropriate, to the President and to those Federal departments and agencies with responsibilities for the provision, management, or allocation of telecommunications resources, during those crises or emergencies in which the exercise of the President's war power functions is not required or permitted by law;

(3) The Director of the Office of Science and Technology Policy shall establish a Joint Telecommunications Resources Board (JTRB) to assist him in the exercise of the functions specified in this subsection. The Director of the Office of Science and Technology Policy shall serve as chairman of the JTRB; select those Federal departments, agencies, or entities which shall be members of the JTRB; and specify the functions it shall perform.

(c) Planning and Oversight Responsibilities.

(1) The National Security Council shall advise and assist the President in:

a. Coordinating the development of policy, plans, programs and standards for the mobilization and use of the Nation's commercial, government, and privately owned telecommunications resources, in order to meet national security or emergency preparedness requirements;

b. Providing policy oversight and direction of the activities of the NCS; and

c. Providing policy oversight and guidance for the execution of the responsibilities assigned to the Federal departments and agencies by this Order.

(2) The Director of the Office of Science and Technology Policy shall make recommendations to the President with respect to the test, exercise and evaluation of the capability of existing and planned communications systems, networks or facilities to meet national security or emergency preparedness requirements and report the results of any such tests or evaluations and any recommended remedial actions to the President and to the National Security Council;

(3) The Director of the Office of Science and Technology Policy or his designee shall advise and assist the President in the administration of a system of radio spectrum priorities for those spectrum dependent telecommunications resources of the Federal government which support national security or emergency preparedness functions. The Director also shall certify or approve priorities for radio spectrum use by the Federal government, including the resolution of any conflicts in or among priorities, under all conditions of crisis or emergency; and

(4) The National Security Council, the Director of the Office of Science and Technology Policy and the Director of the Office of Management and Budget shall, in consultation with the Executive Agent for the NCS and the NCS Committee of Principals, determine what constitutes national security and emergency preparedness telecommunications requirements.

(d) Consultation with Federal Departments and Agencies. In performing the functions assigned under this Order, the National Security Council and the

Director of the Office of Science and Technology Policy, in consultation with each other, shall:

(1)   Consult, as appropriate, with the Director of the Office of Management and Budget; the Director of the Federal Emergency Management Agency with respect to the emergency management responsibilities assigned pursuant to Executive Order No. 12148, as amended; the Secretary of Commerce, with respect to responsibilities assigned pursuant to Executive Order No. 12046; the Secretary of Defense, with respect to communications security responsibilities assigned pursuant to Executive Order No. 12333; and the Chairman of the Federal Communications Commission or his authorized designee; and

(2)   Establish arrangements for consultation among all interested Federal departments, agencies or entities to ensure that the national security and emergency preparedness communications needs of all Federal government entities are identified; that mechanisms to address such needs are incorporated into pertinent plans and procedures; and that such needs are met in a manner consistent, to the maximum extent practicable, with other national telecommunications policies.

(e)   Budgetary Guidelines. The Director of the Office of Management and Budget, in consultation with the National Security Council and the NCS, will prescribe general guidelines and procedures for reviewing the financing of the NCS within the budgetary process and for preparation of budget estimates by participating agencies. These guidelines and procedures may provide for mechanisms for funding, through the budget review process, national security and emergency preparedness telecommunications initiatives which benefit multiple Federal departments, agencies, or entities.

Sec. 3. Assignment of Responsibilities to Other Departments and Agencies. In order to support and enhance the capability to satisfy the national security and emergency preparedness telecommunications needs of the Federal government, State and local governments, private industry and volunteer organizations, under all circumstances including those of crisis or emergency, the Federal departments and agencies shall perform the following functions:

(a)   Department of Commerce. The Secretary of Commerce shall, for all conditions of crisis or emergency:

(1)   Develop plans and procedures concerning radio spectrum assignments, priorities and allocations for use by Federal departments, agencies and entities; and

(2)   Develop, maintain and publish policy, plans, and procedures for the control and allocation of frequency assignments, including the authority to amend, modify or revoke such assignments, in those parts of the electromagnetic spectrum assigned to the Federal government.

(b)   Federal Emergency Management Agency. The Director of the Federal Emergency Management Agency shall:

(1)   Plan for and provide, operate and maintain telecommunications services and facilities, as part of its National Emergency Management System, adequate to support its assigned emergency management responsibilities;

(2)   Advise and assist State and local governments and volunteer

organizations, upon request and to the extent consistent with law, in developing plans and procedures for identifying and satisfying their national security or emergency preparedness telecommunications requirements;

(3) Ensure, to the maximum extent practicable, that national security and emergency preparedness telecommunications planning by State and local governments and volunteer organizations is mutually supportive and consistent with the planning of the Federal government; and

(4) Develop, upon request and to the extent consistent with law and in consonance with regulations promulgated by and agreements with the Federal Communications Commission, plans and capabilities for, and provide policy and management oversight of, the Emergency Broadcast System, and advise and assist private radio licensees of the Commission in developing emergency communications plans, procedures and capabilities.

(c) Department of State. The Secretary of State, in accordance with assigned responsibilities within the Diplomatic Telecommunications System, shall plan for and provide, operate and maintain rapid, reliable and secure telecommunications services to those Federal entities represented at United States diplomatic missions and consular offices overseas. This responsibility shall include the provision and operation of domestic telecommunications in support of assigned national security or emergency preparedness responsibilities.

(d) Department of Defense. In addition to the other responsibilities assigned by this Order, the Secretary of Defense shall:

(1) Plan for and provide, operate and maintain telecommunications services and facilities adequate to support the National Command Authorities and to execute the responsibilities assigned by Executive Order No. 12333; and

(2) Ensure that the Director of the National Security Agency provides the technical support necessary to develop and maintain plans adequate to provide for the security and protection of national security and emergency preparedness telecommunications.

(e) Department of Justice. The Attorney General shall, as necessary, review for legal sufficiency, including consistency with the antitrust laws, all policies, plans or procedures developed pursuant to responsibilities assigned by this Order.

(f) Central Intelligence Agency. The Director of Central Intelligence shall plan for and provide, operate, and maintain telecommunications services adequate to support its assigned responsibilities, including the dissemination of intelligence within the Federal government.

(g) General Services Administration. Except as otherwise assigned by this Order, the Administrator of General Services, consistent with policy guidance provided by the Director of the Office of Management and Budget, shall ensure that Federally owned or managed domestic communications facilities and services meet the national security and emergency preparedness requirements of the Federal civilian departments, agencies and entities.

(h) Federal Communications Commission. The Federal Communications Commission shall, consistent with Section 4(c) of this Order:

(1) Review the policies, plans and procedures of all entities licensed or regulated by the Commission that are developed to provide national security

or emergency preparedness communications services, in order to ensure that such policies, plans and procedures are consistent with the public interest, convenience and necessity;

(2) Perform such functions as required by law with respect to all entities licensed or regulated by the Commission, including (but not limited to) the extension, discontinuance or reduction of common carrier facilities or services; the control of common carrier rates, charges, practices and classifications; the construction, authorization, activation, deactivation or closing of radio stations, services and facilities; the assignment of radio frequencies to Commission licensees; the investigation of violations of pertinent law and regulation; and the initiation of apppropriate enforcement actions;

(3) Develop policy, plans and procedures adequate to execute the responsibilities assigned in this Order under all conditions of crisis or emergency; and

(4) Consult as appropriate with the Executive Agent for the NCS and the NCS Committee of Principals to ensure continued coordination of their respective national security and emergency preparedness activities.

(i) All Federal departments and agencies, to the extent consistent with law (including those authorities and responsibilities set forth in Section 4(c) of this Order), shall:

(1) Determine their national security and emergency preparedness telecommunications requirements, and provide information regarding such requirements to the Manager of the NCS;

(2) Prepare policies, plans and procedures concerning telecommunications facilities, services or equipment under their management or operational control to maximize their capability of responding to the national security or emergency preparedness needs of the Federal government;

(3) Provide, after consultation with the Director of the Office of Management and Budget, resources to support their respective requirements for national security and emergency preparedness telecommunications; and provide personnel and staff support to the Manager of the NCS as required by the President;

(4) Make information available to, and consult with, the Manager of the NCS regarding agency telecommunications activities in support of national security or emergency preparedness;

(5) Consult, consistent with the provisions of Executive Order No. 12046, as amended, and in conjunction with the Manager of the NCS, with the Federal Communications Commission regarding execution of responsibilities assigned by this Order;

(6) Submit reports annually, or as otherwise requested, to the Manager of the NCS, regarding agency national security or emergency preparedness telecommunications activities; and

(7) Cooperate with and assist the Executive Agent for the NCS, the NCS Committee of Principals, the Manager of the NCS, and other departments and agencies in the execution of the functions set forth in this Order, furnishing them such information, support and assistance as may be required.

(j) Each Federal department or agency shall execute the responsibilities assigned by this Order in conjunction with the emergency management activities of the Federal Emergency Management Agency, and in regular consultation with the Executive Agent for the NCS and the NCS Committee of Principals to ensure continued coordination of NCS and individual agency telecommunications activities.

Sec. 4. General Provisions.

(a) All Executive departments and agencies may issue such rules and regulations as may be necessary to carry out the functions assigned under this Order.

(b) In order to reflect the assignments of responsibility provided by this Order,

(1) Sections 2-414, 4-102, 4-103, 4-202, 4-302, 5-3, and 6-101 of Executive Order No. 12046, as amended, are revoked;

(2) The Presidential Memorandum of August 21, 1963, as amended, entitled "Establishment of the National Communications System", is hereby superseded; and

(3) Section 2-411 of Executive Order No. 12046, as amended, is further amended by deleting the period and inserting ", except as otherwise provided by Executive Order No. " and inserting the number assigned to this Order.

(c) Nothing in this Order shall be deemed to affect the authorities or responsibilities of the Director of the Office of Management and Budget, or any Office or official thereof; or reassign any function assigned any agency under the Federal Property and Administrative Services Act of 1949, as amended; or under any other law; or any function vested by law in the Federal Communications Commission.

Sec. 5. This Order shall be effective upon publication in the Federal Register.

RONALD REAGAN, THE WHITE HOUSE, April 3, 1984.

N.2.4   National Security Directive 42[5]
(National Policy for the Security of National Security Telecommunications and Information Systems)

Continuing advances in microelectronics technology have stimulated an unprecedented growth in the demand for and supply of telecommunications and information processing services within the government and throughout the private sector. As new technologies have been applied, traditional distinctions between telecommunications and information systems have begun to disappear.

---

[5]The text presented was released to Marc Rotenberg, Electronic Privacy Information Center, under the Freedom of Information Act and is available on-line at http://snyside.sunnyside.com/cpsr/privacy/computer_security/nsd_42.txt.

Although this trend promises greatly improved efficiency and effectiveness, it also poses significant security challenges.

Telecommunications and information processing systems are highly susceptible to interception, unauthorized electronic access, and related forms of technical exploitation, as well as other dimensions of the foreign intelligence threat. The technology to exploit these electronic systems is widespread and is used extensively by foreign nations and can be employed, as well, by terrorist groups and criminal elements. A comprehensive and coordinated approach must be taken to protect the government's national security telecommunications and information systems (national security systems) against current and projected threats. This approach must include mechanisms for formulating policy, overseeing systems security resources programs, and coordinating and executing technical activities.

This Directive establishes initial objectives of policies, and an organizational structure to guide the conduct of activities to secure national security systems from exploitation; establishes a mechanism for policy development and dissemination; and assigns responsibilities for implementation. It is intended to ensure full participation and cooperation among the various existing centers of technical expertise throughout the Executive branch, and to promote a coherent and coordinated defense against the foreign intelligence threat to these systems. This Directive recognizes the special requirements for protection of intelligence sources and methods.

1. *Objectives.* Ensuring the security of national security systems is vitally important to the operational effectiveness of the national security activities of the government and to military combat readiness. I therefore, direct that the government's capabilities for securing national security systems against technical exploitation threats be maintained or, if inadequate, improved to provide for:

    a.   Reliable and continuing assessment of threats and vulnerabilities, and implementation of appropriate effective countermeasures;

    b.   A technical base within the U.S. Government to achieve this security, and initiatives with the private sector to maintain, complement, or enhance that government technical base and to ensure information systems security products are available to secure national security systems; and;

    c.   Effective and efficient application of U.S. Government resources.

2. *Policies.* In support of these objectives the following policies are established:

    a.   U.S. Government national security systems shall be secured by such means as are necessary to prevent compromises denials or exploitation;

    b.   Federal agencies shall require that national security systems operated and maintained by U.S. Government contractors likewise be secured.

3. *Implementation.* This Directive establishes an NSC Policy Coordinating Committee for National Security Telecommunications and Information Systems, an interagency group at the operating level, an executive agent and a national manager to implement these objectives and policies.

4. *National Security Council/Policy Coordinating Committee for National Security Tele-communications and Information Systems.*

The National Security Council/Policy Coordinating Committee (PCC) for National Security Telecommunications, chaired by the Department of Defense, under the authority of National Security Directives I and 10f assumed the responsibility for the National Security Telecommunications NSDD 97 Steering Group. By authority of this Directive, the PCC for National Security Telecommunications is renamed the PCC for National Security Telecommunications and Information Systems, and shall expand its authority to include the responsibilities to protect the government's national security telecommunications and information systems. When addressing issues concerning the security of national security telecommunications and information systems, the membership of the PCC shall be expanded to include representatives of the Secretary Of State, the Secretary of the Treasury, the Attorney General, the Secretary of Energy, the Secretary of Commerce, and the Director of Central Intelligence. The National Manager for National Security Telecommunications and Information Systems Security shall be invited as an observer. The Policy Coordinating Committee shall:

    a.   Oversee the implementation of this Directive;

    b.   Develop Policy recommendations and provide guidance to the operating level National Security Telecommunications and Information Systems Security Committee (NSTISSC);

    c.   Review and resolve matters referred to it by the NSTISSC in fulfilling the responsibilities outlined in paragraph 5, below; -

    d.   Be subject to the policies of the Director of Central Intelligence on matters pertaining to the protection of intelligence sources and methods; and,

    e.   Recommend for Presidential approval additions or revisions to this Directive as national interests may require.

5. *The National Security Telecommunications and Information Systems Security Committee.*

    a.   The NSTISSC is established to consider technical matters and develop operating policies, procedures, guidelines, instructions, and standards as necessary to implement provisions of this Directive. The Committee shall be chaired by the Assistant Secretary of Defense (Command, Control, Communications and Intelligence) and shall be composed of a voting representative of each of the following:

The Secretary of State
The Secretary of the Treasury
The Secretary of Defense
The Attorney General
The Secretary of Commerce
The Secretary of Transportation
The Secretary of Energy
Director, Office of Management and Budget
Assistant to the President for National Security Affairs

Director of Central Intelligence
Chairman of the Joint Chiefs of Staff
Director, Federal Bureau of Investigation
Director, Federal Emergency Management Agency
Administrator, General Services Administration
The Chief of Staff, United States Army
The Chief of Naval Operations
The Chief of Staff, United States Air Force
Commandant, United States Marine Corps
Director, National Security Agency
Manager, National Communications System
Director, Defense Intelligence Agency

    b.   The NSTISSC shall:

        (1) Develop such specific operating policies, procedures, guidelines, instructions, standards, objectives, and priorities as may be required to implement this Directive;

        (2) Provide systems security guidance for national security systems to Executive departments and agencies;

        (3) Submit annually to the Executive Agent an evaluation of the security status of national security systems with respect to established objectives and priorities;

        (4) Approve the release of cryptologic national security systems technical security material, information, and techniques to foreign governments or international organizations. The concurrence of the Director of Central Intelligence shall be obtained with respect to those activities which he manages;

        (5) Establish and maintain a national system for promulgating the operating policies, instructions, directives, and guidancet which may be issued pursuant to this Directive;

        (6) Establish permanent and temporary subcommittees as necessary to discharge its responsibilities;

        (7) Make recommendations to the PCC for NSTISSC membership and establish criteria and procedures for permanent observers from other departments or agencies affected by specific matters under deliberation, who may attend meetings upon invitation of the Chairman; and,

        (8) Interact, as necessary, with the National Communications System Committee of Principals established by Executive Order 12472 to ensure the coordinated execution of assigned responsibilities.

    c.   The Committee shall have two subcommittees, one focusing on telecommunications security and one focusing an information systems security. The two subcommittees shall coordinate their actions and recommendations concerning implementation of protective measures, which shall combine and coordinate both areas where appropriate.

    d.   The Committee shall have a permanent secretariat composed of personnel of the National Security Agency and such other personnel from Executive departments and agencies represented on the Committee as are requested by the Chairman. The National Security Agency shall provide facilities and support as required. Other Executive departments and agencies shall provide facilities and support as requested by the Chairman.

6. *The Executive Agent of the Government for National Security Telecommunications and Information Systems Security.*

　　a.　　Consistent with the authority for communications security given the Secretary of Defense in Executive Order 12333, the Secretary of Defense shall serve as Executive Agent of the Government for National Security Telecommunications and Information Systems Security and shall be responsible for implementing, under his signature, policies and procedures to:

　　　　(1)　Ensure the development, in conjunction with Committee member departments and agencies of plans and programs to fulfill the objectives of this Directive, including the development of necessary security architectures;

　　　　(2)　Procure for and provide to Executive departments and agencies and, where appropriate, to government contractors and foreign governments, consistent with the laws of the United States such technical security material, other technical assistance, and other related services of common concern as required to accomplish the objectives of this Directive;

　　　　(3)　Approve and provide minimum security standards and doctrine for systems subject to this Directive; (U)

　　　　(4)　Conduct, approve, or endorse research and development of techniques and equipment to secure national security systems; and,

　　　　(5)　Operate, or coordinate the efforts, of U.S. Government technical centers related to national security telecommunications and information systems security.

　　b.　　The Executive Agent shall review and assess the National Manager's recommendations on the proposed national security telecommunications and information systems security programs and budgets for the Executive departments and agencies. Where appropriate, alternative systems security recommendations will be provided to agency heads, to National Security Council Committees and to the OMB. In addition, the Executive Agent shall submit, annually, the security status of national security systems with respect to established objectives and priorities through the National Security Council to the President.

7. *The National Manager for National Security Telecommunications and Information Systems Security.*

The Director, National Security Agency, is designated the National Manager for National Security Telecommunications and Information Systems Security and is responsible to the Secretary of Defense as Executive Agent for carrying out the foregoing responsibilities. In fulfilling these responsibilities the National Manager shall:

　　a.　　Examine U.S. Government national security systems and evaluate their vulnerability to foreign interception and exploitation. Any such activities, including those involving monitoring of official telecommunications, shall be conducted in strict compliance with law, Executive Order and implementing procedures, and applicable Presidential directive. No monitoring shall be performed without advising the heads of the agencies, departments, or services concerned;

b. Act as the U.S. Government focal point for cryptography, telecommunications systems security, and information systems security for national security systems;

c. Conduct, approve, or endorse research and development of techniques and equipment to secure national security systems;

d. Review and approve all standards, techniques, systems, and equipment related to the security of national security systems;

e. Conduct foreign computer security and communications security liaison, including entering into agreements with foreign governments and with international and private organizations regarding national security systems, except for those foreign intelligence relationships conducted for intelligence purposes by the Director of Central Intelligence. Any such agreements shall be coordinated with affected departments and agencies;

f. Operate such printing and fabrication facilities as may be required to perform critical functions related to the provisions of cryptographic and other technical security material or services;

g. Assess the overall security posture of and disseminate information on threats to and vulnerabilities of national security systems;

h. Operate a central technical center to evaluate and certify the security of national security telecommunications and information systems;

i. Prescribe the minimum standards, methods and procedures for protecting cryptographic and other technical security material, techniques, and information related to national security systems;

j. Review and assess annually the national security telecommunications systems security programs and budgets of Executive departments and agencies of the U.S. Government, and recommend alternatives, where appropriate, for the Executive Agent;

k. Review annually the aggregated national security information systems security program and budget recommendations of the Executive departments and agencies of the U.S. Government for the Executive Agent;

l. Request from the heads of Executive departments and agencies such information and technical support as may be needed to discharge the responsibilities assigned herein;

m. Coordinate with the National Institute for Standards and Technology in accordance with the provisions of the Computer Security Act of 1987 (P.L. 100-235); and

n. Enter into agreements for the procurement of technical-security material and other equipment, and their provision to Executive departments and agencies, where appropriate, to government contractors, and foreign governments.

8. *The Heads of Executive Departments and Agencies shall:*

a. Be responsible for achieving and maintaining secure national security systems within their departments or agencies;

b. Ensure that policies, procedures, guidelines, instructions, and standards issued pursuant to this Directive are implemented within their departments or agencies; and

c. Provide to the NSTISSC, the Executive Agent, and the National Manager, as appropriate, such information as may be required to discharge responsibilities assigned herein, consistent with relevant law, Executive Order, and Presidential directive.

9. *Additional Responsibilities.* The Director, Office of Management and Budget, shall:

a. Specify data to be provided during the annual budget review by Executive departments and agencies on program and budgets relating to security of their national security systems;

b. Consolidate and provide such data to the National Manager via the Executive Agent; and

c. Review for consistency with this Directive, and amend as appropriate, OMB policies and regulations which may pertain to the subject matter herein.

10. *Nothing in this Directive shall:*

a. Alter or supersede the existing authorities of the Director of Central Intelligence;

b. Authorize the Committee, the Executive Agent, or the National Manager authority to examine the facilities of other Executive departments and agencies without approval of the head of such department or agency, nor to request or collect information concerning their operation for any purpose not provided for herein;

c. Amend or contravene the provisions of existing law, Executive Order, or Presidential directive which pertain to the protection of sensitive information, to the protection of national security information, to the privacy aspects or financial management of information systems or to the administrative requirements for safeguarding such resources against fraud, waste, and abuse;

d. Provide authority to issue policies, procedure, guidelines, instructions, standards, or priorities or operate programs concerning security of systems other than national security systems;

e. Be intended to establish additional review processes for the procurement of information processing systems;

f. Alter or rescind policies or programs begun under PD-24 or NSDD-145 that may be pertinent to national security systems. Policies or programs retained pursuant to this provision shall not be construed to apply to systems within the purview of the Computer Security Act of 1987 (PL100-235); or

[NOTE: In documents received, approximately two paragraphs of material deleted by redaction of text in this place.]

11. *For the purposes of this Directive the following terms shall have the meanings indicated:*

a. *Telecommunications* means the preparation transmission, communications or related processing of information (writing, images, sounds or other data) by electrical, electromagnetic, electromechanical, electro-optical, or electronic means;

   b.   *Information Systems* means any equipment or interconnected system or subsystems of equipment that is used in the automatic acquisition storage manipulation, management, movement, control, display, switching interchange, transmission, or reception of data and includes computer software, firmware, and hardware;

   c.   *Telecommunications and Information Systems Security* means protection afforded to telecommunications and information systems in order to prevent exploitation through interception, unauthorized electronic access, or related technical intelligence threats, and to ensure authenticity. Such protection results from the application of security measures (including cryptosecurity, transmission security, emission security, and computer security) to systems which generate, store process transfer, or communicate information of use to an adversary, and also includes the physical protection of technical security material and technical security information;

   d.   *Technical security* material means equipment components, devices, and associated documentation or other media which pertain to cryptographic or to the securing of telecommunications and information systems;

   e.   *National security systems* are those telecommunications and information systems operated by the U.S. Government, its contractors, or agents that contain classified information or, as set forth in 10 U.S.C. Section 2315, that involves intelligence activities involves cryptologic activities related to national security, involves command and control Of military forces, involves equipment that is an integral part of a weapon or weapon system, or involves equipment that is critical to the direct fulfillment of military or intelligence missions.

12. *Except for ongoing telecommunications protection activities mandated by and pursuant to PD-24 and NSDD-145, NSDD-145 is hereby rescinded.*

July 5, 1990

N.3   MEMORANDUMS OF UNDERSTANDING (MOU) AND AGREEMENT (MOA)

N.3.1   National Security Agency/National Institute of Standards and Technology MOU

Memorandum of Understanding Between the Director of the National Institute of Standards and Technology and the Director of the National Security Agency Concerning the Implementation of Public Law 100-235

Recognizing that:

A.   Under Section 2 of the Computer Security Act of 1987 (Public Law 100-235), (the Act), the National Institute of Standards and Technology (NIST) has the responsibility within the Federal Government for:
1.   Developing technical, management, physical, and administrative standards and guidelines for the cost-effective security and privacy of sensitive information in Federal computer systems as defined in the Act; and,
2.   Drawing on the computer system technical security guidelines of the National Security Agency (NSA) in this regard where appropriate.
B.   Under Section 3 of the Act, the NIST is to coordinate closely with other agencies and offices, including the NSA, to assure:
1.   Maximum use of all existing and planned programs, materials, studies, and reports relating to computer systems security and privacy, in order to avoid unnecessary and costly duplication of effort; and,
2.   To the maximum extent feasible, that standards developed by the NIST under the Act are consistent and compatible with standards and procedures developed for the protection of classified information in Federal computer systems.
C.   Under the Act, the Secretary of Commerce has the responsibility, which he has delegated to the Director of NIST, for appointing the members of the Computer System Security and Privacy Advisory Board, at least one of whom shall be from the NSA.

Therefore, in furtherance of the purposes of this MOU, the Director of the NIST and the Director of the NSA hereby agree as follows:

I.   The NIST will:
1.   Appoint to the Computer Security and Privacy Advisory Board at least one representative nominated by the Director of the NSA.
2.   Draw upon computer system technical security guidelines developed by the NSA to the extent that the NIST determines that such guidelines are consistent with the requirements for protecting sensitive information in Federal computer systems.
3.   Recognize the NSA-certified rating of evaluated trusted systems under the Trusted Computer Security Evaluation Criteria Program without requiring additional evaluation.
4.   Develop telecommunications security standards for protecting sensitive unclassified computer data, drawing upon the expertise and products of the National Security Agency, to the greatest extent possible, in meeting these responsibilities in a timely and cost effective manner.
5.   Avoid duplication where possible in entering into mutually agreeable arrangements with the NSA for the NSA support.
6.   Request the NSA's assistance on all matters related to cryptographic algorithms and cryptographic techniques including but not limited to research, development, evaluation, or endorsement.

II. The NSA will:

1. Provide the NIST with technical guidelines in trusted technology, telecommunications security, and personal identification that may be used in cost-effective systems for protecting sensitive computer data.

2. Conduct or initiate research and development programs in trusted technology, telecommunications security, cryptographic techniques and personal identification methods.

3. Be responsive to the NIST's requests for assistance in respect to all matters related to cryptographic algorithms and cryptographic techniques including but not limited to research, development, evaluation, or endorsement.

4. Establish the standards and endorse products for application to secure systems covered in 10 USC Section 2315 (the Warner Amendment).

5. Upon request by Federal agencies, their contractors, and other government-sponsored entities, conduct assessments of the hostile intelligence threat to federal information systems, and provide technical assistance and recommend endorsed products for application to secure systems against that threat.

III. The NIST and the NSA shall:

1. Jointly review agency plans for the security and privacy of computer systems submitted to NIST and NSA pursuant to section 6(b) of the Act.

2. Exchange technical standards and guidelines as necessary to achieve the purposes of the Act.

3. Work together to achieve the purposes of this memorandum with the greatest efficiency possible, avoiding unnecessary duplication of effort.

4. Maintain an ongoing, open dialogue to ensure that each organization remains abreast of emerging technologies and issues affecting automated information system security in computer-based systems.

5. Establish a Technical Working Group to review and analyze issues of mutual interest pertinent to protection of systems that process sensitive or other unclassified information. The Group shall be composed of six federal employees, three each selected by NIST and NSA and to be augmented as necessary by representatives of other agencies. Issues may be referred to the group by either the NSA Deputy Director for Information Security or the NIST Deputy Director or may be generated and addressed by the group upon approval by the NSA DDI or NIST Deputy Director. Within days of the referral of an issue to the Group by either the NSA Deputy Director for Information Security or the NIST Deputy Director, the Group will respond with a progress report and plan for further analysis, if any.

6. Exchange work plans on an annual basis on all research and development projects pertinent to protection of systems that process sensitive or other unclassified information, including trusted technology, for protecting the integrity and availability of data, telecommunications security and personal identification methods. Project updates will be exchanged quarterly, and project reviews will be provided by either party upon request of the other party.

7. Ensure the Technical Working Group reviews prior to public disclosure all matters regarding technical systems security techniques to be developed for use in protecting sensitive information in federal computer systems to ensure they are consistent with the national security of the United States. If NIST

and NSA are unable to resolve such an issue within 60 days, either agency may elect to raise the issue to the Secretary of Defense and the Secretary of Commerce. It is recognized that such an issue may be referred to the President through the NSC for resolution. No action shall be taken on such an issue until it is resolved.

        8. Specify additional operational agreements in annexes to this MOU as they are agreed to by NSA and NIST.

        IV. Either party may elect to terminate this MOU upon six months written notice. This MOU is effective upon approval of both signatories.

RAYMOND G. KAMMER, Acting Director, National Institute of Standards and Technology, 24 March 1989

W.O. STUDEMAN, Vice Admiral, U.S. Navy; Director, National Security Agency, 23 March 1989

N.3.2 National Security Agency/ Federal Bureau of Investigation MOU

Memorandum of Understanding Between Federal Bureau of Investigation and National Security Agency

(u) 1. *Purpose.* This Memorandum of Understanding (MOU) implements those portions of the Department of Defense E.O. 12036 replaced by 12333 (see 12333 para. 3.6) procedures that regulate the provision by NSA of specialized equipment, technical knowledge, and expert personnel to the FBI. (The applicable procedures are attached.)

(u) 2. *Background.* The National Security Agency possesses unique skills and equipment developed to support its cryptologic mission. In the past, the Federal Bureau of Investigation has requested, and NSA has provided, assistance related to these skills and equipment for both the Bureau's intelligence and law enforcement functions. Section 2-309(c) of E.O. 12036 permits NSA to continue providing such assistance.

(u) 3. *Agreement.* The undersigned parties, representing their respective agencies, hereby agree to the following procedures for requesting and providing such assistance in the future:

        a. When the FBI determines that the assistance of NSA is needed to accomplish its lawful functions, the FBI shall:

        (1) determine whether the requested assistance involves the Bureau's intelligence of law enforcement missions. Since a counterintelligence or counterterrorism intelligence investigation can develop into a law enforcement investigation, the following guidelines will be used to determine which type of investigation the FBI is conducting. A counterintelligence or counterterrorism investigation which is undertaken to protect against espionage and other clandestine intelligence activities, sabotage, international terrorist activities or assas-

inations conducted for or on behalf of foreign powers does not have a law enforcement purpose until such time as the focus of the investigation shifts from intelligence gathering to prosecution.

(2) coordinate with the appropriate NSA element to determine whether NSA is capable of providing the assistance;

(3) notify the Office of General Counsel, NSA, that a request for assistance is being considered; and

(4) if NSA is able to provide the assistance, provide a certification to the General Counsel, NSA, that the assistance is necessary to accomplish one or more of the FBI's lawful functions. In normal circumstances, this certification shall be in writing and signed by an Assistant Director or more senior official. If the assistance involves provision of expert personnel and is for a law enforcement purpose, the certification must be signed by the Director, FBI, and shall include affirmation of the facts necessary to establish the provisions of Section 4.A., Procedure 16, DoD Regulation 5240.1-R. In an emergency, the certification may be oral, but it shall be subsequently confirmed in writing. If the assistance requested is for the support of an activitiy that may only be conducted pursuant to court order or Attorney General authorization, the certification shall include a copy of the order or authorization. If the requested assistance is to support an intelligence investigation which subsequently develops into a law enforcement investigation, the FBI shall provide the additional supporting data required by Procedure 16.

b. When the FBI requests assistance from NSA, NSA shall:

(1) determine whether it is capable of providing the requested assistance;

(2) determine whether the assistance is consistent with NSA policy, including protection of sources and methods;

(3) agree to provide assistance within its capabilities and when consistent with NSA policy after receipt of the certification discussed in a.(4) above; and

(4) if the assistance requires the detailing of expert personnel, observe the administrative requirements of Procedures 16 and 17, DoD regulation 5240.1-R.

(u) 4. *Effective Date.* This MOU is effective upon signature by the parties below. It remains in effect until superseded by a new MOU or until Section 2-309(c) of E.O. 12036 is revised. Changes to this MOU may be made by joint agreement of the undersigned or their successors.

WILLIAM H. WEBSTER, Director, Federal Bureau of Investigation

B.R. INMAN, Vice Admiral, U.S. Navy, Director, NSA/Chief, CSS

N.3.3   National Security Agency/Advanced Research Projects Agency/Defense Information Systems Agency MOA

Information Systems Security Research Joint Technology Office Memorandum of Agreement Between The Advanced Research Projects Agency, The Defense Information Systems Agency, and The National Security Agency Concerning The Information Systems Security Research Joint Technology Office

Purpose

The Advanced Research Projects Agency (ARPA), the Defense Information Systems Agency (DISA), and the National Security Agency (NSA) agree to the establishment of the Information System Security Research Joint Technology Office (ISSR-JTO) as a joint activity. The ISSR-JTO is being established to coordinate the information systems security research programs of ARPA and NSA. The ISSR-JTO will work to optimize use of the limited research funds available, and strengthen the responsiveness of the programs to DISA, expediting delivery of technologies that meet DISA's requirements to safeguard the confidentiality, integrity, authenticity, and availability of data in Department of Defense information systems, provide a robust first line of defense for defensive information warfare, and permit electronic commerce between the Department of Defense and its contractors.

Background

In recent years, exponential growth in government and private sector use of networked systems to produce and communicate information has given rise to a shared interest by NSA and ARPA in focusing government R&D on information systems security technologies. NSA and its primary network security customer, DISA, have become increasingly reliant upon commercial information technologies and services to build the Defense Information Infrastructure, and the inherent security of these technologies and services has become a vital concern. From ARPA'S perspective, it has become increasingly apparent that security is critical to the success of key ARPA information technology initiatives. ARPA's role in fostering the development of advanced information technologies now requires close attention to the security of these technologies.

NSA's security technology plan envisions maximum use of commercial technology for sensitive but unclassified applications, and, to the extent possible, for classified applications as well. A key element of this plan is the transfer of highly reliable government-developed technology and techniques to industry for integration into commercial off-the-shelf products, making quality-tested security components available not only to DoD but to the full spectrum of government and private sector users as well. ARPA is working with its contractor community to fully integrate security into next generation computing technologies being developed in all its programs, and working with the research community to develop strategic relationships with industry so that industry will develop modular security technologies with the capability of exchanging appropriate elements to meet various levels of required security.

NSA and ARPA now share a strong interest in promoting the development and integration of security technology for advanced information systems applications. The challenge at hand is to guide the efforts of the two agencies in a way that optimizes use of the limited research funds available and maximizes support to DISA in building the Defense Information Infrastructure.

NSA acts as the U.S. Government's focal point for cryptography, telecommunications security, and information systems security for national security systems. It conducts, approves, or endorses research and development of techniques and equipment to secure national security systems. NSA reviews and approves all standards, techniques, systems, and equipment related to the security of national security systems. NSA's primary focus is to provide information systems security products, services, and standards in the near term to help its customers protect classified and national security-related sensitive but unclassified information. It develops and assesses new security technology in the areas of cryptography, technical security, and authentication technology; endorses cryptographic systems protecting national security information; develops infrastructure support technologies; evaluates and rates trusted computer and network products; and provides information security standards for DoD. Much of the work in these areas is conducted in a classified environment, and the balancing of national security and law enforcement equities has been a significant constraint.

ARPA's mission is to perform research and development that helps the Department of Defense to maintain U.S. technological superiority over potential adversaries. At the core of the ARPA mission is the goal to develop and demonstrate revolutionary technologies that will fundamentally enhance the capability of the military. ARPA's role in fostering the development of advanced computing and communications technologies for use by the DoD requires that long term solutions to increasing the security of these systems be developed. ARPA is interested in commercial or dual-use technology, and usually technology that provides revolutionary rather than evolutionary enhancements to capabilities. ARPA is working with industry and academia to develop technologies that will enable industry to provide system design methodologies and secure computer, operating system, and networking technologies. NSA and ARPA research interests have been converging in these areas, particularly with regard to protocol development involving key, token, and certificate exchanges and processes.

One of the key differences between ARPA's work and NSA's is that ARPA's is performed in unclassified environments, often in university settings. This enables ARPA to access talent and pursue research strategies normally closed to NSA due to security considerations. Another difference is that while NSA's research is generally built around developing and using specific cryptographic algorithms, ARPA's approach is to pursue solutions that are independent of the algorithm used and allow for modularly replaceable cryptography. ARPA will, to the greatest extent possible, allow its contractor community to use cryptography developed at NSA, and needs solutions from NSA on an expedited basis so as not to hold up its research program.

DISA functions as the Department of Defense's information utility. Its requirements for information systems security extend beyond confidentiality to include protection of data from tampering or destruction and assurance that data exchanges are originated and received by valid participants. DISA is the first line of defense for information warfare, and needs quality technology for detecting and responding to network penetrations. The growing vulnerability of the Defense information infrastructure to unauthorized access and use, demonstrated in the penetration of hundreds of DoD computer systems during 1994, makes delivery of enabling security technologies to DISA a matter of urgency.

The Information Systems Security Research Joint Technology Office
This MOA authorizes the ISSR-JTO as a joint undertaking of ARPA, DISA, and NSA. It will perform those functions jointly agreed to by these agencies. Each agency shall delegate to the ISSO-JTO such authority and responsibility as is necessary to carry out its agreed functions. Participation in the joint program does not relieve ARPA, DISA, or NSA of their respective individual charter responsibilities, or diminish their respective authorities.

A Joint Management Plan will be developed to provide a detailed definition of the focus, objectives, operation, and costs of the Joint Technology Office. The ISSR-JTO will be jointly staffed by ARPA, DISA, and NSA, with respective staffing levels to be agreed upon by the three parties. Employees assigned to the JTO will remain on the billets of their respective agency. Personnel support for employees assigned to the JTO will be provided by their home organization. The ISSR-JTO will be housed within both ARPA and NSA, except as agreed otherwise by the three parties. To the greatest extent possible, it will function as a virtual office, using electronic connectivity to minimize the need for constant physical colocation. Physical security support will be provided by the party responsible for the specific facilities occupied. Assignment of the ISSR-JTO Director, Deputy Director, and management of other office elements will be made by mutual agreement among the Directors of ARPA, DISA, and NSA upon recommendation of their staffs.

Functions
By mutual agreement of ARPA, DISA, and NSA, the ISSR-JTO will perform the following joint functions:

• Review and coordinate all Information System Security Research programs at ARPA and NSA to ensure that there is no unnecessary duplication, that the programs are technically sound, that they are focused on customer requirements where available, and that long term research is aimed at revolutionary increases in DoD security capabilities.
• Support ARPA and NSA in evaluating proposals and managing projects arising from their information systems security efforts, and maintain a channel for the exchange of technical expertise to support their information systems security research programs.
• Provide long range strategic planning for information systems security research. Provide concepts of future architectures which include security as an integral component and a road map for the products that need to be developed to fit the architectures, taking into account anticipated DoD information systems security research needs for command and control, intelligence, support functions, and

electronic commerce. The long range security program will explore technologies which extend security research boundaries.

• Develop measures of the effectiveness of the information systems security research programs in reducing vulnerabilities.

• Work with DISA, other defense organizations, academic, and industrial organizations to take new information systems security research concepts and apply them to selected prototype systems and testbed projects.

• Encourage the U.S. industrial base to develop commercial products with built-in security to be used in DoD systems. Develop alliances with industry to raise the level of security in all U.S. systems. Bring together private sector leaders in information systems security research to advise the JTO and build consensus for the resulting programs.

• Identify areas for which standards need to be developed for information systems security.

• Facilitate the availability and use of NSA certified cryptography within information systems security research programs.

• Proactively provide a coherent, integrated joint vision of the program in internal and public communications.

Program Oversight and Revisions

The Director, ISSR-JTO, has a joint reporting responsibility to the Directors of ARPA, DISA, and NSA. The Director, ISSR-JTO, will conduct a formal Program Status Review for the Directors of ARPA, DISA, and NSA on an annual basis, and will submit mid-year progress reports between formal reviews. Specific reporting procedures and practices of the JTO to ARPA, DISA, and NSA will be detailed in the Joint Technology Management Plan. This MOA will be reviewed at least annually, and may be revised at any time, based on the mutual consent of ARPA, DISA, and NSA, to assure the effective execution of the joint initiative. Any of the parties may withdraw from participation in the MOA upon six months written notice. The MOA is effective 2 April 1995.

Dr. Gary L. Denman, Director, ARPA
LtGen Albert J. Edmonds, Director, DISA
VADM John M. McConnell, Director, NSA
Dr. Anita K. Jones, Director, DDR&E
Emmett Paige, Jr., Assistant Secretary of Defense for Command, Control, Communications and Intelligence

N.4 REGULATIONS

N.4.1 International Traffic in Arms Regulations (22 CFR, Excerpts from Parts 120-123, 125, and 126)

Part 120
Purpose and Definitions

Sec. 120.1—General authorities and eligibility.

(a) Section 38 of the Arms Export Control Act (22 U.S.C. 2778) authorizes the President to control the export and import of defense articles and defense services. The statutory authority of the President to promulgate regulations with respect to exports of defense articles and defense services was delegated to the Secretary of State by Executive Order 11958, as amended (42 FR 4311). This subchapter implements that authority. By virtue of delegations of authority by the Secretary of State, these regulations are primarily administered by the Director of the Office of Defense Trade Controls, Bureau of Politico-Military Affairs, Department of State.

(b) Authorized Officials. All authorities conferred upon the Director of the Office of Defense Trade Controls by this subchapter may be exercised at any time by the Under Secretary of State for International Security Affairs, the Assistant Secretary of State for Politico-Military Affairs, or the Deputy Assistant Secretary of State for Politico-Military Affairs responsible for supervising the Office of Defense Trade Controls unless the Legal Adviser or the Assistant Legal Adviser for Politico-Military Affairs of the Department of State determines that any specific exercise of this authority under this subsection may be inappropriate.

(c) Eligibility. Only U.S. persons (as defined in Sec. 120.15) and foreign governmental entities in the United States may be granted licenses or other approvals (other than retransfer approvals sought pursuant to this subchapter). Foreign persons (as defined in Sec. 120.16) other than governments are not eligible. U.S. persons who have been convicted of violating the criminal statutes enumerated in Sec. 120.27, who have been debarred pursuant to part 127 or 128 of this subchapter, who are the subject of an indictment involving the criminal statutes enumerated in Sec. 120.27, who are ineligible to contract with, or to receive a license or other form of authorization to import defense articles or defense services from any agency of the U.S. Government, who are ineligible to receive export licenses (or other forms of authorization to export) from any agency of the U.S. Government, who are subject to Department of State Suspension/Revocation under Sec. 126.7 (a)(1)-(a)(7) of this subchapter, or who are ineligible under Sec. 127.6(c) of this subchapter are generally ineligible. Applications for licenses or other approvals will be considered only if the applicant has registered with the Office of Defense Trade Controls pursuant to part 122 of this subchapter. All applications and requests for approval must be signed by a U.S. person who has been empowered by the registrant to sign such documents. . . .

Sec. 120.3—Policy on designating and determining defense articles and services.

An article or service may be designated or determined in the future to be a defense article (see Sec. 120.6) or defense service (see Sec. 120.9) if it:

   (a) Is specifically designed, developed, configured, adapted, or modified for a military application, and
(i)   Does not have predominant civil applications, and
(ii)   Does not have performance equivalent (defined by form, fit and function) to those of an article or service used for civil applications; or
   (b) Is specifically designed, developed, configured, adapted, or modified for a military application, and has significant military or intelligence applicability such that control under this subchapter is necessary.

The intended use of the article or service after its export (i.e., for a military or civilian purpose) is not relevant in determining whether the article or service is subject to the controls of this subchapter. Any item covered by the U.S. Munitions List must be within the categories of the U.S. Munitions List. The scope of the U.S. Munitions List shall be changed only by amendments made pursuant to section 38 of the Arms Export Control Act (22 U.S.C. 2778).

Sec. 120.4—Commodity jurisdiction.

   (a) The commodity jurisdiction procedure is used with the U.S. Government if doubt exists as to whether an article or service is covered by the U.S. Munitions List. It may also be used for consideration of a redesignation of an article or service currently covered by the U.S. Munitions List. The Department must submit a report to Congress at least 30 days before any item is removed from the U.S. Munitions List. Upon written request, the Office of Defense Trade Controls shall provide a determination of whether a particular article or service is covered by the U.S. Munitions List. The determination, consistent with Secs. 120.2, 120.3, and 120.4, entails consultation among the Departments of State, Defense, Commerce and other U.S. Government agencies and industry in appropriate cases.

   (b) Registration with the Office of Defense Trade Controls as defined in part 122 of this subchapter is not required prior to submission of a commodity jurisdiction request. If it is determined that the commodity is a defense article or service covered by the U.S. Munitions List, registration is required for exporters, manufacturers, and furnishers of defense articles and defense services (see part 122 of this subchapter).

(c)   Requests shall identify the article or service, and include a history of the product's design, development and use. Brochures, specifications and any other documentation related to the article or service shall be submitted in seven collated sets.

(d)(1)   A determination that an article or service does not have predominant civil applications shall be made by the Department of State, in accordance with this subchapter, on a case-by-case basis, taking into account:
(i)   The number, variety and predominance of civil applications;
(ii)   The nature, function and capability of the civil applications; and
(iii)   The nature, function and capability of the military applications.
(2)   A determination that an article does not have the performance equivalent, defined by form, fit and function, to those used for civil applications shall be made by the Department of State, in accordance with this subchapter, on a case-by-case basis, taking into account:
(i)   The nature, function, and capability of the article;
(ii)   Whether the components used in the defense article are identical to those components originally developed for civil use.

Note: The form of the item is its defined configuration, including the geometrically measured configuration, density, and weight or other visual parameters which uniquely characterize the item, component or assembly. For software, form denotes language, language level and media. The fit of the item is its ability to physically interface or interconnect with or become an integral part of another item. The function of the item is the action or actions it is designed to perform.

(3)   A determination that an article has significant military or intelligence applications such that it is necessary to control its export as a defense article shall be made, in accordance with this subchapter, on a case-by-case basis, taking into account:
(i)   The nature, function, and capability of the article;
(ii)   The nature of controls imposed by other nations on such items (including COCOM and other multilateral controls), and
(iii)   That items described on the COCOM Industrial List shall not be designated defense articles or defense services unless the failure to control such items on the U.S. Munitions List would jeopardize significant national security or foreign policy interests.

(e)   The Office of Defense Trade Controls will provide a preliminary response within 10 working days of receipt of a complete request for commodity jurisdiction. If after 45 days the Office of Defense Trade Controls has not provided a final commodity jurisdiction determination, the applicant may request in writing to the Director, Center for Defense Trade that this determination be given expedited processing.

(f)   State, Defense and Commerce will resolve commodity jurisdiction disputes in accordance with established procedures. State shall notify Defense and Commerce of the initiation and conclusion of each case.

(g) A person may appeal a commodity jurisdiction determination by submitting a written request for reconsideration to the Director of the Center for Defense Trade. The Center for Defense Trade will provide a written response of the Director's determination within 30 days of receipt of the appeal. If desired, an appeal of the Director's decision can then be made directly to the Assistant Secretary for Politico-Military Affairs. . . .

Sec. 120.6—Defense article.

Defense article means any item or technical data designated in Sec. 121.1 of this subchapter. The policy described in Sec. 120.3 is applicable to designations of additional items. This term includes technical data recorded or stored in any physical form, models, mockups or other items that reveal technical data directly relating to items designated in Sec. 121.1 of this subchapter. It does not include basic marketing information on function or purpose or general system descriptions. . . .

Sec. 120.9—Defense service.

Defense service means:

(1) The furnishing of assistance (including training) to foreign persons, whether in the United States or abroad in the design, development, engineering, manufacture, production, assembly, testing, repair, maintenance, modification, operation, demilitarization, destruction, processing or use of defense articles; or

(2) The furnishing to foreign persons of any technical data controlled under this subchapter (see Sec. 120.10), whether in the United States or abroad.

Sec. 120.10—Technical data.

Technical data means, for purposes of this subchapter:

(1) Information, other than software as defined in Sec. 120.10(d), which is required for the design, development, production, manufacture, assembly, operation, repair, testing, maintenance or modification of defense articles. This includes information in the form of blueprints, drawings, photographs, plans, instructions and documentation.

(2) Classified information relating to defense articles and defense services;

(3) Information covered by an invention secrecy order;

(4) Software as defined in Sec. 121.8(f) of this subchapter directly related to defense articles;

(5) This definition does not include information concerning general scientific, mathematical or engineering principles commonly taught in schools, colleges and universities or information in the public domain as defined in Sec.

120.11. It also does not include basic marketing information on function or purpose or general system descriptions of defense articles.

Sec. 120.11—Public domain.

Public domain means information which is published and which is generally accessible or available to the public:

(1) Through sales at newsstands and bookstores;
(2) Through subscriptions which are available without restriction to any individual who desires to obtain or purchase the published information;
(3) Through second class mailing privileges granted by the U.S. Government;
(4) At libraries open to the public or from which the public can obtain documents;
(5) Through patents available at any patent office;
(6) Through unlimited distribution at a conference, meeting, seminar, trade show or exhibition, generally accessible to the public, in the United States;
(7) Through public release (i.e., unlimited distribution) in any form (e.g., not necessarily in published form) after approval by the cognizant U.S. government department or agency (see also Sec. 125.4(b)(13) of this subchapter);
(8) Through fundamental research in science and engineering at accredited institutions of higher learning in the U.S. where the resulting information is ordinarily published and shared broadly in the scientific community. Fundamental research is defined to mean basic and applied research in science and engineering where the resulting information is ordinarily published and shared broadly within the scientific community, as distinguished from research the results of which are restricted for proprietary reasons or specific U.S. Government access and dissemination controls. University research will not be considered fundamental research if:

(i) The University or its researchers accept other restrictions on publication of scientific and technical information resulting from the project or activity, or
(ii) The research is funded by the U.S. Government and specific access and dissemination controls protecting information resulting from the research are applicable. . . .

Sec. 120.14—Person.

Person means a natural person as well as a corporation, business association, partnership, society, trust, or any other entity, organization or group, including governmental entities. If a provision in this subchapter does not refer exclusively to a foreign person (Sec. 120.16) or U.S. person (Sec. 120.15), then it refers to both.

Sec. 120.15—U.S. person.

U.S. person means a person (as defined in Sec. 120.14 of this part) who is a protected individual as defined by 8 U.S.C. 1324b(a)(3). It also means any corporation, business association, partnership, society, trust or any other entity, organization or group that is incorporated to do business in the United States. It also includes any governmental (federal, state or local) entity. It does not include any foreign person as defined in Sec. 120.16 of this part.

Sec. 120.16—Foreign person.

Foreign person means any natural person who is not a protected individual as defined by 8 U.S.C. 1324b(a)(3). It also means any foreign corporation, business association, partnership, trust, society or any other entity or group that is not incorporated or organized to do business in the United States, as well as international organizations, foreign governments and any agency or subdivision of foreign governments (e.g., diplomatic missions).

Sec. 120.17—Export.

Export means:

(1) Sending or taking a defense article out of the United States in any manner, except by mere travel outside of the United States by a person whose personal knowledge includes technical data; or

(2) Transferring registration, control or ownership to a foreign person of any aircraft, vessel, or satellite covered by the U.S. Munitions List, whether in the United States or abroad; or

(3) Disclosing (including oral or visual disclosure) or transferring in the United States any defense article to an embassy, any agency or subdivision of a foreign government (e.g., diplomatic missions); or

(4) Disclosing (including oral or visual disclosure) or transferring technical data to a foreign person, whether in the United States or abroad; or

(5) Performing a defense service on behalf of, or for the benefit of, a foreign person, whether in the United States or abroad. . . .

Sec. 120.18—Temporary import.

Temporary import means bringing into the United States from a foreign country any defense article that is to be returned to the country from which it was shipped or taken, or any defense article that is in transit to another foreign destination. Temporary import includes withdrawal of a defense article from a customs bonded warehouse or foreign trade zone for the purpose of returning it to the country of origin or country from which it was shipped or for shipment to another foreign destination. Permanent imports are regulated by the Department of the Treasury (see 27 CFR parts 47, 178 and 179).

Sec. 120.19—Reexport or retransfer.

Reexport or retransfer means the transfer of defense articles or defense services to an end use, end user or destination not previously authorized.

Sec. 120.20—License.

License means a document bearing the word license issued by the Director, Office of Defense Trade Controls or his authorized designee which permits the export or temporary import of a specific defense article or defense service controlled by this subchapter.

Sec. 120.21—Manufacturing license agreement.

An agreement (e.g., contract) whereby a U.S. person grants a foreign person an authorization to manufacture defense articles abroad and which involves or contemplates:

(a)   The export of technical data (as defined in Sec. 120.10) or defense articles or the performance of a defense service; or

(b)   The use by the foreign person of technical data or defense articles previously exported by the U.S. person. (See part 124 of this subchapter.)

Sec. 120.22—Technical assistance agreement.

An agreement (e.g., contract) for the performance of a defense service(s) or the disclosure of technical data, as opposed to an agreement granting a right or license to manufacture defense articles. Assembly of defense articles is included under this section, provided production rights or manufacturing know-how are not conveyed. Should such rights be transferred, Sec. 120.21 is applicable. (See part 124 of this subchapter.)

Sec. 120.23—Distribution agreement.

An agreement (e.g., a contract) to establish a warehouse or distribution point abroad for defense articles exported from the United States for subsequent distribution to entities in an approved sales territory (see part 124 of this subchapter). . . .

Part 121
The United States Munitions List

Sec. 121.1—General. The United States Munitions List.

(a) The following articles, services and related technical data are designated as defense articles and defense services pursuant to sections 38 and 47(7) of the Arms Export Control Act (22 U.S.C. 2778 and 2794(7)). Changes in designations will be published in the Federal Register. Information and clarifications on whether specific items are defense articles and services under this subchapter may appear periodically in the Defense Trade News published by the Center for Defense Trade. . . .

Category XIII   Auxiliary Military Equipment. . . .

(b) Information Security Systems and equipment, cryptographic devices, software, and components specifically designed or modified therefor, including:
(1) Cryptographic (including key management) systems, equipment, assemblies, modules, integrated circuits, components or software with the capability of maintaining secrecy or confidentiality of information or information systems, except cryptographic equipment and software as follows:
(i) Restricted to decryption functions specifically designed to allow the execution of copy protected software, provided the decryption functions are not user-accessible.
(ii) Specially designed, developed or modified for use in machines for banking or money transactions, and restricted to use only in such transactions. Machines for banking or money transactions include automatic teller machines, self-service statement printers, point of sale terminals or equipment for the encryption of interbanking transactions.
(iii) Employing only analog techniques to provide the cryptographic processing that ensures information security in the following applications:
(A) Fixed (defined below) band scrambling not exceeding 8 bands and in which the transpositions change not more frequently than once every second;
(B) Fixed (defined below) band scrambling exceeding 8 bands and in which the transpositions change not more frequently than once every ten seconds;
(C) Fixed (defined below) frequency inversion and in which the transpositions change not more frequently than once every second;
(D) Facsimile equipment;
(E) Restricted audience broadcast equipment;
(F) Civil television equipment.

Note: Special Definition. For purposes of this subparagraph, fixed means that the coding or compression algorithm cannot accept externally supplied parameters (e.g., cryptographic or key variables) and cannot be modified by the user.

(iv)   Personalized smart cards using cryptography restricted for use only in equipment or systems exempted from the controls of the USML.

 (v)   Limited to access control, such as automatic teller machines, self-service statement printers or point of sale terminals, which protects password or personal identification numbers (PIN) or similar data to prevent unauthorized access to facilities but does not allow for encryption of files or text, except as directly related to the password of PIN protection.

(vi)   Limited to data authentication which calculates a Message Authentication Code (MAC) or similar result to ensure no alteration of text has taken place, or to authenticate users, but does not allow for encryption of data, text or other media other than that needed for the authentication.

(vii)   Restricted to fixed data compression or coding techniques.

(viii) Limited to receiving for radio broadcast, pay television or similar restricted audience television of the consumer type, without digital encryption and where digital decryption is limited to the video, audio or management functions.

(ix)   Software designed or modified to protect against malicious computer damage (e.g., viruses).

Note: A procedure has been established to facilitate the expeditious transfer to the Commodity Control List of mass market software products with encryption that meet specified criteria regarding encryption for the privacy of data and the associated key management. Requests to transfer commodity jurisdiction of mass market software products designed to meet the specified criteria may be submitted in accordance with the commodity jurisdiction provisions of Sec. 120.4. Questions regarding the specified criteria or the commodity jurisdiction process should be addressed to the Office of Defense Trade Controls. All mass market software products with cryptography that were previously granted transfers of commodity jurisdiction will remain under Department of Commerce control. Mass market software governed by this note is software that is generally available to the public by being sold from stock at retail selling points, without restriction, by means of over the counter transactions, mail order transactions, or telephone call transactions; and designed for installation by the user without further substantial support by the supplier.

(2)   Cryptographic (including key management) systems, equipment, assemblies, modules, integrated circuits, components or software which have the capability of generating spreading or hopping codes for spread spectrum systems or equipment.

(3)   Cryptanalytic systems, equipment, assemblies, modules, integrated circuits, components or software.

(4)   Systems, equipment, assemblies, modules, integrated circuits, components or software providing certified or certifiable multi-level security or user isolation

exceeding class B2 of the Trusted Computer System Evaluation Criteria (TCSEC) and software to certify such systems, equipment or software.
(5)   Ancillary equipment specifically designed or modified for paragraphs (b) (1), (2), (3), (4) and (5) of this category; . . .

Category XXI   Miscellaneous Articles

(a)   Any article not specifically enumerated in the other categories of the U.S. Munitions List which has substantial military applicability and which has been specifically designed or modified for military purposes. The decision on whether any article may be included in this category shall be made by the Director of the Office of Defense Trade Controls.

(b)   Technical data (as defined in Sec. 120.21 of this subchapter) and defense services (as defined in Sec. 120.8 of this subchapter) directly related to the defense articles enumerated in paragraphs (a) of this category. . . .

Part 122
Registration of Manufacturers and Exporters

Sec. 122.1—Registration requirements.

(a)   Any person who engages in the United States in the business of either manufacturing or exporting defense articles or furnishing defense services is required to register with the Office of Defense Trade Controls. Manufacturers who do not engage in exporting must nevertheless register.

(b)   Exemptions. Registration is not required for:
(1)   Officers and employees of the United States Government acting in an official capacity.
(2)   Persons whose pertinent business activity is confined to the production of unclassified technical data only.
(3)   Persons all of whose manufacturing and export activities are licensed under the Atomic Energy Act of 1954, as amended.
(4)   Persons who engage only in the fabrication of articles for experimental or scientific purpose, including research and development.

(c)   Purpose. Registration is primarily a means to provide the U.S. Government with necessary information on who is involved in certain manufacturing and exporting activities. Registration does not confer any export rights or privileges. It is generally a precondition to the issuance of any license or other approval under this subchapter.

Sec. 122.2—Submission of registration statement.

(a) General. The Department of State Form DSP-9 (Registration Statement) and the transmittal letter required by paragraph (b) of this section must be submitted by an intended registrant with a payment by check or money order payable to the Department of State of one of the fees prescribed in Sec. 122.3(a) of this subchapter. The Registration Statement and transmittal letter must be signed by a senior officer who has been empowered by the intended registrant to sign such documents. The intended registrant shall also submit documentation that demonstrates that it is incorporated or otherwise authorized to do business in the United States. The Office of Defense Trade Controls will return to the sender any Registration Statement that is incomplete, or that is not accompanied by the required letter or payment of the proper registration fee.

(b) Transmittal letter. A letter of transmittal, signed by an authorized senior officer of the intended registrant, shall accompany each Registration Statement.
(1) The letter shall state whether the intended registrant, chief executive officer, president, vice-presidents, other senior officers or officials (e.g. comptroller, treasurer, general counsel) or any member of the board of directors:
(i) Has ever been indicted for or convicted of violating any of the U.S. criminal statutes enumerated in Sec. 120.27 of this subchapter; or
(ii) Is ineligible to contract with, or to receive a license or other approval to import defense articles or defense services from, or to receive an export license or other approval from, any agency of the U.S. Government.
(2) The letter shall also declare whether the intended registrant is owned or controlled by foreign persons (as defined in Sec. 120.16 of this subchapter). If the intended registrant is owned or controlled by foreign persons, the letter shall also state whether the intended registrant is incorporated or otherwise authorized to engage in business in the United States.

(c) Definition. For purposes of this section, ownership means that more than 50 percent of the outstanding voting securities of the firm are owned by one or more foreign persons. Control means that one or more foreign persons have the authority or ability to establish or direct the general policies or day-to-day operations of the firm. Control is presumed to exist where foreign persons own 25 percent or more of the outstanding voting securities if no U.S. persons control an equal or larger percentage. The standards for control specified in 22 CFR 60.2(c) also provide guidance in determining whether control in fact exists. . . .

Part 123
Licenses for the Export of Defense Articles

Sec. 123.7—Exports to warehouses or distribution points outside the United States.

Unless the exemption under Sec. 123.16(b)(1) is used, a license is required to export defense articles to a warehouse or distribution point outside the United States for subsequent resale and will normally be granted only if an agreement has been approved pursuant to Sec. 124.14 of this subchapter. . . .

Sec. 123.9—Country of ultimate destination and approval of reexports or retransfers.

(a) The country designated as the country of ultimate destination on an application for an export license, or on a Shipper's Export Declaration where an exemption is claimed under this subchapter, must be the country of ultimate end-use. The written approval of the Office of Defense Trade Controls must be obtained before reselling, transferring, transshipping, or disposing of a defense article to any end user, end use or destination other than as stated on the export license, or on the Shipper's Export Declaration in cases where an exemption is claimed under this subchapter. Exporters must ascertain the specific end-user and end-use prior to submitting an application to the Office of Defense Trade Controls or claiming an exemption under this subchapter.

(b) The exporter shall incorporate the following statement as an integral part of the bill of lading, and the invoice whenever defense articles on the U.S. Munitions List are to be exported:

These commodities are authorized by the U.S. Government for export only to country of ultimate destination for use by end-user. They may not be transferred, transshipped on a non-continuous voyage, or otherwise be disposed of in any other country, either in their original form or after being incorporated into other end-items, without the prior written approval of the U.S. Department of State."

(c) A U.S. person or a foreign person requesting approval for the reexport or retransfer, or change in end-use, of a defense article shall submit a written request which shall be subject to all the documentation required for a permanent export license (see Sec. 123.1) and shall contain the following:
(1) The license number under which the defense article was previously authorized for export from the United States;
(2) A precise description, quantity and value of the defense article;
(3) A description of the new end-use; and
(4) Identification of the new end-user.

(d) The written approval of the Office of Defense Trade Controls must be obtained before reselling, transferring, transshipping on a non-continuous voyage, or disposing of a defense article in any country other than the country of ultimate destination, or anyone other than the authorized end-user, as stated on the Shipper's Export Declaration in cases where an exemption is claimed under this subchapter.

(e)   Reexports or retransfers of U.S.-origin components incorporated into a foreign defense article to a government of a NATO country, or the governments of Australia or Japan, are authorized without the prior written approval of the Office of Defense Trade Controls, provided:

(1)   The U.S.-origin components were previously authorized for export from the United States, either by a license or an exemption;

(2)   The U.S.-origin components are not significant military equipment, the items are not major defense equipment sold under a contract in the amount of $14,000,000 ($14 million) or more; the articles are not defense articles or defense services sold under a contract in the amount of $50,000,000 ($50 million) or more; and are not identified in part 121 of this subchapter as Missile Technology Control Regime (MTCR) items; and

(3)   The person reexporting the defense article must provide written notification to the Office of Defense Trade Controls of the retransfer not later than 30 days following the reexport. The notification must state the articles being reexported and the recipient government.

(4)   In certain cases, the Director, Office of Defense Trade Controls, may place retransfer restrictions on a license prohibiting use of this exemption.

Sec. 123.10—Non transfer and use assurances.

(a)   A nontransfer and use certificate (Form DSP-83) is required for the export of significant military equipment and classified articles including classified technical data. A license will not be issued until a completed Form DSP-83 has been received by the Office of Defense Trade Controls. This form is to be executed by the foreign consignee, foreign end-user, and the applicant. The certificate stipulates that, except as specifically authorized by prior written approval of the Department of State, the foreign consignee and foreign end-user will not reexport, resell or otherwise dispose of the significant military equipment enumerated in the application outside the country named as the location of the foreign end-use or to any other person.

(b)   The Office of Defense Trade Controls may also require a DSP-83 for the export of any other defense articles or defense services.

(c)   When a DSP-83 is required for an export of any defense article or defense service to a non-governmental foreign end-user, the Office of Defense Trade Controls may require as a condition of issuing the license that the appropriate authority of the government of the country of ultimate destination also execute the certificate. . . .

Part 125
Licenses for the Export of Technical Data and Classified Defense Articles

Sec. 125.1—Exports subject to this part.

(a)   The controls of this part apply to the export of technical data and the export of classified defense articles. Information which is in the public domain (see Sec. 120.11 of this subchapter and Sec. 125.4(b)(13)) is not subject to the controls of this subchapter.

(b)   A license for the export of technical data and the exemptions in Sec. 125.4 may not be used for foreign production purposes or for technical assistance unless the approval of the Office of Defense Trade Controls has been obtained. Such approval is generally provided only pursuant to the procedures specified in part 124 of this subchapter.

(c)   Technical data authorized for export may not be reexported, transferred or diverted from the country of ultimate end-use or from the authorized foreign end-user (as designated in the license or approval for export) or disclosed to a national of another country without the prior written approval of the Office of Defense Trade Controls.

(d)   The controls of this part apply to the exports referred to in paragraph (a) of this section regardless of whether the person who intends to export the technical data produces or manufactures defense articles if the technical data is determined by the Office of Defense Trade Controls to be subject to the controls of this subchapter.

(e)   The provisions of this subchapter do not apply to technical data related to articles in Category VI(e) and Category XVI. The export of such data is controlled by the Department of Energy and the Nuclear Regulatory Commission pursuant to the Atomic Energy Act of 1954, as amended, and the Nuclear Non-Proliferation Act of 1978.

Sec. 125.2—Exports of unclassified technical data.

(a)   A license (DSP-5) is required for the export of unclassified technical data unless the export is exempt from the licensing requirements of this subchapter. In the case of a plant visit, details of the proposed discussions must be transmitted to the Office of Defense Trade Controls for an appraisal of the technical data. Seven copies of the technical data or the details of the discussion must be provided.

(b)   Patents. A license issued by the Office of Defense Trade Controls is required for the export of technical data whenever the data exceeds that which is used to support a domestic filing of a patent application or to support a foreign filing of a patent application whenever no domestic application has been filed. Requests for the filing of patent applications in a foreign country, and requests for the filing of amendments, modifications or supplements to such patents, should follow the regulations of the U.S. Patent and Trademark Office in accordance with 37 CFR part 5. The export of technical data to support the filing and processing of patent applications in foreign countries is subject to regulations issued by the U.S. Patent and Trademark Office pursuant to 35 U.S.C. 184.

(c) Disclosures. Unless otherwise expressly exempted in this subchapter, a license is required for the oral, visual or documentary disclosure of technical data by U.S. persons to foreign persons. A license is required regardless of the manner in which the technical data is transmitted (e.g., in person, by telephone, correspondence, electronic means, etc.). A license is required for such disclosures by U.S. persons in connection with visits to foreign diplomatic missions and consular offices. . . .

Sec. 125.4—Exemptions of general applicability.

(a) The following exemptions apply to exports of unclassified technical data for which approval is not needed from the Office of Defense Trade Controls. These exemptions, except for paragraph (b)(13) of this section, do not apply to exports to proscribed destinations under Sec. 126.1 of this subchapter or for persons considered generally ineligible under Sec. 120.1(c) of this subchapter. The exemptions are also not applicable for purposes of establishing offshore procurement arrangements. If Sec. 126.8 of this subchapter requirements are applicable, they must be met before an exemption under this section may be used. Transmission of classified information must comply with the requirements of the Department of Defense Industrial Security Manual and the exporter must certify to the transmittal authority that the technical data does not exceed the technical limitation of the authorized export.

(b) The following exports are exempt from the licensing requirements of this subchapter.
(1) Technical data, including classified information, to be disclosed pursuant to an official written request or directive from the U.S. Department of Defense;
(2) Technical data, including classified information, in furtherance of a manufacturing license or technical assistance agreement approved by the Department of State under part 124 of this subchapter and which meet the requirements of Sec. 124.3 of this subchapter;
(3) Technical data, including classified information, in furtherance of a contract between the exporter and an agency of the U.S. Government, if the contract provides for the export of the data and such data does not disclose the details of design, development, production, or manufacture of any defense article;
(4) Copies of technical data, including classified information, previously authorized for export to the same recipient. Revised copies of such technical data are

also exempt if they pertain to the identical defense article, and if the revisions are solely editorial and do not add to the content of technology previously exported or authorized for export to the same recipient;

(5)   Technical data, including classified information, in the form of basic operations, maintenance, and training information relating to a defense article lawfully exported or authorized for export to the same recipient. Intermediate or depot-level repair and maintenance information may be exported only under a license or agreement approved specifically for that purpose;

(6)   Technical data, including classified information, related to firearms not in excess of caliber .50 and ammunition for such weapons, except detailed design, development, production or manufacturing information;

(7)   Technical data, including classified information, being returned to the original source of import;

(8)   Technical data directly related to classified information which has been previously exported or authorized for export in accordance with this part to the same recipient, and which does not disclose the details of the design, development, production, or manufacture of any defense article;

(9)   Technical data, including classified information, sent by a U.S. corporation to a U.S. person employed by that corporation overseas or to a U.S. Government agency. This exemption is subject to the limitations of Sec. 125.1(b) and may be used only if:

(i)   The technical data is to be used overseas solely by U.S. persons;

(ii)   If the U.S. person overseas is an employee of the U.S. Government or is directly employed by the U.S. corporation and not by a foreign subsidiary; and

(iii)   The classified information is sent overseas in accordance with the requirements of the Department of Defense Industrial Security Manual.

(10)   Disclosures of unclassified technical data in the U.S. by U.S. institutions of higher learning to foreign persons who are their bona fide and full time regular employees. This exemption is available only if:

(i)   The employee's permanent abode throughout the period of employment is in the United States;

(ii)   The employee is not a national of a country to which exports are prohibited pursuant to Sec. 126.1 of this subchapter; and

(iii)   The institution informs the individual in writing that the technical data may not be transferred to other foreign persons without the prior written approval of the Office of Defense Trade Controls;

(11)   Technical data, including classified information, for which the exporter, pursuant to an arrangement with the Department of Defense, Department of Energy or NASA which requires such exports, has been granted an exemption in writing from the licensing provisions of this part by the Office of Defense Trade Controls. Such an exemption will normally be granted only if the arrangement directly implements an international agreement to which the United States is a party and if multiple exports are contemplated. The Office of Defense Trade Controls, in consultation with the relevant U.S. Government agencies, will determine whether the interests of the United States Government are best served by expediting exports under an arrangement through an exemption (see also paragraph (b)(3) of this section for a related exemption);

(12) Technical data which is specifically exempt under part 126 of this sub-chapter; or
(13) Technical data approved for public release (i.e., unlimited distribution) by the cognizant U.S. Government department or agency or Directorate for Freedom of Information and Security Review. This exemption is applicable to information approved by the cognizant U.S. Government department or agency for public release in any form. It does not require that the information be published in order to qualify for the exemption. . . .

Sec. 125.8—Filing of licenses for exports of unclassified technical data.

(a)   Licenses for the export of unclassified technical data must be presented to the appropriate District Director of Customs or Postmaster at the time of shipment or mailing. The District Director of Customs or Postmaster will endorse and transmit the licenses to the Office of Defense Trade Controls in accordance with the instructions contained on the reverse side of the license.

(b)   If a license for the export of unclassified technical data is used but not endorsed by U.S. Customs or a Postmaster for whatever reason (e.g., electronic transmission, unavailability of Customs officer or Postmaster, etc.), the person exporting the data must self-endorse the license, showing when and how the export took place. Every license must be returned to the Office of Defense Trade Controls when the total value authorized has been shipped or when the date of expiration has been reached, whichever occurs first. . . .

Part 126
General Policies and Provisions

Sec. 126.1—Prohibited exports and sales to certain countries.

(a)   It is the policy of the United States to deny licenses, other approvals, exports and imports of defense articles and defense services, destined for or originating in certain countries. This policy applies to: Albania, Armenia, Azerbaijan, Bulgaria, Byelarus, Cambodia, Cuba, Estonia, Georgia, Iran, Iraq, Libya, Kazakhstan, Kyrgyzstan, Latvia, Lithuania, Moldova, Mongolia, North Korea, Romania, Russia, South Africa, Syria, Tajikistan, Turkmenistan, Ukraine, Uzbekistan and Vietnam. This policy also applies to countries with respect to which the United States maintains an arms embargo (e.g., Burma, China, Liberia, Somalia, the Sudan, the former Yugoslavia, and Zaire) or for whenever an export would not otherwise be in furtherance of world peace and the security and foreign policy of the United States. Comprehensive arms embargoes are normally the subject of a State Department notice published in the Federal Register. The exemptions provided in the regulations in this subchapter, except Secs. 123.17 and

125.4(b)(13) of this subchapter, do not apply with respect to articles originating in or for export to any proscribed countries or areas.

(b) Shipments. A defense article licensed for export under this subchapter may not be shipped on a vessel, aircraft or other means of conveyance which is owned or operated by, or leased to or from, any of the proscribed countries or areas.

(c) South Africa. South Africa is subject to an arms embargo and thus to the policy specified in paragraph (a) of this section. Exceptions may be made to this policy only if the Assistant Secretary for Politico-Military Affairs determines that:
(1) The item is not covered by United Nations Security Council Resolution 418 of November 4, 1977; and
(2) The item is to be exported solely for commercial purposes and not for use by the armed forces, police, or other security forces of South Africa or for any other similar purpose.

(d) Terrorism. Exports to countries which the Secretary of State has determined to have repeatedly provided support for acts of international terrorism are contrary to the foreign policy of the United States and are thus subject to the policy specified in paragraph (a) of this section and the requirements of section 40 of the Arms Export Control Act (22 U.S.C. 2780) and the Omnibus Diplomatic Security and Anti-Terrorism Act of 1986 (22 U.S.C. 4801, note). The countries in this category are: Cuba, Iran, Iraq, Libya, North Korea and Syria. The same countries are identified pursuant to section 6(j) of the Export Administration Act, as amended (50U.S.C. App. 2405(j)).

(e) Proposed sales. No sale or transfer and no proposal to sell or transfer any defense articles, defense services or technical data subject to this subchapter may be made to any country referred to in this section (including the embassies or consulates of such a country), or to any person acting on its behalf, whether in the United States or abroad, without first obtaining a license or written approval of the Office of Defense Trade Controls. However, in accordance with paragraph (a) of this section, it is the policy of the Department of State to deny licenses and approvals in such cases. Any person who knows or has reason to know of such a proposed or actual sale, or transfer, of such articles, services or data must immediately inform the Office of Defense Trade Controls. . . .

Sec. 126.5—Canadian exemptions.

(a) District Directors of Customs and postmasters shall permit the export or temporary import without a license of any unclassified defense article or any unclassified technical data to Canada for end-use in Canada by Canadian citizens or return to the United States, or from Canada for end-use in the United States or return to a Canadian citizen in Canada, with the exception of the articles or related technical data listed in paragraph (b) of this section.

(b) Exceptions. The exemptions of this section do not apply to the following articles and related technical data. . . .
(7) Technical data for use by a foreign national other than a Canadian.
(8) Unclassified technical data directly related to a classified defense article. . . .

Sec. 126.7—Denial, revocation, suspension, or amendment of licenses and other approvals.

(a) Policy. Licenses or approvals shall be denied or revoked whenever required by any statute of the United States (see Secs. 127.6 and 127.10 of this subchapter). Any application for an export license or other approval under this subchapter may be disapproved, and any license or other approval or exemption granted under this subchapter may be revoked, suspended, or amended without prior notice whenever:
(1) The Department of State deems such action to be in furtherance of world peace, the national security or the foreign policy of the United States, or is otherwise advisable; or
(2) The Department of State believes that 22 U.S.C. 2778, any regulation contained in this subchapter, or the terms of any U.S. Government export authorization (including the terms of a manufacturing license or technical assistance agreement, or export authorization granted pursuant to the Export Administration Act, as amended) has been violated by any party to the export or other person having significant interest in the transaction; or . . . .

(b) Notification. The Office of Defense Trade Controls will notify applicants or licensees or other appropriate United States persons of actions taken pursuant to paragraph (a) of this section. The reasons for the action will be stated as specifically as security and foreign policy considerations permit. . . .

Sec. 126.9—Advisory opinions.

Any person desiring information as to whether the Office of Defense Trade Controls would be likely to grant a license or other approval for the export of a particular defense article or defense service to a particular country may request an advisory opinion from the Office of Defense Trade Controls. These opinions are not binding on the Department of State and are revocable. A request for an advisory opinion must be made in writing and must outline in detail the equipment, its usage, the security classification (if any) of the articles or related technical data, and the country or countries involved. An original and seven copies of the letter must be provided along with seven copies of suitable descriptive information concerning the defense article or defense service. . . .

N.4.2 Export Administration Regulations

Part 779
Technical Data

Sec. 779.1 Definitions.[6]

(a) Technology, technical data, technical assistance, and software.[7] These terms are defined in Supplement No. 3 to Sec. 799.1 of this subchapter. The terminology used in this part 779 will be changed in the future to conform to the terms and definitions used in Supplement No. 3 to part Sec. 799.1 of this subchapter and in other parts of this subchapter. In the interim, the term "technical data" as used in this part 779, is understood to include both "technology" (i.e., technical data and technical assistance) and "software". If the term "software" is cited separately, the term refers only to software as defined in Supplement No. 3 to Sec. 799.1 of this subchapter.

(b) Export of technical data[8,9]

(1) Export of technical data. "Export of technical data" means

(i) An actual shipment or transmission of technical data out of the United States;[10]

(ii) Any release of technical data in the United States with the knowledge or intent that the data will be shipped or transmitted from the United States to a foreign country; or

(iii) Any release of technical data of U.S.-origin in a foreign country.

(2) Release of technical data. Technical data may be released for export through:

(i) Visual inspection by foreign nationals of U.S.-origin equipment and facilities;

---

[6]See Sec. 770.2 for definitions of other terms used in this part.

[7]The provisions of part 779 do not apply to "classified" technical data, i.e., technical data that have been officially assigned a security classification (e.g., "top secret", "secret", or "confidential") by an officer or agency of the U.S. Government. The export of classified technical data is controlled by the Center for Defense Trade of the U.S. Department of State or the U.S. Nuclear Regulatory Commission, Washington, DC.

[8]License applications for, or questions about, the export of technical data relating to commodities which are licensed by U.S. Government agencies other than the U.S. Department of Commerce shall be referred to such other appropriate U.S. Government agency for consideration (see Sec. 770.10 of this subchapter).

[9]Patent attorneys and others are advised to consult the U.S. Patent Office, U.S. Department of Commerce, Washington, DC 20231, regarding the U.S. Patent Office regulations concerning the filing of patent applications or amendments in foreign countries. In addition to the regulations issued by the U.S. Patent Office, technical data contained in or related to inventions made in foreign countries or in the United States, are also subject to the U.S. Department of Commerce regulations covering the export of technical data, in the same manner as the export of other types of technical data.

[10]As used in this Part 779, the United States includes its possessions and territories.

(ii)   Oral exchanges of information in the United States or abroad; and
(iii)   The application to situations abroad of personal knowledge or technical experience acquired in the United States.

(c)   Reexport of technical data. "Reexport of technical data" means an actual shipment or transmission from one foreign country to another, or any release of technical data of U.S. origin in a foreign country with the knowledge or intent that the data will be shipped or transmitted to another foreign country. Technical data may be released for reexport through:
(1)   Visual inspection of U.S.-origin equipment and facilities abroad;
(2)   Oral exchanges of information abroad; and
(3)   The application to situations abroad of personal knowledge or technical experience acquired in the United States.

(d)   Direct product. The term "direct product" means the immediate product (including processes and services) produced directly by the use of technical data.

Sec. 779.2   Licenses to export.

Except as provided in Sec. 770.3(a) of this subchapter, an export of technical data must be made under either a U.S. Department of Commerce general license or a validated export license. (See Secs. 771.1 and 772.2 of this subchapter for definitions of "general" and "validated" licenses.) General Licenses GTDA and GTDR (see Secs. 779.3 and 779.4) apply to specific types of exports of technical data. A validated license is required for any export of technical data where these general licenses do not apply, except in the case of certain exports to Canada.[11,12]

Sec. 779.3   General License GTDA: Technical data available to all destinations.

Note: In this Sec. 779.3 the word information means "technical data" as used in this part (i.e., "technology" and "software" as defined in Supplement No. 3 to Sec. 799.1 of this subchapter).

---

[11]An export of technical data to Canada may be made without either a validated or general license, unless a validated license is required to Canada by a specific subcategory D or E ECCN on the CCL.

[12]Although the Bureau of Export Administration may provide general information on licensing policies regarding the prospects of approval of various types of export control actions, including actions with respect to technical data, normally it will give a formal judgement respecting a specific request for an action only upon the actual submission of a formal application or request setting forth all of the facts relevant to the export transaction and supported by all required documentation. Advice is always available, however, regarding any questions as to the applicability of a general license. Such questions should be submitted by letter to the U.S. Department of Commerce, Bureau of Export Administration, P.O. Box 273, Washington, DC 20044.

(a) Establishment of general license. A General License GTDA is hereby established authorizing:

(1) Unrestricted export to any destination of information that is already publicly available or will be made publicly available as described in paragraph (b) of this section;

(2) Unrestricted export to any destination of information arising during or resulting from fundamental research, as described in paragraph (c) of this section;

Note: Paragraphs (a)(1) and (a)(2) of this section do not authorize the export of data contained in a patent application for purposes of filing and/or publishing for opposition abroad. Such exports are controlled by the U.S. Patent and Trademark Office and must be licensed by that office. See EAR Sec. 770.10(j).

(3) Release of educational information, as described in paragraph (d) of this section; and

(4) Export of information in connection with certain patent applications, as described in paragraph (e) of this section.

Note 1: See paragraph (f) regarding Government sponsored research covered by contractual national security controls and the note following this section regarding consulting and training. Use of General License GTDA is subject to the prohibitions of Sec. 771.2(c) (1), (4), and (9), but not to the other prohibitions of Sec. 771.2(c).

Note 2: Supplement No. 5 to part 779 contains explanatory questions and answers about the use of General License GTDA. Certain paragraphs of this Sec. 779.3 are followed by references to relevant questions and answers in supplement No. 5.

(b) Publicly available. Information is made public and so becomes "publicly available" when it becomes generally accessible to the interested public in any form, including:

(1) Publication in periodicals, books, print, electronic, or any other media available for general distribution to any member of the public or to a community of persons, such as those in a scientific or engineering discipline, interested in the subject matter either free or at a price that does not exceed the cost of reproduction and distribution (see Questions A(1) through A(6));

(2) Ready availability at libraries open to the public or at university libraries (see Question A(6));

(3) Patents available at any patent office; and

(4) Release at an open conference, meeting, seminar, trade show, or other open gathering.

(i) A conference or other gathering is "open" if all technically qualified members of the public are eligible to attend and attendees are permitted to take notes or otherwise make a personal record (not necessarily a recording) of the proceedings and presentations.

(ii) All technically qualified members of the public may be considered eligible to attend a conference or other gathering notwithstanding:

(A)   A registration fee reasonably related to costs and reflecting an intention that all interested and technically qualified persons be able to attend, or
(B)   A limitation on actual attendance, as long as attendees either are the first who have applied or are selected on the basis of relevant scientific or technical competence, experience, or responsibility (see Questions B(1) through B(6)).

This General License GTDA authorizes submission of papers to domestic or foreign editors or reviewers of journals, or to organizers of open conferences or other open gatherings, with the understanding that the papers will be made publicly available if favorably received. (See Questions A(1) and A(3).)

(c)   Information resulting from fundamental research—
(1)   Fundamental research. Paragraphs (c)(2) through (c)(4) and paragraph (f) of this section provide specific operational rules that will be used to determine whether research in particular institutional contexts qualifies as "fundamental research." The intent behind those operational rules is to identify as "fundamental research" basic and applied research in science and engineering, where the resulting information is ordinarily published and shared broadly within the scientific community. Such research can be distinguished from proprietary research and from industrial development, design, production, and product utilization, the results of which ordinarily are restricted for proprietary reasons or specific national security reasons as defined in Sec. 779.3(f). (See Question D(8).)
(2)   University-based research.
(i)   Research conducted by scientists, engineers, or students at a university normally will be considered fundamental research, as described below. ("University" means any accredited institution of higher education located in the United States.)
(ii)   Prepublication review by a sponsor of university research solely to ensure that publication would not inadvertently divulge proprietary information that the sponsor has furnished to the researchers does not change the rule described in paragraph (c)(2)(i) of this section. However, General License GTDA does not authorize the release of information from a corporate sponsor to university researchers where the research results are subject to prepublication review. See other sections in this part 779 for provisions that may authorize such releases without a validated license. (See Questions D(7), D(9), and D(10).)
(iii)   Prepublication review by a sponsor of university research solely to ensure that publication would not compromise patent rights does not change the rule described in paragraph (c)(2)(i) of this section, so long as the review causes no more than a temporary delay in publication of the research results.
(iv)   However, General License GTDA does not authorize the initial transfer of information from an industry sponsor to university researchers where the parties have agreed that the sponsor may withhold from publication some or all of the information so provided. (See Question D(2).)
(v)   University based research is not considered "fundamental research" if the university or its researchers accept (at the request, for example, of an industrial sponsor) other restrictions on publication of scientific and technical information resulting from the project or activity. Scientific and technical information resulting from the research will nonetheless become subject to General License GTDA

once all such restrictions have expired or have been removed. (See Questions D(7) and D(9).)

(vi)   The provisions of paragraph (f) of this section will apply if a university or its researchers accept specific national security controls (as defined in paragraph (f) of this section) on a research project or activity sponsored by the U.S. Government. (See Questions E(1) and E(2).)

(3)   Research based at Federal agencies or FFRDCs. Research conducted by scientists or engineers working for a Federal agency or a Federally Funded Research and Development Center (FFRDC) may be designated as "fundamental research" within any appropriate system controlling release of information by such scientists and engineers devised by the agency or the FFRDC. (See Questions D(8) and D(11).)

(4)   Corporate research.

(i)   Research conducted by scientists or engineers working for a business entity will be considered "fundamental research" at such time and to the extent that the researchers are free to make scientific and technical information resulting from the research publicly available without restriction or delay based on proprietary concerns or specific national security controls as defined in paragraph (f) of this section.

(ii)   Prepublication review by the company solely to ensure that the publication would compromise no proprietary information provided by the company to the researchers is not considered to be a proprietary restriction under paragraph (c)(4)(i) of this section. However General License GTDA does not authorize the release of information to university researchers where the research results are subject to prepublication review. See other sections in this part 779 for provisions that may authorize such releases without a validated license. (See Questions D(8), D(9), and D(10).)

(iii)   Prepublication review by the company solely to ensure that prepublication would compromise no patent rights will not be considered a proprietary restriction for this purpose, so long as the review causes no more than a temporary delay in publication of the research results.

(iv)   However, General License GTDA does not authorize the initial transfer of information from a business entity to researchers where the parties have agreed that the business entity may withhold from publication some or all of the information so provided.

(5)   Research based elsewhere. Research conducted by scientists or engineers who are not working for any of the institutions described in paragraphs (c)(2) through (c)(4) of this section will be treated as corporate research, as described in paragraph (c)(4) of this section. (See Question D(8)).

(d)   Educational information. The release of "educational information" referred to in paragraph (a)(3) of this section is release by instruction in catalog courses and associated teaching laboratories of academic institutions. Dissertation research is treated in paragraph (c)(2) of this section. (See Question C(1) through C(6).)

(e)   Patent applications. The information referred to in paragraph (a)(4) of this section is:

(1)   Information contained in a patent application prepared wholly from foreign-origin technical data where the application is being sent to the foreign inventor to be executed and returned to the United States for subsequent filing in the U.S. Patent and Trademark Office;

(2)   Information contained in a patent application, or an amendment, modification, supplement, or division of an application, and authorized for filing in a foreign country in accordance with the regulations of the Patent and Trademark Office, 37 CFR part 5 (see Sec. 770.10(j)); or

(3)   Information contained in a patent application when sent to a foreign country before or within six months after the filing of a United States patent application for the purpose of obtaining the signature of an inventor who was in the United States when the invention was made or who is a co-inventor with a person residing in the United States.

(f)   Government-sponsored research covered by contract controls.

(1)   If research is funded by the U.S. Government, and specific national security controls are agreed on to protect information resulting from the research, paragraph (a)(2) of this section will not apply to any export of such information in violation of such controls. General License GTDA as described in paragraph (a)(2) of this section is nonetheless available for any export of information resulting from the research that is consistent with the specific controls.

(2)   Examples of "specific national security controls" include requirements for prepublication review by the Government, with right to withhold permission for publication; restrictions on prepublication dissemination of information to non-U.S. citizens or other categories of persons; or restrictions on participation of non-U.S. citizens or other categories of persons in the research. A general reference to one or more export control laws or regulations or a general reminder that the Government retains the right to classify is not a "specific national security control". (See Questions E(1) and E(2).)

(g)   Advice concerning uncontrolled information. Persons may be concerned that an export of uncontrolled information could adversely affect U.S. national security interests. Exporters who wish advice before exporting such information can contact the appropriate Government scientific or technical personnel by calling the Bureau of Export Administration at (202) 377-4811.

Note: Consulting and training. Technical data can be inadvertently exported in various ways. Consulting and training are especially effective mechanisms of technology transfer. The exporter should be aware that the Department of Commerce maintains controls on exports of technical data that do not qualify for General License GTDA as described in paragraphs (a)(1) through (a)(3) of this section, including application abroad of personal knowledge or technical experience acquired in the United States. (See also paragraph (g) of this section and Question F(1).)

Sec. 779.4   General license GTDR: Technical data under restriction.

A general license designated GTDR is hereby established authorizing the export of technical data that are not exportable under the provisions of General License GTDA, subject to the provisions, restrictions, exclusions, and exceptions set forth below and subject to the written assurance requirement set forth in paragraph (f) of this section.

(a)   Country restrictions. General License GTDR with written assurance may not be used for exports to Country Groups QWYS and Z, the People's Republic of China, Iran, or Syria. General License GTDR without written assurance (GTDU) may not be used for exports to Country Groups S and Z, Iran or Syria of software available at retail outlets as described in the General Software Note.[13] General License GTDR without written assurance (GTDU) as described in any entry on the Commerce Control List (Supplement No. 1 to Sec. 799.1 of this subchapter) may not be used for exports to Country Groups S and Z. This General License is subject to the prohibitions described in Sec. 771.2(c) of this subchapter, including the prohibition on any export to the South African military or police.

(b)   General License GTDR without written assurance authorizes the following exports—
(1)   Operation technical data.
(i)   For definitions and conditions for use of General License GTDR without written assurance for operation technical data, refer to the third paragraph of the General Technology Note as listed in Supplement No. 2 to Sec. 799.1 of this subchapter. As defined in that Note, "operation technical data" is the minimum

---

[13]The General Software Note (GSN) is contained in Supplement No. 2 to Sec. 799.1 of Subchapter C, Chapter VII, Title 15, Code of Federal Regulations. The text of the GSN is as follows:

General License GTDR, without written assurance, is available for release of software that is generally available to the public by being:
a. Sold from stock at retail selling points without restriction by means of:
   1. Over the counter transactions;
   2. Mail order transactions, or
   3. Telephone call transactions; and
b. Designed for installation by the user without further substantial support by the supplier.

General license GTDA is available for software that is publicly available.

The General Software Note does not apply to exports of "software" controlled by other agencies of the U.S. Government.
The phrase "without restriction" clarifies that software is not "generally available to the public" if it is to be sold only with bundled hardware generally available to the public. Software that is both bundled with hardware and "generally available to the public" does qualify for General License GTDR without a written assurance.

necessary for the installation, operations,[14] maintenance (checking), and repair of those products that are eligible for general licenses, or that are exported under a validated export license. The "minimum necessary" excludes from operation technical data development or production technical data and includes use technology only to the extent required to ensure safe and efficient use of the product. Individual entries in the software and technology subcategories of the CCL may further restrict export of "minimum necessary" technical data. (See Supplement Nos. 2 and 3 to Sec. 799.1 of this subchapter for further information and definitions of the terms "development", "production", "use", and "required".)

(ii)   Operation software may be exported under GTDR, without assurance, provided that:

(A)   The operation software is the minimum necessary to operate the equipment authorized for export; and

(B)   The operation software is in object code.

(2)   Sales technical data.

(i)   "Sales technical data" is defined as data supporting a prospective or actual quotation, bid, or offer to sell, lease, or otherwise supply any item controlled by the EAR.

(ii)   Sales technical data may be exported under GTDR, without written assurances, provided that:

(A)   The technical data is a type customarily transmitted with a prospective or actual quotation, bid, or offer in accordance with established business practice; and

(B)   The export will not disclose the detailed design, production, or manufacture, or the means of reconstruction, of either the quoted item or its product. The purpose of this limitation is to prevent disclosure of technical data so detailed that the consignee could use the technical data in production.

Note: Neither this authorization nor its use means that the U.S. Government intends, or is committed, to approve an export license application for any commodity, plant, or technical data that may be the subject of the transaction to which such quotation, bid, or offer relates. Exporters are advised to include in any quotations, bids, or offers, and in any contracts entered into pursuant to such quotations, bids, or offers, a provision relieving themselves of liability in the event that an export license (when required) is not approved by the Bureau of Export Administration.

(3)   Software updates. Software updates that are intended for and are limited to correction of errors ("fixes" to "bugs" that have been identified) qualify for export under General License GTDR, without written assurance, provided the updates are being exported to the same consignee and do not enhance the functional capacities of the initial software package.

(4)   Technical data described in the Commerce Control List. Certain other tech-

---

[14]Exporters of digital computer equipment must describe on their license applications any software, including that shipped under General License GTDR, to be used with the equipment.

nical data may be exported under GTDR without written assurance. Such technical data is identified in the "Requirements" section of the ECCN under the heading "GTDU". The designations "GTDU: Yes" or "GTDU: Yes except . . . ." indicate that General License GTDR without written assurance is available subject to any applicable exceptions. The designation "GTDU: No" indicates that General License GTDR without written assurance is not available. However, the designation "GTDU: No" does not restrict exports under paragraphs (b)(1), (b)(2), or (b)(3) of this section. Exporters have the option of using the term "GTDU" to describe General License GTDR without written assurance for all purposes, including information requirements on the Shipper's Export Declaration.

(c)–(d)   [Reserved]

(e)   Restrictions applicable to the Republic of South Africa—
(1)   General prohibition. Except as provided in Sec. 779.4 (b)(1), (b)(2), and (b)(3), no technical data may be exported or reexported to the Republic of South Africa under this General License GTDR where the exporter or reexporter knows or has reason to know that the data or the direct product of the data are for delivery, directly or indirectly, to or for use by or for military or police entities in South Africa or for use in servicing equipment owned, controlled, or used by or for such entities. In addition, no technical data relating to the commodities listed in Supplement No. 2 to this Part 779 may be exported or reexported under General License GTDR to any consignee in the Republic of South Africa.
(2)   Written assurances. In addition to any written assurances that may or may not be required by paragraph (f) of this section, no export or reexport of technical data may be made to the Republic of South Africa under General License GTDR until the exporter has received written assurance from the importer that neither the technical data nor the direct product of the data will be made available to or for use by or for military or police entities of the Republic of South Africa.

(f)   General License GTDR with written assurances. Except as provided in Sec. 779.4(b) and (f)(5), no export of technical data described in this Sec. 779.4(f) may be made under General License GTDR:
(1)   Until the U.S. exporter has received a written assurance from the foreign importer that, unless prior authorization is obtained from the Office of Export Licensing, the importer will not knowingly:
(i)   Reexport, directly or indirectly, to Country Group Q, S, W,[15] Y, or Z, or the

---

[15]Effective April 26, 1971, Country Group W no longer included Romania. Assurances executed prior to April 26, 1971, that refer to Country Group W continue to apply to Romania as well as Poland. Effective April 25, 1991, Czechoslovakia was added to Country Group W. Assurances executed on or after April 25, 1991, that refer to Country Group W apply to Czechoslovakia as well as Poland. On May 8, 1992, Hungary was removed from Country Group W. Assurances are no longer applicable to Hungary. On January 1, 1993, Czechoslovakia became two separate countries called the Czech Republic and the Slovak Republic. Assurances executed prior to January 1, 1993, that refer to Czechoslovakia continue to apply to the Czech Republic and the Slovak Republic.

People's Republic of China any technical data relating to commodities controlled to Country Group W as described in the paragraph titled "Validated License Required" of any entry of the Commerce Control List;

(ii)   Export, directly or indirectly, to Country Group Z any direct product of the technical data if such direct product is controlled to Country Group "W" in the paragraph of any entry on the Commerce Control List titled "Validated License Required"; or

(iii)   Export, directly or indirectly, to any destination in Country Group Q, S, W, Y, or the People's Republic of China, any direct product of the technical data if such direct product is identified by the code letter "A" following the Export Control Classification Number on the Commerce Control List.

(2)   If the direct product of any technical data is a complete plant or any major component of a plant that is capable of producing a commodity controlled to Country Group "W" in the paragraph of any entry on the Commerce Control List titled "Validated License Required" or appears on the U.S. Munitions List, a written assurance by the person who is or will be in control of the distribution of the products of the plant (whether or not such person is the importer) shall be obtained by the U.S. exporter (via the foreign importer), stating that, unless prior authorization is obtained from the Office of Export Licensing, such person will not knowingly:

(i)   Reexport, directly or indirectly, to Country Group Q, S, W, Y, or Z, or the People's Republic of China, the technical data relating to the plant or the major component of a plant;

(ii)   Export, directly or indirectly, to Country Group Z, the plant or the major component of a plant (depending upon which is the direct product of the technical data) or any product of such plant or of such major component, if such product is identified by the symbol "W" in the paragraph of any entry on the Commerce Control List titled "Validated License Required" or appears on the U.S. Munitions List; or

(iii)   Export, directly or indirectly, to any destination in Country Group Q, S, W, Y, or the People's Republic of China, the plant or the major component of a plant (depending upon which is the direct product of the technical data) or any product of such plant or of such major component, if such product is identified by the code letter "A" following the Export Control Classification Number on the Commerce Control List or appears on the U.S. Munitions List.

Note: Effective April 1, 1964, Sec. 779.4(f)(2)(ii) and (f)(2)(iii) required certain written assurances relating to the disposition of the products of a complete plant or major component of a plant that is the direct product of unpublished technical data of U.S. origin exported under General License GTDR. Except as to commodities identified by the code letter "A" following the Export Control Classification Number on the Commerce Control List, and items on the U.S. Munitions List, the effective date of the written assurance requirements for plant products as a condition of using General License GTDR for export of this type of technical data is hereby deferred until further notice, subject to the following limitations:

1.   The exporter shall, at least two weeks before the initial export of the technical data, notify the Office of Export Licensing, by letter, of the facts required

to be disclosed in an application for a validated export license covering such technical data; and

2. The exporter shall obtain from the person who is or will be in control of the distribution of the products of the plant (whether or not such person is the importer) a written commitment that he will notify the U.S. Government, directly or through the exporter, whenever he enters into negotiations to export any product of the plant to any destination covered by Sec. 779.4(f)(2)(ii), when such product is not identified by the code letter "A" following the Export Control Classification Number on the Commerce Control List and requires a validated license for export to Country Group W by the information set forth in the applicable CCL entry in the paragraph titled "Validated License Required". The notification should state the product, quantity, country of destination, and the estimated date of the shipment.

Moreover, during the period of deferment, the remaining written assurance requirements of Sec. 779.4 (f)(2)(ii) and (f)(2)(iii) as to plant products that are identified by the code letter "A" following the Export Control Classification Number on the Commerce Control List, or are on the U.S. Munitions List, will be waived if the plant is located in one of the following COCOM countries: Australia, Belgium, Canada, Denmark, the Federal Republic of Germany, France, Greece, Italy, Japan, Luxembourg, the Netherlands, Norway, Portugal, Spain, Turkey, and the United Kingdom. This deferment applies to exports of technical data pursuant to any type of contract or arrangement, including licensing agreements, regardless of whether entered into before or after April 1, 1964.

(3)   The required assurance may be made in the form of a letter or other written communication from the importer or, if applicable, the person in control of the distribution of the products of a plant; or the assurance may be incorporated into a licensing agreement that restricts disclosure of the technical data to be used only in authorized destinations, and prohibits shipment of the direct product thereof by the licensee to any unauthorized destination. An assurance included in a licensing agreement will be acceptable for all exports made during the life of the agreement, provided that the obligations of the importer set forth in the assurances survive any termination of the licensing agreement. If such assurance is not received, this general license is not applicable and a validated export license is required. An application for validated license shall include an explanatory statement setting forth the reasons why such assurance cannot be obtained.

(4)   In addition, this general license is not applicable to any export of technical data of the kind described in this Sec. 779.4(f), if at the time of export of the technical data from the United States, the exporter knows or has reason to believe that the direct product to be manufactured abroad by use of the technical data is intended to be exported directly or indirectly to any unauthorized destination.

(5)   The limitations in this Sec. 779.4(f) do not apply to the export of technical data included in an application for the foreign filing of a patent, provided such filing is in accordance with the regulations of the U.S. Patent Office.

(g)   Additional restrictions applicable to chemical or biological weapons. In addition to any other restrictions in Sec. 779.4, the use of General License GTDR is further restricted by Sec. 778.8(a)(5) of this subchapter.

Sec. 779.5   Validated license applications.

(a)   General. No technical data, other than that exportable without license to Canada or under general license to other destinations, may be exported from the United States without a validated export license. Such validated export licenses are issued by the Office of Export Licensing upon receipt of an appropriate export application or reexport request. An application for a technical data license shall consist of:

(1)   Form BXA-622P, Application for Export License, accompanied by;

(2)   A letter of explanation described in Sec. 779.5(d) for technology or description of the capabilities of the software; and

(3)   For shipments to the Czech Republic, Hungary, Poland, and the Slovak Republic, an Import Certificate issued by the appropriate national government. (See Sec. 775.8 and supplement No. 1 to part 775 of this subchapter.)

(b)   Application Form. Form ITA-622P shall be completed as provided in Sec. 772.4, except that Items 9(a) and 11 shall be left blank. In Item 9(b), "Description of Commodity or Technical Data," enter a general statement which specifies the technical data (e.g., blueprints, manuals, etc.). In Purpose."

(c)   [Reserved]

(d)   Letter of explanation. Each application shall be supported by a comprehensive letter of explanation in duplicate. This letter shall set forth all the facts required to present to the Office of Export Licensing a complete disclosure of the transaction including, if applicable, the following:

(1)   The identification of all parties to the transaction;

(2)   The exact project location where the technical data will be used;

(3)   The type of technical data to be exported;

(4)   The form in which the export will be made;

(5)   The uses for which the data will be employed;

(6)   An explanation of the process, product, size, and output capacity of the plant or equipment, if applicable, or other description that delineates, defines, and limits the data to be transmitted (the "technical scope");

(7)   The availability abroad of comparable foreign technical data.

(e)   Special provisions—

(1)   Maritime nuclear propulsion plants and related commodities.[16] These special provisions are applicable to technical data relating to maritime (civil) nuclear propulsion plants, their land prototypes, and special facilities for their construc-

---

[16]See Sec. 779.8(a) which sets forth provisions prohibiting exports and reexports of certain technical data and products manufactured therefrom.

tion, support, or maintenance, including any machinery, device, component, or equipment specifically developed or designed for use in such plants or facilities. Every application for license to export technical data relating to any of these commodities shall include the following:

(i)   A description of the foreign project for which the technical data will be furnished;

(ii)   A description of the scope of the proposed services to be offered by the applicant, his consultant(s), and his subcontractor(s), including all the design data which will be disclosed;

(iii)   The names, addresses and titles of all personnel of the applicant, his consultant(s) and his subcontractor(s) who will discuss or disclose the technical data or be involved in the design or development of the technical data;

(iv)   The beginning and termination dates of the period of time during which the technical data will be discussed or disclosed and a proposed time schedule of the reports which the applicant will submit to the U.S. Department of Commerce, detailing the technical data discussed or disclosed during the period of the license;

(v)   The following certification:

I (We) certify that if this application is approved, I (we) and any consultants, subcontractors, or other persons employed or retained by us in connection with the project thereby licensed will not discuss with or disclose to others, directly or indirectly, any technical data relating to U.S. naval nuclear propulsion plants. I (We) further certify that I (we) will furnish to the U.S. Department of Commerce all reports and information which it may require concerning specific transmittals or disclosures of technical data pursuant to any license granted as a result of this application;

(vi)   A statement of the steps which the applicant will take to assure that personnel of the applicant, his consultant(s) and his subcontractor(s) will not discuss or disclose to others technical data relating to U.S. naval nuclear propulsion plants; and

(vii)   A written statement of assurance from the foreign importer that unless prior authorization is obtained from the Office of Export Licensing, the importer will not knowingly export directly or indirectly to Country Group Q, S, W, Y, or Z, or the People's Republic of China, the direct product of the technical data. However, if the U.S. exporter is not able to obtain this statement from the foreign importer, the U.S. exporter shall attach an explanatory statement to his license application setting forth the reasons why such an assurance cannot be obtained.

(2)   Other license applications. For all other license applications to export technical data identified in an entry with an ECCN ending in the code letter "A" to any destination, other than Country Group Q, S, W, Y, or Z, or the People's Republic of China, an applicant shall attach to the license application a written statement from his foreign importer assuring that, unless prior authorization is obtained from the Office of Export Licensing, the importer will not knowingly reexport the technical data to any destination, or export any national security controlled direct product of the technical data, directly or indirectly, to Country Group Q, S, W, Y, or Z, or the People's Republic of China. However, if the U.S. exporter is not able to obtain the required statement from his importer, the ex-

porter shall attach an explanatory statement to his license setting forth the reasons why such an assurance cannot be obtained.

(f)   Validity period and extension—
(1)   Initial validity. Validated licenses covering exports of technical data will generally be issued for a validity period of 24 months. Upon request, a validity period exceeding 24 months may be granted where the facts of the transaction warrant it and the Office of Export Licensing determines that such action would be consistent with the objectives of the applicable U.S. export control program. Justification for a validity period exceeding 24 months should be provided in accordance with the procedures set forth in Sec. 772.9(d)(2) for requesting an extended validity period with a license application. The Office of Export Licensing will make the final decision on what validity beyond 24 months, if any, should be authorized in each case.
(2)   Extensions. A request to extend the validity period of a technical data license shall be made on Form ITA-685P in accordance with the procedures set forth in Sec. 772.12(a). The request shall include on Form ITA-685P, in the space entitled "Amend License to Read as Follows," whether the license has been previously extended and the date(s) and duration of such extension(s). The Office of Export Licensing will make the final decision on what extension beyond 24 months, if any, should be authorized in each case. (See Sec. 779.8(c)(1) for validity period extensions for reexports of technical data.)

Sec. 779.6   Exports under a validated license.

(a)   Use of validated licenses—
(1)   Retention of license. The validated technical data license need not be presented to the customs office or post office but shall be retained and made available for inspection in accordance with the provisions of Sec. 787.13 of this subchapter.
(2)   Return of revoked or suspended technical data licenses. If the Office of Export Licensing revokes or suspends a technical data license, the licensee shall return the license immediately to the Office of Export Licensing in accordance with the instructions in Sec. 786.2(d) of this subchapter.

(b)   Records. Any person to whom a validated technical data license has been issued shall retain the license and maintain complete records in accordance with Sec. 786.2(d) of this subchapter, including any export licenses (whether used or unused, valid or expired) and all supporting documents and shipping records.

Sec. 779.7   Amendments.

Requests for amendments shall be made in accordance with the provisions of Sec. 772.11. Changes requiring amendment include any expansion or upgrade of the technical scope that was described in the letter of explanation, as approved or modified on the export license.

Sec. 779.8   Reexports of technical data and exports of the product manufactured abroad by use of United States technical data.

(a)   Prohibited exports and reexports. Unless specifically authorized by the Office of Export Licensing, or otherwise authorized under the provisions of paragraph (b) of this section, no person in the United States or in a foreign country may:

(1)   Reexport any technical data imported from the United States, directly or indirectly, in whole or in part, from the authorized country(ies) of ultimate destination;

(2)   Export any technical data from the United States with the knowledge that it is to be reexported, directly or indirectly, in whole or in part, from the authorized country(ies) of ultimate destination; or

(3)   Export or reexport to Country Group Q, S, W, Y or Z, the People's Republic of China or Afghanistan any foreign produced direct product of U.S. technical data, or any commodity produced by any plant or major component thereof that is a direct product of U.S. technical data, if such direct product or commodity is covered by the provisions of Sec. 779.4(f) or Sec. 779.5(e)(1); or

(b)   Permissive reexports—

(1)   Exportable under General License GTDA or GTDR. Any technical data which have been exported from the United States may be reexported from any destination to any other destination provided that, at the time of reexport, the technical data may be exported directly from the United States to the new country of destination under General License GTDA or GTDR and provided that all of the requirements and conditions for use of these general licenses have been met.

(2)   COCOM authorization. Separate specific authorization by the Office of Export Licensing to reexport any U.S. origin technical data is not required if all of the following conditions are met:

(i)   The data being exported are identified by the suffix "A" on the CCL;

(ii)   The export or reexport is from a COCOM participating country, i.e., Australia, Belgium, Canada, Denmark, France, the Federal Republic of Germany, Greece, Italy, Japan, Luxembourg, the Netherlands, Norway, Portugal, Spain, Turkey, or the United Kingdom;

(iii)   The export or reexport is made in accordance with the conditions of the licensing authorization issued by the applicable COCOM participating country; and

(iv)   The export or reexport is to a country in Country Group Q, W, or Y or the People's Republic of China.

(3)   Direct product. Separate specific authorization by the Office of Export Licensing to export or reexport the direct product of U.S. origin technical data is not required if the direct product, were it of U.S. origin, could be shipped under any of the permissive reexport provisions of Sec. 774.2 of this subchapter.

(4)   People's Republic of China. Separate specific authorization by the Office of Export Licensing is not required to reexport software from a COCOM participating country, Austria, Finland, Hong Kong, Ireland, New Zealand, Sweden, or Switzerland to the People's Republic of China that meets the requirements set forth in Advisory Notes for the People's Republic of China or for Country Groups

Q, W, Y in the Commerce Control List (Supplement No. 1 to Sec. 799.1 of this subchapter) and are licensed for shipment by the country from which reexported.

(c)   Specific authorization to reexport—
(1)   Submission of request for reexport authorization. Requests for specific authorization to reexport technical data or to export any product thereof, as applicable, shall be submitted on Form ITA-699P, Request To Dispose of Commodities or Technical Data Previously Exported (OMB approval No. 0625-0009), to: Office of Export Licensing, P.O. Box 273, Washington, DC 20044.

(See Supplement No. 1 to Part 774 for instructions on completing the form.) If Form ITA-699P is not readily available, a request for specific authorization to reexport technical data or to export any product thereof, as applicable, may be submitted by letter. The letter shall bear the words "Technical Data Reexport Request" immediately below the heading or letterhead and contain all the information required by Sec. 779.5(d). Authorization to reexport technical data or to export the product thereof, if granted, will generally be issued with a validity period of 24 months on Form ITA- 699P, or by means of a letter from the Office of Export Licensing. Any request for extension of the validity period shall be requested in accordance with Sec. 774.5(b), and shall specify the period for which additional validity is required. The Office of Export Licensing will make the final decision on what validity beyond 24 months, if any, should be authorized in each case.

(2)   Return of reexport authorization. If the Office of Export Licensing revokes or suspends a reexport authorization, the licensee shall return the reexport authorization immediately to the Office of Export Licensing.
(3)   Records. Any person to whom a reexport authorization has been issued shall retain and make available for inspection records in accordance with the provisions of Sec. 787.13 of this subchapter, including any reexport authorizations (whether used or unused, valid or expired) and all supporting documents and shipping records.

(d)   Effect of foreign laws. No authority granted by the U.S. Office of Export Licensing, or under the provisions of the U.S. Export Administration Regulations, to reexport technical data or export a product thereof shall in any way relieve any person from his responsibility to comply fully with the laws, rules, and regulations of the country from which the reexport or export is to be made or of any other country having authority over any phase of the transaction. Conversely, no foreign law, rule, regulation, or authorization in any way relieves any person from his responsibility to obtain such authorization from the U.S. Office of Export Licensing as may be required by the U.S. Export Administration Regulations.

Sec. 779.9   Commercial agreements with certain countries.

Pursuant to section 5(j) of the Export Administration Amendments Act of 1979, as amended, any non-governmental U.S. person or firm that enters into an agreement with any agency of the government of a controlled country (Country Groups Q, W, Y, and the People's Republic of China), which agreement encourages technical cooperation and is intended to result in the export from the U.S. to the other party of U.S.-origin technical data (except under General License GTDA or General License GTDR as provided under the provisions of Sec. 779.4(b)), shall submit those portions of the agreement that include the statement of work and describe the anticipated exports of data to the Office of Technology and Policy Analysis, Room 4054, P.O. Box 273, Washington, DC 20044. This material shall be submitted no later than 30 days after the final signature on the agreement.

(a) This requirement does not apply to colleges, universities and other educational institutions.

(b) The submission required by this section does not relieve the exporter from the licensing requirements for controlled technical data and goods.

(c) Acceptance of a submission does not represent a judgment as to whether Export Administration will or will not issue any authorization for export of technical data.

Sec. 779.10 Other applicable provisions.

As far as may be consistent with the provisions of this part, all of the other provisions of the Export Administration Regulations shall apply equally to exports of technical data and to applications for licenses and licenses issued under this part.

Supplement No. 1 to Part 779—Technical Data Interpretations

1. Technology based on U.S.-origin technical data. U.S.-origin technical data does not lose its U.S.-origin when it is redrawn, used, consulted, or otherwise commingled abroad in any respect with other technical data of any other origin. Therefore, any subsequent or similar technical data prepared or engineered abroad for the design, construction, operation, or maintenance of any plant or equipment, or part thereof, which is based on or utilizes any U.S.-origin technical data, is subject to the same U.S. Export Administration Regulations that are applicable to the original U.S.-origin technical data, including the requirement for obtaining Office of Export Licensing authorization prior to reexportation.

2. Distinction between General and Validated License requirements for shipment to QWY destinations of technical data and replacement parts.

A number of exporters have recently asked where the line is drawn between general license and validated license exports to PQWY destinations of technical data related to equipment exports.

The export of technical data under validated license is authorized only to the extent specifically indicated on the face of the license. The only data related to equipment exports that can be provided under general license is the publicly available data authorized by General License GTDA, or the assembly, installation, maintenance, repair, and operation data authorized by General License GTDR.

771.20   General License GLX; exports to Country Groups QWY and the People's Republic of China.

(a)   Scope.   A general license designated GLX is established, authorizing exports to civil end-users in Country Group QWY and the People's Republic of China (PRC) of certain specified items.

(b)   Eligible exports.   The items eligible for this general license are those described in the Advisory Notes in the CCL that indicate likelihood of approval for "Country Groups QWY and the PRC," except items described in the notes to ECCNs 1C18A and 2B18A. Likelihood of approval notes that apply only to the PRC, or to specified destinations in Country Group Y also qualify for this general license to eligible destinations (however, those notes indicating Country Group Q or W only, are specifically *not* eligible). In addition, those entries and sub-entires listed in Supplement No. 1 to this Part 771 are eligible to export under this general license. However, this general license is not available for items that are also subject to missile technology (MT), nuclear nonproliferation (NP), or foreign policy (FP) controls to the recipient country.

(c)   Eligible consignees.   This general license is available only for exports to civil end-users for civil end-uses. Exports under this general license may not be made to military end-users or to known military uses. Such exports will continue to require an individual validated license and be considered on a case-by-case basis. In addition to conventional military activities, military uses include any proliferation activities described in Part 778 of this subchapter. Retransfers to military end-users or end-uses in eligible countries are strictly prohibited, without prior authorization.

The relevant part of the Commerce Control List is the "Information Security" category, as described below (taken from Supplement Number 1 to Section 799.1 of the Code of Federal Regulations).

II. "Information Security"

NOTE: The control status of "information security" equipment, "software", systems, application specific "assemblies", modules, integrated circuits, components, technology or functions is defined in the "information security" entries in this Category even if they are components or "assemblies" of other equipment.

NOTE: "Information security" equipment, "software", systems, application specific "assemblies", modules, integrated circuits, components, technology or functions that are excepted from control, not controlled, or eligible for licensing under an Advisory Note are under the licensing jurisdiction of the Department of Commerce. For all other, exporters requesting a validated license from the Department of Commerce must provide a statement from the Department of State, Office of Defense Trade Control, verifying that the equipment intended for export is under the licensing jurisdiction of the Department of Commerce.

A. Equipment, Assemblies and Components

5A11A Systems, equipment, application specific "assemblies", modules or integrated circuits for "information security", as described in this entry, and other specially designed components therefor.

List of Items Controlled

Systems, equipment, application specific "assemblies", modules or integrated circuits for "information security," as follows, and other specially designed components therefor:

a. Designed or modified to use "cryptography" employing digital techniques to ensure "information security";

b. Designed or modified to perform cryptanalytic functions;

c. Designed or modified to use "cryptography" employing analog techniques to ensure "information security", *except:*

c.1. Equipment using "fixed" band scrambling not exceeding 8 bands and in which the transpositions change not more frequently than once very second;

c.2. Equipment, using "fixed" band scrambling exceeding 8 bands and in which the transpositions change not more frequently than once every ten seconds;

c.3. Equipment using "fixed" frequency inversion and in which the transpositions change not more frequently than once every second;

c.4. Facsimile equipment;

c.5. Restricted audience broadcast equipment;

c.6. Civil television equipment;

d. Designed or modified to suppress the compromising emanations of information-bearing signals;

NOTE: 5A11.d does not control equipment specially designed to suppress emanations for health and safety reasons.

e. Designed or modified to use cryptographic techniques to generate the spreading code for "spread spectrum" or hopping code for "frequency agility" systems;

f. Designed or modified to provide certified or certifiable "multilevel security" or user isolation at a level exceeding Class B2 of the Trusted Computer System Evaluation Criteria (TCSEC) or equivalent;

g. Communications cable systems designed or modified using mechanical, electrical or electronic means to detect surreptitious intrusion.

5B11A Equipment specially designed for the development of equipment or functions controlled by the "information security" entries in this Category, including measuring or test equipment.

5B12A Equipment specially designed for the production of equipment or functions controlled by the "information security" entries in this Category, including measuring, test, repair or production equipment.

5B13A Measuring equipment specially designed to evaluate and validate the "information security" functions controlled by the "information security" entries in 5A or 5D.

C. Materials [Reserved]

D. "Software"

5D11A "Software" specially designed or modified for the "development", "production", or "use" of equipment controlled by "information security" entries 5A11, 5B11, 5B12, or 5B13 or "software" controlled by "information security" entries 5D11, 5D12, or 5D13.

5D12A "Software" specially designed or modified to support technology controlled by "information security" entry 5E11.

5D13A Specific "software" as follows.

NOTE: Exporter must have determined that the software is not controlled by the Office of Defense Trade Control, Department of State, before using this general license.

List of Items Controlled

a. "Software" having the characteristics, or performing or simulating the functions of the equipment controlled by the "information security" entries in 5A or 5B.
b. "Software" to certify "software" controlled by 5D13.a;
c. "Software" designed or modified to protect against malicious computer damage, e.g., viruses.

E. Technology

5E11A Technology according to the General Technology Note for the "development", "production", or "use" of equipment controlled by "Information Security" entries 5A11, 5B11, 5B12, or 5B13 or "software" controlled by "information security" entries 5D11, 5D12, or 5D13.

NOTES for "Information Security":

NOTE 1: "Information security" entries in this Category do not control:
a. "Personalized smart cards" using "cryptography" restricted for use only in equipment or systems released from control under 5A11.c.1 to c.6, by this Note or as described in "Information Security" Advisory Notes 3 and 4 below;

b.   Equipment containing "fixed" data compression or coding techniques;

c.   Receiving equipment for radio broadcast, pay television or similar restricted audience television of the consumer type, without digital encryption and where digital decryption is limited to the video, audio or management functions;

d.   Portable (personal) or mobile radio-telephones for civil use; e.g., for use with commercial civil cellular radiocommunications systems, containing encryption, when accompanying their users;

e.   Decryption functions specially designed to allow the execution of copy-protected "software", provided that the decryption functions are not user-accessible.

NOTE 2: "Information Security" entries in this Category do not control:

a.   "Software" "required" for the "use" of equipment released by "Information Security" Note 1;

b.   "Software" providing any of the functions of equipment released by "Information Security" Note 1;

ADVISORY NOTE 3:   Licenses are likely to be approved, as administrative exceptions, for exports to Country Group W or cellular radio equipment or systems specially designed for cryptographic operation, provided any message traffic encryption capability that is within the scope of the control of the "information security" entries in Category 5 and that is contained in such equipment or systems is irreversibly disabled.

N.B.:   Provided message traffic encryption is not possible within such a system, the export of mobile or portable cellular radio subscriber equipment containing cryptographic capabilities is permitted under this Advisory Note.

ADVISORY NOTE 4: Licenses are likely to be approved, as administrative exceptions, for exports to satisfactory end-users in Country Groups QWY and the PRC of the following cryptographic equipment, provided that the equipment is intended for civil use:

a.   Access control equipment, such as automatic teller machines, self-service statement printers or point of sale terminals, that protects password or personal identification numbers (PIN) or similar data to prevent unauthorized access to facilities, but does not allow for encryption of files or text, except as directly related to the password of PIN protection;

b.   Data authentication equipment that calculates a Message Authentication Code (MAC) or similar result to ensure no alteration of text has taken place, or to authenticate users, but does not allow for encryption of data, text or other media other than that needed for the authentication;

c.   Cryptographic equipment specially designed, developed or modified for use in machines for banking or money transactions, such as automatic teller machines, self-service statement printers, point of sale terminals or equipment for the encryption of interbanking transactions, and intended for use only in such applications.

ADVISORY NOTE 5:   (Eligible for GTDR). Licenses are likely to be approved as administrative exceptions, for exports to satisfactory end-users in Country Groups QWY and the PRC of the following cryptographic "software";

a.   "Software" required for the "use" of equipment eligible for administrative exceptions treatment under Advisory Notes 3 and 4 in the Notes for "Information Security" (Category 5);

b.   "Software" providing any of the functions of equipment eligible for administrative exceptions treatment under Advisory Notes 3 and 4 in the Notes for "Information Security" (Category 5). *[End of Notes for "Information Security."]*

III. Other Equipment, Materials, "Software" and Technology

A. Equipment, Assemblies and Components

5A20B Telemetering and telecontrol equipment usable as launch support equipment for unmanned air vehicles or rocket systems.

5A80D Communications intercepting devices; and parts and accessories therefor. (Specify by name.) (Also see S776.13 of this subchapter.)

NOTES: 1. These items are subject to the United Nations Security Council arms embargo against Rwanda described in S785.4 (a) of this subchapter.
              2. Controls on this equipment are maintained in accordance with the Omnibus Crime Control and Safe Streets Act of 1968 (Pub. L. 90-351).

Index

A

Access, 353
  control, 26–27
    defined, 55–56, 94n, 353
    facilitators, 60–65
    see also Back door access
    inhibitors, 58–60
Advanced Research Projects Agency
  (ARPA), 237n
  Memorandum of Agreement with
    Defense Information Systems
    Agency and National Security
    Agency (text of), 633–636
AECA, *see* Arms Export Control Act (AECA)
Algorithm, 378
  and key length, 353
America Online, 42–43n, 148
American National Standards Institute
  (ANSI), 486
Anonymity, 43, 59, 480
ANSI, *see* American National Standards
  Institute (ANSI)
Applications programming interfaces, *see*
  Cryptographic applications
  programming interfaces (CAPI)
Arms Export Control Act (AECA), 114–116,
  118, 255
  text of, 558–573

ARPA, *see* Advanced Research Projects
  Agency (ARPA)
Assurance, 353
Asymmetric cryptography, 53–54, 63, 75,
  313n, 353, 365–367, 375–377, 385–
  388
AT&T, 60, 70n, 419
  Clipper phones, 174–175
  Secure Telephone Unit (STU), 74–75,
    235
  Surity Telephone Device, 175
Attacks on cryptographic systems
  for asymmetric cryptography, 63
  brute-force search, 62–63, 124, 276, 287,
    381
  chosen plaintext, 381–382
  ciphertext only, 287, 381
  exploitation of design factors, 60–62
  exploitation of operational errors, 383
  known ciphertext, 390
  known plaintext, 381
  shortcuts, 63
  for symmetric cryptography, 63
  timing attacks, 63
  work factor, 64n, 181, 214, 288
  see also Information warfare (IW);
    Strong encryption
Audit trails, 3, 354, 370

Auditing, 354
Authentication
    of an identity, 354, 367–370, 374, 450, 468
    defined, 354
    of digital cash tokens, 478–479
    of a file, 354
    infrastructure for, 338–339
    of a message, 354, 367
    uses of, 42–43, 47, 123–125
    see also Audit trails
Authenticity, 354
Authorization, 354, 368n
Availability, 354

B

Back door
    access, 56
    defined, 354
    hidden, 201–201n, 203, 277
    open, 276–277
    see also Escrowed encryption
Banking and finance services, vii, 23, 35–
        36n, 57, 123, 179, 312, 455–458,
        470; *see also* Credit cards; Digital
        cash
Binary digit, 354
Biometric identifiers, 368–369
Bit, 354
Bit stream, 355
Bollinger, Lee, 344
Bush, President George, 100; *see also*
        National Security Directive 42

C

CALEA, *see* Communications Assistance
        for Law Enforcement Act of 1995
        (CALEA)
Cantwell bill, 254–255
CAPI, *see* Cryptographic applications
        programming interfaces (CAPI)
Capstone chip, 176, 355
Capstone/Fortezza initiative, 10, 176–177,
        179, 355
Caracristi, Ann, 344
CCL, *see* Commerce Control List (CCL)
Cellular phones, 11, 67, 217, 295, 327–328
Central Intelligence Agency (CIA), 91n, 95,
        100, 403, 422–423, 428–429; *see*

    also Executive Order 12333 and
        Executive Order 12472
CERT, *see* Computer Emergency Response
        Team (CERT)
Certificate
    authorities, 75–77, 355, 450–454
    infrastructure, 232–234
Certification, 355
Certification authority, 355
Checksum, 367
CIA, *see* Central Intelligence Agency (CIA)
Ciphertext, 172n, 355, 374
Circumventing laws against unescrowed
        encryption, 269, 330
Civil liberties, viii, 44n, 44–46
Civiletti, Benjamin R., 344–345
CJ, *see* Commodity jurisdiction (CJ)
Cleartext, 355
Clinton, President William, 95, 100
Clinton Administration, 41, 170, 235, 265–
        266, 303, 376
Clipper
    chip, xii, 171–174, 230, 355
    initiative, 356, 376, 445n
    see also Escrowed Encryption Standard
        (EES)
CMVP, *see* Cryptographic Module
        Validation Program (CMVP)
CoCom, *see* Coordinating Committee
        (CoCom) nations
Code grabbers, 42n
Collateral cryptography, 356
Commerce Control List (CCL), 8n, 115, 117,
        122, 125n, 135, 160n, 260; *see also*
        Export controls
Commerce Department, *see* Department of
        Commerce
Commodity jurisdiction (CJ), 8n, 115, 165,
        260, 638–640
Communications, xii, 20, 53–54
Communications Assistance for Law
        Enforcement Act of 1995
        (CALEA), 216–221, 278, 281, 503,
        510–511
    text of, 540–550
Competitive access providers, 356
Compuserve, 148, 431–432n
Computer Emergency Response Team
        (CERT), 241–242
Computer Science and
        Telecommunications Board
        (CSTB), xviii–xix, 20n, 73n

Computer Security Act of 1987, 235–236
    text of, 551–557
Computer System Security and Privacy
        Advisory Board (CSSPAB), 242
Conference on Computers, Freedom, and
        Privacy, xvii, 45n, 219n
Confidentiality, 17, 53–54, 123–125, 371–373
    of communications, 356
    of data, 356, 374
    defined, 3, 79–81, 108
    relative levels of, 181, 183, 254, 314
    reliance upon authentication, 373
    see also Cryptography; encryption
Congress, *see* U.S. Congress
Constitutional issues regarding laws on
        encryption, viii, 7, 85n, 160–161n,
        271–273, 304
Coordinating Committee (CoCom) nations,
        231, 251n, 310, 356, 434–436, 442,
        639
Cordless phones, 218, 398n
Countermeasure, 356
Credit cards, 22, 76, 481
Crime prevention, xv, 10, 47, 323, 472–473,
        480
Criminalizing use
    of cryptography for criminal purposes,
        12, 94, 273–274, 332–333
    of unescrowed cryptography, 192, 265–
        273
Crook, Colin, 345
Cryptanalysis, 62, 379n, 380n
    of 40-bit encryption algorithms, 8n, 63,
        73n, 115–117, 120–124, 276, 314–
        317
    of 56-bit encryption algorithms, 8, 63,
        71n, 121, 172, 288–289, 312, 316–
        318
    defined, 356
    see also Data Encryption Standard
        (DES); Strong encryption
Cryptographic
    algorithms, 62–64, 159
        defined, 356
        secret, 171, 201–204
    applications programming interfaces
        (CAPI), 259–262, 311, 474–476
    sockets, 66, 127
    systems, 374–377
        attacks on, 378–383
    see also Modularity; Key

Cryptographic Module Validation Program
        (CMVP), 233
Cryptography
    for authentication, 3–4, 10, 55–56, 176,
        324–327, 469–472
    for confidentiality, 3–4, 8–9, 54, 176, 296,
        470–472
    for criminal purposes, 3–4, 10–11, 43–
        43n, 84, 91, 303–304
    for data integrity, 3–4, 10, 55, 176, 324–
        327, 472–473
    defined, 356
    domestic availabilty of, 72–74, 135, 138,
        299, 310
    foreign availabilty of, 4, 214, 308
    history of, xii–xiii, 52–54, 149–150, 202,
        364–365
    in information security products, 65–66,
        476
        foreign, 132–133
    market for, xii, 66–72, 135–136, 145–152,
        310
    for nonrepudiation, 55
    as one element of information security,
        10, 296, 298
    regulations relevant to (text of), 637–677
    strength of, 63, 152–153, 250
    see also Encryption
Cryptography policy, 16
    adopting standards, 7, 222, 290, 316
    committee recommendations on, viii–
        xvii, 1, 5–13, 303–339
    current U.S. policies, xi, 6, 15, 111–112,
        249, 298, 301
    history of, 414–420
    international dimensions of, 243–244,
        430–431, 438–449
    process of formulating, viii, 226
        public debate over, xvii, 4, 7, 297–298
        urgency regarding, xv–xvi, 39–40,
        151–152
    proper objectives for, 57, 68, 297–303
    role of executive and legislative
        branches, 7, 305
    see also Executive branch; Legislative
        branch; Standards; U.S. Congress
CSSPAB, *see* Computer System Security
        and Privacy Advisory Board
        (CSSPAB)
CSTB, *see* Computer Science and
        Telecommunications Board
        (CSTB)

D

Dam, Kenneth W., Committee Chair, xv–xix, 343
DARPA, *see* Defense Advanced Research Projects Agency (DARPA)
Data
    aggregation, 459–460
    communications, 199, 441–442n
        versus data storage, 323–324, 528–529
    compression, 270–270n, 304
    integrity, 365–367, 374
Data Encryption Standard (DES), 72, 207, 223, 228–232, 288, 314–318, 334, 357, 365, 388–389, 417–420
    triple-DES, 178, 203n, 214–215
Date/time stamping, 57, 357, 371n
Decompiling, 204, 357
Decryption, 185, 357; *see also* Back door access; Cryptanalysis
Decryption algorithm, 374
Defense Advanced Research Projects Agency (DARPA), 241
Defense Department, *see* Department of Defense
Defense Information Systems Agency (DISA), 237–237n
Defense Intelligence Agency (DIA), *see* Executive Order 12333
Denial of service, 357
Department of Commerce, 73, 117, 128n, 173, 176; *see also* Executive Order 12472; Commerce Control List (CCL)
Department of Defense, 158, 187n, 237–238, 487n; *see also* Executive Order 12333; Executive Order 12472
Department of Energy, *see* Executive Order 12333
Department of Justice, 274
Department of State, 114–117, 121–122, 126, 142–144, 162, 321; *see also* Executive Order 12333; Executive Order 12472
Department of the Treasury, 173, 176, 190, 468; *see also* Executive Order 12333
DES, *see* Data Encryption Standard (DES)
Deutch, John, 97–98
DIA, *see* Defense Intelligence Agency (DIA)

Differential work factor cryptography, 264, 287–288; *see also* Attacks on cryptographic systems
Digests, 357
Digital
    cash, 339, 477–482
    information, 220, 280
    signatures, 57, 226–227, 261, 326, 357, 367, 370
    stream, 355
Digital Signature Standard (DSS), 176, 222–223, 225n, 229–230, 259, 301, 357, 418, 488
Digital Telephony Act, 357; *see also* Communications Assistance for Law Enforcement Act (CALEA)
DISA, *see* Defense Information Systems Agency (DISA)
Disassembly, 156n, 204, 215, 357
Disclosure of data, 357
DNA computing, 393–394
DOD, *see* Department of Defense
Double encryption. *See* Multiple encryption
DSS, *see* Digital Signature Standard (DSS)
Dual-use system, 358

E

EAA, *see* Export Administration Act (EAA)
EAR, *see* Export Administration Regulations (EAR)
Economic
    competitiveness
        of U.S. industry and businesses, 1–2, 37–40, 99
        of U.S. information technology industry, x, 38–39, 73, 128–129, 155–156
    espionage, 3, 46, 98
ECPA, *see* Electronic Communications Privacy Act (ECPA)
EES, *see* Escrowed Encryption Standard (EES)
Electromagnetic emissions, monitoring, 64, 397–398
Electronic
    commerce, vii, 24–26, 413, 478
    surveillance
        defined, 587
        history of, 218, 410–413

legal requirements for, 84–88, 396–410

and minimization requirement, 218n, 219, 400–401, 513

see also Foreign Intelligence Surveillance Act of 1978; U.S.Intelligence Activities; Wire and Electronic Communications Interception and Interception of Oral Communications Act

Electronic Communications Privacy Act (ECPA), 396–403, 412–413

Elliptic curve cryptographic systems, 394

E-mail, 403–403n, 469

Encryption, 15–16

defined, 53, 58–59, 90n, 372

technicalities in legal definitions of, 269–270, 273–274, 303, 332

see also Confidentiality

Encryption algorithm, 374

Error-correction, 366n

Escrow

agents, 77

affiliation of, 180, 189–193, 444

certification of, 175

liability of, 191, 197–198, 330, 452–454

number of, 180, 183n, 188n, 189–194, 212

responsibilities of, 180, 194–198, 330, 444–447, 452

trustworthiness of, 190

binding, 210–211, 215

Escrowable encryption products, 182, 262

Escrowed encryption, 15–16, 61, 81, 298, 359

benefits of, 170

contract-based, 191–193, 263–264

defined, 167–169

economic implications, 177–182, 271, 330

government control of, 158, 266–268, 328–332

law enforcement benefits, 4, 9, 11, 184–187

liabilities, 184, 329

mandatory versus voluntary use, 185–188, 199, 265, 320–321

policy issues associated with, 170

proper escrowing, 177–178, 188, 213–214, 250n

and signals intelligence, 175, 202–203

versus strong encryption, 169

weaknesses of, 183

see also Unescrowed encryption

Escrowed Encryption Standard (EES), xvi, 9, 168–175, 181, 223, 301, 358, 419–420, 488

Evaluation, 358

Exceptional access, 16, 80–81, 109

business or corporate, 104–107

defined, 169n, 250, 358

end-user, 106–107, 320

government, 81–104, 297

time scale of operations, 94, 103

voice versus data communications, 281–284

Executive branch, role of, 7, 189–190, 231, 291–292, 305

Executive Order 12333 (U.S. Intelligence Activities), 573-589

Executive Order 12472 (Assignment of National Security and Emergency Preparedness Telecommunications Functions), 612-620

Executive Order 12958 (Classified National Security Information), 589-612

Export Administration Act (EAA), 114–115, 118, 255, 415

Export Administration Regulations (EAR), 115, 415–416

Part 779, Technical Data (text of), 656–677

Export controls, 7–9, 15, 249–251, 298, 307–322

circumvention of, 133

corporate perceptions of, 152–153

cryptography exemptions from, xi, 120–125, 144, 188, 256

description of, 114–122

dimensions of choice in, 252–253

of dual-use items, 8, 118, 162, 264, 310

economic impact of, 40, 153–154

effect on national security, 157–165

effect on sales, 145–153

effectiveness of, 127–134

elimination of, 251, 254

and end-use certification, 320

export defined, 142

foreign policy considerations, 162–163, 170

history of, 414–415

impact on authentication products, 123–125

international harmonization of, 8, 243–244, 256–257, 443, 447–449

and liberal consideration, 117, 256–262, 317–318

licensing practices, current, 117, 122–127, 249–250

licensing process for, 9, 114, 142–144, 647–653, 667–669

limiting domestic availability, 7, 12, 134–138

of other nations, 257, 434–436

providing technical data, 9, 159–161, 313–314

rationale for, 113–114

stimulating foreign competition, 8, 155n, 155–159, 309

threshold between CCL and USML, 118–121, 138, 141, 254–255, 310–312, 415

of transnational corporations, 126

uncertainty of, 138–144, 251, 321–322

see also Arms Export Control Act (AECA); Commerce Control List (CCL); Export Administration Regulations (EAR); Foreign ownership, control or interest (FOCI); International Traffic in Arms Regulations (ITAR)

Export defined, 641

F

Facsimile communications, 2, 149

FAR, see Federal Acquisition Regulations (FAR)

FBI, see Federal Bureau of Investigation (FBI)

FCC, see Federal Communications Commission (FCC)

Fear, uncertainty, doubt, 225–227

Federal Acquisition Regulations (FAR), 187n

Federal Bureau of Investigation (FBI), 82–83, 88–90, 138n, 184, 236–237, 334n, 399, 423; see also Executive Order 12333

Federal Communications Commission (FCC), 220–221, 493; see also Executive Order 12472

Federal Emergency Management Agency (FEMA), see Executive Order 12472

Federal government, information security for, 289–292, 328–332; see also Computer Security Act of 1987

Federal Information Processing Standards (FIPS), 485–488

defined, 358

development of, 222–224

NIST role in, 222, 289–290

related to cryptography, 173, 176, 223, 418

Federal Reserve Board, 290–291

FEMA, see Federal Emergency Management Agency (FEMA)

Fermat numbers, 386–387

FIPS, see Federal Information Processing Standards (FIPS)

Firmware, 358

First party, 358

FISA, see Foreign Intelligence Surveillance Act (FISA) of 1978

FOCI, see Foreign ownership, control or interest (FOCI), U.S. companies under

Foreign Intelligence Surveillance Act (FISA) of 1978, 87–88, 173, 189, 403–410, 494

text of, 511–526

Foreign ownership, control or interest (FOCI), U.S. companies under, 126n

Fortezza cards, 176–177, 225, 259–260, 468

Freeh, Louis, 92n–93n, 93–94, 268, 281

Freeware, 129n, 272; see also Internet

Fuller, Samuel H., 345–346

Functionality, 358

G

Gelb, Leslie H., 346

General Services Administration (GSA), see Executive Order 12472

GII, see Global information infrastructure (GII)

Global information infrastructure (GII), 439–441n, 483

Globalization, 27–29, 38, 50, 188, 308, 430

GOSIP, see Government Open Systems Interconnect (OSI) Profile (GOSIP)

Government classification, xiii, 4, 238, 307; *see also* Executive Order 12958
Government Open Systems Interconnect (OSI) Profile (GOSIP), 224–225
Government procurement, 225, 487n
Graham, Ronald, xxxii, 346–347
GSA, *see* General Services Administration (GSA)

H

Hackers, 67n
Hardware
    product implementations in, 65, 74, 205, 296, 369n
    security advantages of, 130
    security disadvantages of, 206–209
Hashes, 367; *see also* One-way hash function; Secure hash algorithm; Secure Hash Standard
Health care industry, 256, 457, 459–461
Hellman, Martin, 347
Hewlett-Packard, 261n
Homologation laws, 437

I

IBM, 228–229, 417–418
IDEA block cipher, 229
Identification, 358
Identification key, 358
IITF, *see* Information Infrastructure Task Force (IITF)
Implementation, 358
Import controls, 114–115, 436–438
Information
    proprietary
        potential value of, 153–154
    security, 15, 66–68, 294–295
        government needs for, 10, 12, 46–48, 157–159, 240, 267, 302
        private sector needs for, vii–viii, 12–13, 30–31, 40–46, 152–153, 302, 335–338
        threats to, xii, 2–3, 32–38, 153–154, 239, 299
    technologies, viii, xii, 19–21
        need for research and development, 12
        speed of change in, xv, 5, 281, 300–302

technology industry
    and economic security, 22–23, 46, 67–68
    and national security, vii, xv, 3–4, 9–11, 47–48, 94–104, 157–159
    U.S. leadership in, x, 38–39, 73, 128–129, 155–156, 299, 308–311
theory, 364
vulnerability, 15–50, 293–296
warfare (IW), 35, 49, 108
Information Infrastructure Task Force (IITF), 41, 242, 335, 483
Inman, Bobby, xiii, 267
Integrated product, 358
Integrity, 359
Integrity check, 359, 366
Intellectual property, protecting, 228–230, 465, 482–484
Intelligence community
    and the intelligence cycle, 10, 425–429
    mission of, 95, 423–425
    regulation of, 87, 404–405n, 408, 423
    see also Central Intelligence Agency (CIA); Executive Order 12333; Federal Bureau of Investigation (FBI); Foreign Intelligence Surveilllance Act (FISA) of 1978; National Security Agency (NSA); SIGINT
Interception, 286–289, 359, 399, 490, 492–510
Internal Revenue Service (IRS), 466–467
International aspects of cryptography policy, 243
    similar and different national interests, viii–x, xiv–xv, 104, 431–434
    U.S. cooperation with other nations, 102, 231–232, 331–332
    see also Export controls; Import controls; Use controls
International Traffic in Arms Regulations (ITAR), 114–116, 120, 127, 133–137, 142, 159–161, 256, 359, 415–416, 476
    excerpts from Parts 120-123, 125, and 126 (text of), 637–655
Internet, 21, 34–35, 59, 64, 86n, 106n, 221, 282, 432n
    growth of, 293
    loan application by, 458
    and networks, 52, 149
    protocols, 224–225, 280–281

software distributed on, 129–132, 268
see also Netscape Navigator; World
Wide Web
Interoperability, 150, 178, 439, 443; *see also*
Standards
Interpretation of digital streams, 220
IRS, *see* Internal Revenue Service (IRS)
ITAR, *see* International Traffic in Arms
Regulations (ITAR)
IW, *see* Information warfare (IW)

J

Judicial branch, role of, 190
Justice Department, *see* Department of
Justice

K

Katz, Ambassador Julius L., 347
KEAs, *see* Escrow agents
Key
defined, 202, 359, 378
distribution, 359
distribution center (KDC), 377
escrow. *See* Escrowed encryption
escrow agents (KEAs). *See* Escrow
agents
escrow encryption, 359
generation, 211–213, 454
length, 63, 214–215, 287–288, 319, 353, 380
management, 53, 74–75, 133, 173, 223,
280, 359, 376–377
retrieval, 284–285
revocation, 105n, 213, 452
Key Exchange Algorithm, 176

L

Latent demand, for cryptography products,
149–151
Law enforcement, 302
central decryption facility for, 285–286
impact of cryptography on, 3–4, 9–10,
90–94, 184–187, 322–335
impact of information technologies on,
viii, 46–47, 333–335
infringing on civil liberties, viii, 45n, 93
requirements for escrowed encryption,
180, 194–197

and seizure of records, 81–83
technical center for, 334
wiretapping/electronic surveillance, *see*
Electromagnetic emissions;
Wiretapping
see also Communications Assistance for
Law Enforcement Act of 1995
(CALEA); Federal Bureau of
Investigation (FBI); Executive
Order 12333
Law enforcement access field (LEAF), 171–
173
Layered encryption, 277; *see also* Multiple
encryption
LEAF, *see* Law enforcement access field
(LEAF)
Legislative branch, role of, 7, 199
Link encryption, 11–11n, 274–276, 279, 327–
328
Lost sales, 146–148, 214

M

Manufacturing industry, 461–463, 469–470;
see also Vendors
Market
development, 151–152
forces, xv, 7, 305–307
Master Card, *see* Credit cards
Microsoft Windows NT, 135, 259–260
Modularity, 140–142, 223
Monitoring, 359
Moore's law, 63, 276, 385n
Multiple encryption, 58–59, 178, 215,
383
Mutual Law Enforcement Assistance
Treaties, 331, 446

N

NACIC, *see* National Counterintelligence
Center (NACIC)
National Communications System (NCS),
see Executive Order 12472
National Computer Security Center
(NCSC), 232–233
National Counterintelligence Center
(NACIC), 2, 242–243
National information infrastructure (NII),
235, 483

National Institute of Standards and
Technology (NIST), 228, 235–238,
335–337, 365, 418–420, 485–488
public-key infrastructure requirements,
450–454
see also Federal Information Processing
Standards (FIPS)
National Security Act of 1947, *see* Executive
Order 12333
National Security Agency (NSA), xi, xiv,
158, 227–228, 235–241, 289, 335,
338, 416–420, 422–423
role in export licensing, 123n, 126, 128n,
141–144, 162, 256
role in Skipjack/Clipper, 173n, 174
see also Executive Order 12333
National Security Council (NSC), *see*
National Security Directive 42;
Executive Order 12333
National Security Directive 42 (text of),
620–628
National Security Telecommunications and
Information Systems Security
Committee (NSTISSC), *see*
National Security Directive 42
NCS, *see* National Communications System
(NCS)
NCSC, *see* National Computer Security
Center (NCSC)
Netscape Navigator, 73n, 76, 124, 132n,
135, 208
Network Working Group, 280n
Network-based encryption, 199, 278–281
Networks, 149
applications of, 282–284
backward compatibility issues, 151n
vulnerabilities of, 52, 195, 274
Neumann, Peter G., 347–348
New Forum nations, 442; *see also* CoCom
nations
NII, *see* National information infrastructure
(NII)
NIST, *see* National Institute of Standards
and Technology (NIST)
Node, 359
Nonrepudiation, 359, 365, 370–371, 479
NSA, *see* National Security Agency (NSA)
NSTISSC, *see* National Security
Telecommunications and
Information Systems Security
Committee (NSTISSC)

O

Object code, 360
Object linking and embedding (OLE), 360,
475
OECD, *see* Organization for Economic
Cooperation and Development
(OECD) nations
Office of Management and Budget (OMB),
335, 486–487; *see also* Executive
Order 12958
OLE, *see* Object linking and embedding
(OLE)
OMB, *see* Office of Management and
Budget (OMB)
Omnibus Crime Control and Safe Streets
Act, 396–397
One-way hash function, 360, 367
Online services, 217–218, 221; *see also*
America Online; Compuserve;
Netscape Navigator; Prodigy;
World Wide Web
Operating system, 360
Oral communications, *see* Wire and
Electronic Communications
Interception and Interception of
Oral Communications Act
Organization for Economic Cooperation
and Development (OECD)
nations, 244, 331, 442, 448
OSI, *see* Government Open Systems
Interconnect (OSI) Profile
(GOSIP)
Ozzie, Raymond, 348

P

Parallel processing, 63
Partial key escrow, 180
Password, 360
Patent and Trademark Office (PTO), 230
Patents, xii, 228–230
PCMCIA card (or PC-card), 176, 360, 468;
see also Fortezza cards
Pen Register and Traffic Analysis Act (text
of), 526–540
Pen registers, 62, 84, 402
defined, 360, 540
Perry, William, 310
Personal identification number (PIN), 360
Petroleum industry, 463–465

PGP, *see* Pretty Good Privacy (PGP)
Pharmaceutical industry, 200, 465–466
PIN, *see* Personal identification number (PIN)
Plaintext, 9, 53, 270, 355, 360, 374
Plug-in cryptography, *see* Cryptographic sockets
Pretty Good Privacy (PGP), 76, 163–164, 182
Private-key cryptography, 360, 375
Prodigy, 148
Products
    certification and evaluation of, 70
    cryptography, 148, 201–208
    defaults, 250, 258
    integrated or general-purpose, 65–66
    stand-alone or security-specific, 65, 149, 208–211
    weaknesses in, 74
Proper escrowing, *see* Escrowed encryption
Proprietary algorithms, 70, 174, 203
    verifying, 207n
Protocol, 73
    analyzers, 62
    negotiation, 71
Pseudorandom function, 367
PSTN, *see* Public switched telecommunications network (PSTN)
PTO, *see* Patent and Trademark Office (PTO)
Public Cryptography Study Group, 267–268
Public Law 103-160, ix, xiv
Public switched telecommunications network (PSTN), 11
    counterintelligence access to, 534–535
    national security/emergency preparedness (NS/EP) network, 35
    vulnerability of, 34–37, 327–328
    see also National Security Directive 42
Public-key certificate, 360–361
Public-key cryptography, 53, 70, 290, 296, 313, 353, 360, 375; *see also* NIST

Q

Quantum
    computing, 392–393
    cryptography, 394–395

R

RC2/RC4 algorithms, 361
Reagan, President Ronald, 99, 423; *see also* Executive Order 12333; Executive Order 12472
Real-time surveillance, 89–90, 103
Reliability, 361
Remailer, 361
Reverse engineering, 205, 210, 230, 361
Risks addressed by cryptography, 361, 469–473
RSA algorithm, 182, 227–229, 313n, 325, 361, 376
RSA Data Security Conference, 141n

S

Safety margins in key length, 361, 384–385
Satellite uplinks, 438
Schmults, Edward C., 348
Schneier, Bruce, 160n, 163–165
Second party, 361
Secrecy, xiii–xiv, 201–208, 307, 378
Secret-key
    cryptography, 53, 171, 366, 375
    cryptosystem, 361, 383–384
Secure hash algorithm, 361–362, 370n
Secure Hash Standard, 176, 223, 362
Secure Sockets Layer protocol, 124
Secure Telephone Unit (STU), 74–75, 235
Security, 362
Security Policy Board (SPB), 241
Security-specific cryptography product, 362
SED, *see* Shipper's Export Declaration (SED)
Shannon, Claude, 364
Shareware, 362
Shipper's Export Declaration (SED), 119
SIGINT (Signals intelligence)
    and cryptography, 101–102, 114, 317, 335, 428
    historical examples of, 96–99, 427
    utility of, 87–88, 100–101, 174–175, 421–423, 470–471
Signaling System 7, 34
Skipjack algorithm, 171–172, 176, 201, 212n, 230, 362, 383, 391, 420
Slippery slope, 266
Smith, W.Y., Committee Vice Chair, 343–344

Software
advantages of, 191–192
backward compatibility, 151n, 151–152
disadvantages of, 62, 64, 130
integrated, 148
object-oriented, 137n, 140, 165
product implementations in, 20–21, 65, 204–205
Source code, 362
Sovereign immunity, 189, 199
SPB, *see* Security Policy Board (SPB)
Specification, 362
Spillover effect, 123–125
Spoofing, 362, 367
Stand-alone cryptography product, 362
Standards, 70–71, 197, 222, 232–234, 254, 306, 485–486n, 551–556
State Department, *see* Department of State
Steganography, 270n, 372–372n
Stone, Elliot M., 348–349
Strategic intelligence, 97–101
Strong encryption, 101–102, 114, 123, 170, 254, 296, 382–383
STU, *see* Secure Telephone Unit (STU)
STU-III, 362
Superencryption, 269, 438
Symmetric
cryptography, 53–54, 172n, 362, 375–376
cryptosystem, 362
System, 362

T

Tactical intelligence, 96–97
Taxation, 482
TCP/IP, 225
Telephony, *see* Facsimile communications; Voice communications
TEMPEST techniques, 64
Third party access, 362–363; *see also* Exceptional access
Threat, 363
Time stamping, 357
Title III intercept, *see* Wire and Electronic Communications Interception and Interception of Oral Communications Act
Token, 363
TPEP, *see* Trusted Product Evaluation Program (TPEP)

Traffic analysis, *see* Pen Register and Traffic Analysis Act
Translucent cryptography, 277–278
Transparency, 185
Trap-and-trace devices, 84, 402
defined, 363, 540
see also Pen Register and Traffic Analysis Act
Treasury Department, *see* Department of the Treasury
Trojan horses, 56n, 64–65n, 363
Trust, 363, 480–482
Trusted Product Evaluation Program (TPEP), 233
Trustworthiness, 363, 379
Turner, Stansfield, 98

U

Unescrowed encryption, 7, 181–183, 186–187, 199, 268–273, 303–304
United States Postal Service (USPS), 468
U.S. Code, Title 18, Chapter 119, *see* Wire and Electronic Communications Interception and Interception of Oral Communications Act (text of)
U.S. Code, Title 18, Chapter 121 and 206, *see* Pen Register and Traffic Analysis Act (text of)
U.S. Code, Title 22, Chapter 39, *see* Arms Export Control Act (AECA)
U.S. Code, Title 50, Chapter 36, *see* Foreign Intelligence Surveillance Act of 1978 (text of)
U.S. Congress, viii, 162, 187, 231, 305, 332–333
oversight by, 587
reports to, 508, 524–525, 539, 550, 561
see also Legislative branch, role of
U.S. Munitions List (USML), 114–117, 125–127, 135–137, 140, 162–163, 389, 644–646
separating cryptography products on, 264
Use controls on cryptography, 436–438
USML, *see* U.S. Munitions List (USML)
USPS, *see* United States Postal Service (USPS)

V

Vendors, role of, 140, 149–153, 191, 206, 274
VeriSign, 76
Viruses, 64, 206
Visa, *see* Credit cards
Voice communications, secure, 174, 278–280
    vs data communications, 199, 221, 280–281
Vulnerabilities, 24, 57, 293–296, 363

W

Ware, Willis H., 349
Weak encryption, 29, 61–62, 101, 257–258, 276
Web of trust, 75–76
Windows NT, *see* Microsoft Windows NT

Wire and Electronic Communications Interception and Interception of Oral Communications Act (text of), 489–511
Wireless communications, vii–viii, 61, 275, 279–280; *see also* Cellular phones; Cordless phones
Wiretapping, 62, 103, 218–220, 439
    legal framework governing, 84–88, 170
    and protection of civil liberties, 44n, 285n, 285–286
    utility of, 82–84
    see also Electronic surveillance
Work factor, 64n, 363
World Wide Web, 65n

Z

Zimmerman, Philip, 163–164